"Based on data collected from nearly 3,000 employed partnered parents across 10 diverse countries, Project 3535 represents a significant contribution to the study of cross-national work-family issues. By detailing the process used to conduct this ambitious project and sharing the lessons learned, the researchers have provided the international research community with an invaluable resource for conducting cross-national research. This volume is a must have for any researcher interested in cross-cultural research collaborations."

—**Tammy D. Allen**, Department of Psychology, University of South Florida, USA

"*The Work-Family Interface in Global Context* represents a culmination of years of exemplary cross-cultural collaborative research on the cultural and social/organizational policy underpinnings of the operation of the work-family interface. The book is unique in its comprehensiveness of coverage, methodological rigor and approaches, and the integrated theoretical framework which underpins the chapters. It is a delightfully rich source of intellectual wealth to students of cross-cultural/international management and of actionable knowledge to organizations and policy makers concerned to enhance the wellbeing of their employees and citizens."

—**Samuel Aryee**, Surrey Business School, University of Surrey, UK

"This is an outstanding exemplar of work-family research across cultures. The studies presented in this book are conceptually sound and methodologically rigorous, and they provide a solid foundation for future scholars interested in understanding work-family issues around the world."

—**Margaret A. Shaffer**, Michael F. Price Chair of International Business, University of Oklahoma, USA

THE WORK-FAMILY INTERFACE IN GLOBAL CONTEXT

Based on a sweeping, ten-country study known as Project 3535, *The Work-Family Interface in Global Context* comprises the most comprehensive and rigorous cross-cultural study of the work-family interface to date. Just as work-family conflict is associated with negative consequences for workers, organizations, and societies, so too can the work and family domains interact positively to enhance or enrich one another. Drawing on qualitative, quantitative, and policy-based data, chapters in this collection explore the influence of culture on the work-family interface in order to help researchers and managers understand the applicability of work-family models in a variety of contexts and further conceptualize work-family interactions through the development of a more universal knowledge.

Karen Korabik, University of Guelph, Canada.

Zeynep Aycan, Koç University, Turkey.

Roya Ayman, Illinois Institute of Technology, USA.

Artiawati, University of Surabaya, Indonesia.

Anne Bardoel, Monash University, Australia.

Anat Drach-Zahavy, University of Haifa, Israel.

Leslie B. Hammer, Portland State University, USA.

Ting-Pang Huang, Soochow University, Taiwan.

Donna S. Lero, University of Guelph, Canada.

Tripti Pande-Desai, New Delhi Institute of Management, India.

Steven Poelmans, EADA Business School, Spain.

Ujvala Rajadhyaksha, Governors State University, USA.

Anit Somech, University of Haifa, Israel.

Li Zhang, Harbin Institute of Technology, China.

Karen Korabik is Professor Emeritus of Psychology at the University of Guelph, Canada, where she is affiliated with the Centre for Families, Work, and Well-Being. Her research centers on leadership, gender dynamics in organizations, and work-family integration.

Zeynep Aycan is Professor of Psychology and Management at Koç University, Turkey. She received her Ph.D. from Queen's University, Canada and conducted post-doctoral studies at McGill University. Her research focuses on the impact of culture on leadership, human resource management, and work-life balance. She is a Fellow of SIOP and APS.

Roya Ayman is Professor and the Director of the Industrial and Organizational Psychology Program at the Illinois Institute of Technology, United States. She received her Ph.D. from the University of Utah. Her research focuses on leadership and the work-family interface considering gender and cultural impacts. She is a Fellow of the Leadership Trust, United Kingdom.

THE WORK-FAMILY INTERFACE IN GLOBAL CONTEXT

Edited by
Karen Korabik
Zeynep Aycan
Roya Ayman

NEW YORK AND LONDON

First published 2017
by Routledge
711 Third Avenue, New York, NY 10017

and by Routledge
2 Park Square, Milton Park, Abingdon, Oxon, OX14 4RN

Routledge is an imprint of the Taylor & Francis Group, an informa business

Library of Congress Cataloging-in-Publication Data
Names: Korabik, Karen, editor. | Aycan, Zeynep, editor. | Ayman, Roya, editor.
Title: The work-family interface in global context / edited by Karen Korabik, Zeynep Aycan, Roya Ayman.
Description: 1 Edition. | New York, NY : Routledge, 2017. | Includes bibliographical references and index.
Identifiers: LCCN 2016049524 | ISBN 9781138841574 (hardback : alk. paper) | ISBN 9781138841581 (pbk. : alk. paper) | ISBN 9781315732084 (ebook)
Subjects: LCSH: Work and family.
Classification: LCC HD4904.25 .W727 2017 | DDC 306.3/6—dc23
LC record available at https://lccn.loc.gov/2016049524

ISBN: 978-1-138-84157-4 (hbk)
ISBN: 978-1-138-84158-1 (pbk)
ISBN: 978-1-315-73208-4 (ebk)

Typeset in Bembo
by Apex CoVantage, LLC

We dedicate this book to the next generation of collaborative cross-cultural work-family researchers.
The Project 3535 Team

To my daughter, Michelle, who during this project grew from a young girl to a working woman, as we traveled the world together and taught each other about balancing work and family.
Karen Korabik

To my son, Ata, for giving me the privilege of being his mother.
Zeynep Aycan

To my parents Lily and Iraj Ayman.
Roya Ayman

CONTENTS

ACKNOWLEDGMENTS

An endeavor of this magnitude would not be possible without the help and support of many people who were either directly or indirectly involved. We would like to begin by extending a special thanks to our editorial assistant, Grace Ewles, who worked long and hard to meet very tight deadlines under very trying circumstances. Grace provided instrumental support through her excellent ability to copyedit, check consistency, and coordinate the efforts of the contributors to this book with those of the editors and the publisher. As well, she was a tremendous source of emotional support to the editors.

We are grateful to our project coordinator, Allyson McElwain, for her enormous help with collecting the data in Canada, synchronizing the data collection across countries, merging the individual country data files, and administering the project website, among many other tasks too numerous to mention. In addition, we wish to thank Carolyn Pletsch for her input in designing the project website (www.workfamilyconflict.ca).

We are very appreciative of the efforts of the many individuals who assisted with this research in a multitude of different ways, including helping with literature reviews, data collection, and data analyses. In particular, we would like to thank Taniesha Burke, Dara Chappell, Christina Costa, Shannon Ellis Cunningham, Chester Kam, Thomas Oliver, Steven Risavy, Tricia van Rhijn, and Melissa Warner from Canada; Mr. Dhruva Desai from India; Teguh Wijaya Mulya, Syafitri Desnawati, Luh Kusuma Dewi, and many students from the Faculty of Psychology, University of Surabaya in Indonesia; Yen-yu Chou and Sy-bang Yeh from Taiwan; Ayse Burçin Erarslan-Baskurt and Salome Shelia from Turkey; and Shujaat Ahmed, Amy Antani Logue, Ruoqi Pei, Kahtera Sahibzada, Maggie Shafiro, and Chenxuan Zhou from the United States.

We are especially grateful to Nazli Baydar, Alan Mead, and Tricia van Rhijn for their invaluable statistical expertise and assistance in conducting the measurement equivalence/invariance analyses. We would also like to recognize Nazli Baydar, Saba Colakoglu, Hayat Kabasakal, Mila Lazarova, and Arzu Wasti for their excellent job in reviewing drafts of the chapters.

Finally, this project would not have been possible without the financial support and funding that we received from many sources. First and foremost, we are extremely appreciative of the generous funding given by the Koç University College of Social Sciences and Humanities Research Fund and the Koç Holding Chair Fund in Management and Strategy to Zeynep Aycan, which made it possible to carry out the research in Turkey and to hold several team meetings in Istanbul. We are also very grateful for the funding provided by the Social Science and Humanities Research Council of Canada (SSHRC) to Karen Korabik and Donna S. Lero through a SSHRC Grant (# 410-2004-0204) and a SSHRC International Opportunities Fund Grant (# 861-2007-1036) and for the financial support given to Donna S. Lero by the Centre for Families, Work, and Well-Being and the Jarislowsky Chair in Families and Work at the University of Guelph. These funds made it possible to conduct the research in Canada, to set up and maintain the project website, and to prepare the manuscript for this book. The research in Taiwan was partially based on a research project supported by a research grant to Ting-Pang Huang from the National Science Council (Ministry of Science and Technology) of R.O.C. (Taiwan) (NSC-101-2410-H-031-043). Funds for data collection in India (except for New Delhi) were made available through a fellowship provided to Ujvala Rajadhyaksha by the Center for Women's Intercultural Leadership at Saint Mary's College, Notre Dame, Indiana. In addition, funding for data collection in Indonesia was provided by Prof. Dr. Yusti Probowati Rahayu, the Dean of Faculty of Psychology, University of Surabaya, and the Community Service and Research Centre of the University of Surabaya under the leadership of Prof. Dr. Jatie K. Pudjibudojo.

ABBREVIATIONS

Country names were abbreviated according to their two-letter ISO codes as follows:

Australia = AU
Canada = CA
China = CN
India = IN
Indonesia = ID
Israel = IL
Spain = ES
Taiwan = TW
Turkey = TR
United States = US

Work-Family Variables

Work-family = W-F
Work-family conflict = WFC
Work-family guilt = WFG
Work interference with family conflict = WIF, except for Chapter 17 where WIFC
Family interference with work conflict = FIW, except for Chapter 17 where FIWC
Time-based and strain-based WIF and FIW = TB and SB WIF and FIW
Work interference with family guilt = WIFG
Family interference with work guilt = FIWG

Work-family positive spillover = WFPS
Work-to-family positive spillover = WTFS
Family-to-work positive spillover = FTWS
Work-family enrichment (WFE)/work-family facilitation (WFF)
Work-to-family enrichment/facilitation (WTFE/WTFF)
Family-to-work enrichment/facilitation (FTWE/FTWF)
Work-Life Balance = WLB
Family-Friendly = FF
Flexible Work Arrangements = FWAs

Cultural Variables

Individualism-Collectivism = I-C
Vertical collectivism = VC
Vertical individualism = VI
Individualistic-Egalitarian = I-E
Mid Collectivist-Mid Traditional = MC-MT
Collectivist-Traditional = C-T
Polychronic time orientation = PTO
Gender-role ideology = GRI
National gender equity culture = NGE

CONTRIBUTORS

* indicates core team member

***Artiawati**, Ph.D., University of Surabaya, Indonesia. Dr. Artiawati is a Lecturer in the Department of Psychology at the University of Surabaya. She completed her bachelor and doctoral degrees in Industrial-Organizational Psychology from Padjadjaran University, Indonesia and received a Master in Applied Psychology from Murdoch University, Western Australia.

***Zeynep Aycan**, Ph.D., Koç University, Turkey. Dr. Aycan is a Professor of Psychology and Management at Koç University. Her research focuses on the impact of culture on leadership, HRM, and work-life balance. She received her Ph.D. from Queen's University, Canada and conducted post-doctoral studies at McGill University.

***Roya Ayman**, Ph.D., Illinois Institute of Technology, United States. Dr. Ayman is a Professor and the Director of the Industrial and Organizational Psychology program at the Illinois Institute of Technology. She has conducted research in leadership and the work-family interface considering gender and cultural impacts.

***Anne Bardoel**, Ph.D., Monash University, Australia. Dr. Bardoel is an Associate Professor of Management at Monash University. She has an international profile as a work-family researcher and is an advisor to the Australian Workplace Gender Equity Agency.

Ayse Burçin Erarslan-Baskurt, Koç University, Turkey. Ms. Erarslan-Baskurt is a Ph.D. Candidate in social and organizational psychology at Koç University. Her doctorate research concentrates on career shift intentions of young people in Turkey.

Barbara Beham, Ph.D., Berlin School of Economics and Law, Germany. Dr. Beham is a Professor of Organizational Psychology at the Berlin School of Economics and Law. Her research focuses on the work-family interface in diverse national and cultural contexts.

***Anat Drach-Zahavy**, Ph.D., University of Haifa, Israel. Dr. Drach-Zahavy is an Associate Professor at the University of Haifa. Her research focuses on health care organizations, particularly in the areas of quality service, safety, and employee's health.

***Leslie B. Hammer**, Ph.D., Portland State University, United States. Dr. Hammer is a Professor of Psychology in the Department of Psychology at Portland State University and a Senior Scientist in the Oregon Institute of Occupational Health Sciences at Oregon Health & Science University.

***Ting-Pang Huang**, Ph.D., Soochow University, Taiwan. Dr. Huang is an Associate Professor in the Department of Business Administration at Soochow University. He received his Ph.D. degree in Industrial and Organizational Psychology from Illinois Institute of Technology in 1994.

Nahren Ishaya, M.S., Illinois Institute of Technology, United States. Ms. Ishaya is currently pursuing her doctorate in Industrial-Organizational Psychology at the Illinois Institute of Technology. Her research has focused on various antecedents and moderators of the work-family interface.

***Karen Korabik**, Ph.D., University of Guelph, Canada. Dr. Korabik a Professor Emeritus in the Department of Psychology at the University of Guelph where she is affiliated with the Centre for Families, Work, and Well-Being. Her research centers on leadership, gender dynamics in organizations, and work-family integration.

***Donna S. Lero**, Ph.D., University of Guelph, Canada. Dr. Lero is a Professor in the Department of Family Relations and Applied Nutrition at the University of Guelph. She leads a program of research on public policies, workplace practices, and community supports at the Centre for Families, Work, and Well-Being.

***Tripti Pande-Desai**, Ph.D., New Delhi Institute of Management, India. Dr. Pande-Desai is a Professor of Organizational Behavior and Human Resource Management. She has over 30 years of teaching, training, consulting, and research experience and has consulted with some of the Big Five in India.

***Steven Poelmans**, Ph.D., EADA Business School, Spain. Dr. Poelmans is Co-Director and Professor of the EADA MILCO (Leadership & Coaching) and MARD (High Performance) programs and a partner of WorkItOut (WIO). With

WIO he developed the NeuroTrainingLab™, a leadership development methodology using competencies assessment and neurophysiologic indicators.

***Ujvala Rajadhyaksha**, Ph.D., Governors State University, United States. Dr. Rajadhyaksha currently serves as full-time faculty in the College of Business at Governors State University. Her previous affiliations include the Indian Institute of Technology in Bombay, India, and Saint Mary's College, Notre Dame, United States.

***Anit Somech**, Ph.D., University of Haifa, Israel. Dr. Somech is a Professor and Head of the Department of Educational Leadership at the University of Haifa where she serves as the President's Advisor for the Advancement of the Status of Women. Her research is in the areas of teamwork, management (participative management), work motivation (OCB), and stress from a multilevel and cross-cultural perspective.

***Li Zhang**, Ph.D., Harbin Institute of Technology, China. Dr. Zhang is a Professor and Associate Dean in the School of Management at the Harbin Institute of Technology. Her research interests include organizational behavior and human resource management, leadership, work-family balance, etc.

PART I

Examining the Impact of Culture on the Work-Family Interface

Zeynep Aycan

Part 1 of this book consists of three chapters. Chapter 1, authored by Zeynep Aycan, is entitled "Introducing Project 3535: Lessons Learned from a Multicultural Collaborative Research Project on the Work-Family Interface." Aycan describes the development of Project 3535—why and how it started, where the name came from, and how the team was formed. The main purpose of the chapter is to present the lessons learned from the efforts to implement the "best practices" approach in conducting a multicultural collaborative research project. Chapter 2, authored by Karen Korabik, is entitled "Methodology, Measurement, and Country Classification" provides a detailed description of the multimethod, multilevel methodology used in Project 3535. The chapter describes the three types of data collected in the project: social policy data, qualitative focus group data, and quantitative survey data. Methods and validity estimates in country classification and in measurement of constructs are described in detail. Chapter 3, co-authored by Donna S. Lero and Anne Bardoel, is entitled "The Impact of National Context and Organizational Policies: A Cross-Cultural Analysis." Based on Project 3535 survey data and policy documents from each country, the authors identify variations on socioeconomic and labor conditions, as well as institutional policies related to maternity and parental leave and public provisions for child care. The authors provide empirical support for the association between employees' use of workplace policies and practices and W-F balance, reduced turnover intention, and improved psychological well-being.

1

INTRODUCING PROJECT 3535

Lessons Learned from a Multicultural Collaborative Research Project on the Work-Family Interface

Zeynep Aycan

Work-family balance is at the top of the agenda for leaders in the business, politics, and policy domains. World leaders realize that lack of work-family balance is not only a threat to individual and organizational well-being, but also to the sustainability of societies at large. Singapore's Prime Minister attributed alarmingly low birth rates to families' difficulties balancing work and family responsibilities. In the 2016 meeting of the World Economic Forum, a global survey revealed that work-life balance was the top priority in choosing a job, second only to salary/benefits/financial incentives (Enderby, 2016). In this age of globalization, the information gained from cross-cultural research on the work-family interface has important implications both for the success of multinational organizations and for local businesses with diverse workforces.

The primary aim of Project 3535 was to investigate "universal" and "culture-specific" correlates of positive and negative interfaces between the work and family domains (i.e., work-family *conflict* and work-family *positive spillover*, respectively). In the extant literature, various aspects of work-family interface have been investigated in different countries (e.g., Pal & Saksvik, 2008, for Norway; Tang, Siu, & Cheung, 2014, for China) and in multi-country comparisons (e.g., Lyness & Judiesch, 2014; Spector et al., 2004; Yang et al., 2012). However, Project 3535 represents the first comprehensive, integrative, multidisciplinary, multiphase, multimethod effort aimed specifically at understanding the cultural forces that impact the work-family interface. The many specific theoretical and empirical contributions of Project 3535 to closing knowledge gaps in the existing literature and answering practical questions are described in detail throughout this book and summarized in Chapter 20.

In the current chapter, we will focus on the ways in which Project 3535 represented a "best practices" approach in cross-cultural research with respect to *theory and methodology* as well as *team processes*. This project has been conceived and conducted as a truly collaborative work among 14 scholars from 10 countries. We gave the utmost care to avoid creating a team climate dominated by a few "idea generators" in the *center* and "data collectors" in the *periphery* (Shils, 1961). In this chapter, we would like to focus specifically on the team processes and present lessons learned from managing a multicultural collaborative research team.

Project 3535: Origins and Mandate

I was a young cross-cultural psychologist when I initiated Project 3535 in 2002. At the time, I remember feeling frustrated with the way cross-cultural research was conducted by international teams. First, there was hardly ever a project led or initiated by a researcher from a so-called developing country. Second, the majority of teams had a core research group leading the project (mainly from the United States), while those in the periphery were simply data providers in exchange for co-authorship. I questioned this hierarchical model and decided to initiate a genuinely collaborative environment, where learning and growth opportunities were all around, rather than one-directional. I had the opportunity to meet work-family scholars from India, Indonesia, Canada, and Israel during the International Congress of Applied Psychology in Singapore in 2002. At the time, international and cross-cultural comparisons in work-life interface were not common. Therefore, the idea of initiating a cross-cultural project was well-received. During the conference, we discussed possible countries and team members to include in our project. The criteria for inclusion were: (1) being a work-family researcher, (2) being a local researcher in a country fitting into theoretical sampling criteria (see Figure 1.1), and (3) having the will and ability to work in a *collaborative* international research team; that is, actively participate in and engage with the project in every phase, not just the data collection phase. With these criteria in mind, we invited scholars to join the project. Our colleague from Ukraine had to leave the project due to personal reasons. In her place, we invited a colleague from China.

Project 3535 included 10 countries and 14 researchers. The members had a wide spectrum of academic ranks when they joined the project, ranging from one advanced level Ph.D. student to full professors working on the work-family interface. Members were local researchers in their respective countries; therefore, they were subject-matter-experts of their country's cultural context and policies. Various fields of psychology, management, and social policy were represented in the team. Some members adopted dual cultural identities (e.g., Iranian-American, Turkish-Canadian). There was wide diversity in age and research experience. Gender distribution was not balanced; there were only two male members.

Team science has increasingly becoming a norm, rather than an exception, as stated by Williams (2013), who is a member of the Scientific Careers Research and Development Group:

> The science of the twenty-first century looks very different to the science of the Enlightenment or even to the science of the 20th century. The days

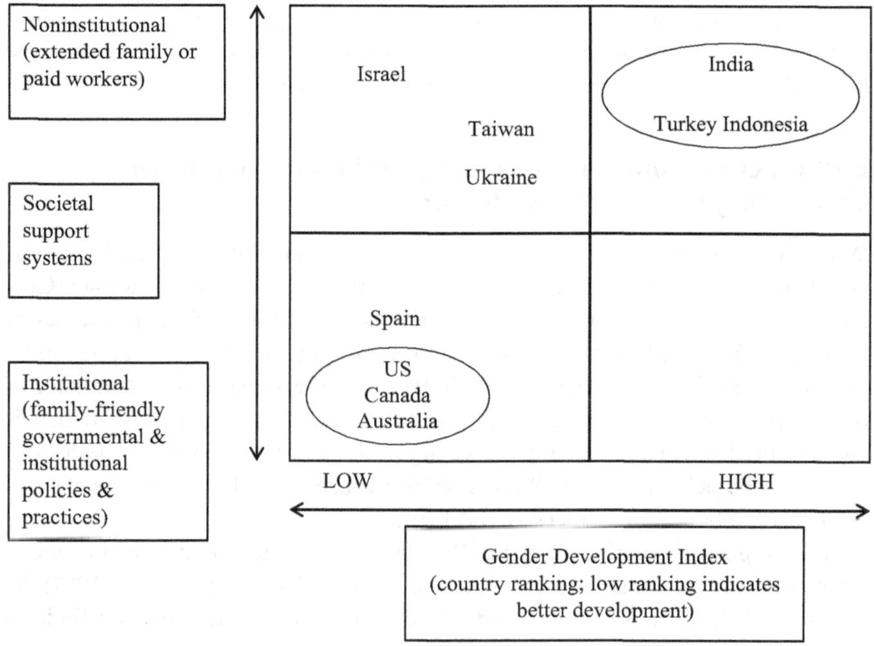

FIGURE 1.1 Initial theoretical sampling of countries.

Source: Korabik, Lero, & Ayman, 2003, p. 295.

> of the lone scientist, immersed in their laboratory, locked in their disciplinary silo, narrowly focused on basic research problems is rapidly becoming a thing of the past. In their place, we see the emergence of a new breed of team science, where large, cross-disciplinary teams focus on complex, applied and translational problems.

In the early 1980s, publications with over 100 authors were rare, whereas by 2010 more than 100 physics papers had more than 1,000 authors (Adams, 2012). The same trend is observed in almost all areas of scientific inquiry. Katz and Martin (1997) define research collaboration as the working together of researchers to achieve the common goal of producing new scientific knowledge. An indication of collaborative research is the number of authors in major publications. However, there is a growing consensus that co-authorship does not imply *collaborative* team processes. The common goal shared by members of Project 3535 was indeed "producing new scientific knowledge," but achieving it in a genuinely collaborative teamwork environment. Therefore, there was special care and attention to team processes along with team outcomes.

Our guiding principles as presented in our website were: (1) use of best practices approach for conducting cross-cultural research (Gelfand, Raver, & Ehrhart,

2002), (2) operate in a value system of collaboration, egalitarianism, and support, and (3) seek for consultative and consensus-oriented decision making. We followed these guiding principles closely throughout the project.

Best Practices Approach in Theory and Methodology of Conducting Cross-Cultural Research

With respect to the first principle, we took Gelfand and colleagues' guidelines for conducting cross-cultural research to heart in our theory and methodology (Gelfand et al., 2002). The theoretical perspectives and methodological approaches of Project 3535 were publicly announced in the early onset of the project in a publication (Korabik, Lero, & Ayman, 2003). Based on this publication, a summary of the project cornerstones is provided in the following few paragraphs. More details are presented in Chapters 2 and 13. We are proud that the theoretical model and research approach adopted by Project 3535 was named as the *best practice of work-family research* by Joplin, Francesco, and Lau (2012).

The original theoretical basis for Project 3535 was the model of the work-family interface by Frone and colleagues (e.g., Frone, Yardley, & Markle, 1997). As we proceeded, we updated this model based on the latest meta-analytic findings in the work-family literature. We also added several sociocultural variables to the model in an attempt to address emic concerns, such as gender-role ideology, vertical and horizontal individualism/collectivism, and monochronic/polychronic time orientation. In cross-cultural research, there is a danger of cultural reductionism—that is, attributing observed differences to culture only. To avoid that, we also added other macro-level institutional contextual variables: public policy support and service provision available to assist individuals to reconcile work and family responsibilities. In our policy analysis (Chapter 3), we focus on the range of policies and programs that affect gender roles, family income, and supports and opportunities for flexibility in integrating work and family responsibilities. Each local researcher(s) compiled information about demographic and labor force trends, relevant labor market and social policies, and provisions for services such as child care and elder care.

In a recent review of cross-national work-life research, Ollier-Malaterre and Foucreault (2017) cited Project 3535 as the only project that has systematically investigated the effects of both cultural and institutional context on work-family interface: "A handful of studies include selected cultural dimensions and structural factors (e.g., Poelmans & Sahibzada, 2004), yet none except the ongoing Project 3535 has offered an integrative framework (see Korabik, Lero, & Ayman, 2003)" (p. 20). The sociocultural context and policy variables in our research were conceptualized both as having *main effects* that directly influence demands and supports, as well as *moderators* that influence the magnitude of relationships between demands, supports, and WFC (see Figure 1.2).

Methodologically, we sought a balance between emic and etic orientations and allowed ideas from both exogenous and indigenous researchers to merge (Ayman, 1994). As recommended by Gelfand et al. (2002), when forming international

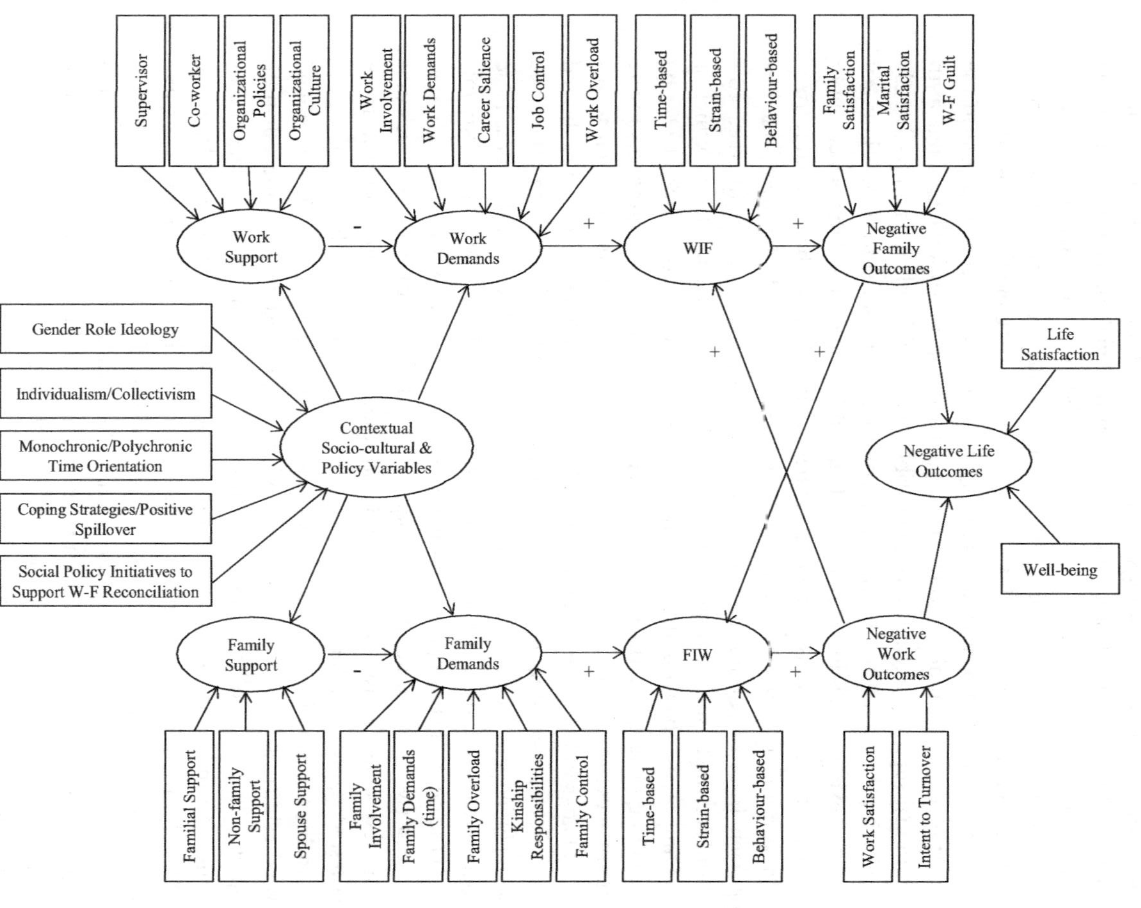

FIGURE 1.2 Initial conceptual model of Project 3535.

Source: Korabik, Lero, & Ayman, 2003, p. 292.

research teams, the members of the team represent countries or cultures that make unique contributions to the research question. Therefore, we developed an a priori classification of countries on two key dimensions that are critical for work-family research. In determining these dimensions, we paid close attention to two design requirements. First, the dimensions had to be discrete from one another as much as possible. Second, the classification of countries had to yield at least two contrasting groups that are different from another and yet homogeneous within themselves. The first dimension was societal "gender egalitarianism." For this, we used the Gender Development Index of UNDP as a general measure (United Nations Development Programme, 2003; www.undp.org). The second dimension is based on the support mechanisms available to reconcile paid and unpaid work. These range from institutional supports (e.g., government, labor, and social policies; family-friendly organizational policies and practices; and community supports) to noninstitutional ones (e.g., extended family support, paid helpers). We determined the placement of countries on the basis of the expert assessment of members of the research team.

Measurement invariance was another requirement of the best practices approach in cross-cultural research. Prior to distributing surveys for data collection, we made sure that our measures had conceptual equivalence, which is more important than linguistic equivalence (van de Vijver & Leung, 1997) by conducting focus group discussions in seven countries. The focus group data were extremely useful in making sure that concepts we used meant the same across cultures. Thanks to the insights gained from the focus group discussions, we adjusted some of our pre-existing measures by adding new items or modifying others. We also included some culture-specific explanations to qualify even the most basic concepts we used, such as spouse/partner, family, and work. We, therefore, followed the derived etic approach proposed by Berry (1997). Our survey was tested in at least two pilot studies in each country to make sure that items were relevant to the respondents, easy to understand and respond to. Measurement invariance was tested rigorously after the survey data were collected (see Chapter 2).

Finally, for sample equivalence (van de Vijver & Leung, 1997), we applied several criteria across cultures for respondent characteristics: (1) being full-time employee in white-collar occupations (not self-employed), (2) being married or having a partner living together who was also employed, (3) having at least one child at home living with parents. Criteria 1 and 2 had to be relaxed in some cases, where not all partners were employed and not all nonmanagerial employees were white collar. To minimize the confounding effect of industry, we recruited samples from the health, manufacturing, finance, and educational sectors, wherever possible. We stratified our sample for gender and job level so that our overall sample contained approximately equal numbers of men and women and managerial and nonmanagerial employees.

Overall, it is fair to state that the majority of our goals to achieve "best practices in theory and methodology of cross-cultural research" were met. The role of culture was stated a priori in our theoretical framework. We sampled countries theoretically, rather than just conveniently. We determined respondent characteristics also a priori and conducted sampling accordingly. We published our theoretical framework and methodological specifications in the second year of the project, before starting to collect data. This way, we were able to receive feedback from reviewers and readers and incorporate them into our design. We paid utmost care to make our measurement culturally appropriate (conceptually and linguistically), relevant and valid to represent the social and cultural context, and practical to respond to.

Designing the theory and methodology in accordance to the best practices guidelines paid off, for the most part. The theoretical framework (see Figure 1.2) was quite ambitious in scope (i.e., the number of variables included), but we managed to keep it comprehensive and yet parsimonious. There were times when inclusion or exclusion of variables in the model spurred heated discussions in the team (e.g., policy-oriented members wanted to have more variables capturing social policies). Thanks to the collaborative spirit in the team, we agreed upon a model that satisfied all of us after some minor compromises from each member. Despite our efforts to keep the survey to a manageable size, we ended up having a long survey (16 pages). But because we worked hard to make questions relevant and easy to comprehend, we had a high response rate and good quality data.

There were some outcomes we did not expect to obtain and some compromises we had to make. As examples of the unexpected outcomes, the grouping of countries was not fully supported and complete measurement invariance of some of the variables was not achieved. We made compromises in data collection, because we underestimated the time it would take to conduct a cross-cultural research with the best practices approach. We initially planned to administer the survey in two waves with the two questionnaires sent out approximately three months apart for two reasons: (1) to eliminate common method bias, and (2) to increase our ability to make causal inferences among study variables (Korabik et al., 2003). We were able to collect two-wave data in Turkey, India, and Canada. Because of the time it took to collect data from all countries in the first wave, we decided not to pursue the second-wave data collection.

According to our judgment, there was a relatively small gap between what we promised to achieve in this project as reported by Korabik and colleagues in 2003 and what we did achieve. Therefore, we propose that Project 3535 is an example of the best practices in theory and methodology in cross-cultural research.

Best Practices Approach in Team Processes in Cross-Cultural Research

Managing multicultural and multidisciplinary research teams like this one required knowledge transfer from the literature on best practices in managing diverse virtual teams in a business context (e.g., Lurey & Raisinghani, 2001). We tried to apply the best practices approach in Project 3535.

FIGURE 1.3 Team meeting in a conference in Athens, July 2006. From left to right: Ting-Pang, Steven, Ujvala, Zeynep, Roya, Karen, Donna, Leslie, Tripti.

Our guiding principles dictated that we operated in a value system of collaboration, egalitarianism, support, consultation, and consensus-oriented decision making. Our aim for the *team processes* was to create an environment of mutual learning, empowerment, and psychological safety. I am extremely proud to say that there was no single member or subgroup of members overpowering the team. We experienced shared leadership—Karen and I were the most active members to keep the team abreast and moving forward. Junior members or those from developing countries felt valued and appreciated (see Figure 1.3). Korabik and colleagues (2003) described the unique features of our project in the following way.

> One thing that distinguishes our project from most cross-national research studies on this topic is that almost all international research teams get their funding from one country and that country's researchers have the ultimate say regarding the study's design and measures. In such circumstances, there are often concerns about the domination of one country with resources over others, and an egalitarian and collaborative atmosphere may be jeopardized by the power of finance. We have tried our best to avoid this situation and to make our team a consultative and consensus driven entity. The coordinator is very attentive to maintaining both quality and representation

> in our consultations. All members have access to e-mail and we have set up a website to facilitate communication between team members.
>
> *(Korabik et al., 2003, p. 298)*

> Being in a multicultural team, with each researcher being indigenous to her/his country, was like living in "diversity," experiencing and learning about different cultures while researching and working together in a pan-cultural study. What we collectively learnt and individually gained was truly synergistic with moments of almost serendipitous insights with relaxed bonhomie and developing friendships thrown in. While working together was mutually beneficial in learning and contributing to our research, the different cultural ideologies and professional differences taught us, in real time, methods and tactics to work collaboratively and respectfully with one another.
>
> *(Project 3535 team member)*

We worked in a spirit of fun; our name Project 3535 even emerged from a funny episode during one of our workshops. It was the end of one of our two-day intensive project workshops in Istanbul. Some team members had to go to the airport to catch their flight. We were all very tired and worried too, because there were no taxis to take people to the airport due to heavy snow (see Figures 1.4 and 1.5). The best strategy was to call the security of Koç University campus and

FIGURE 1.4 Project meeting in Istanbul, February 2004. From left to right: Ujvala, Tripti, Karen, Artiawati, Roya, Zeynep

FIGURE 1.5 Project meeting in Istanbul, February 2004. From left to right: Michelle (Karen's daughter), Anne, Ting-Pang, Tripti, Roya, Karen, Steven, Zeynep, Artiawati

tell them to arrange taxis. I was busy getting meeting notes together and saying goodbye to people. I asked Roya (Roya Ayman) to call the campus security. Roya was at the end of the meeting room and I had to speak loud, so that she could hear me. I was saying, "Roya, dial 3535" (the extension of the office of security). There was a lot of cross-talk in the room and Roya could not hear me. I repeated several times. Finally, she said, "What? How can I dial Turkey Turkey from this phone?" We all broke into laughter! I said, "Not Turkey Turkey, 3535." The joke stayed with us and we decided to make the campus security's phone extension our project's name. Until now, this was the best-kept secret of our project. Many people asked us about it, thinking that the name represented a mysterious code or sophisticated ideology of some sort!

> *The first team meeting in Istanbul where I met all the team members is indelibly etched in my memory. Istanbul is such an amazing city and then to stay at the Villa on the Bosphorus was a great venue to meet the team from all over the world. The members of the team have become my friends and some have visited me in Australia. The focus on the cultural differences in work-family conflict has been a never-ending well of information and insights. I feel privileged to have met the men and women of the team and to be involved in such an ambitious and interesting project.*

> *I have always found the relationships between the members of the team very positive and supportive, particularly in terms of emotional connection and trust—which are often casualties of global teams. The main challenges involved the usual problems around virtual teams—limited opportunities to meet face to face, limitations of e-mail communication, coordination of tasks and meeting deadlines.*
>
> (*Project 3535 team member*)

There were certainly times when we experienced "process losses." Operating in a genuinely collaborative international research team may be costly. The biggest cost of making sure that there were opportunities for equal participation from *each member* at *each phase* of the project was time. The project took 14 years from inception to production of its major publication—this book. Coordination and maintenance was another challenge, because we did not have a dedicated "administrator" or "secretary." Lack of funding could have caused process losses, but we were lucky to have funding to hold four face-to-face project workshops over the years (three in Istanbul and one in Guelph) and to build a dedicated website to disseminate our findings as they emerged (http://www.workfamilyconflict.ca/). We were also able to hold project meetings during international conferences we attended. As a team, we experienced many positive and negative life events that influenced our own work-family balance, including deaths of loved ones, births, retirements, marriages, divorces, natural disasters, health problems, promotions, and so on. Because we were work-family researchers, we knew what these events meant for those who experienced them, and we supported each other by not putting performance pressure to deliver results. It was the right thing to do which we never regretted.

Lessons Learned from Project 3535

The key lesson learned from Project 3535 was that it was not only desirable, but also *possible* to apply the best practices approach in cross-cultural research. By best practices, we refer to both theoretical and methodological aspects as well as collaborative team processes in a cross-cultural project. This project has started with a burning question: "Is it possible to create a 'dream' cross-cultural research, which I truly want to be part of?" I think we came very close to answering this question with a firm "yes." To me, this was one of the best cross-cultural research projects I personally was involved in. It certainly consumed time and energy to manage the process, and it was far from being perfect. But we made every attempt to make it a "dream" project and (to me personally) it was worth the effort. Here are some lessons learned for future cross-cultural research.

Theoretical and Methodological Rigor Takes Time, but It Pays Off

Cross-cultural organizational research has gained ground over the previous half-century. The time of "safari researchers" visiting exotic places but staying aloof to the local culture has passed (Peterson, 2001). We now have accumulated a great deal of knowledge about cross-cultural differences to develop and test a priori hypotheses/models concerning the role of culture in observed phenomena. However, quality of the scales to measure cultural constructs has lagged behind (see Gelfand, Aycan, Erez, & Leung, in press). Our project suffered from lack of measurement invariance of cultural measures, which prevented us from rigorously testing our hypotheses concerning the role of culture in work-family interface. Our recommendation for future research is to pay extra attention to the measurement of cultural constructs. Research teams should not start data collection for the main study, unless they are absolutely sure that cultural measures work. Vas Taras's (2013) Culture Survey Catalogue comprising 121 instruments measuring dimensions of culture would be an excellent resource to refer to (http://www.vtaras.com/instcatalogues). Alternative measures of culture proposed by scholars in the recent special issue of *Journal of International Business Studies*, "What Is Culture and How Do We Measure It?", guest edited by Carpar, Devinney, Kirkman, and Caliguiri (2015), is also highly recommended.

Collaborative Team Processes Are the Essence of Good Cross-Cultural Research

It is hard to imagine a good cross-cultural research not fully utilizing the potential and wisdom of local researchers. We recommend that future cross-cultural research compose the team without a distinction between those in the center (i.e., the "brain"/"key decision makers") and those in the periphery (i.e., the "laborers"/"data collectors") (see Shils, 1975). Project 3535 benefited greatly from the collaborative learning team environment. There were several factors that acted as the glue in the team. First, face-to-face meetings increased the commitment of team members to the project and trust among them (Lurey & Raisinghani, 2001). We held four dedicated project meetings and several subgroup meetings during international conferences. In all these meetings, we spent considerable time socializing and going over team processes. We developed a nice habit of gift giving (almost like a ritual in every meeting); members gave each other small local gifts from their countries. I believe having a female-dominated team helped in attending to the social and interpersonal aspects of the team processes. Second, the dedicated website of the project (http://www.workfamilyconflict.ca/) gave us the "sense of presence" and "sense of growth." The website was updated every year with the activities of the team. It now reports 46 conference papers, five journal articles, one book chapter, and two technical reports produced out of Project 3535. Seeing these outcomes from the Project 3535 motivated members and increased commitment. We intuitively followed the guidelines of best practices in virtual teams provided by Lurey and Raisinghani (2001; see Appendix A. Virtual Teams Survey as a guideline). Cross-cultural research teams are destined to be virtual collaborative teams. Therefore, following these guidelines is highly recommended for future projects.

The Output of Project 3535

The question of "What should be the publication output of Project 3535?" spurred some discussions in the team. We jointly decided to publish our results in a book, rather than in several research articles. There were various reasons behind this decision. First, because the project took longer to complete than what we had expected, we did not want to keep the scholarly community waiting any longer by pushing for journal publications, which would have taken at least several more years. Second, we felt that our results had to be presented in a holistic and integrated way, which could only be achieved in a book format. The advantage of the book is that one can go back and forth among chapters to fill gaps, form links, and place discussions in the right context while reading each chapter. Although journal articles make research more visible and thus more cited, it is hard to integrate the findings published in separate articles. Third, we felt that it was necessary to give each team member a voice to tell a part of Project 3535's story. In journal articles, it is usually the lead author whose voice is most strongly heard. We did not want this to happen; we wanted to give each member freedom to frame and contextualize the results in his or her own scholarly style.

Conclusion

This book is divided into three parts. Part 1 introduces Project 3535, describes its methods and methodology, and presents the findings from the social policy analysis that formed Phase 1 of the project. Part 2 consists of nine chapters that summarize the results from Phase 2, which was aimed at delineating the emic context in each country through the collection of qualitative data via focus group discussions. Part 3 of the book includes eight chapters that center on the quantitative survey results that were obtained from Phase 3 of the project. The chapters in this part pertain to different aspects of how culture intersects with the work-family interface, including an examination of the universal versus culturally contingent antecedents and outcomes of WFC and positive spillover, as well as how these are related to issues like coping, social support, work-family guilt, gender, and context.

Because of its reliance on best practices in theory, methodology, and team processes, Project 3535 constitutes the most comprehensive and rigorous study of the work-family interface conducted to date. By collecting data from participants in 10 countries on four continents, we have been able to offer a more culturally contextualized understanding of the work-family interface, which adds tremendously to our knowledge about the applicability of work-family models outside of Western, industrialized cultures. The results of our research, as detailed in this book, provide important information for researchers, managers, human resource professionals, and policy makers.

References

Adams, J. (2012). Collaborations: The rise of research networks. *Nature, 490*(7420), S335–S336. doi:10.1038/490335a

Ayman, R. (1994, June). *Beyond imperialism in cross-cultural research: A jigsaw puzzle model.* Paper presented at the annual meeting of SIETAR, Ottawa.

Berry, J.W. (1997). An ecocultural approach to the study of cross-cultural industrial/organizational psychology. In P. C. Earley & M. Erez (Eds.), *New perspectives on international industrial/organizational psychology* (pp. 130–147). San Francisco: New Lexington Press.

Caprar, D. V., Devinney, T. M., Kirkman, B. L., & Caligiuri, P. (2015). Conceptualizing and measuring culture in international business and management: From challenges to potential solutions. *Journal of International Business Studies, 46*(9), 1011–1027.

Enderby, L. (2016). *Which countries have the best work-life balance?* Retrieved from https://www.weforum.org/agenda/2016/02/which-countries-have-the-best-work-life-balance/

Frone, M. R., Yardley, J. K., & Markle, K. S. (1997). Developing and testing an integrative model of the work-family interface. *Journal of Vocational Behavior, 50*(2), 145–167. doi:10.1006/jvbe.1996.1577

Gelfand, M.J., Aycan, Z., Erez, M. & Leung, K. (2017). Cross-cultural industrial organizational psychology and organizational behavior: A hundred-year journey. *Journal of Applied Psychology*

Gelfand, M. J., Raver, J. L., & Ehrhart, K. H. (2002). Methodological issues in cross-cultural organizational research. In S. G. Rogelberd (Ed.), *Handbook of research methods in industrial and organizational psychology* (pp. 216–246). Malden, MA: Blackwell.

Joplin, J. R. W., Francesco, A. M., & Lau, T. (2012, June). *The identification and use of etic and emic constructs in cross-cultural work-family research.* Paper presented at the Work-Family Researchers Network Conference, New York, NY.

Katz, J. S., & Martin, B. R. (1997). What is research collaboration? *Research Policy, 26*(1), 1–18. doi:10.1016/S0048-7333(96)00917-1

Korabik, K., Lero, D. S., & Ayman, R. (2003). A multi-level approach to cross cultural work-family research: A micro and macro perspective. *International Journal of Cross Cultural Management, 3*(3), 289–303. doi:10.1177/1470595803003003003

Lurey, J. S., & Raisinghani, M. S. (2001). An empirical study of best practices in virtual teams. *Information & Management, 38*(8), 523–544. doi:10.1016/S0378-7206(01)00074-X

Lyness, K. S., & Judiesch, M. K. (2014). Gender egalitarianism and work-life balance for managers: Multisource perspectives in 36 countries. *Applied Psychology, 63*(1), 96–129. doi:10.1111/apps.12011

Ollier-Malaterre, A., & Foucreault, A. (2017). Cross-national work-life research: Cultural and structural impacts for individuals and organizations. *Journal of Management, 43*(1), 1–26. doi:10.1177/0149206316655873.

Pal, S., & Saksvik, P. Ø. (2008). Work-family conflict and psychosocial work environment stressors as predictors of job stress in a cross-cultural study. *International Journal of Stress Management, 15*(1), 22–42. doi:10.1037/1072-5245.15.1.22

Peterson, M. F. (2001). International collaboration in organizational behavior research. *Journal of Organizational Behavior, 22*(1), 59–81. doi:10.1002/job.61

Poelmans, S., & Sahibzada, K. (2004). A multi-level model for studying the context and impact of work-family policies and culture in organizations. *Human Resource Management Review, 14*(4), 409–431. doi:10.1016.j.hrmr.2004.10.003

Shils, E. (1961). Centre and periphery. In Polanyi Festschrift Committee (Ed.), *The logic of personal knowledge: Essays presented to Michael Polanyi on his seventieth birthday, 11th March 1961* (pp. 117–131). London, UK: Routledge & Kegan Paul.

Shils, E. (1975). *Center and periphery: Essays in macrosociology*. Chicago, IL: The University of Chicago Press.

Spector, P. E., Cooper, C. L., Poelmans, S., Allen, T. D., O'Driscoll, M. I., Sanchez, J. I., . . . Lu, L. (2004). A cross-national comparative study of work-family stressors, working hours, and well-being: China and Latin America versus the Anglo world. *Personnel Psychology, 57*(1), 119–142. doi:10.1111/j.1744-6570.2004.tb02486.x

Tang, S. W., Siu, O. L., & Cheung, F. (2014). A study of work-family enrichment among Chinese employees: The mediating role between work support and job satisfaction. *Applied Psychology, 63*(1), 130–150. doi:10.1111/j.1464-0597.2012.00519.x

Taras, V. (2013). *Culture survey catalogue comprising 121 instruments measuring dimensions of culture*. Retrieved from http://www.vtaras.com/ Culture_Survey_Catalogue.pdf

United Nations Development Programme. (2003). *Human development report 2003: Millennium development goals: A compact among nations to end human poverty*. Retrieved from http://hdr.undp.org/sites/default/files/hdr_2003_summary_en.pdf

Van de Vijver, F., & Leung, K. (1997). *Methods and data analysis for cross-cultural research*. Thousand Oaks, CA: Sage.

Williams, S. (2013, March 15). *Team science—the science of collaborative research* [Web log post]. Retrieved from http://blogs.nature.com/soapboxscience/2013/03/15/team-science-the-science-of-collaborative-research/

Yang, L. Q., Spector, P. E., Sanchez, J. I., Allen, T. D., Poelmans, S., Cooper, C. L., . . . Woo, J. M. (2012). Individualism—collectivism as a moderator of the work demands—strains relationship: A cross-level and cross-national examination. *Journal of International Business Studies, 43*(4), 424–443. doi:10.1057/jibs.2011.58

2

METHODOLOGY, MEASUREMENT, AND COUNTRY CLASSIFICATION

Karen Korabik

This chapter discusses the methodology and measurement used for Project 3535. In making methodological decisions, we were guided by best practices in conducting cross-cultural organizational and work-family (W-F) research (Bagger & Love, 2010; Gelfand, Raver, & Erhart, 2002; Shaffer & Riordan, 2003). We employed multiple methodologies, both qualitative and quantitative (Greenhaus & Parasuraman, 1999), both emic and etic,[1] and that captured both micro- and macro-level processes (Gelfand et al., 2002). Moreover, we paid careful attention to sampling (Bagger & Love, 2010) and selected our constructs based on theory. Finally, we took steps to ensure the reliability and validity of both our qualitative and quantitative findings.

The data collection was conducted in three phases. The first phase, which was carried out concurrently with the second and third phases, consisted of a social policy analysis. The second phase consisted of the collection of qualitative data. In the third phase, quantitative survey data were collected.

Phase One: Social Policy Methodology

In the first phase of the project, an extensive social policy analysis was carried out under the direction of Donna Lero and Anne Bardoel to complement and contextualize the findings. Archival information on macro-level variables was compiled from national and international sources. These included data and analytical reports obtained from national statistical agencies as well as comparative data and reports from the Organization for Economic Cooperation and Development (OECD), the International Labour Organization (ILO), and the United Nations (UN). The national data sources provided comparable data about women's employment, education, and fertility, among other factors. Comparative reports and indices, such as the UN Human Development, Gender Development, and

Gender Empowerment Index were useful for identifying how the Project 3535 countries were similar and different. In particular, rankings from the UN Gender Empowerment Index and policy data that reflected the extent of institutional and organized community support available to working parents were used to identify discrete clusters among the Project 3535 countries.

Information about national policies relevant to work and family reconciliation was obtained with the assistance of Project 3535 researchers, who often were able to identify relevant policy documents and legislation. Additional sources included journal articles and book chapters that provided useful ways to theorize how policy data relate to welfare regimes, and gender equality commitments. This full compilation of policy data allowed a rich description and comparative policy analysis of the institutional factors that affect women's employment and the opportunities available for men and women to balance work and family responsibilities. Key domains included statistics on women's and mothers' education and labor force participation; dual-earner couples; gender equality policies; family income; government financial support to families; and work-family reconciliation policies including leave policies, child and elder care provision, and policies related to part-time work and flexible work scheduling. Labor market and welfare policies that constrain or expand women's and men's involvement in paid employment and in unpaid family work can be theorized as providing the critical political-economic and social contexts that frame both employment conditions and the experience of the W-F interface.

In conducting this analysis we tried to strike a balance between emic and etic concerns. For example, information regarding the social policies in each country was collected on a country-by-country basis and used both to help understand the specific situation that existed in each country and for purposes of cross-country comparisons. In addition, the multilevel design of our research allowed us not only to use the social policy data to examine macro-level effects, but also to look at cross-level effects (i.e., whether national policy and aspects of culture, such as gender-role ideology and collectivist vs. individualistic values, moderated the relationship between micro- and macro-level variables). This is something that few, if any, other studies have been able to do. The results from the social policy analysis are reported in Chapter 3.

Phase Two: Qualitative Methodology

In the second phase of the project, qualitative data were collected to elucidate the primary themes that were pertinent to the W-F interface in each country. The qualitative data served several purposes. First, they helped to identify some of the emic issues that were unique to particular cultural contexts. Second, they were useful in guiding the creation of supplemental items to be included in the survey. Third, they complemented the survey findings by giving more depth to their interpretation.

TABLE 2.1 Number of focus group participants by gender and country.

Country	*Women*	*Men*
Canada	15	5
India	16	6
Indonesia	10	–
Israel	32	–
Turkey	12	–
Taiwan	11	5
United States	10	8

Qualitative data were collected in all countries except for Australia, Spain, and China. It was felt that qualitative data collection could be dispensed with in Australia and Spain because comparable studies recently had been conducted there. Semi-structured interviews with men and women in dual-career couples had been carried out in Spain in 1999 (Poelmans, 2001) and 2002–2003 (Poelmans, 2004) and an extensive qualitative study of employed mothers in Australia had been done in 2000 (Pocock, 2001). Qualitative data were not collected in China because the survey had been fully developed by the time that China joined Project 3535.

The qualitative data were obtained via focus groups (Kruger & Casey, 2000). The number of focus group participants from each country is displayed in Table 2.1. In most countries, data were obtained from both men and women, but in some countries (i.e., Indonesia, Israel, and Turkey), only women were sampled. Each focus group consisted of about four to six same-sex participants. A face-to-face focus group format was utilized in all countries except Canada. In Canada, an online procedure was used whereby a moderator posted a series of questions to a website. Participants were asked to go online for 10 minutes each day for a one-week period at any time that was convenient to them and to respond to the moderator's questions and to comments posted by the other focus group members (see McElwain, Chappell, & Korabik, 2005, for a complete description of the methodology used).

A semi-structured format was used where the moderator focused the conversation around certain topics, using probes where necessary. Examples of the types of questions that were asked are:

1) How do you handle your work and family responsibilities?
2) What factors contribute to your feelings of role overload in the work and family domains?
3) In what ways does work interfere with your family responsibilities? What are the key reasons for that? What are the key outcomes of it?
4) In what ways does family interfere with your work responsibilities? What are the key reasons for that? What are the key outcomes of it?

5) When there is difficulty balancing work and family life, how do you cope with it?
6) What are your primary work and family roles? To what extent are your roles integrated or compartmentalized? What strategies do you use to maintain the boundaries between your roles?
7) How hard/easy is it to combine work with being a parent? Does it make a difference whether one is a mother or father? What is the ideal norm of motherhood in your country?
8) What social supports do you use to try to attain W-F balance? What are the advantages and disadvantages of using different types of supports?
9) In what ways does work enhance or enrich your family life? In what ways does family life enhance or enrich your work life?
10) Are there any changes that could help reduce your WFC at home? In the workplace? What changes would make life better for working parents?
11) Are there any specific workplace or government policies that particularly help working parents reduce WFC?

We employed several of the procedures that Lincoln and Guba (1985) have proposed for assuring the reliability and validity (i.e., the credibility, dependability, confirmability, and trustworthiness) of interview/focus group data. First, because the researchers were indigenous to the cultures studied and had spent extensive time living in them, the criteria of prolonged engagement was satisfied. Second, purposive sampling was used to obtain information-rich data from a small number of select informants in each country. Third, team members practiced reflexivity by reflecting upon and acknowledging any potential biases they might have held. Fourth, thick descriptions were collected from each informant. Fifth, an audit trail was left by having all data recorded and transcribed. Sixth, the results were triangulated by comparing them to what was known from other sources (referential adequacy materials) and to the quantitative survey results. Lastly, peer debriefing was undertaken through the sharing of findings with other team members. The data were analyzed by identifying important themes supplemented by illustrative narrative quotes. The results pertaining to the qualitative data for the individual Project 3535 countries are presented in Part 2 of this book.

Phase Three: Survey Methodology

Participants

The participants for Phase 3 of the project were married/cohabiting parents with at least one child under the age of 21 living at home with them. They were employed by organizations (i.e., not self-employed) in a wide variety of industries. They came from 10 countries: Australia (AU), Canada (CA), China (CN), India (IN), Indonesia (ID), Israel (IL), Spain (ES), Taiwan (TW), Turkey (TR), and the

United States (US). In countries with subcultures, following the procedure used by GLOBE (House, Hanges, Javidian, Dorfman, & Gupta, 2004) sampling was generally done from among individuals in the economically dominant subculture. Exceptions to this were Israel, where both Jewish and Arabic participants were sampled, and Canada, where 25% of the sample was Francophone. Table 2.2 presents demographic information on the survey sample by country.

The total sample consisted of 2,830 individuals. Individual country samples ranged from 150 to 561 with an average of 283 participants per country. This compares favorably with the data from Phase 2 of the GLOBE study where some countries had as few as 27 participants and the average number of participants per country was 251 (House et al., 2004).

To examine whether there were between-country differences in the type of participants sampled, analyses of variance were computed with Country as the independent variable and various demographics as the dependent variables. There was a significant difference among the countries in the job level of the participants in their samples, $F(9, 2820) = 11.17, p < .001$. The samples from India and Turkey had a significantly lower percentage of managers than those from Indonesia, Israel, and Spain. There was a significant difference among countries in the organizational tenure of employees, $F(9, 2757) = 46.33, p < .001$. Organizational tenure was significantly higher in China than it was in all other countries. By contrast, organizational tenure was significantly lower in Turkey than it was in India, Indonesia, Spain, and the United States, and also significantly lower in Taiwan than it was in Indonesia and the United States.

There was a significant difference among countries in the gender of the participants, $F(9, 2797) = 13.66, p < .001$. The samples from Taiwan and the United States had a significantly lower percentage of men than did those from Canada, India, Israel, and Turkey. There was a significant difference among countries in the age of participants, $F(9, 2817) = 13.47, p < .001$. Participants in the United States were significantly older than those in all countries except Australia and Canada.

TABLE 2.2 Sample demographics by country.

Country	*N*	*% men*	*% manager*	*Age (mean)*	*# children (mean)*	*Organizational Tenure (mean)*
Australia	200	41	47	40.37	2.1	8.36
Canada	315	62	50	39.90	2.0	10.08
China	240	48	49	39.24	1.0	18.79
India	561	48	36	37.30	1.6	10.13
Indonesia	306	44	58	37.66	1.9	11.79
Israel	229	50	58	38.14	2.9	11.18
Spain	150	44	60	38.44	2.0	11.13
Taiwan	281	28	38	38.74	1.7	8.08
Turkey	325	51	36	38.15	1.7	7.22
USA	223	25	46	42.86	2.2	12.23
Total	2830	45	40	38.81	1.9	10.55

Countries differed significantly in the number of children participants had, $F(9, 2818) = 66.10, p < .001$. Participants in China had significantly fewer children than those in all other countries, whereas those in Israel had significantly more children than those in all other countries. In addition, participants in India had significantly fewer children than those in Australia, Canada, and the United States. Participants in Turkey and Taiwan also had significantly fewer children than those in the United States.

Procedure

Construct Specification

We began the process of constructing the survey by specifying the general constructs that were theoretically important to the research. This was done during a team meeting in Istanbul, Turkey and via e-mail exchanges.

Relevant constructs were chosen based on the currently available literature and models pertaining to the W-F interface. We first chose WFC and W-F positive spillover as our focal constructs. Then, we selected a range of constructs that had been identified in the literature as being important antecedents and outcomes of these constructs. The antecedents included work and family overload and involvement, job and family control, and social support. The outcomes included job, family, and life satisfaction; turnover intent; and psychological distress. Next, we selected a number of constructs related to cultural values. These included vertical and horizontal individualism and collectivism, gender-role ideology, and time management orientation (i.e., polychronicity).

Selection of Specific Measures and Items

Most measures that were selected for inclusion in the survey were derived-etic in nature. That is, they had been used successfully in prior W-F research and their reliability and validity had been established for the North American context. In general, many of the measures included in this study can be categorized as imposed-etic (Berry, 1997), as they are standardized scales that were designed and validated in one of the participating countries, such as the United States, Israel, or Spain, and were administered in other countries. The preliminary survey went through several iterations. Due to concerns about survey length, items were deleted to create shorter versions of several scales, and where possible, the instrument was consolidated by eliminating item redundancies.

Some new items were added to established scales to address emic concerns that were raised by individual team members or that came out of the qualitative data collected as part of Phase 2, making them more derived-etic (Berry, 1997) in nature. An example of this is our social support measure, which was modified to distinguish between nuclear and extended family support. In addition, some new measures were added to the survey (e.g., coping strategies, W-F guilt) to capture frequent themes arising in the focus group data. This helped to make the measures more culturally relevant (Berry, Poortinga, Segall, & Dasen, 1992).

A preliminary English version of the survey was created during a second team meeting in Istanbul, Turkey. This version was then reviewed by the individual team members to ensure that the wording of the items, the format, and the instructions and response format were appropriate for the respondents in each country.

Translation

If necessary, the final English version of the survey was translated by a bilingual individual into the native language of each of the participating countries. Each team member was responsible for the translation process in their own country. In all, the survey was translated from English into the following languages: French (Canadian), Chinese, Hebrew, Hindi, Bahasa Indonesian, Spanish, and Turkish. These surveys were then independently back-translated into English by individuals who were fluent in both English and the particular country's native language (van de Vijver & Leung, 1997), with any differences being resolved through discussion (Brislin, 1980). There were two exceptions to this. In India, some of the data was collected only in English and the remainder was collected using an English version of the survey with a side by side Hindi translation. In Indonesia, no back-translation procedure was used.

Pilot Studies

The surveys were pilot tested in every country except China. Pilot testing was carried out in stages. First, the team members from each country completed the survey themselves and noted any potential problems. Next, a small number of individuals from each country ($N < 50$ per country) completed the survey and provided feedback on the experience. The surveys were then fine-tuned based on this feedback and the results of internal consistency reliability analyses on the scales. A second pilot study was then conducted in which the revised survey was administered to a small number of participants ($N < 50$ per country) either in a paper-and-pencil or online format depending on the country. Internal consistency reliability analyses were conducted, and correlations among constructs were computed to provide preliminary evidence of validity.

Collection of Survey Data

For the primary data collection, researchers in each country were responsible for recruiting participants following a standardized sampling framework that was designed to result in a large, heterogeneous sample of at least 200 participants per country from a broad range of companies and industries. A stratified sampling technique was used to ensure representation by both men and women and both managers and nonmanagers. A variety of strategies was used to recruit participants (e.g., partnering with organizational representatives or alumni associations, hiring a survey research firm). Sometimes this was supplemented by snowball or convenience sampling. In Australia, Canada, and the United States married parents comprise a minority of those in the workforce. To facilitate data collection in these countries, all employees of participating organizations were surveyed, but only married parents who met the study criteria were included in the sample reported in this volume.

Participants in China, Indonesia, India, Israel, Turkey, and Taiwan filled out the survey in paper-and-pencil format. Participants in Australia, Canada, Spain, and the United States were given the choice of completing the survey either online or by paper and pencil. Survey response rates ranged from 55% in Taiwan to between 78% and 90% for India, Indonesia, Israel, and the United States. However, due to the procedures used to recruit samples and the methodological restrictions imposed by ethics committees, precise response rates were not able to be calculated for several countries (i.e., Australia, Canada, Spain, and Turkey).

The survey (see Appendix) was comprised of a variety of multiple- and single-item measures that assessed WFC and positive spillover, their antecedents and outcomes in the work and family domains, cultural and other moderating variables, and demographic and contextual factors.

Multi-Item Measures

The specific multi-item measures included in the survey are summarized in Table 2.3 and described in the text following. Unless otherwise specified, all scale items were rated using a six-point scale ranging from 1 (*strongly disagree*) to 6 (*strongly agree*) with higher scores indicating higher levels of the construct of interest.

TABLE 2.3 Multi-Item Measures

Construct	*Source*	*Subscales*	*# items*
W-F Conflict	Carlson, Kacmar, & Williams (2000)	Time based WIF	3
		Time based FIW	3
		Strain based WIF	3
		Strain based FIW	3
W-F Positive Spillover	Grzywacz & Marks (2000)	WTFS	4
		FTWS	4
Ease of Balancing	Project 3535 team		5
Work Overload	4 items from Peterson et al. (1995); 1 item from Project 3535 team		5
Family Overload	4 items adapted from Peterson et al. (1995); 1 item from Project 3535 team		5

(*Continued*)

TABLE 2.3 (Continued)

Construct	*Source*	*Subscales*	*# items*
Job Control	Centre for Families, Work, & Well-Being, University of Guelph		5
Family Control	Adapted from job control scale		5
Job Involvement	Frone & Rice (1987)		4
Family Involvement	Frone & Rice (1987)		4
Social Support	Antani (2007)	7 sources	9
Job Satisfaction	Hackman & Oldham (1975)		2
Family Satisfaction	3 items adapted from Hackman & Oldham (1975); 1 item from Project 3535 team		4
Satisfaction with Role Performance	Project 3535 team		6
Life Satisfaction	Diener, Emmons, Larsen, & Griffin (1985)		5
Intention to Turnover	Camman, Firchman, Jenkins, & Klesh (1979, as cited in Cook et al., 1981)		3
Psychological Well-Being	Santor & Coyne (1997)		9
W-F Guilt	McElwain (2008)	WIFG FIWG	4 3
Vertical Individualism	Singelis, Triandis, Bhawuk, & Gelfand (1995)		7
Vertical Collectivism	4 items adapted from Triandis & Gelfand (1998) and 1 from Singelis et al. (1995)		5
Horizontal Individualism	2 items adapted from Singelis et al. (1995); 3 items adapted from Triandis & Gelfand (1998)	at home at work	5 5
Horizontal Collectivism	Adapted from Singelis et al. (1995)	at home at work	8 8
Gender-role Ideology	5 items from Treas & Widmer (2000); 6 items from Mason & Bumpass (1975); 5 items from Project 3535 team		16
Time Orientation	Bluedorn, Kalliath, Strube, & Martin (1999)		5

W-F Conflict

Four constructs were used from Carlson, Kacmar, and Williams' (2000) scale: time- and strain-based work interference with family (TB & SB WIF) and time- and strain-based family interference with work (TB & SB FIW). The behavior-based subscales were not included because the conceptualization and psychometric properties of the behavior-based conflict dimension has been questioned (Milkie, Denny, Kendig, & Schieman, 2010).

W-F Positive Spillover

This was measured by two four-item subscales from a scale developed by Grzywacz and Marks (2000). One subscale assessed work-to-family positive spillover (WTFS) and the other assessed family-to-work positive spillover (FTWS). The response scale ranged from 1 (*never*) to 5 (*always*) with higher scores indicating more positive spillover.

Ease of Balancing

Five items were constructed by the Project 3535 team to assess the ease or difficulty of balancing the work role with different family roles (i.e., spouse/partner, child care, household duties, care of parent/parents-in-law, and care of extended family). Participants responded using a scale ranging from 1 (*very difficult*) to 6 (*very easy*), with an option for not applicable.

Work and Family Overload

Peterson et al.'s (1995) four-item scale was used. This scale was developed using a sample from 21 countries and had previously been employed in cross-cultural research. A fifth item was added by the Project 3535 team. An adaptation of Peterson et al.'s (1995) four-item work overload scale was used to assess family overload. A fifth item was added by the Project 3535 team.

Job and Family Control

Job control was measured using an adaptation of an unpublished five-item measure of job control developed by the Centre for Families, Work, and Well-Being at the University of Guelph. Family control was measured using a five-item scale of family control based on the job control measure.

Job and Family Involvement

Job and family involvement were each assessed with four items from Frone and Rice (1987).

Social Support

The Social Support measure (Antani, 2007, see Appendix in Chapter 16) assessed the support received from each of seven sources (i.e., partner/spouse; child(ren); parents/parents-in-law; paid household helper; neighbors, relatives, and friends; job supervisor; and coworkers/subordinates). The amount of received support from each source was rated for nine issues in both the work and family domains including: child care, help with household tasks, and work-related duties, using a four-point scale ranging from 1 (*Never*) to 4 (*Frequently*), with an option for items that were not applicable.

Job and Family Satisfaction

Job satisfaction was examined using two items from the Job Diagnostics Survey (Hackman & Oldham, 1975). For family satisfaction, three items were adapted from Hackman and Oldham's (1975) job satisfaction measure. A fourth item was created by the Project 3535 research team.

Satisfaction with Role Performance

Four questions were asked regarding respondents' degree of satisfaction in their roles as: (1) an employee, (2) spouse/partner, (3) parent, and (4) caregiver to parents and in-laws. Two additional questions asked about their marital/relationship satisfaction and their satisfaction with the care of their physical and mental health needs. The response scale ranged from 1 (*very dissatisfied*) to 5 (*very satisfied*).

Life Satisfaction

A five-item scale by Diener, Emmons, Larsen, and Griffin (1985) was used to measure life satisfaction.

Turnover Intent

Turnover intent was assessed by three items adapted from Camman, Firchman, Jenkins, and Klesh (1979, as cited in Cook, Hepworth, Wall, & Warr, 1981).

Psychological Well-Being

Psychological well-being was examined using the short version of the Center for Epidemiologic Studies Depression Scale (Santor & Coyne, 1997). This nine-item scale is a self-report measure of depression. The response options were either (0) *none of the time to a little of the time (less than 1 to 2 days)* or (1) *a moderate amount of time to most of the time (3–7 days)*, with higher scores indicating higher levels of psychological distress.

Work-Family Guilt

The Work-Family Guilt Scale (WFGS; McElwain, 2008) assessed the intensity of the negative feeling associated when an individual was unable to fulfill incompatible work and family roles. This measure included seven items; four of these assessed work interference with family guilt (WIFG) and three assessed family interference with work guilt (FIWG).

Individualism-Collectivism

This construct was measured by six subscales. Vertical individualism was assessed with seven items adapted from Singelis, Triandis, Bhawuk, and Gelfand (1995). Vertical collectivism was assessed with five items, four adapted from Triandis and Gelfand (1998) and one from Singelis et al. (1995). Horizontal individualism and collectivism were measured separately in relation to the home and work contexts. Horizontal individualism at home and at work consisted of five items each. Two of these were adapted from Singelis et al. (1995) and three were adapted from Triandis and Gelfand (1998). Horizontal collectivism at home and at work consisted of eight items each. These items were adapted from Singelis et al. (1995).

Gender-Role Ideology

Gender-role attitudes were assessed with 16 items. Five were from Treas and Widmar (2000), six were from Mason and Bumpass (1975), and five were added by the Project 3535 team. The scale was scored so that higher scores indicated a more egalitarian gender-role ideology.

Time Orientation

Time management orientation was assessed via five items from the Inventory of Polychronic Values, modified to refer to individual values as suggested by Bluedorn, Kalliath, Strube, and Martin (1999). Higher scores indicated a more polychronic time orientation.

Single-Item Measures

Work and Family Hours

Participants were asked to indicate the number of hours that they spent per week on: (1) work-related duties, (2) caring for child(ren), (3) helping a parent/parent-in-law, and (4) household related duties.

Opinions About Gender Roles

Two questions were used to compare participants' opinions about gender roles with those of the majority of the people in their country. The first was: "How similar or different are your personal opinions about men and women's roles from the opinions of the majority of people in your country?" The response scale for this item ranged from 1 (*very dissimilar*) to 6 (*very similar*). The second was: "How much stress do you feel due to the fact that your opinions are similar or dissimilar from those of the majority of people in your country?" The response scale for this item ranged from 1 (*none*) to 6 (*a great deal*).

Coping Strategies

This variable was measured by a shortened version of a scale developed by Somech and Drach-Zahavy (2007) specifically to demonstrate how individuals manage work and family roles. The eight individual items each assessed one of eight subcategories of coping strategy: *super at home* ("I insist on doing, on my own, all family duties perfectly, from the least important to the most important."); *good enough at home* ("I lower my performance of family responsibilities to a less than perfect level."); *delegation at home* ("I manage my family duties by delegating some to others."); *priorities at home* ("I don't take responsibility for family duties that are not important to me."); *super at work* ("I insist on doing on my own all my work duties perfectly from the least important to the most important."); *good enough at work* ("I don't volunteer to undertake what I consider extra work duties."); *delegation at work* ("I manage my work duties by delegating some to others."); and *priorities at work* ("I eliminate work duties that are the least important.").

Satisfaction With Social Support

The social support scale developed by Antani (2007) also contained a question asking: "In general, how satisfied are you with the support you receive from . . .?" Satisfaction with support was assessed as it pertained to each of seven sources (i.e., partner/spouse; child(ren); parents/parents-in-law; paid household helper; neighbors, relatives, and friends; job supervisor; and coworkers/subordinates). The response scale ranged from 1 (*very dissatisfied*) to 5 (*very satisfied*) with an option for items that were not applicable.

Helpfulness of Organizational Policies

The effects of nine organizational policies designed to enhance flexibility, support dependent care, and promote employee health were examined. These were: (1) flextime, (2) the opportunity to work reduced hours, (3) telecommuting, (4) emergency absence, (5) maternity/parental leave beyond legislation, (6) leave to care for sick family member, (7) on-site child care facilities or fee subsidies, (8) provision of health insurance, and (9) availability of on-site health facilities. Policy users rated how helpful each policy was for improving their work-family balance on a scale ranging from 1 (*not at all helpful*) to 5 (*extremely helpful*). Nonusers (those who had not used the policy or for whom it was not available) rated how helpful each policy would have been for improving their W-F balance on a similar scale.

Satisfaction With Policies

Two single-item questions were used to assess policy satisfaction. One asked how satisfied respondents were with the family-friendly organizational policies in their company. The other asked respondents how satisfied they were with the family-friendly government policies in their country. The response scale for both of these questions ranged from 1 (*very dissatisfied*) to 5 (*very satisfied*).

Demographics

Single-item questions were collected to assess variables such as age, gender, ethnicity, years of residence in country, education, income, importance of religious beliefs, number and ages of children, family living arrangements, spouse/partner's employment status, job type (managerial or nonmanagerial), length of job and organizational tenure, job schedule (full- or part-time), and size of company.

Measurement Equivalence/Invariance

Procedure

An analysis of measurement equivalence/invariance (ME/I) of the multiple item measures was carried out to ensure that the measures were equivalent in meaning across cultures. In the absence of ME/I, comparisons between cultures may be meaningless because one cannot determine if any differences found are due to differing psychometric responses to the scale items instead of to true differences on the construct of interest (Chueng & Rensvold, 2002). Therefore, it is now commonly accepted that ME/I be verified prior to doing cross-national comparisons (Milfont & Fischer, 2010; Oreg et al., 2008).

ME/I for culture was established through multisample confirmatory factor analysis. In cross-cultural research, the process involves the imposition of increasingly stringent constraints on a measurement model (Steenkamp & Baumgartner, 1998). Although many different types of ME/I exist, only configural and weak (metric) invariance (Steenkamp & Baumgartner, 1998) were assessed, as they were sufficient preconditions for examining the structural relationships among the constructs cross-culturally (Oreg et al., 2008).

Configural invariance demonstrates that the data from each sample have the same factor structure. This indicates that the participants from the different groups (i.e., cultures) conceptualize the construct in the same way (Milfont & Fischer, 2010). Weak (or metric) invariance indicates that the magnitude of all factor loadings (or weights) is equivalent across cultures. If metric invariance exists it shows that participants from the different groups are responding similarly to the items (Milfont & Fischer, 2010). That is, the association of each item with the underlying latent constructs is equal across samples. In other words, how closely each item represents the underlying construct does not vary across samples.

Following Coovert and Craiger (2000) evidence for model fit was determined by examining the χ^2, the CFI ($> .9$), and the RMSEA ($< .08$). Less emphasis was put on the χ^2 value, however, because it is almost always significant in studies with large samples, as is the case in cross-cultural research.

In addition to each model having good fit, the fit for the weak model should not be significantly worse than that of the configural model. Traditionally, the difference in fit between the two models is assessed using the Likelihood Ratio Test (the difference in $\chi 2$ between the two nested models). However, researchers have demonstrated that differences in $\chi 2$ are dependent on sample size in the same way that the chi-square fit statistic itself is (Kelloway, 1995). Cross-cultural research deals with very large sample sizes, so the $\Delta\chi^2$ statistic is almost always significant in cross-cultural studies, making it almost impossible to establish ME/I if this goodness-of-fit criterion is used. Because of this, many authors have proposed alternatives. One of the most widely used is the ΔCFI. According to Oreg et al. (2008), a value of $\leq .01$ indicates that invariance exists and a value $> .02$ indicates a lack of invariance. Values between .01 and .02 suggest that some differences may exist. Following Cigularov and Thronton (2011) we adopted the criteria of $\Delta CFI \leq .02$.

Results

The ME/I of some measures (i.e., job satisfaction) was not assessed due to their having too few items (< 3) per factor. In addition, the ME/I of the psychological well-being measure was not assessed due to the restricted range of its response format.

ME/I at the configural level was obtained for the WFC and W-F guilt scales as originally conceptualized (see Table 2.4). For other constructs, however, modification indices suggested that model fit could be improved if some items were eliminated from some of the scales. Based on this, the following changes were made. One item each was dropped from WTFS and FTWS subscales of the positive spillover measure. The items added by the Project 3535 team to the work and family overload scales were dropped. In addition, one item from Peterson et al. (1995) was eliminated from the work overload scale. One item was dropped from the vertical collectivism scale ("It is important to me that I respect the decisions of groups that I feel that I belong to"). One item was dropped from the horizontal individualism at home subscale ("My personal identity, independent of others, is very important to me").

In addition, due to failure to initially find configural ME/I for some constructs, exploratory factor analysis was used to try to find alternative factor structures for those constructs. Based on the results of these analyses, items from scales with similar meanings were combined to create new measures of particular constructs. For example, a six-item family satisfaction composite variable was created using

TABLE 2.4 Measurement Equivalence/Invariance for Culture

Construct	*Subscales*	*Configural*				*Weak*				
		χ^2 *(df)*	*CFI*	*RMSEA*	*ME/I*	χ^2 *(df)*	*CFI*	*RMSEA*	*ΔCFI*	*ME/I*
W-F Conflict	TB & SB WIF	335.8 (80)	.964	.034	Yes	424.8 (116)	.957	.031	.007	Yes
	TB & SB FIW	296.3 (80)	.967	.032		414.3 (116)	.955	.031	.012	
W-F Positive Spillover	WTFS- 3 items FTWS- 3 items	142.8 (70)	.977	.02	Yes	211.6 (16)	.966	.019	.011	Yes
Ease of Balancing		50.4 (20)	.993	.023	Yes	305.9 (56)	.944	.04	.049	No
Work Overload	3 items	33.0 (10)	.996	.029	Yes	207.3 (37)	.973	.041	.023	Marginal
Family Overload	4 items	60.1 (10)	.992	.04	Yes	221.9 (37)	.971	.042	.021	Marginal
Job Control		119.8 (30)	.969	.03	Yes	289.9 (66)	.922	.036	.047	No
Family Control		104.0 (40)	.975	.024	Yes	210.65 (76)	.948	.025	.027	No
Job Involvement		24.7 (10)	.991	.023	Yes	144.8 (37)	.933	.032	.058	No
Family Involvement		30.5 (10)	.992	.027	Yes	155.1 (37)	.956	.034	.036	No
Family Satisfaction	6 items	325.8 (70)	.952	.037	Yes	405.6 (115)	.945	.03	.007	Yes
Satisfaction with Role Performance		251.7 (80)	.959	.028	Yes	399.2 (125)	.935	.028	.024	Marginal
Life Satisfaction		450.4 (55)	.93	.05	Yes	511.7 (87)	.924	.04	.005	Yes
Turnover Intent		22 (10)	.99	.01	Yes	215.6 (37)	.97	.08	.02	Marginal
W-F Guilt	WIFG FIWG	474.3 (130)	.957	.031	Yes	623.1 (175)	.944	.031	.013	Yes
Vertical Individualism	7 items	587.8 (90)	.859	.044	No	990.6 (114)	.761	.046	.098	No

(*Continued*)

TABLE 2.4 (Continued)

Construct	*Subscales*	*Configural*				*Weak*				
		χ^2 *(df)*	*CFI*	*RMSEA*	*ME/I*	χ^2 *(df)*	*CFI*	*RMSEA*	*ΔCFI*	*ME/I*
Vertical Collectivism	4 items	48. (10)	.955	.037	Yes	91. (37)	.936	.023	.019	Yes
Horizontal Individualism	at home 4 item	13.6 (10)	.997	.011	Yes	88.2 (37)	.963	.022	.034	No
	at work 5 item	19.1 (16)	.998	.01	Yes	89.1 (44)	.977	.021	.021	Marginal
Horizontal Collectivism	at home	453.3 (160)	.946	.025	Yes	556.56 (223)	.937	.023	.009	Yes
	at work	499.4 (150)	.933	.03	Yes	3434.9 (285)	.4	.03	.053	No
Gender-role Ideology	GRI1- 3 items GRI2- 3 items GRI3- 3 items	646.6 (220)	.95	.027	Yes	912.8 (274)	.931	.028	.019	Yes
Time Orientation		177.7 (40)	.952	.035	Yes	692.1 (76)	.787	.054	.165	No
Supervisor Support for Work	4 items	34.1 (22)	.997	.015	Yes	118.9 (46)	.981	.026	.016	Yes
Coworker/Subordinate Support for Work	4 items	25.3 (10)	.995	.023	Yes	119.7 (37)	.973	.028	.022	Marginal

three of the four items from the original family satisfaction measure ("I frequently think I would like to change my family situation" was eliminated) and three items from the satisfaction with role performance measure (i.e., spouse/partner, parent, and marriage/relationship). Similarly, a four-item intent to turnover composite was created from the three original intent to turnover items plus one reverse coded item from the job satisfaction scale. Moreover, two four-item composites were created that pertained to social support for work-related issues from supervisors and coworkers/subordinates, respectively.

Seven items were dropped from the gender-role ideology scale: three from the Mason and Bumpass (1975) measure, two from the Treas and Widmar (2000) measure, and two from those added by the Project 3535 team. The remaining nine items were found to load onto three factors, each of which consisted of three items. The first factor (GRI1) pertained to issues concerning division of labor (i.e., beliefs that husbands should be employed, whereas wives should stay at home). The second factor (GRI2) consisted of three items from Mason and Bumpass (1975) regarding the importance of men's careers. Items on the third factor (GRI3) concerned the issue of women's employment being detrimental to family well-being.

In addition, the modification indices indicated that model fit for some of the constructs could be improved by correlating the error terms for some items. This was done only if the items were conceptually related and involved some redundancy in their content. This procedure was used for the following variables: FTWS positive spillover, family overload, job and family control, job and family involvement, supervisor and coworker support, family satisfaction, turnover intent, life satisfaction, satisfaction with role performance, vertical individualism and collectivism, horizontal individualism at work, horizontal collectivism at home and at work, and gender-role ideology. Each modification that resulted in a significant improvement in model fit based on the Sartorra-Bentler-scaled chi-square difference test was retained in the final CFA model.

After these modifications were made, configural ME/I was found for all of the variables except vertical individualism (see Table 2.4). Moreover, as Table 2.4 shows, weak (metric) ME/I was found for the following variables: WFC, positive spillover, family and life satisfaction, W-F guilt, vertical collectivism, horizontal collectivism at home, supervisor support for work, and gender-role ideology.

Additionally, some of the variables were deemed to have marginal weak ME/I because their ΔCFI values just slightly exceeded the .02 cut-off. These included work and family overload, satisfaction with role performance, turnover intent, horizontal individualism at work, and coworker/subordinate support for work. Even once the modifications had been made, however, the following variables did not meet the criteria for weak ME/I: ease of balancing, job and family control, job and family involvement, vertical individualism, horizontal individualism at home, horizontal collectivism at work, and time orientation. Caution should be used when interpreting the findings from analyses using these variables as one cannot differentiate whether any between-group differences found are due to culture instead of to the fact that respondents from different cultures attribute different meanings to the survey items.

Reliability of Measures

In order to assess internal consistency, Cronbach alphas were calculated for all of the multi-item constructs. The results can be found in Table 2.5. For the total sample, the alphas were > .67 except for four constructs (i.e., vertical individualism and collectivism, horizontal individualism at home, and time orientation). All of these measures were related to cultural values. In addition, certain constructs displayed a pattern of fairly weak internal consistency reliabilities for

TABLE 2.5 Internal consistency reliabilities of multi-item measures by country.

Scale	*AU*	*CA*	*CN*	*IN*	*ID*	*IL*	*ES*	*TW*	*TR*	*US*	*Total*
WIF time-based	.86	.88	.79	.63	.76	.79	.80	.83	.84	.85	.82
WIF strain-based	.84	.81	.82	.68	.68	.75	.90	.84	.76	.87	.74
FIW time-based	.80	.66	.72	.73	.47	.67	.66	.84	.77	.72	.80
FIW strain-based	.91	.85	.85	.77	.67	.79	.87	.85	.78	.89	.84
WTFS	.66	.65	.59	.60	.57	.69	.68	.66	.68	.70	.69
FTWS	.67	.61	.61	.72	.59	.63	.60	.71	.63	.63	.67
Ease of balance	.80	.66	.74	.84	.78	.78	.63	.82	.71	.78	.78
Work overload	.90	.90	.83	.88	.88	.86	.83	.89	.84	.92	.88
Family overload	.90	.90	.81	.89	.80	.67	.84	.87	.85	.91	.86
Job control	.83	.76	.56	.73	.56	.80	.78	.66	.63	.78	.67
Family control	.76	.69	.56	.74	.72	.73	.73	.79	.60	.72	.67
Job involvement	.74	.66	.64	.50	.51	.59	.71	.75	.67	.63	.67
Family involvement	.67	.73	.72	.60	.57	.66	.86	.77	.70	.69	.70
Supervisory support	.88	.83	.84	.80	.74	.82	.85	.88	.84	.81	.82
Coworker support	.81	.78	.81	.76	.69	.80	.82	.86	.60	.80	.76
Family satisfaction	.86	.82	.72	.81	.82	.55	.80	.83	.74	.80	.79
Satisfaction with role perf.	.75	.67	.76	.83	.81	.47	.73	.79	.70	.75	.73
Life satisfaction	.90	.88	.81	.70	.81	.80	.85	.87	.82	.89	.84
Turnover intention	.89	.88	.63	.79	.68	.85	.75	.85	.82	.88	.82
Psychological well-being	.70	.67	.54	.58	.64	.67	.65	.66	.58	.68	.74
W-F guilt	.81	.74	.75	.89	.88	.69	.84	.83	.74	.82	.84
Vertical individualism	.73	.82	.58	.57	.53	.66	.79	.73	.66	.73	.64
Vertical collectivism	.47	.53	.66	.65	.57	.50	.62	.57	.50	.49	.55
Horizontal Individ. @ home	.65	.72	.51	.70	.64	.74	.70	.58	.46	.75	.62
Horizontal Individ. @ work	.67	.77	.54	.73	.73	.74	.69	.59	.56	.74	.67
Horizontal Collect. @ home	.76	.78	.81	.78	.57	.85	.83	.80	.67	.82	.91
Horizontal Collect. @ work	.81	.80	.56	.77	.64	.62	.84	.78	.71	.81	.85
Gender-role Ideology 1	.84	.79	.76	.71	.67	.87	.74	.74	.67	.78	.87
Gender-role Ideology 2	.77	.61	.56	.68	.70	.78	.62	.59	.54	.66	.80
Gender-role Ideology 3	.83	.86	.59	.62	.67	.84	.72	.71	.74	.88	.78
Time orientation	.72	.75	.42	.52	.30	.80	.88	.62	.84	.67	.65

many counties. For example, the alphas for WTFS and FTWS were marginal (i.e., .59–.71) for all 10 countries. In addition, for several countries, $\alpha < .7$ for: (1) time-based FIW conflict, (2) job and family control, (3) job and family involvement, (4) psychological well-being, (5) horizontal collectivism at home and at work, (6) horizontal individualism at work, and (7) gender-role ideology 2 and 3.

Country Classification

Societies differ from one another in a myriad of ways. Among the most important features that distinguish them are their geography, language, ethnicity, history of colonization/immigration, religion, political system, and economic development (House et al., 2004). There is an advantage to conducting cross-cultural research so that one can understand the uniqueness of each individual country that is part of a research project. The results from Phase 2 of Project 3535, as reported in Chapters 4 through 12, speak to this need.

There are also times, however, when it is desirable to condense data so as to reduce complexity and better understand general trends and wide-ranging effects. To facilitate this latter aim, many attempts have been made to group individual countries into broader categories. Table 2.6 presents a comparison of how the Project 3535 countries would be categorized using some of these previously developed classification systems.

One approach to country classification has been the culturalist approach (Ollier-Malaterre & Foucreault, 2017). Here countries are grouped based on the similarity of their cultural attitudes and values. Researchers using this approach typically employ only a single values dimension (most often individualism-collectivism) and then infer the values of those in the countries studied from secondary source data (most often Hofstede, 1980) rather than by directly measuring the dimensions of interest (Shaffer & Riordan, 2003). Moreover, once countries have been grouped using this method, researchers assign labels to the groups that reflect not the underlying cultural values, but rather the region of the world in which the countries are located.

Such an approach was taken by Hill, Yang, Hawkins, and Ferris (2004). They conducted a study of the W-F interface using a sample of IBM employees from 48 countries. Their grouping system is the least differentiated of those presented here; it consists of only three categories. Hill et al. (2004) first used Hofstede's individualism-collectivism scores to divide countries into the broad categories of East (collectivistic) versus West (individualistic). They then further subdivided the West category into West-Developing versus West-Affluent based on the countries' GDPs. As can be seen from Table 2.6, using Hill et al.'s (2004) classification, nine of the Project 3535 countries can be placed into the two categories of East versus West (they did not have data for Turkey). It should be noted that Project 3535 did not have any countries that fell into the West-Developing category (primarily

TABLE 2.6 Country classification systems.

Country	*Hill et al. (2004)*	*GLOBE (House et al., 2004)*	*Shaffer et al. (2011)*	*Ronen & Shankar (2013)*	*UN HDI (2005)*	*UN GDI (2005)*	*UN GEI (2005)*	*GLOBE GEV (2004)*	*GLOBE IGCP (2004)*	*Project 3535 GRI*	*Project 3535 VC*	*Project 3535*
AU	West	Anglo	Anglo	Anglo	3	2	8	5.2	4.17	4.99	3.64	I-E
CA	West	Anglo	Anglo	Anglo	4	1	1	5.11	4.26	4.92	3.76	I-E
US	West	Anglo	N/A	Anglo	12	16	15	5.6	4.25	4.94	3.76	I-E
ES	West	Latin Europe	West Europe	Latin Europe	13	12	13	4.82	5.45	4.97	3.56	I-E
IL	West	Latin Europe	West Europe	Latin Europe singleton	23	21	28	4.71	4.7	4.29	3.88	MC-MT
TW	East	Confucian Asian	Asian	Confucian Asian	N/A	N/A	N/A	4.6	5.6	3.91	3.85	MC-MT
CN	East	Confucian Asian	Asian	Confucian Asian	81	73	57	3.68	5.8	3.48	3.95	C-T
TR	N/A	Middle East	East Europe	Near East	84	79	90	4.5	5.88	3.4	4.34	C-T
ID	East	South Asian	N/A	Far East	107	94	N/A	3.38	5.68	3.48	4.2	C-T
IN	East	South Asian	Asian	Far East singleton	128	113	N/A	4.51	5.92	3.1	4.37	C-T

Notes: *UN = United Nations; HDI = Human Development Index; GDI = Gender Development Index; GEI = Gender Empowerment Index; GEV = gender egalitarian values; IGCP = ingroup collectivism practices; VC = vertical collectivism; GRI = gender-role ideology; I-E = individualistic-egalitarian; MC-MT = mid collectivist-mid traditional; C-T = collectivist-traditional* those in South America and Eastern Europe), so all of the Project 3535 countries in the West category can be considered West-Affluent.

A different approach was used in the GLOBE leadership study (House et al., 2004). First, 10 a priori regional categories were proposed based on past literature. For example, countries were grouped together into an Anglo cluster due to their ethnic and linguistic similarities and past migration patterns. Turkey was placed in the Middle East cluster because of common language (Arabic) and religion (Islam) with other nations in the region. Surprisingly, Israel was placed in the Latin European cluster, together with Spain, despite a religious difference with the other countries in the cluster. This was based on previous migration patterns to Israel from Europe, as well as current business connections. Following this, the societal practices and societal values scores on the nine cultural dimensions derived from the GLOBE data collected in 62 societies were subjected to a discriminant analysis with a holdout sample to confirm the placement of the countries into the 10 clusters. As Table 2.6 shows, the 10 Project 3535 countries fell into five of the 10 GLOBE regional clusters—Anglo (the United States, Canada, Australia), Latin European (Spain, Israel), Middle Eastern (Turkey), Confucian Asian (China, Taiwan), and East Asian (India, Indonesia).

Shaffer, Joplin, and Hsu (2011) reviewed 219 studies on the work-family interface that were conducted in 37 countries. They organized the studies into six categories using a condensed version of GLOBE's classification system. As can be seen from Table 2.6, because no studies from the United States or Indonesia were reviewed, the remaining eight Project 3535 countries fell into four of their six categories: Anglo (Canada, Australia), Western/Latin Europe (Spain, Israel), Eastern Europe (Turkey), and Asian (India, Taiwan, and China).

The final values-based system to be discussed here was developed by Ronen and Shenkar (2013). They conducted a cluster analysis on a wide variety of work attitude and values dimensions using secondary data from 70 countries. They found evidence for 11 global clusters, 15 consensus clusters, and 6 singletons. As can be seen in Table 2.6, the 10 Project 3535 countries were represented on five of the global clusters: Anglo (Australia, Canada, the United States), Latin Europe (Spain, Israel), Near East (Turkey), Far East (India, Indonesia), and Confucian Asian (China, Taiwan). Similar to GLOBE, Ronen and Shenkar found that Israel clustered with Spain. However, Israel was a singleton in the Latin European cluster, indicating a lack of cohesiveness with the other countries in that cluster. Similarly, India was a singleton within the Far East cluster. Interestingly, in contrast to GLOBE's results, Turkey did not fall within the Arab cluster, but rather into the Near East category along with Greece. Ronen and Shenkar (2013) found that the Far East and Confucian Asian categories had a great deal of empirical overlap with one another and could be combined if necessary.

There is agreement among all four of these culturalist classification systems that Australia, Canada, and the United States belong in the Anglo cluster. Spain and Israel are also generally categorized together into a cluster labeled as Western or Latin European. Despite this, Israel appears not to fit into this category as well as Spain does. GLOBE (House et al., 2004) and Ronen and Shenkar (2013) place China and Taiwan in the Confucian Asian cluster and India and Indonesia in the South Asian or Far Eastern cluster. However, Ronen and Shenkar's data indicate that all four of these countries can be grouped together into a single broader category that has been labeled East (Hill et al., 2004) or Asian (Shaffer et al., 2011). It should be noted that very little work-family research has been done in Indonesia and also that India was found to be a singleton by Ronen and Shenkar and may, therefore, differ from the remaining countries in its cluster. Turkey has often been difficult to classify (Ronen & Shenkar, 2013). It has been variously categorized as Eastern European, Near Eastern, or Middle Eastern. Overall, however, the consistency among the results of these classification systems is remarkable because many factors, including the type of values on which they are based, the characteristics of their samples, and the particular countries included, can influence the results.

A second approach to country classification is the structuralist perspective (Ollier-Malaterre & Foucreault, 2017) which focuses on where countries fall on indices of economic or human development. The next three columns of Table 2.6 portray the rankings of the Project 3535 countries on various UN development indices (i.e., human development, gender development, and gender empowerment). One can see that, based on these criteria, the five Western countries (i.e., those in the Anglo and Latin European clusters) have rankings indicative of greater development, whereas the five Eastern countries have rankings indicative of lesser development (see also Ronen & Shenkar, 2013).

The next columns of Table 2.6 depict the mean scores of the Project 3535 countries on the two cultural value dimensions of vertical or ingroup collectivism and gender egalitarianism. The scores from both GLOBE and Project 3535 are presented for comparison purposes. As noted previously, most researchers: (1) classify countries based on a single value dimension and (2) rely on proxy scores obtained from secondary source data to do so. We did not employ this approach. Instead, we used the data we ourselves had collected to place the Project 3535 countries into categories.

Team members Anit Somech and Anat Drach-Zahavy carried out a cluster analysis on individuals' scores on vertical collectivism and gender-role ideology. Under the K-means algorithm (Hartigan, 1975; Hartigan & Wong, 1979), a three-group model provided the best fit. Group 1, labeled individualistic-egalitarian (I-E), consisted of four countries (Australia, Canada, the United States, and Spain) that had high scores on individualism and high scores (egalitarian) on gender-role ideology. Group 2 (MC-MT) consisted of two countries (Israel and Taiwan) that had average ratings on both dimensions. Group 3, collectivistic-traditional (C-T), consisted of four countries (China, India, Indonesia, and Turkey) that had high scores on collectivism and low scores (traditional) on gender-role ideology.

A comparison between the GLOBE and the Project 3535 data indicates that for both, the five Western countries are the most egalitarian (with the Anglo countries being more egalitarian than the Latin European ones), whereas the five Eastern countries are the most traditional. The results are similar for collectivism.

In general, the five Western countries are lower in collectivism than the five Eastern countries. The exception is that for the Project 3535 data, Israel was similar to Taiwan in collectivism, resulting in these two countries being clustered together into the MC-MT category.

As can be seen from the preceding discussion of country classification, those counties categorized as Western by Hill et al. (2004) tend to be more developed and to embrace more egalitarian and less collectivistic values, whereas those classified as Eastern tend to be less developed and to embrace more traditional and more collectivistic values. This can present a problem when interpreting the results of research, as it is difficult to disentangle whether the findings are attributable to factors associated with region (e.g., geography, climate, or history), degree of development, or cultural values.

In Project 3535 we left it up to each researcher on the team to choose whatever classification system they wished to adopt depending on whatever made the most sense for the particular purpose at hand. The categorization of cultures in the literature is admittedly arbitrary (Minkov & Hofstede, 2011). In most cases, classification systems are theoretically driven. Those which are empirically driven are based on actual measures of some value or belief dimensions. We adopted the latter approach and measured value dimensions with the hope that we would arrive at an empirically verified categorization of cultures in Project 3535. However, we obtained only partial measurement equivalence for the scales used to measure the cultural dimensions. Therefore, we let researchers use value dimensions to group countries or not for the specific purposes of the framework with which they were working. As you will see throughout this book, a variety of approaches were employed. Sometimes, as in the case of Chapters 15 and 19, an a priori system was used, where for example, countries were categorized as I-E, C-T, and MC-MT or as East versus West, respectively, prior to data analysis. In other instances (e.g., Chapter 17), the data analysis was carried out for each country separately and then post hoc categories were utilized to aid the interpretation of the results. Yet another approach (see Chapter 14) was to completely avoid placing countries into categories and to rely instead on continuous scores on values dimensions, such as vertical collectivism or polychronicity.

Conclusion

Project 3535 is one of the only large-scale cross-cultural research endeavors to focus specifically on the W-F interface. It is notable for its multilevel, multimethod, and multisource approach. A fairly large number of countries, spanning four continents, was included and country selection was theoretically based. There was an emphasis on both emic and etic concerns and on both micro- and macro-level and both culturalist and structuralist processes. We formulated a state-of-the-art model that included a full range of W-F interface constructs, as well as multiple dimensions of cultural values. This model was tested with a large, heterogeneous sample composed of employed parents, with roughly equal proportions of both men and women and managers and nonmanagers, in a variety of occupations. We utilized procedures that would help to ensure the reliability and validity of both our qualitative and quantitative data and conducted an extensive ME/I analysis to ensure the equivalency of the meaning of our measures across countries.

As with any research project of this scale, many compromises had to be made. We were unable to include countries from many regions (e.g., Nordic, Germanic, and Eastern Europe) and continents (Africa, South America) of the world. Our sample sizes, although sufficient, could have been larger and more representative. This is particularly true for the qualitative data collected in Phase 2, which for some countries came only from women. Despite our best efforts, the participants from the different countries are likely not equivalent to one another in a number of ways.

Due to considerations about length, we had to make some hard decisions about what would/would not be included in our Phase 3 survey. We eliminated some items from standardized measures in an attempt to shorten them. However, this often resulted in an attenuation of their reliability. Furthermore, we assessed job satisfaction with only two items and psychological distress with a binary response scale which meant that ME/I for culture could not be calculated for these constructs.

Because all of our Phase 3 data were collected from a survey completed by a single source, common source and common method biases cannot be ruled out as explanations for the effects found. In addition, the survey data were cross-sectional in nature. This limits the extent to which causal conclusions can be drawn from our findings. Future longitudinal research is necessary to address this issue.

A massive research project like this one necessarily takes a long time to complete. This raises legitimate concerns that due to changing societal conditions over time the findings reported here may have become obsolete. There is no way to assess to what extent this may be the case. In presenting our results, we have tried to be sensitive to this by laying out the conditions that were in place at the time the data were collected and explaining how the context may have changed since then. For example, in Chapter 3 both the social policies that were in place in each country at the time of data collection and those that presently exist are discussed.

In preparing the chapters in this book, individual team members were given the freedom to make their own methodological decisions about the research questions they wanted to address, the constructs they wanted to include in their analyses, and the types of analyses they wanted to carry out, with the caveat that they discuss the implications of their choices.

Project 3535 was founded upon a set of best practices for carrying out cross-cultural organizational and W-F research (Bagger & Love, 2010; Gelfand et al., 2002; Shaffer & Riordan, 2003). We have tried as much as possible to remain true to that vision. As a result, Project 3535 represents the most comprehensive and methodologically rigorous cross-cultural study of the work-family interface conducted to date.

Note

1 For a discussion of emic and etic approaches see Shaffer and Riordan (2003).

References

Antani, A. K. (2007). *The role of social support and work-family conflict on turnover intentions* (Unpublished doctoral dissertation). Illinois Institute of Technology, Chicago.

Bagger, J., & Love, J. (2010). Methodological considerations in conducting cross-national work-family survey research. In S. Sweet & J. Casey (Eds.), *Work and family encyclopedia*. Chestnut Hill, MA: Sloan Work and Family Research Network.

Berry, J. W. (1997). An ecolocultural approach to the study of cross-cultural industrial/organizational psychology. In P. C. Earley & M. Erez (Eds.), *New perspectives on international industrial organizational psychology* (pp. 130–147). San Francisco: The New Lexington Press.

Berry, J. W., Poortinga, Y. H., Segall, M. H., & Dasen, P. R. (1992). *Cross-cultural psychology: Research and applications*. New York: Cambridge University Press.

Bluedorn, A. C., Kalliath, T. J., Strube, M. J., & Martin, G. D. (1999). Polychronicity and the Inventory of Polychronic Values (IPV): The development of an instrument to measure a fundamental dimension of organizational culture. *Journal of Managerial Psychology, 14*(3/4), 205–230. doi:10.1108/02683949910263747

Brislin, R. W. (1980). Translation and content analysis of oral and written material. In H. C. Triandis & J. W. Berry (Eds.), *Handbook of cross-cultural psychology* (Vol. 2, pp. 389–344). Boston: Allyn & Bacon.

Carlson, D. S., Kacmar, K. M., & Williams, L. J. (2000). Construction and initial validation of a multidimensional measure of work-family conflict. *Journal of Vocational Behavior, 56*(2), 249–276. doi:10.1006/jvbe.1999.1713

Chueng, G. W., & Rensvold, R. B. (2002). Evaluating goodness-of-fit indexes for testing measurement invariance. *Structural Equation Modeling, 9*(2), 233–255. doi:10.1207/S15328007SEM0902_5

Cigularov, K. P., & Thronton, J. C., III. (2011, April). *Achievement motivation in Bulgaria and the US: Cross-country comparison*. Paper presented at the annual meeting of the Society for Industrial/Organizational Psychology, Chicago, IL.

Cook, J. D., Hepworth, S. J., Wall, T. D., & Warr, P. B. (1981). *The experience of work*. New York, NY: Academic Press.

Coovert, M. D., & Craiger, J. P. (2000). An expert system for integrating multiple fit indices for structural equation models. *New Review of Applied Expert Systems and Emerging Technologies, 6*, 39–55.

Diener, E., Emmons, R. A., Larsen, R. J., & Griffin, S. (1985). The satisfaction with life Scale. *Journal of Personality Assessment, 49*(1), 71–75. doi:10.1207/s15327752jpa4901_13

Frone, M. R., & Rice, R. W. (1987). Work-family conflict: The effect of job and family involvement. *Journal of Occupational Behavior, 8*(1), 45–53. doi:10.1002/job.4030080106

Gelfand, M. J., Raver, J. L., & Erhart, K. H. (2002). Methodological issues in cross-cultural organizational research. In S. Rogelberg (Ed.), *Handbook of research methods in industrial/organizational psychology* (pp. 216–246). Malden, MA: Blackwell.

Greenhaus, J. H., & Parasuraman, S. (1999). Research on work, family, and gender. In G. N. Powell (Ed.), *Handbook of gender and work* (pp. 391–412). Thousand Oaks, CA: Sage.

Grzywacz, J. G., & Marks, N. F. (2000). Reconceptualizing the work-family interface: An ecological perspective on the correlates of positive and negative spillover between work and family. *Journal of Occupational Health Psychology, 5*(1), 111–126. doi:10.1037/1076-8998.5.1.111

Hackman, J. R., & Oldham, G. R. (1975). Development of the job diagnostic survey. *Journal of Applied Psychology, 60*(2), 159–170. doi:10.1037/h0076546

Hartigan, J. A. (1975). *Clustering algorithms*. New York: John Wiley & Sons.

Hartigan, J. A., & Wong, M. A. (1979). Algorithm AS136: A k-means clustering algorithm. *Applied Statisticsi, 28*(1), 100–108. doi:10.2307/2346830

Hill, E. J., Yang, C., Hawkins, A. J., & Ferris, M. (2004). A cross-cultural test of the work-family interface in 48 countries. *Journal of Marriage and Family, 66*(5), 1300–1316. doi:10.1111/j.0022-2445.2004.00094.x

Hofstede, G. (1980). *Culture's consequences: International differences in work related values* (2nd ed.). Thousand Oaks, CA: Sage.

House, R. J., Hanges, P. J., Javidian, M., Dorfman, P. W., & Gupta, V. (2004). *Culture leadership, and organizations: The GLOBE study of 62 societies*. Thousand Oaks, CA: Sage.

Kelloway, E. K. (1995). Structural equation modelling in perspective. *Journal of Organizational Behavior, 16*(3), 215–224. doi:10.1002/job.4030160304

Kruger, R. A., & Casey, M. A. (2000). *Focus groups: A practical guide for applied research* (3rd ed.). Thousand Oaks, CA: Sage.

Lincoln, Y. S., & Guba, E. G. (1985). *Naturalistic inquiry*. Newbury Park, CA: Sage.

Mason, K. O., & Bumpass, L. L. (1975). U.S. women's sex-role ideology, 1970. *American Journal of Sociology, 80*(5), 1212–1219.

McElwain, A. (2008). *An examination of the reliability and validity of the Work-Family Guilt Scale* (Unpublished doctoral dissertation). University of Guelph, Guelph, ON, Canada.

McElwain, A., Chappell, D. B., & Korabik, K. (2005, June). *Online focus groups: A new technology for research on gender*. Section on Women and Psychology pre-convention workshop on qualitative research and women, Canadian Psychological Association, Montreal, QC.

Milfont, T. L., & Fischer, R. (2010). Testing measurement invariance across groups: Applications in cross-cultural research. *International Journal of Psychological Research, 3*(1), 2011–2084. doi:10.21500/20112084.857

Milkie, M. A., Denny, K. E., Kendig, S., & Schieman, S. (2010, April). Measurement of the work-family interface. In S. Sweet & J. Casey (Eds.), *Work and family encyclopedia*. Chestnut Hill, MA: Sloan Work and Family Research Network.

Minkov, M., & Hofstede, G. (2011). Is national culture a meaningful concept? Cultural values delineate homogeneous national clusters of in-country regions. *Cross-Cultural Research*. doi:10.1177/1069397111427262

Ollier-Malaterre, A., & Foucreault, A. (2017). Cross-national work-life research: Cultural and structural impacts for individuals and organizations. *Journal of Management, 43*(1), 111–136. doi:10.1177/0149206316655873

Oreg, S., Bayazit, M., Vakola, M., Arciniega, L., Armenakis, A., Barkauskiene, R., . . . van Damn, K. (2008). Dispositional resistance to change: Measurement equivalence and the link to personal values across 17 nations. *Journal of Applied Psychology, 93*(4), 935–941. doi:10.1037/0021-9010.93.4.935

Peterson, M. F., Smith, P. B., Akande, A., Ayestaran, S., Bockner, S., Callan, V., . . . Viedge, C. (1995). Role conflict, ambiguity and overload: A 21 nation study. *Academy of Management, 38*(2), 429–452. doi:10.2307/256687

Pocock, B. (2001). *Having a life: Work, family, fairness and community in Australia 2000*. Adelaide, South Australia: Adelaide University, Centre for Labor Research.

Poelmans, S. (2001). *A qualitative study of work-family conflicts in managerial couples. Are we overlooking some fundamental questions?* (Report No. 445). Barcelona, Spain: IESE Publishing.

Poelmans, S. (2004, April). *Individual experiences of work-family conflict and institutional responses in Spain*. Paper presented at the annual meeting of the Society for Industrial/Organizational Psychology, Chicago, IL.

Ronen, S., & Shenkar, O. (2013). Mapping world cultures: Cluster formation, sources and implications. *Journal of International Business, 44*(9), 867–897.

Santor, D.A., & Coyne, J. C. (1997). Shortening the CES-D to improve its ability to detect cases of depression. *Psychological Assessment, 9*(3), 233–243. doi:10.1037/1040-3590.9.3.233

Shaffer, B. S., & Riordan, C. M. (2003). A review of cross-cultural methodologies for organizational research: A best practices approach. *Organizational Research Methods, 6*(2), 169–215. doi:10.1177/1094428103251542

Shaffer, M. A., Joplin, J. R. W., & Hsu, Y.-S. (2011). Expanding the boundaries of work-family research: A review and agenda for future research. *International Journal of Cross Cultural Management, 12*(2), 221–268. doi:10.1177/1470595811398800

Singelis, T. M., Triandis, H. C., Bhawuk, D. P. S., & Gelfand, M. J. (1995). Horizontal and vertical individualism and collectivism: A theoretical and methodological refinement. *Cross-Cultural Research, 29*(3), 240–275. doi:10.1177/106939719502900302

Somech, A., & Drach-Zahavy, A. (2007). Strategies for coping with work-family conflict: The distinctive relationships of gender role ideology. *Journal of Occupational Health Psychology, 12*(1), 1–29. doi:10.1037/1076-8998.12.1.1

Steenkamp, J. E. M., & Baumgartner, H. (1998). Assessing measurement invariance in cross-national consumer research. *Journal of Consumer Research, 25*(1), 78–90. doi:10.1086/209528

Treas, J., & Widmar, E. D. (2000). Married women's employment over the life course: Attitudes in cross-national perspective. *Social Forces, 78*(4), 1409–1437. doi:10.1093/sf/78.4.1409

Triandis, H. C., & Gelfand, M. J. (1998). Converging measurement of horizontal and vertical individualism and collectivism. *Journal of Personality and Social Psychology, 74*(1), 118–129. doi:10.1037/0022-3514.74.1.118

van de Vijver, F. J. R., & Leung, K. (1997). *Methods and data analysis for cross-cultural research*. Thousand Oaks, CA: Sage.

Appendix: Work-Family Balance International Research Project Survey

Dear Participant,

Thank you for taking time to fill out the questionnaire designed to study how people manage their work and family life in different parts of the world.

In order to participate in the study, you need to meet the following criteria:

1. Married/having a partner living together
2. With at least one unmarried child living with you
3. Employee of an organization (not self-employed)

Your participation in this study is voluntary, and your contribution to our research is very valuable.

Please read each question carefully. There are no right or wrong answers. Your candid answers are the most useful for us.

We require that you complete the questionnaire within a week, if possible.

Should you have any questions, please do not hesitate to contact the Researcher.

This is a study of work-family balance around the world. Although some questions may not seem relevant to you, we ask that you please bear with us and respond to the questions as best you can. In order to make comparisons across different countries, we need to obtain answers to all of the scales.

[Unless otherwise noted, the following response scale was used.]

Please use the scale below to respond to the following statements as they pertain to your WORK AND FAMILY LIFE.

1	2	3	4	5	6
Strongly Disagree	Disagree	Somewhat Disagree	Somewhat Agree	Agree	Strongly Agree

Items marked with an * are reverse coded.

SECTION A: HOW YOU MANAGE YOUR WORK AND FAMILY RESPONSIBILITIES

Q1, Items 1–12 (Work-Family Conflict); time- and strain-based WIF and FIW items from Carlson, Kacmar, and Williams (2000).

Q2 (Coping). Please indicate your typical coping strategies with your multiple daily family and work duties.

1. I lower my performance of family responsibilities to a less than perfect level.
2. I insist on doing, on my own, all family duties perfectly, from the least important to the most important.
3. I manage my family duties by delegating some to others.
4. I don't take responsibility for family duties that are not important to me.
5. I don't volunteer to undertake what I consider extra work duties.
6. I manage my work duties by delegating some to others.
7. I eliminate work duties that are the least important.
8. I insist on doing on my own all my work duties perfectly from the least important to the most important.

Q3 (Ease of Balancing). Circumstances differ and some people find it easier than others to balance working with family responsibilities. In general, how easy or difficult is it for you to balance the following? Please use the scale below to respond. Use "Not Applicable" only for situations that do not apply to you (i.e., you do not have an extended family).

Response scale: 1 = very difficult; 2 = difficult; 3 = somewhat difficult; 4 = somewhat easy; 5 = easy; 6 = very easy; 7 = not applicable

1. Work and child care?
2. Work and marriage/relationship with your partner?
3. Work and household chores?
4. Work and care of parents/parents-in-law?
5. Work and care of extended family?

Q4, items 1–8 (Positive Spillover); from Grzywacz and Marks (2000).

SECTION B: YOUR OPINIONS AND ATTITUDES

Q5, items 1–5 (Time Orientation); from Bluedorn, Kalliath, Strube, and Martin (1999).

1. I like to juggle several activities at the same time.
2. I would rather complete an entire project than complete parts of several projects.*
3. I believe that people should try to do as many things as possible at once.

4. I prefer to do one thing at a time.*
5. I believe that people do their best work when they have many tasks to complete.

Q5, items 6–17 (Vertical Individualism and Collectivism); adapted from Singelis, Triandis, Bhawuk, and Gelfand (1995) and Triandis and Gelfand (1998).

6. Parents and children must stick together to no matter what.
7. Competition is the law of nature.
8. Even when I have to sacrifice what I want, it is my duty to take care of others.
9. It is important to me that I respect the decisions made by groups I feel that I belong to.
10. It annoys me when other people perform better than I do.
11. Children should be taught to place duty before pleasure.
12. It is important that I do my job better than others.
13. Winning is everything.
14. Group members should stick together, no matter what sacrifices are required.
15. When another person does better than I do, I get tense and aroused.
16. I enjoy situations involving competition with others.
17. Some people emphasize winning; I am not one of them.*

Q6 (Horizontal Individualism and Collectivism Family) and Q7 (Horizontal Individualism and Collectivism Work); adapted from Singelis, Triandis, Bhawuk, and Gelfand (1995) and Triandis and Gelfand (1998).

	In My Family	*In My Work Life*
1. I'd rather depend on myself than people around me.	1 2 3 4 5 6	1 2 3 4 5 6
2. I often do my own thing.	1 2 3 4 5 6	1 2 3 4 5 6
3. Being a unique individual is important to me.	1 2 3 4 5 6	1 2 3 4 5 6
4. I would feel proud, if people around me get recognition.	1 2 3 4 5 6	1 2 3 4 5 6
5. The well-being of people around me is important to me.	1 2 3 4 5 6	1 2 3 4 5 6
6. I rely on myself most of the time; I rarely rely on others.	1 2 3 4 5 6	1 2 3 4 5 6
7. To me, pleasure is spending time with people around me.	1 2 3 4 5 6	1 2 3 4 5 6
8. I feel good when I cooperate with others.	1 2 3 4 5 6	1 2 3 4 5 6
9. I would help within my means, if people around me were in financial difficulty.	1 2 3 4 5 6	1 2 3 4 5 6
10. It is important to me to maintain harmony.	1 2 3 4 5 6	1 2 3 4 5 6

	In My Family	*In My Work Life*
11. My personal identity, independent of others, is very important to me.	1 2 3 4 5 6	1 2 3 4 5 6
12. I like sharing little things with others.	1 2 3 4 5 6	1 2 3 4 5 6
13. My happiness depends very much on the happiness of those around me.	1 2 3 4 5 6	1 2 3 4 5 6

Q8 (Gender-Role Ideology); items 1 and 10–13 from Treas and Widmar (2000); items 2–9 from Mason and Bumpass (1975).

1. A working mother can establish just as warm and secure a relationship with her children as a mother who does not work.
2. It is more important for a wife to help her husband's career than to have a career herself.*
3. It is much better for everyone involved if the man is the achiever outside the home and the woman takes care of the home and family. *
4. Men should share the work around the house, such as doing the dishes, cleaning, and so forth.
5. Men make better supervisors on the job than women do.*
6. A father should be as involved in caring for the children as a mother, such as taking them to the doctor, changing their diapers, etc.
7. Even if there is limited number of jobs, it is all right for a married woman to hold a job when her husband is able to support her.
8. Women are expected to change their behavior after they are married and have children.*
9. Housekeeping is the woman's primary responsibility and should not be delegated.*
10. Child care is the woman's primary responsibility and should not be delegated.*
11. A young child is likely to suffer if his or her mother works.*
12. All in all, family life suffers when the woman has a full-time job.*
13. A job is all right, but what most women really want is a home and children.*
14. A man's job is to earn the money; a woman's job is to look after the home and family.*
15. A good wife tolerates family conflicts in the interest of family harmony.*
16. Women's employment causes harm to children's development and academic achievement.*

Q9 and 10 (Similarity of Opinions to Society)

Q9. How similar or different do your personal opinions on men and women's roles from the opinions of the majority of people in your society?

1 = very dissimilar; 2 = dissimilar; 3 = somewhat dissimilar; 4 = somewhat similar; 5 = similar; 6 = very similar

Q10. How much stress do you feel due to the fact that your opinions are similar or dissimilar from those of the majority of the people in your society?

1 = none; 2 = very little; 3 = some; 4 = a moderate amount; 5 = quite a bit; 6 = a great deal

SECTION C: YOUR WORK AND FAMILY SITUATION

Q11, items 1–5 (Job Control) and items 6–10 (Family Control); adapted from Centre for Families, Work, and Well-Being measure

1. I have influence over the things that happen to me at work.
2. I am satisfied with the amount of involvement I have in the decisions that affect my work.
3. At work, I can modify my daily schedule if needed.
4. I get as much out of my job as I put into it.
5. I am in charge of how my work gets done.
6. I have influence over the things that happen to me at home.
7. I am satisfied with the amount of involvement I have in the decisions that affect my family life.
8. At home, I can modify my daily schedule if needed.
9. I get as much out of my family life as I put into it.
10. I am in charge of how things run in my family.

Q11, items 11–14 (Job Involvement) and items 15–18 (Family Involvement); from Frone and Rice (1987).

Q12, items 1–5 (Job Overload) and Q13, items 1–5 (Family Overload); items 1–4 adapted from Peterson et al. (1995).

	At My Workplace	*At Home*
1. There is a need to reduce some parts of my role.		
2. I feel overburdened in my role.		
3. I have been given too much responsibility.		
4. My workload is too heavy.		
5. The amount of work I have to do interferes with the quality I want to maintain.		

Q14–17 (Work and Family Hours)
[Please type your answers into the spaces provided below the following questions]

Q14 Indicate the average number of hours PER WEEK spent on all WORK-RELATED DUTIES. This may include hours spent at work, hours spent during the evening and weekends, hours spent working from home or when on vacation, hours spent travelling for work-related purposes, etc. Please type the number of hours into the box below.

Q15 Indicate the average number of hours PER WEEK spent CARING FOR CHILD(REN). This may include everything that you do to assist your child(ren), such as preparing and taking child(ren) to school or child care, playing with your child(ren), working with child(ren) on homework, making arrangements for care, making meals, bathing, etc.

Q16 Indicate the average number of hours PER WEEK spent HELPING A PARENT/PARENT-IN-LAW. This may include everything that you do to assist a parent, such as shopping, home maintenance, transportation to appointments, providing emotional support, financial management, checking on them by phone, making arrangements for care, making meals, bathing, time spent traveling to them, etc.

Q17 Indicate the average number of hours PER WEEK spent on all other HOUSEHOLD RELATED DUTIES. This may include cooking, paying bills, washing dishes, doing yard work, shopping, and all other household maintenance activities.

SECTION D: YOUR FEELINGS ABOUT YOUR WORK AND FAMILY LIFE

Q18–26 (Social Support); from Antani (2007); please see Appendix in Chapter 16 for a copy of this measure.

Q27 (Satisfaction with Support)

Response scale: 1 = Very Dissatisfied; 2 = Dissatisfied; 3 = Neutral; 4 = Satisfied; 5 = Very Satisfied

How satisfied are you with the support you receive from your:

Partner/Spouse
Child(ren)
Parents or parents-in-law
Paid household helper
Neighbors, friends, or relatives
Job supervisor
Coworkers or subordinates

Q28, items 1–3 and 14 (Family Satisfaction), items 4 and 5 (Job Satisfaction); adapted from Hackman and Oldham (1975)

1. Overall I am very satisfied with the way my children are growing up.
2. I frequently think I would like to change my family situation.*

3. I am generally satisfied with the role I play in my family.
4. Generally speaking, I am very satisfied with my present job.
5. I am generally satisfied with the kind of work I do in my present job.
14. Generally speaking, I am very satisfied with my family.

Q28, items 6–8 (Turnover Intent) from Camman, Firchman, Jenkins, and Klesh (1979, as cited in Cook, Hepworth, Wall, & Warr, 1981).

6. I will actively look for a new job in the next year.
7. I often think about quitting my job.
8. I will probably look for a new job in the next year.

Q28, items 9–13 (Life Satisfaction); from Diener, Emmons, Larsen, and Griffin (1985).

Q29, items 1–6 (Satisfaction with Role Performance)

Response scale: 1 = very dissatisfied; 2 = dissatisfied; 3 = neutral; 4 = satisfied; 5 = very satisfied; 6 = not applicable
How satisfied are you with your role as:

1. an employee?
2. a spouse/partner?
3. a parent to your child(ren)?
4. a caregiver to your parents or parents-in-law?
5. How satisfied are you with your marriage/relationship with your partner?
6. How satisfied are you with taking care of your own physical and mental health needs?

Q30, items 1–7 (Work-Family Guilt); from McElwain (2008)

1. I regret not being around for my family as much as I would like to.
2. I feel guilty for not being able to take care of my child(ren) as well as I would like to.
3. I feel bad because I frequently have to take time away from my family to deal with issues happening at work.
4. I feel guilt for not showing as much interest in my spouse/partner as I wish.
5. I am worried about the quality of my work because I often put my family before my job.
6. I regret missing work due to family responsibilities.
7. I feel bad because I frequently have to take time away from work to deal with issues happening at home.

Q31, items 1–9 (Psychological Well-Being); from Santor and Coyne (1997).

SECTION E: POLICIES AND PRACTICES AT YOUR ORGANIZATION

Part 1, Q32–42 (Helpfulness of Organizational Policies)

Please consider whether or not you have used each of the following company policies and practices and then use the scale provided to evaluate each policy as to its helpfulness for reducing work-family conflict. For each type of policy or procedure, please indicate EITHER how helpful it was if you have used it, OR if you have not used it, how helpful you think it would be.

If you HAVE USED this, how helpful was it in improving work and family balance?

OR

If you HAVE NOT USED this, or it is not available to you, how helpful do you think it would be to improve work and family balance?

Response scale: 1 = not helpful at all to 5 = extremely helpful

Q32. FLEXIBLE WORK SCHEDULE: This means that employees have to work an official number of hours, but can choose when to start and end the work day

Q33. EMERGENCY ABSENCE: This means that an employee has the autonomy to leave work for a couple of hours or leave earlier to attend a family emergency, after consulting with the supervisor, but without asking official permission.

Q34. REDUCED WORK SCHEDULE: This means that employees can work fewer hours (e.g., half a day).

Q35. TELECOMMUTING: This means that employees—after consulting their supervisor—have the flexibility to work from home some days of the week.

Q36. MATERNITY/PARENTAL LEAVE BEYOND LEGISLATION: This means that employees can take a leave beyond the period specified by law, to attend to their baby. They are guaranteed their job upon their return.

Q37. LEAVE TO CARE FOR SICK FAMILY MEMBERS: This means that employees can take a leave to take care of sick or disabled family members (child(ren)/parents), if they renounce their salary during that period. They have the guarantee to have the job upon their return from leave.

Q38. CHILD CARE FACILITIES: This means that the employer provides child care facilities in-company or close to the company during office hours. It also includes child care subsidies, financial support to child(ren)'s education, etc.

Q39. HEALTH INSURANCE FOR DEPENDENTS: This means that the company not only covers the health insurance of the employee, but also of his or her family members (spouse/child(ren)).

Q40. HEALTH FACILITIES:This means that the company provides health facilities (company doctor/nurse) in-company or close to the company during office hours.

Q41. WELFARE ACTIVITIES:This means that the company organizes activities such as picnics, sports day functions, activities on special occasions such as religious holidays, etc. to create a feeling of belonging among employees and for the general well-being of the employees' family and community.

Q42 and 43 (Satisfaction with Organizational and Government Policies)

Response scale: 1 = very dissatisfied; 2 = dissatisfied; 3 = neither satisfied nor dissatisfied; 4 = satisfied; 5 = very satisfied

Q42. In general, how satisfied are you with the ORGANIZATIONAL family-friendly policies and practices available in your company?

Q43. In general, how satisfied are you with the GOVERNMENT family-friendly policies and practices available in your country (e.g., maternity leave)?

SECTION F: DEMOGRAPHIC INFORMATION

Q44. Age: _____

Q45. Gender: a. Male b. Female

Q46. How many years have you lived in this country? _____

Q47.	What is the highest level of education that you have attained?
	High School (or equivalent)
	Technical School
	College Degree
	University Bachelor's Degree
	Master's Degree
	Doctorate

Q48. What is your ethnicity?

Q49. How many children do you have?

Q50. Indicate the ages of the children living with you at least 3 days per week.

_________, _________, _________, _________, _________.

Q51. Do you have children with special needs/disabilities? a. yes b. no

Q52. What is your occupation?

Q53. What is your position title?

Q54. What type of job do you hold? a. Managerial b. Nonmanagerial
Q55. How many years have you been working for your present organization?
Q56. How many years have you been working in your present job?
Q57. What is the type of organization that you are working in?

a. Multinational corporation b. Local firm c. Private d. Public

Q58. Is your job: a. Union b. non-union
Q59. What is the schedule of your job? a. Part-time b. Full-time
Q60. What is the size of your organization?
a. less than 100 employees
b. 101–1000 employees
c. 1001–5000 employees
d. 5001–10,000 employees
e. over 10,000 employees

Q61. In which sector are you working?

a. Education b. Manufacturing c. Health d. Finance e. Other

Q62. What is the occupation of your spouse/partner?
Q63. What type of job does your spouse/partner hold?

a. Managerial b. Nonmanagerial

Q64. What is the schedule of your spouse's/partner's job?

a. Part-time b. Full-time

Q65. If you belong to a religious group, how important are your religious beliefs?

a. very important b. somewhat important c. not at all important

Q66. Considering the average income level of your country, which income group would you consider your family's total income?

a. low income b. lower-middle income c. middle income
d. upper-middle income e. upper income

Q67. Considering the average income level of your country, which income group would you consider the income of the family you come from?

a. low income b. lower-middle income c. middle income
d. upper-middle income e. upper income

Q68. What are your living arrangements?

a. In our household, there is only my spouse/partner and our children (please go to the next question)

b. If you are living with your extended family:

____ we live in our residence
____ we live in their residence
____ we live close by

Q69. Please check all the relatives who are alive and/or who need elder care:

	Alive	*Need Elder Care*
Mother	____	____
Father	____	____
Mother-in-law/partner's mother	____	____
Father-in-law/partner's father	____	____

Q70. What was the "family" concept in your mind while answering the questions on "family" in the questionnaire?

____ me, my spouse/partner, and my children only (i.e., my nuclear family).
____ my nuclear family plus my parents and parents-in-law/parents of my partner.
____ my nuclear family, my parents and in-laws, and my relatives (e.g., uncles, aunts, nephews, etc.).

3

THE IMPACT OF NATIONAL CONTEXT AND ORGANIZATIONAL POLICIES

A Cross-Cultural Analysis

Donna S. Lero and Anne Bardoel

Introduction

A growing number of work-family (W-F) researchers are engaging in the challenging work of conducting cross-national and cross-cultural analyses of how various national contextual factors influence work-life policies, practices, and outcomes at the organizational and individual levels. In particular, Ollier-Malaterre, Valcour, Den Dulk, and Kossek (2013) have been instrumental in promoting scholarship that includes analysis of how such macro-level factors as country-specific cultural, institutional, societal, and economic influences affect employers' expectations, motivations, the provision of workplace policies and supports, and workplace culture. In turn, both macro-level and organizational-level influences affect employees' work experiences and WFC and enrichment—ultimately impacting on individuals' life satisfaction and family well-being.

Cross-national policy research complements the large body of research on organizational policies and programs that can help reduce negative outcomes experienced by individuals related to strain, stress, and conflict between work and family roles. Many factors have been identified as contributors to heightened workplace stress, including factors that increase work demands (long work hours and high workloads distributed in 24/7 operating systems; a sharpened pace and intensity of work; and increased financial, market, and job insecurity) and others that deplete employees' resources to cope with those demands effectively, including lack of control over work schedules and workload, and increased WFC (Kossek, Pichler, Bodnar, & Hammer, 2011). Processes that compromise employees' physical and mental health, engagement, and motivation affect not only individual employees, but also organizational-level business outcomes including absenteeism, productivity losses, the quality of customer/client services, and the organization's ability to attract and retain talented employees, as well as the financial costs associated with these outcomes (Kelly et al., 2008; Lero, Richardson, & Korabik, 2009).

In light of this, strategies to reduce WFC are an increasing focus of policy initiatives at government and organizational levels around the world. Cross-national research, such as Project 3535, can help identify the variety of national contextual factors that influence the availability and use of employer work-life policies and programs, and their effectiveness in influencing attitudes towards work and experiences of WFC.

This chapter will first provide an overview of the key findings from recent cross-national work-life research and then introduce the cultural, institutional, and labor force variables we used for contextualizing cross-national comparisons in the present study. More detailed examples of government policy initiatives are provided in the country-specific chapters. Our aim here is to provide a conceptual framework that incorporates salient differences between the Project 3535 countries in national contextual factors and social policies that can be used to help interpret our analyses of cross-national differences in the use of family-friendly policies.

Current Approaches in Cross-National Work-Life Policy Research

The most recent studies build on the work of scholars in the 1980s and 1990s who critiqued concepts of welfare state regimes (most notably Esping-Andersen's work) and emphasized that the choices made when selecting particular institutional features for analysis can limit or expand interpretations in cross-national research (see O'Reilly, 2006, for a review). The last two decades have seen considerable expansion of cross-national studies by major organizations such as the OECD (2007) and by multinational research teams such as the Project GLOBE studies (House, Hanges, Javidan, Dorfman, & Gupta, 2004) and the Cranet network (Parry, Stavrou, & Morley, 2011). These efforts underscore the importance attached to effective W-F reconciliation approaches at the national level for achieving societal goals such as increasing women's employment, promoting gender equality, and ensuring the well-being of families (OECD, 2007, 2011) and at the organizational level to support employee engagement and effectiveness, reduce avoidable costs, and help sustain a resilient workforce (Butts, Casper, & Yang, 2013; Eby et al., 2005; Kossek & Ollier-Malaterre, 2013). Though much of the research is still focused on advanced industrial countries, particularly OECD and EU countries, there is considerable interest and some progress in extending cross-national research on the W-F interface to a wider range of countries (e.g., Bardoel & De Cieri, 2014).

Several authors (Den Dulk, Groenveld, Ollier-Malaterre, & Valcour, 2013; Kossek & Ollier-Malaterre, 2013; Ollier-Malaterre et al., 2013) have argued that work-life researchers must address a number of challenges to advance future research and theorizing in this area. Among those challenges is the need to carefully consider which factors (or set of factors) at the macro level are the most important and salient dimensions of "national context" that link to organizational policies and practices and, ultimately, to individual and family outcomes. In addition, these authors challenge us to avoid functioning in silos characterized by either an organizational or national policy focus, instead engaging in multilevel research that bridges institutional, cross-cultural, and systems/organizational theory approaches to assess the impacts of policies at different levels, including unintended consequences.

Cultural Influences

Two cultural dimensions pertinent to understanding WFC and enrichment across countries are individualism/collectivism (I-C) and gender egalitarianism. I-C has become particularly salient as a way of distinguishing how work is perceived—either as a way of supporting a family or as a way of enhancing one's self. Building on the Project GLOBE studies, researchers have found differences in the relationship between work demands and WFC and between family demands and family-work conflict in individualistic versus collectivistic countries (e.g., House et al., 2004; Lu, Gilmour, Kao, & Huang, 2006; Spector et al., 2007). More recently, Masuda et al. (2012) found that I-C differentiated between countries in the extent to which flexible work arrangements were made available to managers, with managers in more individualistic countries reporting greater access to flextime options than managers in more collectivistic countries. Moreover, I-C moderated the relationship between flextime availability and WFC, job satisfaction, and turnover intentions, with relationships between these variables noted primarily among managers in individualistic (Anglo) countries.

Gender egalitarianism has been studied in several ways, and has long been identified as a critical cultural dimension (Aycan, 2008). Most studies are consistent in finding that in more egalitarian countries, men and women experience WFC similarly, reflecting societal expectations for both partners in couple families to be employed and to share care responsibilities (Strandh & Nordenmark, 2006). Lyness and Kropf (2005) found that national gender equality was positively related to the provision of flexible work arrangements and a supportive work culture and, in turn, to reported W-F balance among managers in 20 European countries. Importantly, these authors recommended that both national values related to gender equality and organizational practices be considered in association with the availability of institutional policies and local services, in part accounting for differences noted in the relative influence of organizational family-supportive culture for managers located in headquarter companies and the influence of flexible work options for managers located in host countries. More recently, Kassinis and Stavrou (2013) utilized the UN Gender Empowerment Index (GEI) in a study of 15 countries that spanned diverse clusters based on Project GLOBE characteristics. They found that senior HR representatives' reports of the extent to which employees used flexible work arrangements in large organizations was more strongly related to GEM scores (a cultural measure) than to public expenditures on parental leave or an index of employment laws and protections. These authors remind us that firm practices are influenced by both cultural context and institutional pressures.

Institutional Influences

Institutional approaches in cross-national research focus on the impact of national social policies on employees' experiences of the work-life interface and on the extent to which organizations implement work-life policies and programs. The social policies that have been of most interest to researchers are maternity, parental, and other forms of family leave (Allen et al., 2014; Gornick & Meyers, 2003; Ray, Gornick, & Schmitt, 2010), with lesser attention paid to the impacts of child care provision and tax system components that affect families with children or low-income families. In many ways, institutional policies and mechanisms constitute the processes by which shared values are reinforced and transmitted. Of particular interest is the extent to which public provisions are linked to employer-sponsored work-life programs (Den Dulk, 2005; Ollier-Malaterre, 2009). Den Dulk et al. (2013), building on institutional theory, note the complex ways organizations respond to societal and institutional influences. In particular, these authors posit that large organizations and those in the public sector are more sensitive to societal and institutional pressures and that in countries with high levels of institutional support for combining work and family, firms may expand or augment what is available through state provision. In more individualistic countries with low levels of state support for W-F reconciliation, such as the United States, larger firms may compensate for the lack of provision (for example, through employer-provided paid leave or, more rarely, on-site day care), but do so unevenly, in large part based on organizational or industry characteristics and a perceived competitive advantage for recruiting and retaining top talent. These observations remind us of the complexity of interactions between influences at the macro, institutional, and organizational levels.

Women's Labor Force Characteristics

To date, few researchers have incorporated observed variations in women's or mothers' labor force patterns and other aspects of labor markets and industrial relations (such as the extent to which sector-wide bargaining or unions influence employers' provision of work-life programs and practices) into cross-national work-life studies. Crude measures of women's labor force participation mask other important features, such as the extent to which women are employed part-time and the extent of gendered occupational segregation in low-wage jobs. Although women's labor force participation patterns may reflect efforts to promote gender egalitarianism and specific institutional policies, we argue that it is an important part of national context in its own right. For example, we might hypothesize that in countries in which mothers are commonly employed on a full-time basis, there may be more developed child care provision or pressure on governments and employers to address child care issues to reduce WFC. In countries with more part-time and low-wage employment for women, employers may not feel or respond to such pressures, assuming that part-time employment is a sufficient vehicle for addressing family care needs.

Project 3535 is a unique research program that was designed to incorporate a multilevel approach to the study of work-life experiences (Korabik, Lero, & Ayman, 2003). It includes a number of measures of national cultural and institutional factors, including an examination of national female labor force variables. Among the 10 countries in our study are several (India, Indonesia, Israel, and Turkey) that are rarely included in existing cross-national work-life research. Our sample includes both managers and employees in organizations who do not have managerial responsibilities.

Our primary goals for the remainder of this chapter are: (1) to provide rich, multidimensional information about the national contexts in each country; (2) to identify important similarities and differences between countries in this study and to determine the utility of clustering countries based on global composite measures of human development, gender inequality, individualism-collectivism, and observed patterns of female employment; and (3) to examine how these factors, embedded in cross-national comparisons, are related to employees' use of employer-provided work-life policies and programs; measures of WFC, job satisfaction, and intent to turnover; and to employees' satisfaction with government and organizational supports. At this point, our analyses are largely descriptive and exploratory. We plan to utilize more complex multivariate, multilevel tests of relationships between national and organizational factors in the future.

National Contextual Data

Measures of Human Development and Gender Inequality

We utilized two well-known composite global measures to "locate" 3535 countries in terms of their economic and societal development and gender egalitarianism. Each measure is briefly described here, and our countries' relative standing on each measure is shown in Table 3.1.

The first measure is the Human Development Index (HDI) developed by the United Nations in 1990. It is a widely used composite index based on three dimensions: life expectancy, adult literacy and participation in education at each of three levels, and national economic development/standard of living as measured by GDP per capita in US dollars. We utilized overall scores and rankings from the *2007/2008 Human Development Report*, as it provides data coincident with our period of data collection (UN Development Programme 2007).

The second measure is the Global Gender Gap Index Rankings (GGG). In 2006, the World Economic Forum began estimating global gender gaps using

TABLE 3.1 Composite human development and gender gap scores.[1]

Country	*Human Development Index (HDI) Rank*[a]	*HDI Value*[a]	*Global Gender Gap (GGG) Index Rank*[b]	*GGG Composite Score*[b]	*GGG Economic Participation & Opportunity Subindex Rank*[b]	*GGG Economic Participation & Opportunity Subindex Score*[b]
Australia	3	.962	21	.724	22	.731
Canada	4	.961	31	.714	15	.744
China	81	.777	57	.688	43	.692
India	128	.619	113	.606	125	.399
Indonesia	107	.728	93	.647	90	.571
Israel	23	.932	56	.690	55	.659
Spain	13	.949	17	.728	89	.577
Taiwan[c]	–	–	–	–	–	–
Turkey	84	.775	123	.585	124	.412
United States	12	.951	27	.718	12	.752

[1]A lower rank on the Human Development Index Ranking signifies a higher score. A lower rank on the GGG Index and the Economic Participation and Opportunity Sub-Index indicates greater gender equality.

a Human Development Index ranks and scores as per the *UN Human Development Report 2007/2008*. Most data refer to 2005–2006.

b Global Gender Gap Index ranks and scores and Economic Participation and Opportunity Subindex ranks and scores as reported in the World Economic Forum *Global Gender Gap Report, 2008*. http://www3.weforum.org/docs/WEF_GenderGap_Report_2008.pdf

c Note: No data recorded for Taiwan. 2012 estimates developed by the government of the Republic of China (Taiwan) suggest that Taiwan has an estimated HDI rank of 23 and ranks among the top five countries on the UN's Gender Inequality Index. (https://en.wikipedia.org/wiki/Gender_Inequality_Index#Countries_not_included.5B12.5D.5B13.5D)

Source: Data is sourced from Table 1, pp. 229–232 in http://hdr.undp.org/sites/default/files/reports/268/hdr_20072008_en_complete.pdf

a new measure, in part because of criticisms of the available UN measures, specifically, the Gender Development Index and Gender Empowerment Index. (In 2010, a new measure, the Gender Inequality Index [GII] was developed by the UN and included in its *2010 Human Development Report*. It includes indicators of women's reproductive health, empowerment based on women's national parliamentary representation and attainment of secondary and tertiary education, and women's labor market participation. GII scores have been interpreted by the UN as reflecting percentages of loss in achievement in human development due to gender inequality. In light of criticisms of the GII for its mix of well-being and inequality indicators and its complexity, we decided on the GGG as a more appropriate measure of gender equality.) GGG index rankings are based on indicators representing four domains: (1) economic participation and opportunity (gaps between men and women in labor force participation, income, and opportunities for the advancement of women); (2) gaps in educational attainment; (3) gaps in health (life expectancy and survival of women based on sex ratio at birth); and (4) gaps in political participation. We provide overall, composite GGG scores from the 2008 *Global Gender Gap* report in Table 3.1, as well as scores and rankings calculated for the Economic Participation and Opportunity subindex. This subindex score is based on ratios of women's to men's labor force participation; estimated wage equality for similar work; estimated earned income; representation as legislators, senior officials, and high-ranking government managers; and employment as professional and technical workers. These ratios are measures of inequality; however, the report also provides information about the level of women's participation in these areas. Selected information is included in Table 3.2, reflecting women's employment and economic activity in each of the 3535 countries.

According to the UN, five of the 10 Project 3535 countries (Australia, Canada, the United States, Spain, and Israel) are considered to have high Human Development scores, and four countries (China, Turkey, Indonesia, and India) have scores that are described as indicative of medium human development. Scores on the World Economic Forum's Global Gender Gap measure follow a similar pattern with less gender inequality evident among countries ranked high on the HDI. No data are reported for Taiwan from the UN or the World Economic

TABLE 3.2 Selected labor force statistics.*

Country	*Labor Force Participation Rate*[1]		*Percentage of Women in Non-Agricultural Paid Labor Force*[2]	*Percentage of Women Employed Part-Time*[3]	*Percentage of Women among Professional and Technical Workers*[4]
	Women	*Men*			
Australia	68	81	49	38	56
Canada	73	83	49	26	56
China	75	88	41	–	52
India	36	84	17	–	21
Indonesia	53	87	31	–	42
Israel	59	65	50	24	54
Spain	58	81	42	21	48
Taiwan	50[5]	67[6]	–	12[7]	–
Turkey	29	80	20	17	33
United States	70	81	49	18	57

* Data pertain to 2006 or closest year.

[1] Population age 15 and older. Source: World Economic Forum. *Global Gender Gap Report, 2008.*

[2] As a percentage of total labor force. Source: World Economic Forum. *Global Gender Gap Report, 2008.*

[3] Source: *OECD Labour Force Statistics, 2012* for the year 2006. Based on International Labour Organization Key Indicators of the Labour Market Database.

[4] Source: World Economic Forum. *Global Gender Gap Report, 2008.*

[5] As of 2008. Source: http://www.statista.com/statistics/319819/taiwan-female-labor-force-participation-rate/

[6] As of 2008. Source: http://www.statista.com/statistics/319818/taiwan-male-labor-force-participation-rate/

[7] Information provided by Dr. Ting-Pang Huang.

Forum; however, the Republic of China (ROC) government calculated its HDI in 2012 as equivalent to a rating of 23 (high) among ranked countries. Similarly, the ROC reported a calculated score of .223 on the criteria used by the UN for its Gender Inequality Index (GII) in 2008, which would rank Taiwan as 4th (indicating low gender inequality) in its standing on this measure (Gender Inequality Index, 2015).

Scores on the Economic Participation and Opportunity subindex reflect higher levels of gender inequality on this dimension for several Project 3535 countries relative to their composite GGG standings, indicative of larger gaps between women and men in labor force participation, wage equality and earnings, and opportunities in government and in professional occupations than is observed on other dimensions, notably educational attainment and health indicators. In particular, India, Turkey, Indonesia, and Spain demonstrate this pattern (see Figure 3.1).

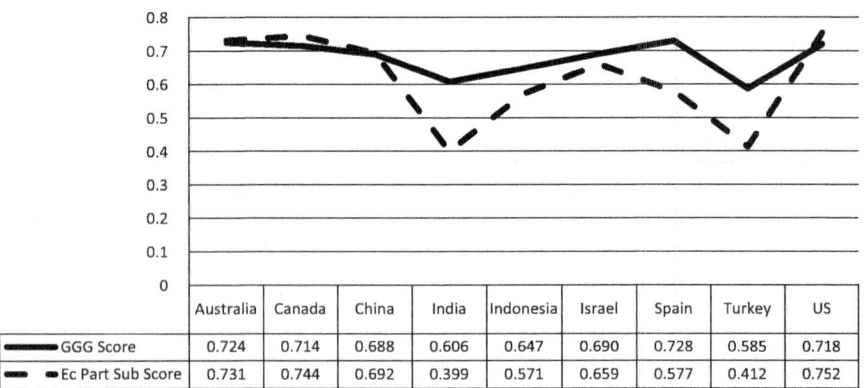

FIGURE 3.1 Global gender gap and economic participation and opportunity gap scores, 2008.

Source: Hausmann, R., Tyson, L.D. & Zahidi, S. (2008). *The Global Gender Gap Report 2008*. World Economic Forum. Geneva, Switzerland.

Women's Labor Force Patterns

Data on women's labor force patterns are routinely collected by national statistical agencies, but not always in the same way. To ensure comparability, we selected information published in the World Economic Forum's *Global Gender Gap Report, 2008*, supplemented when available by data from individual countries. Table 3.2 summarizes data from these sources.

This descriptive information provides a broad snapshot of women's labor force characteristics. High rates of labor force participation among women are noted in China, the United States, Canada, and Australia; moderate levels are evident in Indonesia, Israel, Spain, and Taiwan; and lower rates are characteristic of India and Turkey. A higher proportion of women in India, Turkey, and Indonesia are engaged in work in the agricultural sector. Typically, a small proportion of women (but considerably more than men) is employed part-time when employed. Higher proportions of part-time employment among women were evident in Australia, Canada, and Israel, an option that may be used particularly when children are young or there are higher family care demands. In five of the nine countries for which data were available (China, Israel, Australia, Canada, and the United States), women comprised more than half of those employed in professional and technical jobs, indicative of women's advancement and position within the labor market.

Institutional Policies That Support Women's Employment and Parental Employment

Two major policy domains in the cross-national literature are indicative of institutional supports for combining earning and parenting. These are parental leave policies and public funding for affordable, accessible early child care. Paid maternity leave has a long history in many countries. Multiple purposes and benefits are noted, including enhanced maternal and child health, increased labor force attachment, potentially increased fertility, enhanced job security, and reduced WFC for new parents. Opportunities for sharing parental leave and more recent advancements in providing designated periods of paternity leave are seen as an essential tool for promoting greater gender equality and for supporting fathers' role in the care of young children (Moss & Deven, 2015; Ray, Gornick, & Schmitt, 2010).

The literature on parental leave indicates substantial variation in the duration of leave available, especially paid leave, and whether or not there are provisions for sharing a period of parental leave or for a designated period of paternity leave (Moss, 2014). Paid maternity leave is widely available. Limited paid leave options (such as in Australia at the time of data collection and in the United States) can result in lower workforce attachment, longer periods of unpaid leave, and more uneven patterns of employment, earnings, and advancement among women. Gaps in the availability of affordable child care, particularly for very young children, are likely to result in longer periods out of the workforce for women and/or greater stress upon returning to work related to ensuring high-quality, consistent care when an immediate family member is not available. In Canada, research suggests that some mothers opt for a period of self-employment as a way of combining work and care, but not without economic costs and unique stresses related to blurred boundaries between work and nonwork roles (Hilbrecht & Lero, 2014).

Table 3.3 provides a summary of leave provisions among the 3535 countries that were in place in 2004 (the year or two preceding data collection in most countries). Based on the policies that were in place at that time,[1] one can say that China, Spain, Israel, and Canada had the most generous statutory paid maternity leave policies; Turkey, India, and Taiwan had moderate policies (with an effective

TABLE 3.3 Employment-protected statutory maternity, parental, and paternity leave arrangements, 2004.[1]

Country	*Type of Leave*	*Name & Total Leave (Weeks)*	*Paid*	*Payment*	*Effective Total Leave (Weeks)*[2]	*Eligibility Criteria for Payments*
Australia	Maternity	52 weeks (unpaid)[3]	No	Federal public employees also entitled to 12 weeks full pay[4] maternity leave (Commonwealth) or 6–12 weeks (states) and some private sector employees also have paid leaves.[5]	0	12 months of continuous employment, all parents. Also for adopted children. Employment type either full-time or part-time (not casual). Parents may share.
	Parental	Fathers can share the 12 months unpaid parental leave entitlement with the child's mother.	No		0	To a limit of the child's first birthday. Father needs to take on the role of primary carer.[6]
	Paternity	No legal requirement.[7]	–	–	–	–
Canada (excluding Québec)	Maternity	Employment Insurance:[3] 15 weeks benefits (leave varies across provinces, 15–18 weeks).	Yes	55% of average insured earnings up to a maximum; up to 65% for low income.	8.25	Paying premiums to employment insurance plan (not available for self-employed). 600 hours in last 52-week period. Two-week unpaid waiting period.
	Parental	Employment Insurance: 35 weeks benefits (job-protected leave varies across provinces from shared 37 weeks to 52 weeks each parent[4]).	Yes	Same as maternity.	19.25	Same as maternity. Parents may share if both are eligible.

	Paternity	0				
Canada—Québec (Québec Parental Insurance Plan (QPIP), as of Jan. 1, 2006)[8]	Maternity	18 weeks (basic) 15 weeks (special)	Yes	Basic plan: 70%. Special plan: 75%.	12.6 (basic) 11.25 (special)	All employees (available to self-employed) with a minimum $2000 insurable income in 52-week reference period.
	Parental	32 weeks (basic) 25 weeks (special)	Yes	Basic plan: 70% first 7 weeks; 55% remaining 25. Special plan: 75%.	18.65 (basic) 18.75 (special)	Same as maternity. Parents may share.
	Paternity	5 weeks (basic) 3 weeks (special)	Yes	Basic plan: 70%. Special plan: 75%.	3.5 (basic) 2.25 (special)	Same as maternity.
China	Maternity	Maternity allowance:[9] 90 days	Yes	100%	18	If covered under maternity insurance, maternity allowance is administered by local government. Otherwise, employer must provide the equivalent of full salary.
	Parental					
	Paternity	3–14 days, varying by region	No		0	
India	Maternity	12 weeks[10] Includes maximum of 6 weeks prior to expected date of birth. Can be extended by 4 weeks for medical reasons.	Yes	100% of average earnings (based on wage class). Minimum daily benefit is 10 rupees.	12	Monthly earnings of 6500 rupees or less. Available to workers in power-using manufacturing establishments with 10+ workers or non-power-using establishments with 20+ workers (includes shops, hotels, restaurants, cinemas, road transport agencies, newspaper establishments).

(*Continued*)

TABLE 3.3 (Continued)

Country	Type of Leave	Name & Total Leave (Weeks)	Paid	Payment	Effective Total Leave (Weeks)[2]	Eligibility Criteria for Payments
						Must work in insured employment for 70 days during two designated and consecutive 6-month periods. Excluded: self-employed workers, seasonal workers (less than 7 months of the year), agricultural workers.
	Parental					
	Paternity	15 days[11]	Yes	100% of salary immediately prior to leave.	2	Workers in Central Government only. Less than 2 surviving children. May be taken up to 15 days before or up to 6 months from the date of delivery.
Israel	Maternity	12 weeks paid and job-protected maternity leave, 6 of which may be taken prior to birth.	Yes	100% of wages equal to last 3 months of paid employment.	12	Mother contributed to insurance fund for minimum of 6 months. By law, full-time working mothers are eligible to work an hour less per day during the four months following the completion of their maternity leave.
	Parental	Mothers may take 9 months unpaid leave supplementing the paid maternity leave period. Father may take 7–12 weeks of paid leave in lieu of mother.[12]	No/ Part			Since 1995, fathers may take parental leave instead of the mother, from the 7th week following the birth, they are also eligible for a parental allowance for a period of up to 42 days.[13]

	Paternity					Parents are also granted up to 6 days/year fully paid sick leave to care for sick children under the age of 16. The parents can choose which of them takes leave for this task.
Spain	Maternity	16 weeks (extended by 2 weeks in the case of disabled children or if more than 3 children).[14]	Yes	100% of earnings with ceiling.	16	To be entitled to cash maternity benefits, employees should be affiliated to the general social security scheme and have made contributions for 180 days in the 5 years preceding the date of birth, adoption or foster care.
	Parental	Part-time parental leave; reduction in daily work time of 30–50%. If child is < 6, reduced working hours. 36 months (including maternity leave) up to child's 3rd birthday.[15]	No	No compensation.	0	Three years/parent/child, with age limit up to 3 or 6 years if part-time. Each successive child entitles the worker to a new period of leave which marks the end of the current period of leave. Only 1 parent may exercise this right when they both work for the same employer.[16]
	Paternity	2 days (paid) + 4 weeks transferable from mother (extended to 13 days).[17]	Yes	100% of earnings.		The worker shall give advance notice and provide evidence of the birth of the child before taking this 2 day-leave.[18]
Taiwan	Maternity	Employer-paid leave[19]: 8 weeks.	Yes	Employer-paid leave: 100%. Additional 1–2 months of childbirth allowance.	8	6 months service = full pay, less than 6 months = half pay. 4 different social insurance plans cover the majority of workers.
	Parental	104 weeks[20]	No		0	Up to 2 years unpaid until child reaches 3 years of age, eligible if working for more than 1 year at a company with 30 or more employees.

(*Continued*)

TABLE 3.3 (Continued)

Country	*Type of Leave*	*Name & Total Leave (Weeks)*	*Paid*	*Payment*	*Effective Total Leave (Weeks)*[2]	*Eligibility Criteria for Payments*
	Paternity	3 days[21]	Yes	Employer-paid leave: 100%.	0.3	Leave to be taken on day child is born and one day within 2 to 5 days before or after childbearing day. If this occurs during regular off day, no supplementary leave will be given.
Turkey	Maternity	16 weeks (12 weeks paid). Can extend additional 24 weeks.[22]	Yes No	66.7%	8	All insured women: social insurance program. Leave taken 8 weeks before and 8 weeks after giving birth, on request (and doctor's approval) women may work until 3 weeks prior to birth.
	Parental	0				
	Paternity	3 days[23]				Public sector only.
United States	Maternity	0				Maternity covered by temporary disability insurance (TDI) in California, Hawaii, New Jersey, New York, Rhode Island, & Puerto Rico. Ranges from 26–52 weeks.[24]
	Parental	Family and Medical leave Act:[25] 12 weeks	No		0	Firms with 50 or more employees. Employed for 12 months and at least 1250 hours.
	Paternity	0				
US—California (Paid Family Leave, as of July 1, 2004)[26]	Maternity/ Paternity	6 weeks	Yes	55% of earnings, up to a maximum of USD 728 per week	3.3	Paying premiums to State Disability Insurance Program. Seven-day unpaid waiting period. Can be taken at one time or in hourly, daily, or weekly increments over the course of the year.

[1] For more recent statutory provisions and international comparisons, readers are referred to the International Labour Organization's publication, *Maternity and Paternity at Work: Law and Practice across the World, 2014* and the annual review of leave policies published by the International Parental Leave and Policy Research Network.

[2] Effective parental leave is calculated by weighing the length of parental leave by the level of payment. Effective parental leave = [(maternity leave in weeks−unpaid waiting period) × % payment benefit] + (parental leave in weeks × % payment benefit)

[3] Any paid maternity leave is available through enterprise bargaining agreements and select awards.

[4] http://www.ilo.org/dyn/travail/travmain.sectionReport1?p_lang=en&p_structure=3&p_countries=AU&p_year=2009&p_sc_id=2000

[5] http://www.childpolicyintl.org/countries/australiahi.pdf

[6] Whitehouse, G., Baird, M., Diamond, C., & Soloff, C. (2007). Parental leave in Australia: Beyond the statistical gap. *Journal of Industrial Relations 49*(1), 103–112.

[7] There is no legal requirement for paid paternity leave, though about one-third of working men get some form of paid paternity leave from their employers. The average duration is 14 days. Whitehouse et al. (2007).

[8] Québec Parental Insurance Plan, http://www.rqap.gouv.qc.ca/index_en.asp

[9] *China Briefing*. "Expecting in China: Employee Maternity Leave and Allowances." http://www.china-briefing.com/news/2014/11/11/maternity-leave-allowance-china.html

[10] Social Security Programs Throughout the World: Asia and the Pacific, 2004 http://www.ssa.gov/policy/docs/progdesc/ssptw/2004–2005/asia/index.html

[11] No. 13018/1/97-Est.(L) Government of India Ministry of Personnel, P.G. & Pensions (Department of Personnel & Training), New Delhi, Dated October 7, 1997.

[12] http://www.childpolicyintl.org/countries/israelhi.pdf

[13] Ben-Arieh, A., Zionit, Y., & Krizak, G. (2003). *The state of the child in Israel: A statistical abstract*. Jerusalem: National Council for the Child.

[14] Aybars, Ayse Idil. (2007). Work-life balance in the EU and leave arrangements across welfare regime. *Industrial Relations Journal, 38*(6), 569–590 (see Table 5 on page 586).

[15] Aybars (2007).

[16] http://www.ilo.org/travaildatabase/servlet/maternityprotection?pageClass=org.ilo.legislation.work.web.ReferencePage&LinkId=9123

[17] Aybars (2007).

[18] http://www.ilo.org/travaildatabase/servlet/maternityprotection?pageClass=org.ilo.legislation.work.web.ReferencePage&LinkId=9127

[19] Ministry of Labor, Republic of China (Taiwan). Law Source Retrieving System of Labor Laws and Regulations. http://laws.mol.gov.tw/Eng/EngContent.aspx?msgid-44.

[20] Ibid.

[21] Ibid.

[22] Labour Act of Turkey, Article 74 http://www.ilo.org/public/english/region/eurpro/ankara/legislation/law4857.htm

[23] International Labour Organization—Conditions of Work and Employment Programs http://www.ilo.org/public/english/protection/condtrav/family/reconcilwf/specialleave.htm

[24] Institute for Women's Policy Research. (2007). Maternity Leave in the United States. http://www.iwpr.org/publications/pubs/maternity-leave-in-the-united-states-paid-parental-leave-is-still-not-standard-even-among-the-best-u.s.-employers

[25] U.S. Family and Medical Leave Act. http://www.dol.gov/whd/regs/compliance/whdfs28.htm

[26] California Paid Family Leave. http://www.paidfamilyleave.org/

total of less than 12 weeks of paid maternity leave or restrictions on eligibility); and Australia and the United States had no public provision for paid maternity leave, relying on employers to provide leave and income replacement.[2]

Provisions for paid parental leave (a period of leave that follows maternity leave or a period that can be shared by both parents if desired) are notably absent among Project 3535 countries with the exception of Canada and minor provisions in Israel, in contrast to the availability of paid parental leave in many European countries. A period of unpaid parental leave was available to parents in Australia, Spain, Taiwan, and the United States. Only the Province of Québec in Canada had a designated period of three to five weeks of generous paid paternity leave reserved for fathers. By contrast, Spain, Indonesia, and Taiwan provided 2–3 days of paid paternity leave.

Provisions for publicly funded early childhood education and care (ECEC) programs, especially for children under 3 years of age, and data about their availability are not widely available, yet are a critical element in family policies (OECD, 2011). In their absence, parents make a variety of private arrangements with family or friends if available, or with private providers (often unregulated) that may or may not be of high quality or sustainable. Concerns about the availability and quality of child care arrangements can result in parents delaying their return to work following maternity/parental leave, leaving the labor force, or experiencing considerable worry about their children while at work (Barnett, 2004). Low-income mothers are particularly vulnerable, thwarting efforts to be economically self-sufficient. Consequently, ECEC policy has become a greater policy priority in many countries, especially given the wide range of social and economic benefits than can result for children, women, families, and society. In the last decade, a number of countries have introduced kindergarten or pre-kindergarten programs, often in communities with higher populations of low-income families, while others are expanding provisions for early childhood education more universally in line with recommendations from the OECD Network on Early Childhood Education and Care.

Table 3.4 provides a summary of the main institutional arrangements for the provision of ECEC and the extent to which children participated in those arrangements among the Project 3535 countries that were in place around the time of data collection. Several countries have committed to major expansions in ECEC programs since that time.

Little information was available about the extent to which children under 3 or 4 years of age participate in nonparental care arrangements in many countries, both because care by family members is expected and because no data systems are in place to collect such information. ECEC programs for children ages 4–5 are more common, especially in Israel, Spain, Canada, the United States, and Australia, and they are more accessible in urban areas. Many of these programs are offered part-time, however, and are only partly publicly funded, other than programs specifically targeted to low-income groups. In many studies of ECEC, affordability

TABLE 3.4 Main institutional arrangements for provision of ECEC, 2004 or closest year.[1*]

Age of children	*0 (birth)*	*1*	*2*	*3*	*4*	*5*	*6*
Australia	15%[2] in approved day care and occasional care centers.				Preschool classes with out-of-school hours care. Kindergarten About half of over-3-year-olds enrolled in pre-primary education.[3]		Compulsory and minimum school starting ages are determined in each state and territory. 6 is the most common compulsory age.[4]
Canada[5]	Little data available for children under 5 years. Primarily private and unsupervised arrangements. Québec exception: offers subsidized child care, enrolls 38% of 0–4s. 24% of children 0–6 years in center-based and family day care.				Junior K: 40% of 4–5s in Ontario; 50% in Québec. Kindergarten: 95% of 5- to 6-year-olds enrolled.		Compulsory school at 6.
China	Little data available. Traditionally grandparents have had strong involvement in infant care.[6]				Preschool education for children age 4–€, mostly privately funded and operated.[7] 36% of children enrolled in 2003–2004[6] Major differences in availability and enrollment between large urban centers and remote and rural areas[8]		Compulsory school at 6 or 7 years of age.
India	Unrecorded in official statistics, however Day care is available from birth to 3 years of age.[9]				The main arrangement of poor mothers (54%) is to bring their babies to work, whereas 85% of the better-off group had house-girls.[10] Pre-primary education not a fundamental right: very low percentage of children receiving preschool educational facilities. Pre-primary school includes: Lower Kindergarten (LKG) for children 3–4 years of age and Upper Kindergarten (UKG) children 4–5 years of age.[11]		Primary school includes children of ages 6–11, organized into classes 1 through 5. Upper Primary and Secondary school pupils aged 11–15 are organized into classes 6 through 10, and higher secondary school students ages 16–17 are enrolled in classes 11 through 12.[12]

(Continued)

TABLE 3.4 (Continued)

Age of children	*0 (birth)*	*1*	*2*	*3*	*4*	*5*	*6*
Indonesia	Data not available for the group under 3 years.[13]				In 2003, less than 20% of 3- to 5-year-olds enrolled in pre-primary school education.[14] In 2004, 31% of total children aged 3–6 participated in any type of ECED.[15] Approx. 40% of working women care for their children while working, 37% rely on female relatives (esp. grandmothers), and 10% use older female siblings to help. In rural areas, older female siblings are the primary caregivers for young children.[16] Kindergarten (*Taman Kanak-kanak*) beginning at 5 but not compulsory. Approximately 60% of children enrolled in grade 1 have not participated in any form of ECED service[17] In 2005, 24.4% of children aged 4–6 were enrolled in formal services and 10% in non-formal services.[18]		Children ages 7–12 attend Sekolah Dasar (SD) (literally Elementary School). Compulsory for all Indonesian citizens.[19]
Israel	Some 30% at the age of 2.[20] Among Arab families, unlike many Jewish Israeli families, it is rare to find babies who are left with caregivers, babysitters, or other strangers. Members of the extended family often help parents fulfill the basic tasks of disciplining and taking care of children.[21]				About 90% of over-3-year-olds enrolled in pre-primary education.[22]		Compulsory school at 5. (Strong involvement in youth movements, community centers and after school programs.)
Spain	5%[23] Education pre-scholar (center-based). Culturally there is a high reliance on family networks for care.				Education infantile (preschool) with primary school More than 90% of over-3-year-olds enrolled in pre-primary education.[24]		Compulsory school at 6.

Taiwan	No findings of public arrangements for care for children under age 4; Care mostly provided by grandparents.	2 year preschool education optional, 27% enrolment in 2001.[25]	Compulsory school at 6.
Turkey	Center, community-based care, and day cares.	16% of children 3–5 enrolled in preschool education programs, including kindergartens, nursery classes, and practical nursery classes. Ministry funded; parental contribution for meals & cleaning materials.[26]	Compulsory school at 6.
United States[27]	Primarily private child care centers and family day care; 50% of children 0–3 (38% of these in licensed services).	40% of children 3- to 4-years-old, and 70% of 4–5s enrolled in educational programs, including pre-K, private kindergartens, Head Start, purchase-of-service. Head Start covers 11% of 3- and 4-year-olds. From age 5, over 80% of children are enrolled in state-funded kindergarten (education auspices).	Compulsory school at 6.

* Most ECEC services for children 0–4 are described as family day care, social welfare, health, or family services.

Preschool and other services are most often administered under an Education ministry or education. Services for 5-year-olds are mixed, with some administered within schools or by school boards typically under an education ministry or agency; others are part of a community-based mix of preschool services.

Free and compulsory primary or preschool educational services are typically under an education ministry or agency.

1 Based on OECD *Starting Strong II*, Table 4.1, page 76, OECD. (2006). Starting Strong II: Early Childhood Education and Care. http://www.oecd.org/edu/school/startingstrongiiearlychildhoodeducationandcare.htm

2 As at 1998–2000. http://www.undp.or.id/pubs/ihdr2004/ihdr2004_full.pdf

3 As at 1998–2000. http://www.undp.or.id/pubs/ihdr2004/ihdr2004_full.pdf

4 http://www.oecd.org/dataoecd/37/14/39676760.pdf (see page 15)

5 *Starting Strong II*, Table 4.1.

6 UNESCO (2006). China Early Childhood Care and Education (ECCE) programmes: Country profile prepared for the Education for All Global Monitoring Report 2007 Strong Foundations: Early Childhood Care and Education. http://unesdoc.unesco.org/images/0014/001471/147175e.pdf

7 Stanford University Rural Education Action Plan and Institute for International Studies. (n.d.) Educational Challenges—Early Childhood Education. http://reap.fsi.stanford.edu/docs/early_childhood_education

8 According to the UNESCO report cited in note 6, "In March 2003, the State Council enacted the "Recommendations on Early Childhood Education Reform and Development," which promoted the early childhood education reform and development in marketing economy implemented by China and set the milestone for ECCE. Goals for development of ECCE that assuring the enrolment rate of children in preschool education to 55% by 2007, one-year-before primary education enrollment rate to 80%, universalizing three-year-before primary education in major cities and capacity building for parents and child care staffs have been put forward in the Recommendations."

[9] As at 1998–2000. http://www.undp.or.id/pubs/ihdr2004/ihdr2004_full.pdf

[10] As at 1998–2000. http://www.undp.or.id/pubs/ihdr2004/ihdr2004_full.pdf

[11] Early childhood education activities remained scattered, concentrated in urban settings, restricted to certain regions in the country, and confined to those who could afford such services. http://www.childpolicyintl.org/

[12] http://countrystudies.us/india/37.htm

[13] As at 1998–2000. http://www.undp.or.id/pubs/ihdr2004/ihdr2004_full.pdf

[14] http://www.childpolicyintl.org/ecectables/figure127.pdf

[15] http://siteresources.worldbank.org/INTINDONESIA/Resources/Publication/280016–1152870963030/ReportECED.pdf See Table A2.1

[16] Kamerman, 2002, as quoted in Hein, 2005, "Reconciling work and family responsibilities: practical ideas from global experience" ILO, Geneva p17

[17] http://siteresources.worldbank.org/INTINDONESIA/Resources/Publication/280016–1152870963030/ReportECED.pdf, see page 9 of report.

[18] http://siteresources.worldbank.org/INTINDONESIA/Resources/Publication/280016–1152870963030/ReportECED.pdf, see Figure 14

[19] http://education.stateuniversity.com/pages/662/Indonesia-EDUCATIONAL-SYSTEM-OVERVIEW.html

[20] As at 1998–2000 http://www.undp.or.id/pubs/ihdr2004/ihdr2004_full.pdf

[21] Katz, R. & Lavee, Y. (2005). Families in Israel. In B.N. Adam and J. Trost, J. (Eds.), *Handbook of world families* (Ch. 23). Thousand Oaks, CA: Sage.

[22] As at 1998–2000. http://www.undp.or.id/pubs/ihdr2004/ihdr2004_full.pdf

[23] As at 1998–2000. http://www.undp.or.id/pubs/ihdr2004/ihdr2004_full.pdf

[24] As at 1998–2000. http://www.undp.or.id/pubs/ihdr2004/ihdr2004_full.pdf

[25] Ministry of the Interior, Taiwan. http://www.moi.gov.tw/outline2007.e5.htm

[26] Turkey Early Childhood Care and Education (ECCE) programmes, UNESCO 2006

[27] *Starting Strong II*, Table 4.1

and accessibility are major barriers, and parents may use multiple arrangements to cover their work hours, especially when their children are below school age.

Among the countries in Project 3535, Israel has a history of collective care for children on kibbutzim and an early recognition of the values of group care and education. Australia has developed a variety of high-quality early childhood education (preschool) programs, most of which focus on children 3–5 years of age, with some serving infants and toddlers. Since 1997, Québec has worked to develop a province-wide system of affordable, licensed, home-based child care and child care centers as a component in its family policy; in other parts of Canada, regulated child care for children under 18 months is rare and very expensive. The Canadian Province of Ontario implemented universal junior kindergarten for 4-year-olds, which is publicly funded, but until recently was provided only part day or part week. In the United States and Canada most child care is privately purchased with tax deductions (and employer-administered pre-tax child care expense plans in the United States), providing some relief with high child care costs. Programs for young children in low-income families in the United States are administered separately (e.g., through federally funded Head Start initiatives, and over the last 15–20 years have been expanding downward to include programs for children 2 years of age and younger and more gradually to include pre-kindergarten programs in designated schools). Overall, the available data indicate that whereas some countries, such as Israel and Spain, have well-developed programs for 3- to 5-year-olds, others such as India, Indonesia, Turkey, and Taiwan are in the early stages of implementing a system of early childhood education and care that can provide stimulating early education for children and support for working parents. Other than in Québec in Canada, no country in this sample has developed the public system available in several European countries which ensures that many parents who work during their child's preschool years have access to affordable, high-quality child care.

An Integrated Picture: Putting Together Information about Cultural Differences, Labor Force Patterns, and Institutional Supports

Composite rankings based on the UN's Human Development Index, the World Economic Forum's Global Gender Gap Index and its subindex that focuses on Economic Participation and Opportunity provide a fairly consistent picture of the relative standing of Project 3535 countries on these measures. Countries that ranked high on the HDI also had scores on the GGG that indicated less gender inequality in economic participation and opportunity, education, health, and political participation (the latter often considered an indicator of women's empowerment). We adopted the UN's approach of considering rankings below 80 as indicating high human development and gender equality and rankings above 80 as indicating medium human development and gender equality. Doing so suggests that Australia, Canada, the United States, Israel, and Spain can be grouped together as having high rankings on both composite measures; similarly, India, Indonesia, and Turkey have medium rankings on both measures. China's HDI ranking of 81 places it in the medium range on human development, but it remains in the top half of countries ranked on the composite GGG measure. The information available about Taiwan (which is not a member country of either organization and for which figures are based on its own government's calculations) suggests that it would be considered in the first group.

Consideration of the GGG subindex on Economic Participation and Opportunity brings greater attention to gaps in labor force participation, earnings, and opportunities for women to participate as professionals and managers. Based on this measure, the countries ranked as high or medium on the HDI and GGG composite measure retain their relative standing except for Spain. There were also notable gaps between GGG composite scores and those obtained on this subindex for India and Turkey in particular, with less striking but observable differences noted among scores for Indonesia and Spain; these patterns suggest there is more gender inequality in economic opportunities than in other areas of life.

Observations based on employment data indicate very high rates of women's labor force participation in China, Canada, the United States, and Australia, with particularly lower rates of employment noted among women in Turkey and India. In these countries and in Indonesia, a large proportion of women are engaged in agricultural work, and fewer are engaged in industries and the service sector. Among those women who are employed, a higher percentage works part-time in Australia, Canada, and Israel than in Taiwan, Turkey, or the United States. Part-time work likely reflects a variety of factors—including the structure of the labor force and the jobs available, and the choice to work part-time to manage caregiving demands. Also of note is that over 50% of employed women were classified as professional or technical workers in half of the Project 3535 countries—the United States, Australia, Canada, China, and Spain. Smaller proportions of employed women were professional or technical workers in India and Turkey.

Are institutional mechanisms in place to support women's labor force participation and advancement, gender equality, and less WFC for parents, especially when children are young? The data suggest that other than Canada, and particularly in Québec, Project 3535 countries have room to improve statutory provisions for paid maternity and parental leave, especially in contrast to many European countries. A particular contrast is the lack of public provisions for any paid maternity and parental leave in the United States and Australia, despite the high levels of women's labor force participation. In these countries, employers play a substantial role in providing paid time off for parents around the birth or adoption of a child and there are likely to be considerable inequities in access to such leave. In several other Project 3535 countries, there are provisions for paid maternity leave, but no or limited provisions for paid or unpaid parental leave. Paternity leave (other than a few days or when taken in lieu of mother's leave) is rare.

Similarly, other than in Québec, there are limited public provisions for the care of children below three years of age other than by family members or private arrangements. Well-developed programs for children age 4–5 were observed in Israel, Spain, Canada, the United States, and Australia and in most cases, such programs have a dual role, providing educational experiences for children and child care for working parents.

Figure 3.2 provides a schematic view of Project 3535 countries based on their standing on the GGG subindex on Economic Participation and Opportunity and a rudimentary index that combines information about the availability of paid maternity and parental leave and early childhood education and care. We see Project 3535 countries as falling within three of the four quadrants of this graph and comprising three "clusters" that may relate to patterns of use of workplace programs that provide flexibility and support and also to satisfaction with organizational practices and government policies. Readers should note that our

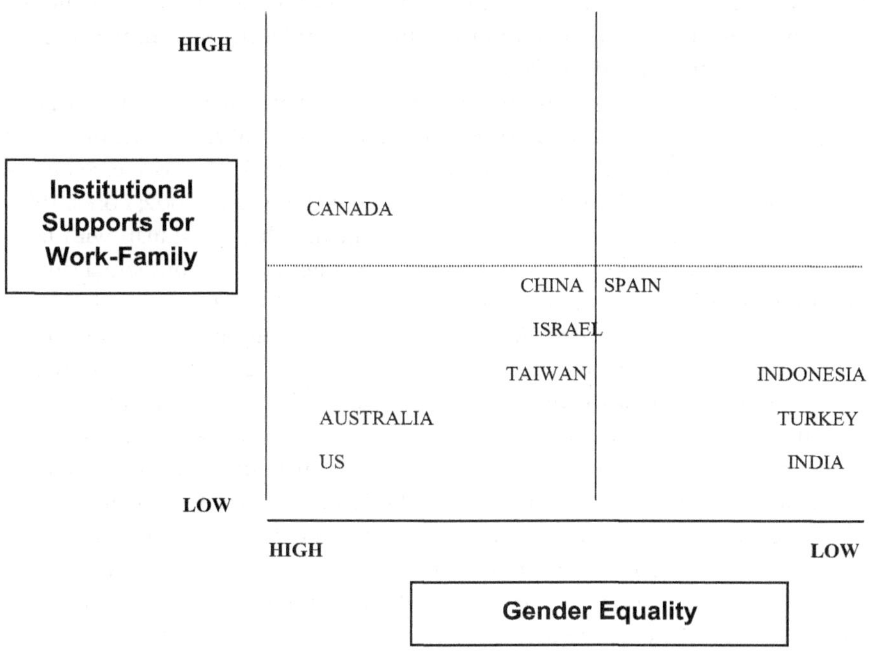

FIGURE 3.2 Clusters of 3535 countries based on gender equality and institutional supports.

Notes: 1. The Gender Equality Axis reflects scores on the World Economic Forum's Global Gender Gap Index. An adjustment was made for Spain given greater gaps in women's economic and social participation than in other areas.

2. The Institutional Support Axis reflects a combined standing based on policies related to paid maternity and parental leave and the availability of publicly funded early child care and education services.

schematic conceptualization of clusters is specific to the 10 countries involved in this project and that a broader international comparison of countries such as Norway, Sweden, and the Netherlands, as well as developing countries in Africa, South America, and Asia might suggest a different grouping of countries than presented here.

Survey Data

Organizational Policies, Programs, and Supports

An extensive body of research confirms that well-designed human resource management (HRM) policies and programs and improvements in workplace culture can improve both individual employee outcomes and organizational effectiveness and return on investment (Attridge, 2009). "HR programs such as performance management, selection, and training can reflect fair treatment, respect for collective association rights, and work-family balance, and reward not only economic performance, but also community involvement or reduced environmental emissions" (Boudreau & Ramstad, 2005, p. 131).

Family-friendly human resource initiatives have been shown to have a positive impact on individuals and organizations, including enhanced organizational commitment, job satisfaction, performance, and productivity, and decreased stress, WFC, absenteeism, and turnover (Kelly et al., 2008; Lero et al., 2009; Lobel, 1999; Rosin & Korabik, 2003). Moreover, there is evidence that individuals with family responsibilities are increasingly seeking companies that demonstrate a sincere commitment to helping them balance their work and family lives, and also are more likely to stay with them (Allen, Herst, Bruck, & Sutton, 2000). Still, little is known about the mechanisms through which these policies bring about favorable outcomes or the extent to which they affect men and women differently.

Until recently, much of the research on the impact of workplace policies and practices on employees and on organizational sustainability has been carried out in single country settings, particularly in the United States. A growing number of studies that compare different countries and cultures suggest both common concerns and outcomes, at least among the larger organizations represented in the research (e.g., Hill, Yang, Hawkins, & Ferris, 2004). However, international studies of the work and family interface must also be sensitive to the effects of different national contexts, welfare regimes, gender-role ideologies, and values such as individualism-collectivism (Blair-Loy & Frenkel, 2005; Lu, Gilmour, Kao, & Huang, 2006). The current emphasis on global competition means it is necessary to find out the extent to which these effects are cross-nationally generalizable. One purpose of the present study, therefore, was to examine the impact of national context on employees' use of and satisfaction with organizational policies and programs and how this is related to employees' attitudes to the workplace, WFC, and life satisfaction—all of which are related to individual engagement and resilience.

A second purpose of this study is to examine the effects of gender. Previous research has demonstrated that men and women may have different experiences of WFC, that their utilization of family-friendly organizational policies may be different, and that the policies may have a differential impact on them (Rosin & Korabik, 2003). For example, research has shown that policy availability and use have a more positive impact on women's organizational commitment than they do on men's (Greenberger, Goldberg, Hamill, O'Neal, & Payne, 1989; Scandura & Lankau, 1997). Similarly, Hill (2005) and Batt and Valcour (2003) find that positive perceptions of W-F culture and supervisor support are more strongly associated with the degree of reported WFC for mothers/women than for fathers/men. These findings suggest that workplace practices and support may be more critical for women's capacity to balance work and family and for their opportunities for continued career advancement than it is for men—a factor that is especially important in countries where economic growth depends on an increasing proportion of women in the workforce and skill shortages loom, as well as for gender equity more broadly.

In particular, the analyses in this chapter address the following questions:

(1) To what extent are cross-national differences evident in employees' use of and satisfaction with organizational policies that can help employees integrate work and family responsibilities or promote their health and well-being?
(2) To what extent are there gender differences in policy use and in satisfaction with organizational policies?
(3) How is satisfaction with family-friendly organizational policies related to individual outcomes (WFC, intent to turnover, and life satisfaction)?
(4) To what extent are there cross-national differences in satisfaction with family-friendly government policies and programs, and are there differences in satisfaction between men and women? Are employees more satisfied with organizational family-friendly practices in countries with more limited institutional supports?

To answer these questions, we focus on self-reported use and the perceived helpfulness of nine organizational policies designed to enhance flexibility, support dependent care, and promote employee health. We analyze use and perceived helpfulness of workplace programs and practices rather than availability for several reasons, the most important of which are: (1) employees may not be aware of what policies and programs are available to them; (2) availability can vary greatly within an organization based on specific job characteristics or supervisor discretion; and (3) even when available, employees may not feel comfortable using flexible work-life arrangements if they fear it will affect their job security or career advancement or if use is discouraged by a supervisor (Williams, Blair-Loy, & Berdahl, 2013). Similarly, if available options are not seen as helpful or appropriate, they will not be used or will not have the desired effects on such measurable outcomes as job satisfaction, absenteeism, or WFC (Rosin & Korabik, 2003).

TABLE 3.5 Percentage policy use by country.

Country	*Flex Schedule*	*Reduced Hours*	*Telecom-muting*	*Emergency Absence*	*Extended Maternity/ Parental Leave*	*Family Leave*	*Child Care*	*Health Insurance*	*Health Facilities*
Australia[1]	65.0	37.0	–	67.5	39.0	52.0	–	–	9.0
Canada	61.0	34.3	37.0	70.8	21.6	16.5	9.8	85.7	14.6
China	81.7	80.1	77.9	89.6	82.9	83.3	85.0	82.1	87.5
India	58.6	68.0	56.5	62.2	74.5	78.6	65.2	67.6	66.7
Indonesia	52.6	40.2	28.4	76.8	51.3	41.2	24.8	52.6	67.6
Israel	76.1	62.9	57.6	79.5	66.8	69.9	53.7	61.6	60.7
Spain	44.0	20.7	12.7	64.7	7.3	4.0	6.0	22.7	36.7
Taiwan	37.4	33.9	12.8	64.5	26.7	37.0	19.9	49.8	38.1
Turkey	25.5	9.5	8.9	91.7	15.7	40.0	12.0	68.0	37.2
USA	64.1	46.6	39.0	63.2	23.8	22.4	18.4	81.2	32.3

[1] Data were not collected in Australia related to the use of telecommuting, child care, and health insurance.

The Use of Organizational Policies and Programs

The data on the percentage of employees who used each of the nine organizational policies by country are presented in Table 3.5. As shown, use of individual workplace practices that provide employees with opportunities to better balance work and family responsibilities or promote employee health varies considerably across countries. The most widely used workplace practices are permission to leave work in a personal or family emergency, employer-provided health insurance, and flexible scheduling. The least commonly used practice across all countries is working from home (telecommuting), which can reflect not only more limited workplace acceptance of this option, but also realistic constraints based on the nature of specific jobs. Comparisons across countries indicate that, except for emergency leave and health insurance, other family-friendly workplace practices are used least often by employees in Turkey, Spain, and Taiwan, and most often by employees in China, India, and Israel.

Perceived Helpfulness of Organizational Policies and Practices

Separate country-by-gender comparisons of helpfulness ratings for each organizational policy were carried out with age and job level (manager/nonmanager) as covariates. The control for job level was necessary because research has shown that family-friendly policies have differential effects on managerial and nonmanagerial employees (Oliver, Korabik, McElwain, & Lero, 2008). Age was used as a proxy for several factors including life stage, family stage (age of youngest child), and job tenure/career advancement. We present our findings first for organizational policies that provide more flexibility over the timing or location of work, then those pertaining to time away from work for family care (emergency absence, extended maternity/parental leave, and time off to care for a sick family member), and finally for assistance with child care and access to health insurance and health facilities.

Flexible Hours, Reduced Hours, and Telecommuting

There are significant cross-national differences in perceptions of the helpfulness of each practice pertaining to flexibility among those who used these practices. The main effect of country for those who used flexible scheduling is highly significant, F (9, 1516) = 8.97, $p < .0001$. Users in Turkey, Spain, the United States, and Australia rated flextime as significantly more helpful for improving their W-F balance than those who used flexible scheduling in India, China, and Indonesia (see Figure 3.3). There is also a significant main effect for gender, F (1, 1516) = 5.79, $p < .02$, and a significant gender-by-country interaction, F (9, 1516) = 3.11, $p < .001$. Women rated flexible scheduling as more helpful to them in improving their W-F balance than men did except in India, Indonesia, China, and Taiwan where men rated it as more helpful than women did.

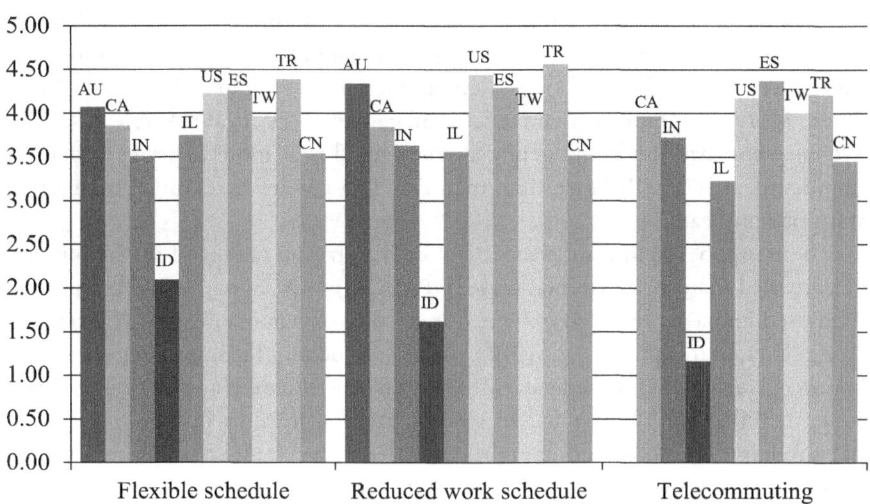

FIGURE 3.3 Mean helpfulness ratings for users of flexible schedules, reduced schedules, and telecommuting by country.

Note: Data are not available on telecommuting for Australia

There is also a main effect for country for reduced hours, F (9, 1236) = 5.39, $p < .0001$. Users in Turkey, Spain, the United States, and Australia rated using reduced hours as significantly more helpful for W-F balance than those in India, China, Indonesia, Israel, and Canada. Analyses of covariance revealed a significant main effect for gender, F (1, 1236) = 5.39, $p < .0001$, and a significant gender-by-country interaction, F (9, 1236) = 4.73, $p < .0001$. Women rated reduced work hours as more helpful to them in improving their W-F balance than men did except in India and Taiwan, where men rated it as more helpful than women.

For telecommuting (work at home), there is a significant main effect for country, F (8, 970) = 6.91, $p < .0001$. Users in Spain, Turkey, the United States, and Taiwan rated telecommuting as more helpful than did those in Israel and China. There is also a significant main effect for gender, F (1, 970) = 9.63, $p < .0001$, such that women rated telecommuting as more helpful to them in improving their W-F balance than men did. The country-by-gender interaction was not significant.

Leave Policies

Leave policies included emergency absence, extended maternity/parental leave, and time off to care for a sick family member. Significant country differences were noted on ratings of helpfulness for W-F balance among users of each leave policy (see Figure 3.4). For emergency absence, there is a significant main effect for country, F (9, 1996) = 34.6, $p < .0001$. Users of emergency leave in Turkey, Spain, the United States, Canada, and Australia rated this practice as significantly more helpful than those who used emergency leave in India, China, and Israel. There is also a significant main effect for gender, F (1, 1996) = 7.1, $p < .008$. Women who had used emergency absence rated it as more helpful to them in improving their W-F balance than men did. The gender by country interaction was not significant.

There is also a significant main effect of country on ratings of the helpfulness of extended maternity/parental leave, F (9, 1215) = 3.73, $p < .0001$. Employees who used employer-granted extended maternity or parental leave in Turkey and Australia rated this practice as significantly more helpful for improving their W-F balance than those who used extended leave in the other eight countries, whereas those in India and China rated maternity/parental leave to be significantly less helpful than those in the other eight countries. There was also a significant main effect for gender, F (1, 1215) = 12.47, $p < .0001$, and a significant gender-by-country interaction, F (9, 1215) = 3.8, $p < .0001$. Women rated maternity/parental leave as more helpful to them in improving their W-F balance than men except in Taiwan where men rated having extended parental leave as more helpful than women.

Cross-national differences were also evident when employers rated the helpfulness of being able to take time off to care for a sick family member, F (9,

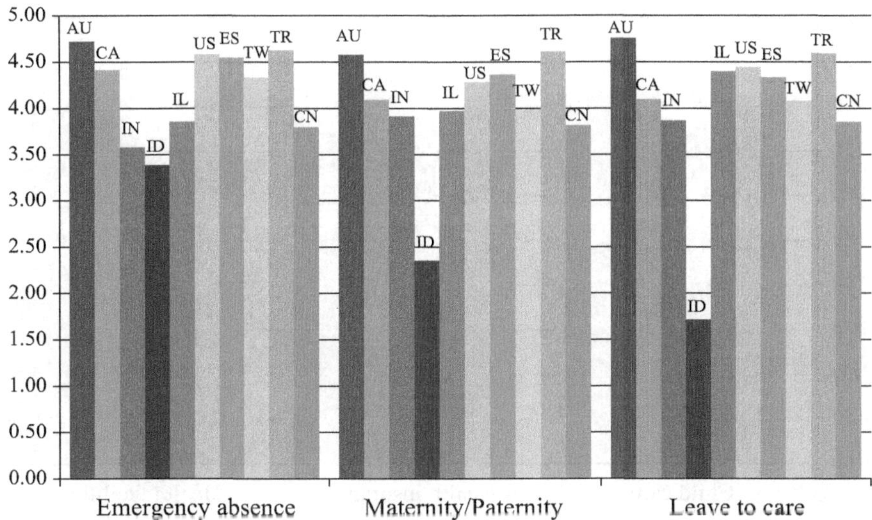

FIGURE 3.4 Mean helpfulness ratings for users of emergency family leave, maternity or parental leave, and caregiving leave policies by country.

1325) = 11.64, $p < .0001$. Those who availed themselves of this practice in Turkey and Australia rated family leave as significantly more helpful than those who utilized this practice in China, India, and Indonesia. Neither the main effect for gender nor the gender-by-country interaction was significant.

Assistance With Child Care and Access to Health Insurance and Health Facilities

There are significant cross-national differences in employees' perceptions of the helpfulness of employer support for child care provision or subsidies, F (8, 905) = 5.64, $p < .0001$. Those who utilized employer-provided child care support in Turkey, Taiwan, the United States, and Indonesia rated this organizational support as significantly more helpful for improving W-F balance than those in Canada and Spain (see Figure 3.5). The main effect for gender was not significant, $p > .05$; however, there was a significant gender-by-country interaction, F (8, 905) = 2.17, $p < .03$. Women rated child care as more helpful to them than men did except in China, Taiwan, and Turkey, where men rated it as more helpful than women did.

Comparisons across countries in ratings of the helpfulness of employer-provided health insurance are also significantly different across countries, F (8, 1670) = 23.59, $p < .0001$. Those who used this company benefit in Turkey, Canada, the United States, and Indonesia rated health insurance as being significantly more helpful than did individuals in India, China, and Israel. Neither the gender nor the gender-by-country interaction was significant.

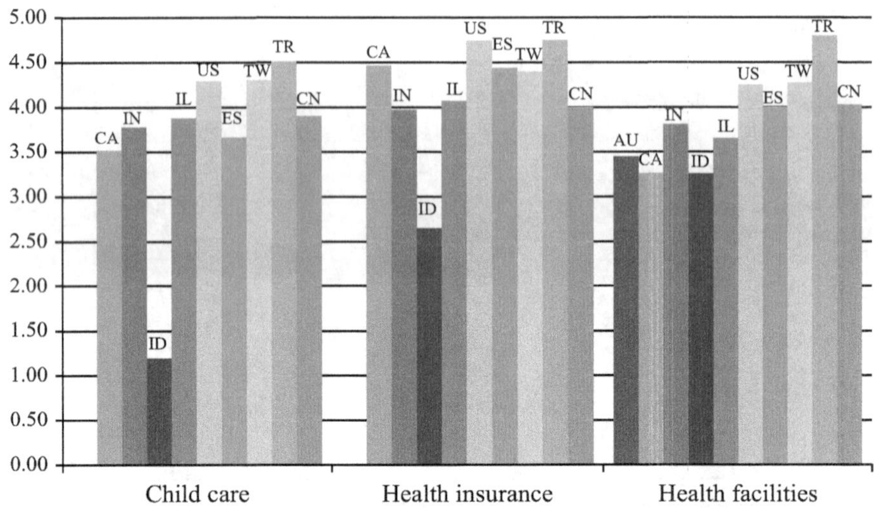

FIGURE 3.5 Mean helpfulness ratings for users of child care provisions and employer-provided health insurance and health facility policies by country.

Note: Data are not available on child care, and health insurance for Australia

Finally, there are cross-national differences in ratings of the helpfulness of employer-provided health facilities (an on-site or near-site doctor or nurse during office hours), F (9, 1301) = 15.92, p < .0001. Users in Turkey, Indonesia, Taiwan, and the United States rated availability of health facilities as being significantly more helpful than those in India, Canada, Australia, and Israel. There was also a significant main effect for gender, F (1, 1301) = 11.46, p < .0001. Women who had used company-provided health facilities rated them as more helpful in improving their W-F balance than men did. The gender-by-country interaction was not significant.

In summary, there were substantial cross-national differences in the extent of use of each organizational policy or practice and in the extent to which users rated these policies as helpful to them for improving their work-life balance. Differences in use could reflect differences in availability, perceived appropriateness or need, support/discouragement of use from supervisors, and the availability of other alternatives (e.g., a family member at home who can provide child care or attend to an ailing family member). Differences in the perceived helpfulness of these policies/practices for W-F balance among those who use them should be explored further. Finally, we note that were significant differences between men and women in the rated helpfulness of six of the nine organizational practices studied (all but leave for a sick family member, employer-provided child care, and health insurance). Among those who used these policies, women were significantly more likely to say that flexible scheduling, reduced work hours, telecommuting, emergency absence policies, extended maternity/parental leave, and access to on-site or near-site health facilities were helpful for improving their W-F balance.

Desired Access to Organizational Policies and Programs

Data were also collected about the extent to which non-users of each policy thought that having access to these forms of organizational support would be helpful to them (see Figure 3.6, Figure 3.7, and Figure 3.8). Cross-national differences were significant for each policy/practice, with the strongest interest evident in having access to flexible scheduling and reduced hours options, emergency absence, and leave to care for a sick family member. Significant gender differences were clear for all organizational policies/practices except for health insurance. Women who were not using these practices were significantly more likely than male non-users to believe that they would be helpful for improving W-F balance in each case.

Satisfaction With Organizational Policies and Practices

All respondents were asked to rate their overall satisfaction with the organizational family-friendly policies and practices available in their company on a scale ranging from 1 (*very dissatisfied*) to 5 (*very satisfied*). Average ratings ranged from a low of 2.79 for China to 3.75 for India (see Figure 3.9 for means). When analyses were

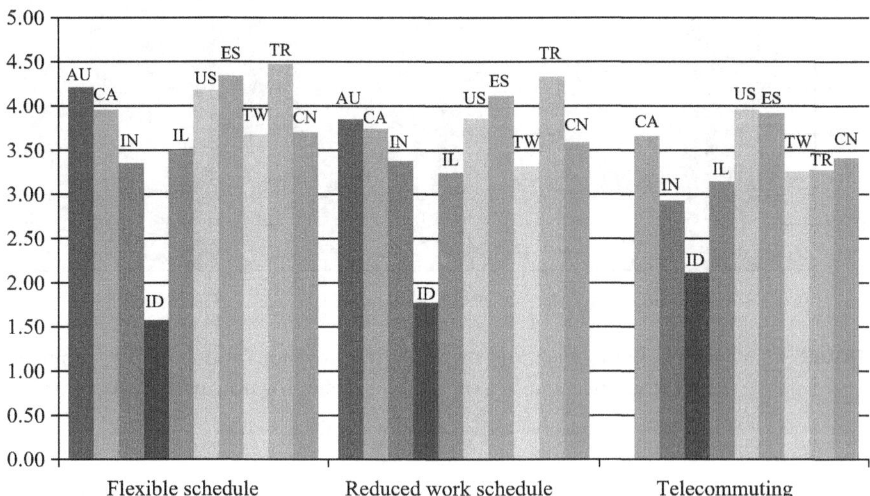

FIGURE 3.6 Mean helpfulness ratings of flexible schedule, reduced schedule, and telecommuting policies for non-users by country.

Note: Data are not available on telecommuting for Australia

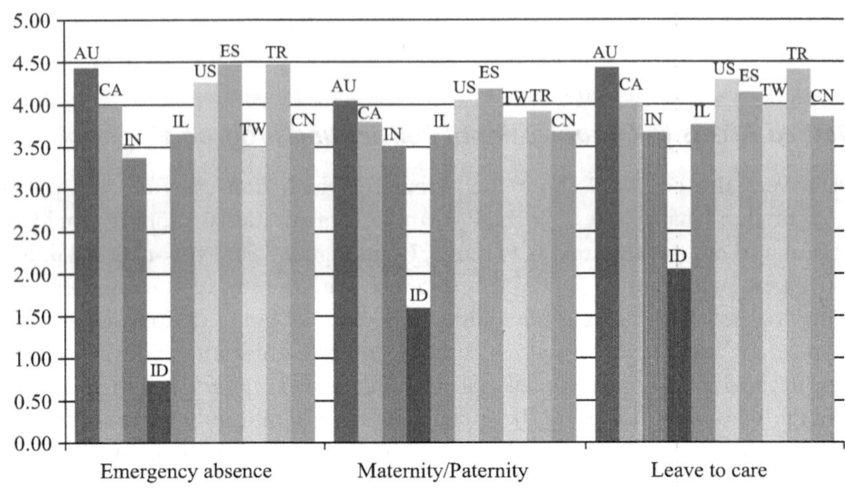

FIGURE 3.7 Mean helpfulness ratings of emergency family leave, maternity or paternity leave, and caregiving leave policies for non-users by country.

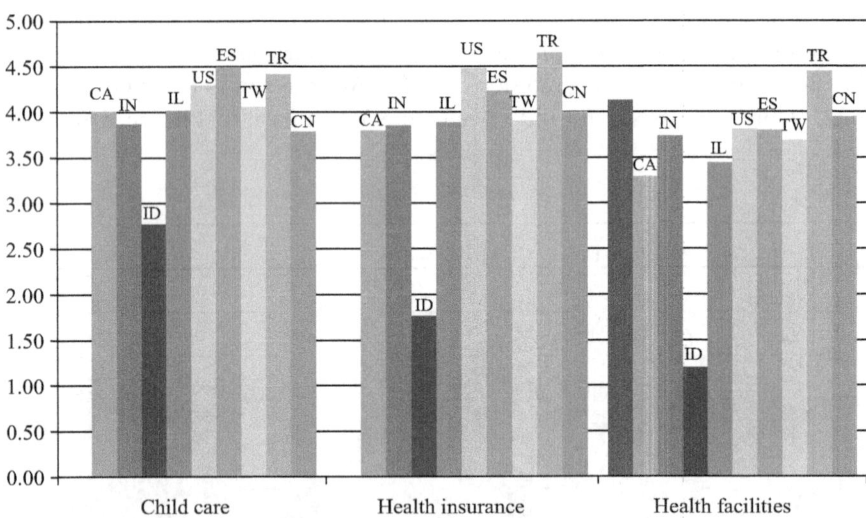

FIGURE 3.8 Mean helpfulness ratings of child care provisions and employer-provided health insurance and health facility policies for non-users by country.

Note: Data are not available on child care and health insurance for Australia

carried out with age and job level as covariates, there is a significant main effect for country, $F = (9, 2674) = 34.13, p < .0001$. Respondents in Australia, India, and the United States are the most satisfied, with those in Canada, Indonesia, Israel, and Turkey less so. Satisfaction with organizational policies is significantly lower among respondents in Spain, Taiwan, and China.

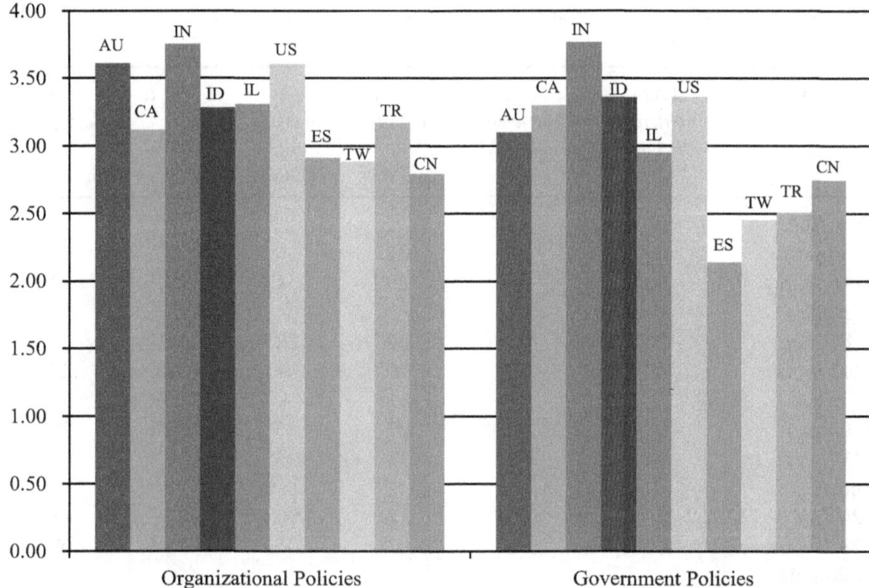

FIGURE 3.9 Mean ratings of satisfaction with organizational policies and practices and satisfaction with government policies by country.

There is also a significant main effect for gender, $F = (1, 2674) = 6.49, p < .01$ and a significant gender-by-country interaction, $F = (9, 2674) = 5.85, p < .0001$. Overall, women reported significantly greater satisfaction with organizational policies than men except in India, China, and Taiwan, where men were more satisfied than women.

Relationship Between Satisfaction With Organizational Policies and Practices and the W-F Interface and Outcome Variables

Correlations between satisfaction with organizational policies and W-F interface and outcome variables can be found in Table 3.6.

Greater satisfaction with organizational policies and practices is significantly associated with lower work interference with family conflict (WIF) for both men and women in Australia, Canada, Indonesia, and the United States. This relationship also held for men in Israel and women in Spain and Turkey. Greater satisfaction with organizational policies was also significantly associated with higher work-to-family positive spillover (WTFS) for both genders in Canada and Turkey. This relationship also held for men in China and women in Australia, Israel, Taiwan, and the United States.

TABLE 3.6 Correlations between satisfaction with organizational policies and work-family interface and outcome variables by country and gender.

Country (n)	*Work Interference with Family*	*Family Interference with Work*	*Work to Family Positive Spillover*	*Family to Work Positive Spillover*	*Intent to Turnover*	*Life Satisfaction*
Australia						
(79 men)	-.43**	-.06	.07	.15	-.37**	.17
(116 women)	-.42**	-.08	.29**	.34**	-.29**	.32**
Canada						
(186 men)	-.38**	-.03	.27**	.22**	-.39**	.42**
(115 women)	-.47**	-.20*	.20*	.04	-.32**	.27**
China						
(103 men)	-.14	.02	.27*	.26*	-.22*	.29*
(117 women)	-.15	.07	.11	.05	-.29**	.18
India						
(262 men)	.06	.06	-.12	-.09	-.21**	.15*
(282 women)	-.03	.03	.03	-.002	-.23**	.07
Indonesia						
(135 men)	-.21*	-.07	.08	.07	-.47**	.30**
(171 women)	-.22**	-.17*	.13	.10	-.19*	.32**
Israel						
(111 men)	-.24*	-.04	-.05	.09	-.34**	.33**
(113 women)	-.14	-.05	.20*	.11	-.38**	.34**
Spain						
(60 men)	-.12	-.12	.11	.19	-.30*	.25
(74 women)	-.33*	.13	.25*	-.06	-.36*	.22
Taiwan						
(76 men)	.004	-.04	-.03	-.01	-.24*	.18
(195 women)	-.06	-.19**	.21**	.34**	-.22**	.25**
Turkey						
(164 men)	-.05	.04	.24**	.16*	-.02	.31**
(161 women)	-.25**	-.16*	.31**	.14	-.07	.21**
USA						
(47 men)	-.53**	-.19	.27	.28	-.45**	.57**
(159 women)	-.37**	-.07	.29**	.03	-.35**	.21*

Note: * $p < .05$; ** $p < .01$.

Satisfaction with organizational policies was also significantly associated with lower turnover intent for both men and women in every country except Turkey—an important finding given the costs to employers of replacing talented employees and losing investments made in training and firm-specific knowledge. In addition, satisfaction with organizational policies was significantly associated with higher life satisfaction for both men and women in Canada, Indonesia, Israel, Turkey, and the United States. This relationship also held for men in China and India and for women in Australia and Taiwan.

Satisfaction With Government Policies

Respondents also were asked to rate their overall satisfaction with the family-friendly government policies available in their country on a scale from 1 (*very dissatisfied*) to 5 (*very satisfied*). Average ratings ranged from a low of 2.14 (Spain) to 3.77 in India (see Figure 3.5). Statistical comparisons revealed that rated satisfaction with government policies was significantly higher for participants in India than for all other countries. Following India, and not significantly different from each other, were Indonesia, the United States, Canada, and Australia. Respondents from Israel, China, Turkey, and Taiwan were relatively less satisfied; however, employees in Spain were significantly less satisfied with government policies than those from all other countries. In contrast to ratings of organizational policies and practices, there was no statistical difference between men and women on average ratings of satisfaction with government policies or gender-by-country interactions. The average rating of satisfaction with government policies was 3.09 for men and 3.06 for women.

Relationship Between Satisfaction With Government Policies and the W-F Interface and Outcome Variables

The most consistent correlations between satisfaction with government policies and outcome variables were observed with ratings of life satisfaction (see Table 3.7). Greater satisfaction with government policies is significantly associated with higher life satisfaction for both men and women in Canada, China, India, and Indonesia. This relationship also held for men in Australia and the United States and for women in Israel. Satisfaction with government policies is less consistently related to intent to turnover, with the strongest correlations evident for men in the United States, women in Spain, and both men and women in Israel.

Discussion

One of the main purposes of the present study was to determine whether there were cross-national differences in employees' use of and satisfaction with organizational policies that can help employees integrate work and family responsibilities or promote their health and well-being, or both. We also examined whether satisfaction with family-friendly organizational policies was related to individual outcomes, including WFC and positive spillover, intent to turnover, and life satisfaction. The findings revealed significant cross-national differences in policy use, policy helpfulness ratings by users and non-users, and satisfaction with family-friendly organizational policies and practices. The most commonly used policies were permission to leave work in a personal or family emergency, employer-provided health insurance or benefits, and flexible scheduling. Comparisons across countries indicated that other family-friendly workplace practices were used significantly less often by employees in Turkey, Spain, and Taiwan and most often in

TABLE 3.7 Correlations between satisfaction with government policies and work-family interface and outcome variables by country and gender.

Country (n)	*Work Interference with Family*	*Family Interference with Work*	*Work to Family Positive Spillover*	*Family to Work Positive Spillover*	*Intent to Turnover*	*Life Satisfaction*
Australia						
(79 men)	-.18	-.25*	.07	.03	-.08	.39**
(116 women)	-.21*	-.11	-.10	-.04	-.23*	.04
Canada						
(186 men)	-.15*	-.06	.27**	.21**	-.16*	.24**
(115 women)	-.15	-.19*	.05	.04	-.05	.27**
China						
(103 men)	-.13	.04	.27**	.29**	-.13	.31**
(117 women)	-.06	.14	.23**	.13	-.13	.35**
India						
(262 men)	-.04	-.004	-.21**	-.28**	-.16*	.14*
(282 women)	.04	.18*	-.15*	-.16*	-.01	.13*
Indonesia						
(135 men)	-.21*	-.12	.13	.10	-.24*	.31**
(171 women)	-.16*	-.10	-.01	.02	-.01	.23**
Israel						
(111 men)	-.03	.08	.23*	.04	-.35**	.16
(113 women)	.09	.18	.07	.20*	-.27**	.24*
Spain						
(60 men)	-.03	-.03	.08	.09	-.06	-.04
(74 women)	-.35*	-.14	.27*	.05	-.35**	.17
Taiwan						
(76 men)	-.07	.02	-.09	-.26	-.18	.17
(195 women)	.13	.01	.14	.16*	.01	.11
Turkey						
(164 men)	-.20**	.03	.08	-.11	.22**	.07
(161 women)	-.10	-.10	.02	.01	-.09	-.11
USA						
(47 men)	-.38*	.10	.23	.25	-.44**	.32*
(159 women)	-.08	-.18*	-.02	-.01	-.01	-.02

Note: * $p < .05$; ** $p < .01$.

China, India, and Israel. We note that use reflects many factors: availability, accessibility, awareness, need/perceived benefit, and whether the workplace culture and supervisor attitudes support policy use.

As Rosin and Korabik (2003) and others have noted, satisfaction with policies used or available is a separate and important factor to assess than simply availability or even use per se. Though there was variation across specific family-friendly practices, in general, those who used family-friendly employer-provided flexibility and leave options in Turkey, Spain, the United States, and Australia were significantly more likely to say that their use of these policies was helpful in supporting their work-life balance. Among non-users, employees in most countries rated these practices' potential usefulness as fairly high, with average ratings generally exceeding 3.5 out of 5. Non-users in Spain and Turkey were most likely to indicate that family-friendly initiatives would be helpful to better balance W-F responsibilities. In some cases, such as employer-provided child care support and having additional job-protected maternity/parental leave, the findings partially reflect limited support available through public policies. Researchers such as den Dulk, Peters, and Poutsma (2012) have noted the interplay between institutional arrangements and organizational conditions that can affect the availability of W-F supports. More subtle interactions between country, practice, and gender require further inquiry to better explain how and why certain HRM practices are perceived as helpful by men and women in different circumstances.

Significant differences were also noted in participants' overall satisfaction with organizational policies. Employees in Spain, Taiwan, and China were least satisfied, while those in Australia, India, and the United States were most satisfied.

Does satisfaction with organizational policies that support W-F integration predict positive outcomes? Our results suggest that in all countries except Turkey, the more both men and women are satisfied with the family-friendly policies in their organizations, the lower their intent to turnover. Satisfaction with organizational policies was also positively associated with life satisfaction, not quite as consistently, but significantly. This was especially so for women, but with high correlations for men in the United States, Canada, and Israel. These findings are consistent with a large body of studies conducted mostly in the United States in the last two decades that indicate that workplace supports (including specific policies and a family-friendly workplace culture, as well as supervisors who support W-F integration practices) can have particular positive impacts on employees' attitudes towards their workplace (including higher organizational commitment and less intent to turnover) as well as on WFC as a result of reducing demands or enabling employees to better manage demands without compromising their health and the quality of family life (Allen et al., 2014; Eby et al., 2005; Hill, 2005; Kossek et al., 2011; Kossek & Ollier-Malaterre, 2013).

A second purpose of this study was to examine the effects of gender. Our findings confirmed that among both policy users and non-users, women were significantly more likely than men to feel that organizational supports that allow greater flexibility and additional support for their family roles (longer maternity/parental leave, child care support, leave to care for sick family members) are beneficial or would be beneficial in helping them attain greater work-life balance. Women were also significantly more satisfied with the organizational policies that were available to them. Finally, satisfaction with organizational policies was significantly related to both turnover intention and life satisfaction in most of the countries in this study. Some of the unique variation observed in country-by-gender interactions will require further study. Our finding that use of most family-friendly organizational policies was perceived as more helpful for W-F balance among women aligns well with other studies that have demonstrated that such organizational policies (along with greater supervisor support and positive perceptions of W-F culture) have stronger impacts on women's organizational commitment and WFC (Batt & Valcour, 2003; Greenberger et al., 1989; Hill, 2005; Rosin & Korabik, 2003; Scandura & Lankau, 1997).

We also examined the extent to which satisfaction with organizational policies and, particularly, satisfaction with government policies could be interpreted in the context of national differences in culture, gender equality, differences in women's labor force patterns, and specific institutional policies (paid maternity and parental leave and publicly funded child care). Specifically, are employees more satisfied with the provision of employer-provided policies and benefits in countries with limited public policies? Is there evidence of greater satisfaction with government policies in countries that demonstrate greater gender equality or that have more developed institutional policies and public programs to support working parents?

The pattern of findings in the present study are somewhat mixed and difficult to interpret, but do not suggest strong linkages between the national contextual variables we utilized and satisfaction with government policies. Australia, Canada, and the United States had the highest scores on both the UN's Human Development Index and the World Economic Forum's Global Gender Gap subindex on Economic Participation and Opportunity. Yet average ratings of satisfaction with government family-friendly policies were considerably higher for respondents from India, which ranked among medium development countries on the HDI and 125th out of 130 countries on the GGG subindex on Economic Participation and Opportunity. As well, overall ratings of satisfaction with government policy among respondents from Australia, Canada, and the United States were not significantly different from the average satisfaction rating provided by respondents in Indonesia, a country with considerably lower rankings on both of the measures just discussed. Also puzzling was that there was no significant difference in overall ratings of satisfaction with government policies between men and women, even though policy analyses have consistently found that women are far more likely to benefit from institutional policies such as paid maternity/parental leave and publicly supported child care (e.g., Hegewisch & Gornick, 2011).

There may be several explanations for the observed lack of a relationship between national contextual variables and satisfaction with government family-friendly policies. One possibility is that national scores and ratings are based on the whole population of a country while respondents in this study may be better educated, with higher income, and in some cases have achieved a level of occupational status that is not typical or representative of their national population.

This explanation may be particularly pertinent to the women in this sample from countries such as India and Indonesia, whose responses may reflect their different status and resources. Another possibility is that government policies related to maternity/parental leave and child care may be less relevant to parents of older children. In its international synthesis of the effects of W-F policies, the OECD has observed that

> Maternity, paternity and parental leaves (and in some countries home-care benefits) are most valuable to parents as part of an overall policy support system supporting the reconciliation of work and family life. All too often, however, policy does not provide a continuum of supports in which case decisions concerning a few months early in a child's life, though very important, do not change much the overall work and family balance that parents face throughout the child-raising years.
>
> *(OECD, 2007, p. 119)*

Allen et al. (2014) found that even though their study of parental leave policies was limited to parents of children 5 years and younger, other policies, such as paid family leave to care for a sick child, might extend over a longer period of time and be more useful to a wider range of families. Both Allen et al. (2014) and Kossek et al. (2011) argue that workplace practices and supervisor supportive behaviors have more proximal relationships to parents' capacities to reconcile work and family demands effectively. Their argument is supported by the findings of our study. Employer-provided flexibility and supports were considered by many of the respondents in this sample who used those policies as helpful to them in improving work-life balance, and satisfaction with employer-provided supports was consistently related to lower intent to turnover, higher scores on life satisfaction, and lower work interference with family, albeit not in China, India, and Taiwan. Whereas broader cultural and economic factors and institutional policies affect the larger context in which people live, including their opportunities for stable employment, our findings support the view that more immediate organizational influences on people's daily lives can have more direct influence on their attitudes towards work, their capacity to manage work and family roles, and their overall life satisfaction.

In conclusion, our findings provide further support for those who believe that HRM practices and perspectives that embrace the value of promoting men's and women's capacities to manage multiple roles and enhance their capacity to be productive workers contribute to organizational engagement and stability. Although there are many other factors besides support for W-F integration that can promote employee health and engagement, supporting a healthy work-life balance is increasingly important to younger employees, and will continue to be a vital means to enable men and women to be successful parents and caring sons and daughters as populations age. Predictions of skill shortages in many countries and competition for global talent are other reasons why organizations should be aware of the opportunities they have to adopt policies that support employee engagement and reinforce organizational sustainability. By providing W-F policies and practices that provide the flexibility, control and resources that employed parents find helpful to them, organizations can help alleviate conflict between work and family life, foster positive spillover, decrease turnover intent, and enhance life satisfaction.

Notes

1 For more recent statutory provisions and international comparisons, readers are referred to the International Labour Organization's publication, *Maternity and Paternity at Work: Law and Practice across the World, 2014* and the annual review of leave policies published by the International Parental Leave and Policy Research Network.
2 Australia introduced a publicly paid parental leave scheme in 2011 (which includes maternity leave), although some form of employer-provided paid parental leave was reportedly available to almost half of new mothers in 2010 (Whitehouse, Baird, Alexander, & Brennan, 2015). In the United States approximately half of employed parents are eligible for 12 weeks of unpaid Family and Medical Leave; five states provide partial payment for birth mothers under Temporary Disability Insurance (TDI) provisions. California was the first state to enact partially paid family leave in 2004 by extending the TDI to cover up to six weeks of leave following childbirth, adoption, or to care for a seriously ill family member.
3 Phipps, S. (2006). Working for working parents: The evolution of maternity and parental benefits in Canada. *IRPP Choices, 12*(2).
4 Ibid.

References

Allen, T. D. (2001). Family-supportive work environments: The role of organizational perceptions. *Journal of Vocational Behavior, 58*, 414–435.

Allen, T. D., Lapierre, L., Spector, P. E., Poelmans, S., O'Driscoll, M., Sanchez, J. I., Cooper, C. L., Walvoord, A. G., Antoniou, A., & Brough, P. (2014). The link between national paid leave policy and work-family conflict among married working parents. *Applied Psychology: An International Review, 63*(1), 5–28. doi:10.1111/apps.12004.

Allen, T. D., Herst, E. E., Bruck, C. S., & Sutton, M. (2000). Consequences associated with work-to-family conflict: A review and agenda for future research. *Journal of Occupational Health Psychology, 5*, 278–308.

Attridge, M. (2009). Measuring and managing employee work engagement: A review of the research and business literature. *Journal of Workplace Behavioural Health, 24*, 383–398.

Aycan, Z. (2008). Cross-cultural approaches to work-family conflict. In K. Korabik, D. S. Lero, & D. L. Whitehead (Eds.), *Handbook of work-family integration: Research, theory and best practices* (pp. 353–370). Boston: Academic Press, Elsevier.

Bardoel, E. A., & De Cieri, H. (2014). A framework for work-life instruments: A cross-national review. *Human Resource Management, 53*, 633–659.

Barnett, R. C. (2004). Women and multiple roles: Myths and reality. *Harvard Review of Psychiatry, 12*, 158–164.

Batt, T., & Valcour, P. M. (2003). Human resources practices as predictors of work-family outcomes and employee turnover. *Industrial Relations, 42*, 189–220.

Blair-Loy, M., & Frenkel, M. (2005). Societal cultural models of work and family: An international perspective. In *Work and family encyclopedia*. Chestnut Hill, MA: Sloan Work and Family Research Network. Retrieved February 16, 2012, from https://workfamily.sas.upenn.edu/wfrn-repo/object/wk1mj65bh8qd7y01.

Boudreau, J. W., & Ramstad, P. M. (2005). Talentship, talent segmentation and sustainability: A new HR decision science paradigm for a new strategy definition. *Human Resource Management, 44*, 129–136.

Butts, M. M., Casper, W. J., & Yang, T. S. (2013). How important are work-family support policies? A meta-analytic investigation of their effects on employee outcomes. *Journal of Applied Psychology, 98*, 1–25.

Den Dulk, L. (2005). Workplace work-family arrangements: A study and explanatory framework of differences between organizational provisions in different welfare states. In Steven A. Y. Poelmans (Ed.), *Work and family: An international research perspective* (pp. 211–238). Mahwah, NJ: Lawrence Erlbaum.

Den Dulk, L., Groeneveld, S., Ollier-Malaterre, A., & Valcour, M. (2013). National context in work-life research: A multi-level cross-national analysis of the adoption of workplace work-life arrangements in Europe. *European Management Journal, 31*, 478–494.

Den Dulk, L., Peters, P., & Poutsma, E. (2012). Variations in adoption of workplace work-family arrangements in Europe: The influence of welfare-state regime and organizational characteristics. *The International Journal of Human Resource Management, 23*, 2785–2808.

Eby, L. T., Casper, W. J., Lockwood, A., Bordeaux, C., & Brinley, A. (2005). Work and family research in IO/OB: Content analysis and review of the literature (1980–2002). *Journal of Vocational Behaviour, 66*, 124–197.

Gender Inequality Index. (2015). *Wikipedia.* Retrieved July 28, 2015, from https://en.wikipedia.org/wiki/Gender_Inequality_Index#Countries_not_included.5B12.5D.5B13.5D.

Gornick, J. C., & Meyers, M. K. (2003). *Families that work: Policies for reconciling parenthood and employment.* New York: Russell Sage Foundation.

Greenberger, E., Goldberg, W., Hamill, S., O'Neal, R., & Payne, C. (1989). Contributions of a supportive work environment to parents' well-being and orientation to work. *American Journal of Community Psychology, 17*, 755–783.

Hausmann, R., Tyson, L. D., & Zahidi, S. (2008). *The global gender gap report 2008.* Geneva, Switzerland: World Economic Forum. Retrieved from http://www3.weforum.org/docs/WEF_GenderGap_Report_2008

Hegewisch, A., & Gornick, J. C. (2011). The impact of work-family policies on women's employment: A review of research from OECD countries. *Community, Work & Family, 14*(2), 119–138.

Hilbrecht, M., & Lero, D. S. (2014). Self-employment and family life: Negotiating work-life balance when you're "always on." *Community, Work and Family, 20*(1), 20–42.

Hill, E. J. (2005). Work-family facilitation and conflict, working fathers and mothers, work-family stressors and support. *Journal of Family Issues, 26*, 793–819.

Hill, E. J., Yang, C., Hawkins, A. J., & Ferris, M. (2004). A cross-cultural test of the work-family interface in 48 countries. *Journal of Marriage and Family, 66*, 1300–1316.

House, R. J., Hanges, P. J., Javidan, M., Dorfman, P. W., & Gupta, V. (Eds.). (2004). *Culture, leadership and organizations: The GLOBE study of 62 societies.* Thousand Oaks, CA: Sage.

Kassinis, G. I., & Stavrou, E. T. (2013). Non-standard work arrangements and national context. *European Management Journal, 31*, 464–477.

Kelly, E. L., Kossek, E. E., Hammer, L. B., Durham, M., Bray, J., Chermack, K., Murphey, L. A., & Kaskubar, D. (2008). Getting there from here: Research on the effects of work-family initiatives on work-family conflict and business outcomes. *The Academy of Management Annals, 2*, 305–349.

Korabik, K., Lero, D., & Ayman, R. (2003). A multi-level approach to cross-cultural work-family research: A micro- and macro-level perspective. *International Journal of Cross-Cultural Management, 3*(3), 289–303.

Kossek, E. E., & Ollier-Malaterre, A. (2013). Work-life policies: Linking national contexts, organizational practice and people for multi-level change. In Steven Poelmans, Jeffrey H. Greenhaus, & Mireira Las Heras Maestro (Eds.), *Expanding the boundaries of work-family research* (pp. 3–31). Basingstoke, UK: Palgrave MacMillan.

Kossek, E. E., Pichler, S., Bodnar, T., & Hammer, L. (2011). Workplace social support and work-family conflict: A meta-analysis clarifying the influence of general and work-family-supervisor and organizational support. *Personnel Psychology, 64*, 289–313.

Lero, D. S., Richardson, J., & Korabik, K. (2009). *Cost-benefit review of work-life balance practices-2009*. Ottawa, Canada: Canadian Association of Administrators of Labour Legislation. Retrieved from http://www.caall-acalo.org/uploads/resource%20library/cost-benefit%20 review.pdf

Lobel, S. A. (1999). Impacts of diversity and work-life initiatives in organizations. In G. N. Powell (Ed.), *Handbook of gender and work* (pp. 453–476). Thousand Oaks, CA: Sage.

Lu, L., Gilmour, R., Kao, S., & Huang, M. (2006). A cross-cultural study of work/family demands, work/family conflict and wellbeing: The Taiwanese vs. British. *Career Development International, 11*, 9–27.

Lyness, K. S., & Kropf, M. B. (2005). The relationships of national gender equality and organizational support with work-family balance: A study of European managers. *Human Relations, 58*(1), 33–60.

Masuda, A. D., Poelmans, S., Allen, T. D., Spector, P. E., Lapierre, L., Cooper, C. L., Abarca, N., Brough, P., Ferreiro, P., & Fraile, G. (2012). Flexible work arrangements availability and their relationship with work-to-family conflict, job satisfaction, and turnover intentions: A comparison of three country clusters. *Applied Psychology: An International Review, 61*(1), 1–29.

Moss, P. (2014). *International review of leave policies and research 2014*. Retrieved from http://www.leavenetwork.org/lp_and_r_reports/

Moss, P., & Deven, F. (2015). Leave policies in challenging times: Reviewing the decade 2004–2014. *Community, Work and Family, 18*(2), 137–144.

OECD (Organisation for Economic Cooperation and Development). (2006). *Starting strong II: Early childhood education and care*. Paris, France: OECD Publishing.

OECD (Organisation for Economic Cooperation and Development). (2007). *Babies and bosses: Reconciling work and family life: A synthesis of findings for OECD countries*. Paris, France: OECD.

OECD (Organisation for Economic Cooperation and Development). (2011). *Doing better for families*. Paris, France: OECD Publishing. Retrieved from http://dx.doi.org/10.1787/9789264098732-en

Oliver, T., Korabik, K., McElwain, A., & Lero, D. S. (2008, June). *Workplace policies and work-interference with family: The effects of job type*. A poster presented at the annual meeting of the Canadian Psychological Association. Halifax, NS.

Ollier-Malaterre, A. (2009). Organizational work-life initiatives: Context matters. France compared to the UK and the US. *Community, Work and Family, 12*, 159–178.

Ollier-Malaterre, A., Valcour, M., Den Dulk, L., & Kossek, E. E. (2013). Theorizing national context to develop comparative work-life research: A review and research agenda. *European Management Journal, 31*, 433–447.

O'Reilly, J. (2006). Framing comparisons: Gendering perspectives on cross-national comparative research on work and welfare. *Work, Employment and Society, 20*(4), 731–750.

Parry, E., Stavrou, E., & Morley, M. (Eds.). (2011). The Cranet international research network on human resource management. Special Issue of *Human Resource Management Review, 21*(1–4).

Phipps, S. (2006). Working for working parents: The evolution of maternity and parental benefits in Canada. *IRPP Choices, 12*(2).

Ray, R., Gornick, J. C., & Schmitt, J. (2010). Who cares? Assessing generosity and gender equality in parental leave policy designs in 21 countries. *Journal of European Social Policy, 20*(3), 196–216.

Rosin, H. M., & Korabik, K. (2003). Do family-friendly policies fulfill their promise? An investigation on work-family conflict and work and personal outcomes. In D. L. Nelson & R. J. Burke (Eds.), *Gender, work, stress, and health* (pp. 211–226). Washington, DC: APA Books.

Scandura, T. A., & Lankau, M. J. (1997). Relationships of gender, family responsibility and flexible work hours to organizational commitment and job satisfaction. *Journal of Organizational Behavior, 18*, 377–391.

Spector, P. E., Allen, T. D., Poelmans, S., Lapierre, L. M., Cooper, C. L., O'Driscoll, M., Sanchez, J. I., Abarca, N., Alexandrova, M., Beham, B., Brough, P., Ferreiro, P., Fraile, G., Lu, C., Lu, L., Moreno-Velazquez, I., & Pagon, M. (2007). Cross national differences in relationships of work demands, job satisfaction and turnover intentions with work-family conflict. *Personnel Psychology, 60*, 805–835.

Strandh, M., & Nordenmark, M. (2006). The interference of paid work with household demands in different social policy contexts: Perceived work—household conflict in Sweden, the UK, the Netherlands, Hungary, and the Czech Republic. *British Journal of Sociology, 57*, 597–617.

United Nations Development Programme (UNDP). (2007). *Human development report 2007/2008*. Retrieved from http://hdr.undp.org/sites/default/files/reports/268/hdr_20072008_en_complete.pdf

Whitehouse, G., Baird, M., Alexander, M., & Brennan, D. (2015). Australia country note. In P. Moss (Ed.), *International review of leave policies and research 2015*. Retrieved from http://www.leavenetwork.org/lp_and_r_reports/

Williams, J. C., Blair-Loy, M., & Berdahl, J. L. (2013). Cultural schemas, social class, and the flexibility stigma. *Journal of Social Issues, 69*(2), 209–234.

PART II

The Work-Family Interface in Different Countries in the World

Zeynep Aycan

Part 2 of this book contains information about the emic context of the countries that participated in the study. The structure of each emic chapter is the same. First, the sociocultural, economic, and demographic characteristics of the respective country are described in detail. Second, the research literature on how the work-family interface is experienced by individuals in the respective country is reviewed. Finally, for those countries in which focus group discussions were conducted, the emic themes that emerged are presented. More specifically, the chapters in this section are: Chapter 4 on the United States by Roya Ayman, Leslie B. Hammer, and Nahren Ishaya; Chapter 5 on Canada by Donna S. Lero and Karen Korabik; Chapter 6 on Australia by Anne Bardoel; Chapter 7 on Israel by Anat Drach-Zahavy and Anit Somech; Chapter 8 on Turkey by Ayse Burçin Erarslan-Baskurt and Zeynep Aycan; Chapter 9 on India by Tripti Pande-Desai and Ujvala Rajadhyaksha; Chapter 10 on Indonesia by Artiawati; Chapter 11 on China by Li Zhang and Karen Korabik, and Chapter 12 on Taiwan by Ting-Pang Huang. In general, many similar themes were brought up by the focus group participants, including the frequent mention of role overload, guilt, and gender roles as factors that impacted on the work-family interface. However, the manner in which these factors manifested themselves often was very different in different cultures. These differences provide an important context that must be taken into account when interpreting the results of our study.

PART I

The Work-Family Interface

4

THE WORK-FAMILY INTERFACE IN THE UNITED STATES

Roya Ayman, Leslie B. Hammer, and Nahren Ishaya

The United States of America Context

Situated on the North American continent, the United States of America is a vast and diverse country. It is a federation of 50 states with a total population of 318,872,000 which makes it the third most populated country in the world (2014 in the United States, n.d.). Urbanization is on the rise with 81% of the population residing in cities and suburbs as of 2014. The fertility rate in the United States per woman is estimated to be 1.87. Although the United States has one of the lowest fertility rates in the world, it has the highest percentage of immigrants ("List of sovereign states," n.d.). The US Census Bureau shows a population increase of .75% for one year. The foreign-born population in metropolitan areas with 5 million or more people as of 2000 ranged from 5.1 to 29.6%.

Statistics pertaining to the diverse population show that the United States had 158.6 million women and 151.4 million men in 2009. The median age was 36.8 years. Women outlived men by two to one and over one-fourth of the population was under 20 years. The diversity of ethnicity and race is complex. Overall a majority of the citizens of the United States are White and English-speaking though there are regional differences. The definition of White includes having origins in Europe, the Middle East, and North Africa. By this definition 72.4% of the US population is White. However, if Hispanics, who consider themselves White, are excluded, Whites constitute 63.7% of the population. Hispanic and Latino Americans accounted for 48% of the national population growth of 2.9 million between 2005 and 2006. Unaffiliated and don't know or refused to respond comprised 16.9%.

Based on Pew's report in September 2016 (Pew Research Center, n.d.), three-quarters of Americans think religion is losing influence in people's lives. Based on this report, the largest affiliation is with Evangelical Protestant churches (26.3%), followed by Catholics (21.9%), mainline Protestant churches (18.1%), and historically Black churches (6.9%); all other traditions and faiths represent about 1 or less percent, other than Mormons with 1.7%.

According to Wikipedia, the most common language is American English with 80% of the population reported in 2007 using that as their sole means of communication. However, there is no official language at the federal level. About 337 languages are spoken or signed by the population of which 176 are indigenous to the area. The second most common language in the United States is Spanish with 35 million people speaking it. Although new Latin American immigrants are less fluent in English, the second generation is fluent, and only half of them still speak Spanish. The United States has the fifth largest Spanish-speaking population in the world. According to the US Census in 2000, those with German ancestry made up the largest ethnic group in the United States, and use of the German language ranks fifth.

Population distribution by age and gender and family structure as reported by the US Census shows that the population is younger in age with most being between 35 and 44. The majority are non-Hispanic Whites, with a growth in Hispanic White and Black demonstrated between 1980 and 2000. The number of individuals with multiracial identification has increased, with the largest group being White and some other race (32.32%), White and American Indian (15.86%), White and Asian (12.72%), and White and Black (11.50%).

Household and family structure was examined in 1990 (about 92 million) and 2000 (105 million). In 1990, 55.15% were married couples of whom 25% lived with children. In 2000, 51.66% were married and 23.55% were living with children. However, married couples without children dropped from 25.55% to 23.55%. Women with no spouse as head of the household in 1990 were about 11.6% and in 2000 were 12.23%. Men with no spouse as head of the household did not change in the 10 years from 3.42% and 4.17%. Households with people living alone (24.56%) were about the same in year 2000 (25.82%). Those with people living together as not a "family" were 5.27% and in 2000 were 6.13%. This information may indicate that more women than men are single parents and that there are more singles in the society than ever before.

According to Wikipedia, the United States is still considered the largest national economy due to many factors such as national resources, well-developed infrastructures, and high productivity. In the last 10 years, based on the Congressional Budget Office, Department of Commerce, Bureau of Economic Analysis, Department of Labor Statistics, and Federal Reserve, the real GDP in the United States, which had emerged as the world's lone economic super power (Young, 2013), experienced a major dip in its growth in 2008. Though it has bounced back to some extent since the crash of 2008, there is a fluctuation of change of about 2.5 to about 1.4.

The unemployment rate was the highest between 2008 and 2009. Following this, unemployment dropped from almost 10% to about 7.9%, with a promising trajectory. It is important to note that most of the data for this project was collected before 2008. The distribution of household incomes in the United States has increased in inequality during the post-2008 economic recovery. The median household wealth dropped 35% in the United States between 2005 and 2011. While the indicators may show a decline in the economic condition of the United States, Wikipedia references Sean Starrs (2013) stating that these indices are a reflection of the globalization of the US economy and that it still owns 46% of the world's top 500 corporations.

The US government is the largest employment sector in the United States with 22 million of the 154.4 million employed in the United States. Small business represents 53% of US workers, and large businesses employ 38%. Americans still have the highest average employee income among OECD nations (US Bureau of Labor Statistics, 2013).

The growth of women in the workforce since 1960 has been steadily increasing and it peaked in 1999. Based on "Women in the Labor Force: A Databook" (US Bureau of Labor Statistics, 2013) the following facts are presented. In 2011, the percentage of women in the labor force was 58.1. The reported unemployment for women in 2011 was 8.1% compared to men's at 9.4%. Women's rate of unemployment varied by race with Asian Americans having the lowest rate and Black women the highest rate. The majority of mothers with children at home was likely to work (76.5% in March 2011). As expected, unmarried mothers had a higher employment rate (74.9%) compared to married mothers (69.1%).

The education of women has risen substantially in the last 40 years from only about 11% with a college education in the 1970s to about 37% in 2011. In 2011, only 7% of women did not have a high school diploma. According to the report, in 2011, of all people employed 51% were women. As for the distribution of women in various occupations, the majority of teachers in elementary and middle school was women (82%), whereas 34% of physicians and surgeons were women, and 62% of accountants and auditors were women. Professions such as construction and manufacturing still have very few women.

More specifically, the ratio of women's to men's median earnings between 2007 and 2009 for health professionals like physicians and surgeons was .64, for nurses .90, and for accountants and auditors .71. Also, the US Census Bureau (2009) reported the percentage of mothers of preschoolers opting out of the labor force in managerial and professional occupations to be 15%. Yet, the gap between the level of education of women and men has been closing, and younger women in recent years are doing better than men in getting a college education. The number of women in management also has increased significantly, from 1970 until 2000 the percentage of women in management moved from 10% to almost 35%. Since 2000 this growth has leveled off. Representation of women in different industries varies, with health care and social assistance having the highest representation at 61.9%, followed by education at 56.4%, management of companies at 13.2%, and construction at 9.5% (US Bureau of Labor Statistics, 2015). Based on the US Census Bureau (2007) report, 69% of women worked less than 40 hours a week and 20.3% of them worked more than 40 hours. In contrast, for men the report shows 49.7% reported less than 40 hours a week and 37.3% more than 40 hours a week (US Bureau of Labor Statistics, 2015).

Since 1990, the United States has been engaged in several major conflicts including the Gulf Wars, the fight against al-Qaida, and now the challenge in Syria. These periods of unrest and military deployment have placed pressures on those responsible for meeting family needs. In January 2013, the United States Department of Defense (DOD) lifted the ban on women participating in combat, which had been a barrier for women's promotion and advancement in the armed forces (Barry, 2013). These increased opportunities benefit women and their families. However, when mothers are deployed, the care of the family can be challenged. This change has been a topic of debate since the American Revolution and has had some turning points, such as in 1948 when women could first join the regular army. The ban from combat, though not intended to create barriers for women's promotion, did inhibit women's advancement. Now that this has been repealed, women have a much more equal presence in military. From a work and family perspective this has good news and bad news. The good news is that women can also bring the opportunities and benefits from the DOD to their families. The bad news is when both mother and father are deployed, the care of the family is challenged.

The United States' terrain represents almost all types of climate and with this also exists all types of life styles. The 50 states in the United States are autonomous and are connected together through a federation. The laws and policies have a federal level of formation and execution and a state level modification and implementation. Thus to draw a picture of understanding the United States' sociopolitical condition toward work and family is complex and beyond the scope of this chapter.

During the post-Industrial Revolution, as the urban centers grew, so did the division of work and family life become ever more distant. For most middle- and upper-class families, the division of labor became clear, and it was drawn on the fault line of gender. Women were to take care of the household and men attend to "work." However, for the lower economic class, men and women, due to necessity, worked since the beginning of the development of this nation. However, the nature of their work was different. This persisted until the 1970s and was challenged by the women's rights movement and the call for equal treatment of women and men. This movement opened the doors for women to receive equal education and employment, which was already represented in earlier sections.

Research on the Work-Life Interface in the United States

Interest by scholars in the United States in how workers manage their work and family roles has only been critically examined over the past 35+ years, yet the problems and difficulties of combining paid work with family work have been in existence much longer. In 1977 Rosebeth Moss Kanter introduced the phrase "myth of separate worlds," which brought more recognition by US scholars to the significant difficulties associated with integrating work and family roles. Kanter's argument was that the workplace could no longer function without consideration of the context within which our larger working society operates and the reality that what was going on at home and outside of work time had a significant impact on behavior at work. The idea that workers needed to leave their family issues at home was debunked (Kanter, 1977). Work-family research exploded in the United States in the 1980s with the publication of several key articles, including Greenhaus and Beutell (1985) in the *Academy of Management Review* on the types/sources of WFC, and the *Harvard Business Review* 1989 article by Felice Schwartz (1989) dubbed the "mommy track." By the 1990s attention had broadened for both academic researchers as well as organizational practitioners to the importance of work-family issues. Furthermore, by 1990 the health of workers and the health of organizations were addressed in two seminal articles contributing to the emphasis of work-life balance in the development of healthy workplaces (i.e., Ilgen, 1990; Zedeck, 1992).

Although the majority of literature in the United States on the work-family interface has focused on the conflict associated with enactment in both work and family roles, as an extension of the Greenhaus and Beutell (1985) paper, a growing body of research suggested that work and family also have beneficial effects on one another (e.g., Crain & Hammer, 2013; McNall, Nicklin, & Masuda, 2010). The degree to which experiences in the work role improve the quality of life in the family role, and vice versa, has been referred to as work-family enrichment (Greenhaus & Powell, 2006), work-family positive spillover (e.g., Hanson, Hammer, & Colton, 2006), and work-family facilitation (e.g., Wayne, Grzywacz, Carlson, & Kacmar, 2007).

Although not elaborated on in this chapter, the dominant theoretical frameworks that have guided scholars' understanding of the relationship between work and family include role theory (Katz & Kahn, 1978), systems theory (Bronfenbrenner, 1977), border theory (Nippert-Eng, 1996), crossover theory (Westman & Vinokur, 1998), conservation of resources theory (Hobfoll, 1989), and boundary theory (Clark, 2000). With this backdrop of research and theory, Frone, Russell, and Cooper (1992) introduced a comprehensive theoretical model of the work-family interface.

The Frone, Yardley, and Markel Model

Frone, Yardley, and Markel (1997) suggested that there are two directions of work-family conflict (WFC) in which work interferes with family (work-to-family conflict) and family interferes with work (family-to-work conflict). Frone et al. (1992) demonstrated that work-related demands are most often associated with work-to-family conflict, and family-related demands are most often associated with family-to-work conflict. More specifically, job stressors were predictive of work-to-family conflict, whereas family stressors and family involvement were predictive of family-to-work conflict (Frone et al., 1992; 1997). However, other researchers (e.g., Grandey & Cropanzano, 1999) demonstrated the effects of the conflict can occur in the opposite domain from the originating stressor. Meta-analyses and reviews have since demonstrated that work interference with family (WIF) may have different antecedents and outcomes from family interference with work (FIW) (Eby, Casper, Lockwood, Bordeaux, & Brinley, 2005).

Definitions of W-F Conflict and Positive Spillover and Work-Life Balance

WFC has been defined as a type of inter-role conflict in which the demands of work and family roles are mutually incompatible (Greenhaus & Beutell, 1985), and is the construct that has received the most research attention from work-life scholars. Greenhaus and Beutell (1985) proposed three sources of WFC: time-based, strain-based, and behavior-based conflict. Time-based conflict arises when time pressures in one role restrict the amount of time that can be devoted to the other role. According to Greenhaus and Beutell (1985), antecedents of time-based conflict include number of hours worked per week, inflexibility with one's work schedule, and the number and age of dependent children at home. Strain-based conflict arises when strain in one role (e.g., family) affects successful performance of role responsibilities in another (e.g., work). Examples of strain-based conflict include role ambiguity, poor supervisory support, family disagreement about gender roles, and absence of familial or spousal support. Behavior-based conflict, the most infrequently studied form of conflict, arises when patterns of behavior in one role are incompatible with behaviors in another. Greenhaus and Beutell (1985) suggest that these pressures will be experienced as stressful only to the degree that the individual experiences negative consequences for not meeting role demands.

Additionally, the positive side of work-life integration leading to healthy workplaces includes positive spillover, enrichment, and facilitation. *Positive spill-over* has been defined as the transfer of positively valenced affect, skills, behaviors, and values from the originating domain to the receiving domain, thus having beneficial effects on the receiving domain (Edwards & Rothbard, 2000; Hanson, Hammer, & Colton, 2006). *Enrichment* occurs when resources (e.g., skills, social capital, flexibility) or positive affect are generated in one role, such as the family domain, that then improve the quality of life in another role, such as work (Greenhaus & Powell, 2006). Finally, *facilitation* refers to the extent to which an individual's involvement in one particular life domain (e.g., family) provides gains (i.e., developmental, affective, capital, or efficiency) that contribute to enhanced functioning in another domain of life (e.g., work; Wayne, Grzywacz, Carlson, & Kacmar, 2007). Each of these constructs has been identified as bidirectional, in that the nonwork domain can influence the work domain, and conversely, the work domain can influence the nonwork domain. More recently, scholars have introduced the concept of work-family *balance*. Greenhaus and Allen (2011) define work-family balance as "an overall appraisal of the extent to which individuals' effectiveness and satisfaction in work and family roles are consistent with their life values at a given point in time" (p. 174).

Meta-Analytic Work

Scholars have attempted to summarize the literature on the work-family interface since the Frone et al. (1992) model, and today we have results from over 15 meta-analyses on the work-family interface since 2005 that have largely been based on US research conducted since the Frone et al. model was introduced. Furthermore, there are countless book chapters and full books devoted to work and family, published especially during the past 10 years. Interestingly, we found only two meta-analyses that were focused on the antecedents and outcomes of work-family enrichment/positive spillover (i.e., McNall et al., 2010b; Michel, Clark, & Jaramillo, 2011), primarily due to the limited availability of research in this area.

Antecedents of W-F Conflict

Byron (2005) conducted a meta-analysis of the antecedents of WIF and found that job stress, schedule inflexibility, job involvement, hours spent at work, work stress, and work support, were key antecedents, whereas key antecedents to FIW were time spent with household activities, family support, family stress, family conflict, number of children, and marital status. However, Byron also found that several of the nonwork variables showed similar relationships to WIF and FIW (i.e., nonwork involvement, family support, family conflict, age of youngest child, and spousal employment). In their meta-analysis of cross-domain relationships, Ford, Heinen, and Langkamer (2007) found that WIF antecedents included job stress, which had the strongest relationship, job involvement, work support, and hours worked per week, and FIW antecedents included family stress, family conflict, family hours, and family support.

Michel, Kotrba, Mitchelson, Clark, and Baltes (2011) conducted a follow-up meta-analysis to Byron (2005) examining the significant antecedents of WFC. Consistent with the prior work, job stressors, work role overload, work role conflict, and work time demands had moderate to large relationships with WIF, while work role ambiguity had a small relationship with WIF. Family stressors, family role conflict, and family role overload had moderate relationships with FIW and family role ambiguity, family time demands, parental demands, and number of children/dependents had small relationships with FIW. Likewise, as task variety increases, so does WIF, and as job autonomy and family-friendly organization perceptions increase, WIF decreases; and as family climate increases, FIW decreases.

Outcomes of W-F Conflict

As far as outcomes, evidence from meta-analyses has demonstrated that WFC is associated with lower self-rated performance and general performance (Gilboa, Shirom, Fried, & Cooper, 2008). In 2010 a meta-analysis conducted by Hoobler, Hu, and Wilson found that both WIF and FIW were negatively related to performance (both self-rated and manager-rated) and career satisfaction. Interesting, they also found that WIF was negatively related to salary, but FIW was positively related to salary.

Amstad, Meier, Fasel, Elfering, and Semmer (2011) conducted a meta-analysis of the relationships between WIF and FIW with work-related outcomes, family-related outcomes, and domain-unspecific outcomes, demonstrating both were related to all types of outcomes with stronger relationships to same-domain outcomes than to cross-domain outcomes (i.e., WIF was more strongly related to work outcomes than family outcomes, and FIW more strongly related to family outcomes than work outcomes), contrary to Frone et al. (1992). The strongest relationships were between WIF and general stress, family stress, and organizational citizenship behaviors (OCBs), whereas FIW had the strongest relationships with general stress, OCBs, work-related stress, marital satisfaction, burnout/exhaustion, and health problems.

Workplace Support and W-F Conflict

Workplace support can come in the form of formal policies and programs or more informal support that develops as part of the work-family culture in an organization. Kossek, Pichler, Bodner, and Hammer (2011) conducted a meta-analysis on the relationship between general and family-specific organizational and supervisor workplace supports with WFC outcomes (both WIF and FIW). The four types of workplace social support examined were perceived organizational support (POS), supervisor support, perceived organizational work-family support, also known as family-supportive organizational perceptions (FSOP), and supervisor work-family support, also frequently known as family supportive supervisor behaviors (FSSB). Results show work-family-specific constructs of supervisor support and organizational support are more strongly related to WFC than general supervisor support and organizational support, respectively, demonstrating that work-family-specific support is more strongly related to individuals' WFCs than more general types of workplace support. Michel et al. (2011) found that organizational support, supervisor support, and coworker support had negative relationships with WIF and family support and spousal support had negative relationships with FIW.

Butts, Casper, and Yang (2013) investigated the relationship between workplace supportive policies and employee work and well-being outcomes. Meta-analysis results showed that both availability and use of work-family supportive policies were positively related to job satisfaction, affective commitment, and intentions to stay, with policy availability more strongly related than policy use. Policy availability was also related to increased family supportive organizational perceptions, while policy use was related to decreased work-to-family conflict.

In another meta-analysis on the relationship between flexible work arrangements and WFC, Allen, Johnson, Kiburz, and Shockley (2013) demonstrated that while flexibility was related to WIF, flexible work arrangements were not related to FIW. Furthermore, similar to the findings of Butts et al. (2013), stronger effects were associated with availability than with use.

Personality and W-F Conflict

A recent meta-analysis directly examined the relationship between personality and WFC, suggesting that personality can serve as both a risk factor and protective factor in the experience of WFC (i.e., Allen, Johnson, Saboe, Cho, Dumani, & Evans, 2012). For example, results demonstrated that negative affect and neuroticism were positively related to WFC (WIF and FIW) and may be seen as risk factors, while positive affect and a high self-efficacy were negatively related to WFC (WIF and FIW) and, thus, may be seen as protective factors from WFC. Meta-analytic structural equation modeling demonstrated that extraversion, agreeableness, conscientiousness, and neuroticism were related to negative work-nonwork spillover (Michel, Clark, & Jaramillo, 2011).

Antecedents of Work-Family Enrichment

As with WFC, antecedents of work-family enrichment can be broadly grouped into the categories of nonwork-related variables, work-related variables, and personal characteristics. Most of this research has focused on identifying work and nonwork antecedents, while less attention has been paid to individual differences. According to Crain and Hammer (2013), nonwork antecedents include family, community, and recreation variables, although family variables have been examined the most. Work-related variables associated with enrichment include perceived control and supervisor support, with both autonomy (e.g., Carlson et al., 2006) and family supportive supervisor behaviors (e.g., Hammer, Kossek, Yragui, Bodner, & Hanson, 2009) being positively related to both directions of work-family enrichment. A recent meta-analysis conducted by Michel et al. (2011) examined the relationship between personality and enrichment and found extraversion, agreeableness, conscientiousness, and openness to experience to be positively related to the overall construct of work-family enrichment.

Outcomes of Work-Family Enrichment

To date, only one meta-analysis has been conducted on the outcomes of the positive side of the work-family interface (McNall, Nicklin, & Masuda, 2010). This review examined six consequences associated with enrichment: job satisfaction, affective commitment, turnover intentions, family satisfaction, life satisfaction, and physical/mental health. Research on the health and well-being outcomes of enrichment has examined various aspects of physical and psychological health. For example, family-to-work enrichment (FTWE) has been positively associated with sleep quality (Williams, Franche, Ibrahim, Mustard, & Layton, 2006) and negatively associated with chronic health problems (Grzywacz, 2000). Furthermore, as mental health outcomes have been positively linked with both directions of enrichment (e.g., Gareis, Barnett, Ertel, & Berkman, 2009), psychological distress has been negatively associated with work-to-family enrichment (WTFE) (Haar & Bardoel, 2008). These results are in line with McNall et al.'s (2010) findings that both directions of enrichment are positively associated with physical and mental health.

Focus Group Study

Participants and Method

Four separate focus groups were conducted, with a total of 18 participants. Focus groups were divided by gender to help make participants feel more comfortable in discussing work-family issues. Two female and two male focus groups were conducted. The female focus groups included five women in each session. Male focus groups included four individuals per group. The demographic makeup of the samples varied. All participants were married, worked in professional settings, and had at least one child living at home under the age of 18.

The format of the sessions was standardized to ensure that the manner in which the focus group was conducted did not affect the findings obtained. There were seven main questions asked in each focus group, not including any follow-up questions that were used within a session. Example questions included: "How do you handle work and family responsibilities?"; "Do you experience that your work interferes with your family responsibilities?"; and, "What support mechanisms do you use when work interferes with your family?"

Results: Major Themes

Managing Work and Family Responsibilities

Both men and women talked about the importance of planning ahead and time management as key to managing work and family responsibilities ("You have to plan ahead . . ."; "I try to be efficient with both my family and work time."). Another method used to manage work and family responsibilities included the utilization of spousal and familial support ("I depend on friends and neighbors. . . ."; "My husband and daughter help me a lot."; "My husband helps me."). Participants across all groups expressed an inability to "handle it all" but that they try to do the best they can in managing work and family responsibilities ("I try and balance both as best I can. . . ."; "It's very hard, but we're trying to do our best.").

Work Interfering With Family

Both men and women discussed experiencing work interference with family conflict (". . . happens all the time."; "Many times you miss family obligations."; ". . . work interferes with family responsibilities more often than I like."). Reasons expressed by participants for this type of conflict included familial events occurring during time at work, coming home stressed and tired, business travel, and work deadlines.

Family Interfering With Work

Women, more so than men, discussed experiencing family interference with work conflict. Women in the focus groups provided specific examples of how family may interfere with their work, including: receiving calls from children, making necessary phone calls to handle any issues (nonwork), paying bills, and meal planning. Men, though, did not experience this phenomenon or experienced it to a lesser extent than work interference with family conflict. Key reasons for family interfering with work conflict occurring as expressed by both men and women included: sick child, change in day care schedule, and changing one's routine/hours to accommodate a change in spouse/partner's schedule.

Preference for Role Integration Versus Role Segmentation

Participants discussed being flexible in managing their work and family roles ("I try to separate the roles but oftentimes you find yourself thinking about the other parts of your life while at work."; "While I can compartmentalize somewhat, everyday family events enter into the equation."; "I think a person that integrates the roles and responsibilities into everyday life is better able to cope both at work and home."). Others talked about segmenting work and family roles to reduce both directions of conflict ("I try to keep work at the office to not interfere with family more than it already does."; "When you're at work you have to concentrate at work. If you think about both at the same time then you can't concentrate so you have to divide your time and identities.").

Role Identity

When focus group participants were asked to describe what their main role identities were, the responses across gender yielded interesting differences. The majority of women in our sample expressed being a "mother" as the main role identity and did not discuss their roles as wage earners/career persons, etc. Men in the sample, though, expressed multiple roles that they fulfilled, including father, spouse, and wage earner.

Focus Group Discussion: Conclusion

As evidenced through the focus group discussions, the experience of WFC is very common in today's workforce for both genders. Men and women from these focus groups shared examples of the extent to which work may interfere with family and the reasons for why this phenomenon occurs. One difference that was found through these focus group discussions was with family interfering with work conflict. Women voiced much greater experience with family interfering with work occurring than the men in our sample did.

A key technique offered by both men and women in this sample to manage work and family responsibilities was "planning." Specifically, having a plan for how work and family role responsibilities would be managed was critical to being successful in reducing conflict. Participants admitted, though, needing to be flexible in managing work and family responsibilities, as things may happen unexpectedly that change the best laid plans.

Although both men and women described the role of parent as being a main role identity, men were much more expressive in discussing the role of worker/wage earner as an additional role identity. The difference in how men and women in this sample perceived their main roles may be due to traditional gender roles. Specifically, men saw their main role identity tied to that of the "breadwinner" and women more so to that of the "caretaker." Women in the focus groups, though, in responding to other questions did express the importance of working to support one's family and lifestyle choices as well as setting a positive example to their children for being a hard worker and taking care of responsibilities.

References

2014 in the United States. (n.d.). Wikipedia. Retrieved January 9, 2017, from https://en.wikipedia.org/wiki/2014_in_the_United_States

Allen, T. D., Johnson, R. C., Kiburz, K. M., & Shockley, K. M. (2013). Work-family conflict and flexible work arrangements: Deconstructing flexibility. *Personnel Psychology, 66*, 345–376.

Allen, T. D., Johnson, R. C., Saboe, K. N., Cho, E., Dumani, S., & Evans, S. (2012). Dispositional variables and work-family conflict: A meta-analysis. *Journal of Vocational Behavior, 80*, 17–26.

Amstad, F. T., Meier, L. L., Fasel, U., Elfering, A., & Semmer, N. K. (2011). A meta-analysis of work-family conflict and various outcomes with a special emphasis on cross-domain versus matching-domain relations. *Journal of Occupational Health Psychology, 16*(2), 151–169.

Barry, B. (April–May, 2013). Women in Combat. *Survival: Global Politics and strategy, 55*(2), 19–30. https://www.iiss.org/publications/survival/sections/2013-94b0/survival—global-politics-and-strategy-april-may-2013-b2cc/55-2-03-barry-0f0c

Bronfenbrenner, U. (1977). Toward an experimental ecology of human development. *American Psychologist, 32*(7), 513–531.

Butts, M. M., Casper, W. J., & Yang, T. S. (2013). How important are work-family policies? A meta-analytic investigation of their effects on employee outcomes. *Journal of Applied Psychology, 98*(1), 1–25.

Byron, K. (2005). A meta-analytic review of work-family conflict and its antecedents. *Journal of Vocational Behavior, 67*, 169–198.

Carlson, D. S., Kacmar, K. M., Wayne, J. H., & Grzywacz, J. G. (2006). Measuring the positive side of the work-family interface: Development and validation of a work-family enrichment scale. *Journal of Vocational Behavior, 68*, 131–164.

Clark, S. C. (2000). Work/family border theory: A new theory of work/family balance. *Human Relations, 53*, 747–770.

Crain, T. L., & Hammer, L. B. (2013). Work-family enrichment: A systematic review of antecedents, outcomes and mechanisms. In Arnold B. Bakker (Ed.), *Advances in positive organizational psychology* (Vol. 1, pp. 303–328). Bingley, UK: Emerald.

Eby, L. T., Casper, W., Lockwood, A., Bordeaux, C., & Brinley, A. (2005). Work and family research in IO/OB: Content analysis and review of the literature (1980–2002). *Journal of Vocational Behavior, 66*, 124–197.

Edwards, J. R., & Rothbard, N. P. (2000). Mechanisms linking work and family: Clarifying the relationship between work and family constructs. *Academy of Management Review, 25*(1), 178–199.

Ford, M. T., Heinen, B. A., & Langkamer, L. (2007). Work and family satisfaction and conflict: A meta-analysis of cross-domain relations. *Journal of Applied Psychology, 92*(1), 57–80.

Frone, M. R., Russell, M., & Cooper, M. L. (1992). Antecedents and outcomes of work-family conflict: Testing a model of the work family interface. *Journal of Applied Psychology, 77*(1), 65–78.

Frone, M. R., Russell, M., & Cooper, M. L. (1997). Relation of work-family conflict to health outcomes: A four year longitudinal study of employed parents. *Journal of Occupational and Organizational Psychology, 70*, 325–335.

Frone, M. R., Yardley, J. K., & Markel, K. S. (1997). Developing and testing an integrative model of the work-family interface. *Journal of Vocational Behavior, 50*(2), 145–167.

Gareis, K. C., Barnett, R. C., Ertel, K. A., & Berkman, L. F. (2009). Work-family enrichment and conflict: Additive effects, buffering, or balance? *Journal of Marriage and Family, 71*, 696–707.

Gilboa, S., Shirom, A., Fried, Y., & Cooper, C. (2008). A meta-analysis of work demand stressors and job performance: Examining main and moderating effects. *Personnel Psychology, 61*, 227–271.

Grandey, A. A., & Cropanzano, R. (1999). The conservation of resources model applied to work family conflict and strain. *Journal of Vocational Behavior, 54*, 350–370.

Greenhaus, J. H., & Allen, T. D. (2011). Work-family balance: A review and extension of the literature. In J. C. Quick & Lois E. Tetrick (Eds.), *Handbook of occupational health psychology* (2nd ed., pp. 165–183). Washington, DC: American Psychological Association.

Greenhaus, J. H., & Beutell, N. J. (1985). Sources of conflict between work and family roles. *Academy of Management Review, 10*(1), 76–88.

Greenhaus, J. H., & Powell, G. H. (2006). When work and family are allies: A theory of work-family enrichment. *Academy of Management Review, 31*(1), 72–92.

Grzywacz, J. (2000). Work-family spillover and health during midlife: Is managing conflict everything? *American Journal of Health Promotion, 14*(4), 236–243.

Haar, J., & Bardoel, A. (2008). Positive spillover form the work-family interface: A study of Australian employees. *Asia Pacific Journal of Human Resources, 46*(3), 275–287.

Hammer, L. B., Kossek, E. E., Yragui, N. L., Bodner, T. E., & Hanson, G. C. (2009). Development and validation of a multidimensional measure of family supportive supervisor behaviors (FSSB). *Journal of Management, 35*(4), 837–856.

Hanson, G. C., Hammer, L. B., & Colton, C. L. (2006). Development and validation of a multidimensional scale of perceived work-family positive spillover. *Journal of Occupational Health and Psychology, 11*(3), 249–265. doi:10.1037/1076-8998.11.3.249

Hobfoll, S. E. (1989). Conservation of resources: A new attempt at conceptualizing stress. *American Psychologist, 44*(3), 513–524.

Hoobler, J. M., Hu, J., & Wilson, M. (2010). Do workers who experience conflict between the work and family domains hit a "glass ceiling?" A meta-analytic examination. *Journal of Vocational Behavior,* 77, 481–494.

Ilgen, D. R. (1990). Health Issues at work. *American Psychologist, 45*(2), 273–283.

Kanter, R. M. (1977). *Men and women of the corporation*. New York, NY: Basic Books.

Katz, D., & Kahn, R. L. (1978). *The social psychology of organizations*. New York, NY: John Wiley & Sons.

Kossek, E. E., Pichler, S., Bodner, T., & Hammer, L. B. (2011). Workplace social support and work-family conflict: A meta-analysis clarifying the influence of general and work-family-specific supervisor and organizational support. *Personnel Psychology, 64,* 289–313.

List of sovereign states and dependent territories by fertility rate. (n.d.). In Wikipedia. Retrieved January 9, 2017, from https://en.wikipedia.org/wiki/List_of_sovereign_states_and_dependent_territories_by_fertility_rate

McNall, L. A., Nicklin, J. N., & Masuda, A. D. (2010). A meta-analytic review of the consequences associated with work-family enrichment. *Journal of Business Psychology, 25,* 381–396. doi:10.1007/s10869-009-9141-1

Michel, J. S., Clark, M. A., & Jaramillo, D. (2011). The role of the five factor model of personality in the perceptions of negative and positive forms of work-nonwork spillover: A meta-analytic review. *Journal of Vocational Behavior, 79,* 191–203.

Michel, J. S., Kotrba, L. M., Mitchelson, J. K., Clark, M. A., & Baltes, B. B. (2011). Antecedents of work family conflict: A meta-analytic review. *Journal of Organizational Behavior, 32,* 689–725. doi:10.1002/job.695

Nippert-Eng, C. (1996). Calendars and keys: The classification of "Home" and "Work". *Sociological Forum, 11*(3), 563–583.

Pew Research Center. (n.d.). *Importance of religion in one's life*. Retrieved January 19, 2017 from http://www.pewforum.org/religious-landscape-study/importance-of-religion-in-ones-life/

Schwartz, F. N. (1989, January–February). Management women and the new facts of life. *Harvard Business Review, 67*(3), 65–76.

Starrs, S. (2013). American economic power hasn't declined—It Globalized! Summoning the data and taking globalization seriously. *International Studies Quarterly, 57*(4), 817–830. doi:10.1111/isqu.12053

US Census Bureau. (2007). Retrieved from https://www.census.gov/population/age/data/2007comp.html.

US Bureau of Labor Statistics. (2009). Women in the Labor Force: A Databook (2009 Edition). Retrieved March 3, 2017 from http://www.bls.gov/cps/wlf-databook2009.htm.

US Bureau of Labor Statistics. (2013). Women in the Labor Force: A Databook. Retrieved January 19, 2017 from http://www.bls.gov/cps/wlf-databook-2012.pdf

US Bureau of Labor Statistics. (2015). Latest Annual Data: Women of Working Age. Retrieved January 19, 2017 from https://www.dol.gov/wb/stats/latest_annual_data.htm#labor

Wayne, J. H., Grzywacz, J. G., Carlson, D. S., & Kacmar, K. M. (2007). Work-family facilitation: A theoretical explanation and model of primary antecedents and consequences. *Human Resource Management Review, 17*, 63–76.

Westman, M., & Vinokur, A. D. (1998). Unraveling the relationship of distress levels within couples: Common stressors, empathic reactions, or crossover via social interaction? *Human Relations, 51*(2), 137–156.

Williams, A., Franche, R. L., Ibrahim, S., Mustard, C. A., & Layton, F. R. (2006). Examining the relationship between work-family spillover and sleep quality. *Journal of Occupational Health Psychology, 11*(1), 27–37.

Young, J. T. (2013). The worst four years of GDP growth in History: Yes, we should be worried. *Forbes*. Retrieved from http://www.forbes.com/sites/realspin/2013/04/12/the-worst-four-years-of-gdp-growth-in-history-yes-we-should-be-worried/#12d23e7b588e

Zedeck, S. (Ed.). (1992). *Work, families, and organizations*. San Francisco, CA: Jossey-Bass.

5

THE WORK-FAMILY INTERFACE IN CANADA

Donna S. Lero and Karen Korabik

Introduction

Canada is a country characterized by increasing diversity in its population and in its functioning as a federated state. The country is officially bilingual (English and French), and includes within its population three recognized Aboriginal groups (First Nations, Métis, and Innuit peoples), a large proportion of citizens originally derived from English and French settlers, and many others who have emigrated from around the globe. According to the last census, 20.6% of current residents are foreign born who have made Canada their home (Statistics Canada, 2014a). National profiles and characterizations of Canada as a liberal welfare state typical of the "Anglo group" of countries (Esping-Andersen, 1990) mask major differences between Québec and the rest of Canada that derive from different legal systems, social and cultural values, and government policies, with a coordinated family policy approach in Québec that more closely resembles a Nordic social welfare regime. Federal and provincial roles in policy making in areas such as health care delivery, labor standards, child care, and income security are divided and complex, resulting in what has been called a "patchwork approach" to family/social policy (Friendly & Prentice, 2009; Rose & Humble, 2014). In addition to concerns about how best to support child and family well-being, three additional issues that frame current policy debates are the challenges associated with rapid population aging, increasing levels of income inequality, and concerns about younger adults who are experiencing financial pressures and difficulties getting established in a labor force that is characterized by more precarious forms of employment.

This chapter is divided into three parts. The first section provides a description of the geographic, demographic, socioeconomic, and cultural context in Canada.

We then summarize the main findings from research literature using Canadian samples on work and family issues. In the last section, we present the results of focus group interviews with 15 women and 5 men about their experiences of work and family conflict, balance, and guilt.

The Canadian Context

Geographic and Demographic Features

Since its founding in 1867, Canada has grown in geographic size and in population. It is the second largest country in the world, stretching over 3.8 million square miles and is bordered by the Atlantic and Pacific Oceans, the Arctic Ocean to its north, and its lengthy border with the United States to the south. Relative to its geographic size, its population density is small in comparison to other countries, with a current population of 35.7 million (Statistics Canada, 2015a). Canada's population is spread over 10 provinces and three northern territories, each of which has unique economic and social characteristics. Most of the population lives within 100 miles of the US border. In 2013, 47% lived in one of Canada's six largest cities, however 30% lived in rural areas or small population centers of less than 30,000 people (Statistics Canada, 2015b). Canada's population continues to grow, with estimates that by 2061, the population could reach 52.6 million (Statistics Canada, 2014a). Migratory increases are expected to remain the key driver of both population and labor force growth, as has been the case since the early 1990s—a result of low fertility (approximately 1.6 children per woman) and active efforts to promote immigration, especially among individuals who have the educational background, language skills, and experience that supports their economic and social integration.

While Canada's population is growing, it is also aging—a consequence of low fertility, delayed childbearing, and longer life spans. In this way, Canada is not unlike other OECD countries; however, the rate of aging of the population is expected to accelerate in the next two decades as the large cohort of baby boomers born between 1946 and 1964 reaches the age of 65. The proportion of Canadians age 65 and older was 8.0% in 1971, 14.4% in 2001, and 16.1% in 2015. For the first time in Canada's history, on July 1, 2015, the proportion of seniors age 65 and older exceeded the proportion of children aged 0–14 years (Statistics Canada, 2015c). By 2036, it is estimated that seniors age 65 and over could account for almost 25% of the population (Statistics Canada, 2014b). Similarly, the proportion of those age 80 years and older is increasing, from 1.9% in 1982 to 4.1% in 2012 and an estimated 9.6% in 2045. The aging of the population, combined with delayed childbearing, has profound effects on families, the labor force, communities, and expenditures on health and social care and pensions. In particular, the proportion of the population of working age will shrink, and the proportion of employees who will have children and/or care responsibilities for aging family members will increase, adding even greater impetus to better address the challenges of combining paid work and care.

Canada's increasing diversity is evident in a number of ways. Currently, Canada is among the top 10 countries with the largest foreign-born population, at approximately 7.5 million (Statistics Canada, 2014a). In addition to the growing number of immigrants to Canada each year, there is greater ethnocultural diversity among newcomers than ever before. In 2012, nearly 6 in 10 (57.9%) immigrants to Canada came from Asia (Statistics Canada, 2014a). There has also been a significant increase in the proportion of Canadians who identify as Aboriginal (1.4 million or 4.3% the population), reflecting higher fertility rates among Aboriginal women. In 2011, two thirds of the population declared their religion as Christian, with Catholics the largest religious group. Slightly more than 7% of the population described their religious affiliation as Muslim, Hindu, Sikh, or Buddhist, and 1% are Jewish. Nearly one quarter of the population said they had no religious affiliation (up from 16.5% in 2001).

Canada was the first country to adopt an official policy of multiculturalism in 1971 and the first to enact legislation in 1988 (The Canadian Multiculturalism Act) that "acknowledged multiculturalism as a fundamental characteristic of Canadian society with an integral role in shaping Canada's future" (Elliott & Fleras, 1990, p. 65). Despite this official policy, recent immigrants to Canada have had more difficulty securing appropriate employment that reflects their educational and professional credentials and business experience, affecting their economic security and family well-being—an issue that is partially being addressed through government actions (Becklumb & Elgersma, 2008; Buzdugan & Halli, 2009). Newcomers to Canada bring richness and vitality to the country and add additional impetus to creating inclusive workplaces and communities.

Economic Context

Canada is a wealthy nation with a developed market economy. It is ranked eighth highest on the United Nations' Human Development Index. It is a member of the Organization for Economic Cooperation and Development (OECD) and the G-7 countries. Canada's GDP was estimated at $1.992 trillion in 2014 (Statistics Canada, 2015d). The World Bank ranks Canada 23rd in the world based on GDP per capita (estimated in 2012 at $42,114 $US)—ratings on a par with Denmark and Germany (Statistics Canada, 2014c). Canada experienced recessions in the early 1980s and again in the early 1990s, in the latter case accompanied by significant increases in government deficits, relatively high unemployment, and a "jobless recovery" that affected individual and family security, confidence in political leadership, and trust in the implicit employer-employee contract for long-term tenure based on good performance (National Forum on Family Security, 1993). The economy improved from about 1997 onward, decreased in 2008–2009, and has resumed growing, but at a lower rate since then, with GDP per capita growth estimated at 2.5% in 2014 (CIA, 2015). Since mid-2014, sharply reduced global oil prices have had a dramatic impact on the energy sector and on government revenues, and there are some fears about Canada's capacity to sustain recent levels of GDP growth in the short term. Despite its wealth, there is continued concern in Canada about the prevalence of child poverty using relative measures of family income (Campaign, 2000, 2014) and about increasing income inequality (Conference Board of Canada, 2013; Government of Canada, 2013). The Gini coefficient for Canada has been calculated as approximately .32 throughout the 2000s (Conference Board of Canada, 2013).

International trade makes up a large part of the Canadian economy with exports particularly strong in the agricultural, energy, and forestry and mining sectors, as well as machinery equipment, automotive products, and other manufacturing. The United States is Canada's largest trading partner by far, and economic and social ties are strong between the two countries. In recent years the Canadian government has successfully negotiated a number of multilateral and bilateral trade agreements and continues to do so. Natural resources and primary industries are a traditional and strong component of the economy, and in some regions of the country are the dominant source of revenues and jobs. Despite their importance, however, these industries employ an increasingly small percentage of the workforce. Over the last few decades, Canada, like many other industrialized countries, has witnessed a trend toward reduced jobs in agriculture and in manufacturing and substantial growth in the large and multifaceted service sector, which employs more than three quarters of Canadians. Major portions of the service sector are retail trade, business and financial services and communications, the education and health sectors, high tech industries, and tourism (Statistics Canada, 2015b).

Canada's Labor Force and Employment Trends

Canada's labor force consists of over 19.1 million Canadians age 15 years and over. In 2014 the participation rate was 66.0% (70.6% for men and 61.6% for women) and the unemployment rate was 6.9%, down from a recent high of 8.3% in 2009 (Statistics Canada, 2015e). In 2014, the workforce consisted of almost 65% employed in the private sector, 19.9% in the public and quasi-public sectors (including those employed directly by government as well as in schools, universities, hospitals, and government-funded social agencies), and 15.3% self-employed (Statistics Canada, 2015f). The labor force contains several generations and in recent years, the proportion of "older workers" age 55 and over has increased to almost 20%. Statistics Canada estimates that the labor force will grow more slowly in coming years and the overall labor force participation rate may decline to 60–62% by 2031 as a result of population aging and the retirement of the large cohort of baby boomers (Statistics Canada, 2014a).

One aspect readers should be aware of is the large proportion of Canadians who are employed in small and medium-sized enterprises. In 2012, Industry

Canada estimated that 7.7 million employees, or almost 70% of the total private labor force, worked in small businesses with fewer than 100 employees (including many companies with 20 employees or less); another 2.2 million employees worked in medium-sized businesses with 100–499 employees (Industry Canada, 2013). The remaining 10% of private sector employees worked in organizations with 500 or more employees, including national and transnational corporations. Small businesses are more likely to offer flexible work arrangements on an informal basis, but typically lack the financial and human resources to offer employees generous employer-provided benefits, including pension plans and paid leaves for family care. In addition, over the last three decades there has been a decline in the number of employees who are represented by unions—from 38% to about 30%. Much of this decline took place in the 1980s and 1990s, and particularly affected men as manufacturing jobs were lost. Among women, the unionization rate has remained stable at around 30%, but union representation is less common among women below the age of 45 (Galarneau & Sohn, 2013).

Women have made up more than 45% of employees since the early 1990s and accounted for 47.3% of the Canadian labor force in 2014. Women comprise 63.4% of those employed in the public and quasi-public sectors and 45.5% of private sector employees (Statistics Canada, 2015f). Despite progress, two thirds of women work in female-dominated occupations such as teaching, nursing and related health occupations, clerical/administrative positions, or sales and service occupations (Statistics Canada, 2013). In comparison to other countries, a large proportion of women are employed on a full-time basis (approximately 73%). In 2014, nearly one third of women who worked part-time did so to care for their children or other family members, but almost as many indicated they wanted to work full-time, but could only find part-time work (Statistics Canada, 2015g). Despite limited publicly funded child care services, the employment rate of women with young children is high; since 2001 more than 60% of women with a child younger than 3 years of age are employed, and more than 80% of those who were employed prior to having a baby return to work within a year after giving birth (Doucet, Lero, McKay, & Tremblay, 2015).

The largest increases in women's participation in the labor force occurred in Canada in the 1980s. In addition to Canadian families becoming smaller and more diverse in composition, including more blended families and same-sex unions, employment patterns of families with children have changed dramatically. In 2014, 69% of couple families with a child or children under 16 were dual-earner families, compared to 36% in 1976. Furthermore, among dual-earner families, almost three quarters have two parents who work full-time, full year. In addition, the percentage of lone parent families has more than doubled, accounting for 20% of families with children in 2014; the majority of lone parents (69% of single mothers and 82% of single fathers) are also employed, most on a full-time basis (Uppal, 2015). Given the substantial involvement of parents in the labor force, there is considerable interest in the topic of work-family balance. More recently, policy makers and researchers have identified the substantial challenges associated with caring for a child or adult family member with a disability or chronic health condition, including aging family members (Turcotte, 2013).

Canada's Political System and Institutional Mechanisms

Canada is a parliamentary democracy, a federation, and a constitutional monarchy. It has enjoyed political stability for most of its history. As a member of the Commonwealth and a former Dominion of the United Kingdom, the Queen of England is the Head of State and is represented in Canada by the Governor General. Canadians elect Members of Parliament through national elections held at least every five years. The Prime Minister is the head of the party that forms either a minority or majority government. Parliament (consisting of elected members of the House of Commons and an appointed Senate) passes legislation and controls the executive branch. In 1982 Canada patriated its constitution, incorporating within it the Canadian Charter of Rights and Freedoms. Québec was not a signatory to this constitutional change, which created considerable stress and political difficulty. That fact and a variety of other influences (political, economic, social, and historical) gave added impetus to the desire for Québec separatists to hold a (second) provincial referendum on Québec sovereignty, which was narrowly defeated in 1995. Since then, Québec has sought additional opportunities for more autonomy in economic, labor, and social policies, opting out of efforts to develop Pan-Canadian initiatives.

Traditionally, federal members have been elected from one of three national parties—the Liberal Party, the Conservative Party of Canada, or the New Democratic Party. In 1991 the Bloc Québécois was formed as a "federal" political party (with members elected only from Québec) devoted to the protection of Québec's interests in the House of Commons of Canada, and to the promotion of Québec sovereignty.

Federal and provincial roles in policy making are complicated, reflecting at various times, and with respect to particular issues, unilateral federal policies, shared policy making, and cooperative or collaborative, multi-lateral initiatives involving the federal, provincial, and territorial governments. In many social policy areas, there is both a federal role (often related to tax policies and funding arrangements with the provinces) and a provincial/territorial role, which can result in variation in policies and programs and their implementation from one jurisdiction to another. Three examples relevant to work-family integration are working conditions and labor standards (minimum wage, overtime hours, etc.), maternity/parental leave and income replacement, and child care policies that affect access and parental costs. The federal government was led by the Conservative Party from 2006 until October 2015. Under Prime Minister Stephen Harper, the Conservative government was considerably less likely to initiate collaborative social policy making. In particular, it opposed the development of a national child care system, dismantling multilateral agreements that were negotiated by the previous government and substituting in their place a taxable, modest monthly benefit paid to families for each child under age 6, which need not be spent on regulated early childhood services. In October 2015, a Liberal majority government was elected, headed by Prime Minister Justin Trudeau. The party's electoral platform promised more collaborative policy making with the provincial/territorial governments, with substantial investments in health care, child care, and public infrastructure. For the first time in Canada's history, the newly sworn in Federal cabinet has an equal number of men and women Cabinet Ministers.

There is no national family policy in Canada, despite the fact that there are individual measures such as paid parental leave and compassionate care leave (for the care of a terminally ill family member). In contrast, beginning in 1997 Québec developed a multipronged family policy specifically designed to support parents in balancing work and family responsibilities and in creating an environment that enhances child development and well-being (Québec, 1997). Québec's family policy includes financial support for lower income families with children, a generous and flexible program of paid maternity, parental, and paternity leave (implemented in 2006), and a universal approach to low-cost child care for all families in that province. Because of the substantial differences in family policies between Québec and the rest of Canada, there is considerable interest in assessing how these policies affect women, families, and children. The differences also require readers of recent research on Canadian work and family integration to be aware that national data can and does mask considerable variation in the context in which individual employees and families manage work and family obligations.

Research on the Work-Family Interface in Canada

Research on work-family integration in Canada has grown substantially in the last two decades and has attracted the attention of policy makers and academics from a variety of disciplines, most particularly in psychology, sociology, economics, political science, and business. The major topics represented in the research are: assessing the relative contributions of work and family characteristics as contributors to work stress, role overload, and perceptions of work-life balance; examining gender differences in role overload and WFC; and examining the availability, accessibility, and outcomes of flexible work arrangements. Additional areas of investigation relate to how the work-life interface is experienced differentially depending on the nature of work in high-status careers versus precarious, low-wage work, in specific occupations/professions, and among the self-employed. Finally, more recent studies highlight the challenges of combining work with care for adult and aging family members with chronic health problems.

The backdrop for much of the research conducted in Canada reflects the significant changes that have taken place in families since the early 1990s (particularly the increase in women's participation in the labor force), changes in workplaces and in the nature of work (less job security, increased work intensity, and the long-term impacts of downsizing), and more blurring of work-life boundaries, in large part as a result of technological advances. Given what appear to be increasing rates of workplace stress and role overload, there is considerable interest in the physical and mental health consequences that may result for individuals and the consequent costs to employers and to the public health system (Dewa, 2007; Duxbury & Higgins, 2001; Mullen, Kelley, & Kelloway, 2008).

Canadian research has utilized secondary data analysis of national time use surveys conducted by Statistics Canada, as well as studies conducted by individual researchers, most of whom collected data through selected workplaces. Although a considerable amount of the research is descriptive in nature, it is evident that researchers have drawn on several theoretical frameworks, most particularly models based on role theory (Greenhaus & Beutell, 1985; Kahn, Wolfe, Quinn, Snoek, & Rosenthal, 1964), job demands and resources (Bakker & Demerouti, 2007), and, more recently, notions of work-life fit (Moen, Kelly, & Huang, 2008). Frone, Yardley, and Markel's (1997) integrative model of the work-family interface has also influenced researchers' conceptualizations of the potential consequences of work stress and WFC and, in at least one case (McElwain, Korabik, & Rosin, 2005), has provided the basis for model testing.

Canadian "Time Use" Surveys: Assessing the Relative Contributions of Work and Family Characteristics to Stress, Role Overload, and Satisfaction With Work-Life Balance

Statistics Canada has conducted time use surveys as part of the General Social Surveys program on a regular basis since 1992. The 1998 and 2005 surveys have been the most widely used by researchers. In addition to detailed information about paid and unpaid work, the surveys incorporated measures of "time crunch," work stress, general stress, and satisfaction with work-life balance—in a single-item, dichotomous measure: "Are you satisfied or dissatisfied with the balance between your job and home life?" A subset of the items used in the original 10-item time crunch measure was utilized by Williams (2008) as a measure of role overload, and Tézli and Gauthier (2009) compared the time crunch measure with an alternative, multi-item "time-related stress" scale based on three of the original time crunch questions plus other items that assessed feeling rushed, feeling the days are too short to do all the things you want, and the general stress question: "How stressful are most of your days?" Analyses of the time use surveys have been widely circulated, particularly in government circles, but also in the media, heightening concern about work stress, role overload, and work-family balance as societal issues. Key findings from a number of studies can be summarized as follows:

1. *General levels of stress* are high among the employed population. In 2010, 27% of all Canadian workers described their daily lives as highly stressful, a proportion similar to results obtained in other national surveys conducted in 2002 and 2005 (Crompton, 2011). Six in 10 highly stressed workers identified work as their main source of stress; time and family were chosen as main sources by 12% and 8% of workers, respectively. There were marginal differences in demographic and socioeconomic characteristics depending on the source of stress. Of note is that those most worried about time were more likely to be parents with children at home and that family-stressed workers were 1.5 times more likely to be women.
2. *Feeling time crunched or experiencing time stress* is common and has increased, particularly among Canadian parents (Burton & Phipps, 2011). Similarly, dissatisfaction with work-life balance (based on the single-item measure used in these surveys) is not a new issue. About 28% of all full-time workers surveyed in 1998 were dissatisfied, a proportion similar to that reported in 2005 (Williams, 2008). In Tézli and Gauthier's analyses, number of work hours (especially working 50 or more hours per week) had the strongest impact on perceived work-life balance of any variable—a finding consistent with the literature generally and with the practice of using the proportion of workers with long work hours as a population indicator of work-life balance by the OECD in its Better Life Index. As well, while Williams found that working a nonstandard shift (especially irregular hours or rotating shifts) contributed to dissatisfaction with work-life balance for men and time stress (described as role overload) for both men and women; Tézli and Gauthier found that the effect of working a nonstandard shift was not significant when total work hours was controlled.
3. Across studies, it is evident that different variables contribute to time stress, role overload, and dissatisfaction with work-life balance. Based on regression models from the 2005 survey data predicting each of the main measures of time-related stress and WFC, Tézli and Gauthier (2009) demonstrated that only gender, a high number of weekly work hours (40 or more, but particularly 50 hours or more), and a strong sense of belonging to one's community (a measure of social support not often included in the literature) predicted all four measures. The fact that women were more likely than men to experience role conflict, time pressure, and dissatisfaction combining paid work and unpaid work when other variables were controlled for is particularly notable. As well, in contrast to Beaujot and Andersen (2007), the number of children under 15 years living in the household was a better predictor of time stress than having a young child. Tézli and Gauthier also found that some work-related variables contributed more to time-related stress than to

dissatisfaction with work-life balance and vice versa. As examples, working from home contributed to time stress, but not to dissatisfaction with work-life balance, while having schedule flexibility or working nonstandard hours affected satisfaction with balance, but not time stress.

4. The approach taken in all of the time use research is one in which the relative contribution of individual variables is assessed (typically in logistic regressions) to predict work-family/well-being outcomes. However, as these researchers themselves note, many of the work-related variables are interrelated; that is, shifts, total work hours per week, access to flexible start and end times, and occupation are linked in ways that are masked by an approach that assumes independence and fails to consider how different packages of job demands and resources can affect an individual's autonomy, stress, and relationships.
5. Similarly, while household income is often used as a covariate, Burton and Phipps (2011) observed that families live in circumstances where time and money are resources that must be considered simultaneously. Taking a more macro approach, they demonstrate that over the period from 1992 to 2005, time crunch has increased relatively more in dual-earner families at different points along the income distribution. Time crunch increased and life satisfaction decreased most among dual-earner parents in the middle and lower income quintiles who, as couples, increased their total number of hours of paid labor, mostly because of women's work involvement, but experienced stagnant household income. In contrast, dual-earner couples in the highest quintile of the income distribution reduced their total number of hours of paid work, but experienced increased incomes. The authors conclude that increases in real incomes have not compensated mothers in low and middle-income families for their increased paid labor, resulting in relatively greater inequality in well-being relative to high-income mothers.

National Work-Life Studies

Another major source of information about Canadians' experiences at the work-life interface is a series of studies conducted by Linda Duxbury, Chris Higgins, and colleagues (2001, 2009, 2012). Duxbury et al. have conducted three major studies. All are based on large samples of employees drawn from public, private, and not-for-profit organizations—mostly medium and large organizations. In comparison to the 1991 and 2001 samples, the 2012 study sample contained more individuals with higher education and income who were employed in a professional position and a smaller proportion (10%) who were employed in the private sector. Sixty percent worked more than 45 hours per week, with the majority regularly taking work home in the evening. Elder care was far more prevalent in this more recent study—23% provided care or support to at least one elder family member on a weekly basis, and one in three respondents were described as sandwich generation, combining paid work with both child care and elder care responsibilities (Duxbury & Higgins, 2012). Taken together, the body of knowledge that has emerged from this program of research has identified key contributors and consequences of role overload and WFC and identified a number of ways organizations can benefit by providing employees with more flexibility, support, and control.

Duxbury and Higgins have focused on three major dimensions of work-life conflict: role overload, work interference with family, and family interference with work, adding caregiver strain as a fourth area in their later work. Importantly, they define role overload similarly to Greenhaus and Beutell, emphasizing the strain and conflict an individual perceives when the "collective demands of multiple roles are so great that time and energy resources are insufficient to adequately fulfill the requirements of those roles to the satisfaction of self and others" (Duxbury, Lyons, & Higgins, 2008, p. 130). Key findings from their research include the following.

Role overload is seen as a serious and systemic issue: 58% of the 2001 sample was assessed as experiencing high role overload (40% in the 2012 study). Key contributors to role overload were found to be work culture (supportive or nonsupportive of work-life balance, focused on face time, a culture of work versus family), increased work demands (both total work hours and time spent in unpaid overtime each month), and, for men, supervisory status and the number of supplemental work hours at home. For women (but not men), role overload increased dramatically with the amount of time spent in job-related travel. Work factors, more than nonwork factors, predominated as contributors to role overload; however, for women only, role overload was also affected by family type (partnered or single parent) and the amount of support received from a spouse/partner. Along with significant impacts evident in the workplace (higher rates of job stress, absenteeism, reduced job satisfaction, and greater likelihood of intent to turnover), high role overload was associated with high levels of burnout, perceived stress, depressed mood, lower levels of life satisfaction, and reported poorer physical health (Duxbury & Higgins, 2009).

Work interference with family (WIF): High rates of WIF were reported by 38% of the 2001 sample, a level similar to 1991, and by 29% of the 2012 sample. As has been found in other studies, work factors contributed most to WIF. Major contributors were: an organizational culture that prioritizes work over family and work demands that directly compete with family time (total hours as well as hours spent in overtime, in supplemental work at home, and on nights spent away from home for business purposes). Employees with heavier work demands (supervisors, managers, and professionals) and lower levels of control experienced the most WIF, and this seemed most problematic for Canadians with more dependent care responsibilities. The consequences of high levels of WIF are similar to those reported for role overload, with particularly strong impacts on job stress, satisfaction, and intent to quit, as well as impacts on life satisfaction and perceived health. In addition, WIF impacts both family satisfaction and satisfaction with parental abilities (Duxbury & Higgins, 2009). These findings (impacts on work, health, and life satisfaction) are consistent with the relationships identified by Frone and colleagues (Frone, Russell, & Cooper, 1997).

Family interference with work (FIW) is reported to a lesser extent than WIF, as is common in the literature, but has been increasing (5% reported high FIW in 1991, 10% in 2001, and 15% in 2012). One in five respondents in the 2012 study reported high levels of caregiver strain. The key predictors of FIW reflect caregiving demands, particularly elder care. Organizational cultures that reflect a culture of hours, as well as those promoting a culture of work or family, contributed to the challenges of meeting higher family demands. High levels of FIW were more weakly associated with organizational commitment, job satisfaction, job stress, and intent to turnover than WIF but were more strongly associated with absenteeism. High FIW was also associated with poorer self-reported physical health, higher rates of burnout and depressed mood, and lower family and life satisfaction scores (Duxbury & Higgins, 2009).

Gender Differences in W-F Conflict and Relationships Within a Comprehensive Model

While, for the most part, gender differences have not been a specific focus of work-family research in Canada, research findings support the conclusion reached by McElwain, Korabik, and Rosin (2005) that gender differences are evident in the relationship between family demands and family interference with work, but are more equivocal in other areas of research. (See Chapter 12 in this volume for in-depth consideration of differences in WFC antecedents, outcomes, and paths pertaining to gender and gender-role ideology.) Canadian research findings indicate that family demands (in combination with paid work hours) more directly affect women's perceptions of stress (Crompton, 2011), time-related stress, and satisfaction with work-life balance than is the case for men (MacDonald, Phipps, & Lethbridge, 2005; Tézli & Gauthier, 2009; Williams, 2008). In their 2001 study, Duxbury and Higgins found that women were more likely to experience role overload while men were more likely to experience work interference with family. These differences were not evident in their most recent study however, leading Duxbury and Higgins to suggest that, perhaps because more women in dual-earner couples are the primary earner or equal partner in the breadwinning role and men appear to be taking on more responsibility for child care, that gender per se is less associated with role overload, WIF, and FIW compared to the involvement in child care or elder care responsibilities (Duxbury & Higgins, 2012). Nonetheless, it appears that men and women may respond to specific situations differently at work and at home, with women more likely to accommodate high or conflicting demands by reducing work hours (Beaujot & Andersen, 2007; Williams, 2008), trading flexibility for less income (Fakih, 2014), or perhaps opting for self-employment as a strategy for being more available to children, though not without additional challenges (Hilbrecht & Lero, 2014).

In 2005, McElwain et al. analyzed data collected over a 20-month period from a sample of married professional men and women, to test a comprehensive model of the relationship between work and family demands; WIF and FIW; and job, life, and family satisfaction based on Frone, Yardley, and Markel's (1997) model of the work-family interface. They also investigated potential gender differences in mean scores and in the relationships between variables in the model. McElwain et al. found no significant mean gender differences on level of work demands or family demands, or on their measure of FIW; however, contrary to expectations, women reported more WIF than men. There were also no significant differences in job satisfaction, family satisfaction, or overall life satisfaction. Path analyses confirmed fit of the model for both men and women. An analysis of potential differences in the path coefficients within the model did demonstrate some significant differences in the relationships between variables. Although there were no differences between men and women in the relationship between work demands and WIF, the relationship between family demands and FIW was stronger for women and FIW was a stronger predictor of job satisfaction for men.

As is true in all research areas, findings can vary based on different samples, measures, and analytical procedures. What appears to be a fruitful area of research, however, is more sensitive analysis of how variables relate to each other, potentially considering how different packages or patterns of variables within the work and family domains affect WIF, FIW, and more distal consequences. As one example, Schieman and Glavin (2011) have described how education moderates the association between WFC and distress, reflecting differences in the nature of WFC experienced by individuals with lower education in more precarious work situations and by those in high status positions, which are characterized by a different set of work demands and more work-family role blurring. Similarly, more sensitive analysis of the nature of involvement in adult and elder care, in interaction with the extent to which employees have access to workplace and community supports, can provide more insight into how demands, resources, and WFC affect employment and health consequences among employed caregivers (Hilbrecht et al. 2015).

The Availability, Accessibility, and Outcomes of Flexible/ Family-Friendly Work Arrangements

A final set of studies that have engaged Canadian researchers assesses employees' access to flexible work arrangements and family-friendly supports and the extent to which they can and do reduce WFC. Earlier studies were based on Statistics Canada's Workplace and Employee Survey (WES) conducted between 1999 and 2003. Comfort, Johnson, and Wallace (2003) found that no more than a third of Canadian employees had some flexibility with respect to work scheduling. These authors and Zeytinoglu, Cooke, and Mann (2010) found that access to other family-friendly work arrangements (including telework and on-site child care and elder care) was very limited. Access to flexible work arrangements was found to be consistently related to establishment characteristics such as industry and firm size rather than to employees' family characteristics. Women were less likely to participate in flexible work arrangements than men. Similarly, Ferrer and Gagné (2006) demonstrated a mismatch between the availability of family-friendly workplace arrangements and employees' needs, with greater availability of such options available for men and for employees who did not have dependent care responsibilities. Zeytinoglu et al. also found that child care and elder care supports, in addition to being available in a very small number of workplaces, were less available to women and to part-time workers.

In 2002 Rosin and Korabik conducted a study of professional workers and found that the availability of flexible workplace arrangements had little impact on employees, but that satisfaction with family-friendly policies was significantly associated with lower WIF and lower FIW scores for both men and women. In their 2001 study, Duxbury and Higgins found that employees who had greater work time and work location flexibility had lower levels of role overload, WIF, and FIW (Duxbury & Higgins, 2009). In their most recent study, Duxbury and Higgins found that there has been limited change in the availability of flexible work arrangements and employee supports. Among their professional sample in larger organizations, 40% could not vary arrival and departure times or arrange their work schedule to accommodate family demands—behaviors that were found to be key determinants of employees' mental health, work-life balance, and absenteeism (Duxbury and Higgins, 2012).

While the "availability" of flexibility in work scheduling and work-from-home arrangements, options to reduce work hours, or the opportunity to take a short period of leave to provide child or elder care depends on a number of organizational characteristics, there is some evidence that even when available, employees may not use these options if they fear that doing so may jeopardize their career prospects or even their job security. Analyses of data from the 2012 General Social Survey on Caregiving revealed that employed caregivers who used flexible work scheduling and short periods of leave for caregiving reported less absenteeism and a lower tendency to reduce work hours; however, almost half of employed caregivers felt they could not use flexible work arrangements without it having a negative impact on their careers (Fast, Lero, DeMarco, Ferriera, & Eales, 2014). Concerns about what has been referred to as "flexibility stigma" appear to be real for many employees. In contrast, two articles, both based on earlier data from the Canadian WES, suggest that employees' use of organizational work-life benefits can be positive. Konrad and Yang (2012) found that employees who used one or more flexibility options (reduced hours, flexible scheduling, or work from home) in 2001 were 14% more likely to receive a promotion by 2002 than their counterparts who did not use a flexibility option, while use of child care supports was unrelated to the probability of receiving a promotion. More refined analyses indicated interactions between gender, the presence of a young child, and benefit use. Specifically, working at home benefited career advancement in mothers of young children, while flexible scheduling and use of a compressed work week was more beneficial for fathers. These authors conclude that using work-life benefits can be beneficial when they enable workers to maximize their performance at work, while reducing potential strain and WIF. A second study, using longitudinal data over the period from 1999 to 2003, found that use of a combination of flexibility options can improve employee productivity as measured by wages and promotions, as well as job satisfaction and morale (Fang & Lee, 2008). The relationship between use of flexible work options and wages and promotions was significant for men, but not for women.

In summary, Canadian research on employees' experiences at the work-family interface contributes to our understanding of how work and family demands, resources, and even community supports can help reduce role overload and WFC. These studies also provide compelling evidence for the business case for employers to support employees' performance through a range of options to support employee engagement, health, and resilience.

Focus Group Discussion Results

Twenty individuals (15 women and 5 men) participated in the focus groups. They were all members of dual-earner couples with at least one child under the age of 18 living at home. On average they had 1.56 children, and their children ranged in age from 1–15 years. The average age of the participants was 41 years (range 23–53). They were employed primarily in managerial and technical occupations and, on average, worked 39 hours per week. Their spouse/partners were employed for an average of 44 hours per week.

Data were collected via six online focus groups with 2–4 same-sex participants in a group. A moderator posted a series of questions to a website on a daily basis. Participants were asked to sign on for 10 minutes each day for a one-week period at any time that was convenient to them and to respond to the moderator's questions and to comments posted by the other focus group members.

Work Interference With Family

Most participants reported that their work frequently interfered with their family lives. As one woman stated, "I would say I experience that almost every day." Work overload was a commonly cited reason for this. For example, many respondents said things like, "The nature of my work is never ending." and "I have more work to do than I can get done in the course of the day." This brought about the need for them to work long hours. Often this meant they had to spend time away from home due to "obligations and responsibilities at my office that extend outside 8 a.m. to 5 p.m." or the need to travel for business. As one woman remarked,

"I need to work late to get things done, or come in to work on the weekend, and that interferes with having dinner with my family or doing things with them. I am away from home a lot." Another commented that, "Evening meetings can be a problem only because of the difficulties with finding a suitable child care provider. Also, training sessions and conferences where I'll be busy all day or perhaps even out of the city for a few days."

One of the effects of work interfering with family time was that, "There are often things that I would like to do with my children (field trips, special days, etc.) that do not happen because of work responsibilities." Another was that, "I don't have time to myself, and even when I do have time to myself, I feel like I don't have time alone with my partner." Work overload also took a physical and emotional toll on the participants. They complained of being tired, distracted, and "cranky."

Family Interference With Work

Most respondents reported that family interference with work was less of a problem for them than work interference with family. They said things like, "My family doesn't interfere with my work; my work interferes with my family." However, despite this, many spoke of specific family demands that interfered with their jobs, often on a daily basis. For example, one woman commented,

> I can almost never be at work before 9:15 or so because I have to get the kids off to school in the morning. In addition, my sons always phone me when they get home from school, so I try hard to be available to them for a few minutes at that time of day. There are also times that I need to do stuff during the day with the kids—appointments, lunch duty, field trips, etc. etc.

Similarly, another responded,

> Family interfering with work responsibilities is hard when I'm trying to get the children up and out of the house on time so I am not late for work, or when I need to pick them up at a certain time after work.

One mother noted, "A major reason is the age of our child and that he is still nursing every 3 hours." Several parents specifically mentioned their children's sports activities, particularly hockey, as being extremely time-consuming.

In addition to family demands, parents spoke of problems related to the inflexibility of family responsibilities. One mother remarked, "It is very difficult to set boundaries. Children need you when they need you; they are not projects to be completed on time and in a predictable task-oriented way." Another said, "My [work] deadlines are flexible, so everything else (i.e., caring for baby, house, and husband) comes before work."

One of the most frequently discussed outcomes was a pervasive sense of guilt. For example, one woman spoke about, "feeling guilty about neglecting my son or husband or mother or dog or . . ." Another woman talked about her intention to quit her job: "I am choosing to leave the workplace in the next year or so, as I do not have the energy to coordinate/delegate or lower my standards."

Difficulty or Ease of Balancing

In terms of their attitudes toward combining work and family, the sentiments expressed by this woman were fairly typical. She remarked, "I want to work—I love the work that I do—and I love my family; I hate balancing work and family." Both women and men had a wide range of opinions in regard to how easy or difficult it was for them to achieve work-family balance. For example, one woman said, "I find it difficult to be a parent . . . I am constantly worried about my kids . . . It is also exhausting work, and we get absolutely not one iota of family support." By contrast, another woman stated, "Overall I think that my partner and I balance things pretty well with the kids. They get a good bit of time with both of us and we make time with them a priority." Men's opinions were similarly variable. One man noted,

> I think that it is hard to be an employee and a father at the same time. By trying to fulfill two roles at one time, there has to be some conflict there—no matter how much or how little . . . I think that nowadays, fathers are taking on more roles in the home while still working, so this is creating more conflict between the role as an employee and the role of a father.

However, another man commented that,

> I don't think that it's hard to be a parent and have a career. Both require effort on your part. I look at both my career and parenting as something that's integral to my identity, how I define myself as an individual. I think that it's within my power to be successful at both. However, in my opinion parenting should always take precedence over one's career.

Work-Family Enrichment

Respondents also noted some ways in which work and family were able to have a positive impact on one another. As one woman so eloquently summed up:

> Positive outcomes would be that the desire to protect home and family time does provide motivation for being very focused and productive. As well, I believe (and my husband shares this view of parenting) that it is good to provide my son with "teachable moments" which allow him to practice

patience, empathy, understanding, unselfishness, and an increased understanding of the adult work world . . . not being able to have our undivided attention on a 24/7 basis allows him to develop skills which will make him happier and stronger in life. I also believe that having a working mom with real and obvious work responsibilities provides him with a realistic and equitable role model for what women are and can be. Hopefully, he will translate this into healthy adult relationships with women later in his life. Another positive impact of work/home life imbalance on an occasional basis is that I believe it strengthens my relationship with my husband when he (and I in my turn) provide support for each other in coping with workplace overload.

Coping Strategies

Many respondents used coping strategies that involved finding ways to reduce their work demands. Often this meant finding jobs that allowed them flexibility. As one woman put it, "My partner and I both actively sought (and luckily found) jobs that provide us with some flexibility and latitude for accommodating family activities/demands." Another mother said,

> I do rely on the flexibility and supportive culture in my workplace to accommodate my occasional need to attend to family responsibilities. For example, I routinely start work at 9:00, so that I can do school drop-off. If I need time away to attend school events, care for my son when he is sick, or leave early when there is early school dismissal, this is accepted and accommodated.

This strategy was not without drawbacks, however. As one woman noted,

> I do have the flexibility to adjust my work schedule, work from home occasionally etc.—That helps, but it also means that I still have to put in the long hours another time to try to keep up with the work.

Participants also spoke about adopting strategies that allowed them to lower their work loads. For example, one woman remarked that she chose "to work less and not worry about getting everything done, to say no when I really can't take something on." Others did this by setting limits on what they hoped to accomplish (e.g., "I try to set realistic objectives for a day.") or by not going above and beyond what was necessary for good performance (e.g., "I will work to get the job done well.").

Similarly, many participants spoke of trying to find ways to reduce their family demands. They said things like, "I tend to reduce my parenting and participation in household duties to really basic maintenance tasks (cooking, cleaning, putting to bed, etc.) with very little playing, reading books, watching soccer games, etc." and "neither of us stresses out too much about having a perfectly kept house, clean car, or extensive roster of entertaining and social obligations . . . we need to focus on our core family responsibilities." In addition, some noted that the way they structured activities was important, "Basically—we do a lot of 'upkeep' (i.e., laundry and other household tasks) on weekends in order to maintain a less stressful work week."

Another coping technique was for spouses to trade off work or family responsibilities with one another. In the work domain this took the form of things like, "my partner and I work opposite shifts in order to share child care responsibilities." In the family domain, it was, "one of us usually stays with the kids when the other goes out to play." The down side of this strategy was that it meant that, "What's lacking still is a regular routine for spending time alone with my partner."

Another common technique was to compartmentalize activities. As one participant said, "One way I keep boundaries is changing the physical environment associated with each role. I think about work when I'm at work and . . . I think about family issues when I'm at home."

Similarly, another noted that, "Given the immense flexibility that my work provides, I am able to get most of my work done while the children are in school, and then I can fulfill my parental responsibilities once they are home." Although the vast majority of men and women indicated that they would prefer to keep their work and home lives separate, most felt that, "It isn't always easy or feasible."

Finally, many respondents spoke about the importance of taking time to attend to their own needs. They said things like, "I do try to practice extreme self-care. . . . yoga, a bit of meditation, walking, gardening, sleeping." and "I've also become better at making time for myself—doing activities such as gardening and reading a novel before bed (even if it's just a couple of pages)."

Social Support

Support from others was a very frequently mentioned topic. The importance of receiving support from one's spouse or partner was noted by most of the respondents. Wives talked about receiving both instrumental and emotional support from their husbands. For example, one said, "My husband does a lot of the child care and child-related stuff (taking kids places, cooking and having dinner with kids, overseeing their homework, etc. etc.)." Another stated, "He listens to me vent and tries to help me in the evenings when he is home." Husbands rarely commented on the support their wives provided to them. Instead, they tended to emphasize the instrumental support that they gave to their wives. As one said, "I share the family responsibilities (day care, cooking, cleaning, playing, etc.) equally with my wife. On a daily basis I typically do a lot of work around the house, such as laundry, cooking, dishes, bedtime, etc."

Some wives commented on how detrimental it was to their well-being when their spouse was unwilling or unable to give them the support they needed. Sometimes they remarked that small changes in support provision made a big impact, as in the following case: "I used to resent hockey season, but then he decided to start doing the laundry, including folding the clothes while watching games, and now I *like* hockey season."

The majority of respondents also talked about the importance of support provided by family members. Those who had family living nearby said things like,

> We both have our families in town which helps us out a lot. We can always count on someone to be home when we are in a pinch. That's what family is for . . . I never realized how important it is to live where you have a support system, because without them it would be impossible.

Respondents who did not have relatives in close proximity often talked about how helpful it would have been to have someone living nearby who could have given them instrumental support.

Friends and neighbors were regularly called upon to provide instrumental support, primarily for child care. One mother noted,

> We are very fortunate to live in a neighborhood that is very supportive and when one of us needs help with picking up or dropping off kids we all pitch in to help each other since we are all in the same boat.

These arrangements were often viewed as mutual obligations, involving as one woman called them, "regular child swaps" and they seemed to operate according to norms of reciprocity and equity. As one mother noted, "I also ask friends, one in particular, but then again I often help her out, so I don't feel I'm imposing asking her." Women also used other women as sources of emotional support. They noted, "I have a network of close women friends who I see daily." and "I use other mothers to cope with the frustrations. Just talking about things always helps."

Several participants mentioned receiving support from paid help, particularly babysitters. As one woman remarked, "I get a lot of support in balancing work and family roles by investing in paid services for housecleaning and after-school child care (a licensed after-school program)."

In the work domain nearly all of the participants spoke about the importance of having supportive supervisors. They said things like,

> I think that having sympathetic managers is very important to working parents. Having the ability to flex work time to accommodate family needs is a major stress-reliever, not just when a specific need arises, but on an ongoing basis (knowing that you will get support and understanding when you need it gives you a more positive and relaxed approach to work all of the time).

One woman noted that this had kept her from quitting her job, "Personally, I work for a person who is extremely flexible and supportive and that has been a major reason that I have stayed at my workplace."

Most respondents also commented on the support they received from their coworkers. As one put it, "Colleagues can actually make or break my workforce participation. Ultimately it is the support that I get from colleagues that are the day-to-day kind of interactions that make working "worth it." Coworker support was certainly not universal. One woman commented that,

> There have still been one or two comments about peoples' 'life choices' that have made me feel that such understanding is at a surface level. I sometimes sense that while it is accepted that parents have unique struggles, I am not considered as dedicated or as serious . . . because I have chosen to have a family.

Another woman spoke of the "perception by coworkers of not being fully committed to the job or profession (especially if the job is male-dominated and most, if not all, of the users of . . . family-friendly policies are women)." However, men were not immune from such reactions. As one man noted,

> Sometimes it's difficult when my colleagues adopt a fairly traditional script for parenting, i.e., man works late and woman tends to the kids, especially when they consciously think that they are nontraditional and progressively fair, and fail to see the subtle ways in which they uphold these traditional roles, values, expectations, etc. This is when the uniqueness of my situation becomes very salient and clear, and I have a little trouble reconciling my career aspirations with my family commitments.

To counteract coworkers' negative attitudes and create a more accepting culture for working parents, one woman noted that, "Ensuring that I am pulling my own weight is a big part of maintaining the support from colleagues." Another observed that, "We need to be very careful not to judge the situations our coworkers are in."

Policies and Practices

Focus group participants were asked to speak about the types of organizational and government policies and practices that would be helpful in reducing WFC for working parents. Nearly all of the women spoke about the necessity of having "universal, affordable, accessible, and high-quality child care." More specifically, this included the need for more care for school-aged children (i.e., before- and after-school programs), care that was more conveniently located, and programs that offered longer and more flexible hours. And, although Canada currently has one of the more generous parental leave policies in the world, there was still the sentiment that this could be improved. For example, one respondent cited a desire for "Longer parental leave, with better benefits . . . to be shared between the couple however they choose."

Many of the other suggestions revolved around instituting more family-friendly workplace policies. The option to telecommute or work from home seemed particularly attractive to men, with three of the five men specifically mentioning that this would be something they wanted. Both men and women frequently mentioned policies directed at providing more workplace flexibility. For example, one respondent pointed to, "Flexible work policies that allow parents to alter their work schedules as long as they are still meeting timelines for deliverables at work." and another noted that, "The ability to take time off more spontaneously would be really helpful." Many parents also advocated for policies that allowed reduced work hours. However, several mentioned that while this was "wonderful for parents who are in the financial position to take advantage," most parents would be "unable to afford the reduced salary that accompanies reduced workload." Some respondents commented that being able to have such policies available to them had had positive effects. For example, one woman said,

> I have been able to adjust my schedule to meet my parenting needs since the day my first child was born—thanks to a very flexible manager. This has included (at different times) moving some hours to evening (at the workplace) and reducing total hours. . . . It makes my position a dream job for many women. I feel respected and trusted as an employee. I also feel that the work that I complete is more important than the number of hours that I spend at my desk.

By contrast, others highlighted the negative consequences of their not being able to access these policies. In the words of one, "In terms of reducing hours, that wasn't an option for me at my old job . . . and the main reason I left. There was no willingness to look at part-time hours, job sharing, or any other option."

Participants also discussed impediments to workers' use of the family-friendly policies that were available to them. Most respondents said things like, "I think that most of the parents in my workplace do take advantage of family-friendly policies when they need them." However, they did acknowledge several barriers to policy use. One of the biggest was a lack of awareness. Several said things like, "I don't think anyone really knows what is available to them," and "I don't think that my workplace has work-life policies . . . if they do, I don't know about them. Neither do I know what the government policies are." Other barriers mentioned were that workers were "discouraged by their managers from taking advantage of these policies" and criticized by their coworkers when they did so. This led to the fear that policy use would diminish participants' career opportunities.

Some participants espoused a broader vision about what changes were needed. As one parent put it, this meant that,

> the value of the parenting work we do be appreciated and valued by others, especially by those who do not have children . . . to have enough time and freedom to feel successful at work and at home . . . to have more fun, to love our jobs, to know that we are making the right choices for our families.

Conclusions

Changes in the economy, technological advances, globalization, and the nature of work, on the one hand, and in family life, reflected particularly in high rates of full-time employment among women, have had dramatic impacts on Canadians over the last few decades. Consistently high rates of role overload and work stress and their potential consequences for employees' health and well-being have attracted the attention of policy makers and academics and led to a significant body of research on antecedents and consequences of work-life conflict. Common to findings from other countries, long work hours, lack of control over workloads, and lack of flexible work arrangements or lack of support for using them contribute to role overload and WFC, especially for those with young children, and increasingly for employees with care responsibilities for aging family members. Unique to Canada are substantial differences between policies in Québec and other provinces that directly affect access to generous parental leave and affordable child care.

Current interests among Canadian work-family researchers include: (1) more specific consideration of how combinations of work demands and resources affect employees and their families (e.g., among managers vs. those in precarious, low-wage work or in particular occupations/professions); (2) impacts of inequitable access to flexible work arrangements for employees with significant care responsibilities, and potential positive and negative impacts of using alternative work options; and (3) potential impacts of policy change or inaction (e.g., with respect to parental leave, child care, home care, and supports for employed caregivers) for employees and employers. Current studies suggest that many Canadians are challenged to adopt private solutions to public problems with variable success. Population aging and a projected shrinking labor force add greater impetus for employers and policy makers to engage in more sustainable approaches to support work-family integration.

References

Bakker, A. B., & Demerouti, E. (2007). The job-demands-resources model: State of the art. *Journal of Managerial Psychology*, *22*(3), 309–328.

Beaujot, R., & Andersen, R. (2007). Time-crunch: Impact of time spent in paid and unpaid work, and its division in families. *Canadian Journal of Sociology, 32*, 295–315.

Becklumb, P., & Elgersma, S. (2008). *Recognition of the foreign credentials of immigrants.* Government of Canada, Library of Parliament. PRB 04–29E. Retrieved from http://www.parl.gc.ca/Content/LOP/researchpublications/prb0429-e.pdf

Burton, P., & Phipps, S. (2011). Families, time and well-being in Canada. *Canadian Public Policy, 37*(3), 395–423.

Buzdugan, R., & Halli, S. (2009). Labour market experiences of Canadian immigrants with a focus on foreign education and experience. *International Migration Review, 43*(2), 366–386.

Campaign 2000. (2014). *2014 Report card on child and family poverty in Canada.* Retrieved from http://www.campaign2000.ca/anniversaryreport/CanadaRC2014EN.pdf

Central Intelligence Agency. (2015). *The world factbook 2013–14.* Washington, DC: Central Intelligence Agency, 2013. Retrieved from https://www.cia.gov/library/publications/the-world-factbook/index.html

Comfort, D., Johnson, K., & Wallace, D. (2003). *Part-time work and family-friendly practices in Canadian workplaces.* Ottawa, ON: Statistics Canada. Catalogue No. 71-584-MIE No. 6. Retrieved from http://publications.gc.ca/Collection/Statcan/71-584-M/71-584-MIE2003006.pdf

Conference Board of Canada. (2013). *How Canada performs—income inequality.* Retrieved from http://www.conferenceboard.ca/hcp/details/society/income-inequality.aspx

Crompton, S. (2011). *What's stressing the stressed? Main sources of stress among workers. Statistics Canada.* Canadian Social Trends. Catalogue No. 11-008-X. October 13, 2011, 44–51.

Dewa, C. S. (2007). Mental illness and the workplace: A national concern. *Canadian Journal of Psychiatry, 52*(6), 337–338.

Doucet, A., Lero, D. S., McKay, L., & Tremblay, D.-G. (2015). Canada country note. In P. Moss (Ed.), *International review of leave policies and research 2015.* Retrieved from http://www.leavenetwork.org/lp_and_r_reports/.

Duxbury, L., & Higgins, C. (2001). *Work-life balance in the new millennium: Where are we? Where do we need to go?* Canadian Policy Research Networks. Paper No W/12. Ottawa, October.

Duxbury, L., & Higgins, C. (2009). *Work-life conflict in Canada in the new millennium: Key findings and recommendations from the 2001 national work-life conflict study.* Health Canada. Retrieved from http://www.hc-sc.gc.ca/ewh-semt/pubs/occup-travail/balancing_six-equilibre_six/index-eng.php

Duxbury, L., & Higgins, C. (2012). *Revisiting work—life issues in Canada: The 2012 national study on balancing work and caregiving in Canada.* Retrieved from http://newsroom.carleton.ca/wp-content/files/2012-National-Work-Long-Summary.pdf

Duxbury, L., Lyons, S., & Higgins, C. (2008). Too much to do, and not enough time: An examination of role overload. In K. Korabik, D. S. Lero, & D. Whitehead (Eds.), *Handbook of work-family integration* (pp. 125–140). San Diego, CA: Elsevier.

Elliott, J. L., & Fleras, A. (1990). Immigration and the ethnic mosaic. In Peter S. Li (Ed.), *Race and ethnic relations in Canada* (pp. 51–76). Toronto: Oxford University Press.

Esping-Andersen, G. (1990). *The three worlds of welfare capitalism.* Princeton, NJ: Princeton University Press.

Fakih, A. (2014). *Availability of family-friendly work practices and implicit wage costs: New evidence from Canada.* Institute for the Study of Labour (IZA). Discussion Paper No. 8190. Retrieved from http://ftp.iza.org/dp8190.pdf

Fang, T., & Lee, B. (2008). *Family-friendly benefits and employee labour market outcomes*. Paper presented at the 2008 Western Academy of Management Meeting, Oakland, CA. Retrieved from http://www.cerforum.org/conferences/200705/papers/FangLee.pdf

Fast, J., Lero, D., DeMarco, R., Ferriera, H., & Eales, J. (2014). *Combining care work and paid work: Is it sustainable?* Research on Aging Policies and Practice. University of Alberta. Retrieved from http://www.rapp.ualberta.ca/~/media/rapp/Publications/Documents/Combining_care_work_and_paid_work_2014–09–16.pdf

Ferrer, A., & Gagné, L. (2006). *The use of family-friendly workplace practices in Canada*. Working Paper Series No. 2006-02. Montreal, QC: Institute for Research on Public Policy.

Friendly, M., & Prentice, S. (2009). *About Canada: Childcare*. Halifax, NS: Fernwood Publishing.

Frone, M., Russell, M., & Cooper, M. (1997). Relation of work-life conflict to health outcomes: A four-year longitudinal study of employed parents. *Journal of Occupational & Organizational Psychology, 70*, 325–335.

Frone, M., Yardley, J., & Markel, K. (1997). Developing and testing an integrative model of the work-family interface. *Journal of Vocational Behaviour, 50*, 145–167.

Galarneau, D., & Sohn, T. (2013). *Long-term trends in unionization*. Insights on Canadian Society. Statistics Canada. Catalogue No. 75-006X.

Government of Canada. (2013). *Income inequality in Canada: An overview*. Report of the Standing Committee on Finance. House of Commons. December, 2013.

Greenhaus, J. H., & Beutell, N. J. (1985). Sources of conflict between work and family roles. *Academy of Management Review, 10*, 76–88.

Hilbrecht, M., & Lero, D. S. (2014). Self-employment and family life: Negotiating work-life balance when you're "always on." *Community, Work and Family, 20*(1), 20–42.

Hilbrecht, M., Lero, D. S., Schryer, E., Mock, S. E., & Smale, B. (2015). Understanding the association between time spent caregiving and well-being among employed adults: Testing a model of work–life fit and sense of community. *Community, Work and Family*. Retrieved from http://dx.doi.org/10.1080/13668803.2015.1112254.

Industry Canada. (2013). *Key small business statistics—August 2013*. Retrieved from http://www.ic.gc.ca/eic/site/061.nsf/eng/02805.html

Kahn, R. L., Wolfe, D. M., Quinn, R. P., Snoek, J. D., & Rosenthal, R. A. (1964). *Organizational stress: Studies in role conflict and ambiguity*. New York, NY: John Wiley & Sons.

Konrad, A. M., & Yang, Y. (2012). Is using work-life interface benefit a career-limiting move? An examination of women, men, lone parents and parents with partners. *Journal of Organizational Behavior, 33*(8), 1095–1119.

MacDonald, M., Phipps, S., & Lethbridge, L. (2005). Taking its toll: The influence of paid and unpaid work on women's well-being. *Feminist Economics, 11*(1), 63–94.

McElwain, A. K., Korabik, K., & Rosin, H. M. (2005). An examination of gender differences in work-family conflict. *Canadian Journal of Behavioural Science, 37*(4) 283–298.

Moen, P., Kelly, E., & Huang, R. (2008). 'Fit' inside the work-family black box: An ecology of the life course, cycles of control reframing. *Journal of Occupational and Organization Psychology, 81*, 411–433.

Mullen, J., Kelley, E., & Kelloway, E. K. (2008). Health and well-being outcomes of the work-family interface. In K. Korabik, D. S. Lero, & D. Whitehead (Eds.), *Handbook of work-family integration* (pp. 191–124). San Diego, CA: Elsevier.

National Forum on Family Security. (1993). *Family security in insecure times*. Ottawa, Canada: National Forum.

Québec, Gouvernement du Québec. (1997). *Nouvelles dispositions de la politique familiale: les enfants au coeur de nos choix*. Québec, QC: Publications du Québec.

Rose, H. A., & Humble, A. M. (2014). Canada's patchwork policy: Family policy in the Canadian context. In M. Robila (Ed.), *Handbook of family policies across the globe* (pp. 357–372). New York, NY: Springer Science+Business Media.

Rosin, H. M., & Korabik, K. (2002). Do family-friendly policies fulfill their promise? An investigation of their impact on work-family conflict and work and personal outcomes. In Debra L. Nelson & Ronald J. Burke (Eds.), *Gender, work stress and health* (pp. 211–226). Washington, DC: American Psychological Association.

Schieman, S., & Glavin, P. (2011). Education and work-family conflict: Explanations, contingencies and mental health consequences. *Social Forces, 89*(4), 1341–1362.

Statistics Canada. (2013). *Portrait of Canada's labour force*. Minister of Industry. Catalogue No. 99-012-X2011002.

Statistics Canada. (2014a). *Canadian demographics at a glance* (2nd ed.). Retrieved from http://www.statcan.gc.ca/pub91-003-x/2014001.

Statistics Canada. (2014b). *Population projections for Canada (2013 to 2063), provinces and territories (2013 to 2038)*. Catalogue No. 91-520-X. Retrieved from http://www.statcan.gc.ca/pub/91-520-x/2014001/section02-eng.htm#a4

Statistics Canada. (2014c). The World Bank International Comparison Program for purchasing power: Overall ranking of countries, 2011. *The Daily*, May 9, 2014.

Statistics Canada. (2015a). Canada's population estimates, first quarter 2015. *The Daily*, June 17, 2015. Retrieved from http://www.statcan.gc.ca/daily-quotidien/150617/dq150617c-eng.pdf

Statistics Canada. (2015b). *Canada at a glance*. Minister of Industry. Catalogue No. 12-581-XIE.

Statistics Canada. (2015c). Canada's population estimates: Age and sex, July 1, 2015. *The Daily*, September 29, 2015.

Statistics Canada. (2015d). *Canada: Economic and financial data*. Retrieved from http://www.statcan.gc.ca/tables-tableaux/sum-som/l01/cst01/dsbbcan-eng.htm

Statistics Canada. (2015e). *Table 282–0002—Labour force survey estimates (LFS), by sex and detailed age group, annual (persons unless otherwise noted)*. CANSIM (database).

Statistics Canada. (2015f). *Table 282–0012—Labour force survey estimates (LFS), employment by class of worker, North American Industry Classification System (NAICS) and sex, annual (persons)*. CANSIM (database).

Statistics Canada. (2015g). *Table 282–0014—Labour force survey estimates (LFS), part-time employment by reason for part-time work, sex and age group*. CANSIM (database).

Tézli, A., & Gauthier, A. H. (2009). Balancing work and family in Canada: An empirical examination of conceptualizations and measurements. *Canadian Journal of Sociology, 34*(2), 433–461.

Turcotte, M. (2013). *Family caregiving: What are the consequences?* Insights on Canadian Society. Statistics Canada. Catalogue No. 75-006-X.

Uppal, S. (2015). *Employment patterns of families with children*. Insights on Canadian Society. Statistics Canada. Catalogue No. 75-006X. June 2015, 1–12.

Williams, C. (2008). *Work-life balance of shift workers*. Perspectives on Labour and Income. Statistics Canada. Catalogue No. 75-001-X. August 2008, 5–16.

Zeytinoglu, I. U., Cooke, G. B., & Mann, S. L. (2010). Employer-offered family support programs, gender and voluntary and involuntary part-time work. *Industrial Relations, 65*(2), 177–195.

6

THE WORK-FAMILY INTERFACE IN AUSTRALIA

Anne Bardoel

Introduction

This chapter first outlines the major contextual conditions affecting the work-family (W-F) interface in Australia, including demographics and the household, women and work, the intersection of work and family, and legal changes over time. Second, Australian research pertinent to WFC is summarized in terms of antecedents and various causal models, as well as limited studies of W-F enhancement. A brief conclusion follows. As indicated in Chapter 2, Australia was one of the countries for which focus group discussions were not conducted.

The Australian Context

Australia, officially known as the Commonwealth of Australia is a stable, democratic, and culturally diverse nation with a highly skilled workforce and a strong performing economy (Department of Foreign Affairs and Trade, 2014). Australia is the sixth largest country in the world by total land area and 12th largest economy of the world (Australian Government, 2014).

Australia is ranked second on the United Nations' Human Development Index and is placed highly with the rest of the world on national performance such as press freedom, political rights, and civil liberties (World Audit Organisation, 2007). Australia is also a member of the United Nations (UN), Group of 20 major economies (G20), World Trade Organization (WTO), East Asia Summit (EAS), Organisation for Economic Co-operation and Development (OECD), Asia-Pacific Economic Cooperation (APEC), Commonwealth, Association of South-east Asian Nations (ASEAN), Indian Ocean Rim Association (IORA), Forum for East Asia–Latin America Cooperation (FEALAC), International climate change negotiations, Asia–Europe Meeting (ASEM), and the Pacific Islands Forum (PIF) (Australian Government, 2014).

Demographics and the Household

Australia's population increased rapidly from the beginning of the 20th century, when the population was just under 4 million, to over 22 million at present (ABS, 2014a). Several components of population growth that impact on WFC are discussed here: immigration, life expectancy, fertility, family structure, and the division of labor in couple households.

Immigration to Australia was historically limited to culturally homogeneous groups under the White Australia Policy, which favored immigration to Australia from Western Europe, the United States, Canada, and South Africa. The policy was phased out between World War II and 1975, when the policy was formally abolished (Department of Immigration and Border Protection, 2009). Given Australia's geographic location, immigration from Asian nations has been substantial since 1975, and between 2007 and mid-2011, 7 of the 10 nations contributing the largest numbers of immigrants were Asian (New Zealand, South Africa, and the United Kingdom rounded out the list; ABS, 2012–2013). As De Cieri and Bardoel (2009) note with regard to multinational corporations operating in Asia, cultural differences may influence the very meaning of WFC and the effectiveness of measures to reduce WFC. The relevance of cultural diversity to Australia will likely expand in the future, given that 60% of population growth since the mid-2000s is accounted for by immigration (ABS, 2014a).

In line with other developed nations, Australia is also undergoing a demographic shift toward an older population, with more elderly and fewer people of working age. At June 2013, the median age of Australian population was 37.3 years, up from 36.9 years at June 2008 (ABS, 2014b). The labor force reflects this shift, with an annual growth rate of only .22% between March of 2010 and March of 2015 (ABS, 2015).

In part, the aging population is related to the population of baby boomers achieving retirement age (Australian Government, 2007), as well as to extended longevity. Due to both factors, between 1994 and 2014, the proportion of people aged 65 years and over increased from 11.8% to 14.7% and the proportion of people aged 85 years and over almost doubled from 1.0% of the total population in 1994 to 1.9% in 2014 (ABS, 2014b).

Together with a world-wide increase in the incidence of chronic diseases (World Health Organization, 2013), the aging population and increased longevity imply that the need for unpaid care by family members has and will continue to increase in Australia. Meeting that need may increase WFC.

On the other hand, fertility has declined, and the proportion of people aged less than 15 years decreased from 21.6% to 18.8% (ABS, 2014b). Akin to many other developed nations, fertility decline is linked to delayed childbearing (ABS,

2008a). Australian demographer Peter McDonald (2000) attributes both low fertility and delayed childbearing to efforts by women to avoid WFC in nations where traditional gender relations hold sway in both the home and in public policy, a point we return to later in the chapter.

Family structure continues to be dominated by couple families in Australia, albeit with fewer children, as previously noted. However, between 1986 and 2011, the number of one-person households increased from 18.8% to 24.3% of all households (Australian Institute of Family Studies, 2013). That trend might continue and, to the extent it involves increasing numbers of the elderly, and particularly elderly women, may expand both the need for family caregiving and, in turn, WFC.

The division of household or unpaid work in Australia is closely related to gender. Hoenig and Page (2012), using 2009–2010 data, estimate that 60% of all unpaid care work in Australia is performed by women, while Craig, Bittman, Brown, and Thompson (2008) report from 1997 time use data that women perform between 22 and 50 hours more unpaid work in the household than men in couple families. This inequality could make WFC particularly acute for women.

Work and Gender

As in many other developed countries, the long-term entry of women into the labor force is central to understanding WFC. In Australia, men's labor force participation declined from 80% in 1978 to just over 70% as of 2014, while women's rate rose from 43% to just under 60% over that same time period (Vandenbroek, 2014).

Also like many other developed nations, Australian institutions were built around the assumption that families are composed of breadwinner fathers and stay-at-home mothers. That assumption was initially enshrined in the "Harvester Judgement" determined by the Commonwealth Court of Conciliation and Arbitration in 1907, which required that most employers pay at least a "basic wage," which would permit an unskilled adult male laborer to support a family of five with full-time employment (Davis & Lansbury, 2000). At that time, base wage for females was pegged at 54% of the male "basic wage." Although equal pay legislation has been in place since 1969 (Young, 2013), the gender wage gap for full-time equivalent work stood at 18.8% as of February 2015 (Workplace Gender Equity Agency, 2015).

In Australia, employees may be classified as full-time (at least 35 hours per week) or part-time, and as permanent or casual. Historically, casual employees did not receive vacation, sick time, or pension benefits, and were subject to employment at will; in return, they received a 20% hourly wage premium called the casual loading (Drago, Pirretti, & Scutella, 2007). A majority of casual employees and of part-time employees are women, and due to labor market liberalization, only around half of current casual employees receive the casual loading (ABS,

2008b). Although women's low wages and part-time and casual employment may support gender inequality in couple families, they might also reduce levels of WFC for men and women by ensuring that one member is relatively unencumbered by employment so therefore can meet family needs as they arise (Bardoel & Grigg, 2010).

Drago and Wooden (2010) compared preferred and usual work hours in Australian and US samples and, using differences of more than five hours to define overwork and underwork, found overwork more than twice as prevalent in the United States (49.5% compared to 23.1% in Australia). Underwork was slightly more prevalent in the United States (14.6% compared to 12.7%). Across groups of women working part-time, overwork is rare in both nations, but underwork is reported more frequently in both nations for mothers but only in Australia for non-mothers. They interpret the latter finding as suggesting that involuntary part-time employment may often be attributable to discrimination against mothers per se in the United States, but due to discrimination against women in general in Australia. Both overwork and underwork may be related to heightened levels of WFC, in the prior case due to time binds and in the latter due to a shortfall of income.

Work and Family

As McDonald (2000) has argued, WFC may be the result of institutions that favor breadwinner fathers and stay-at-home mothers clashing with the reality of women's employment. A compromise of sorts, the neotraditional, or one-and-a-half earner family, is particularly prevalent in Australia, where the OECD reports for samples of women of child-rearing age that rates of part-time employment for the mother of one child are 54% in Australia, with an OECD average of only 29% for a large group of member nations (OECD, 2002, p. 78).

Reliance on neotraditional family form is not irrational for Australian women, given time use data shows the smallest difference in total workload (paid plus unpaid work) for couple families with a breadwinner husband and homemaker wife, and the largest differences where the woman works full-time or beyond at paid work. The woman's total work hours rise from just over 80 hours per week in the prior to over 100 hours in the latter case, while the man's contributions only change minimally (Craig et al., 2008, p. 22). Relatedly, while differences between the unpaid care and housework of men and women exist in both the United States and Australia, Drago et al. (2007) conclude that the difference is more pronounced in Australia. That difference may adversely affect WFC for employed women in Australia.

In addition to care for children, WFC may be related to care for multiple generations. The 2012 Survey of Disability, Ageing, and Carers defined a carer as a person who provides informal assistance to an older person or someone who has a disability or a long-term health condition. The survey identified 2.7 million

Australian carers (12% of the population), with 770,000 (3.4%) identified as primary carers, although care for children was not studied (ABS, 2012). Estimates of simultaneous care for multiple generations in Australia derived from the 2005–2012 waves of the Household, Income and Labour Dynamics Australia (HILDA) data suggest that, by the time they achieve age 65, 59% of women and 36% of men will have experienced simultaneous care for a dependent child and an adult (Bardoel & Drago, 2014).

Government and Legislation

By the turn of the 21st century, the Australian government had put in place few explicit legislative mechanisms to reduce WFC. However, there were increasing pressures to do so, including low fertility, and the fact that Australia remained one of the few nations in the world without paid parental leave (Gornick & Meyers, 2005).

An initial response was found in the (conservative) Howard government's 2004 announcement of the baby bonus, a flat amount paid to all women who bore children, regardless of employment status, which had a mild positive impact on fertility (Drago, Sawyer, Shreffler, Warren, & Wooden, 2011). The policy was intended to respond to low fertility, but not to women's employment.

Calls for more substantial policies continued at this time, particularly with regard to paid parental leave and the right-to-request flexibility (e.g., Australian Human Rights Commission, 2007; Bourke, 2004). By 2009, the Howard government was replaced by a Labor government which, under the Fair Work Act of 2009, guaranteed a statutory right-to-request flexibility for parents of young children or of children with a disability under the age of 18 (Australian Government, 2009). That legislation was amended in 2013 to cover care for virtually any adult with a disability or long-term illness as well (Australian Government, 2013). In between, during 2010, the government introduced universal paid parental leave of 18 weeks (Karvelas, 2010). In either the short-run or long-run (or perhaps both), these policy shifts may function to reduce WFC.

Research on the Work-Family Interface in Australia

In a comprehensive of work-life research conducted in Australia and New Zealand, Bardoel, De Cieri, and Santos (2008) found dominant themes in the research conducted between 2004 and 2007:

- Organizational approaches to work-life issues with a focus on policies, programs, strategies, and support provided by organizations to alleviate employees' WFC and to promote work-family balance;
- Government policy and legislation, mostly related to child care, maternity leave (or parental leave), and caregiving;

- Family structure and children, particularly issues faced by single-parent families, dual-career families, and families with children with disabilities or chronic illnesses;
- Characteristics of the jobs themselves, including the omnipresence of long working hours in the lives of Australian and New Zealand workers;
- Psychological outcomes such as stress, burnout, and other well-being-related aspects.

As is standard, most relevant Australian studies tend to focus on the potential for work to interfere negatively with family commitments, or WIF conflict per se. However, some studies also address reverse directionality, or FIW conflict, and the possibility of positive or enrichment effects, as described later in the chapter.

Antecedents of W-F Conflict

Starting with the causes or antecedents of WFC, using the HILDA data, Reynolds and Aletraris (2007) find that men report significantly higher levels of WIF conflict than women, but that for both groups WIF conflict is positively correlated with preferences for fewer work hours. They also report that women experience significantly higher levels of FIW conflict than men and, oddly, that high levels among women are related to both preferences for greater and for fewer hours. Hosking and Western (2008) also used the HILDA data and found that employed mothers do not report significantly higher levels of WIF conflict than employed fathers, but that mothers employed full-time report significantly elevated levels of conflict relative to those employed part-time, with no significant effects for casual employment. Albeit less direct in terms of WIF conflict, Rose, Hewitt, and Baxter (2013) found to the contrary that part-time as opposed to full-time employment for women was not associated with significant reductions in reported levels of time pressure.

In terms of industry, Lingard and Francis (2004) found that men construction employees working on-site reported significantly higher levels of WIF conflict than those located at a regional or head office, but that no such differences exist for women. They attribute this finding to the long hours of male employees working on-site.

In studies that did not differentiate by gender, a study of lawyers and accountants found no significant difference in perceived WIF across members of dual-career versus single-career couples (Elloy & Smith, 2003). However, in a sample of legal industry employees (including paralegals and administrative employees), Russo and Waters (2006) divided employees into workaholics, enthusiastic workaholics, relaxed, and uninvolved workers, and found both groups of workaholics reporting higher levels of WIF, and that WIF was moderated by access to flexible scheduling among the enthusiastic workaholics. For employees in the construction industry, Lingard, Francis, and Turner (2012) found that high work time demands and low work time control were positively correlated with WIF. Relatedly, for a sample of academic employees, measures of work pressure were positively, and autonomy negatively, correlated with WIF (Winefield, Boyd, & Winefield, 2014). Somewhat differently, in an analysis of employees in construction organizations, it was found that private sector employees reported significantly higher levels of WIF than those in the public sector (Francis, Lingard, Prosser, & Turner, 2013). In a public sector agency only, Yule, Chang, Gudmundsson, and Sawang (2012) found managerial support and flexible and alternative work arrangements positively related to work-life balance (which can be viewed as a rough inverse indicator of WIF), while off-site working exhibited a negative correlation. Using a sample of policewomen and a path model, Thompson, Kirk, and Brown (2005) found that conflict within the family was predicted by supervisor support (negatively) feeding into both role overload and role ambiguity, and then via emotional exhaustion.

In a cross-national study of US and Australian family-owned business owners and employees, similar positive relationships were found for business dissatisfaction and WIF conflict by Smyrnios et al. (2003). In another cross-national comparison, here of managers, Billing et al. (2014) found WIF conflict similarly and positively correlated with cultural values of vertical individualism in the United States and Australia, with milder correlations in samples from Japan and South Korea.

W-F Conflict as Cause

In a sample of lawyers and accountants, Elloy (2001) found no relationship between WIF conflict and reports of stress. However, in a sample of social workers, Kalliath and Kalliath (2013) find evidence positively linking WIF conflict (and FIW conflict) with psychological strain, with job satisfaction mediating some of the relationships. Using a sample of professionals and managers in the construction industry, Lingard and Francis (2006) found that WIF conflict is related to burnout, and that some types of organizational and supervisory support moderated those effects. In the cross-national study of small businesses, Smyrnios et al. (2003) found that WIF moderated the causes of family cohesion.

Using a sample of police officers, Hall, Dollard, Tuckey, Winfield, and Thompson (2010) found evidence for complex causality wherein WIF mediated the relationship between job demands and emotional exhaustion, but also that emotional exhaustion mediated the relationship between job demands and WIF. Similarly, Winefield, Boyd, and Winfield's (2014) study of academics found that WIF mediated the effects of work pressure and autonomy on psychological strain and adverse physical symptoms. Using a broader sample of employed parents of 4- to 5-year-old children, Strazdins, O'Brien, Lucas, and Rodgers (2013) found that reports of WIF by either parent were associated with adverse emotional and behavioral symptoms in the children, and that the effect was stronger when both parents reported WIF; nor was that relationship moderated by W-F facilitation or enrichment.

In a study of cancer workers, Thanacoody, Bartram, and Casimir (2009) found that WIF and FIW conflict were associated with intention to leave the employer, but the relationships were mediated by levels of burnout, with stronger relationships where low levels of supervisor support existed.

W-F Enrichment

In terms of positive effects, Haar and Bardoel (2008) studied positive work-to-family spillover and family-to-work spillover (WTFS and FTWS) and found the prior associated negatively with psychological distress and turnover intentions, and the latter negatively related to psychological distress and positively linked to family satisfaction. Relatedly, Lingard et al. (2012) found that the combination of high work time demands and work time control in the construction industry contributed to W-F enrichment.

Conclusions

Australian researchers, like many of their counterparts elsewhere, have tested whether long work hours, particularly for women; organizational and supervisor support; job autonomy; and family circumstances are linked to WFC. They have also tested for linkages between WFC and various psychological or behavioral outcomes, whether those linkages are cast as direct or as mediating.

Overall, the results are somewhat mixed, particularly in terms of work hours and gender, and surprisingly in terms of the relationship between WFC and stress. Nonetheless, in at least one study the predicted results were found that long work hours have adverse effects on WIF; that part-time as opposed to full-time employment reduces WIF for women; and that organizational or supervisory support, flexible work arrangements, and job autonomy reduce WIF. More generally, most, though not all, of the studies found that WFC is associated with ill effects for employees.

The studies leave a variety of questions unexplored. These include at least the following: "How are immigrants from Asia influencing the causes, levels, and effects of WFC?"; "How are differences in the gendered division of household labor linked to WFC?"; "How is the increasing prevalence of multigenerational caregiving altering WFC?"; and "How are recent policy developments such as paid parental leave and the right-to-request flexibility affecting levels of WFC for women and for men?" McDonald's (2000) research suggests that these policies will help to ameliorate WFC, but further studies are needed to confirm this possibility.

What is probably most surprising about the results is the scarce coverage of gender. Given that studies of WFC were largely motivated by the entry of women into the labor force in the last half-century, these lacunae are particularly notable. It is also to some extent a purposeful choice of the researchers, given that a large number of the studies report the gender breakdown of the sample, but do not test for gender differences (Billing et al., 2014; Elloy, 2001; Elloy & Smith, 2003; Francis et al., 2013; Haar & Bardoel, 2008; Hall et al., 2010; Kalliath & Kalliath, 2013; Lingard & Francis, 2006; Lingard, Francis, & Turner, 2012; Russo & Waters, 2006; Smyrnios et al., 2003; Thanacoody, Bartram, & Casimir, 2009; Winefield, Boyd, & Winefield, 2014; Yule et al., 2012). Admittedly, some of these samples have small numbers of women (e.g., in construction) or men (e.g., in social work). But even in those cases it would have been useful to replicate the analyses after excluding the smaller group to identify any qualitative or quantitative changes in measured effects. It would be useful if future studies rectified this omission.

References

ABS, Australian Bureau of Statistics. (2008a). *Australian social trends, 2008*. No. 4102.0. Canberra, ACT: ABS.

ABS. (2008b). *Australian labour market statistics, October 2008*. No. 6105.0. Canberra, ACT: ABS.

ABS. (2012). *Disability, ageing and carers, Australia: Summary of findings, 2012*. No. 4430.0. Canberra, ACT: ABS.

ABS. (2012–2013). *Reflecting a nation: Stories from the 2011 Census, 2012–2013*. Canberra, ACT: ABS.

ABS. (2014a). *Australian historical population statistics, 2014*. No. 3105.0.65.001. Canberra, ACT: ABS.

ABS. (2014b). *Population by age and sex, regions of Australia, 2013*. No. 3235.0. Canberra, ACT: ABS.

ABS. (2015). *Table 01. Labour force status by sex—trend*. Labour Force, Australia, March 2015, No. 6202.0. Canberra, ACT: ABS.

Australian Government. (2007). *Baby boomers*. Canberra, ACT: Australian Government. Retrieved May 4, 2015, from http://www.australia.gov.au/about-australia/australian-story/baby-boomers

Australian Government. (2009). *Fair Work Act 2009*. Act. No. 28 of 2009. Canberra, ACT: Australian Government.

Australian Government. (2013). *Fair Work Amendment act 2013*. Act. No. 73 of 2013, Canberra, ACT.

Australian Government. (2014). *Australia in brief*. Retrieved February 16, 2015, from http://www.dfat.gov.au/about-us/publications/Documents/australia-in-brief.pdf

Australian Human Rights Commission. (2007). *It's about time: Women, men, work and family, final paper 2007*. Sydney, NSW: AHRC.

Australian Institute of Family Studies. (2013). *Family facts and figures*. Canberra, ACT: AIFS.

Bardoel, E. A., De Cieri, H., & Santos, C. (2008). A review of work/life research in Australia and New Zealand. *Asia Pacific Journal of Human Resources, 46*, 316–333.

Bardoel, E. A., & Drago, R. (2014). *Dual-responsibility caregiving: The sandwich generation in Australia*. Work and Family Researchers Network Conference, New York, June 21.

Bardoel, E. A., & Grigg, K. (2010). Work-life management. In Julia Connell & Stephen Teo (Eds.), *Strategic HRM: Contemporary issues in the Asia Pacific region* (pp. 185–211). Prahran, Australia: Tilde University Press.

Billing, T. K., Bhagat, R., Babakus, E., Srivastava, B. N., Shin, M., & Brew, F. (2014). Work-family conflict in four national contexts: A closer look at the role of individualism-collectivism. *International Journal of Cross Cultural Management, 14*, 139–159.

Bourke, J. (2004). Using the law to support work/life issues: The Australian experience. *Journal of Gender, Social Policy & the Law, 12*, 19–68.

Craig, L., Bittman, M., Brown, J., & Thompson, D. (2008). *Managing work and family*. SPRC Report 6/08. Social Policy Research Centre, Sydney, VIC: University of New South Wales. Retrieved May 3, 2015, from https://www.sprc.unsw.edu.au/media/SPRCFile/Report6_08_Managing_Work_and_Family.pdf

Davis, E., & Lansbury, R. (2000). Employment relations in Australia. In G. Bamber & R. Lansbury (Eds.), *International and comparative employment relations* (pp. 110–143). London, UK: Sage.

De Cieri, H., & Bardoel, E. A. (2009). What does work-life management mean in China and Southeast Asia for MNCs? *Community, Work and Family, 12*, 179–196.

Department of Foreign Affairs and Trade. (2014). *Australia in brief, Australian Government*. Retrieved February 3, 2015, from http://www.dfat.gov.au/about-us/publications/Documents/australia-in-brief.pdf

Department of Immigration and Border Protection. (2009). *Fact sheet 8—Abolition of the 'White Australia' policy*. Canberra, ACT: Australian Government. Retrieved May 2, 2015, from https://www.immi.gov.au/media/fact-sheets/08abolition.htm

Drago, R., Pirretti, A., & Scutella, R. (2007) Work and family directions in the USA and Australia: A policy research agenda. *Journal of Industrial Relations, 49*, 49–66.

Drago, R., Sawyer, K., Shreffler, K. M., Warren, D., & Wooden, M. (2011). Did Australia's baby bonus increase fertility intentions and births? *Population Research and Policy Review, 30*, 381–397.

Drago, R., & Wooden, M. (2010). Work hours mismatch in the United States and Australia. In K. Christensen & B. Schneider (Eds.), *Workplace flexibility: Realigning Jobs for a 21st Century* (pp. 262–275). New York, NY: Cornell University Press.

Elloy, D. F. (2001). A predictive study of stress among Australian dual-career couples. *The Journal of Social Psychology, 141*, 122–123.

Elloy, D. F., & Smith, C. R. (2003). Patterns of stress, work-family conflict, role conflict, role ambiguity and overload among dual-career and single-career couples: An Australian study. *Cross Cultural Management, 10*, 55–66.

Francis, V., Lingard, H., Prosser, A., & Turner, M. (2013). Work-family and construction: Public and private sector differences. *Journal of Management in Engineering, 29*, 393–399.

Gornick, J. C., & Meyers, M. K. (2005). *Families that work: Policies for reconciling parenthood and employment*. New York, NY: Russell Sage.

Haar, J. M., & Bardoel, E. A. (2008). A positive spillover from the work-family interface: A study of Australian employees. *Asia Pacific Journal of Human Resources, 46*(3), 275–287.

Hall, G. B., Dollard, M. F., Tuckey, M. R., Winfield, A. H., & Thompson, B. M. (2010). Job demands, work-family conflict, and emotional exhaustion in police officers: A longitudinal test of competing theories. *Journal of Occupational and Organizational Psychology, 83*, 237–250.

Hoenig, S. A., & Page, A. R. E. (2012). *Counting on care work in Australia*. Report prepared by AECgroup Limited for economic Security4Women, Australia.

Hosking, A., & Western, M. (2008). The effects of non-standard employment on work-family conflict. *Journal of Sociology, 44*, 5–27.

Kalliath, P., & Kalliath, T. (2013). Does job satisfaction mediate the relationship between work-family conflict and psychological strain? A study of Australian social workers. *Asia Pacific Journal of Social Work and Development, 23*, 91–105.

Karvelas, P. (2010). Australia gets first national paid parental leave scheme. *The Australian*, June 17. Retrieved May 3, 2015, from http://www.theaustralian.com.au/news/australia-gets-first-national-paid-parental-leave-scheme/story-e6frg6n6-1225881031472

Lingard, H., & Francis, V. (2004). The work-life experiences of office and site-based employees in the Australian construction industry. *Construction Management and Economics, 22*, 991–1002.

Lingard, H., & Francis, V. (2006). Does a supportive work environment moderate the relationship between work-family conflict and burnout among construction professionals? *Construction Management and Economics, 24*, 185–196.

Lingard, H., Francis, V., & Turner, M. (2012). Work time demands, work time control and supervisor support in the Australian construction industry. *Engineering Construction and Architectural Management, 19*, 647–665.

McDonald, P. (2000). Gender equity, social institutions and the future of fertility. *Journal of Population Research, 17*, 1–16.

OECD, Organisation for Economic Cooperation and Development. (2002). Women at work: Who are they and how are they faring? In *Employment outlook 2002—Surveying the jobs horizon* (pp. 70–84). Geneva, Switzerland: OECD Publishing.

Reynolds, J., & Aletraris, L. (2007). Work-family conflict, children, and hour mismatches in Australia. *Journal of Family Issues, 28*, 749–772.

Rose, J., Hewitt, B., & Baxter, J. (2013). Women and part-time employment: Easing or squeezing time pressure? *Journal of Sociology, 49*, 41–59.

Russo, J. A., & Waters, L. E. (2006). Workaholic work type differences in work-family conflict: The moderating role of supervisor support and flexible work scheduling. *Career Development International, 11*, 418–439.

Smyrnios, K. X., Romano, C. A., Tanewski, G. A., Karofsky, P. I., Millen, R., & Yilmaz, M. R. (2003). Work-family conflict: A study of American and Australian Family Businesses. *Family Business Review, 16*, 35–51.

Strazdins, L., O'Brien, L.V., Lucas, N., & Rodgers, B. (2013). Combining work and family: Rewards or risks for children's mental health. *Social Science & Medicine, 87*, 99–107.

Thanacoody, P. R., Bartram, T., & Casimir, G. (2009). The effects of burnout and supervisory social support on the relationship between work-family conflict and intention to leave: A study of Australian cancer workers. *Journal of Health Organization and Management, 23*, 53–69.

Thompson, B. M., Kirk, A., & Brown, D. E. (2005). Work based support, emotional exhaustion, and spillover of work stress to the family environment: A study of policewomen. *Stress and Health, 21*, 199–207.

Vandenbroek, P. (2014). *Labour stats 101 labour force: A quick guide*. Parliament of Australia: Canberra, ACT. Retrieved May 3, 2015, from http://www.aph.gov.au/About_Parliament/Parliamentary_Departments/Parliamentary_Library/pubs/rp/rp1314/QG/LabourForce

Winefield, H. R., Boyd, C., & Winefield, A. H. (2014). Work-family conflict and well-being in university employees. *The Journal of Psychology, 148*, 683–697.

Workplace Gender Equity Agency. (2015). *Gender pay gap statistics*. Canberra, ACT: Australian Government. Retrieved May 3, 2015, from https://www.wgea.gov.au/sites/default/files/Gender_Pay_Gap_Factsheet.pdf

World Audit Organisation. (2007). *Australia: World democracy profile*. Retrieved February 24, 2015, from http://www.worldaudit.org/countries/australia.htm

World Health Organization. (2013). *Global action plan for the prevention and control of noncommunicable diseases 2013–2020*. Geneva, Switzerland: WHO.

Young, N. (2013). Gender pay inequality is still holding Australia back. *ABC News*. Retrieved May 3, 2015, from http://www.abc.net.au/news/2013-10-16/young-gender-pay-gap/5026096

Yule, C., Chang, A., Gudmundsson, A., & Sawang, S. (2012). The role of life friendly policies on employees' work-life balance. *Journal of Management & Organization, 18*, 53–63.

7

THE WORK-FAMILY INTERFACE IN ISRAEL

Anat Drach-Zahavy and Anit Somech

The Israeli Context

Israel was founded in 1948 as a Jewish state, and is a parliamentary democracy. Elections are normally held every four years, whereby the Knesset—the Israeli parliament—is elected. Israel has undergone many elections (19 parliaments in 66 years), but has had only 13 prime ministers. Its population is 8.2 million people: 75.0% Jews, 20.7% Arabs (mostly Muslims), and the remaining 4.3% Druze, Circassians, and no religious affiliation (Israel Central Bureau of Statistics, 2014a).

From biblical times to the present days there has been uninterrupted settlement of Jews in Israel, although the country was ruled by various regimes: Persian, Roman, Arab, Ottoman, British, and more. The age-old Jewish settlement in Israel has created a strong connection of this nation to the land. The 20th-century wave of Jewish immigration established a new and unique way of settlement, called the kibbutz. This is a collective community traditionally based on agriculture and a cooperative way of living.

Some may say that the most significant event in Jewish history is the Holocaust. From the ascent to power of the Nazi regime in Germany in 1933 to the defeat of Germany in the Second World War in 1945, about six million Jews were murdered all over Europe. The collective memory of the Jewish genocide increased the significance of the family concept in Israel. In 66 years, since its establishment, Israel has been involved in seven wars and six military operations. This regularity of armed conflict has caused Israelis to strengthen the family unit and elevate its value.

Israel is a developed market economy with substantial, though diminishing, government participation. The main drivers of the economy are science and the high-technology sectors. Accordingly, manufacturing and agriculture, despite the country's limited natural resources, is highly developed and sophisticated. Israel's economy is growing rapidly, at an average of about 4.5% annually (IMF) and its per capita GDP continuously rose from 2003 (USD 23,100) to 2013 (USD 32,774) (OECD, 2014). However, the Gini ratio indicates that inequalities in Israel are among the highest in the OECD, standing at 37.6 in 2012 (Central Intelligence Agency, 2012).

Regarding the workforce, 55% of women are employed (64% of Jewish women, 23% of Arab women) (Israel Central Bureau of Statistics, 2014b). Half of the women are employed in traditional jobs such as teaching, secretarial, and care-giving. As for managerial positions, only 7.3% of CEOs are women, and 32% serve as senior managers. Women's average salary is approximately 40% less than men's (Israel Central Bureau of Statistics, 2014b), despite women having an average of 14.2 years of education, as against 13.8 years for men. Hence women account for 67.3% of the workers in the lower deciles, and only 23.3% in the upper deciles.

A 2007 survey showed that husbands in double-income households spend weekly 49 hours at work, 21 hours on child care, 8 hours on care for the elderly, and 7 hours on housekeeping. Wives spend 43 hours at work, 33 hours on child care, 7 hours on care for the elderly, and 16 hours on housekeeping. Moreover, due to today's demanding workplace, 20.4% of Israeli employees engage in work duties at home after work hours. Of these, 55% are women. Parents, mostly mothers, are those who take work home (63%). On average, women spend 10 hours a week working from home.

Despite the relatively high ratio of women in the workforce, most still seem to maintain their traditional roles as mothers, wives, and housekeepers, along with the additional demands of paid employment, and women still experience discrimination in various aspects of work. As a result, the Israeli government has invested resources to promote women's status in workforce-related matters.

For example, the Equal Employment Opportunities Commission, established in the Ministry of Industry, Trade, and Labor in 2006, filed its first complaint: government resolution no. 1134, "Steps to Reduce Social Gaps and Increase Participation in the Labor Force." The resolution directed resources to day care center services for children up to age three years and the provision of lunches for children younger than six. Additional funding is earmarked for three purposes: lowering the cost of child care through higher subsidy payments, subsidizing afternoon child care facilities (previously not eligible for funding by the Ministry of Industry, Trade, and Labor), and improving service by lengthening day care operating hours according to parental needs. In June 2014, the government (Strauber committee) introduced new objectives in reducing the gap between women and men in the labor force (Strauber, 2014). These objectives include (1) setting standards for appointing women to directorial positions in government corporations until equal representation of men and women is achieved, (2) setting goals in reducing wage gaps between men and women, (3) approval for overtime work from home, and (4) strengthening pregnancy and maternity protection for women in the workplace. The most noteworthy change is extending maternity leave from 12 to 14 weeks, and the option to extend the maternity leave by an extra unpaid 12 weeks. Fathers can also take paternity leave if their partner has declined this option.

On the face of it, the government's many new policies to foster a work-family balance seem adequate. However, in fact, many problems remain. There are serious discrepancies between government policies and what workers encounter in their workplaces. More effort should evidently be directed to the enforcement of government's policies and laws. However, for the development of a more equal society, passing and enforcing laws, though crucial, is not enough. Society needs to assimilate norms of equity, so intervention programs are vital for the education of individuals and organizations alike in an effort to alter informal norms of the traditional gender-role segregation.

Research on Work-Family Interface in Israel

The work-family interface in Israel has been of scholarly interest over the past two decades. Characteristics of Israeli culture, such as individualistic as well as collectivistic tendencies, population diversity, and particular values (emic) in Israeli culture make it possible for researchers to contribute to the vast literature on work-family conflict (WFC). We reviewed the literature through a search of the main sociology and psychology databases, focusing on main keywords such as WFC, work-family spillover, and work-family interface specifically in the Israeli context. The results are presented in Table 7.1. It is seen that most studies adopted the common Western models (e.g., the Frone, Yardley, & Markel, 1997 model) for better understanding the interface of work and family in Israel. As indicated by Frone et al.'s model, WFC was examined in Israel as bidirectional: work interferes with family (WIF) and family interferes with work (FIW) (e.g., Al-Yagon & Cinamon, 2008; Cinamon & Rich, 2002a, 2002b, 2010, 2014; Cohen & Liani, 2009; Heilbrunn & Davidovitch, 2011; Kulik & Liberman, 2013; Kulik & Rayyan, 2006).

Overall, similar to findings from other Western countries, men reported higher levels of WFC (WIF and FIW) than women, and men and women alike reported higher levels of WIF than FIW. Several studies also examined the interplay of the work and family domains as facilitating each other (e.g., Al-Yagon & Cinamon, 2008; Cinamon & Rich, 2014). Hence, domain-specific antecedents and consequences of WFC were tested. Among the antecedents, research has focused on social support—spouse support as a family antecedent, and to a lesser degree managers and colleagues' support as a work antecedent. Similarly, regarding the consequences, more research focused on family outcomes, such as attachment relationships, family cohesion, and family satisfaction, than on work consequences such as burnout and vigor. These findings might reflect the emphasis on family in Israeli culture. However, in general, findings support the "Western" model of

TABLE 7.1 Summary of the Israeli literature review.

Author(s)	*Aims*	*Participants (Sector, Gender, Family Status, Etc.)*	*Study Design (Qualitative/ Quantitative)*	*Main Findings*
Al-Yagon and Cinamon (2008)	To examine WIF, FIW, and WFF of mothers of children with learning disabilities.	48 mothers of children with learning disabilities and 48 mothers of typically developing children.	Quantitative	Mothers of children with learning disabilities reported higher levels of FIW and WFF than mothers of typically developing children.
Chen, Shaffer, Westman, Chen, Lazarova, and Reiche (2014, 190–218)	To develop a theoretically based and psychometrically sound measure of family role performance.	Study 1: 15 Israelis and 11 US respondents. Study 2: 211 US and 165 Israeli respondents. Study 3: 30 clients from a European relocation company. Study 4: 158 alumni of a European business school. Study 5: 200 US business travelers.	Qualitative/ Quantitative	Family role performance represents a multi-dimensional construct, consisting of family role task performance and family role relationships.
Cinamon (2006a)	To assess the effects of gender, gender role, and self-efficacy on levels of anticipated WFC.	358 unmarried students without children at two universities.	Quantitative	Students reported high levels of anticipated WIF and FIW and low-efficacy to manage that conflict. Women anticipated higher levels of WIF and FIW, and lower efficacy in managing these conflicts than men. Exposure to an egalitarian child care model correlated with lower anticipated levels of WIF; self-efficacy correlated negatively with WIF and FIW.

Cinamon (2006b)	To test the effectiveness of a culturally appropriate career intervention program for increasing Israel-Arab adolescents' self-efficacy to manage work and family roles.	15 Israeli-Arab adolescents (8 females and 7 males) from a mixed Arab and Jewish neighborhood of low socioeconomic status in the Tel Aviv area.	Post-intervention evaluation	93% reported the workshop contributed to their self-awareness of their work and family plans. 80% noted the contribution of the workshop to their career plans. 60% recommended that future programs also work with adolescents' parents.
Cinamon (2010)	To investigate the link of self-efficacy and role salience to anticipated WFC.	387 unmarried students without children at two universities in central Israel.	Quantitative	Four profiles relating to the centrality of the work of family domains emerged: work-oriented, family-oriented, dual-oriented, and no orientation. Work-oriented participants anticipated the highest levels of WFC and demonstrated the lowest efficacy to manage this conflict. In contrast, family-oriented participants anticipated the lowest levels of WFC and demonstrated the highest efficacy to manage it.
Cinamon and Hason (2009)	To examine the work-family plans of an at-risk youth population.	15 at-risk Israeli youth interviewees.	Qualitative	Work and family proved central in at-risk youths' future plans: They thought they could have a family only after earning enough money. Work was perceived as serving the family by providing money.
Cinamon, Most, and Michael (2008)	To assess the impact of disability (hearing status) on role salience and anticipated work-family relations.	101 unmarried young adults: 35 with hearing loss and 66 hearing.	Quantitative	The deaf participants (who used spoken language and sign language simultaneously) demonstrated a significantly higher level of commitment to work, but anticipated the significantly lowest level of conflict.

(Continued)

TABLE 7.1 (Continued)

Author(s)	*Aims*	*Participants (Sector, Gender, Family Status, Etc.)*	*Study Design (Qualitative/ Quantitative)*	*Main Findings*
Cinamon and Rich (2002a)	To explore between- and within-gender differences in the importance of life roles and their implications for WFC.	126 married men and 87 married women employed in computer or law firms.	Quantitative	More women than men fit the family-oriented profile, while more men than women fit the work-oriented profile. No gender differences were found for the dual profile.
Cinamon and Rich (2002b)	To examine the link between the relative importance ascribed to the family and work domains and WFC.	213 married computer workers and lawyers (126 men; 87 women) from Tel Aviv.	Quantitative	Participants with work-oriented and dual-oriented profiles demonstrated higher levels of WIF conflict than those with a family-oriented profile. No significant differences in FIW were found among the different groups. High spousal support correlated positively with WIF conflict in work-profile participants only.
Cinamon and Rich (2010)	To investigate the impact of different types of social support on WIF, FIW, WTFF, and FTWF and consequently on professional burnout and vigor.	322 married female teachers working in 40 Israeli-Jewish schools.	Quantitative	Family conflict and family facilitation had unique social support antecedents, but also shared some common variance. In contrast, conflict and facilitation in the work domain were unrelated. WIF and FIW predicted burnout.

Cinamon and Rich (2014)	To investigate the link between the centrality of work and family roles and anticipation of WFC and WFF among at-risk Israeli adolescents.	At-risk Israeli male and female adolescents.	Quantitative/ Qualitative	Both sexes anticipated greater facilitation than conflict and demonstrated little exploration and unsophisticated understanding of the work domain. Females' exploration of family roles was widespread. Both sexes understood work as a means to financially support the family.
Cinamon, Weisel, and Tzuk (2007)	To investigate couples' crossover effects of WIF and FIW, and their effect on parents' self-efficacy.	120 Israeli-Jewish working adults (60 couples), each couple having at least one child.	Quantitative	WIF and FIW crossed over from one spouse to the other. Mothers experienced more WFC and lower self-efficacy than fathers.
Cohen (2009)	To examine the relationship of the individual's values, using Schwartz's theory, and WIF and FIW to coping strategies.	122 employees at two Israeli high-tech companies.	Quantitative	Schwartz's 10 values (especially power) explained a relatively large percentage of the variation in WIF, FIW, and coping strategies.
Cohen and Liani (2009)	To examine the antecedents of WIF and FIW in Israeli health care administrators.	168 female employees in two public hospitals.	Quantitative	A strong relationship between work attitudes, particularly job satisfaction, and WIF and FIW; income was negatively related to WIF and FIW; surprisingly, stronger organizational support for nonwork activities were found to increase FIW.
Eran-Jona (2011)	To examine attitudes to family life and differences in work-family practices of male and female military personnel.	965 male and female spouses of IDF military personnel, as well as in-depth interviews with combat officers and their wives.	Quantitative/ Qualitative	Servicemen adopted a "traditional" role division model that placed the entire burden of family-work on their wives. Servicewomen adopted a more "egalitarian" role division model demonstrating a more equal relationship pattern between the spouses.

(*Continued*)

TABLE 7.1 (Continued)

Author(s)	*Aims*	*Participants (Sector, Gender, Family Status, Etc.)*	*Study Design (Qualitative/ Quantitative)*	*Main Findings*
Feldman, Masalha, and Nadam (2001)	To examine the work and family functioning of dual-earner Arab and Jewish couples.	100 Israeli-Jewish couples and 62 Israeli-Arab couples with their firstborn children.	Quantitative	Arab parents reported better adaptation to work following the first childbirth, while the triadic interactions (i.e., family processes involving father, mother, and a child) in Jewish families were more cohesive. Generally, child care arrangements, part-time employment, easier infant temperament, and lower separation anxiety predicted maternal re-adaptation to work. Traditional sex-role attitudes, career centrality, full-time employment, and marital satisfaction predicted fathers' work adaptation. Parents' family focus, marital satisfaction, and responsive parenting correlated with a cohesive triadic interaction process.
Frenkel (2008)	To explore gender differences in coping with work-family issues in the high-tech sector.	Ten focus groups (five composed only of women, two of men only, and three mixed) in the high-tech sector.	Qualitative	Israeli high-tech women enacted and constructed a "new femininity" that simultaneously challenged both the discourse of the "ideal high-tech worker" and that of traditional Israeli femininity. These women maintained their high-profile careers and functioned as mothers caring for their families by using work-family practices at the workplace (e.g., working from home).

Heilbrunn and Davidovitch (2011)	To explore factors influencing the intensity of WFC among Israeli Arabs, Israeli Jews, and Jewish immigrants.	111 women entrepreneurs in Israel (Israeli-born; Israeli-Arab; immigrants from FSU.	Quantitative	Having more children younger than 18 was positively associated with WFC for women entrepreneurs from FSU; family support was negatively associated with WFC for all groups; size of business and scope of investment were negatively associated with WFC, with Jewish women experiencing it more.
Kulik and Liberman (2013)	To understand the impact of WFC on mothers' experience of distress.	227 Israeli working mothers with children.	Quantitative	WIF and FIW mediated the relationship between social support and distress; demands of one domain spilled over to the other; contrary to what was hypothesized, the more roles the women performed the less distress they experienced at work.
Kulik and Rayyan (2006)	To examine whether educated Jewish and Arab-Muslim women differed in their attitudes to gender role, division of domestic labor, and perceived spousal support, and how these attitudes affected their emotional well-being.	Jewish and Arab-Muslim women from dual-earner families, employed in the education system and in municipalities.	Quantitative	Jewish women had more liberal attitudes to gender roles and division of labor than Arab women. With respect to coping strategies, though both groups invested considerable efforts to meet conflicting demands, Jewish women were more likely to seek help from family members or colleagues than their Arab-Muslim counterparts. Yet both groups reported receiving support from their husbands and this had a similar positive effect on women's emotional well-being.

(Continued)

TABLE 7.1 (Continued)

Author(s)	*Aims*	*Participants (Sector, Gender, Family Status, Etc.)*	*Study Design (Qualitative/ Quantitative)*	*Main Findings*
Lavee and Ben-Ari (2007)	To examine the relation of work-related stress of both spouses and daily fluctuations in their affective states to their dyadic closeness.	169 Israeli dual-earner couples.	Quantitative	Work stress had no direct effect on dyadic closeness but was mediated by the spouses' negative mood. Evidence was found for spillover of stress from work to home, as well as negative crossover in couples with higher marital quality, resulting in greater distance on stressful days.
Malach-Pines, Hammer, and Neal (2009)	To compare how Israeli and American "sandwich generation" couples address work and family issues.	40 Israeli "sandwich generation" couples living on a kibbutz, 80 Israeli couples living in small towns, and 75 American couples.	Quantitative	Americans reported more WIF than Israelis, while Israelis reported more FIW than Americans; Israelis reported greater satisfaction with work and family than Americans and men reported greater satisfaction with work than women. With respect to social support, Israelis received more help from their spouse than Americans, and kibbutz members reported receiving more help than Israeli city dwellers. Burnout correlated negatively with spouse's support.

Malach-Pines, Neal, Hammer, and Icekson (2011).	To explore the levels of and relationship between job and couple burnout reported by dual-earner couples in the "sandwich generation."	100 "sandwich generation" couples from Israel and 64 "sandwich generation" couples from the US.	Quantitative/ Qualitative	"Sandwich couples" experienced lower levels of job and couple burnout. Focus group supported the finding that those with spousal support in caring for aging parents reduced their couple burnout. Israelis reported lower levels of job and couple burnout than Americans, though they experience higher levels of stress in both their work and their family. Women had higher levels of job and couple burnout than men. Crossover effects of work stressors also indicated that the higher one's job stressors, the higher one's couple burnout.
O'Brien, Yoo, Del Pino, Cinamon, and Han (2014)	To test the link between work-family management and psychological distress among employed mothers in three different cultures.	Employed mothers in three countries: Israel, Korea, and the US.	Quantitative	No differences in the levels of WFC across countries were found. Korean mothers had the lowest levels of W-F enrichment and of spousal and employer support, and highest level of depression, as against Israeli and American mothers; spousal support mediated the relationship between WFC and depression in all three countries.
Snir, Harpaz, and Ben-Baruch (2009)	To examine the effect of men's and women's parenthood on the centrality of and investment in work and family issues in the high tech industry.	319 Israeli high tech workers.	Quantitative	Fathers showed higher work centrality than childless men, whereas mothers showed lower relative work centrality than childless women. Mothers evinced higher relative family centrality, and invested more weekly hours in child care and core housework tasks, than did fathers.

(Continued)

TABLE 7.1 (Continued)

Author(s)	*Aims*	*Participants (Sector, Gender, Family Status, Etc.)*	*Study Design (Qualitative/ Quantitative)*	*Main Findings*
Somech and Drach-Zahavy (2007)	To develop a typology of strategies coping with work and family issues, and to test their effectiveness in reducing WIF and FIW, with respect to sex and gender role ideology.	Employed professional parents from various organizational sectors.	Quantitative/ Qualitative	Eight coping strategies were identified for interviews: four for coping at home and four for coping at work. The effectiveness of these strategies in decreasing WIF and FIW was moderated by sex and gender-role ideology; both men and women experience higher levels of WFC than FWC.
Somech and Drach-Zahavy (2012)	To test the role of personal coping strategies and organizational family-friendly supports in reducing WIF and FIW.	474 employees in Israel having a partner and children and representing diverse professions and organizations.	Quantitative	Personal coping was significantly associated with decreasing WIF and FIW. However, the findings also suggested that the role of organizational support is important in decreasing WFC when employees lack the personal coping strategies required or when they perceive the organization's efforts to be unfair in relation to their own coping efforts.
Westman (2002)	To identify crossover mechanisms.	–	Literature review	Three main crossover mechanisms were identified: common stressors, empathic reactions, and an indirect mediating process.

WFC. That is, the higher the support and/or the lower the demands, the lower WFC. In addition, the higher the WFC, the higher the negative work, family, and life outcomes.

Another stream of research focused on parents' strategies to handle WFC (e.g., Cinamon, 2010; Cohen, 2009; Eran-Jona, 2011; Kulik & Rayyan, 2006; Somech & Drach-Zahavy, 2007, 2012). Most of these studies relied on Lazarus and Folkman's (1984) typology of coping strategies, developed for coping with stress in general. These studies generally found problem-focused coping and social support the most effective ways for decreasing WFC, largely owing to the importance of psychological control and self-efficacy for effective stress management. A novel approach was introduced by Somech and Drach-Zahavy (2007), who developed a typology specific to the context of coping with WFC. The typology has eight coping strategies: super at home, good enough at home, delegation at home, priorities at home, super at work, good enough at work, delegation at work, priorities at work. The researchers found that no coping style was universally appropriate; rather, the effectiveness of the coping strategy in lessening WFC largely depended on gender and gender role ideology.

It is notable that most previous coping research in the work-family domain in Israel has focused on personal coping, with only scant research on the role of the organization as a source of support to manage WFC. One example of the latter is Somech and Drach-Zahavy's (2012) study. These researchers found the role of organizational support important in decreasing WFC when employees lack the necessary personal coping strategies or when they perceive the organization's efforts as unfair in relation to their own coping efforts.

Several studies examined WFC from a cross-cultural perspective, reflecting Israel's multicultural nature (e.g., Heilbrunn & Davidovitch, 2011; Kulik & Rayyan, 2006). For example, Kulik and Rayyan (2006) compared Muslim-Arab and Jewish women in dual-earner families. Several cultural differences emerged: Jewish women expressed more liberal gender-role attitudes and reported a more egalitarian division of domestic labor. Yet both groups of women tended to use the behavioral coping strategy of concerted efforts to reduce role conflict. And while cultural differences were found regarding the relation of the division of domestic labor to emotional well-being, no differences were found regarding spousal support. Heilbrunn and Davidovitch (2011) examined WFC of women entrepreneurs and compared Arab, Israeli-born, and immigrant Jewish women. They found that the degree of family support influenced intensity of the WFC for all three groups of women entrepreneurs, but those from the former Soviet Union experienced the lowest intensity of the conflict, which can be explained in terms of particularities of gender status in their country of origin.

Finally, other studies (e.g., Malach-Pines, Hammer, & Neal, 2009; Malach-Pines, Neal, Hammer, & Icekson, 2011;) investigated cross-cultural differences across nations. Malach-Pines and colleagues (2009) compared US couples, Israeli couples living in a kibbutz, and Israeli couples living in small towns and found cross-cultural differences: Americans reported higher WIF than Israelis, whereas Israelis reported higher FIW than Americans. Israeli kibbutz members received the highest level of help from their spouse with both home and work problems, followed by the Israelis living in small towns; the Americans received the least help. O'Brien and colleagues (2014), comparing Korean, Israeli, and American mothers, found that WFC levels were similar. In all three countries spousal support mediated the relation of WFC to depression. However, Korean women had the lowest levels of work-family enrichment and the highest level of depression as against Israeli and American mothers.

This research concentrated on work-family conflict/facilitation as a *within-person* across-domain transmission of demands. By contrast, some research in Israel drew attention to dyadic, *inter-individual* transmission of stress or strain, which they labeled crossover. Specifically, Westman's (2002) pioneering work suggests that crossover involves transmission across individuals, whereby demands and their consequent strain cross over between closely related persons. So crossover stress experienced in the workplace by an individual may lead to stress being experienced by the individual's partner at home. For example, Cinamon, Weisel, and Tzuk (2007) investigated 60 married couples and found that family conflict of one spouse correlated positively with family-work conflict of the other.

A somewhat different viewpoint, presented by Cinamon (2010) and Cinamon and Hason (2009), concentrated on anticipated WFC compared with experienced WFC, which was the focus of most studies reviewed. Cinamon and Hason (2009) examined adolescents' work and family plans and the perceived barriers and resources affecting their realization. For example, Cinamon (2010) found that the work-oriented participants anticipated the highest levels of WFC and demonstrated the lowest efficacy in managing this conflict. The family-oriented participants anticipated the lowest levels of WFC and demonstrated the highest efficacy in managing it.

Finally, from a methodological perspective, the literature review reveals that most studies conducted in Israel are akin to the major Western literature. First, the samples consist mainly of white-collar professionals from sectors such as high tech (Cohen, 2009; Snir, Harpaz, & Ben-Baruch, 2009), law firms (Cinamon & Rich, 2002a), entrepreneurs (Heilbrunn & Davidovitch, 2011), teachers (Cinamon & Rich, 2010), and health care employees (Cohen & Liani, 2009). Secondly, the research applied quantitative and qualitative methods, while the quantitative studies had mainly cross-sectional, one-source self-report designs, although there are some exceptions. Thirdly, the most measures in these studies were adopted from Western studies, and hence, do not necessarily capture the emic nature of Israeli context. Fourthly, most of this research typically focused on the employee level, overlooking the more multilevel perspectives for understanding the WFC phenomenon. Obviously, employees are nested within teams, organizations, and sectors, which might influence the way they experience the interface of work and family.

Focus Group Results

Thirty-two employed mothers (21 Jewish, 11 Arab) participated in our focus groups. All selected individuals were mothers who lived with a spouse and worked full-time. Participants were randomly selected from four types of organization in Israel: industrial, health care, educational, and financial. Participants were randomly divided into three groups of Jewish women and two groups of Arab women. Each group was heterogeneous in age, marital status, number of children, and occupation. Average age was 33.6 years ($SD = 7.2$); 83% were married. Seven participants were managers. Of the sample, 25% were in care professions (e.g., nurses, psychologists), seven were secretaries, four were physicians, seven were teachers, two were accountants, two were lawyers, and two were engineers. Each focus group semi-structured interview lasted approximately 110 minutes. Discussions addressed the research questions of work-family interface, its antecedents, and consequences. The main themes along with representative quotes are presented in Table 7.2, which reveals several important insights.

TABLE 7.2 Results of the Israeli focus groups: Jewish vs. Arab women.

Theme	*Jewish Sample*	*Arab Sample*
WIF vs. FIW	WIF (21/21) "I was reading my daughter a bedtime story, and the phone rang. When I came back she was asleep. I felt awful . . ." FIW (9/21), spontaneously "I can't leave home for a two-day psychology conference . . ." "The home blocks me . . ."	WIF (3/11) "It is stressful when my routine is interfered with, for example, when one of the children is sick." FIW (3/11) only when asked "Can't stay after 5 p.m. even though the training is very interesting."
Conflict vs. Positive Spillover	Positive spillover (21/21) "Every facet of life complements the others."	Positive spillover (11/11) "I can't view myself only as a mother; nor can I see myself as a working woman solely."
Conflicting Social Roles	Parent-job (21/21)	Parent-job (11/11) Housekeeper-job (11/11) Social woman-job (11/11)
Types of Conflict	Time-based conflict (21/21) "The conflict is mainly technical, to arrange transportation for after school activities . . ." Strain-based conflict. (6/21)	Time-based conflict (4/11) Strain-based conflict (0/11) Behavior-based conflict (11/11) "I have an aunt who cooks for me, and it makes me feel bad as a woman."

(Continued)

TABLE 7.2 (Continued)

Theme	*Jewish Sample*	*Arab Sample*
	"When I come home I feel emotionally exhausted, and I can't deal with my children's problems." Behavior-based conflict (0/21)	
Coping Strategy	Good enough (18/21) "My perception has changed. If in the past I believed that I had to do everything perfectly, today I do mainly what I like, and to a minor degree what I ought . . ." Delegation (21/21) "In the morning, I ask my husband to take the children to after-school activities." Priorities (15/21) "It's really my decision whether I'm here to serve my husband, my children, my parents."	Superwoman at home (11/11) "I have to be perfect in all facets of life. So I get up at 4 a.m. to bake bread. . ." Family and community support (11/11) "On my way back home I take dishes that my mother-in-law cooked for me . . ."
Spouse's Support	Instrumental (12/21) helping with parental responsibilities Emotional support as sharing (20/21) "My husband is my best friend. I share the dilemmas that arise at work with him."	Instrumental (4/11) helping with parental responsibilities Emotional support as backing (11/11) "My husband always tells his friends: What do you want? That's her work."
Extended Family's Support	Instrumental (3/21) "My mother looks after my children when I am at work . . ."	Instrumental (11/11) Viewed as a source of instrumental support, but also causes emotional stress "I come back from work tired, and my neighbors come in to drink coffee and to check how I manage my home duties . . ." Emotional backing from fathers (11/11) "I studied abroad, and he stood up for me against the whole community."
Motives for Engagement With Paid Work	Self-actualization (21/21) Economic gain (15/21)	Self-actualization (11/11) Economic gain (11/11)

Theme	Jewish Sample	Arab Sample
	Message from parents (3/21) "My mother always said: a woman needs a profession, so that she can be independent." Dominant figure: mother (9/21)	Message from parents (9/11) "My parents lack any formal education, so they always encouraged me to learn. . ." Dominant figure: father (11/11)

Note: Numbers in parentheses indicate the number of respondents indicating the idea proportionate to the number of total respondents in each subsample.

Experience of the Interplay of Work and Family

All 21 Jewish women experienced the interplay between work and family simultaneously as a conflict and as a positive spillover experience. The Arab women tended to experience it more as a positive spillover than as a conflict; all the Jewish women defined the conflict in terms of work interferes with family, but only nine of the 21 defined it in terms of family interferes with work. All the Jewish women perceived the conflict as time-based, one third of them as strain-based, and none as behavior-based. The Arab women evinced a mirror image: All of them perceived the conflict as behavior-based, some as time-based, and none as strain-based.

As for the type of the role conflict, all Jewish women noted only the parent-job conflict. The Arab women also referred to the housekeeper-job conflict and to the social woman-job conflict (namely her responsibility to be involved in the social life of the extended family and the community).

Coping With Work and Family Conflict

The focus group results identified several coping strategies for managing the conflict. The Jewish women referred to three strategies: *good enough*, namely lowering the performance of family/work responsibilities to a less-than-perfect level; *balancing by delegation*, namely managing one's own family/work duties by delegating some to others; *priorities*, namely arranging family/work duties in order of priority and undertaking only those with high priority. In comparison, the Arab women identified two other strategies: *superwomen*, namely insisting on doing all family/ work duties single handedly and perfectly; *relying on family and community support*. Finally, women from both sectors mentioned spouse's instrumental and emotional support as important resources for coping with the conflict.

Motives for Engagement in Paid Work

As for their motives to engage with paid work, women from both sectors noted self-actualization as a major driving force. However, all the Arab women also mentioned economic gain as an important motive while only 70% of the Jewish women did so. The Arab women also referred to their parents' messages, especially their fathers', as a crucial factor in shaping their careers; among the Jewish women, the mother was found to be the dominant figure.

Conclusions

The last two decades have galvanized intensive research, greater regulatory efforts, as well as public interest in issues of work and family in Israel. Israel is a multicultural nation but most studies conducted in this country yielded results supporting the usual Western work and family models. This approach ignores the potential differences among subcultures. A closer inspection of the scant research that did study work-family issues as a context-related phenomenon, as well as the focus group findings presented here, emphasized the need to refine our models to better capture how the specific context impacts employees' experience of the interplay between work and family. A further trend in the Israeli research concerns the dominance of individual-level models by focusing on personal antecedents and consequences of the WFC. Specifically, most research focused on the individual's responsibility to cope with the conflict, thereby disregarding the role of organizations, communities, and the society as a whole in equipping the individual with family-friendly resources for coping. These gaps in the Israeli research opens new research agendas for scholars.

References

Al-Yagon, M., & Cinamon, R. G. (2008). Work-family relations among mothers of children with learning disorders. *European Journal of Special Needs Education, 23*, 91–107. doi:10.1080/08856250801946202

Central Intelligence Agency. (2012). *The world factbook*. Retrieved October 19, 2014, from https://www.cia.gov/library/publications/the-world-factbook/fields/2172.html

Chen, Y., Shaffer, M., Westman, M., Chen, S., Lazarova, M., & Reiche, S. (2014). Family role performance: Scale development and validation. *Applied Psychology: An International Review, 63*(1), 190–218. doi:10.1111/apps.12005

Cinamon, R. G. (2006a). Anticipated work-family conflict: Effects of gender, self-efficacy, and family background. *The Career Development Quarterly, 54*, 202–215.

Cinamon, R. G. (2006b). Preparing minority adolescents to blend work and family roles: Increasing work-family conflict management self-efficacy. *International Journal of Advancement of Counselling, 28*(1), 79–94. doi:10.1007/s10447-005-9006-x

Cinamon, R. G. (2010). Anticipated work-family conflict: Effects of role salience and self-efficacy. *British Journal of Guidance & Counselling, 38*(1), 83–99. doi:10.1080/03069880903408620

Cinamon, R. G., & Hason, I. (2009). Facing the future: Barriers and resources in work and family plans of at-risk Israeli youth. *Youth & Society, 40*, 502–525. doi:10.1177/0044118X08328008

Cinamon, R. G., Most, T., & Michael, R. (2008). Role salience and anticipated work-family relations among young adults with and without hearing loss. *Journal of Deaf Studies and Deaf Education, 13*, 351–361. doi:10.1093/deafed/enm065

Cinamon, R. G., & Rich, Y. (2002a). Gender differences in the importance of work-family roles: Implications for work-family conflict. *Sex Roles*, *47*, 531–541. doi:0360-0025/02/1200-0531/0

Cinamon, R. G., & Rich, Y. (2002b). Profiles of attribution of importance to life roles and their implications for the work-family conflict. *Journal of Counselling Psychology*, *49*, 212–220. doi:10.1037//0022-0167.49.2.212

Cinamon, R. G., & Rich, Y. (2010). Work family relations: Antecedents and outcomes. *Journal of Career Assessment*, *18*(1), 59–70. doi:10.1177/1069072709340661

Cinamon, R. G., & Rich, Y. (2014). Work and family plans among at-risk Israeli adolescents: A mixed-method study. *Journal of Career Development*, *41*, 163–184. doi:10.1177/0894845313507748

Cinamon, R. G., Weisel, A., & Tzuk, K. (2007). Work-family conflict within the family: Crossover effects, perceived parent-child interaction quality, parental self-efficacy, and life role attributions. *Journal of Career Development*, *34*(1), 79–100. doi:10.1177/0894845307304066

Cohen, A. (2009). Individual values and the work/family interface. *Journal of Managerial Psychology*, *24*, 814–832. doi:10.1108/02683940910996815

Cohen, A., & Liani, E. (2009). Work-family conflict among female employees in Israeli hospitals. *Personnel Review*, *38*, 124–141. doi:10.1108/00483480910931307

Eran-Jona, M. (2011). Married to the military: Military-family relations in the Israel defense forces. *Armed Forces & Society*, *37*(1), 19–41. doi:10.1177/0095327X10379729

Feldman, R., Masalha, S., & Nadam, R. (2001). Cultural perspective on work and family: Dual-earner Israeli-Jewish and Arab families at the transition to parenthood. *Journal of Family Psychology*, *15*, 492–509. doi:10.1037/0893-3200.15.3.492

Frenkel, M. (2008). Reprogramming femininity? The construction of gender identities in the Israeli high tech industry between global and local gender orders. *Gender, Work and Organization*, *15*, 352–374. doi:10.1111/j.1468-0432.2008.00398.x

Frone, M. R., Yardley, J. K., & Markel, K. S. (1997). Developing and testing an integrative model of the work-family interface. *Journal of Vocational Behavior*, *50*, 145–167. doi:10.1006/jvbe.1996.1577

Heilbrunn, S., & Davidovitch, L. (2011). Juggling family and business: Work-family conflict of women entrepreneurs in Israel. *The Journal of Entrepreneurship*, *20*(1), 127–141. doi:10.1177/097135571002000106

Israel Central Bureau of Statistics. (2014a). *Population & demography*. Retrieved October 19, 2014, from http://www.cbs.gov.il/reader/?MIval=cw_usr_view_SHTML&ID=705

Israel Central Bureau of Statistics. (2014b). *Labor force survey*. Retrieved October 19, 2014, from http://www.cbs.gov.il/reader/?MIval=cw_usr_view_SHTML&ID=417

Kulik, L., & Liberman, G. (2013). Work-family conflict, resources, and role set density: Assessing their effects on distress among working mothers. *Journal of Career Development*, *40*, 445–465. doi:10.1177/0894845312467500

Kulik, L., & Rayyan, F. (2006). Relationships between dual-earner spouses, strategies for coping with home-work demands and emotional well-being. *Community, Work and Family*, *9*, 457–477. doi:10.1080/13668800600925100

Lavee, Y., & Ben-Ari, A. (2007). Relationship of dyadic closeness with work-related stress: A daily diary study. *Journal of Marriage and Family*, *69*, 1021–1035. doi:10.1111/j.1741-3737.2007.00428.x

Lazarus, R. S., & Folkman, S. (1984). *Stress, appraisal, and coping*. New York, NY: Springer.

Malach-Pines, A., Hammer, L., & Neal, M. (2009). "Sandwiched generation" couples: A cross-cultural, cross-gender comparison. *Pratiques psychologique*, *15*, 225–237. doi:10.1016/j.prps.2008.09.010

Malach-Pines, A., Neal, M. A., Hammer, L., & Icekson, T. (2011). Job burnout and couple burnout in dual-earner couples in the sandwiched generation. *Social Psychology Quarterly, 74*, 361–386. doi:10.1177/0190272511422452

O'Brien, K. M., Yoo, A., Del Pino, H.V. G., Cinamon, R. G., & Han, Y. (2014). Work, family, support, and depression: Employed mothers in Israel, Korea, and the United States. *Journal of Counseling Psychology, 61*, 461–472. doi:10.1037/a0036339

OECD. (2014). *Selected indicators for Israel.* Retrieved October 19, 2014, from http://data.oecd.org/israel.htm

Snir, R., Harpaz, I., & Ben-Baruch, D. (2009). Centrality of and investment in work and family among Israeli high-tech workers. *Cross-Cultural Research, 43*, 366–385. doi:10.1177/1069397109336991

Somech, A., & Drach-Zahavy, A. (2007). Strategies for coping with work-family conflict: The distinctive relationships of gender role ideology. *Journal of Occupational Health Psychology, 12*(1), 1–19. doi:10.1037/1076-8998.12.1.1

Somech, A., & Drach-Zahavy, A. (2012). Coping with work-family conflict: The reciprocal and additive contributions of personal coping and organizational family-friendly support. *Work & Stress, 26*(1), 68–90. doi:10.1080/02678373.2012.660361

Strauber, D. (2014). Committee report on women in the civil service. *Hebrew.* Retrieved November 18, 2014, from http://www.csc.gov.il/databases/reports/documents/reportwomencommittee2014.pdf.

Westman, M. (2002). Crossover of stress and strain in the family and in the workplace. In P. L. Perrewé & D. C. Ganster (Eds.), *Research in occupational stress and well-being* (Vol. 2, pp. 143–181). Greenwich, CT: JAI Press.

8

THE WORK-FAMILY INTERFACE IN TURKEY

Ayse Burçin Erarslan-Baskurt and Zeynep Aycan

Introduction

Turkey is renowned for its cultural richness and diversity, given that it influenced and has been influenced by many civilizations for over millennia. Being the cradle of many civilizations, such as the Byzantine, Roman, and Ottoman Empires, Turkey embraces diverse influences. According to Hofstede's (1980) framework, Turkish culture is characterized as a collectivistic, high power distance, feminine, and high uncertainty avoidance culture. The location of the country, as a bridge between the East and the West, adds to its cultural richness. This diversity in its culture and values is also reflected in the practices and experiences of work-family relationships in daily life.

In this chapter, there are four parts. In the first part, the geographic, demographic, socioeconomic, and cultural contexts of Turkey are described. Then, a summary of the main findings from research with Turkish samples on the work-family interface is presented. In the third part, the results of focus group discussions with 12 Turkish women are outlined, and finally a conclusion on general work-family research is reached in light of this literature review and focus group discussion.

The Turkish Context

Geographic and Demographic Features

Turkey is located between Europe and the Middle East. The border countries on the European side are Greece and Bulgaria, which are Christian countries. In the eastern side both Christian and Muslim countries such as Georgia, Azerbaijan,

Armenia, Iran, Iraq, and Syria have borders with Turkey. Turkey has been a bridge between East and West throughout history. The analysis of work-family interface conveys the simultaneous influence of Eastern and Western cultures in the Turkish context.

According to the recent statistics, Turkey's population is 78.7 million (Turkish Statistical Institute, 2015). According to the Central Intelligence Agency (CIA) *World Factbook*, 70–75% of the population is Turkish. Kurds make up 19% of the population, and other ethnic minorities such as Caucasians, Armenians, and Jews make up the rest of the country (CIA, 2016). With recent crises in neighboring countries, the number of refugees and asylum-seekers in Turkey in 2015 is expected to rise to nearly 1.9 million, including 1.7 million Syrian refugees (The UN Refugee Agency, 2015). Besides Turkish, Kurdish and several other minority languages are spoken in Turkey. The Turkish population is spread across seven regions, each of which has unique social and economic characteristics, the eastern parts being relatively less developed in terms of economy, education, and social facilities.

The Turks won the independence war under the leadership of Mustafa Kemal Ataturk, and the Republic of Turkey was established in 1923 upon the demise of the Ottoman Empire. A series of reforms in social, political, linguistic, and economic areas were carried out, and the values of secularism, nationalism, and modernism were promoted, which encouraged rapid westernization of the society. During the early years of the Republic in the 1930s a whole new society with a new mindset, new Latin alphabet, new laws, new dress codes, and new codes of conduct was created. Women had a special meaning in the nation-building process and they were assigned an important role in this modernization project. Their progress was interpreted as a measure of success in reaching modernity, westernization, and development of the nation (Arat, 1994, 1999). In the post-1980 period, the symbolic meaning of Turkish women as mothers of the nation emphasized a more individualistic motivation to be present in the labor force instead of a collectivist sense of fulfilling a national duty. Later on, as a result of economic and social developments, as well as changing values and cultural influences, some conflicting and traditional roles continued to be simultaneously present in the Turkish society.

Since its establishment, the Republic of Turkey has had a secular government that differentiates religious and governmental activities. Located in a critical borderland between Europe and Asia, Turkey is positioned to play an influential role in areas with which it shares ethnic and religious affinities (Mastny & Nation, 1996). Because of its location, Turkey combines diverse elements from European, Middle Eastern, and Central Asian traditions, and hence combines East and West in its overall culture. These influences are apparent in work-family practices, as will be seen both in the literature review and focus group discussions.

Socioeconomic and Cultural Context

Turkey is a developing country. It is ranked eighth highest on the United Nations' Human Development Index. Turkey is a member of the Organization for Economic Cooperation and Development (OECD), North Atlantic Treaty Organization (NATO), and the G20 major economies. The GDP of the country was estimated to be around $800 billion in 2014, which made Turkey the 18th largest economy globally (IMF, 2015).

The growth model of Turkey mostly depends on demographic growth and consumption. According to the Turkish Statistical Institute (TUIK), in 2014, 66% of GDP came from private spending. This consumption-driven economy runs a structural current account deficit and has an extremely low savings ratio. In the past, Turkey experienced a number of recessions and most of them can be associated with current account deficits accompanied with high budget deficits. The most important recessions in the near past occurred during 1980, 1994, 1999, 2001, and 2008–2009. Economic development gained pace after the liberalization efforts in the 1980s and during the single party era of 2001. Most recently, political uncertainty in the country combined with the global economic slowdown has had an impact on the stability of the Turkish economy. However, the country still manages to grow with growth rates close to 3%.

One of the most structural changes that the country is having is related to labor force participation. Especially, the participation for women has been increasing drastically in the last five years, from 26% to 32%. TUIK's 2015 statistics demonstrate that the male employment rate is 66.2% and the female employment rate is 28.6%. Among the young population, the employment rate is 17.7% and the unemployment rate reached 9.6% in 2015. Entrepreneurship has also been on the rise in Turkey. According to the Small and Medium Enterprises Development Organization in Turkey (KOSGEB) the entrepreneur rate is approximately 32% (KOSGEB, 2013). However, only a small percent of it consists of women. As of 2012, small- and medium-sized enterprises in Turkey represented 99.8% of all enterprises, 75.8% of total employment, 54.5% of salary and wages, and 63.3% of gross revenues (Turkish Statistical Institute, 2014). According to the report of Global Entrepreneurship Monitor (2013), the average level of early-stage entrepreneurial activity in Turkey rose from 5.9% for the period of 2006–2008 to 10.9% for the period of 2010–2012.

With major social and economic processes, such as urbanization, rapid growth of industrial and service sectors after the 1960s, and migration from rural to urban areas, the Turkish labor force has gone through major changes (Ozar, 1994). A drop especially in the agricultural employment rate led to a steady decline in women's percentage in the total labor force afterwards. While women constituted 43.1% of the total labor force in 1955, this ratio had decreased to 30.3 in 2014 (Turkish Statistical Institute, 2007, 2014), which is far below the OECD and European Union-28 rates of 51.5% and 51.8% in 2014, respectively (OECD, 2014).

Gender statistics are recently alluding to low representation, although some groups continue to do well in terms of educational and work careers leading to within-gender variation of Turkish women. In the World Economic Forum's Global Gender Gap Index (2014) Turkey ranked 125 out of 142 countries and even lower, 127th, on the economic participation of women index. Turkey is the lowest performing country from the region on the economic participation and opportunity subindex, ranking 132nd. The country ranks 128th overall on the labor force participation indicator and is part of the 20 lowest-ranked countries on the legislators, senior officials, and managers' indicator.

Although for Western countries economic development coincides with increasing numbers of women entering the labor force, the associations between development variables, such as socioeconomic development, urbanization, and women's status with respect to education, and workforce participation shows great variation across cultures. An example of this diverging pattern of relationship between economic development and women's labor force development was found in an earlier comparative analysis of 49 countries, in which less-developed countries, including Turkey, had higher proportions of women in the professions (Blitz, 1975). In the case of Turkey, deliberate policies to increase the number of women in professions in the early years of the Republic as part of an equality ideology and national plan for westernization and modernization led to greater numbers of women even in "masculine" jobs. In the index for doctors, lawyers, architects, and engineers, women's percentage in Turkey was 25%, whereas the United States had 2.3%, Canada had 2.6%, the United Kingdom had 4.3%, Germany had 8.5%, and Sweden had 13.3% (Blitz, 1975). However, it is important to note that only a particular group of women, who were relatively elite and privileged, benefited from these policies (Bolak-Boratav, 2011; Ozbilgin & Healy, 2004).

This interaction between state policies and women's entrance into professions led Turkish women, especially those who had higher social class backgrounds, not to experience as much sexism as their counterparts in the United States (Bolak-Boratav, 2011). However, Turkish women were increasingly socialized into gender roles and clustered in more female jobs later on. In other words, employment opportunities for women have recently been generally concentrated in certain sectors paying low-wage rates.

The gender discrepancy in labor force participation has many things to do with the socioeconomic and cultural context of Turkey. Socially assigned gender roles of women, such as responsibility for doing the housework and child care/elder care and the norms of patriarchal society, play an influential role in shaping women's decisions to enter the labor market (Dayioğlu, 2000; Dayioğlu & Kirder, 2009). Recent findings of the Household Labor Force Survey (Turkish Statistical Institute, 2013) showed that the labor force participation rates of women (age 29–45) with children (29.9%) are significantly lower than for those without children (45.5%).

All these matters related to women's status and employment statistics in the Turkish context have an impact on the work-family experiences of men and women in Turkey. Most women still seem to maintain their traditional roles as mothers, wives, and housekeepers, along with the additional demands of paid employment. In addition to traditional values prevailing, for professional women, too, there are barriers for their career advancement, such as negative attitudes toward women managers in organizations and difficulties in achieving work-family balance (Aycan, 2009). Urban women who are relatively more well off try to buffer these high demands of roles from the family with the aid of extended family members or paid caregivers at their homes. This shows unequal conditions for different groups of women in Turkey. The current Turkish government invests resources not to promote women's status in workforce-related matters, but to encourage them to stay at home and care for their children through initiatives for marriage and childbirth. Day care center services for working mothers are lacking, and paternal leave is very short. A recent initiative to provide families with additional funding for each newborn child and ongoing popular debates about banning abortion are some of the issues that frame current policy discussions about women. The right-wing ruling party, Justice and Development Party, that has been in power since the early 2000s, promotes segregation of gender roles, and the role of women as mothers and wives has replaced the state feminism of the early Republican era. Some people are cynical in their approach to these policy debates and practices, suggesting that all these debates and policies are in favor of keeping women at home. But some people think of these initiatives as enabling women to give a break to their work lives and experience their early motherhood period smoothly, which would ultimately help population growth, thus benefiting the whole society.

Research on the Work-Family Interface in Turkey

As in many countries, in Turkey structural changes such as a shift toward nuclear families, the entrance of increasing numbers of women into the labor force, hard living conditions in cities, higher expectations from work and family, lack of support for child care, and household activities seem to pose some problems in the work-family relationship that matter both to individuals and organizations. Scholars have been investigating antecedents, correlates, and consequences of this relationship and providing policy implications. In order to grasp the main issues in work-family interface in Turkey, main psychology databases have been searched with the main keywords including WFC, work-family spillover, work-family interface, and work-family enrichment.

The work-family interface has received considerable research attention in Turkey over the past two decades. However, use of different work-family measures and diverse samples from different parts of Turkey and different occupational groups partly account for the inconsistent findings. Although this inconsistency makes generalizable results less likely, some major areas of study in this topic reveal antecedents, correlates, and consequences of work-family interface in the Turkish context.

The major areas of study represented in this research topic include *gender differences in WFC* (e.g., Adak, 2007; Bolak, 1997), coping strategies including *social support in reducing WFC* (e.g., Aycan & Eskin, 2005; Karatepe & Kilic, 2005; Karatepe & Uludag, 2008a; Yildirim & Aycan, 2008), and *psychological and work-related outcomes* of this interface (e.g., Burke, Koyuncu, & Fiksenbaum, 2013; Karatepe & Uludag, 2008b).

Major samples used in the Turkish studies include hotel employees, nurses, physicians, managers, entrepreneurs, employees in the tourism and hospitality sector (e.g., frontline employees), health care professionals, defense sector employees, and bankers. A considerable amount of research has been done either with hotel employees or doctors and nurses. One reason for using samples from hotel employees is that Turkey is one of the most attractive tourism places, and delivering quality of service is very important in such a globally competitive sector despite problems such as long work hours, job insecurity, irregular and inflexible work schedules, role stress, heavy workloads, limited weekend time off, and low wages. The reason for selecting samples from doctors and nurses is similar because of the analogous working conditions, such as long working hours, limited qualified personnel, heavy workloads, and limited incentives to retain qualified doctors and nurses in hospitals. In addition to these samples, some studies used heterogeneous groups of employees in a single study, such as male, female, married, single, professionals, and managers (e.g., Ozutku & Altindis, 2013); some used samples from different occupational groups such as academics, doctors, nurses, policemen, and bankers in a single city (Akdogan & Polatci, 2013); and some studies were only confined to women (e.g., Yildirim & Aycan, 2008) or married employees (e.g., Aycan & Eskin, 2005).

Research in the Turkish context has mostly utilized studies conducted by individual researchers, most of whom collected data through selected workplaces and occupational groups in selected cities. Although a considerable amount of the research is descriptive in nature, it is evident that researchers have drawn on several theoretical frameworks, most particularly, models based on studies conducted in the Western countries.

In most of the studies conducted in Turkey work-to-family conflict (WIF) and family-to-work conflict (FIW) have been found to be two independent but correlated constructs that impact time, strain, and behaviors of individuals in these two roles (Burke, Koyuncu, & Fiksenbaum, 2013). In a study conducted with a large sample of frontline service workers in the hospitality sector in Turkey, the findings revealed a higher level of WIF was experienced compared to FIW, but the levels of both were moderate (Burke et al., 2013). This result that WIF is experienced more than FIW has been found in many of the samples in various studies (e.g., Anafarta, 2011; Erdamar & Demirel, 2014; Giray & Ergin, 2006). These findings supported Pleck's (1977) theory of asymmetric boundary permeability such that greater interference from work-to-family than from family-to-work is experienced by many of the Turkish samples.

With respect to gender differences in experiencing the work-family interface and its antecedents, research findings have been inconsistent. In a study conducted with dual-earner couples in five different cities in Turkey, for women, age, work-related life events, and other life events were significantly related to WIF, and number of children and managerial position were significantly related to FIW conflict. However, for men, a significant relationship was found between work-related life events and WFC only (Giray & Ergin, 2006). Some other studies found no gender differences in the experience of WFC between men and women (e.g., Ozutku & Altindis, 2013). There were some gender differences in the antecedents and consequences of work-family interface which are summarized in the following sections.

Antecedents

Among the antecedents of the work-family interface, demographic variables (e.g., Karapinar, Ilsev & Ergeneli, 2006), personality (e.g., Karatepe & Uludag, 2008b), social support (e.g., Aycan & Eskin, 2005; Gurbuz, Turunc, & Celik, 2013; Karatepe & Uludag, 2008a; Turunc & Celik, 2010; Turunc & Findikli, 2015), and work-related factors such as work stress (Ozafsarlioglu & Kilic, 2013), work intensity (Ozutku & Altindis, 2013), and organizational commitment (e.g., Benligiray & Sönmez, 2012) have been used in the studies conducted with Turkish samples.

Demographic Variables

Among demographic variables, presence and number of young children, age, and education level were found to have some significant effects on the experience of work-family interface. In a study conducted in Ankara (the capital city) with 300 public sector employees, it was found that the heaviest burdens of working individuals were the responsibilities of being parents and married couples. Related to the effect of family life on work life, it was found that respondents who had many children felt the effect of family life on work life more severely; on the other hand married individuals evaluated the effect of working life on family life as being more severe than single individuals (Ozmete & Eker, 2012). In another study, presence of younger children was found to be the only source of both WIF conflict and FIW conflict (Ozutku & Altindis, 2013). In another study, being an older individual, presence of younger children and being a single career couple predicted FIW conflict (Karapinar, Ilsev, & Ergeneli, 2006). In a study conducted with 462 health care professionals who were working in 25 different state hospitals across 12 cities in Turkey, there was a significant effect of number of children on the WFC levels of health care professionals (Ozutku & Altindis, 2013).

Nonetheless, there is also a study which found no difference between work stress and WFC in terms of demographic variables, gender, marital status, age, income, and number of children (e.g., Ozafsarlioglu & Kilic, 2013). Yet, it is important to note that this particular study was conducted with sugar factory employees and not the predictors but only level of WFC differed among these sugar factory employees. Employees working three shifts had relatively more WFC when compared with those working a day shift on a permanent basis. Overall, these results indicate that being married and having children seem to add the most extra burden to Turkish couples' WFC. However, the findings are inconsistent.

Personality Variables

With respect to personality variables, the number of studies looking at the relationship between personality and work-family interface is limited. Research conducted both in and outside Turkey mostly tested relationships between situational variables and the work-family interface. However, empirical research on the effects of dispositional variables on the work-family interface has been less frequent. One study from Turkey mainly focused on two dispositional personality variables, and found that positive affectivity (PA) ameliorated both WIF and FIW, while negative affectivity (NA) exacerbated only WIF (Karatepe & Uludag, 2008b). This finding only partly supported Frone's (2003) finding that both NA and PA are the common causes of WIF and FIW. This means that for the case of Turkish frontline hotel employees in Karatepe and Uludag's study, those who are high in NA experience higher conflicts between work and family, whereas those who have more enthusiasm, energy, and concentration (high in PA) are better able to cope with WIF and FIW. In another study, savoring was negatively related to WFC, indicating that individuals who were high in the capacity for overall savoring, experienced lower levels of WFC than did those low in that capacity (Camgoz, 2014). This is the empirical evidence illustrating the impact of individuals' beliefs about their ability to savor positive circumstances on WFC.

Social Support

The role of social support has been extensively examined in the literature. Some studies only focused on one type of support; others focused on different types and sources of support, and social support has been used in the research models, both as a moderator and a main effect. Spousal support and child care support have been considered as family antecedents, and supervisory support as a work antecedent, and all have been investigated with work and family outcomes (e.g., Aycan & Eskin, 2005).

Turkey generally has a family-friendly organizational culture where superiors are concerned with and involved in the professional as well as personal lives of their subordinates (Aycan, 2004). In many of the studies conducted in Turkey, organizational support was found to be negatively related to WIF and FIW in different samples from banks, small and medium-sized enterprises, hotel employees, and defense sector employees (e.g., Aycan & Eskin, 2005; Gurbuz et al., 2013; Karatepe & Uludag, 2008a, 2008b; Turunc & Celik, 2010). Turkey has paternalistic practices both in families and organizations such that individuals holding the authority are obliged to offer protection to the ones under their care, and in return they expect loyalty and respect. So, similar to the father role in a family, managers are expected to apply their powers for providing protection and improvement for their employees. In one of these studies conducted by Aycan and Eskin (2005), some gender differences were found with respect to the ameliorating effects of social support. Spousal support was related to WFC for women, whereas both spousal and organizational support were related to WFC for men (Aycan & Eskin, 2005). This conclusion can be interpreted as men's expectation to have protection, care, and guidance from their superiors at work in matters that concern their family life, just like women expect the same from their husbands, who are perceived to be in an authority position. That is why organizational support seems to be a more important source of support for men than it is for women (Aycan & Eskin, 2005). Other studies found some moderating variables in the relationship between supervisory support and WFC such that only when organizational commitment was low was supervisory support found to have a negative effect on WFC (Turunc & Findikli, 2015). Another study with female Turkish nurses used supervisory support as a moderating variable between work demands, work-to-family conflict, and satisfaction with job and life, but no significant effect was found for supervisory support (Yildirim & Aycan, 2008). Overall, main and moderating effects of social support variables seem to be significant, yet the effects vary across samples.

Work-Related Factors

Among the work-related antecedents, the impact of organizational commitment and its sub-dimensions (affective commitment, continuance commitment, and normative commitment) revealed a positive effect on WFC in a study conducted with doctors and nurses employed at seven state hospitals and three medical faculties of universities in Ankara (Benligiray & Sönmez, 2012). The more committed they were to the hospital they worked for, the more general WFC they experienced (Benligiray & Sönmez, 2012). This finding is important, especially because this population has a large workload and they are limited in quality and quantity in Turkey. There is also a regional imbalance of retention of qualified personnel in hospitals, and because of the physical, psychological, and social pressures, doctors and nurses are very likely to experience WFC. In this respect, organizational commitment is one of the key factors to ameliorate their work conditions. In another study conducted with employees in the pharmaceutical industry, organizational commitment as an outcome variable was found to be not affected by

WFC experienced by these employees (Efeoglu & Ozgen, 2007). Direction of the relationship mattered in these studies, so models tested in different research studies gave different findings.

Work intensity factors were also investigated in a study conducted with 462 health care professionals who were working in 25 different state hospitals across 12 cities in Turkey (Ozutku & Altindis, 2013). The significant predictors of WIF for Turkish health care professions included job-emotion demand and time demand factors, which were among the work intensity factors, and they had a negative and significant effect on behavior-based WIF.

Consequences

Among the consequences of the work-family interface, research has focused mainly on affective and performance outcomes. Generally, affective outcomes included satisfaction and well-being (e.g., Burke et al., 2013; Karatepe & Uludag, 2008a), intention to leave (e.g., Karatepe & Azar, 2013), exhaustion and burnout (Karatepe, 2010), whereas performance outcomes included job performance (Akdogan & Polatci, 2013).

Generally two contrasting views prevail in this scholarship on the consequences of multiple roles. One view, which is based on the scarcity hypothesis, suggests that multiple roles consume energy and lower performance (Rothbard, 2001); another view based on role accumulation theory suggests that multiple roles boost energy and create alternative strategies to make use of resources (Marks, 1977). These views are also apparent in the terms used in this scholarship. WFC and negative work-family spillover are the main constructs that connote negative consequences of having multiple roles in work and family. In contrast, recent scholarship on work-family enrichment, enhancement, and facilitation connotes more positive consequences where participation in one role increases the quality or performance in another role or has a positive effect on it (Greenhaus & Powell, 2006; Grzywacz & Marks, 2000; Wayne, Randel, & Stevens, 2006). Research in the Turkish context mainly utilized the scarcity hypothesis and most of the studies investigated work-family relationship from a conflict perspective.

Affective outcomes have been of more interest to the scholars in Turkey. Satisfaction is one of the outcome variables which has been extensively investigated. Different types of satisfaction, including life satisfaction, career satisfaction, marital satisfaction, and family satisfaction, have been used as important outcome variables in work-family research.

In the literature, marital satisfaction is suggested to be one of the role-related outcomes of WIF conflict, but not FIW conflict (Frone, 2003). However, some studies conducted in Turkey (e.g., Karatepe & Uludag, 2008b) found that employees who have elevated levels of conflicts between the family and work domains are dissatisfied with their marital life. In other words, role-related consequences of FIW conflict may also reside in the family domain. Research findings coming from frontline employee samples in Turkey support the negative relationship between conflict and satisfaction, such that both WIF and FIW conflict diminished family, career, job, and life satisfaction outcomes in different samples (Karabay, 2015; Karatepe & Sokmen, 2006; Karatepe & Tekinkus, 2006; Karatepe & Uludag, 2008a; Yildirimalp, Oner, & Yenihan, 2014). WFC was found to have a negative effect on job and life satisfaction for women-only samples as well (Dursun & Istar, 2014; Ergeneli, Ilsev, & Karapınar, 2010). WFC generally predicted both work and psychological well-being outcomes, work interfering with family being a consistently stronger predictor of well-being outcomes than family interfering with work in a managerial sample of women (Koyuncu, Burke, & Wolpin, 2012).

Intention to quit is another outcome variable that has been frequently used in work-family interface research. Employees experiencing WFC have been found to have intentions to leave their organizations. In much of the research conducted in Turkey, satisfaction, work-family, and intention to leave variables were analyzed in the same conceptual model (e.g., Karabay, 2015). WFC was found to have positive relationship with turnover intentions (Karabay, 2015; Karatepe & Uludag, 2008b) and negative relationship with work, family, and life satisfaction (Karabay, 2015).

Emotional exhaustion and burnout are other outcome variables that have been studied in Turkish samples. In a study conducted with 151 employees in public and private banks, the effects of perceived workload and WFC on burnout were investigated, and findings revealed that as employees experienced more WFC and believed workload to be more than they could handle, they were more likely to feel emotionally exhausted and become cynical and indifferent toward the work in response to adverse conditions. Especially in this sector, workload was perceived to be very high, and it supported the previous findings that workload led to higher levels of work stress which eventually resulted in emotional exhaustion. In addition, high work load was found to increase WFC, which in turn increased emotional exhaustion and cynicism (Tayfur & Arslan, 2012). In a study conducted with physicians working at private and public hospitals in Antalya and Istanbul, Turkey, predictors of emotional exhaustion were found to be high workload, lack of reciprocity, and lack of supervisory support (Tayfur & Arslan, 2013).

With respect to performance outcomes, job performance has been used both as a predictor of job satisfaction and turnover intention and as an outcome of WFC. Apart from these variables, a study in Turkey investigated the effect of psychological capital, which is composed of high self-efficacy, optimism, hope, and resiliency (Luthans, Avolio, Avey, & Norman, 2007). It was found that psychological capital of individuals significantly affected performance, and this effect was increased by the effect of positive and negative work-family spillover and psychological well-being. In addition to the mediating role of positive and negative work-family spillover, researchers also found a positive correlation between positive and negative spillover (Akdogan & Polatci, 2013). This pointed to the fact that the construct of work-family spillover encompassed both positive and negative experiences, and negative experiences in one domain might have positive effects in another domain.

Although most empirical research in Turkey has been limited to the Turkish national context, several studies examined WFC from a cross-cultural perspective. A 10-country study for the Project 3535 investigated cross-cultural similarities and differences in work-family interface experiences of employees in dual-earner families with at least one child living at home. In Turkey women reported higher WIF and FIW conflict than men (Korabik, Lero, Aycan, & Bardoel, 2012). For women in Turkey, greater satisfaction with organizational policies was associated with lower WFC (Korabik et al., 2012). However, greater satisfaction with organizational policies had different effects on turnover intent and life satisfaction in Turkey, leading to lower turnover intent (only in Turkey) and higher life satisfaction for both genders (Korabik et al., 2012). With respect to work-family positive spillover, women reported higher work-family positive spillover than men in all countries except China, Spain, and Indonesia and greater satisfaction with organizational policies was associated with higher work-family positive spillover for both genders in Canada and Turkey (Korabik et al., 2012).

Another multicountry study conducted in Australia, Ireland, New Zealand, Portugal, South Africa, Sweden, Turkey, and the United Kingdom examined cross-cultural perspectives of gender and management in higher education institutions (Ozkanli, 2010). In each country interviews were conducted with both male and female senior managers, including current and former rectors and vice rectors. Results from the Turkish data revealed that being a top level academician conflicted with family roles. Women presidents and vice presidents underlined the limited number of women in top positions in universities which stemmed from the existing organizational cultures and lack of support both from organizations and spouses to lessen their WFC. Although cross-cultural studies that include Turkey are very much limited in number, they give some clues about particular characteristics in Turkey.

Overall, the literature on the work-family interface in Turkey as reviewed here mainly concentrates on antecedents and consequences of WFC and only a few studies used a cross-cultural perspective. Gender differences as well as some mediating and moderating processes in this relationship have been investigated. The reason why researchers focused mainly on these issues may be driven from the aspects of sociocultural context of Turkey, such as women's entrance into the labor force, marriage, family, paternalism, social support, institutions, and values in the Turkish culture. Many researchers tested models that included these variables.

Focus Group Results

In our focus groups, 12 women participated and shared their experiences. All selected women except for two were mothers, and all but one worked full-time.

Participants were selected from a research company's roster. Their professions ranged from nurse to kindergarten teacher, to public servant. Our focus group discussions addressed the following questions: how frequently they experienced WFC/imbalance; when and under which conditions this conflict/imbalance appeared most, that is, antecedents of WFC; and consequences of this conflict/imbalance in the sense of how it affected them and their families.

Theme 1: Conflict Revolves Around Spouse, Children, and Work

When asked about their experience of work-family balance or conflict, all women talked about their roles as wives, mothers, and workers. Some women also discussed their roles as daughters and daughter-in-laws. But, the main role conflict seemed to happen between the roles of wife, worker, and mother. Most of the husbands were criticized as being nonsupportive, such that women had an extra duty to cook after they came home, whereas husbands were believed to assume the single role of a breadwinner. In this sense, women expected more emotional support from their husbands. For most women in the discussion group, husbands in general and their nonsupportive behaviors were seen as the antecedents of WFC.

Theme 2: Bidirectionality of the Work-Family Interface

Spillover from family to work seemed to be more concerning for the interviewed women. The reason for this spillover was mostly related to their husbands, and their reluctance to equally share household and child care responsibilities. But other than that mother-in-laws were usually involved in household activities and child care, and women said they had a hard time maintaining smooth relationships with their mother-in-laws. But still, they believed mother-in-laws were better caregivers than babysitters, because they could give unconditional love to their grandchildren. Spillover from work to family also occurred for many women. Some of the women said they reflected their anxiety at home if they had a hard day at work, and this affected their relationships with their husbands.

Theme 3: Consequences of Conflicts

Consequences of these bidirectional conflicts included becoming a nervous person; leaving good jobs because of spouse's worries and jealousy; having some health problems; and having effects on children such as unhappiness, ill-temperedness, and excessive addiction to moms. Most of the mothers felt guilty for working and leaving their kids to grandparents or child care centers. They usually tried to work in relatively flexible jobs where they could leave early, take leaves, and visit home at lunch. But, the majority of them said they had sacrificed their previous good jobs, which they had loved and where they had earned good money. In other words, for the sake of their family life many women changed their previous jobs despite their satisfaction. They interpreted this as limiting their career development with their own hands.

Theme 4: Women Divided in Pieces

Women compared themselves to their husbands in terms of their well-being, and they concluded that even if they were dual-earner couples, men shut down their work when they came home, but women kept on working at home by doing household and child care work. Serving food to their husbands and spending time with their children were seen as extra burdens to these women especially to those who had more perfectionist and conscientious personalities. They felt as if they were divided in pieces to maintain a clean home, raise well-behaving children, and be good wives to their husbands and good daughters or daughter-in-laws to their parents. Women felt divided in pieces not only because the division of labor between their husbands and themselves was unequal, but also because they felt themselves as owning everything, such as wanting to do everything themselves, including shopping for their husbands and wanting to have things done in a short period of time without delegating chores to someone else. Still, some of these "divided women" found that relaxing techniques such as playing music, watching soap operas, and chatting with their husbands helped them to cope with their divided state.

Theme 5: Generational Differences in Child-Raising Styles

Women suggested that men were raised differently than women in Turkey. Men were believed to be more relaxed and less obsessed with details, whereas women were raised as more emotional, more respectful to men, and more attentive to details, so they wore out more easily. Being aware of this difference in styles, these women said they tried to raise their sons and daughters in a more gender neutral way, assigning less distinct roles to them.

Overall, despite their complaints and dissatisfaction with some aspects of their work-family relationship, when asked about their opinions about working women in general, all of these women unequivocally agreed that it was necessary for a woman to work, but their reasons differed. Some said it was a financial necessity, whereas others said it led to women's freedom. They said working women were more planned, conscious, able to care for themselves, and could make sure they had their own money in case of a possible future conflict in their marriage. None of these women were forced to work; they all said they worked of their own will, and none of them wanted to stop working. This shows that despite conflicts, complaints, and regrets, women believed in the importance of working both financially and psychologically. In order to cope with such conflicts, they mainly tried to delegate some of their housework to their husbands or other family members such as mother-in-laws. Working mothers with children seemed to have more difficulty compared to those who did not yet have children, because their conflicts both in terms of limited time and excessive expectations revolved around their multiple roles as wives and mothers.

Conclusion

The work-family interface has been of interest to many Turkish scholars in the past two decades. This interest stems not only from the increasing presence of women in the workforce, but also from the changing values that accompany economic and social changes in the society. Turkey's strategic location between the East and the West makes its culture a mixture of both Eastern and Western values with modernity, traditionalism, and Islamic values existing side by side at all layers of society, organizations, and individuals. As in many practices, in their work-family relations Turkish people combine the traditional values of familialism and collectivism with modern, egalitarian, and individualistic values. In that sense, research in the Turkish context has the potential to reveal unique mechanisms in the work-family relationship. However, as compared to work-family research coming from the West, work-family research in Turkey is limited in amount and scope. This chapter aimed to introduce the Turkish context and review the relevant literature in light of these contextual characteristics and finally to support some of the themes in the literature with focus group discussions.

Given that the status of women has been a major issue in the Turkish context since the early Republican era, work-family research has gained more attention with the entrance of women into the labor force. However, in research conducted in the Turkish context, gender has been considered only physical gender, and mostly treated as a biologically determined variable. Therefore, within-gender variation in the experience of work-family relationship has not been captured very well. Especially in the Turkish context where gender inequality is high—as the statistics show—it is very likely that there may be greater within-gender variation than across-gender variation in roles. Although gender differences in the experience of WFC did not differ drastically in the previously mentioned studies, there were some gender differences in the antecedents associated with reduced work-family conflict, such as social support (e.g., Aycan & Eskin, 2005).

In the research literature conducted in Turkey, antecedents of work-family interface included broad categories of demographics and work domain variables, and consequences mainly included satisfaction and performance variables. Many of the findings can be comparable to those found in other countries, such as a negative relationship between WFC and satisfaction, and a positive relationship between WFC and turnover intention. Being married and having children are the two demographic factors that were also specifically emphasized in the focus group discussions. Given that family is a very important institution in Turkey, it creates a source of support, and of conflict and concern at the same time. Therefore, more research is needed to cope with conflict arising from this domain, both at the individual level and the organizational level.

As a methodological note, all these studies, which generally investigated antecedents and outcomes of the work-family interface, were quantitative studies and they used work-family scales that had mostly been taken from the Western researchers (e.g., Netemeyer et al., 1996). This poses some problems with respect to explanation of the emic characteristics of work-family issues in Turkey. But still, antecedents such as social support come as a coping strategy, which can be understood better within the context of paternalistic Turkish culture. There were also few qualitative studies conducted with Turkish employees (Turk, Davas, Tanik, & Montgomery, 2014; Ufuk & Özgen, 2001), which also revealed similar predictors and outcomes of WIF and FIW conflict. Still, it can be suggested that more qualitative studies, especially on the meaning of work and family, and conflict and enhancement in this relationship, can give a better understanding of the unique practices and experiences in the Turkish context.

More research also is necessary in the domain of work-family enrichment in Turkey, because demands and resources are very likely to have influences both on the experience of conflict and enrichment. This gap in the Turkish work-family literature needs to be filled both with qualitative and quantitative studies. Moreover, research in Turkey reveals that WFC is applicable to various occupational groups, but more application of this construct in different cultural contexts might underline emic characteristics of the Turkish culture. In that sense, more cross-cultural studies are needed to understand the meaning and experience of work-family relations. Furthermore, going beyond the analyses of antecedents and consequences of the work-family interface, choice of variables and conceptual models in the Turkish research need to consider mediating and moderating processes more. These gaps in the work-family research conducted in Turkey open new venues for exploration and suggest new theoretical mechanisms to explain the dynamics of the work-family relationship in this particular cultural context.

References

Adak, N. (2007). Kadınların ikilemi: Iş ve Aile Yaşamı / The women dilemma: Between work and family life. *Journal of Sociology, 17*, 137–152.

Akdogan, A., & Polatci, S. (2013). Psikolojik sermayenin performans üzerindeki etkisinde iş aile yayılımı ve psikolojik iyi oluşun etkisi. *Atatürk Üniversitesi Sosyal Bilimler Enstitüsü Dergisi, 17*(1), 273–293.

Amaros, J. E., & Bosma, N. (2013). *Global Entrepreneurship Monitor 2013 Global Report.* Retrieved from http://www.gemconsortium.org/report

Anafarta, N. (2011). The relationship between work-family conflict and job satisfaction: A structural equation modeling approach. *International Journal of Business and Management, 6*(4), 168–177.

Arat, Z. (1994). Liberation or indoctrination: Women's education in Turkey. *Boğaziçi Journal: Review of Social, Economic and Administrative Studies, 8*(1–2), 83–105.

Arat, Z. (1999). *Deconstructing images of the Turkish woman.* New York, NY: Palgrave MacMillan.

Aycan, Z. (2004). Key success factors for women in management in Turkey. *Applied Psychology: An International Review, 53*(3), 453–477.

Aycan, Z. (2009). Career development of professional women in Turkey. In S. Bekman, A. Aksu-Koç, S. Bekman, & A. Aksu-Koç (Eds.), *Perspectives on human development, family, and culture* (pp. 284–297). New York, NY: Cambridge University Press. doi:10.1017/CBO9780511720437.020

Aycan, Z., & Eskin, M. (2005). Relative contributions of childcare, spousal support, and organizational support in reducing work-family conflict for men and women: The case of Turkey. *Sex Roles, 53*(7–8), 453–471. doi:10.1007/s11199-005-7134-8

Benligiray, S., & Sönmez, H. (2012). Analysis of organizational commitment and work-family conflict in view of doctors and nurses. *International Journal of Human Resource Management, 23*(18), 3890–3905. doi:10.1080/09585192.2012.665063

Blitz, R. C. (1975). An international comparison of women's participation in the professions. *The Journal of Developing Areas, 9*(4), 499–510.

Bolak, H. (1997). When wives are major providers: Culture, gender and family work. *Gender & Society, 11*, 409–443.

Bolak-Boratav, H. (2011). Searching for feminism in psychology in Turkey. In A. Rutherford, R. Capdevila, V. Undurti, & I. Palmary (Eds.), *Handbook of international feminisms: Perspectives on psychology, women, culture, and rights* (pp. 17–36). New York, NY: Springer.

Burke, R. J., Koyuncu, M., & Fiksenbaum, L. (2013). Gender differences in work experiences, satisfactions and wellbeing among physicians in Turkey. *Gender in Management: An International Journal, 24*(2), 70–91.

Camgoz, S. M. (2014). The role of savoring in work-family conflict. *Social Behavior and Personality, 42*(2), 177–188.

Central Intelligence Agency (2016). *Turkey*. In *The World Factbook*. Retrieved from https://www.cia.gov/library/publications/the-world-factbook/geos/tu.html.

Dayıoğlu, M. (2000). Labor market participation of women in Turkey. In F. Acar & A. Güneş-Ayata (Eds.), *Gender and identity construction: Women of Central Asia, Caucasus and Turkey* (pp. 44–74). Leiden: Brill.

Dayıoğlu, M., & Kırdar, M. G. (2009). *Determinants of and trends in labor force participation of women in Turkey*. Middle East Technical University Working Paper No: 5, Ankara.

Dursun, S., & Istar, E. (2014). Kadın çalışanların yaşamış oldukları iş aile yaşamı çatışmasının iş ve yaşam doyumu üzerine etkisi. *Ataturk University Journal of Economics & Administrative Sciences, 28*(3), 127–138.

Efeoglu, D. E., & Ozgen, P. H. (2007). İş aile yaşam çatışmasının iş stresi iş doyumu ve örgütsel bağlılık üzerindeki etkileri: İlaç sektöründe bir araştırma. *Çukurova Üniversitesi Sosyal Bilimler Enstitüsü Dergisi, 16*(2), 237–254.

Erdamar, G., & Demirel, H. (2014). Investigation of work-family, family-work conflict of the teachers. *Procedia—Social and Behavioral Sciences, 116* (5th World Conference on Educational Sciences), 4919–4924. doi:10.1016/j.sbspro.2014.01.1050

Ergeneli, A., Ilsev, A., & Karapınar, P. B. (2010). Work-family conflict and job satisfaction relationship: The roles of gender and interpretive habits. *Gender, Work & Organization, 17*(6), 679–695. doi:10.1111/j.1468-0432.2009.00487.x

Frone, M. R. (2003). Work-family balance. In J. C. Quick & L. E. Tetrick (Eds.), *Handbook of occupational health psychology* (pp. 143–162). Washington, DC: American Psychological Association.

Giray, M. D., & Ergin, C. (2006). Çift kariyerli ailelerde bireylerin yaşadıkları iş-aile ve aile-iş çatışmalarının kendini kurgulama davranışı ve Yaşam olayları ile ilişkisi [The effects of stressful life events and self-monitoring behavior on work-family conflict in dual career families]. *Türk Psikoloji Dergisi, 21*(57), 83–101.

Greenhaus, J. H., & Powell, G. N. (2006). When work and family are allies: A theory of work-family enrichment. *Academy of Management Review, 31*, 72–79.

Grzywacz, J. G., & Marks, N. F. (2000). Reconceptualizing the work-family interface: An ecological perspective on the correlates of positive and negative spillover between work and family. *Journal of Occupational Health Psychology, 5*(1), 111–126.

Gurbuz, S., Turunc, O., & Celik, M. (2013). The impact of perceived organizational support on work-family conflict: Does role overload have a mediating role? *Economic & Industrial Democracy, 34*(1), 145–160. doi:10.1177/0143831X12438234

Hofstede, G. (1980). *Culture's consequences: International differences in work related values*. Beverly Hills, CA: Sage.

IMF World Economic Outlook Database. (2015). *Report for selected countries and subjects, April 14, 2015*. Retrieved from http://www.imf.org/external/pubs/ft/weo/2015/01/weodata/weorept.aspx?sy=2008&ey=2014&scsm=1&ssd=1&sort=country&ds=.&br=1&c=186&s=NGDPD%2CNGDPDPC%2CPPPGDP%2CPPPPC&grp=0&a=&pr.x=63&pr.y=3

Karabay, M. E. (2015). Sağlık personelinin iş stresi, iş- aile çatışması ve iş-aile-hayat tatminlerine yönelik algılarının işten ayrılma niyeti üzerindeki etkilerinin belirlenmesi üzerine bir araştırma. *Yonetim Bilimleri Dergisi* [*Journal of Administrative Sciences*], *13*(26), 113–134.

Karapinar, P. B., Ilsev, A., & Ergeneli, A. (2006). Demographic variables affecting work-family and family-work conflict and the relationship between work-family and family-work conflict. *Hacettepe Üniversitesi İktisadi ve İdari Bilimler Fakültesi* Dergisi, *2*(22), 85–109.

Karatepe, O. M. (2010). The effect of positive and negative work-family interaction on exhaustion: Does work social support make a difference? *International Journal of Contemporary Hospitality Management, 22*(6), 836–856.

Karatepe, O. M. & Azar, A. K. (2013). The effects of work-family conflict and facilitation on turnover intentions: The moderating role of core self-evaluations. *International Journal of Hospitality and Tourism Administration, 14*(3), 255–281.

Karatepe, O.M., & Kilic, H. (2007). Relationships of supervisor support and conflicts in the work-family interface with the selected job outcomes of frontline employees. *Tourism Management, 28*, 238–252.

Karatepe, O. M., & Sokmen, A. (2006). The effects of work role and family role variables on psychological and behavioral outcomes of frontline employees. *Tourism Management, 27*(2), 255268. doi:10.1016/j.tourman.2004.10.001

Karatepe, O. M., & Tekinkus, M. (2006). The effects of work-family conflict, emotional exhaustion, and intrinsic motivation on job outcomes of front-line employees. *International Journal of Bank Marketing, 24*(2/3), 173–193. doi:10.1108/02652320610659021

Karatepe, O. M., & Uludag, O. (2008a). Supervisor support, work-family conflict, and satisfaction outcomes: An empirical study in the hotel industry. *Journal of Human Resources in Hospitality & Tourism*, 7(2), 115–134. doi:10.1080/15332840802156824

Karatepe, O. M., & Uludag, O. (2008b). Affectivity, conflicts in the work-family interface, and hotel employee outcomes. *International Journal of Hospitality Management, 27*(1), 30. doi:10.1016/j.ijhm.2007.07.001

Korabik, K., Lero, D. S., Aycan, Z., & Bardoel, A. (2012, December). *HR policies to enhance work-family balance: Fostering organizational sustainability in global context*. Paper presented at the Research Colloquium on Creating Sustainable Organizations: The Human and Social Dimensions, Deakin Management Centre, Victoria, AU.

KOSGEB (2013). Turkish Entrepreneurship Strategy and Action Plan 2014–2016. Retrieved from http://www.kosgeb.gov.tr/site/tr/genel/detay/349/plan-raporlar-ve-mali-tablolar

Koyuncu, M., Burke, R. J., & Wolpin, J. (2012). Work-family conflict, satisfactions and psychological well-being among women managers and professionals in Turkey. *Gender in Management, 27*(3), 202–213. doi:10.1108/17542411211221286

Luthans, F, Avolio, B. J., Avey, J. B., & Norman, S. M. (2007). Positive psychological capital: Measurement and relationship with performance and satisfaction. *Personnel Psychology, 60*, 541–572.

Marks, S. R. (1977). Multiple roles and role strain: Some notes on human energy, time and commitment. *American Sociological Review, 42*(6), 921–936.

Mastny, V., & Nation, R. C. (1996). *Turkey between east and west: New challenges for a rising regional power.* Boulder, CO: Westview Press.

Netemeyer, R. G., Boles, J. S., & McMurrian, R. (1996). Development and validation of work-family conflict and family-work conflict scales. *Journal of Applied Psychology, 81*(4), 400–410.

OECD. (2014). *LFS by sex and age—Indicators: Labour force participation rate.* Retrieved from http://stats.oecd.org/#.

Ozafsarlioglu, S., & Kilic, R. (2013). The influence of stress sources in organizations on the work- family conflict of employees. *Uşak Üniversitesi Sosyal Bilimler Dergisi, 1267*, 208–237.

Ozar, S. (1994). Some observations on the position of women in the labor market in the development process of Turkey. *Bogazici Journal: Review of Social, Economic and Administrative Studies, 8*(1–2), 21–43.

Ozar, S. (2007). *Women entrepreneurs in Turkey: Obstacles, potentials and future prospects.* Retrieved from http://www.genderclearinghouse.org/Ar/Ar/upload/Assets/Documents/pdf/Comp%20I%20Prop%2043%20Full%20Draft%20Turkey%20copy.pdf

Ozbilgin, M., & Healy, G. (2004). The gendered nature of career development of university professors: The case of Turkey. *Journal of Vocational Behavior, 64*, 358–371.

Ozkanli, O. (2010). Türkiye'de üniversitelerde üst düzey kadın yöneticilerin karşılaştıkları kültürel ve yapısal engeller. *Mülkiye Dergisi, 34*(268), 267–281.

Ozmete, E., & Eker, I. (2012). Iş-aile yaşamı çatışması ve roller: Kamu sektörü örneğinde bir değerlendirme [Work-family conflict and roles: Assessment of the public sector]. *Çalışma Ilişkileri Dergisi* [*Journal of Labour Relations*], *3*(2), 1–23.

Ozutku, H., & Altindis, S. (2013). The relations between work intensity and work-family conflict in collectivist culture: Evidence from Turkish health care professionals. *Journal of Health Management, 15*(3), 361. doi:10.1177/0972063413492049

Pleck, J. H. (1977). The work-family role system. *Social Problems, 24*(4), 411–421.

Rothbard, N. P. (2001). Enriching or depleting? The dynamics of engagement in work and family roles. *Administrative Science Quarterly, 46*, 655–684.

Tayfur, O., & Arslan, M. (2012). Algılanan iş yükünün tükenmişlik üzerine etkisi: Iş-aile çatışmasının aracı rolü [The effect of perceived workload on burnout: The mediating role of work-family conflict]. *Hacettepe Universitesi Iktisadi Ve Idari Bilimler Fakultesi Dergisi* [*Hacettepe University Journal of Economics and Administrative Sciences*], *30*(1), 147–172.

Tayfur, O., & Arslan, M. (2013). The role of lack of reciprocity, supervisory support, workload and work-family conflict on exhaustion: Evidence from physicians. *Psychology, Health & Medicine, 18*(5), 564–575. doi:10.1080/13548506.2012.756535

Turk, M., Davas, A., Tanik, F. A., & Montgomery, A. J. (2014). Organizational stressors, work-family interface and the role of gender in the hospital: Experiences from Turkey. *British Journal of Health Psychology, 19*(2), 442–458. doi:10.1111/bjhp.12041

Turkish Statistical Institute. (2007). *Statistical indicators 1923–2011*. Retrieved from http://www.turkstat.gov.tr/IcerikGetir.do?istab_id=158

Turkish Statistical Institute. (2013). *Household labor force survey statistics*. Retrieved from http://www.turkstat.gov.tr/PreTablo.do?alt_id=1007

Turkish Statistical Institute. (2014a). *Labour force statistics*. Retrieved from http://www.tuik.gov.tr/PreTablo.do?alt_id=1007

Turkish Statistical Institute. (2014b). *Small and medium size enterprises statistics*. Retrieved June 15, 2015, from http://www.turkstat.gov.tr/PreHaberBultenleri.do?id=18521.

Turkish Statistical Institute. (2015). *The results of address based population registration system, 2015*. Retrieved from http://www.turkstat.gov.tr/PreHaberBultenleri.do?id=21507.

Turunc, O., & Celik, M. (2010). Algılanan örgütsel desteğin çalışanların iş-aile, aile-iş çatışması, örgütsel özdeşleşme ve işten ayrılma niyetine etkisi: Savunma sektöründe bir araştırma. *Atatürk Üniversitesi Sosyal Bilimler Enstitüsü Dergisi, 14*(1), 209–232.

Turunc, O., & Findikli, M. A. (2015). Algılanan lider desteği ile iş-aile çatışması ilişkisinde kendini işletmeden Hissetmenin düzenleyici etkisi: Turizm. *Kafkas Üniversitesi Iktisadi Ve Idari Bilimler Fakültesi Dergisi* [*Kafkas University, Journal of Economics & Administrative Sciences Faculty*], *6*(10), 113–134. doi:10.18025/kauiibf.6.10.2015.31045

Ufuk, H., & Özgen, Ö. (2001). Interaction between the business and family lives of women entrepreneurs in Turkey. *Journal of Business Ethics, 31*(2), 95–106.

The UN Refugee Agency. (2015). *2015 UNHCR country operations profile—Turkey*. Retrieved from http://www.unhcr.org/pages/49e48e0fa7f.html

Wayne, J. H., Randel, A. E., & Stevens, J. (2006). The role of identity and work-family support in work-family enrichment and its work-related consequences. *Journal of Vocational Behavior, 69*, 445–461.

Yildirim, D., & Aycan, Z. (2008). Nurses' work demands and work-family conflict: A questionnaire survey. *International Journal of Nursing Studies, 45*(9), 1366–1378. doi:10.1016/j.ijnurstu.2007.10.010

Yildirimalp, S., Oner, M., & Yenihan, B. (2014). Hemşirelerin iş-aile çatışması ve yaşam tatmini düzeyleri: Demografik özellikler açısından bir değerlendirme. *Siyaset, Ekonomi Ve Yönetim Arastirmalari Dergisi* [*Research Journal of Politics, Economics & Management*], *2*(3), 165–182.

9

THE WORK-FAMILY INTERFACE IN INDIA

Tripti Pande-Desai and Ujvala Rajadhyaksha

Socioeconomic and Cultural Context of India

India is the seventh largest country in the world and occupies the second rank among the world's most populated countries. The current population of India is around 1.21 billion (Census, 2011). It is estimated that India will surpass China and will soon be the most populous country of the world. Thus, India represents almost 17.31% of the world's population; that is, one out of six people in the world is Indian. The population growth rate is 1.58%; more than 50% of India's current population is below age 25, and over 65% of its population is below the age of 35 years.

India is composed of 29 states and stretches 3,214 km from north to south and 2,933 km from east to west. To the south of India lies the Indian Ocean, the Arabian Sea is on the west, and the Bay of Bengal is on the southeast. The northern most part of India has the Himalayan mountain range. The countries of China, Bhutan, and Nepal lie along the northern border and on India's west is Pakistan.

With the vastness comes huge diversity. Each state is like another country with its own music, food, and language. There are 22 major languages with 2,000 dialects and approximately 420 million English language speakers. English seems to have become the *de facto* language for trade and business. The official Indian language is Hindi. The major religion of India is Hinduism, and Islam is the next largest. India has the third largest Muslim population in the world. Buddhism, Jainism, Sikhism, and Christianity contribute to less than 2% of the population.

India has always been an agrarian society where most of its population is occupied in agricultural activities and lives in villages. The numbers of people in the villages is going down, however, and currently only 72.2% of the population lives in villages while the rest live in towns and urban conglomerations. India has 10 of the 30 fastest growing urban areas in the world (Goldman Sachs, 2003). However, in all its vastness, there is unity in its diversity.

The literacy rate in India is 74.08% with male literates being 82.14% and female literates being 65.4%. Girls in the villages are not encouraged to study, and it is assumed that they will marry and leave their homes for childbearing and rearing. India is an inegalitarian society where disparity between the sexes is great, and girls are not welcome in many states. Until 1991, India was following a closed economy with a strong tendency toward protectionism, emphasis on import substitutes, and a large public sector with tough controls on the private sector. In the 1990s the economic liberalization plan was initiated by decreasing government control over many domestic industries and thereby increasing its openness to the world. Tax reforms and inflation control measures were started during this time, and with the opening up of foreign investments, the initial major steps to the globalization of India began. According to a report by Citigroup (2011), India may be on a path to surpass China as the world's largest economy by 2050. The middle class in India is increasing, and India is being seen as a ripe country for tapping into a new market of millions of potential consumers. Currently the GDP of India is 1876.80 billion USD and represents 3.03% of the world economy (India, n.d.). The annual GDP growth rate had reached an all-time high of 11.45% in the first quarter of 2010 (Ministry of Statistics and Programme Implementation, 2010).

India's young population and the educated middle class is creating a whole new India, which is nudging India's growth story and also it's entrepreneurial activity. It constitutes two thirds of the total population; thus, nearly 800 million Indians will be under 35 and will be a primary engine of India's economic future. This young population, often referred to as India's demographic dividend has the possibility to translate itself into a huge literate workforce and contribute to raising the GDP and growth rate of an erstwhile "developing" country.

India is the world's most populous democracy. A parliamentary republic with a multiparty system, it has six recognized national parties, including the Indian National Congress and the Bharatiya Janata Party (BJP), and more than 40 regional parties. India is a federation with a parliamentary system governed under the Constitution of India, which serves as the country's supreme legal document. The country is a constitutional republic with a representative democracy, in which majority rule is tempered by minority rights protected by law. It is a federal democracy and the power distribution between the federal government and the states is controlled by the constitution. The Constitution of India, which came into effect on 26 January 1950, states in its preamble that India is a sovereign, socialist, secular, democratic republic. With the opening up of the economy in 1991, the center has become stronger. Liberalization has changed the power structures and, with the new government of 2014, even more.

Many of India's states are very large, as large as some nations, and though New Delhi, the capital and center, controls the budget for the needed reforms, the implementation strategies for important issues are largely left to the states. In 2014, with a new central government and a newly elected prime minister who is committed to economic well-being as opposed to the building up of social welfare programs of the earlier government, the current feeling of the country seems upbeat about its economy. Internationally too, there seems to be increased confidence, corroborated by increased FII's (Foreign Institutional Investment) inflows. India however, has huge challenges, which involve dealing with the ongoing corruption scandals, weak physical and social infrastructure, poor quality and quantity of educational options, and an unclear and inconsistent regulatory environment that creates significant roadblocks to what could be a vibrant economic growth story.

Indian civilization dates back to more than 3,000 years. Another reason for its huge diversity also comes from the foreign influences comingling with domestic Hindu life. Foreign contact came from trade connections as well as through various foreign invasions (Thapar, 1990). Understanding the diversity of the postcolonial context, marked by economic, social, religious, and linguistic diversity is the starting point to understand WFC and balance in India (Cooke & Saini, 2010).

Culturally, as per the GLOBE index, India ranks among the five highest countries on the in-group collectivism and the five lowest on the gender egalitarianism. Traditionally, Indian society was hierarchically ordered through the caste system, an important aspect of Hinduism, the major religion of India (Basham, 1954). Usually the individual's caste was defined at birth and governed all aspects of life, including professions that could be practiced, method of cooking, and even whom one could marry. Upper castes enjoyed more privileges than lower caste groups in India, thereby creating a high "power distance" culture where status differences are tolerated (Chhokar, 2007). As a consequence, status and titles are important sources of motivation in the Indian work environment (Kanungo & Mendonca, 1994).

The family system in India has been a "joint family" system where extended families live together; however, nuclear families are increasing exponentially in urban areas (Roy, 2000). Children are a very important aspect of the Indian families, and in a patriarchal setup, there is encouragement to bear male children in order to carry forward the lineage and perform death rites that can only be done by male children.

The status of women in India has witnessed many changes over its long history (Devi, Pruthi, & Pruthi, 2003). The women of ancient India enjoyed huge freedom, were educated, and indulged in public debate and discourses. In more recent history, they have been relegated to a much lower status than men in most spheres, and Hindu widows are the worst affected. Thus, India, as previously stated, has become very low on the egalitarian index. The government of India has attempted to restore the balance by the recent Women's Reservation Bill of 2010 which ensures that 33% women get reservation in the parliament and state legislative bodies (Rajadhyaksha, 2012).

India's sex ratio is heavily skewed in favor of men (914 females for 1,000 males; John, 2011). Even in education the gender gap is significantly large; 82% of the men and 65% of the women are literate. Although the number of women students in science, engineering, and management fields has increased from 1% in 1971 to 20% in 2000, it is still small compared to men (Parikh & Sukhatme, 2004). Also, the educational qualifications do not translate to job experiences and career, due to India's traditional social and cultural traditions. Women form about a third of India's working population. A majority (90%) of these women are employed in unorganized sectors. The percentage of women in the organized sector has increased from 12.2% in 1981 to 17.2% in 1999, according to the latest census figures available. In 2004–2005, 36% of women in urban India were in the workforce or studying (Bhalla & Kaur, 2011).

Thus, India, in its vast diversity with multilayered caste and class systems and a rapidly changing psycho-sociocultural and economic profile, presents a unique combination of endemic factors, a large informal sector, and swift economic growth. Collectively, these create a kaleidoscope of complex realities. Understanding the interconnections between these varied realities is the key to addressing work and family problems in India.

Formal and Informal Child Care Systems/Provisions in India

To understand child care systems, which are tied in with the leave policies, it becomes necessary to view them from two sectors: the government (including the public sector) and the private sector. While the government of India changed and upgraded its older policies in September 2008, the private sector is still operating on an individual organization-to-organization basis and does not have a common policy for all. Consequently, some private organizations have progressive policies, while some are still operating with their old policies without making any changes to keep up with the changing scenario of an urban and globalized India.

The employees of the central government, namely, those working directly under the government of India are governed by the Central Civil Service (Leave) Rules, 1972. Under these rules, women employees are entitled to maternity leave for a period of 180 days for their first two live born children. During maternity leave, employees will be paid equal to the pay drawn by them immediately before the delivery. For child care, the Sixth Central Pay Commission recommended progressive policies to help women fulfill family responsibilities. Thus, child care leave was granted to women employees having minor children below the age of 18 years, for a maximum period of two years (i.e., 730 days). The leave can be availed during their entire service, for taking care of up to two children whether for rearing or to look after any of their needs, like examinations, sickness, etc.

In totality, including the paid leave period, women employees can avail child care leave for a period of three years. All the benefits here will be admissible only in respect of their two eldest surviving children. With a notification in 1999, the government of India also made provisions for the new father to help and be with his wife and newborn child, where he can avail paternity leave up to 15 days before or within 6 months from the date of delivery of the child. If he does not avail this leave during this period, it is treated as lapsed (Central Service Leave Rules 551(A)). For this leave, the male employee shall be paid a salary equal to the last pay drawn just before he proceeded on leave. Following the central government's move, many state governments of India have also implemented similar provisions for their employees.

The child care policy also requires that any organization that has more than 30 women laborers working for it has to have an in-house day care. However, as usual, the gap between policy and practice is large, and organizations have a way to beat this policy—they do not keep more than 25 permanent women employees and depict the rest as temporary or contract labor. This way they beat a perfectly progressive policy. Even when they do run day cares, they are poorly equipped and mainly notional. In the private sector, day cares and toddler schools are mushrooming, but either they are hugely expensive or do not adhere to strict quality control. Thus, one can safely say that formal child care is still in its infancy in India. New parents still depend on parents, in-laws, and the extended social support from friends and family.

Research Literature on the Work-Family Interface in India

WFC research is fairly new to India, but has grown with the rapid influx of women into the workforce, especially in urban areas. In a study tracing the timeline of work-family research, Rajadhyaksha and Smita (2004) reported that two kinds of work-family research have been conducted in India. One stream of research, conducted mainly within women's studies departments in universities, has focused on underprivileged women, structures of patriarchy, and their contribution to subordination of women at work and home. The other path of research, conducted within social sciences and management departments, has examined work-family relations within urban settings from a role theory perspective. In this chapter we review work-family studies in India set within the second stream of research focusing on negative and positive aspects of the work-family interface, its causes and outcomes, and the role of gender and support for work-family balance of employees in formal paid work.

Early Phase of Work-Family Research: Women and Work

Early focused research on work and family in India can be traced to the 1970s with the establishment of women's studies centers across the country. This was followed by the declaration of 1975 as International Women's Year, the 1970s as the

Women's Decade, and the release of the first ever Report of the Committee on the Status of Women in India (Government of India, 1974) that officially recorded the subordination of women by summarizing statistics of imbalanced child and adult sex ratios (Jain & Rajput, 2003). Because women's studies centers in India were based on the premise of a critical inquiry into structures that upheld subordination of women, a large number of early studies on work and family described terrible working conditions for women in different sectors of the economy and discussed the structuring of family relations that subjugated women at home (e.g., Krishna Raj, 1983).

It can be said that early work and family research in India was synonymous with women and work research, and its predominant focus was on the rural and unorganized sector. At the same time, given concerns about the low status of women in the country, psychosocial studies that focused on work and family roles of urban working women in India were conducted in social sciences/psychology departments in universities. The concern of these studies was the changing status of urban working woman in society and their ability to take on work roles without compromising on home responsibilities or negatively impacting their own well-being, as well as that of family members, especially children (Bharat, 2000).

P. Kapur's book (1970) *Marriage and the Working Women in India* compared the lives of women who worked with pay and women without paid work and found that the former were largely aimed toward making more assertive choices for themselves in the midst of rigid family expectations and roles. Other early studies by K. Rani (1976) and Unwalla (1977) looked at an early generation of urban working women who had few role models, especially when it came to balancing work and family roles. They attempted to understand the motivations for middle-class urban women from somewhat conservative circles to enter the paid workforce. Reasons that were uncovered included economic necessity, a need to feel important, social recognition, and other personal factors. Unwalla's (1977) study was perhaps among the first that identified work spillover into family in the urban Indian context, as she found that for 65% of the women executives, work remained in their thoughts even after they returned home. Her study did not explore for family spillover into work (perhaps because family work continued to be seen as the primary and nonnegotiable responsibility of women). Unwalla's study further found that commuting time did not have any bearing on stress, and conflict and work did not directly affect marital relationships of working women in the sample. Similar studies conducted by Narayana (1982) and Shukla (1987) found that employed women still considered their dominant role to be that of a homemaker. It appeared that the working status of urban women did not alter their gender-role perceptions, and many times women themselves played a role in perpetuating gender-role stereotypes depending on the distance between their work identity and their internalized gender identity as homemakers (e.g., Kumar, 1986).

Middle Phase of Work-Family Research: Two Income Families and Gender Differences

In the decades since the mid-1980s the deficiency of male respondents in work and family studies conducted in urban settings was addressed to a degree. As the number of urban educated married or willing to be married women increased, there was also a corresponding increase in the number of working couples in urban areas, and studies on dual-earner wives and dual-earner couples abounded (e.g., Bharat, 1995; Ramu, 1987, 1989; Rani & Khandelwal, 1992; Sekaran, 1982; Shukla, 1987; Shukla & Kapoor, 1990). Most of the studies found that employment status of women was not a guarantee of significant change in division of work and family responsibilities within the family. Overall, important financial decisions were still generally made by husbands (Shukla, 1988). Further, women in dual-earner families tended to perpetuate gender-role stereotypes by socializing their children, especially daughters, to take up traditional roles (Ramu, 1987, 1989). Rani and Khandelwal (1992) found that both husbands and wives in dual-earner families in India perceived men mainly in the provider role and that employed wives more than the nonemployed wives were the most conservative in their perception of husband's roles and continued to bear the lion's share of household responsibilities, even within presumably egalitarian dual-earner marriages. Shukla (1987) reported that dual-earner couples experienced maximum satisfaction in performing their gender-defined roles. Srivastava and Srivastava (1989) and Rao (1990) found that it was not the wife's employment per se that determined marital adjustment, but the extent of agreement between spouses on attitudes toward work and family roles; thus, spousal conflict depended on the personality, attitude, and gender identity of the partners, especially the wife. Families in which the wife was more androgynous in her gender-role identity tended to be less husband-dominated.

Given a small but noticeable presence of married women in professional and high-status jobs, work-family studies from the 1990s began to distinguish between career- and job-oriented women (e.g., Parikh & Shah, 1994) and dual-career as opposed to dual-earner families (e.g., Pande-Desai, 2000; Rajadhyaksha, 1996). Bhatnagar and Rajadhyaksha (2001) and Rajadhyaksha and Bhatnagar (2000) reported results from an exploration of attitudes toward work and family roles of 92 husband-wife pairs from salaried, upper middle-class, dual-career families in India. They found that attitudes toward occupational and homemaker roles, instead of varying across age as per propositions of adult development theories, varied by gender in a stereotypic manner, with mean values for the occupational role being higher for men and mean values for the homemaker role being slightly higher for women. There was no reversal in attitudes toward work and family roles after midlife. Rather there was some reversal in attitudes between the marital and parental role over the life-span. Both men and women invested more heavily in the parental role and less in the marital role after midlife. The authors explained their results in terms of pervasive gender norms and the expectation that "marriage is for life" within the Indian cultural context. Using the same sample of dual career couples, Rajadhyaksha (2004a) reported results of an examination of mean levels of WFC across gender and across stages of the work-family life cycle. Overall, levels of WFC were highest in the early stage of the work-family life cycle as compared to the middle and late stages. There were no significant gender differences in mean levels of overall WFC, though gender differences emerged for different types of conflict. Women experienced more conflict between their job and home roles, while men experienced more conflict between their job and spousal roles.

Liberalization and Postliberalization Phase of Work-Family Research: Work-Family Interface, Gender, Social Support, and Family-Friendly Benefits

The decade of the 1990s marked the liberalization and globalization of the Indian economy. Although work and family research continued in this environment along the two independent research trajectories developed in previous decades (Rajadhyaksha & Smita, 2004) with women's studies centers focusing on the impact of globalization on female workforce participation (Sonpar & Kapur, 2001) and feminization of poverty (Desai, 1994), research from a psychosocial perspective continued its focus on the work-family interface within urban settings (Vindhya, 2007). Studies during this phase largely focused on antecedents and outcomes of positive and negative aspects of the work-family interface, the role of gender, and social and organizational support for work-life balance.

Antecedents and Outcomes

Aryee, Srinivas, and Tan (2005) studied antecedents and outcomes and the moderating role of gender for the facilitation and conflict elements of the work-family balance using a sample of full-time employed parents in India. Antecedents included personality correlates, overload, involvement, and support from the work and family domains. Results for the facilitation aspect of the work-family balance found that family support was significantly related to family-to-work facilitation. The personality dimension of neuroticism and work overload were significantly positively related both to the work-to-family (WIF) and family-to-work (FIW) elements of conflict. Job involvement had a significant negative, instead of positive, influence on FIW conflict. With regard to outcomes, work-to-family facilitation, not WIF conflict, was significantly positively related to job satisfaction and affective organizational commitment. Overall, the role of gender as moderating variable was not very strong.

In a causal test of WFC, its antecedents, and outcomes, based on a sample of married working men and women from two Indian cities taken from the Project

3535 database, Rajadhyaksha and Ramadoss (2013) found that work demands measured by work overload and family demands measured by family overload were significantly and positively related to WIF and FIW, respectively. At the same time, work and family demands were significantly negatively related to negative work and family outcomes such as WIF guilt and FIW guilt. Rajadhyaksha and Ramadoss explained these results in terms of the "high power distance" in the Indian context. Here, work is seen as the means for a better life, and therefore higher work demands from the boss or workplace, even if they contribute to conflict, are tolerated and do not necessarily have negative outcomes in the work and family domain. However, higher job demands could lead to high stress and strain for individuals and negatively impact health as was found by a recent study by Ramadoss (2013b). Results of this study resonated with results of a previous study by Pal and Saksvik (2008) comparing doctors and nurses in Norway and India, where they found that low job control was responsible for the job stress of Indian doctors and low social support, and high FIW conflict was responsible for the high job stress of Indian nurses.

Role of Gender

Over the last decade, conversation about the role of gender in work-family research in India appears to have moved beyond exploring for significant differences in mean levels of conflict to exploring for the moderating role of gender. This may have had to do with the overbearing evidence of gender inequality in the Indian context despite results of previous studies such as those conducted on dual-career couples in the 1980s and early 1990s reporting no significant difference in levels of conflict between comparable samples of men and women.

In Aryee et al.'s (2005) study reported earlier in the chapter, gender moderated the relationship between the personality dimension of optimism and job involvement on family-to-work facilitation such that the relationship was stronger for men. Other than that, gender played no moderating role. Rajadhyaksha and Pande-Desai (2006) using Project 3535 data from three Indian cities—New Delhi, Mumbai, and Bengaluru (Bangalore)—found that gender moderated the relationship between antecedents and WFC. High job overload was associated with higher FIW conflict for women than for men and high work hours were similarly associated with higher WIF conflict for women than for men. Further, high child care hours were associated with similar levels of WIF conflict for men and women, while low child care hours were associated with higher levels of WIF conflict for women as compared to men. Low as well as high child care hours were associated with higher FIW conflict for women as compared to men. Rajadhyaksha and Velgach (2009) using Indian data from Mumbai and Bengaluru from the Project 3535 database studied the impact of gender and gender-role ideology and the interaction between the two on WFC. They found no significant difference in the levels of WIF conflict between men and women, but FIW conflict was significantly higher for women than for men, as hypothesized. Respondents with a "traditional" gender-role ideology reported more of both forms of conflict than respondents with an "egalitarian" gender-role ideology. Women with a "traditional" gender-role ideology experienced higher FIW conflict than men "traditionals."

Support for Work-Family Balance

Since the mid-1990s, the Information Technology/Information Technology Enabled Services/Business Process Outsourcing (IT/ITES/BPO) sectors grew rapidly in India and employed women workers in ever increasing numbers, especially in urban areas. According to the National Association of Software and Services Companies (NASSCOM—the country's industry association for the IT/ITES/BPO sector) HR survey of 2010–2011, almost 37% of the BPO workforce in India was women (NASSCOM, 2011). As an attestation of this change, NASSCOM began a diversity and inclusion initiative, which included an industry award in 2006 (NASSCOM, 2011), and many organizations in this sector began to offer family-friendly benefits.

In initial growth years of this sector, work-family benefits appeared to be offered as a hybrid or imitation of practices of developed country multinational corporations (MNCs) (Rajadhyaksha & Smita, 2004). However as evidence gathered that a "call center culture" of working the graveyard shift and taking on of "fake" western identities different from one's own national identity to service client calls (Das, Dharwadkar, & Brandes, 2008) has a negative impact on employee's physical and mental well-being and employee turnover (e.g., Machado, Sathyanarayanan, Bhola, & Kamath, 2013; Ranganathan & Kuruvilla, 2008), the clamor for supportive workplace practices has become more strident and heartfelt within the Indian context over the last decade. As a result of this change a fresh slew of studies emerged that focused on women and the work-life interface in the IT industry and other growing sectors of the Indian economy, sources of support for balancing work and family responsibilities including organizational support and family-friendly benefits (e.g., Baral & Bhargava, 2009; Buddhapriya, 2009; Ramadoss, 2013a).

Traditionally, support for work and family balance in India has come from a noninstitutional family context and has been provided by extended family members, such as grandparents and in-laws (if they are close at hand and in good health), paid help (which is relatively cheap in India, but oftentimes unorganized and unreliable), and the spouse (depending on the attitude of the spouse toward work and family roles and only when all other sources of support have been exhausted) (Rajadhyaksha, 2004b; Sekaran, 1982; Valk & Srinivasan, 2013). Child care centers, though increasing in urban areas, are still quite uncommon and not always professionally managed (Datta, 1999).

The relative paucity and unreliability of support for child care often causes urban working parents to leave their children in the care of grandparents who are viewed as a more legitimate and trusted source of care within Indian society. Sometimes, working parents may choose to keep children with grandparents in another city instead of relying on substandard paid help from maids and nannies or day care centers closer to home. In return for this (usually unpaid) service, grandparents benefit from less loneliness and more respect and concern and involvement from their own children, especially as they age and face health issues (e.g., Sreedharan, 2013). Centers for the care of the elderly or assisted-living facilities are limited in India since elder care is viewed as the responsibility of family members as per Hindu family norms and often falls on women's shoulders. "Old-age homes" tend to serve as a last option for destitute aged persons. Recently there has been a trend of "Indianized" elderly residences (Lamb, 2007) targeted toward relatively healthy and affluent senior citizens (Yadav, 2013). However, these are few and far between and do little to significantly alleviate the burden of elder care in the country on working parents. Formal hospice care facilities are virtually absent within India.

Rajadhyaksha (2012) refers to the complexity of social support in the Indian context as a "web of reciprocal relationships of dependence and counter-dependence" (p. 150) and offers it as an explanation for the significant positive as opposed to negative relationship between family support and family demands and family support and work-family guilt observed in a test of a causal model of WFC conducted on a sample of Indian working men and women from the Project 3535 dataset (mentioned earlier in the chapter). Since social support in India comes with strings attached and operates as a two-way street, it probably does not play an alleviating role in the work-family interface.

In other studies on the relationship between social support and the work-family interface, Ramadoss and Rajadhyaksha (2012) reported, based on a sample of 92 dual-career couples, that men reported significantly more supervisor, coworker, and extended family support than women in managing work and family responsibilities. Ganesh and Ganesh (2014) conducted a study on 308 bank employees in India and found that social support was positively related to quality of work life. Based on a study of 148 police personnel in India, Rathi and Barath (2013) reported that social support from coworkers significantly moderated the relationship of WIF and FIW conflict with family satisfaction, while Baral and Bhargava (2009) reported that job characteristics and supervisor support were positively related to work-family enrichment. Aryee et al.'s (2005) study (mentioned earlier) found family support was positively associated with family-to-work facilitation. However, social support did not have a significant relationship with the conflict aspect of work-family balance.

Buddhapriya (2009) in a study of 121 women professionals working in government services, public sector, private sector, and NGOs across different levels found that commitment to family responsibilities and lack of gender sensitive policies by the employers were perceived by women as being major barriers to their career advancement. The top three provisions preferred by respondents included wellness and personal development programs (50%), child care facilities and emergency care for children and elders (45%), and flexible working hours (40%). Ramadoss (2013b) in a study of IT sector employees found that organizational support moderated the relationship between high job demands and high WFC in such a way that employees who perceived their organizations to be supportive of their work and family issues also reported better health. However, Baral and Bhargava (2009) reported no significant association between work-life benefits and policies and job outcome measures, even though in the same study they reported that a supportive work-family culture was positively related to job satisfaction and affective commitment. This contrary result could be explained by the fact that many workplaces in India tend to offer limited formal work-life balance measures, but they may offer a supportive approach even if this approach is steeped in patriarchal "family" values (e.g., employee welfare programs) (Rajadhyaksha, 2012).

Focus Group Discussion Findings

Demographic Characteristics

Twenty-two participants were gathered for the focus group discussion (FGD). It included 16 women and 6 men. Eleven women came from the finance industry and five from the IT industry. Out of the six men, three were from finance, one from IT, and the remaining two from manufacturing organizations. All the participants except for three of the women and three of the men had a child or children at home. They all belonged to dual-career families with an average of two children. None of the children were above the age of 18; in other words, none of them was an adult. The average age of the participants was 38 years. All the participants had a college degree; 90% of them had a postgraduate degree.

Participants of the FGD were asked to discuss their work-family conflict. The process was the following: the discussion began with a brief introduction about each participant, including the work-life-cycle stage they were in, their number of children, and any specific challenge they were facing at and around the time of the discussion. The next step involved the moderator asking a question and leaving it open to the participants to talk among themselves, as well as with the moderator. Some of the questions put forth for the discussion were: "What are your major responsibilities at work?"; "What are your major responsibilities in your family?"; "How much time do you spend on family responsibilities?"; "In what ways does your work interfere with your family responsibilities?"; "In what way do your family responsibilities interfere with your work?"; "How do you cope with these problems?"; "What kind of differences do you see between a working mother and working father/working man or working women?" (where the participant did not have children); and "Do you think that a form of equality can be or should be achieved between a working man and a working woman?"

Major Themes

The main themes that emerged from the FGDs were as follows. All the women experienced conflict between work and family, and they also felt that they had to do much more than their working husbands at home. The two women who did not have children also expressed conflict between work and family. Women from the IT workplace defined the conflict in terms of work interfering with family, whereas 70% of the women in finance defined the conflict as family interfering with work. Eighty percent of the men defined the conflict in terms of family interfering with work.

Seven women perceived the conflict as time-based; the rest perceived it as strain-based. The role conflict that was common to all the mothers was the parent-job conflict; however, there was a lot of discussion on other family roles, like keeping relationships and family commitments, especially during festival time. Even women with young children (who did not go to secondary schools) had grave anxiety about admission and educational future of their offspring already!

Percentage-wise, women working in the IT sector talked more about guilt than those from the finance sector. Without exception, the mothers of school-going children talked of the increase in pressure from schools for parents to get involved in school activities and increase real time engagement with their children in class and outdoor activities, which took a toll on their worklife. Education was uppermost when it came to discussion about their children among both men and women.

Another theme that emerged during the FGD was elder care. It was clear that the responsibility of elder care rested more with women than men. In India, where old age homes are a rarity, aged parents stay in their sons' and increasingly their daughters' homes; in both cases, the responsibility for caregiving tends to fall more upon the woman than on her male counterpart.

A recurring theme that also emerged during the FGD was festivals—planning, related shopping, and food/cooking. India, being a land of rituals and festivals, once again puts the onus of celebrating festivals on the woman. Thus, the women in the FGD talked a lot about what they had to do on festival days and their roles as daughter, daughter-in-law, or wife, irrespective of their having children, with special reference to special dishes associated with different festivals! This was not echoed by the men. It was clear that religious, ritualistic, and festival responsibilities fell on the women, regardless of their work responsibilities, in a very gender inegalitarian India. The women complained about activities such as buying gifts, making special festival food, etc., which are time-consuming and—as echoed by many—irrelevant. At the time of the FGDs, online buying had not become popular.

When it came to work, women from the finance sector complained less about family interfering with work as compared to the women from the IT sector. The timings of the IT professionals were irregular and project based, rather than fixed timings like the women from finance.

Men reported more FIW than WIF in the IT and finance sector, and the "manufacturing" men expressed general dissatisfactions with the long working hours and not being able to spend enough time with the family. They also mentioned that their spouses were unhappy with their lack of contribution not only to home chores, but also their lack of involvement with children's educational activities.

Overall, FGD findings suggest that women were more stressed, had much more to do, and were running double shifts. Despite having a good support structure from family and friends, because good child care facilities are still few and far between, working women felt they always needed extra hands. Perhaps the small number of men and their level of engagement (two arrived late, and two more were distracted throughout) indicates the level of seriousness they or their organization accord this issue, or perhaps indicates the lack of time they have available to address things that are not directly linked to their work. However, men did experience conflict within themselves for not "being there." Helping with school activities of the children was a recurring theme across gender, and with schools being linked to individual parents via the internet, personal involvement can almost be measured by the schools, thereby increasing pressure on the parents.

Coping was an issue that generated a lot of discussion and it was quite clear that there were gender differences as far as coping mechanisms were concerned. Women just ploughed on and used the web of support that they had developed over a period of time, which included friends, domestic help, mothers, mother-in-laws, etc. They worked harder and longer hours, and 80% of the women were resentful that their spouses didn't help. However, they still carried on their responsibilities to completion by being "superwomen"—staying up late, getting up earlier than their spouses, etc. Twenty percent accepted this as a part of life and had few expectations of help from their spouses, citing acceptable gender differences while growing up. These were, understandably, older women who perhaps had grown up with societal acceptance of inequality and power distance. They also gave up their work time to family issues, whereas the younger women gave up more of their family time to work issues and used more of the social support. One working mother had decided to stay on with her in-laws for the sake of her job and child, opposing the trend of nuclearization of families.

Men, on the other hand, coped more by denial and rationalization by staying late in the office and rationalizing the legitimacy of their work demands. Their statements were: "If my wife can't do so much, she can quit anytime," or "No one tells her to do so much," and "If the house is dirty, let it, there is no compulsion for it to be cleaned everyday," or "If there is no cooked food, we can always order in." All these statements were not in keeping with what the women felt needed to be done to run a home or bring up children. When it came to perception of differences between working mothers and fathers, women found stark differences, whereas the men thought there were not too many differences between the genders.

Conclusions

The sociocultural context, literature review, and FGD results from India suggest that WFC exists to a greater degree in the working woman than the working man. India is a secular state and straddles many cultures and religions and is home to vast economic, social, religious, and linguistic diversity. In this context the status of women has changed across history from an egalitarian society with equal status in ancient India to the current highly inegalitarian society due, in part, to various invasions over a period of time from different races and regions of the world. In contemporary India, despite a family-oriented culture and the availability of paid help, women in the workplace are struggling to handle both domestic and professional responsibilities. Women's advancement in their careers gets inhibited due to domestic responsibilities, forcing a lot of women to drop out of the workforce and the rest to make compromises on their career tracks. Age among women seemed to be a moderating factor, where older women were more inclined to believe that commitment to family hinders professional growth. The reality of working women bearing the responsibility of child care and elder care is echoed by men in discussions and at most times is accepted by women, albeit resentfully in the younger generation. With the men of the current generation helping in the home and with children's education, a significant area of concern for all parents in India, there is some small relief for the women—however, the ultimate responsibility of the domestic sphere and its allied responsibilities still rests primarily with the woman. Thus, despite the fast changing socio-psychological and economic profile of India, things haven't really changed when it comes to gender equality between working men and working women.

Future research on the work-family interface in India should focus on various issues that are unique to India. Researchers have not yet looked into the connections between the work-family behaviors of employees in lower and upper strata of the economy. A need exists to examine differences in WFC in these strata. Another area of differentiation is the organized and unorganized sector, since a large proportion of working women belong to the unorganized sector. WFC for men has also to be researched in more detail, an aspect largely unresearched thus far, with a focus needed on questions like "Do men attain work-life balance at the expense of women's work-life balance?" Another important question to be asked is "Do urban educated women attain work-life balance at the expense of low-income women's (maids') work-life balance?" The latter is an important area to be looked at since India has cheap uneducated labor that is exploited for and by dual-career couples. Since future research needs to be cognizant about the manner in which income inequalities in India affect work-life balance of all employees across the organized and unorganized sectors, more cross-disciplinary research work in the work-family field needs to be done. The economic status and disparity needs to be factored in more researches, and the ambit of work-family research needs to be broadened to include not just the urban educated.

To reduce WFC at national, regional, and organizational levels, policies and practices need to be developed to be more inclusive in their scope and keep the reality of India in mind. The current status is that though Indian organizations are more open to the idea of having more women at their top and senior management levels, the talent pool of women candidates at the top level is very shallow. The reasons are obvious. This sector understands, but turns a blind eye to, the fact that societal expectations and family responsibilities come in the way of the women professionals and their career decisions. Some men, too, are affected by WFC, which may be exhibited in health-related issues. Thus, organizations need to develop robust policies and make sure that these policies are translated into practice.

The approach to dealing with work and family issues in India is an indirect one and appears to be steeped in a patriarchal style of functioning. The assumption is that if the worker is male, WFC will be tackled as a health issue. With women it became an issue of dealing with family issues and allowing them flexibility to deal with work and family issues.

Women, until as recent as 1995, were not working late into the night or working night shifts in manufacturing or any other sectors. As per the Factories Act of 1948, women could not be employed on the night shift. However this has changed with the entry of the ITeS (Information Technology enabled Services) sector. The number of women who work in this sector and thereby work night shifts has tripled and led the Ministry of Labour and Employment of the government of India to make some amendments. Unfortunately, a lacuna exists in law which does not cover the right to shared family responsibilities, part-time workers, and domestic workers, even though India is a signatory to the Conventions of the International Labour Organization (Convention nos. 156 in 1981, 175 in 1994, and 177 in 1996, respectively). This is an area where extensive work needs to be done so that the requisite policy can be formulated.

India has been fairly progressive as far as its policies go. The MNCs brought with them their workplace family-friendly policies. The government of India has its own skewed, yet healthy, leave structure for child rearing and child care. Some Indian private companies, too, have some flexibility in their work hours. However, these are fragmented and do not cover the wider issue of WFC. The private sector must develop, as a policy, more paid maternity and child care leave, mirroring the healthy leave policy that the government of India has promulgated for its own employees. Thus, parental leave must be regularized and not be given on a case-to-case basis, as is the norm in many private sector organizations. It needs to be a right as per policy rather than a perk for performance. An act to prevent discrimination because of family responsibilities can be passed. Another act that needs to be developed is equal opportunity for both men and women to reconcile both work and family life along the lines of some Scandinavian countries. For a country that has limited professional help for elders and where old age homes are something people shun and look down upon, official leave and provisions for care of aged parents must be factored in while creating work-family policies. Instances where women and men can take career breaks must be looked into for greater work-family balance. Flextime and flexibility at work needs to be included in organizational policy and not left hanging in a vague space dependent on performance and team leads.

Last but not least, practitioners and researchers must keep in mind that the problem in reducing WFC in organizations is not limited to adding and improving policy. Emphasis must be laid on implementing these policies. Many of the existing laws lack effective implementation, as organizations find ingenious ways of circumventing them. For instance, employers bypass the legislation requiring them to provide child care facilities if 30 or more women are employed in the workplace by employing fewer than 30 women as permanent employees and the rest as part-time or contract labor. Another implicit organizational negative is holding back the men and women who avail themselves of work-family leave by taking them off the professional fast track. This serves to discourage men and women from using the family leave available to them.

Thus, India is still a long way from turning WFC into a strategic concern. Governmental, nongovernmental, and private organizations need to not only develop good policy, but also to create ways and means to ensure smooth and sure implementation of these policies, some of which are already progressive and timely. Lastly, new initiatives need to be carefully planned and must consider the nature of industry, profile of workforce, and the local culture and environment.

References

Aryee, S., Srinivas, E. S., & Tan, H. H. (2005). Rhythms of life: Antecedents and outcomes of work-family balance in employed parents. *Journal of Applied Psychology*, *90*(1), 132–146.

Baral, R., & Bhargava, S. (2009). Work-family enrichment as a mediator between organizational interventions for work-life balance and job outcomes. *Journal of Managerial Psychology*, *25*(3), 274–300. doi:10.1108/02683941011023749

Basham, A. L. (1954). *The wonder that was India: A survey of the history and culture of the Indian sub-continent before the coming of the Muslims*. London, UK: Sidgwick Jackson.

Bhalla, S., & Kaur, R. (2011). *Labour force participation of women in India: Some facts, some queries*. Working Paper No. 40. Asia Research Centre, London School of Economics and Political Science, London, UK. Retrieved from http://eprints.lse.ac.uk/38367/

Bharat, S. (1995). Attitude and sex-role perception among working couples in India. *Journal of Comparative Family Studies*, *26*(3), 371–388.

Bharat, S. (2000). On the periphery: The psychology of gender. In J. Pandey (Ed.), *Psychology in India revisited: Developments in the discipline*. New Delhi: Sage.

Bhatnagar, D., & Rajadhyaksha, U. (2001). Attitudes towards work and family roles and their implications for the career growth of women: A report from India. *Sex Roles, 45*(7–8), 549–565.

Buddhapriya, S. (2009). Work-family challenges and their impact on career decisions: A study of Indian women professionals. *Vikalpa, 34*(1), 31–45.

Census Survey of India 2011, Office of the Registrar General & Census Commissioner, Ministry of Home Affairs, New Delhi.

Central Service Leave Rules. http://epaper.timesofindia.com/Repository/ml.asp?Ref=QkdNSVIvMjAxMS8wNS8wOCNBcjAwNjAw&Mode=HTML

Chhokar, J. S. (2007). India: Diversity and complexity in action. In J. S. Chhokar, F. C. Brodbeck & R. J. House (Eds.), *Culture and leadership across the world: The GLOBE book of in-depth studies* (Vol. 2, pp. 971–1020). Mahwah, NJ; London: Lawrence Erlbaum.

Citigroup. (2011). *Citigroup Global Markets holdings incorporated annual report.* Retrieved from http://www.citigroup.com/citi/investor/quarterly/2012/ar11c_en.pdf.

Cooke, F. L., & Saini, D. S. (2010). Diversity management in India: A study of organizations in different ownership forms and industrial sectors. *Human Resource Management, 49*(3), 477–500.

Das, D., Dharwadkar, R., & Brandes, P. (2008). The importance of being 'Indian': Identity centrality and work outcomes in an off-shored call center in India. *Human Relations, 61*(11), 1499–1530. doi:10.1177/0018726708096636

Datta, V. (1999). *Child care in India: Issues and challenges for the 21st century.* Proceedings of the 7th Early Childhood Convention, Vol. 2, pp. 99–108. Nelson, New Zealand.

Desai, N. (1994). Research in women's studies in India: An overview. *Indian Journal of Social Sciences*, 7(3/4), 377–394.

Devi, R., Pruthi, R., & Pruthi, R. K. (Eds.). (2003). *Indian women: Present status and future prospects.* Jaipur, India: Mangal Deep Publications.

Ganesh, S., & Ganesh, M. P. (2014). Effects of masculinity-femininity on quality of work life. *Gender in Management: An International Journal, 29*(4), 229–253.

Goldman Sachs. (2003). *Investor relations and financials. Annual reports.* Retrieved from http://www.goldmansachs.com/investor-relations/financials/archived/annual-reports/2003-annual-report.html

Government of India. (1974). http://pldindia.org/wp-content/uploads/2013/04/Towards-Equality-1974-Part-1.pdf

India. (n.d.). In the World Bank. Retrieved January 19, 2017 from http://www.worldbank.org/en/country/india.

Jain, D., & Rajput, P. (Eds.). (2003). *Narratives from the women's studies family.* New Delhi, India: Sage.

John, M. E. (2011). Census 2011, Governing populations and the girl child. *Economic and Political Weekly, 46*(16), 10–12.

Kanungo, R., & Mendonca, M. (1994). Culture and performance improvement. *Productivity, 35*(4), 447–453.

Kapur, P. (1970). *Marriage and the working women in India.* New Delhi, India: Vikas Publications.

Krishna Raj, M. (1983). *Research on women and work in the seventies—Where do we go from here?* Bombay, India: Research Centre for Women's Studies, SNDT University.

Kumar, U. (1986). Indian women and work: A paradigm for research. *Psychological Studies, 31*(2), 147–160.

Lamb, S. (2007). Lives outside the family: Gender and the rise of elderly residences in India. *International Journal of Sociology of the Family, 33*(1), 43–61.

Machado, T., Sathyanarayanan, V., Bhola, P., & Kamath, K. (2013). Psychological vulnerability, burnout, and coping among employees of a business process outsourcing organization. *Industrial Psychiatry Journal, 22*(1), 26–31.

Ministry of Statistics and Programme Implementation, Government of India. (2010). "Infrastructure Statistics - 2010." Retrieved January 19, 2017 from http://mospi.nic.in/publication/infrastructure-statistics-2010

Narayana, G. (1982). Job analysis of workload assessment of female workers in India. *ASCI Journal of Management, 11*(2), 99–109.

NASSCOM. (2006). *Diversity and inclusivity summit.* Retrieved April 9, 2012, from http://www.nasscom.in/disummit/overview

NASSCOM. (2011). *HR survey of 2010–11.* Retrieved April 7, 2012, from http://epi.nasscom.in/upload/docs/annualreport_201011/NASSCOM_Annual_Report_2010–11.pdf.

Pal, S., & Saksvik, P. (2008). Work-family conflict and psychosocial work environment stressors as predictors of job stress in a cross-cultural study. *International Journal of Stress Management, 15*(1), 22–42.

Pande-Desai, T. (2000). *Organisational role stress and coping among dual career couples along the work family life cycle* (Unpublished Ph.D. dissertation). Department of Psychology, University of Delhi.

Parikh, I., & Shah, N. A. (1994). Women managers in transition: From homes to corporate offices. *The Indian Journal of Social Work, 55*(2), 143–160.

Parikh, P. P., & Sukhatme, S. P. (2004). Women engineers in India. *Economic and Political Weekly, 39*(2), 193–201.

Rajadhyaksha, U. (1996). *Work-family conflict across the work-family life cycle: A study of dual career couples* (Unpublished Ph.D. Dissertation). Indian Institute of Management, Ahmedabad.

Rajadhyaksha, U. (2004a). Work-family balance and dual career couples: What do organizations of the future need to know? In R. Padaki, N. M. Agarwal, C. Balaji, & G. Mahapatra (Eds.), *Emerging Asia: An HR agenda* (pp. 333–356). New Delhi: McGraw-Hill.

Rajadhyaksha, U. (2004b). *Sources of non-institutional support and work-family conflict in India.* Paper presented at the International Congress of Cross-Cultural Psychology, Xi'an, China, August 2–6.

Rajadhyaksha, U. (2012). Work-life balance in South East Asia: The Indian experience. *South Asian Journal of Global Business Research, 1*(1), 108–127.

Rajadhyaksha, U., & Bhatnagar, D. (2000). Life role salience: A study of dual career couples. *Human Relations, 53*(4), 489–511.

Rajadhyaksha, U., & Pande-Desai, T. (2006). *Antecedents of work-family conflict in India.* Paper presented at the International Congress of Applied Psychology, Athens, Greece.

Rajadhyaksha, U., & Ramadoss, K. (2013). Work-family conflict in India: Test of a causal model. In D. M. Pestonjee & S. Pandey (Eds.), *Stress and work: Perspectives on understanding and managing stress* (pp. 129–155). New Delhi, India: Sage.

Rajadhyaksha, U., & Smita, S. (2004). Tracing a timeline for work and family research in India. *Economic and Political Weekly of India, 39*(17), 1674–1680.

Rajadhyaksha, U., & Velgach, S. (2009). *Gender, gender-role ideology and work-family conflict in India.* Paper presented at the Annual Meeting of the Academy of Management, Chicago, IL.

Ramadoss, K. (2013a). Availability and use of work-family policies by call center employees in India. *International Journal of Business and Social Science, 4*(9), 29–36.

Ramadoss, K. (2013b). Work stress, work-family conflict and health: A multi-level perspective. In D. M. Pestonjee and Satish Pandey (Eds.), *Stress and work: Perspectives on understanding and managing stress* (pp. 156–179). New Delhi, India: Sage.

Ramadoss, K., & Rajadhyaksha, U. (2012). Gender difference in commitment to roles, work-family conflict and social support. *Journal of Social Sciences, 33*(2), 227–233.

Ramu, G. N. (1987). Indian husbands: Their role perception and performance in single- and dual-earner families. *Journal of Marriage and the Family, 49*(4), 903–915.

Ramu, G. N. (1989). *Women, work and marriage in urban India: A study of dual and single-earner couples.* New Delhi, India: Sage.

Ranganathan, A., & Kuruvilla, S. (2008). Employee turnover in the business process outsourcing industry in India. In D. Jemielniak & J. Kociatkiewicz (Eds.), *Management practices in high-tech environments* (pp. 110–132). Hershey, PA: Ideas Group.

Rani, K. (1976). *Role conflict in working women.* New Delhi, India: Chetana Publications.

Rani, V., & Khandelwal, P. (1992). Family environment and interpersonal behaviour: A comparative study of dual career and single career families. *The Indian Journal of Social Work, 53*(2), 232–243.

Rao, M. H. (1990). Employment of wife and husband's participation in housework. *The Indian Journal of Social Work, 51*(3), 447–456.

Rathi, N., & Barath, M. (2013). Work-family conflict and job and family satisfaction. *Equality, Diversity and Inclusion: An International Journal, 32*(4), 438–454.

Roy, P. K. (Ed.) (2000). *The Indian Family: Change and Persistence.* Delhi: Gyan Publications.

Sekaran, U. (1982). An Investigation of the career salience of men and women in dual-career families, *Journal of Vocational Behavior, 20*(1), 111–119.

Shukla, A. (1987). Decision making in single and dual career families in India. *Journal of Marriage and the Family, 49*(3), 621–629. doi:10.2307/352207

Shukla, A., & Kapoor, M. (1990). Sex-role identity, marital power, and marital satisfaction among middle class couples in India. *Sex Roles, 22*(11/12), 693–706.

Sonpar, S., & Kapur, R. (2001). Non-conventional indicators: Gender disparities under structural reforms. *Economic and Political Weekly, 36*(1), 66–78.

Sreedharan, D. (2013). A labour of love. *The Hindu*, Sunday Magazine, November 3.

Srivastava, K., & Srivastava, A. K. (1989). Job stress, marital adjustment, social relation and mental health of dual career and traditional couple: A comparative study. *Perspectives in Psychological Researches, 8*(1), 28–33.

Thapar, R. (1990). *A history of India.* London, UK: Penguin.

Towards Equality: Report of the Committee on the Status of Women in India, Department of Social Welfare, Government of India, 1974, New Delhi.

Unwalla, J. M. (1977). *Beyond the household walls—A study of women executives at work and at home* (Unpublished Ph.D. Dissertation). Tata Institute of Social Sciences (TISS), Mumbai.

Valk, R., & Srinivasan, V. (2013). Work-family balance of Indian women software professionals: A qualitative study. *IIMB Management Review, 23*(1), 39–50.

Vindhya, U. (2007). Quality of women's lives in India: Some findings from two decades of psychological research on gender. *Feminism & Psychology, 17*(3), 337–356. doi:10.1177/0959353507079088

Yadav, S. (2013). Why India's elderly are moving to retirement homes. *BBC News India*, July 4. Retrieved from October 9, 2014, http://www.bbc.com/news/world-asia-india-23176206.

10

THE WORK-FAMILY INTERFACE IN INDONESIA

Artiawati

Introduction

The headline in *Kompas*, the most popular daily newspaper in Indonesia, with the picture of Karen Agustiawan, the President Director of PT. Pertamina, the prominent gasoline and oil company owned by the government of Indonesia, attracted my attention and inspired me to start writing this chapter. Karen looked so sad reaching her hands out to her employees, who also looked very sad wanting to give her a farewell handshake. Under the picture there was a note saying:

> "*Karen mengundurkan diri per 1 Oktober 2014 dengan alasan ingin mengurusi keluarga dan meniti karier sebagai pengajar*"
>
> (Karen voluntarily quit as of 1 October 2014 due to her desire to care for family and to start a career as a lecturer).

Karen, 55 years old and a mother of three children, is a very famous woman in Indonesia. She was the first woman President Director of PT. Pertamina. Since she started her job as a director in the year 2009, she impressed many people, not only in Indonesia, but beyond, especially in leading giant gasoline and oil business corporations. Karen led PT. Pertamina to outstanding performance in many aspects.

Karen successfully acquired some famous oil companies in the world and brought PT. Pertamina into the group of the 500 richest companies in the world. PT. Pertamina is in the rank of 123, beating PepsiCo in the rank of 137, Unilever in the rank of 140, and Google in the rank of 162 (Wicaksono, 2014, reporting for *Liputan 6*, a famous portal newspaper in Indonesia, on 30 September 2014, 11.37).

Even though many rumors were heard about Karen's resignation from the position of the President Director of PT. Pertamina, the fact of quitting jobs by women in Indonesia due to family reasons had always been accepted and even respected. In Wicaksono's report it was said that the Minister of State Owned Enterprises (*Badan Usaha Milik Negara*/BUMN), Dahlan Iskan, could not refuse Karen's resignation because she had already asked for it for several times and was willing to focus on her family life.

Success in a career does not seem meaningful when it is not aligned with success in family. A woman who prioritizes her family life is highly respected in Indonesia. It seems that a single type of a woman well accepted by the society in Indonesia is the one who is "married, has a child (children), and stays at home." If you happen not to meet one or any of these criteria, people often bother you with questions like: "Why don't you get married?"; "Why are you not pregnant yet?"; and "Why do you have to work? What are you looking for?" Being a working woman seems to be not fully appreciated, especially when it is not accompanied by success in family life.

My curiosity to study the work-family interface actually started to emerge in 1993 when I first got a full-time job as an academic employee in the University of Surabaya, where I still work. To become permanent staff, I had to pass a one-year probation period, in which I could not take a leave, even for a day. At that time, I had just given birth to my first daughter; therefore, my husband and I decided to move to a new house which was closer to my workplace. In short, my husband took a leave, and my mother-in-law came from Bandung, a city in West Java 750 km away from my place, and helped us with arranging the house. One day when I had just arrived to the office, my superior called me. I rushed in to her office and found myself in front of the Dean (female) and the Vice Dean (male). I was feeling uncomfortable seeing their firm expressions, while wondering what mistakes I had made. The Dean said:

"I heard you're moving your house . . . and your husband and your mother-in-law are arranging that matter. I disagree with your attitude; it is very bad for a woman to do that."

The Vice Dean, who had a main duty as the Human Resource Manager then said:

"Now you go home and take your responsibility to care for your family."

(I said I was still on probation), but then he said: "Don't worry . . . I allow you to go home and I guarantee that it will not be a problem for your employment."

While going home, I kept wondering why the dedication of a woman to her work seemed to be not respected, whereas dedication to her family was expected. Just before writing this part, I checked my son's bag (he's nine years old, a fourth grader in the primary school). He had a homework assignment for the subject of *Bahasa Indonesia* (Indonesian Language) about the rights and responsibilities of a mother and a father. It is written in the handbook that the rights of mothers and fathers are the same, and those are: being loved and being respected by the children. However, regarding the responsibilities, there were different statements that came in different numbers. The responsibility of fathers was only one, that was "to work," while the responsibilities of mothers were three: "take care of family, love children, and look after children."

Traditional gender-role ideology and patriarchal culture have been deep-rooted in Indonesian society and are being taught to younger generations through the formal education system. Traditional gender-role ideology and patriarchal culture play a vital role in understanding WFC issues in Indonesia. Furthermore, as a collectivist culture, understanding the individual life of an Indonesian cannot be separated from an understanding of the societal belief systems influencing the belief system of that individual. I am often annoyed when men say: "A woman works just to avoid responsibility of doing domestic chores." In addition, I often hear a husband warn his working wife saying: "You may work, but don't forget about your responsibility to take care of the family." Juggling the demands of work and family often results in WFC.

This chapter describes the unique dynamics of the work-family interface occurring in Indonesia. The socioeconomic and cultural context of Indonesia and the summary of research on work and family issues in the country are provided in the beginning. The results of the focus group discussion with 10 Indonesian women workers are presented later, and finally, conclusions about the unique dynamics of work-family interface are discussed.

Socioeconomic and Cultural Context of Indonesia

Indonesia is a country in Southeast Asia, located between the Indian and Pacific Oceans. Having the total area of 1,904,569 km^2, Indonesia is now the sixteenth largest country in the world. Furthermore, there are 17,508 islands in Indonesia, out of which only 6,000 islands are utilized. This makes Indonesia the only archipelago country in the world. Indonesia is divided into 33 provinces with two special regions and one special capital city area.

In 2003 Indonesia's population was 220 million, comprising 51% female and 49% male. The latest population census in the year 2010 identified the number of population growth as 237,641,326 and the composition of female and male as 49.8% and 50.2%, respectively. Even though the number of female citizens decreased, the composition of male and female citizens stayed relatively equal. Indonesia is fourth among the most populous countries in the world. In terms of age distribution, the majority of the population is 15–64 years old (66%), and the remaining population is 10–14 years old (28.1%) or above 65 years old (6%) (*Kementerian Pemberdayaan Perempuan dan Perlindungan Anak*, 2012a).

The majority of people in Indonesia (60%) live on Java Island, which is relatively small (138,794 km^2) compared to some other bigger islands such as Kalimantan

(539,460 km^2), Sumatra (443,066 km^2), and Papua (421,982 km^2). Indonesians with the Javanese ethnic background are around 41% (around 100 million) of the total population. The influence of the Javanese culture, which is represented by beliefs of patriarchy and traditional gender-role ideology can be seen in many aspects of life of the Indonesian people. Not only Javanese, but most ethnicities in Indonesia, have adopted the same beliefs in different magnitudes. However, there is an ethnic group in Indonesia that is well known for adopting a matriarchy—the Minangkabau of West Sumatra. However, matriarchy in the Minangkabau ethnic group mainly encompasses two matters: the marriage process and inheritance issues. In most ethnic groups in Indonesia, the groom and his family propose to the bride. Conversely, in the Minangkabau ethnic group, the bride and her family should propose to the groom. Furthermore, in most ethnic groups in Indonesia men get a larger inheritance than women, while in Minangkabau women get the bigger portion.

Although Indonesia has more than 1,000 ethnic groups and more than 700 local languages, it has one national language, which is called Bahasa Indonesia (Indonesian language). Bahasa Indonesia was declared an official language of Indonesia on the 28 October 1928 in Sumpah Pemuda (Youth Pledge), at the Indonesian nationalist youth congress. Since then, every 28th of October the Indonesian people celebrate Youth Pledge Day to remember that we have one nation, one language, and one motherland—Indonesia. Most Indonesians speak Bahasa Indonesia more fluently than other local or foreign languages.

The Indonesian basic law and philosophy require all Indonesians to believe in God. Six religions are practiced in Indonesia: Islam, Catholicism, Protestant Christianity, Buddhism, Hinduism, and Confucianism. Most citizens of Indonesia are Muslims, despite a significant change in the last two decades. In the 1980s the number of Muslims in Indonesia was above 90%, which decreased to 88.2% in the year 2000, and 85.1% in the year 2010. Religious life matters are arranged by the Ministry of Religion. However, as Islam in Indonesia has various streams, Majelis Ulama Indonesia (MUI/Indonesia Ulema Council), which comprises the representatives of various Muslim groups in Indonesia, plays a role in advising the Muslim community on existing issues by producing fatwa (legal opinion of qualified jurist pertaining to Islamic law) to avoid conflict among the streams.

Indonesia is still considered a developing country. Data from the Indonesian Statistic Body shows that GNP per capita in the year 2000 was Rp. 6,325,722, which increased in the year 2010 to Rp. 29,762,690, and in the year 2013 to Rp. 35,378,758. In the period between 2000 and 2010 the currency exchange rate was relatively stable (1 USD = 9,000 rupiahs); however, in the year 2013 the currency rate changed to 1 USD = 12,000 rupiahs, and remains relatively stable up to now.

The economic growth rate in Indonesia was increasing every year in the last decade. From 4.8% in the year 2000 to 6.1% in the year 2010. In the year 2010 economic growth occurred in all sectors; the highest growth was in the communication and transportation sectors (13.5%) and the lowest in the agricultural sector (2.9%). The economic growth rate stayed relatively stable at around 6% until 2012 (the pick number was 6.33%); however, for the last two years it has been decreasing (as low as 5.21% in the year 2014).

As an agricultural country, employment in Indonesia is predominantly provided by the agricultural sector. However, in the years 2000–2010 there was a significant decrease, from 45.3% to 38.1%. A slight decrease also occurred in the manufacturing sector, from 13.0% to 12.8%. Conversely, an increase in employment numbers occurred in other areas, such as mining and quarrying (0.5%–1.2%); construction (3.9%–5.2%); electricity, gasoline, and water (0.1%–0.2%); communication and transportation (5.1%–5.2 %); finance, insurance, real estate, and business services (1.0–1.6%); and personal, social, and community services (10.7%–14.7%).

Data from ILO Indonesia (2013) shows that most of the workforce in Indonesia was from three islands—Java, Bali, and Sumatera (in the middle to the west part of Indonesia)—accounting for 81.2% in the year 2012. Employment is still not well distributed, as the eastern part is still poor. However, the unemployment rate has tended to decrease over the last decade, from 9.06% in the year 2002 to 6.4% in the year 2012.

The majority of the workforce in Indonesia still works in the informal sectors. Workforce in the informal sector from the year 2001 to 2009 was relatively stable, accounting for 61%–66%. However, this number decreased for three years after, to 59% in the year 2010, 54.7% in the year 2011, and 53.6% in the year 2012. A significant decrease in numbers occurred in the female workforce. In the year 2001 the share of women who worked in the informal sector was 67% and of men 57%, while in the year 2012 it changed to 57% for women and to 51.2% for men.

Participation in the labor force in the year 2003 was 43.5% for women and 70% for men. This increased in the year 2010 and became 51.76% for women and 83.76% for men. Nevertheless, there are still not many women in managerial positions. The only woman governor existed in the year 2007. In the year 2011 there were only 16 female mayors out of a total of 497 mayors in Indonesia. Even though the number of women in managerial positions is growing, as in 2003 it was only around 1.2%, the number of woman managers is still low, around 3% in the year 2012. A significant move in this direction was made by the seventh president of Indonesia, Joko Widodo, who was inaugurated in October 2014. Eight female ministers now assist him. Previously, in the period of 2009–2014, there were only four female ministers out of a total of 34 ministers in Indonesia (Kementerian Pemberdayaan Perempuan dan Perlindungan Anak, 2012b).

The Republic of Indonesia has been independent since the year 1945. Throughout the era of independence, the most tragic situation happened in the year of 1998, in which the Soeharto (the second president) regime fell after 32 years of Indonesia under his command. Accompanied by the worst monetary crisis, in that period Indonesia was in the hardest political and economic situation. Nevertheless, since then the more democratic era of Indonesia began.

All Indonesian laws refer to the 1945 Constitution Basic Law and State Philosophy *Pancasila* (5 Basics), which are: (1) believe in the One Supreme God, (2) fair and civilized humanity, (3) unity of Indonesia, (4) deliberative democracy, and (5) social justice. These laws and philosophies guarantee equal rights to Indonesian citizens in the fields of education, law, health, political participation, and employment. Since the year 1983, Indonesia has had the Ministry of Women role arrangement, which, in the year 1999, after the Soeharto regime era ended, changed into the Ministry of Women Empowerment. As of 2009 the name has been modified to the Ministry of Women Empowerment and Children Protection. Nonetheless, inequality is still present in many sectors. Particularly in employment, women are still underpaid. Men can be paid as much as three times more than women.

The Indonesian law on workforce no. 13/2003 states that working more than 48 hours/week is excessive. However, data from the ILO (2012) found that in the year 2012, 55.96% of the Indonesian workforce worked for more than 40 hours/week (29.4% worked for 40–48 hours/week, 15.09% worked for 49–59 hours/week, and 11.44% worked for more than 60 hours/week).

Economic reasons are a predominating factor for women to work in Indonesia. As a developing country, poverty is still experienced by 11.37% of the population, which makes it understandable that meeting their financial needs is challenging for many families. *"Kemiskinan berwajah perempuan"* (Poverty is represented by a woman's face). This statement is known in Indonesia to mean that when there is poverty, there is a woman making sacrifices, for example, going abroad as a migrant laborer.

As a country with highly traditional gender-role ideology and patriarchal culture, women in Indonesia are actually expected to stay at home, doing domestic chores and taking care of children. Having permission and support from their husbands is not that easy for many Indonesian women. When support is given, it is mostly because there is no other choice for the family to survive. The religious factor plays an important role in understanding the beliefs of Indonesian people in terms of banning women from work. As a Muslim majority country, people in Indonesia are very influenced by Islamic values, which support traditional gender-role attitudes. Indonesia is also a collectivistic culture, where family is a priority adopted by male and female workers (Artiawati, 2012).

The size of a family tends to be bigger after the fall of the Soeharto regime. In his period of presidency the family planning program was tightly controlled, as each family was suggested to have no more than two children. Nowadays, fewer people participate in the family planning program, although the mean size of a family in the year 2013 was still 3.9.

Research on the Work-Family Interface in Indonesia

It is not easy to find literature about work-family (W-F) life in the Indonesian context, especially any that was published internationally. However, research at the graduate and postgraduate levels pertaining to the W-F interface has been growing, and that helps us better understand the dynamics of WFC in Indonesia.

The first interesting research about working women I found a long time ago in the works of my lecturer, Dr. Parwati Soepangat, when I was an undergraduate student. Soepangat (1986), for her doctoral dissertation, conducted a study on 370 working women in Java. Results from this study showed that the level of education had no impact on self-awareness of women's empowerment due to the pervasiveness of sociocultural background. Furthermore, having a higher level of education did not influence the traditional gender-role ideology adopted by the women. Working women with different levels of formal educational background in this study adopted traditional gender-role beliefs.

Ten years later, Nainggolan, Candra, and Widyastuti (1996) conducted a study on four working women in Yogjakarata. The participants of this study had quit their jobs after delivering their first children. Causes for quitting were due to the WFC they experienced, a lack of support for child care, and their religious beliefs, which suggested that it was better for women to stay home and care for children.

Dewi, Artiawati, and Suvianita (2007) conducted a study of the dynamics of WFC among teachers. Using a qualitative approach and in-depth interviews, this study aimed at revealing the sources of WFC, the consequences of WFC, and the strategies to handle WFC experienced by the teachers. Participants of this study were six teachers in Surabaya (three women and three men).

Guru is an Indonesian term for teacher. *Guru iku digugu omongane lan di tiru kelakoane*, in Javanese language, means that the speech of a teacher is always copied, and the behavior of a teacher is always an example (model) for everybody, particularly for the student. In the Dutch colonial era, Indonesian people were proud to be called *guru* (teacher), as it was equal to *priyayi* (aristocrat). However, in this 21st century, most people think that the career of a teacher is not very promising, and salaries are low. Suroso (2002) reported that there still were primary school teachers receiving salaries of Rp. 94,000 (10 USD) per month, which was under the minimum regional wage in Jakarta, which was Rp. 320,000 (35 USD) at that time. Therefore, to cover the daily expenses of a family, most teachers, to find additional income, gave private classes to students. This situation led to work interference with family (WIF) conflict, as the time meant for family was spent for work after school time. Another source of WIF conflict included work overload, especially for teachers with structural positions. The teachers complained about occupying these positions as they did not receive more salary for undertaking the job. Family interference with work (FIW) conflict was also experienced by teachers and was caused by several factors, such as demands to care for children, especially those under five years old and teenagers, responsibilities to do domestic chores, and social activities for the family. A domestic helper was also a source of strain, as the attitude and character of the helper did not always match with teachers' expectations.

The impact of the WFC experienced by the teachers was mainly expressed in losing concentration at work due to physical fatigue after working hard the day before. Coming late to school and withdrawal from work due to sickness were also impacts of WFC in the work domain. On the other hand, impacts on the family domain were complaints from the family members (spouse and children) because of the lack of time for family, physical problems (e.g., high blood pressure), being preoccupied by concerns for family and children, and feeling worried about the condition of the children.

Coping strategies applied to handle WFC were: getting support from parents and using domestic helpers. However, most respondents only used support from a domestic helper when their children were ages 2–11 years. Above 11 years old, children could be more independent and could even be a source of support themselves. They could help parents to sweep and clean the floor, and wash clothes using a washing machine. The financial issue also became a reason to stop using a domestic helper, as the expenses for raising elder kids grew, especially for their education.

Research about WFC in Indonesia has been conducted by researchers from various fields. Alteza and Hidayati (2009), researchers in the Economic and Social Sciences Department of State University of Yogjakarta, employed a case study approach utilizing in-depth interviews and participative observation. They conducted an interesting study on six working women in Yogjakarta, Indonesia. They investigated the sources and impact of WFC and coping strategies used to reduce WFC. Results from the study found that the sources of WFC were divided into areas of family and work. Sources coming from family included: a nonsupportive husband, difficulties managing children, nonavailability of a domestic helper, the role of a single parent, too many family demands, the responsibility to manage domestic chores, and demands for involvement in social activities.

Sources of WFC coming from the work context included: frequent schedules of meetings and supervision in the field, long distance from home to work (also problems of traffic jams), long work hours, work overload, nonconducive work environments, work overtime, and duty to work out of town.

The impacts of WFC were divided into three domains, encompassing impacts on the individual, family, and work domain. Impacts on individuals included: stress, lower concentration, over-sensitivity, gloominess, irritability, health disturbances (e.g., headache, tight muscles, vertigo), feeling sick and tired, limited interaction with spouse that led to misunderstandings, lack of intense kinship relationships, child becoming closer to the domestic helper, and speech problems of the child. Furthermore, impacts on the family domain included: learning difficulties for children, uncontrolled emotions, conflict among family members, frequent anger toward the domestic helper and children, arguing with extended family (parents) about the ways to teach children, children becoming spoiled, limited time for family gatherings, and insufficient time to care for children. In addition, impacts on the work domain were stress, low concentration on work, low performance, inhibition of finishing tasks, and not focusing at work.

Coping strategies to reduce WFC were divided into two types, which were emotion-based and problem-based. Among emotion-based strategies, it was found that working women more frequently engaged in religious activities, avoided conflict with extended family (parent), shared problems with friends, relaxed in a beauty salon, engaged in hobbies, and engaged in recreation activities out of town with family. On the other hand, problem-based coping strategies utilized included making rules in the family, employing a domestic helper and a driver, maintaining good communication with a spouse, trying to be firm with the children, asking for support from the workplace, using outside family services (food catering and laundry), work scheduling, daily scheduling and prioritizing, consulting with an expert counselor, doing karaoke with the family, asking for support from the extended family, asking for support from coworkers, and spoiling kids at holiday times.

Kesumaningsari and Simarmata (2014), researchers in the faculty of psychology and faculty of medicine at Udayana University, Bali, conducted research to examine the correlation between WFC and work engagement. Participants were 121 working women in the banking sector who were 22–55 years old. Results from this study showed that there was a significant negative correlation between WFC and work engagement—the higher the WFC, the lower work engagement and vice versa. However, the level of WFC tended to be low.

The Balinese people have some different characteristics compared to the majority of Indonesians. Unlike the majority of Indonesians, who are Muslim, most Balinese are Hindu. Furthermore, Balinese women are commonly working in public; many of them are even breadwinners. The role of Balinese women is very complex. Upon getting married, a Balinese woman automatically becomes *krama adat istri* (women members of *desa adat)*custom village, in which Balinese people group). The intensity of custom ceremonies of Balinese Hindi is quite high, wherein married women have to fully participate as representatives of their families. All preparation and ceremonial activities become the responsibility of Balinese women, especially preparing *sesaji* (gift for God). Responsibility for domestic chores and as *krama adat istri* cannot be avoided by working mothers in Bali. Social sanctions will be applied if the working mothers do not meet those responsibilities. A Balinese woman will be seen as *luh luu* (misbehaved and rubbish women) by the society if she does not fulfill her domestic responsibilities, even if she has a high-level position in the workplace (Suatha, cited in Kesumaningsari & Simarmata, in press). Similarly, if Balinese women are often not present at custom/religious activities and ceremonies, they have to pay fines and will be alienated by the society (Saskara, Pudjihardjo, Maskie, & Suman, cited in Kesumaningsari & Simarmata, 2014).

High demands from the family domain, which create WFC, can be met by Balinese women using social support. The collectivist culture, which is present in the Balinese society, facilitates finding support for child care and doing domestic chores for Balinese working mothers. Husbands and extended family in Bali can be relatively easily asked to provide emotional and/or instrumental support. Received social support can lower the level of workload, and therefore reduce WFC. WFC, which tended to be low in this study, may also be influenced by the status of its participants, which was 90% staff. The work demands of staff are not as high as those of managers (Kesumaningsari & Simarmata, 2014).

Desnawati (2008), the first student in the Master of Psychology Program, University of Surabaya, who did her master's thesis about W-F life found some interesting results. The study was aimed at improving the W-F balance of employees of the University of Surabaya. Desnawati first did an assessment of the conditions of employees, before creating intervention programs. She applied the qualitative as well as the quantitative approach to collect the data. She first conducted a focus group discussion with eight employees (six men and two women). She found that even though the participants expressed their ideas in different statements when asked about ideas of work and family, all could be summarized in one idea—that they worked for their families. They were aware that spending time for work would reduce time available for family; however, all work activities and results were for the continuity of the family life. Although all respondents felt that on the weekdays they spent more time on work activities than on family activities, they tried to have time for families during weekends.

It was interesting that when asked about WIF conflict, they could identify the source of WIF conflict, which was mostly long work hours. However, when they were asked about FIW conflict, at first they expressed ideas such as: "I don't feel so . . . in principle, there is none . . . family interferes with work . . . as a matter of fact, family supports work." "For me . . . family never disturbs work."

But then a male respondent said that he felt preoccupied and could not concentrate when his child was sick. His wife was taking care of the child, but often contacted him while his child was sick. Female respondents got support from their extended families (the grandmothers) for taking care of children while the mothers worked. In general, the respondents said that they received full support from (extended) families, therefore they seldom experienced FIW conflict. The findings of the qualitative approach can complement and give clues to understanding the results from the quantitative approach.

Of 509 employees who were married with/without child(ren), 86 became participants (24 women and 62 men) for the quantitative study. Desnawati (2008) examined the roles of WFC and W-F guilt in predicting job satisfaction, family satisfaction, and life satisfaction. WFC was found to be a significant predictor of job satisfaction and family satisfaction. However, only family satisfaction, and not job satisfaction, was a predictor of life satisfaction. Furthermore, although WIF guilt was a significant predictor of job satisfaction and family satisfaction, FIW guilt predicted neither job satisfaction nor family satisfaction. Most respondents had low levels of WFC (only 2.3% respondents had high WFC), because most respondents received social support, especially from their families, which could reduce WFC.

A study about WFC and social support was also done by Leofianti (2013). She conducted a study on 70 nurses to find correlation between social support and WFC. Social support in her study came from three sources: superior, coworker, and husband. Leofianti found that nurses in Yogjakarta, Indonesia, experienced WFC, both WIF and FIW. In her preliminary study, she found a nurse, namely Mawar (42 years old, work experience 17 years), who experienced WIF conflict because of the fixed shift schedule imposed by the management of the hospital. Mawar said: "I felt annoyed because if there was a family gathering, I could not make it because I had to stand by in the hospital. The schedule for shift work was arranged by the hospital management, I could not choose." On the other hand, FIW conflict in Leofianti's study occurred due to problems with child care. Siti (35 years old, 10 years of work experience) said: "I really wanted to rush home when my child was sick. I had no heart . . . if I left my child only with *'mbah' nya* (the kid's grandmother)."

Surprisingly, Leofianti (2013) found there was no correlation between social support and WFC. However, some interesting results showed that WFC experienced by the participants tended to be low, while social support received tended to be high. In addition, the location of the hospital where the participants worked was different from the preliminary study. The location for the preliminary study was in Yogjakarta city (urban), while the actual study was carried out in Bantul (a rural part of Yogjakarta). Demands from work were relatively low, as the hospital was in the rural area. Furthermore, the hospital in Bantul was more flexible in arranging work schedules. The hospital in Bantul had a system that enabled nurses to take leaves without jeopardizing the schedule. There were some nurses who only worked when the nurse in charge took a long leave, such as a maternity leave.

Collectivism was also strongly seen in Bantul society. The extended family could not only be asked for help for undertaking domestic chores, but also neighbors could provide support, particularly in child care. In addition, when we look into the belief system of Javanese (Yogjakarta is part of Java), it is known that the Javanese adopt the philosophy of *nrimo ing pandum*, which means "always accept every condition through feeling blessed." The study also found that there were different levels of WFC experienced by junior and senior nurses. Senior nurses had higher levels of WFC (particularly strain-based WIF conflict) than junior nurses. This could be caused by the different workloads of senior and junior nurses. Many senior nurses also occupied managerial positions. Furthermore, doctors preferred to be assisted by senior nurses, as they were more skillful and the nurses were reluctant to refuse their requests. Javanese people are also known to have personal characters such as *sungkanan* and/or *ewuh pakewuh* (hesitation to refuse/to frankly speak about feelings, also could be said as less assertive). Furthermore, senior nurses had to also teach junior nurses, and they all too often felt annoyed when working with unskilled coworkers. All this increased their workload and strain.

To more comprehensively examine the antecedents and outcomes of WFC, Artiawati (2009) conducted a study with the Project 3535 data from Indonesia using the model proposed by Aycan (2006), in which work and family support and work and family demands play a role as antecedents for WFC. On the other hand, negative work, family, and life outcomes are consequences of WFC. The study was done using 268 workers (150 women and 118 men) from education, health, manufacturing, and finance sectors. The results of this study were different from Aycan's study, in which the model fit the Turkish sample. For the Indonesian sample the model did not meet the criterion of goodness of fit. However, some interesting findings could be seen through the dynamics of the results. Work and family support were significantly associated with work and family demands; however, work and family demands were not significantly associated with WFC. Furthermore, WFC was significantly associated with negative work and family outcomes. Nevertheless, similar to Desnawati (2008), life outcomes were only associated with family outcomes.

Rajadyaksa, Huang, and Artiawati (2011) also used the data from Project 3535 to examine the model of antecedents and consequences of WFC in three countries—India, Taiwan, and Indonesia. Gender-role ideology (GRI) and work and family overload played a role as antecedents for WFC, while work and family guilt played a role as the consequence of WFC. Three different samples, 561 Indians, 281 Taiwanese, and 306 Indonesians, participated in this study. Results from this study showed that all the path coefficients in the model were in the hypothesized direction for the three countries, indicating that GRI predicted WFC in the same manner among the three Asian countries. More traditional GRI was associated with higher W-F demands, higher WFC, and higher W-F guilt.

Results did not vary for men and women within the three countries; however, some specific dynamics in each country could be identified. In Taiwan and Indonesia, higher work demands (overload) did not significantly increase W-F guilt, which could be explained by work and family demands (overload), both being perceived as part of the responsibility toward family. Nevertheless, unlike India and Taiwan, for Indonesia traditional GRI was not associated with higher W-F overload. The role of social support, which is relatively easy to get in a collectivist culture such as in Indonesia, needs to be considered to understand this result. Social support can significantly reduce W-F overload (Artiawati, 2009). Furthermore, as mentioned in Leofianti (2013), the acceptance attitude of Indonesians may have influence so that work overload is seen as something to be accepted and feel blessed with, also taking traditional gender orientation for granted. Research from Artiawati (2012) can explain the dynamics occurring among Indonesians more clearly.

Artiawati (2012) examined the model of antecedents and consequences of WFC on 360 journalists (100 women and 254 men, 6 missing) in six provinces located in Java and Bali. The following were considered as antecedents of WFC: GRI, work and family role overload, social support (from superior and spouse), and personality (Big Five). On the other hand, work and family guilt, and psychological well-being were consequences of WFC. Results from this study represent the uniqueness of Indonesian culture, which is strongly influenced by patriarchal beliefs and high collectivism.

Using path analysis, the model met the criterion of the goodness of fit, where GRI, W-F overload, social support, and personality were the antecedents of WFC, while W-F guilt and psychological well-being were the outcomes of WFC. Furthermore, this study showed traditional GRI was not significantly associated with role overload and WFC. In addition, support from the spouse and superior were high. Triandis, Bontempo, Villareal, Asai, and Lucca (1988) mention that the psychological level of allocentrism, as the dimension of collectivism, is positively correlated with social support; therefore, in the collectivist society like Indonesia, support is relatively easy to find. However, this study showed that while support from a spouse could effectively reduce family role overload, support from a superior could not reduce work role overload. Journalists in managerial positions tended to have higher work role overload and needed support more from coworkers (for coordination) and subordinates (for doing tasks related to reporting and editing processes). As coworkers could not well coordinate and subordinates did not meet deadlines, journalists in managerial positions tended to take over their tasks, which made them work overtime or take work home. This condition caused WIF conflict.

Agreeableness was the only trait that was significantly correlated with WIF conflict. The correlation was positive, which meant that higher agreeableness was associated with higher WIF conflict experienced by the respondents. Lack of assertiveness, difficulty to refuse, and difficulty to express disagreement are representing the agreeableness trait. Workers, especially the managers (editors), were less assertive in refusing work overload, therefore they were in the end taking too many responsibilities. In family domain, the only trait significantly associated with FIW conflict was neuroticism. The correlation was in the positive direction, which means the higher neuroticism, the higher the FIW conflict experienced. Family is the primary concern of Indonesian life.

The meaning and appreciation of traditional gender-role ideology by male and female workers in Indonesia may be different. However, both male and female workers experienced WFC. Even though in this study both genders experienced low WFC, WFC in men was slightly higher than it was among women. It was almost similar to the condition in India, wherein female workers had prepared themselves for juggling many tasks (due to the belief system about women's duties), while male workers were not prepared to deal with the complexity of W-F life (Desai, 2005).

Artiawati (2012) also conducted a qualitative study conducting three sessions of focus group discussions with six journalists (four women, two men) in Bandung (west Java), three journalists (two women, one man) in Yogjakarta (near central Java), three journalists (four women, one man) in Bali; and seven interview sessions with journalists (three women, four men) representing all six provinces. Of the male journalists involved in the FGD and interviews, only two felt that women should work. Both of them had working wives. Another three journalists said it was fine for women to work, but their wives were not working women. One male journalist firmly disagreed with women working. He said: "It is so sad for her children if she works." However, this journalist had a wife working as a nurse. The reason why his wife worked was because of the financial demands of family, which could not be fulfilled if he were the only one who worked in the family. From these results, it seems that women in Indonesia are expected to play a role in the domestic domain more than in the public domain.

Triandis et al. (1988) mention,

"Conformity may occur more frequently in collectivist cultures when the norms are clear, and sanctions are likely to be imposed for deviant behavior."

"*Saya ini perempuan tradisional lo mbak . . .*" (I'm such a traditional woman . . . sister.)

This sentence was often said by female respondents.

In a more detailed explanation, Helia, a woman editor with three children said:

"I never have a helper . . . all domestic chores are done by myself *(sounds very proud of herself)*, my hobby is also cooking . . . I'm a traditional woman . . . so . . . even though I'm working . . . children and housekeeping are handled by me . . . children . . . husband . . . respect me . . . although actually my husband feels pity . . . he actually doesn't like *(disagree)* that I work . . . but see . . . you can see my house *(her house looks neat, beautiful, and comfortable, with the touch of uniqueness of traditional Java design)* . . . many of my friends . . . especially expatriates . . . are pleased to stay in my house."

Conformity to traditional gender orientation, is a safe choice for women in Indonesia, and complying to norms as a traditional woman will help avoid social sanctions. It could be understood from the results of the study that showed that traditional gender-role ideology was positively correlated with psychological well-being.

Results of Focus Group Discussions

Two sessions of focus group discussions (FGD) were conducted to find out the following: (1) how often participants experienced WIF and FIW, (2) sources of WIF and FIW, (3) outcomes of WIF and FIW, (4) coping strategies applied to reduce WFC. Participants of this study were 10 working women. Each session of focus group discussions had five participants and took around two hours to discuss the issues. All participants were married at the time of FGD, but varied in terms of other demographic characteristics. More detailed information about the participants can be found in Table 10.1.

TABLE 10.1 Demographic characteristics of participants in focus group discussions.

Demographic Characteristics	*Number of Participants*
Age (in years)	
Under 30	2
30–40	6
Above 40	2
Education	
Bachelor's Degree	3
Master's Degree	6
Doctoral Degree	1
Religion	
Muslim	4
Catholic	5
Protestant Christian	1
Ethnicity	
Javanese	4
Chinese Javanese	6
Occupation	
Lecturer	3
Lecturer with Managerial Experience	6
Business and Development Manager	1
Work experience (in years)	
Under 5	2
5–10	3
Above 10	5
Number of children	
No children	1
Pregnant	1
1–2 children	7
3 children	1
Husband's education	
Bachelor's Degree	8
Master's Degree	2

(*Continued*)

TABLE 10.1 (Continued)

Demographic Characteristics	*Number of Participants*
Husband's occupation	
Staff	2
Manager	4
Entrepreneur	4
Length of marriage (in years)	
Under 5	2
5–10	5
Above 10	3

All participants were very enthusiastic and actively participated in the process of discussion. The situation was very conducive to making all participants open to sharing their feelings and ideas. The laughter and expression of sadness happened interchangeably during the discussion session. At the end of the session, the participants were expressing feelings of relief. They felt relief to have shared many things that they had kept in themselves for so long. They were also happy to know that they were not alone in experiencing WFC.

Results from the focus group discussion revealed some interesting themes. Most importantly, all participants mentioned that they experienced WIF conflict more often than FIW conflict. It seems work life is more difficult to manage, and therefore, it is more challenging when considering the effort for balancing the work and family life. In the next part, antecedents and outcomes of WIF and FIW conflict, as well as coping strategies to balance work and family life, are discussed.

Antecedents and Outcomes of WIF Conflict

The source of WIF conflict came from work demands, which were identified as: ineffective management (meeting after work hours), lack of reliable administrative supports, indecisive leadership from superiors, and unskilled coworkers/subordinates. This all ended up in work overload due to taking too many responsibilities.

One of the participants, namely Tita (44 years old, manager), mentioned that she often brought her work home because otherwise she would come home very late if she did all the work at the office. She said laughing, but with sadness showed in her expression:

> "I have one experience . . . I did not know that my husband had been waiting for me till late at night in the bedroom, I thought he already slept. He started screaming when I entered the bedroom bringing lots of my paperwork. What? You still keep working? And he went to sleep with anger. I felt discomfort and guilt, but the deadline for submitting the work was the next day."

The outcomes of WIF conflict are feeling guilt, sleep deprivation, and exhaustion.

Antecedents and Outcomes of FIW Conflict

The source of FIW conflict came from family demands, which included problems of caring for children and providing education for them, caring for the elderly, unequal distribution of handling domestic chores with a spouse, unavailable or incompetent domestic helpers, demands from extended family, and jealousy and conflict with a spouse. A young manager, Yani (30 years old), who looked desperate while talking, said:

> "My husband always scowls if I have a telephone call from my male subordinate . . . who is only calling to consult about urgent things . . . but my husband seems very jealous him . . . My husband thinks that my subordinate just tries to find reasons to contact me at home. My coworkers and subordinates are not as capable as I would like, and as a result it makes more work for me. In addition, my boss is indecisive. And my home life is impacted by my husband's jealousy of the phone calls from my male subordinate."

The extended family can also become a source of strain. Nita (34 years old, staff) talked expressively and felt annoyed when sharing her experience. She said:

> "I get stressed when facing my husband's family. They often come to my house and spend a long time at my house. Especially my sister-in-law, she doesn't care whether I'm busy or not. She insists on me accompanying her just for sightseeing and shopping."

Outcomes of FIW conflict were: low work motivation, difficulty concentrating on the job, withdrawal from work, distress, irritability, and guilty feelings. Panic and sadness were also often felt when having sick children at home.

Strategies Used to Cope with W-F Conflict

Coping strategies to reduce WFC can be divided into three domains: personal, family, and organizational. For the personal domain the strategy of coping was aimed at reducing distress and strain. All participants had a unique way to release their distress. They tried to find a "me time" by doing an activity alone, including going to the beauty salon and spa or a bookstore, driving a car and turning favorite music a bit loud, and religious activities such as praying and reading the holy book (the Qur'an). In the family domain, coping strategies applied included asking for support from the extended family, a neighbor, a coworker, and a domestic helper;

using equipment at home to make the domestic chores easier (washing machine and microwave); subscribing to daily food catering services; and living in a house close to the office.

On the organizational level, child care is available, but people still hesitate to use it. As much as they can, they are not sending their children to child care. They prefer their children to be looked after by the extended family or relatives (including coworkers). Yanti again said: "*Anak kok dititip-titip . . . memangnya barang*" (it is difficult to find an exact translation, but the meaning is about wondering and complaining about why people send their children to an external agent; it is like depositing stuff). On the organizational level, it is also relatively easy to ask permission for handling urgent domestic demands. Taking the child to the workplace when no one can look after him/her at home is a common and acceptable practice in many organizations in Indonesia. Even though child care and elder care facilities are now available, they are rarely utilized. Sending children to child care or a family member to elder care causes humiliation and resentment in Indonesia.

Special Themes Found in the FGDs

Extended family could be a source of support as well as a source of strain. The situation was similar with domestic helpers; they could be a source of support when they are skillful and cooperative, but when they are not skillful and not cooperative, this could be a source of strain to working women. Domestic helpers staying at home are commonly found in many families. Yanti (38 years old, manager) shared her experience in handling problems with her domestic helper.

> "My servant is not skillful, so I have to teach her all the time. She is now pretty good about handling the domestic chores. . . . However, another problem appeared when she had a boyfriend . . . she often disappeared . . . so I made a schedule for her when she could leave home for dating . . . I asked her for cooperation to obey the schedule. Not only that, I also asked her to introduce her boyfriend so I could be sure with whom she went out. Her relatives also often come to visit her, to take her salary or ask permission to take her home for a couple of days. So I have to also get in contact with her family circle to handle them so that they don't bother us so often."

WFC experienced was also causing some participants to intend to quit their job and marriage, but it was difficult to do because of social and religious sanctions. Santi (33 years old, staff, with two children) mentioned that her decision to work was based on her bad experience when she was not financially independent due to not working. She said:

> "I was feeling that I'm in the lowest point of my life when I asked money from my husband for daily needs of family . . . and my husband said angrily . . .

where is the money I gave to you yesterday? You used it all? . . . At that time I swore that I would work and keep working no matter what. Since I work, my husband started complaining and keeps complaining. He allows me to work, but he imposed on me to do all the domestic chores and care for my two kids. I feel a burden arguing every time with him . . . and frankly I really, really don't like doing domestic chores. I want him to do some of the domestic chores . . . at least we can share. I'm thinking of divorce but still confused . . . what will people say if I get divorced?"

Even though Santi disliked doing domestic chores, other participants enjoyed doing domestic chores. Moreover, they sometimes experienced the feeling of being "lost" when they could not do some domestic chores. Doing domestic chores made women happy because they received appreciation from family, especially from their spouse. Tita again said:

"I get up early every morning and before sunrise I already go to the traditional market near my house preparing all stuff for cooking. My husband likes my cooking, and it makes me happy . . . but when I'm sweeping outside my house, suddenly my daughter calls me loudly . . . Mom, get in please . . . I don't like people seeing you sweeping to think you are a housewife, my mom is a manager."

It seems there is a shifting perspective in how the younger generation see the value of working woman, especially from the female perspective. Being a working woman will increasingly be a preference for young women.

Conclusion

Women in Indonesia are faced with demands to carry more responsibilities in the domestic life due to traditional gender-role ideology adopted by the majority of the Indonesian society. There is no excuse for women who work in public sectors not to take responsibility in domestic life. Juggling demands from work and family causes work conflict for working women in Indonesia. Nevertheless, as a collectivist culture, it is relatively easy to find social support that can decrease the occurrence of WFC. Caring for children and doing domestic chores are highly respected parts of women's roles, as it's seen as dedication to the family. Conformity to the beliefs in traditional gender-role ideology is a safe choice for women in Indonesia to avoid social sanctions, and one which, in the end, can increase well-being. Work-family conflict is also experienced by male workers, as the well-being and life satisfaction of Indonesian people are predominantly influenced by the family domain (family satisfaction). This occurs due to the collectivist culture in Indonesia, in which belongingness to the group (in-groups), particularly a family, is very strong. Family is the first priority for Indonesian people. Further research is needed to explore more about the dynamics of work-family interface issues as Indonesia has many subcultures.

References

Alteza, M., & Hidayati, L. N. (2009). *Work-family conflict pada wanita bekerja: Studi tentang penyebab, dampak dan strategi coping* [Work-family conflict on working women: Study about source, impact and coping strategy]. Research report for Faculty of Economic and Social Sciences, Universitas Negeri Yogjakarta, Indonesia.

Artiawati. (2009). *Anteseden dan konsekuensi konflik kerja-keluarga pada manajer dan pekerja di Indonesia* [Antecedents and consequences of work-family conflict on managers and workers in Indonesia]. *Simposium Kebudayaan Indonesia-Malaysia* (Symposium of Indonesia-Malaysia Culture) IX, Bandung, Indonesia.

Artiawati. (2012). *Konflik kerja-keluarga pada jurnalisi di Jawa dan Bali (Model konflik kerja-keluarga dengan ideologi peran gender, beban peran berlebih, dukungan sosial dan kepribadian sebagai anteseden; rasa bersalah dan kesejahteraan psikologis sebagai konsekuensi) [Work-family conflict among journalists in Java and Bali (the model of work-family conflict with gender role orientation, role overload, social supports and personality as antecedents; guilty feeling and psychological well-being as consequences)]* (Doctoral dissertation). Doctoral Program in Psychology, Universitas Padjadjaran, Bandung, Indonesia.

Aycan, Z. (2006). *Work-family conflict in Turkey: Societal change and policy implications*. Paper presented at the International Conference of Applied Psychology, Athens, Greece.

Badan Pusat Statistik Indonesia (the Statistic Central Body of Indonesia), retrieved from http://www.bps.go.id/

Desai, T. P. (2005). *India: At multiple crossroads of work-family conflict*. Paper presented at the First International Conference: Community, Work and Family, Change and Transformation, Manchester, United Kingdom.

Desnawati, S. (2008). *Upaya meningkatkan keseimbangan kehidupan kerja-keluarga di Universitas Surabaya* [Effort on improving work-family life balance in University of Surabaya] (Postgraduate thesis). Master of Psychology Program, Universitas Surabaya, Indonesia.

Dewi, L. K., Artiawati, & Suvianita, K. (2007). Dinamika konflik kerja-keluarga pada guru [The dynamic of work-family conflict on teacher]. *Anima Indonesian Psychological Journal, 2*(3), 263–275.

ILO Indonesia. (2012). *Tren Ketenagakerjaan dan Sosial Indonesia 2011: Mempromosikan pertumbuhan lapangan kerja di tingkat provinsi, Kantor Perburuhan Internasional Jakarta* [Labour and Social tends in Indonesia: Promoting job-rich growth in provinces]. International Labour Office, Jakarta, Indonesia.

ILO Indonesia. (2013). *Tren Ketenagakerjaan dan Sosial Indonesia 2012: Upaya untuk menciptakan ekonomi yang adil dan berkelanjutan, Kantor Perburuhan Internasional Jakarta* [Effort to build economic fairly and continuously]. International Labour Office, Jakarta, Indonesia.

Kementerian Pemberdayaan Perempuan dan Perlindungan Anak. (2012a). *Pembangunan Manusia Berbasis Gender 2012*. Jakarta: Kementerian Pemberdayaan Perempuan dan Perlindungan Anak (Ministry of women empowerment and children protection).

Kementerian Pemberdayaan Perempuan dan Perlindungan Anak. (2012b). *Profil Perempuan Indonesia 2011* [Profile of Indonesian Women 2011]. Jakarta: Kementerian Pemberdayaan Perempuan dan Perlindungan Anak (Ministry of women empowerment and child protection).

Kesumaningsari, N.P.A., & Simarmata, N. (2014). *Konflik kerja keluarga* dan *work engagement karyawati Bali pada Bank di Bali* [Work-family conflict and work engangement on Balinese women employees in Bali). *Journal Psikologi Indoonesia, 1*(3), 493–506, Program Studi Psikologi, Fakultas Psikologi Universitas Udayana.

Leofianti, A. R. (2013). *Hubungan antara dukungan sosial atasan, dukungan sosial rekan kerja dan dukungan sosial pasangan terhadap work-family conflict pada perawat rumak sakit swasta di Yogjakarta [Correlation between social support from superior, co-worker, spouse and work-family conflict on nurses in a private hospital in Yogjakarta].* (Udergraduate thesis). Faculty of Psychology, Universitas Gadjah Mada, Yogjakarta, Indonesia.

Nainggolan, C., Candra, P., & Widyastuti, A. (1996). Studi kasus tentang faktor-fator yang mempengarungi keputusan untuk berhenti bekerja pada wanita setelah kelahiran anak pertama [The case study of factors influencing decision to quit job on women after first child's birth]. *Jurnal Psikologi dan Masyarakat, 2*, 75–109.

Rajadyaksa, U., Huang, T., & Artiawati. (2011). *Gender role ideology, work-family overload, conflict and guilt: Examining a path analysis model in three Asian countries.* Paper presented in Regional Conference International Association of Cross-Cultural Psychology, Istanbul, Turkey.

Soepangat. (1986). *Pengaruh lingkungan budaya terhadap keibuan dan emansipasi sebagai bentuk aktualisasi diri wanita: Studi kasus para ibu-ibu pekerja di beberapa kota di Jawa; Suatu Pendekatan melalui teori psikologi budaya. [The influence of cultural environment towards mothering and emancipation as a form of the women's self-actualization: A case study of working mothers at several places in Java: A cultural psychology approach]* (Doctoral Dissertation). Universitas Padjadjaran, Bandung, Indonesia.

Suroso (2002). *In memorium guru.* Yogjakarta: Jendela.

Triandis, H. C., Bontempo, R., Villareal, M. J., Asai, M., & Lucca, N. (1988). Individualism and collectivism: Cross-cultural perspectives on self–ingroup relationships. *Journal of Personality and Social Psyhology, 54*(2), 323–338.

Wicaksono, P. E. (2014). *Karen Agustiawan Mundur dari Dirut Pertamina pada 1 Oktober 2014*) [Karen Agustiawan quits as the President Director of Pertamina on 1 October 2014], liputan6.com, Jakarta.

11

THE WORK-FAMILY INTERFACE IN THE PEOPLE'S REPUBLIC OF CHINA

Li Zhang and Karen Korabik

The Chinese Context

China has one of the world's oldest civilizations. Before the advent of the Communist government in 1949, however, China was still a largely feudal society characterized by high rates of poverty, illiteracy, and premature mortality. Since then sweeping social, political, and economic changes have taken place, resulting in a dynamic economy that is currently undergoing an unprecedented transformation (Joplin, Shaffer, Francesco, & Lau, 2003).

Geography, Population, and Demographics

The People's Republic of China is located in East Asia. China is one of the world's largest countries, second only to Russia and Canada in its land mass. It has 14,500 km of coastline and shares borders with many nations—Afghanistan, Bhutan, Burma, India, Kazakhstan, North Korea, Kyrgyzstan, Laos, Mongolia, Nepal, Pakistan, Russia, Tajikistan, and Vietnam. Its diverse climate ranges from subarctic in the north to tropical in the south.

China is the world's most populous country. Based on United Nations estimates, its population currently exceeds 1,380,000,000, which is equivalent to nearly 19% of the world's total population. Overall, there are 56 recognized ethnic groups in China. However, the predominant Han group makes up over 90% of the population. China's official language is Mandarin, but many dialects are spoken, and Cantonese is commonly used in the south.

Political and Economic Context

In recent decades, China has experienced dramatic changes in its economy and policies that provide a unique backdrop against which to understand the work-family (W-F) interface. The modern day Communist government, the People's Republic of China, was established in 1949. It has a unicameral legislature and an executive branch that consists of the president, who is the head of state, and the premier, who is the head of government. China's administrative units include 23 provinces, four municipalities (Beijing, Tianjin, Shanghai, Chongqing), five autonomous regions (Guangxi, Inner Mongolia, Tibet, Ningxia, Xinjiang), and two special administrative regions (Hong Kong, Macau).

During its early years, the focus of the Communist government was on bringing about modernization primarily through policies aimed at land reform (collectivization) and the abolition of private ownership. There was also an effort to eliminate class and gender inequities and to improve women's status through transforming a social system that was patriarchal, patrilocal, and patrilineal in nature (Chen, 2004). Despite radical social reorganization, extensive legislation, and constant ideological crusades aimed at promoting gender equality, the government has been unable to completely eradicate long-standing cultural beliefs about male superiority or stereotyped views about the nature of the sexes (Korabik, 1994).

Starting in the late 1970s China began a series of economic reforms. These were aimed at decentralizing planning and decision making, decollectivizing agriculture, emphasizing individual accountability for production, promoting technological advancement, and encouraging entrepreneurship and foreign investment (Korabik, 1994). During this period, less emphasis was placed on directly improving women's welfare. Instead, women were expected to benefit by having benefits from general economic development "trickle down" to them from above (Korabik, 1994).

The most recent series of economic reforms has been directed at moving to a more market-oriented economy, including the reform of State-Owned Enterprises and Urban Collective-owned Enterprises, through the privatization and contracting out of much state-owned industry and the lifting of price controls, protectionist policies, and regulations. This has involved the eradication of lifelong employment contracts (Joplin et al., 2003) which has increased feelings of job insecurity and forced employees to adapt to increased work demands (Ling & Powell, 2001).

Cultural and Policy Context

Cultural Values

Historically, the three philosophical traditions of Confucianism, Taoism, and Buddhism have played an important role in shaping Chinese cultural values. Chinese cultural beliefs and traditions have been deeply engrained over the course of many centuries and continue to critically affect people's cognitions and their responses to the W-F interface (Tang, Siu, & Cheung, 2014). For example, China is a collectivist country that ranked 58 on the Individualism Index among the 76 countries and regions in Hofstede's research (Hofstede, Hofstede, & Minkov, 2010). The need to maintain harmonious relationships within organizations and families dominates the Chinese mindset. Organizations are seen as families, requiring employees to obey rules and keep loyal to their firms. Specifically, Guanxi (i.e., a network of interpersonal relationships) applies not only to personal social activities, but also to work and family demands, and is essential for success (Ling & Powell, 2001). Additionally, shame culture (i.e., face) can affect the turnover decisions of employees in China. Changing work situations frequently is not a personal decision, but rather is seen by others as an infringement of family obligations, representing the failure to meet essential requirements dictated by the social position that people occupy.

What's more, filial piety, regarding the care for one's parents as an obligation, is also a core concept of traditional Confucianism (Laidlaw, Wang, Coelho, & Power, 2010). Laidlaw and colleagues (2010) found that compared to residents of the United Kingdom, older adults in China had a much greater expectation that their adult children had a duty to take care of them. In China, adult children are indoctrinated to provide physical, financial, and emotional care for their aging parents (Zhan, Feng, Chen, & Feng, 2011). This means that adult children must spend considerable time and energy giving instrumental and emotional support to their elderly parents (Ling & Powell, 2001), which intensifies their family demands and WFC.

Internal Migration

One result of China's economic reforms has been that surplus rural labor has been driven to urban areas, changing China from a primarily rural economy to a primarily urban one in a very short period of time (Hu, 2012). Because of this, China has had one of the highest rates of internal migration in the world (Hu, 2012). Most migration from rural to urban areas is by young people seeking better job opportunities for themselves and so they can help their families left behind (Hu, 2012). The Chinese policy of Hukou (the household registration system that categorizes citizens based on their place of residence and eligibility for local socioeconomic benefits), however, has produced obstacles for these migrant workers and made it less attractive for professional workers to move from one location to another (Russell, 2008). In response to the increasing need for an urban workforce, the government recently has loosened restrictions on the Hukou system.

One consequence of internal migration is that adult children who reside in cities far away from their parents in rural areas face increasing difficulty in fulfilling their obligations to visit their parents and provide parental care. To address the growing problem of elder neglect, the government has recently imposed regulations that dictate filial visits.

The One-Child Family Policy

The policy that undoubtedly has had the most dramatic impact on the W-F interface in China, however, is the one-child family policy. Starting in 1979 the government mandated a one-child limit for families in both rural and urban areas, with a maximum of two children in special circumstances and higher limits for minority nationalities and ethnic groups with very small populations. The policy has been enforced through a combination of public education, social pressure, fines, rewards for compliance, and at times coercion. By 2014, the one-child policy had prevented over 400 million births and reduced fertility levels to 1.55 children/woman. Lately, to cope with an ageing population, the policy has been revised to allow two children per family.

One of the foremost effects of the one-child family policy has been the creation of a society with unbalanced sex ratios. Due to a long-standing cultural preference for boys, particularly in rural areas, families often resorted to a variety of strategies to ensure that they had a son. Because of this, in 2010, there were 118 boys to every 100 girls, and presently there are about 9 million more boys than girls in China. This has had some advantageous consequences for women, improving their prospects for marriage and making the household division of labor more equitable (Fong, 2002).

Because of the one-child policy and urban migration, family structure in China has been transformed from extended families to nuclear families. Families consisting of two adults and one child are now the prevalent family type, especially in urban areas. However, in most of these the generations still reside near to one another (Fong, 2002) with grandmothers often acting as caregivers of their grandchildren (Chen, 2004). The close ties between extended family members who can provide both material and social support for family responsibilities (Ling & Powell, 2001) helps to attenuate family demands and reduce WFC.

One effect of the one-child family policy was that families invested all of their time, energy, and money into a single child instead of spreading their resources among many. The education of children was given an extremely high priority (Zhang & Liu, 2011). In addition to the nine years of compulsory education, the number of people receiving senior secondary school and college education sharply increased. Education is seen as an asset because it is an avenue to obtaining a good job and it brings honor to the extended family (Russell, 2008).

The one-child family policy specifically benefited women and girls in a number of ways (Fong, 2002). Women were able to spend less of their time on child rearing (Siu et al., 2010) and less significance was given to patrilineal lineage (Zhou, Dawson, Herr, & Stukas, 2004). There also has been a greater pressure for the gender equality of children, giving daughters greater status than before, and along with this daughters have been encouraged to make nontraditional career choices, as these are associated with higher wages and greater prestige (Zhou et al., 2004).

China's Labor Force and Employment Trends

China's economic reforms have brought with them many changes to the nature of the workplace. Along with increased business opportunities and more entrepreneurship has come an end to guaranteed lifetime employment (Joplin et al., 2003). The new competition for jobs has resulted in a situation where employees have had to adjust to conditions characterized by increased work demands and job insecurity (Zhao, Qu, & Ghiselli, 2011). Factors like the increased prevalence of dual-career families, more urban employees living apart from their rural elders, and single children having the sole responsibility for looking after their elders have resulted in higher levels of WFC for Chinese workers and brought about greater HR challenges for their firms (Zhao et al., 2011).

For women workers, the effects of the economic reforms must be understood in the context of the dual paradoxical forces of Confucianism and Communism. According to Confucian beliefs, the ideal woman was supposed to be subservient to the men in her life: a dutiful daughter to her father, wife to her husband, and mother to her son(s). Women's roles were confined to the domestic sphere (Aaltion & Huang, 2007; Zhang, Yip, Chi, Chan, Cheung, & Zhang, 2012). Under Communism, many policies and programs aimed at promoting gender equity were adopted and women were said to "hold up half the sky." The Communist ideal was for all women to be both good workers and good mothers. Today, China has one of the highest rates of women employed in full-time jobs in the world (Aaltion & Huang, 2007; Zhang, Yip, et al., 2012) and 51% of businesses have a woman in senior management (Thornton, 2007). Women management students appear to have overcome the lack of confidence and assertiveness they displayed in the past (Korabik, 1994) and are now equivalent to men in leadership style, self-efficacy, and motivation to manage (Ebrahimi, Young, & Luk, 2002; Frank, 2001).

Despite this, due to remnants of Confucian thinking, negative stereotypes about women's capabilities abound, and there is still a "glass ceiling" that hampers their advancement (Aaltion & Huang, 2007; Frank, 2001). What's more, in today's job market instead of job assignments being handed out by the State, obtaining a good job depends on having an advanced education and using Guanxi to persuade a personnel manager to hire you (Granrose, 2007). Because women still have fewer of the necessary connections and resources than men, their workforce opportunities lag behind those of men (Granrose, 2007).

In addition, as the power of the State as the primary employer has decreased, discrimination against women has risen (Honig & Hershatter, 1998; Leung, 2003). There is much evidence of gender discrimination in hiring, job placement, wages, and layoffs. More specifically, compared to their male counterparts: (1) women have lower income levels due to pay inequity, (2) women face greater job segregation and are found at lower occupational levels, (3) women are subject to forced early retirement, and (4) women have a higher proportion of lay-offs (Wikipedia, n.d.). Furthermore, in China the physiological differences between men and women have been used to justify giving women certain privileges in the workplace (Korabik, 1993). For example, women are entitled to rest periods during menstruation, pregnancy, and breast feeding and to maternity leave during confinement. These privileges, along with regulations requiring employers to supply day care, have been a double-edged sword for women. Making women more expensive to employ than men has resulted in a bias against female employees (Matthews & Nee, 2000).

Research on the Work-Family Interface in China

Early research on the W-F interface in China consisted primarily of qualitative interview studies with small samples composed mostly of women (Korabik, 1992, 1993, 1994). Over the years there has been a rapid proliferation of studies on the W-F interface in China. Today large sample investigations with multi-wave data collection and sophisticated methodologies and statistical analyses are the norm.

W-F Conflict

There is evidence that the rapid changes in the structure of both work and family life have fostered greater WFC among Chinese working parents (Lu, Shi, & Lawler, 2002; Siu, Spector, Cooper, & Lu, 2005). Role demands are one of the most important precursors of WFC. Chinese workers are currently subject to high levels of demands in both the work and the family domains (Coffey, Anderson, Zhao, Liu, & Zhang, 2009).

Compared to men, however, women have greater role demands. In China, gender-based division of labor is prevalent (Leung, 2003), with most women, despite being employed full-time, carrying the predominant responsibility for housework and child care (Lai, 1995). Choi and Chen (2006) collected data from 153 married Chinese employees. The results indicated that although Chinese women reported the same level of work demands as men, their perceptions of family demands were higher than those of Chinese men. On the other hand, because the primary role identity of Chinese men is as workers, they tend to report higher levels of work-to-family interference and higher spillover effects from the work-to-family domains than do women (Choi & Chen, 2006).

Today's Chinese urban professionals, who were born during the era of the one-child family policy and economic reforms, may have a different approach to dealing with role demands than those in their parents' generation. Coffey and colleagues (2009) studied MBA students and found that, unlike their parents, over 30% of their participants mentioned hiring a housekeeper to help them manage their domestic demands. Moreover, these young workers had more of an expectation that both their spouses and their organizations would provide them with the support they needed to achieve W-F balance.

Lu, Siu, Spector, and Shi (2009) sampled 189 employed parents and found that several indicators of role demands (i.e., child care responsibilities, working hours, and monthly salary) were positively related to WFC. Along the same line, a study by Zhang, Yip, et al. (2012) indicated that the highest levels of WFC were reported by the segments of the population who would likely be experiencing the highest W-F demands (i.e., middle-aged married adults and those with dependent children).

A comparison of the United States and China (Yang, Chen, Choi, & Zou, 2000), however, showed that work demands had a greater effect on WFC in the United States than they did in China. Yang et al. attributed this to the fact that Chinese employees place a different priority on work versus family than those in the West. In China, employees put work before family because work is seen as being carried out to enhance the welfare of the family. Therefore, spending extra time at work after official hours and on weekends to meet work demands is legitimized as a way to obtain honor and income for family well-being. This is consistent with other research indicating that WFC is less detrimental to individuals in collectivistic than in individualistic cultures (Lu, Gilmour, Kao, & Huang, 2006; Spector et al., 2004, 2007).

Outcomes of W-F Conflict

Several studies have examined the impact of WFC on outcome variables such as organizational commitment; job, career, and life satisfaction; and turnover intentions. Lu et al. (2009) found that higher WFC was related to greater organizational commitment and job satisfaction, but that there was no significant relationship with career satisfaction. Higher WFC, however, was predictive of lower life satisfaction.

In a study of 121 hotel sales managers Zhao et al. (2011) looked at how the affective and cognitive components of job satisfaction were related to work interference with family (WIF) and family interference with work (FIW) conflict. Their findings differed from those of Lu et al. (2009) in that they found the relationship between WFC and job satisfaction to be negative instead of positive. More specifically, Zhao et al.'s (2011) findings indicated that while both WIF and FIW were negatively related to the affective component of job satisfaction, the cognitive component was only negatively associated with FIW. Moreover, greater life satisfaction was associated with lower FIW and higher affective job satisfaction. A follow-up study (Qu & Zhao, 2012) showed that life satisfaction had positive spillover effects on job satisfaction when WIF and FIW were low, but not when WIF and FIW were high.

Wang, Lawler, Walumbwa, and Shi (2004) examined 394 employees from the banking sector in the United States and China. They found that WIF was more positively related to job withdrawal intentions among those in the United States than those in China, whereas FIW was more positively related to job withdrawal intentions for those in China than those in the United States.

Family Resources as a Buffer

Work and family roles tend to be highly blurred in Chinese societies, leading people to feel obligated to conscientiously fulfill both work and family responsibilities (Wu, Kwan, Liu, & Resnick, 2012). This can result in higher levels of WFC. Ling and Powell (2001) have proposed, however, that within a Confucian cultural tradition, interpersonal traits and resources can assist individuals to build and maintain harmonious relationships in both the family and the workplace. These resources can act as buffers against family and work stress. Research has also shown that there are crossover effects such that resources generated in the family can have a positive impact on what transpires at work, particularly when working conditions are stressful.

An example of this comes from a two-wave longitudinal study of 279 Chinese female nurses (Lu, Siu, Chen, & Wang, 2011). The findings indicated that having greater family control (family mastery) at Time 1 predicted higher work engagement at Time 2. Furthermore, family mastery had a greater impact on work engagement when job demands were high.

Two studies have demonstrated that the ability to segment work and home can act as a buffer against the negative effects of work stressors spilling over into the family. Wu et al. (2012) examined the effects of boundary strength (the tendency to separate the work and family domains with an inflexible boundary) using a three-wave survey. They found that employees with high boundary strength at home were less likely to experience WIF and to let the negative effects of abusive work supervision spill over into the family domain. In a similar three-wave study, Liu, Kwan, Lee, and Hui (2013) found that while workplace ostracism decreased family satisfaction, this relationship was mediated by WIF. Moreover, work-home segmentation preferences attenuated the mediating effect of WIF on the relationship between workplace ostracism and family satisfaction.

W-F Facilitation, Enhancement, and Enrichment

The positive side of the W-F interface has variously been called W-F facilitation, enhancement, and enrichment. In contrast to WFC, these concepts have invariably been associated with positive W-F outcomes. In the Chinese context, social support is a very important precursor of this linkage. For instance, Lu et al. (2009) found that W-F facilitation was a function of the support received from one's spouse, as well as from family-friendly supervisors and coworkers. Moreover, both work-to-family (WTFF) and family-to-work (FTWF) facilitation were related to higher job satisfaction and WTFF was related to higher life satisfaction.

Some multiwave research has been directed at examining the interrelationships among work and family support, W-F enrichment, and outcomes. Exchange theory predicts that employees who receive support at work will reciprocate with high levels of job satisfaction. Tang et al. (2014) postulated that

W-F enrichment was the mechanism through which this occurred. In support of their hypothesis, they found that W-F enrichment fully mediated the relationship between supervisor and organizational support and job satisfaction. This was true both for those who were single and living with extended family and for those who were married, but the effect was stronger for women than for men (Tang et al., 2014).

In contrast to the exchange theory perspective, Greenhouse and Powell's (2006) affective pathway model of W-F enrichment postulates a different causal sequence. Here, affective reactions like satisfaction and engagement are viewed as mediators of the relationships between work and family support and W-F enrichment. Siu et al. (2011) examined this using a three-wave design. Their results demonstrated that job satisfaction partially mediated the relationship between supervisor support and WTFE whereas family satisfaction partially mediated the relationship between family support and FTWE. In a similar study, Siu et al. (2010) showed that work engagement fully mediated the relationships between family-friendly organizational policies and WTFE as well as between job autonomy and FTWE. What's more, work engagement partially mediated the relationships between supervisor support and job autonomy and WTFE, and also between family support and FTWE.

Joint Effects of W-F Conflict and Enhancement/Enrichment

Some investigations have examined the effects of both the positive and the negative sides of the W-F interface within the same study. For example, Ho, Chen, Cheung, Liu, and Worthington (2013) looked at crossover effects in dual-earner couples. For both husbands and wives both family orientation and family support had positive effects. Namely, greater family orientation and higher perceived family support predicted lower WFC and higher FTW enhancement. The findings for work support, however, followed a different pattern. Higher perceived work support was related to greater FTW enhancement for wives, but to lower WIF for husbands. In addition, work support did not always produce positive outcomes. So, when husbands had more support at work, their wives reported greater WTF enhancement, but when wives had more support at work, their husbands reported greater FIW. In addition, the more family oriented a husband was, the less WTF enhancement his wife reported experiencing.

Jin, Ford, and Chen (2013) carried out a comparison of North American and Chinse workers. Their results indicated that WTF spillover effects were stronger in North America, whereas FTW spillover effects were stronger in China. Moreover, role overload was a stronger predictor of WFC in North America, whereas it was more strongly related to W-F enrichment in China. More specifically, high work overload was associated with higher WIF and lower job satisfaction more so for North American than for Chinese workers. Similarly, higher W-F support was related to higher WTF enrichment and greater job satisfaction more so in North America than in China. By contrast, having a lower work overload was associated with greater WTFE more so for those in China than for those in North America.

Contrary to expectations, higher family overload was more strongly related to higher FIW and higher family support was more strongly related to higher FTWE more so in North America than in China. In contrast, higher family support was related to lower FIW more so in China than in North America (Jin et al., 2013). Jin et al. speculate that because ties to extended family are so predominant in China, Chinese workers not only gain more resources from their family that are useful for work, but also expend more resources due to their family obligations.

Chen and Powell (2012) used data from 1,052 Chinese employees to examine the proposition that work and family role experiences simultaneously generate and deplete resources. In line with this, they postulated that work role resource gain and loss separately mediate the paths from work role engagement to WFC and from work role engagement to W-F enrichment. Their results confirmed these hypotheses. A follow-up study (Chen, Powell, & Cui, 2014) examined 382 employees of Chinese firms at two points in time one year apart. The results indicated that work resource gain at Time 1 weakened the positive relationship between WFC at Times 1 and 2, whereas work resource loss at Time 1 weakened the positive relationship between W-F enrichment at Times 1 and 2. However, WFC at Time 1 strengthened the positive relationship between work resource gain at Time 1 and family resource gain at Time 2. Overall, these results suggest the existence of complementary forces whereby high resource losses reduce the transfer of gains and high resource gains reduce the transfer of losses, but also that unexpected gains may result from individuals having to cope with stressful circumstances.

Summary and Conclusion

In China, work is given priority over the family since working is seen as a way to enhance family well-being (Yang et al., 2000). Because of this, Chinese workers place a high value on persistence and are more tolerant of heavy work demands and WFC than are those in North America (Jin et al., 2013). Chinese employees also have less of an expectation of enrichment among their life roles. This has the effect of mitigating the effects of role conflict and enrichment on work- and family-related well-being (Jin et al., 2013).

In China, work and family roles tend to be blurred rather than segmented (Wu et al., 2012). Social support, particularly from family members, acts as an important role resource that can buffer the effects of stressful work events. Chinese workers tend to have larger social support networks and more support from elders at home, reducing need for the workplace to provide family supports.

The rapidly changing societal conditions in China will continue to have a dramatic impact on the interplay of work and family life for some time to come. Although the situation in China represents a unique opportunity for researchers, many more studies are necessary to attain a complete understanding of the complex forces shaping the W-F interface.

References

Aaltion, I., & Huang, J. (2007). Women managers' careers in information technology in China: High flyers with emotional costs? *Journal of Organizational Change, 20*(2), 227–244. doi:10.1108/09534810724775

Chen, F. (2004). The division of labor between generations of women in rural China. *Social Science Research, 33*(4), 557–580. doi:10.1016/j.ssresearch.2003.09.005

Chen, Z., & Powell, G. N. (2012). No pain, no gain? A resource-based model of work-to-family enrichment and conflict. *Journal of Vocational Behavior, 81*(1), 89–98. doi:10.1016/j.jvb.2012.05.003

Chen, Z., Powell, G. N., & Cui, W. (2014). Dynamics of the relationships among work and family resource gain and loss, enrichment, and conflict over time. *Journal of Vocational Behavior, 84*(3), 293–302. doi:10.1016/j.jvb.2014.02.006

Choi, J., & Chen, C. C. (2006). Gender differences in perceived work demands, family demands, and life stress among married Chinese employees. *Management and Organization Review, 2*(2), 209–229. doi:10.1111/j.1740-8784.2006.00041

Coffey, B. S., Anderson, S. E., Zhao, S., Liu, Y., & Zhang, J. (2009). Perspectives on work-family issues in China: The voices of young urban professionals. *Community, Work & Family, 12*(2), 192–212. doi:10.1080/13668800902778967

Ebrahimi, B. P., Young, S. A., & Luk, V. W. M. (2002). Motivation to manage in China and Hong Kong: A gender comparison of managers. *Sex Roles, 45*(5/6), 433–453. doi:10.1023/A:1014369817131

Fong, V. L. (2002). China's one-child policy and the empowerment of urban daughters. *American Anthropologist, 104*(4), 1098–1109.

Frank, E. J. (2001). Chinese students' perceptions of women in management: Will it be easier? *Women in Management Review, 16*(7), 316–324. doi:10.1108/EUM0000000006113

Granrose, C. S. (2007). Gender differences in career perceptions in the People's Republic of China. *Career Development International, 12*(1), 9–27. doi:10.1108/13620430710724802

Greenhouse, J. H. & Powell, G. N. (2006). When work and family are allies. *Academy of Management Review, 31*(1), 72–92.

Ho, M. Y., Chen, X., Cheung, F. M., Liu, H., & Worthington, E. L., Jr. (2013). A dyadic model of the work-family interface: A study of dual-earner couples in China. *Journal of Occupational Health Psychology, 18*(1), 53–63. doi:10.1037/a0030885

Hofstede, G., Hofstede, G. J., & Minkov, M. (2010). *Cultures and organizations*. New York, NY: McGraw-Hill.

Honig, E., & Hershatter, G. (1998). *Personal voices: Chinese women in the 1980s*. Stanford, CA: Stanford University Press.

Hu, Xiaochu. (January 2, 2012). China's "new generation" rural-urban migrants: Migration motivation and migration patterns. *Migration Information Source*, 2012. Available at SSRN: https://ssrn.com/abstract=1978546 or http://dx.doi.org/10.2139/ssrn.1978546.

Jin, F. J., Ford, M. T., & Chen, C. C. (2013). Asymmetric differences in work-family spillover in North America and China: Results from two heterogeneous samples. *Journal of Business Ethics, 113*(1), 1–14. doi:10.1007/s10551-012-1289-3

Joplin, J. R. W., Shaffer, M. A., Francesco, A. M., & Lau, T. (2003). The macro-environment and work-family conflict development of a cross cultural comparative framework. *International Journal of Cross Cultural Management, 3*(3), 305–328. doi:10.1177/1470595803003003004

Korabik, K. (1992). Women hold up half the sky: The status of managerial women in China. In W. Wedley (Ed.), *Advances in Chinese industrial studies* (Vol. 3, pp. 197–211). Greenwich, CT: JAI Press.

Korabik, K. (1993). Women managers in the People's Republic of China: Changing roles in changing times. *Applied Psychology: An International Review, 42*(4), 353–363. doi:10.1111/j.1464-0597.1993.tb00750.x

Korabik, K. (1994). Managerial women in the People's Republic of China: The long March continues. In N. J. Adler & D. N. Izraeli (Eds.), *Competitive frontiers: Women managers in a global economy* (pp. 114–126). Cambridge, MA: Blackwell.

Lai, G. (1995). Work and family roles and psychological well-being in urban China. *Journal of Health and Social Behavior, 36*(1), 11–37.

Laidlaw, K., Wang, D., Coelho, C., & Power, M. (2010). Attitudes to ageing and expectations for filial piety across Chinese and British cultures: A pilot exploratory evaluation. *Aging & Mental Health, 14*(3), 283–292. doi:10.1080/13607860903483060

Leung, A. S. M. (2003). Feminism in transition: Chinese culture, ideology and the development of the women's movement in China. *Asia Pacific Journal of Management, 20*(3), 359–374. doi:10.1023.A:1024049516797

Ling, Y., & Powell, G. N. (2001). Work-family conflict in contemporary China. *International Journal of Cross Cultural Management, 1*(3), 357–373. doi:10.1177/147059580113006

Liu, J., Kwan, H. K., Lee, C., & Hui, C. (2013). Work-to-family spillover effects of workplace ostracism: The role of work-home segmentation preferences. *Human Resource Management, 52*(1), 75–94. doi:10.1002/hrm.21513

Lu, C., Siu, O, Chen, W., & Wang, H. (2011). Family mastery enhances work engagement in Chinese nurses: A cross-lagged analysis. *Journal of Vocational Behavior, 78*(1), 100–109. doi:10.1016/j.jvb.2010.07.005

Lu, J. F., Shi, K., & Lawler, J. (2002). A preliminary model of work-family conflict. *Chinese Journal of Applied Psychology, 8*, 45–52.

Lu, J. F., Siu, O., Spector, P. E., & Shi, K. (2009). Antecedents and outcomes of a fourfold taxonomy of work-family balance in Chinese employed parents. *Journal of Occupational Health Psychology, 14*(2), 182–192. doi:10.1037/a0014115

Lu, L., Gilmour, R., Kao, S. F., & Huang, M. T. (2006). A cross-cultural study of work/family demands, work/family conflict and wellbeing: The Taiwanese vs. British. *Career Development International, 11*, 9–27. doi:10.1108/13620430610642354

Matthews, R., & Nee, V. (2000). Gender inequality and economic growth in rural China. *Social Science Research, 29*(4), 606–632. doi:10.1006/ssre.2000.0684

Qu, H., & Zhao, X. (2012). Employees' work-family conflict moderating life and job satisfaction. *Journal of Business Ethics, 65*(1), 22–28. doi:10.1016/j.jbusres.2011.07.010

Russell, G. (2008). *Work and life in China*. Boston, MA: Boston College Center for Work & Family. Retrieved from http://www.bc.edu/content/dam/files/centers/cwf/research/publications/pdf/China_Policy_Paper_Final.pdf

Siu, O., Lu, J., Brough, P., Lu, C., Bakker, A. B., Kalliath, T., . . . Shi, K. (2010). Role resources and work-family enrichment: The role of work engagement. *Journal of Vocational Behavior*, 77(3), 470–480. doi:10.1016/j.jvb.2010.06.007

Siu, O., Lu, J., Lu, C. Q., Wang, H., Brough, P., Timms, C., . . . O'Driscoll, M. (2011). Testing a model of work-family enrichment: The effects of social resources and affect. *Academy of Management Proceedings, 1*, 1–6. doi:10.5465/AMBPP.2011.65869671

Siu, O., Spector, P. E., Cooper, C. L., & Lu, C. (2005). Work stress, self-efficacy, Chinese work values, and work well-being in Hong Kong and Beijing. *International Journal of Stress Management, 12*(3), 274–288. doi:10.1037/1072-5245.12.3.274

Spector, P. E., Allen, T. D., Poelmans, S.A.Y., Lapierre, L. M., Cooper, C. L., Michael, O. D., . . . Widerszal-Bazyl, M. (2007). Cross-national differences in relationships of work demands, job satisfaction, and turnover intentions with work-family conflict. *Personnel Psychology, 60*(4), 805–835. doi:10.1111/j.1744-6570.2007.00092.x

Spector, P. E., Cooper, C. L., Poelmans, S., Allen, T. D., O'Driscoll, M., Sanchez, J. I., . . . Lu, L. (2004). A cross-national comparative study of work-family stressors, working hours, and well-being: China and Latin America versus the Anglo world. *Personnel Psychology, 57*(1), 119–142. doi:10.1111/j.1744-6570.2004.tb02486.x

Tang, S., Siu, O., & Cheung, F. (2014). A study of work-family enrichment among Chinese employees: The mediating role between work support and job satisfaction. *Applied Psychology: An International Review, 63*(1), 130–150. doi:10.1111/j.1464-0597.2012.00519.x

Thornton, G. (2007). *Four in ten businesses worldwide have no women in senior management.* Retrieved from http://www.gti.org/pressroom/articles/pr_03082007.asp

Wang, P., Lawler, J. J., Walumbwa, F. O., & Shi, K. (2004). Work-family conflict and job withdrawal intentions: The moderating effect of cultural differences. *International Journal of Stress Management, 11*(4), 392–412. doi:10.1037/1072-5245.11.4.392

Wikipedia. (n.d.) *Gender inequality in China.* Retrieved from https://en.wikipedia.org/wiki/Gender_inequality_in_China

Wu, L., Kwan, H. K., Liu, J., & Resnick, C. J. (2012). Work-to-family spillover effects of abusive supervision. *Journal of Managerial Psychology, 27*(7), 714–731. doi:10.1108/02683941211259539

Yang, N., Chen, C. C., Choi, J., & Zou, Y. (2000). Sources of work-family conflict: A Sino-US comparison of the effects of work and family demands. *Academy of Management Journal, 43*(1), 113–123. doi:10.2307/1556390

Zhan, H. J., Feng, Z., Chen, Z., & Feng, X. (2011). The role of the family in institutional long-term care: Cultural management of filial piety in China. *International Journal of Social Welfare, 20*(s1), S121–S134. doi:10.1111/j.1468-2397.2011.00808.x

Zhang, H., Yip, P. S. F., Chi, P., Chan, K., Cheung, Y. T., & Zhang, X. (2012). Factor structure and psychometric properties of the work-family balance scale in an urban Chinese sample. *Social Indicators Research, 105*(3), 409–418. doi:10.1007/s11205-010-9776-3

Zhang, J., & Liu, Y. (2011). Antecedents of work-family conflict: Review and prospect. *International Journal of Business and Management, 6*(1), 89–103.

Zhang, M., Griffeth, R. W., & Fried, D. D. (2012). Work-family conflict and individual consequences. *Journal of Managerial Psychology, 27*(7), 696–713. doi:10.1108/02683941211259520

Zhao, X., Qu, H., & Ghiselli, R. (2011). Examining the relationship of work-family conflict to job and life satisfaction: A case of hotel sales managers. *International Journal of Hospitality Management, 30*(1), 46–54. doi:10.1016/j.ijhm.2010.04.010

Zhou, I. Y., Dawson, M. L., Herr, C. L., & Stukas, S. K. (2004). American and Chinese students' predictions of people's occupations, housework responsibilities, and hobbies as a function of cultural and gender influences. *Sex Roles, 50*(7), 547–563. doi:10.1023/B:SERS.0000023074.30947.92

12

THE WORK-FAMILY INTERFACE IN TAIWAN

Ting-Pang Huang

Socioeconomic and Cultural Context

Taiwan, or the Republic of China, is located in eastern Asia, some 180 km (112 mi.) off the southeastern coast of China across the Taiwan Strait. It has an area of 35,883 km^2 (13,855 sq. mi.) and spans the Tropic of Cancer. It has a population size about 23,433,000 (DGBAS, 2014). The Taiwanese population basically consists 95% Han Chinese, which includes early immigrants from the Holo and Hakka ethnic groups and late immigrants at the end of the Chinese Civil War in 1949, and 5% aborigines who now mostly live in the mountainous eastern part of the island. The main ethnic group, Holo, immigrated from southern Fujian province of mainland China after the 17th century. Hakka people from eastern Guangdong arrived later and settled the foothills further inland. A further 1.3 million people from throughout mainland China entered Taiwan at the end of the Chinese Civil War in 1949 (GIO, 2012; Wikipedia, 2014).

The gender distribution of the population of Taiwan is 49.95% male to 50.05% female. The age distribution is skewed with the old age group increasingly comprising a larger percentage, for instance, the percentage of the 60–79 age group increased from 13.21% in 2011 to 15.16% in 2014. According to the most recent governmental statistics in June 2014 (DGBAS, 2014), the percentages of the 0–14, 15–64, and over 65 age groups are 14.14%, 74.11%, and 11.75%, respectively. The majority of people in Taiwan (93%) have a religion that is a mixture of Buddhist and Taoist. The others include 4.5% Christian and 2.5% all other religions.

The official language of Taiwan is Mandarin Chinese, but because many Taiwanese are from the southern part of Fujian province, a local dialect from there, Min-nan (or Holo) is also widely spoken in Taiwan. The smaller groups of Hakka people and aborigines also have their own languages. Many elderly people can also speak some Japanese, because they were subjected to Japanese education before Taiwan was returned to Chinese rule in 1945 after the Japanese occupation for a half century. The most popular foreign language in Taiwan is English, which is part of the regular school curriculum.

Economic and Workforce Information

The basic economic and workforce information of Taiwan for the last 10 years is listed in Table 12.1. The industrial structure of Taiwan and the percentage of GDP of each industry sector in 2012 are as follows: service sector (69.1%), industry sector (29.0%), which includes 24.2% manufacturing, others (4.8%), and agriculture sector (1.9%) (Council for Economic Planning and Development (CEPD), 2013).

Political System and Developments

The Republic of China (ROC) was established at first in mainland China in 1912. After the Chinese Civil War in 1949, the Chinese communist party took over mainland China, and the ROC government retreated to Taiwan. The ROC government in Taiwan had been officially asserting itself to be the sole legitimate government of all China until 1991. Now, the Taiwanese ROC government is a multiparty democratic regime headed by a popularly elected president with a unicameral legislature. The president appoints the premier, who wields considerable power because the premier is the head of Taiwan's many ministries that oversee the large bureaucracy.

The relationship of the ROC, Taiwan, with the People's Republic of China, and the related issues of Taiwan's independence and Chinese reunification continue to dominate Taiwanese politics.

TABLE 12.1 Basic economic and workforce characteristics in Taiwan.

Year	*Economic Growth Rate (%)*	*Per Capita GNP in US Dollars*	*Unemployment Rate (%)*	*Percentage of Women in Workforce (%)*	*Percentage of Men in Workforce (%)*
2004	6.19	15,503	4.44	47.71	67.78
2005	4.70	16,449	4.13	48.12	67.62
2006	5.44	16,911	3.91	48.68	67.35
2007	5.98	17,596	3.91	49.44	67.24
2008	0.73	17,833	4.14	49.67	67.09
2009	-1.81	16,901	5.85	49.62	66.40
2010	10.76	19,090	5.21	49.89	66.51
2011	4.19	20,625	4.39	49.97	66.67
2012	1.48	21,082	4.24	50.19	66.83
2013	2.09	21,588	4.18	50.46	66.74

Note. Source: Directorate General of Budget, Accounting and Statistics (DGBAS), 2014, Executive Yuan, ROC.

However, many people in Taiwan have been asking the government of Taiwan to improve economic and cultural relationships with mainland China, and open direct transportation links with mainland China, including direct flights. Now, Taiwan and Mainland China have made a lot of improvement in their relationships, and in 2008 they resumed regular direct flights or cross-strait relations after six decades of tense relations between them.

The Gender Equality in Employment Act and its Influence on Work and Family

To protect gender equality of right to work and promote the spirit of substantial gender equality, the Gender Equality in Employment Law was passed and enacted in 2002, and the law was amended and renamed as the Gender Equality in Employment Act in 2007. This Act stipulates that all employees regardless of gender or sexual orientation shall enjoy equal rights at their places of employment, and that the principle of equal pay for equal work is to be respected. Employers demonstrating gender discrimination or failing to set up mechanisms to prevent sexual harassment in the workplace are subject to large fines. The act also ensures women employees the right to eight weeks of paid maternity leave and men employees the right to three days of paid paternity leave. Each parent is entitled to up to one year of unpaid parental leave that is not concurrent with the other parent. The law has resulted in a great deal of influence on human resource management practices for business organizations, and has significantly helped employees in facing their work and family problems, especially for women employees (Liu, 2008; Shih, 2008).

Sociocultural Characteristics in Relation to Work and Family

The majority of research has found that traditional Chinese culture is related to social orientation, familial collectivism, or in-group collectivism (Li, Lam, & Fu, 2000; Schwartz & Bilsky, 1990; Triandis, 1988; Triandis, Bontempo, Villareal, Asai, & Lucca, 1988; M.C. Yang, 1972, K.S. Yang, 1986). Taiwanese under traditional Chinese culture generally consider family to be the basic and most important in-group (Yang, 1986). The teachings of Confucius stress the obligations of people toward one another based on their relationship and the ethic of the relationship. Confucius proposed five principal relationships: ruler and minister, father and son, elder brother and younger brother, husband and wife, and friend and friend. In terms of the three relationships occurring in a family (husband and wife, father and son, and elder brother and young brother), the wife, son, and younger brother owe obedience and respect to the husband, the father, and the elder brother, respectively. The social relationships outside of the family are typically developed and established in a similar manner as the relationships within a family. A business organization is typically considered as a big family; coworkers of similar ages are considered as brothers and sisters, and coworkers with ages close to those of parents are considered as uncles or aunts. Confucius in fact devised a social system with stable relationships based on the relationships within a family. This social system created a kind of social hierarchical structure based on ethics and obligations defined for each different relationship between family members.

As a result, traditional Chinese culture can be considered to be a vertical and in-group or family collectivism. Vertical collectivism stresses the integrity of the in-group, such as the family and the friendship groups, and expects individuals in the group to emphasize the benefits of the group and may ask group members to sacrifice themselves for the in-group if necessary. Furthermore, vertical collectivism promotes competition between different in-groups (Triandis & Gelfand, 1998). According to the results of Project 3535 in Taiwan, it was shown that Taiwan has the highest average value of vertical collectivism (M = 4.80), and the second-highest average value of horizontal collectivism (the average of horizontal collectivism at home plus horizontal collectivism at work; M = 4.72). These values are followed by horizontal individualism (M = 4.04) and finally vertical individualism (M = 3.62). In addition, when considering the second-highest value of horizontal collectivism in Taiwan, it is important to note that this value includes a much higher value of horizontal collectivism at home (M = 4.89) compared with the value of horizontal collectivism at work (M = 4.55). These results in Taiwan reveal that Taiwanese value vertical collectivism with an emphasis on family as the most important in-group and stress the inequality in the family and among groups. These findings are consistent with past research on Chinese culture (Li et al., 2000; Schwartz & Bilsky, 1990; Triandis, 1988; Triandis et al., 1988; M.C. Yang, 1972; K.S. Yang, 1986).

Although the majority of individuals in Taiwan are influenced by traditional values based on Confucian ethics, in modern times pressures from industrialization and globalization have been challenging traditional values. Due to industrialization and modernization, women and children enjoy greater freedom and a higher social status, family sizes have decreased, and most families have become nuclear in structure (DGBAS, 2014). Furthermore, relationships between family members have become more egalitarian, and more emphasis has been placed on respecting each other. This change in social culture may have some influence on traditional Chinese culture in Taiwan, prompting culture in Taiwan to change from vertical collectivism to horizontal collectivism.

Research on the Work-Family Interface in Taiwan

Development of Work and Family Research

Before the year 2000, very little research on work and family was conducted and published in Taiwan (Chen, Wang, & Chiu, 2013). Early research about work and family mostly focused on stress issues for dual-career women. Married female workers in the past were likely to feel more pressure from both work and family duties because, according to traditional culture, women are responsible for the majority of house work, even if they have a job (Cheng & Chen, 1994; Hsu, 1993). In addition, early research starting to focus on work and family conflict (WFC) was mostly unpublished theses or dissertations (Chen et al., 2013).

After the year 2000, there has been an increasing number of studies focusing on WFC. A recent review of WFC research in Taiwan (Chen et al., 2013) included 36 WFC research papers published between 2000 and 2013. However, that review did not include research published in foreign periodicals, especially studies published in the United States or England. In addition, the positive aspects of work and family, such as work-family enrichment (WFE) and facilitation (WFF), have not been reviewed. Moreover, many WFC research studies were published after that WFC review was released. Hence, the literature review of work and family research in Taiwan presented in this chapter includes all the work and family research in Taiwan containing WFC, WFE, or WFF research papers. The present literature review will include papers published abroad (seven papers) or published in Taiwan after the Chen et al. (2013) review (five papers). Furthermore, this literature review also includes the research on the positive aspects of work and family (six papers) published before or after the Chen et al. (2013) review, either in Taiwan or abroad (two papers). Thus, this review actually includes 16 more papers for review, in addition to the 36 papers previously reviewed by Chen et al. (2013).

The recent review of WFC research (Chen et al., 2013) used a review framework similar to that in several meta-analyses on WFC research completed in the United States (Allen, Herst, Bruck, & Sutton, 2000; Amstad, Meier, Fasel, Elfering, & Semmer, 2011; Byron, 2005; McNall, Nicklin, & Masuda, 2010; Michel, Kotrba, Mitchelson, Clark, & Baltes, 2011). The review framework typically includes the antecedents of WFC: the work domain, the nonwork or family domain, and demographic or individual difference variables. Additionally, the framework includes the outcomes of WFC that can be classified into work-related, nonwork or family-related, and stress-related variables, and finally the moderators of WFC. The significant findings are classified and presented in the following sections.

Antecedents of W-F Conflict

The antecedents of WFC examined in Taiwan included a large number of variables. In Taiwan, research has been mostly focused on WFC as a global variable, and less focused on separately examining the two different directions of WFC, work interference with family (WIF) and family interference with work (FIW). Based on the work and family categories in the meta-analysis of Michel et al. (2011), the antecedents of WFC in Taiwan can be classified as role stressors, role involvement, social support, and work characteristics. First, in the work domain, the work role stressors include work demands, work expectations, role conflict, role ambiguity, and work overload (Chen et al., 2013; Lu, Hwang, & Kao, 2005; Lu, Kao, Chang,

Wu, & Cooper, 2008); work role involvement includes job involvement and job identification (Chang, Liou, & Huang, 2010; Chen et al., 2013); social support includes supervisor support, organizational support, and mentoring (Chang et al., 2010; Chen et al., 2013); and work characteristics include work flexibility, family-friendly policy, work resource gain or loss (Chang & Lu, 2009), and organizational justice (Lin, Kao, & Feng, 2013).

In the nonwork domain, the family role stressors include family expectations, family pressure, family demands, family resource loss, and family conflict. Family role involvement includes time for housework and time for family or children. Nonwork social support includes spouse support and family support (Chen et al., 2013). Finally, the family characteristics include family resources (Chang & Lu, 2009).

The individual difference variables and demographics associated with WFC examined in Taiwan contain a larger number of variables. The demographic variables include gender, age, marital status, educational degree, number of children, work hours, tenure, and job position (Chen et al., 2013; Lu, Gilmour, Kao, & Huang, 2006; Lu et al., 2008, 2009). Individual variables include parents' health, workaholic tendencies, emotional exhaustion (Huang & Wang, 2013), learning resources (Kau & Cho, 2013), person-organization value congruence, person-supervisor value congruence (Pan & Yeh, 2012), perception of gender equality, and self-concept (Chen et al., 2013).

Outcomes of W-F Conflict

The outcomes of WFC can be classified into work-related, nonwork-related, and stress-related variables. Work-related outcomes include turnover intention, job satisfaction, job exhaustion, job performance (Chen et al., 2013), organizational commitment (Liao, 2011), and organizational citizenship behaviors (Yen, 2013). Nonwork-related outcomes include life satisfaction, family satisfaction, marital satisfaction, and well-being (Chen et al., 2013; Wu, Chang, & Zhuang, 2010). Stress-related outcomes include emotional exhaustion (Huang & Wang, 2013).

Moderators of the Relationship of W-F Conflict With Antecedents and Outcomes

Moderators of the relationships between antecedents and WFC include age, self-concept, supervisor support (Chou, Chang, & Lee, 2012), coworker support, time loss for work, organizational family support policy (Chen et al., 2013), self-efficacy (Chang & Lu, 2013), conscientiousness, position level, industries (Huang & Wang, 2013), and perceived procedure justice (Lin et al., 2013). Moderators of the relationships between WFC and outcomes include family support, supervisor support, coworker support, friend support, Type A personality, work flextime, time loss for work (Chen et al., 2013), and self-efficacy (Chang & Lu, 2013).

The Positive and Negative Aspects of Work and Family Interface

Research on the positive aspects of work and family, such as WFE and WFF, has not been published and reviewed in Taiwan until recently. Three papers have examined WFE in Taiwan (Chang, Lu, & Pan, 2012; Chang et al., 2010; Lu, 2011). Chang, Liou, and Huang (2010) examined and found a structure model that workplace spirituality influenced work-family balance through work identity and work-to-family enrichment (WTFE), and through family identity and family-to-work enrichment (FTWE), respectively. Lu (2011) used a longitudinal design with a three-wave panel sample. She found that WTFE was both an antecedent and a consequence of work role satisfaction over time; similarly, FTWE was both an antecedent and a consequence of family role satisfaction over time. Chang et al. (2012) found that resources (supervisory support) and family resources were positively related to WTFE and FTWE. WTFE was related to increased work satisfaction, and FTWE was related to increase family satisfaction. Both WTFE and FTWE positively affected happiness. In particular, the interdependent self was found to moderate the effect of work resources (flexible leave) on WTFE and FTWE, and also moderate the effect of family resources on WTFE and FTWE.

Three papers examined both WFC and WFE (Lu & Chang, 2014; Wang, 2014) or both WFC and WFF (Chou, 2012) in Taiwan. The Chou (2012) study found that WFC and WFF were different and independent factors. WFC was found to have two dimensions, WIF and FIW; however, WFF was found to be a unidimensional factor. Chou (2012) actually used a scale for measuring the positive aspects of work and family interface, WFF. This may be related to Chou's (2012) unexpected findings of the unidimensional factor. This issue needs further examination. Chou (2012) also found that Taiwanese parents experienced significantly higher levels of WFF than WFC. It was also revealed that the WFC and WFF affected life satisfaction.

Lu and Chang (2014) examined the mediating roles of four dimensions of the work and family interface, including both directions of WFC and both directions of WFE. The authors actually investigated a structural equation model, which treated workload, supervisory support, parental workload, and couple cohesion as antecedents of the four dimensions of the work and family interface, and then how the four dimensions of work and family interface affected job satisfaction, burnout, and family satisfaction.

Wang (2014) conducted a qualitative study aimed at exploring the WFC (both WIF and FIW) and WFE (both WTFE and FTWE) experiences of dual-career adults. Both WTFE and FTWE were related to obtaining resources or benefits from work or family to aid the other domain, and enhance spiritual meaning in both the work and family realms.

The studies reviewed here found that WFC and WFE were different and independent factors. Their findings were the same as those found in Western countries, which revealed that the positive and negative aspects of work and family interface could occur simultaneously in Taiwan (Aryee, Srinivas, & Tan, 2005; Grzywacz & Marks, 2000). As for the two quantitative researches on both WFC and WFE or WFF (Chou, 2012; Lu & Chang, 2014), both studies show that WFE or WFF are significantly higher than WFC in Taiwan.

As to the quantitative research papers including studies on WFE or WFF, the review framework and variable categories used for reviewing WFC also can be used for reviewing WFE and WFF. The antecedents of WFE or WFF in Taiwan can also be classified into role stressors, including workload and parent load (Lu & Chang, 2014); role involvement including work identification and family identification (Chang et al., 2010); social support including supervisor support (Chang et al., 2012; Lu, 2014); work or family characteristics including work resource, family resource, and couple cohesion (Chang et al., 2012; Lu, 2014); and demographic or individual variables including gender, age, marital status, educational degree, number of children, tenure, and job position (Chang et al., 2012; Chou, 2012). The outcomes of WFE or WFF can also be classified into work-related variables, including work satisfaction (Chang et al., 2012; Lu, 2014); nonwork-related variables, including family satisfaction and life satisfaction (Chang et al., 2012; Lu, 2011, 2014); and stress-related variables, including burnout, happiness, and work and family balance (Chang et al., 2010, 2012; Lu, 2014). The Interdependent self was found "marginally" significant as a moderator of the relationships between family resources and WTFE, and between family resources and FTWE (Chang et al., 2012).

The Characteristics of Work and Family Research

Theories, Variables, and Samples of Work and Family Research

The review framework and variable categories used in meta-analyses of W-F research in the United States (Allen et al., 2000; Amstad et al., 2011; Byron, 2005; McNall, Nicklin, & Masuda, 2010; Michel et al., 2011) can generally be applied to the classification and categorization of W-F research in Taiwan. Except for several qualitative studies, most theories and variables used for W-F research in Taiwan are similar to those used in Western countries, especially the United States. No specific emic construct or variable was found in this review. In fact, some emic issues or constructs related to work and family in Taiwan have been found and have contributed to the construction of those cross-cultural variables, such as vertical and horizontal individualism and collectivism, independent and interdependent self, etc. (Li et al., 2000; Schwartz & Bilsky, 1990; Triandis, 1988; Triandis et al., 1988; M.C. Yang, 1972; K.S. Yang, 1986). This W-F research review also included a study that looked at independent and interdependent self as moderator variables (Chang et al., 2012). There are probably some other unidentified emic issues about work and family in Taiwan. Those unidentified emic issues need further research in the future.

The most frequently used theory is role theory (Kahn et al., 1964; Marks, 1977; Sieber, 1974), and WFC research is generally based on the resource scarcity perspectives of the theory. WFE or WFF research is generally based on resource expansion-enhancement perspectives of the theory. The next most frequently used theory is conservation of resource (COR) theory (Hobfoll, 1989). COR theory proposes that people seek to acquire and maintain resources, and avoid a loss of resources. When people are faced with a loss of resources, they feel stressed. Role theory was described more clearly in its statements and logic. If COR theory can make a distinction between two kinds of resources, scarcity or finite resources, such as time, body energy, personal assets etc., and expansive or accumulative resources, such as experiences, skills, knowledge etc., COR theory might be used for explaining WFC and WFE more appropriately and clearly.

The samples used in W-F research include a large variety of participants in Taiwan, including participants from different areas, industries, businesses, occupations, professions, ethnicities, marital status, and other demographic variables. According to the analyses of the recent review of 36 WFC research papers by Chen et al. (2013), three industries, including education, public sector, and high-tech, have more WFC research examined.

Methodological Issues in W-F Research and Implications for Future W-F Research

Almost all the W-F research in Taiwan used and translated Western scales. There were generally no critical problems reported in the research using the Western scales. Only a few studies made some revisions to their W-F scales based on some Western scales. More qualitative research would facilitate the examination of cultural features and the emic constructs in the work and family interface in Taiwan. Consequently, based on the findings of the emic constructs from qualitative research, the emic variables and scales can be constructed.

There are no consistent gender differences found in WFC. Chen et al. (2013) suggest that future studies may use gender as a moderator to examine the other possible variables that might interact with gender and have a significant influence on WFC. Similarly, the possible gender moderating effect should also be examined in WFE or WFF domains.

Most W-F research in Taiwan has employed a cross-sectional design, a self-report survey to collect data, and did not check or prevent common method biases with valid procedural or statistical techniques (Podsakoff, MacKenzie, Lee, & Podsakoff, 2003). Future W-F research using a cross-sectional design in Taiwan should use valid procedural or statistical techniques in order to control the possible method biases. If more and more valid quantitative research on work and family is published in Taiwan, a meta-analysis of W-F research can then be implemented for obtaining more accurate and integrative findings on the work and family interface in Taiwan. Moreover, additional research with a longitudinal design or employing a qualitative method is also required in Taiwan.

W-F issues have become one of the major social issues in Taiwan. Due to advancement in information technology and globalization, most business companies of Taiwan need to enlarge their foreign markets or establish more foreign subsidiaries, and extend their service to 24 hours. The W-F interface therefore will become a more serious problem for many employees in the business companies. As a result, WFC and W-F balance would become a major concern for HRM in most companies in Taiwan. In the academic field, more researchers in HRM, OB, and I-O should become interested in W-F issues, and hence more research on W-F issues would be done in the future.

Focus Group Results

Demographic Characteristics and Procedure of the Focus Groups

Two focus group discussions were conducted at different times within approximately two months. The first focus group included five women and three men; the second focus group included six women and two men. In all, 11 women and 5 men participated in the two focus groups. The majority of the participants worked in the commerce industry. The families of the participants were all dual-earning families with one to three children. The average age of participants in the first focus group was 34.8 years; the average age of participants in the second focus group was 39.2 years. The average age of the all participants was 37.0 years. The majority of the participants had a college degree. More detailed information about the demographics of the focus group participants can be found in Table 12.2.

TABLE 12.2 Demographic characteristics of focus groups.

Focus Group	*Participant*	*Gender*	*Age*	*Educational level*	*Occupation*
1	1	Female	25	College	Assistant pharmacist
1	2	Female	36	College	Restaurant service
1	3	Female	54	College	Accountant
1	4	Female	40	College	Commerce
1	5	Female	35	College	Commerce
1	6	Male	26	College	Sales service
1	7	Male	28	College	Sales service
1	8	Male	35	High school	Information service
2	1	Female	34	College	Commerce

Focus Group	*Participant*	*Gender*	*Age*	*Educational level*	*Occupation*
2	2	Female	38	College	Commerce
2	3	Female	30	College	Finance
2	4	Female	47	High school	Clothing manufacture
2	5	Female	32	College	Commerce
2	6	Female	40	High school	Commerce
2	7	Male	38	Master's degree	Commerce
2	8	Male	55	College	Commerce

Participants in the focus groups were asked to discuss their own work and family conflict issues for an hour. The moderator, this author, first proposed questions and then led the participants in a discussion. The following questions were proposed in the discussion:

1. In what ways does your work interfere with your family responsibilities? What are the key reasons for this situation? What are the key outcomes? How do you cope with this problem?
2. In what ways does your family interfere with your work responsibilities? What are the key reasons for this situation? What are the key outcomes? How do you cope with this problem?
3. Are there differences between being a mother and being a father? What are the ideal norms for a mother and father, respectively?

General Themes and Subthemes

The primary antecedents of WIF were:

1. Long work hours: working until very late, working on weekends
2. Work overload: going on business trips, frequently needing to work overtime, needing to work for long overtime hours during the busy season
3. Busy with business meetings: busy with a lot of different kinds of meetings, attending work-related events or business parties

The main consequences of WIF were:

1. Lack of time for family members: less time to talk with children, less time to take care of children and elders
2. Poor relationships with children and other family members: complaints and criticism from spouses, elders, and children
3. Feeling guilty about not caring about one's family
4. Child behavioral problems: problems may be caused by less time spent caring for and educating children at home

The primary antecedents of FIW were:

1. Child or elder care problems: more child care needed, children get sick, accidents or emergencies involving children or elders
2. Children exhibit deviant behaviors: children show inappropriate behaviors, poor performance in school, wandering and playing on the street, and not coming home until very late
3. Social and family events: a death in the family, festivals and ceremonies, attending weddings or funerals

The main consequences of FIW were:

1. Poor performance or mistakes on the job: not able to concentrate on one's job due to worrying about one's family, making serious mistakes on the job
2. Work pressure: worrying about not completing the job, receiving a poor job evaluation, being anxious about losing one's job

Many different strategies for work and family conflict were discussed. These included:

1. Using sources of social supports including parent support, spouse support, coworker support, neighbor support, supervisor support, or a paid household helper, etc.
2. Building trust and reciprocal relationships and negotiating roles with one's partner: doing housework or caring duties in turn, setting schedules for household duties
3. Using electronic appliances to help oversee baby care: Using a monitor to oversee a baby while doing household chores or working at home
4. Using after-school child care services provided by private institutes: Children are bought to a child care center after they are dismissed from the school. The children generally stay in the center for several hours to do their homework or take some classes there until they are brought home by their parents.
5. Managing one's own emotional frustration in order not to lose one's temper at home or at work
6. Negotiating with companies to have more flexibility and benefits for doing the job or caring for one's family such as bringing children to the company during work hours or being able to put aside jobs or housework temporarily and then return to them later
7. Communicating with children to help solve their problems and training children to be more independent
8. Giving up the job or changing to a new job for a better work and family balance

Special Themes Found in the Focus Groups

Women Spend More Time at Home Doing Housework and Caring for Children and Elders

In traditional Chinese culture in Taiwan, more traditional obligations exist for women to take care of the housekeeping and their children, their parents-in-law, or even their own parents. The women in the groups expressed more FIW conflicts and more serious FIW outcomes than the men. The FIW conflicts and outcomes are listed in the preceding section. The survey results of Project 3535 support these focus group discussion results. The female participants surveyed in Taiwan spent more time per week caring for children (M = 34.32 vs. 24.52, $p <$ .001) and doing other household-related duties except caring for children and elders (M = 15.92 vs. 11.05, $p <$.01) than the male participants. In addition, the female participants reported significantly lower job involvement than the male participants (M = 3.97 vs. 3.71, $p <$ .05). The additional finding may be related to the fact that women generally spend more time at home and have less time to be involved in their jobs.

Women Are Traditionally Supposed to Sacrifice Their Career for Their Families if Necessary

Some mothers said that if their dual-earning family had problems balancing work and family, they would likely give up their job or change to a new job in order to balance work and family. Traditional Chinese culture in Taiwan generally considers family to be the basic and most important in-group (Triandis et al., 1988; M.C. Yang, 1972; K.S. Yang, 1986). The teachings of Confucius stress the obligations of people toward one another based on their relationship and the ethic of the relationship. Confucius proposed five principal relationships: One of the five relationships is the husband and wife relationship. According to the ethic of the relationship defined between the husband and the wife, the wife owes obedience and respect to the husband. In addition, there is a traditional ethic for the division of labor between men and women. Wives as women are responsible for housekeeping and husbands as men are responsible for working out of the family and earning a living for the family. Therefore, even women nowadays in Taiwan are still more likely than their husbands to give up their job or change to a new job in order to balance their work and family life.

Different Attitudes Toward Gender Inequality Between Older and Younger Generations of Women

Women frequently have different attitudes toward unequal gender situations that women face in work and family. Older generations of women in Taiwan are generally more willing to accept inequality than younger generations of women. Older generations of women tend to consider the WFC as challenges to their duties as women. However, younger generations of women tend to consider the inequality as being unfair to them, so they are more likely to ask for help from their husbands or other social supports in order to reduce their WFC.

Conclusion

In general, the problem of WFC in Taiwan is quite similar to the conflicts revealed in other countries. Thus, parents experience pressures from work and family demands; these pressures gradually create their own problems of WFC. Finally, the conflicts result in negative family and work outcomes. The general themes and subthemes were shown to be similar to the implication of the general WFC theory. However, there may be a few subthemes or illustrative instances unique to Taiwan, such as coping strategies: Taiwanese individuals may use after-school child care services provided by private institutes in Taiwan.

Three special themes were found in the focus groups, which include: (1) women spend more time at home doing housework and caring for children and elders, (2) women are traditionally supposed to sacrifice their careers for their families if necessary, and (3) different attitudes exist toward gender inequality between older and younger generations of women in Taiwan. These three themes actually reveal a common unique theme of social culture in Taiwan that the family ethics and conduct of Taiwanese individuals have been mainly influenced by traditional Chinese culture, especially Confucianism. Due to these traditional cultural influences on Taiwanese behaviors in family, women are more likely to take on more household responsibilities and are supposed to sacrifice their careers for their families. Older and younger generations of women are likely to have different attitudes toward gender inequality because older generations of women have been more influenced by traditional culture.

References

Allen, T. D., Herst, D. E., Bruck, C. S., & Sutton, M. (2000). Consequences associated with work-to-family conflict: A review and agenda for future research. *Journal of Occupational Health Psychology*, *5*, 278–308.

Amstad, F. T., Meier, L. L., Fasel, U., Elfering, A., & Semmer, N. K. (2011). A meta-analysis of work-family conflict and various outcomes with a special emphasis on cross-domain versus matching-domain relations. *Journal of Occupational Health Psychology*, *16*(2), 151–169.

Aryee, S., Srinivas, E. S., & Tan, H. H. (2005). Rhythms of life: Antecedents and outcomes of work-family balance in employed parents. *Journal of Applied Psychology*, *90*(1), 132–146.

Byron, K. (2005). A meta-analytic review of work-family conflict and its antecedents. *Journal of Vocational Behavior*, *67*, 169–198.

Chang, H. T., Liou, J. W., & Huang, M. Y. (2010). 職場靈性影響工作家庭平衡之研究: 整合模式的驗證 [The effects of workplace spirituality on work family balance: The Integrating model]. 台灣管理學刊, *10*(l), 79–102.

Chang, T., & Lu, L. (2009). 資源損失與資源獲得對職家衝突之影響：資源保存理論的觀點 [The effects of resource loss and resource gain on work-family conflict: The perspective of resource conservation]. *臺大管理論叢, 20*(1), 69–98.

Chang, T., Lu, L., & Pan, C. (2012). 工作與家庭的雙向增益：前因、後果及互依我的調節作用 [The bi-directional enrichment of work and family: Antecedents, consequences, and interdependent self as a moderator]. *中華心理學刊, 54*(4), 471–493.

Chang, Y., & Lu, L. (2013). 自我效能於家庭對工作衝突及其前因後果的調節作用 [The moderating effects of self-efficacy in the family-to-work conflict process]. *應用心理研究, 57*, 117–154.

Chen, W., Wang, Y., & Chiu, Y. (2013). 台灣工作家庭衝突研究之回顧與展望 [Review and prospection of studies on work-family conflict in taiwan]. *人力資源管理學報, 13*(4), 79–106.

Cheng, J., & Chen, J. (1994). 已婚職業婦女的生活壓力與自我狀態對身心健康之影響 [The effects of life stress and ego state on health of married working women]. *婦女與兩性學 刊, 5*, 47–67.

Chou, H. W., Chang, H. H., & Lee, C. Y. (2012). Work-family conflict and work exhaustion for IT employees: The moderating effect of social support. *Journal of Human Resource Management, 12*(2), 67–89.

Chou, L. (2012). 雙工作家庭的生活滿意：工作-家庭衝突與互利的影響 [Life satisfaction of dual-income families: The effect of work-family conflict and facilitation]. *中華心理衛生學刊, 25*(3), 377–418.

Council for Economic Planning and Development (CEPD). (2013). *Taiwan statistical data book*. Taipei, Taiwan: Executive Yuan, ROC. Retrieved October 10, 2014, from file:///C:/Users/tph/Downloads/Taiwan%20Statistical%20Data%20Book%20 2013%20(pdf)%20(3).pdf

Directorate General of Budget, Accounting and Statistics (DGBAS). (2014). *National Statistics Taiwan, ROC* [Data file]. National Statistics Information Service. Retrieved from http://www.stat.gov.tw/ct.asp?xItem=15408&CtNode=3623&mp=4

Government Information Office (GIO). (2012). *The Republic of China yearbook 2012*. Taipei, Taiwan: Executive Yuan, Taiwan. Retrieved October 12, 2014, from http://www.ey.gov.tw/en/MetaData.aspx?n=575a019c0a39897d

Grzywacz, J. G., & Marks, N. F. (2000). Reconceptualizing the work-family interface: An ecological perspective on the correlates of positive and negative spillover between work and family. *Journal of Occupational Health Psychology, 5*(1), 111–126.

Hobfoll, S. E. (1989). Conservation of resources: A new attempt at conceptualizing stress. *The American Psychologist, 44*(3), 513–524.

Hsu, Tsung-Kuo. (1993). *女人和男人的工作與家庭—攸關時間* [Women and men's work & family—Concerning time]. *婦女與兩性學刊, 4*, 175–206.

Huang, J. C., & Wang, Y. H. (2013). 工作狂與情緒耗竭、工作—家庭衝突之關係：個體間差異的調 節效果 [The relationships between workaholism, emotional exhaustion, and work-family conflict: The moderating effects of individual differences]. *東吳經濟商學學報, 83*, 1–42.

Kahn, R. L., Wolfe, D. M., Quinn, R. P., Snoek, J. D., & Rosenthal, R. A. (1964). *Organizational stress: Studies in role conflict and ambiguity*. New York, NY: John Wiley & Sons.

Kau, S., & Cho, K. (2013). 個人資源對在職進修者職家學衝突及後果之影響 [Antecedents and consequences of work, family, and learning conflict among adult learners]. 應用心理研究, *57*, 81–115.

Li, J., Lam, K., & Fu, P. P. (2000). Family-oriented collectivism and its effect on firm performance: A comparison between overseas Chinese and foreign firms in China. *The International Journal of Organizational Analysis, 8*(4), 364–379.

Liao, P.-Y. (2011). Linking work-family conflict to job attitudes: The mediating role of social exchange relationships. *International Journal of Human Resource Management, 22*(14), 2965–2980.

Lin, H., Kao, S., & Feng, H. (2013). 同酬也要同工：組織公平知覺對國小教師的職家衝突 與後果之調節 [Equal pay with equal obligation: Effects of perceived organizational justice on work-to-family conflict among elementary school teachers]. 商略學報, *5*(2), 137–152.

Liu, Y. (2008). 影響企業提供工作/家庭平衡措施之因素探討 *[The research on influencing factors of providing work/family balance programs]* (Unpublished master's thesis). 臺灣大學國家發展研究所學位論文, 臺北市, Taipei, Taiwan.

Lu, L. (2011). A Chinese longitudinal study on work/family enrichment. *Career Development International, 16*, 385–400.

Lu, L. (2014). 職家平衡在台灣：一個發展中國家的現況 [The dynamism of balancing work and family in a developing society: Evidence from Taiwan]. *應用心理研究, 59*, 49–79.

Lu, L., & Chang, Y. (2014). An integrative model of work/family interface for Chinese employees. *Career Development International, 19*(2), 162–182.

Lu, L., Gilmour, R., Kao, S. F., & Huang, M. T. (2006). A cross-cultural study of work/family demands, work/family conflict, and well-being: The Taiwanese vs. British. *Career Development International, 1*(11), 9–27.

Lu, L., Hwang, M., & Kao, S. (2005). 工作與家庭的雙向衝突：前因、後果及調節變項之探討 [The bi-directional conflict of work and family: Antecedents, consequences and moderators]. *應用心理研究, 27*, 133–166.

Lu, L., Kao, S. F., Chang, T., Wu, H., & Cooper, C. L. (2008). Work/family demands, work flexibility, work/family conflict, and their consequences at work: A national probability sample in Taiwan. *International Journal of Stress Management, 15*(1), 1–21.

Lu, L., Kao, S. F., Cooper, C. L., Allen, T. D., Lapierre, L. M., O'Driscoll, M., Poelmans, S.A.Y., Sanchez, J. I., & Spector, P. E. (2009). Work resources, work-to-family conflict, and its consequences: A Taiwanese-British cross-cultural comparison. *International Journal of Stress Management, 16*, 25–44.

Marks, S. R. (1977). Multiple roles and role strain: Some notes on human energy, time and commitment. *American Sociological Review, 42*(6), 921–936.

McNall, L. A., Nicklin, J. M., & Masuda, A. D. (2010). A meta-analytic review of the consequences associated with work-family enrichment. *Journal of Business & Psychology, 25*, 381–396.

Michel, J. S., Kotrba, L. M., Mitchelson, J. K., Clark, M. A., & Baltes, B. B. (2011). Antecedents of workfamily conflict: A meta-analytic review. *Journal of Organizational Behavior, 32*, 689–725.

Pan, S., & Yeh, Y. (2012). Impact of value congruence on work-family conflicts: The mediating role of work-related support. *Journal of Social Psychology, 152*(3), 270–287.

Podsakoff, P. M., MacKenzie, S. B., Lee, J. Y., & Podsakoff, N. P. (2003). Common method biases in behavioral research: A critical review of the literature and recommended remedies. *Journal of Applied Psychology, 88*, 879–903.

Schwartz, S. H., & Bilsky, W. (1990). Toward a theory of the universal content and structure of values: Extensions and cross cultural replications. *Journal of Personality and Social Psychology, 58*, 878–891.

Shih, Yin-Ho. (2008). 性別工作平等法實施現況與展望 [Implementation and prospects of gender equality in Employment Act]. *研考雙月刊, 32*(4), 22–31.

Sieber, S. D. (1974). Toward a theory of role accumulation. *American Sociological Review. 39*(4), 567–578.

Triandis, H. C. (1988). Collectivism and individualism: A reconceptualization of a basic concept in cross-cultural psychology. In G. K. Verma & C. Bagley (Eds.), *Personality, attitudes, and cognitions* (pp. 60–95). London, UK: Palgrave MacMillan.

Triandis, H. C., Bontempo, R., Villareal, M. J., Asai, M., & Lucca, N. (1988). Individualism and collectivism: Cross-cultural perspectives on self-ingroup relationships. *Journal of Personality and Social Psychology, 54*, 323–338.

Triandis, H. C., & Gelfand, M. J. (1998). Converging measurement of horizontal and vertical individualism and collectivism. *Journal of Personality and Social Psychology, 74*(1), 118–128.

Wang, Y. (2014). 雙生涯成人工作家庭角色衝突與優勢經驗之探究 [Work-family conflict and enrichment: An exploratory study of dual-career adults' experience]. *中華輔導與諮商學報, 39*, 151–182.

Wikipedia. (2014). Geography of Taiwan. Retrieved October 15, 2014, from http://en.wikipedia.org/wiki/Geography_of_Taiwan

Wu, M., Chang, C., & Zhuang, W. (2010). Relationships of work-family conflict with business and marriage outcomes in Taiwanese copreneurial women. *The International Journal of Human Resource Management, 21*(5), 742–753.

Yang, K. S. (1986). Chinese personality and its change. In M. H. Bond (Ed.), *The psychology of the Chinese people* (pp. 106–170). Hong Kong: Oxford University Press.

Yang, M. C. (1972). 中國的家族主義與國民性 [Chinese familism and nationalities]. In 李亦園 & 楊國樞 (Eds.), *中國人的性格* (pp. 133–179). 台北：桂冠.

Yen, H. (2013). 心有餘，而力不足？「家庭對工作衝突」對教師組織公民行為的影響 [The spirit is willing, but the flesh is weak? Investigate the impact of family-to-work conflict on teachers' organizational citizenship behaviors]. *教育經營與管理研究集刊, 9*, 31–60.

PART III

Work-Family Issues in Global Context

Zeynep Aycan

While Parts 1 and 2 of this book set the stage, Part 3 delves into the specific results from the quantitative survey that pertain to different aspects of how culture affects the work-family (W-F) interface, including relationships with coping, social support, guilt, gender, and context. Chapter 13, by Zeynep Aycan and Karen Korabik, is entitled "An Integrative Model of Work-Family Conflict: Pan-Cultural Effects and Cross-Cultural Differences." The authors present a bird's-eye view of the within- and cross-domain relationships in the theoretical model of Project 3535. Findings of the nested model testing with data from all 10 countries are presented. The most important contribution of this chapter is to illuminate "universal" as well as "culture-specific" relationships among WFC and its antecedents and consequences. Chapter 14, "Positive Spillover of the Work and Life Domains," by Barbara Beham, Anne Bardoel, and Steven Poelmans, focuses on the relationship of work-family positive spillover with well-being at work and at home. This chapter contributes to the relatively thin literature on positive spillover between work and family from a cross-cultural perspective. The cultural dimensions of vertical collectivism and monochronic-polychronic time orientation are treated as moderators in these relationships. Findings based on hierarchical linear modeling reveal several cross-level interactions indicating the significant role of culture as a moderator.

Chapter 15, "Understanding the Role of Personal Coping Strategy in Decreasing Work and Family Conflict: A Cross-Cultural Perspective," discusses the role of coping strategies in reducing WFC. The authors, Anit Somech and Anat Drach-Zahavy, provide an expert analysis that groups countries along two cultural dimensions: individualism-collectivism and gender-role ideology. The results suggest distinct patterns of coping strategies in different cultural groups. Chapter 16, by Roya Ayman, entitled "Social Support and the Work-Family Interface from a Cross-Cultural Perspective," examines the interaction between social support and culture. Findings based on multilevel linear modeling suggest that the most important sources of support to alleviate WFC were spouse and paid help, whereas the most important sources of support to increase positive spillover were spouse and children. This chapter is among a few empirical studies focusing exclusively on the role of social support in the positive and negative interface between work and family, and possibly the first cross-cultural study in the literature.

The next chapter, Chapter 17, "The Role of Work-Family Guilt in the Work-Family Interface: A Cross-Cultural Analysis," by Karen Korabik presents findings pertaining to a rarely studied and yet pervasive phenomenon: W-F guilt. Korabik found that in all countries, guilt arising from WIF is greater than that arising from FIW. The chapter provides a detailed description of cross-cultural similarities and differences in W-F guilt. Chapter 18, by Ujvala Rajadhyaksha, is entitled "Work-Family Conflict and Positive Spillover: Examining the Interaction of Gender, Gender-Role Ideology, and National Gender Equity Culture." This chapter presents a unique emphasis on gender and gender-related issues in the W-F interface. Based on a series of MANCOVA analyses, the author investigates the main and interaction effects of gender, three aspects of gender-role ideology (attitudes toward division of work and family roles, attitudes toward importance of men's careers, and attitudes toward women's employment), and national gender equity on WFC and positive spillover. Chapter 19, also by Ujvala Rajadhyaksha, is entitled "Exploring the Interaction of Culture and Contextual Factors on the Work-Family Interface." This chapter focuses on "contextual variables," including demographics, work context, and family context. Most contextual variables interacted with culture to impact the W-F interface and psychological well-being outcomes. The most influential contextual moderators were the family variables of spouse's job schedule and living arrangements. Finally, Chapter 20 provides a summary of the results of the research and highlights their implications for researchers, practitioners, and policy makers.

13

AN INTEGRATIVE MODEL OF WORK-FAMILY CONFLICT

Pan-Cultural Effects and Cross-Cultural Differences

Zeynep Aycan and Karen Korabik

Introduction

"We want work-life balance, we encourage people to have work-life balance"
—(Prime Minister Loong of Singapore, National Day speech, 2012).

"President Obama Models Work-Life Balance as Dad-in-Chief"
—(Pynchon, Forbes Magazine, 2011).

Work-family conflict (WFC) has been identified as an important issue occupying the agenda of even the highest level government officials in the world. Over the past two decades, research on WFC has proliferated, and increasingly complicated models have been postulated. The fast-growing research in this area has inspired several meta-analyses (e.g., Michel, Mitchelson, Kotrba, LeBreton, & Baltes, 2009; Shockley & Singla, 2011). Scholars around the world have investigated various aspects of the phenomenon in different countries (e.g., Pal & Saksvik, 2008, for Norway; Tang, Siu, & Cheung, 2014, for China). There are also large-scale cross-country comparisons (e.g., Hill, Yang, Hawkins, & Ferris, 2004; Lyness & Judiesch, 2014; Spector et al., 2004; Yang et al., 2012) and a special issue on international perspectives on work and family (Casper, Allen, & Poelmans, 2014).

The purpose of this study was to extend the current literature on WFC. We did so by first starting with a basic model of WFC, in which it was viewed as a bidirectional (i.e., work-interfering family, WIF, and family-interfering work, FIW) and multidimensional (i.e., time- and strain-based conflict) construct mediating the relationships between demands and outcomes in the work and family domains and work and family outcomes. Second, based on the results of several meta-analytic reviews (e.g., Allen, Herst, Bruck, & Sutton, 2000; Kossek & Ozeki, 1998,

1999; Mesmer-Magnus & Viswevaran, 2005) and meta-analytic path analyses (e.g., Byron, 2005; Ford, Heinen, & Langkamer, 2007; Michel et al., 2009; Shockley & Singla, 2011), we formulated a more comprehensive and integrated model that included both within-domain (e.g., work antecedents predicting WIF) and cross-domain (e.g., work antecedents predicting FIW) effects. Third, we tested the validity of this state-of-the-art model in 10 countries, which allowed us to identify both pan-cultural and culture-specific relationships. Fourth, we tested theory-driven hypotheses regarding cross-cultural differences. Last but not least, we went through a rigorous test of measurement equivalence across countries for all study variables prior to conducting cross-cultural comparisons.

Integrative Model of Bidirectional and Multidimensional W-F Conflict: Within- and Cross-Domain Effects

WFC is a form of inter-role conflict where the role demands in one domain (work or family) are incompatible with those in the other domain (Greenhaus & Beutell, 1985). The model we tested treats WFC as a bidirectional and multidimensional construct. The proposed model (see Figure 13.1) also focuses on both within- and cross-domain effects of WFC on outcome variables in the work and family domains.

Research has shown that WFC is bidirectional in nature, consisting of work interference with family conflict (WIF) and family interference with work (FIW) conflict. Much research has demonstrated that although WIF and FIW are related to one another (e.g., Aryee, Fields, & Luk, 1999; Frone, Russell, & Cooper, 1992; Mesmer-Magnus & Viswesvaran, 2005; Michel et al., 2009), they are associated with unique outcomes and explain incremental variance over one another (e.g., Korabik,

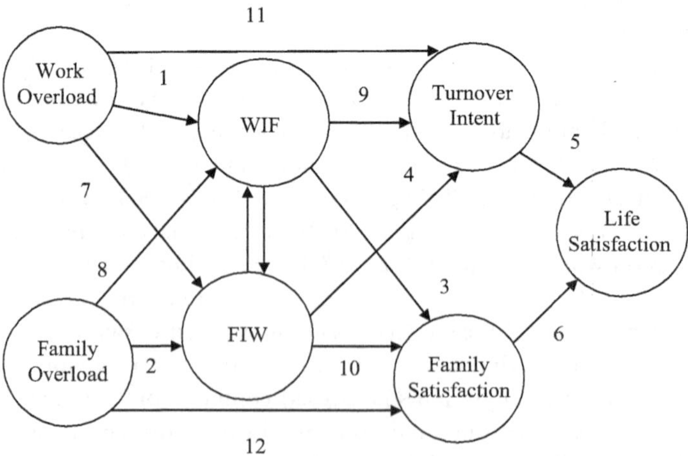

FIGURE 13.1 Conceptual model.

Lero, & Whitehead, 2008; Michel et al., 2009). Research has also shown that WFC is multidimensional. Greenhaus and Beutell (1985) proposed that WFC is composed of three components: time-, strain-, and behavior-based conflict. Because there have been problems regarding the conceptualization and psychometric properties of the behavior-based conflict dimension (Milkie, Denny, Kendig, & Schieman, 2010), we examined only time- and strain-based conflict in this study.

Basic Model of W-F Conflict

We began by articulating a basic model of WFC. In most such models, WIF and FIW are viewed as mediators between antecedents in the work and family domains and outcomes in the work, family, and life domains (Michel et al., 2009). For example, the models tested in earlier influential studies (i.e., Aryee, Fields, & Luk, 1999; Frone et al., 1992; Frone, Yardley, & Markle, 1997) share certain core features: (1) antecedents in the work domain predict WIF, whereas antecedents in the family domain predict FIW, and (2) WIF predicts family-related outcomes, whereas FIW predicts work-related outcomes. In developing our model, we started with a basic model similar to these (e.g., Aryee et al., 1999; Frone et al., 1992, 1997).

These models postulate that there will be within-domain effects between stressors and WFC. This has been supported by meta-analytic findings demonstrating that job stressors have a stronger influence on WIF than on FIW, whereas family stressors tend to be more related to FIW than to WIF (Byron, 2005; Mesmer-Magnus & Viswesvaran, 2005). Evidence that job stressors are positively related to WIF and family stressors are positively related to FIW is very compelling (Aryee et al., 1999, Byron, 2005; Ford et al., 2007; Frone et al., 1992, 1997; Mesmer-Magnus & Viswevaran, 2005; Michel et al., 2009). Using meta-analytic path analysis, Byron (2005) and Ford et al. (2007) compared the magnitude of the relationships between different types of job and family stressors to WIF and FIW. They both found that work overload was the strongest predictor of WIF, whereas family overload was the strongest predictor of FIW. In addition, the overload constructs explained significantly more of the variance in WFC than hours spent in the work or family domains (see also, Spector et al., 2007). Because of this, and the fact that role overload can be seen as both a time- and strain-based predictor of WFC (Frone et al., 1997), we used work and family overload as our measures of job and family role stressors, respectively. As depicted in Figure 13.1, it was predicted that work overload would be positively associated with WIF (path 1) and family overload would be positively associated with FIW (path 2).

According to the models just cited (Aryee et al., 1999; Frone et al., 1992, 1997) there should be cross-domain relationships between WIF and FIW and outcomes. Thus, WIF should produce negative outcomes in the family domain, whereas FIW should produce negative outcomes in the work domain. In the literature, outcomes related to satisfaction (i.e., job, family, life) are the most frequently investigated (Ford et al., 2007). Thus, there is a large body of research showing that WIF is associated with marital and family dissatisfaction (Allen et al., 2000; Ford et al., 2007; Michel et al., 2009; Mullen, Kelley, & Kelloway, 2008). Based on this we expected that there would be a significant negative relationship between WIF and family satisfaction (path 3).

Similarly, much research has indicated that FIW is negatively related to job satisfaction (Aryee et al., 1999; Dorio, Bryant, & Allen, 2008; Ford et al., 2007; Frone et al., 1997; Mesmer-Magnus & Viswevaran, 2005; Michel et al., 2009) and positively related to turnover intentions (Dorio et al., 2008; Kossek & Ozeki, 1999; Mesmer-Magnus & Viswevaran, 2005). In the present study we chose turnover intention rather than job satisfaction as the job-related outcome variable. Meta-analysis has established that there is a significant negative relationship between job satisfaction and turnover intention (Hellman, 1997). We focused on turnover intent, because it was of greater practical value to organizations, as intent to quit is considered to be one of the most reliable predictors of voluntary turnover (Hom & Griffeth, 1995; Mueller, Price, Boyer, & Iverson, 1994; Price & Mueller, 1986). We expected that there would be a significant positive relationship between FIW and turnover intent (path 4).

Aryee et al. (1999) demonstrated that life satisfaction was a function of both work and family satisfaction. Michel et al.'s (2009) meta-analytic path analysis supported this by establishing that both job satisfaction and family satisfaction were strong predictors of life satisfaction. Based on this we expected that there would be a significant negative relationship between turnover intent and life satisfaction (path 5) and a significant positive relationship between family satisfaction and life satisfaction (path 6).

Integrative Model of W-F Conflict

Over time, studies have indicated that WFC is a more complicated and intricate phenomenon than originally conceptualized. This has led researchers to formulate increasingly elaborate models. Three of the issues that have been addressed most frequently are: (1) whether in addition to within-domain effects, there are also cross-domain relationships between work and family overload and WFC, (2) whether in addition to cross-domain effects, there are also within-domain relationships between WFC and outcomes, and (3) whether direct relationships between role overload and within-domain outcomes exist or whether these relationships are fully or partially mediated by WFC. In developing our hypothesized integrative model, we examined the literature on each of these issues to see if postulating additional paths was warranted.

Additional Cross-Domain Effects

In Michel et al.'s (2009) meta-analytic path analysis the addition of cross-domain paths from work role conflict to FIW and family role conflict to WIF to basic models of WFC led to improved model fit. Based on this, we predicted that work overload would have a significant positive relationship with FIW (path 7) and family overload would have a significant positive relationship with WIF (path 8).

As previously noted, basic models specify that WFC will be associated with cross-domain outcomes (i.e., when work interferes with family it results in negative outcomes in the family and when family interferes with work it results in negative outcomes at work). By contrast, an alternative theory, the source attribution approach, has been proposed whereby WFC will lead individuals to attribute the blame for it to the domain that was the source of the conflict (Shockley & Singla, 2011). Source attribution effects should be accentuated when outcomes are of an affective nature, like satisfaction. According to this perspective, when work interferes with family, because the source (work) is blamed, it should result in decreased job satisfaction. Likewise, when family interferes with work, it should result in decreased family satisfaction (Shockley & Singla, 2011).

There is empirical support for source attribution predictions. Research has demonstrated that WIF is significantly negatively related to job satisfaction and positively related to turnover intent (Allen et al., 2000; Dorio et al., 2008; Kossek & Ozeki, 1998; Mesmer-Magnus & Viswevaran, 2005; Michel et al., 2009). Similarly, research supports a link between FIW and family satisfaction (Michel et al., 2009; Mullen et al., 2008). Both Michel et al.'s (2009) and Shockley and Singla's (2011) meta-analytic path analyses found that WIF and FIW were better predictors of same domain satisfaction than cross-domain satisfaction. Based on this, we predicted that there would be a significant positive relationship between WIF and turnover intent (path 9) and a significant negative relationship between FIW and family satisfaction (path 10).

Direct and Indirect Relationships of Role Overload

There is evidence to suggest that role overload may be directly related to within-domain outcomes. For example, using a sample drawn from 21 countries, Peterson et al. (1995) found that work overload was negatively correlated with job satisfaction. Likewise, work overload has often been cited as an antecedent of voluntary turnover (Hom & Griffeth, 1995; Mueller, Price, Boyer, & Iverson, 1994). By inference, one could expect a similar pattern for the effect of family overload with family satisfaction. Moreover, Michel et al.'s (2009) meta-analytic path analysis indicated that work role conflict and family role conflict had direct relationships with job and family satisfaction, respectively. Based on this, we expected that there would be a significant direct positive relationship between work overload and turnover intent (path 11) and a significant direct negative relationship between family overload and family satisfaction (path 12).

A related issue has to do with the extent to which WIF and FIW mediate the relationships between role overload and within-domain outcomes. Some evidence in regard to this comes from Michel et al.'s (2009) meta-analytic path analysis. Their results indicated that role stressors directly explained nearly 40% of the variance in the same domain satisfaction and that the incremental variance explained by the indirect effects (mediated through WIF or FIW) was very small (only 1–2%). However, Michel et al. did not include role overload among their job stressor variables. We examined mediation by comparing the direct paths from work and family overload to turnover intent and family satisfaction, respectively, as well as the indirect paths from domain specific overload to within domain satisfaction as mediated by WFC.

Cross-Cultural Differences in the Integrative Model

According to Russell and Bowman (2000), "global organizations have realized that there is a need to understand variations in work/family issues from one country or region to another, and what the key drivers of these variations are" (p. 124). Understanding cultural differences in WFC is necessary not only for global organizations (e.g., MNCs), but also for domestic organizations with a multicultural workforce. To effectively manage diversity, these organizations must seek to develop policies to balance work and family that are sensitive to cultural differences. Studying the influence of culture on WFC also will help managers in non-Western contexts (e.g., emerging economies) to understand the applicability of WFC models and policies that are developed in Western industrialized societies. Cross-cultural studies, therefore, will contribute to practice and policy development, and enhance theory building by introducing boundary conditions (i.e., cultural contingencies) in conceptualizing the WFC phenomenon and arriving at a more universal knowledge (Gelfand & Knight, 2005; Powell, Francesco, & Ling, 2009).

Shaffer, Joplin, and Hsu (2011) reviewed the results of 219 studies that used non-US samples. They classified them by region into the following categories: Anglo, East Europe, West Europe, Nordic Europe, Latin America, and Asia. They found that in the Anglo, Asian, Nordic, and Western European country clusters, work demands predicted both WIF and FIW. Family stressors were positively related to WFC for countries in the Anglo cluster, to both WIF and FIW for countries in the Asian cluster, and to FIW for counties in the Western European cluster. In terms of work-related consequences, WIF and FIW were generally negatively related to affective reactions (e.g., job dissatisfaction) and positively related to withdrawal outcomes in all country clusters. The results for family-related outcomes were more mixed. WIF and FIW were often, but not always, negatively related to family attitudes (e.g., satisfaction) in Anglo, Asian, Nordic, and East and West European country clusters.

In one of the few existing multinational studies, Steibler (2009) examined dual-earner couples in 23 European countries using archival data. She employed a demands-resource perspective to look at how work and family antecedents were related to time- and strain-based WIF. It was found that although country-level effects were not strong, the European countries with the highest levels of WIF were those characterized by greater affluence, more egalitarian gender-role attitudes, and better child care infrastructures. In another study, Hill et al. (2004) used structural equation modeling to test a basic model of WFC with job satisfaction as the only outcome variable. The sample was composed of men and women from 48 countries, all of whom were employed by IBM. The results indicated that the effects of corporate culture outweighed those of national culture.

Spector and colleagues (2004) examined relationships among W-F stressors, time spent at work, and well-being among managers in three geographical regions: Anglo, Chinese, and Latin American. Their results showed that in all three country clusters, W-F stressors were negatively related to job satisfaction and well-being. However, there was a stronger relation between weekly work hours and W-F pressure for Anglo participants than for Chinese or Latin American participants. In a follow-up study, Spector and colleagues (2007) looked at the relationships among WIF, job satisfaction, and turnover intention in a sample of managers in four country clusters (Anglo, Asia, Eastern Europe, and Latin America). The results were similar to their previous study in that the association between work demands and WIF and between WIF and job satisfaction/turnover intention was stronger for the Anglo countries than for the other country clusters.

Most research on WFC and its correlates has been carried out in single countries (Aycan, 2008; see Shaffer et al., 2011, for a review). However, there also have been some studies that compared multiple cultures (e.g., Hill et al., 2004; Lyness & Judiesch, 2014; Spector et al., 2004; Steibler, 2009; Yang et al., 2012). None of these studies, however, examined an integrative model of WFC that included both antecedents and consequences in both the work and family domains. Most of them looked only at WIF and not at FIW (Spector et al., 2004, 2007; Steibler, 2009) and/or only at job-related outcomes (Hill et al., 2004; Spector et al., 2004, 2007). In addition, the range of participants in these studies had been limited due to their sampling from a single organization (Hill et al., 2004), a single geographic region (Steibler, 2009), or individuals with certain demographic characteristics. For example, the participants in the Spector et al. (2004, 2007) studies were all managers, the majority of whom were men and who were not parents. Furthermore, most of these studies have relied on convenience samples of countries and ad hoc explanations of cross-country differences. The present research extends the literature by testing the integrative model previously described with a theoretically justified selection of countries with a priori hypotheses concerning cross-cultural differences.

We selected the 10 Project 3535 countries to vary on individualism-collectivism and gender egalitarianism, which have been the cultural characteristics most frequently cited to account for variance in WFC and its relationships with antecedents and consequences (e.g., Aycan, 2008; Powell et al., 2009; Yang et al., 2012). Individualism-collectivism captures how individuals construe themselves (as unique and independent persons vs. connected to others) and how they attribute importance to personal interests versus shared pursuits (Triandis, 1995; Wagner, 1995). In individualistic cultures people have a higher tendency to keep work and family relationships separate, compared to those in collectivistic ones (e.g., Smith, Dugan, & Trompenaars, 1996). Therefore, it is likely that role overload in the work and family domains would upset individuals more in individualistic compared to collectivistic cultures (Yang et al., 2012). The collectivist culture legitimizes giving priority to work, and investing extra effort in work is considered self-sacrifice for the benefit of the family rather than sacrifice of the family for the selfish pursuit of one's own career as in an individualistic culture (Lu, Gilmour, Kao, & Huang, 2006).

Gender egalitarianism as a cultural characteristic concerns the enactment of men's and women's roles in society (Emrich, Denmark, & Den Hartog, 2004; House, Hanges, Javidian, Dorfman, & Gupta, 2004). In gender egalitarian cultures, there is less adherence to the traditional division of labor between men and women in which men are viewed as primary earners and women are viewed as primary caregivers. Gender egalitarianism, although not as widely used as individualism-collectivism, has recently been considered an important cultural characteristic accounting for variation in WFC experiences across cultures (e.g., Lyness & Judiesch, 2014; Powell et al., 2009). It is expected that in cultures with less, compared to more, gender egalitarianism, role overload in work and family domains will be associated with stronger WFC and its negative consequences.

In the present study, we theoretically classified the 10 countries into three groups based on previous findings of their placement on individualism-collectivism and gender egalitarianism (e.g., Hofstede, 1990; House et al., 2004). We further empirically verified this grouping through cluster analysis of the scores on vertical collectivism and gender-role ideology from our survey, as reported in Chapter 2. Accordingly, the 10 countries were classified into three groups: (1) high on individualism and high on gender egalitarianism (Australia, Canada, Spain, and the United States); (2) high on collectivism and low on gender egalitarianism (China, India, Indonesia, and Turkey); (3) average on both dimensions (Israel and Taiwan). We refer to these groups as I-E (individualistic and egalitarian), C-T (collectivistic and traditional), and MC-MT (medium collectivistic and medium traditional).

The primary purpose of this chapter was to test an integrative model in 10 countries and to examine cross-cultural differences in the paths proposed in the model (see Figure 13.1). We adopted the Type II approach in cross-cultural research by treating culture as the moderator (rather than the main effect) (Brett, Tinsley, Janssens, Barsness, & Lyttle, 1997; see also, Chapter 1). This approach acknowledges that constructs may be related in non-uniform ways across cultures. We expect that the relationships in the hypothesized paths would be strongest in the I-E country group, followed by MC-MT and C-T.

Results

Analytic Approach

Measurement and structural model testing were carried out using AMOS (Arbuckle, 2006). Multiple goodness-of-fit indices were reviewed to asses model fit including Chi square (χ^2), comparative fit index (CFI), Tucker-Lewis Index (TLI), and root mean square error of approximation (RMSEA). Although good fitting models will have nonsignificant ($p < .05$) chi-square values, models with large sample sizes will almost always be statistically significant (Milfont & Fischer, 2010; Vandenberg & Lance, 2000), not necessarily indicative of a lack of fit. Values close to 1 for the CFI and TLI are considered to signify a very good fit, while models with fit indices < .9 require substantial improvement (Arbuckle, 2006). The RMSEA should ideally be < .05; however, values up to .08 are acceptable (Vandenberg & Lance, 2000).

Test of the Integrative Baseline Model

After establishing the measurement equivalence/invariance of all of the constructs in our model (see Chapter 2), we proceeded to test the hypothesized integrative model (Figure 13.1) with the combined data from 10 countries. This model was treated as the baseline model to build nested models onto. The exploratory evaluation involved post hoc fitting of the model to determine the best fitting and the most parsimonious model (Byrne, 2012). First, instead of a reciprocal path between WIF and FIW, the path went from FIW to WIF. Second, the modification indices suggested a correlation between two exogenous variables (work overload and family overload). These modifications, were considered to be substantively meaningful and were supported by previous research (Michel et al., 2009). The overall fit of this baseline model was adequate: χ^2 (140) = 355.17, $p < .001$; CFI = .975; TLI = .935; RMSEA = .024. The standardized path coefficients presented in Table 13.1 (column named "Baseline Model") suggested that the data confirmed all relationships proposed in Figure 13.1, except for that between WIF and family satisfaction (path 3). For this path, the relationship was nonsignificant.

Two mediation pathways were examined in the baseline model. The first was from work overload to WIF to turnover intent, and the second was from family overload to FIW to family satisfaction. In order to evaluate the mediation effects, the direct and indirect effects of the paths and standard errors of the indirect effects were simultaneously estimated using a bias-corrected bootstrapped standard error with 1,000 draws. This approach was selected as other methods for testing for mediation (e.g., Baron & Kenny, 1986) have been shown to be statistically underpowered compared to this method (MacKinnon, Lockwood, Hoffman, West, & Sheets, 2002; MacKinnon, Lockwood, & Williams, 2004). The

TABLE 13.1 Nested model testing for cross-cultural differences and similarities.

			Theoretical Grouping				*Type A Modification*			*Type B Modification*		*Type C Modification*	
	Path number Figure1	*Baseline Model*	*I-E*	*MC-MT*	*C-T*	*CFI*	*All, but IN, CN*	*IN, CN*	*CFI*	*All countries equal*	*CFI*	*All countries free*	*CFI*
WO-WIF	1	40 (02)	44 (02)	37 (04)	26 (02)	**.973**							
FO-FIW	2	30 (02)	15 (02)	27 (04)	25 (02)	**.970**							
FIW-TI	4	22 (04)	08 (08)	35 (10)	27 (06)	**.969**							
WIF-FSAT	3	-03 (02), ns				.950	-15 (02)	21 (07)	**.966**				
TI-LSAT	5	-11 (01)				.944			.945		.948	§	**.966**
FSAT-LSAT	6	82 (02)				.943			.947	80 (06)	**.966**		
WO-FIW	7	14 (01)				.950	07 (01)	22 (03)	**.965**				
FO-WIF	8	10 (02)	06 (03)	10 (04)	19 (02)	**.965**							
WIF-TI	9	15 (02)	34 (07)	17 (09)	01 (06)	**.964**							
FIW-FSAT	10	-09 (03)	-16 (04)	-05 (05)	-18 (04)	**.964**							
WO-TI	11	15 (02)				.943			.940		.940	§	**.963**
FO-FSAT	12	-11 (01)	-14 (02)	-12 (03)	03 (02)	**.962**							

Note. Numbers in parentheses are SE of the unstandardized beta weights. Decimal points in standardized path coefficients and SE are omitted. I-E: Individualistic and Egalitarian; C-T: Collectivistic and Traditional; ME-MT: Mid-level Collectivism and Mid-level Traditionalism; IN: India; CN: China; CFI: Comparative Fit Index; WO: Work Overload; FO: Family Overload; WIF: Work Interfering Family; FIW: Family Interfering Work; TI: Turnover Intention; FSAT: Satisfaction with Family; LSAT: Life Satisfaction. §. Beta weights for each country can be obtained from the first author.

TABLE 13.2 Unstandardized estimates of the direct and indirect effects of the two mediation pathways.

Mediation Pathways	*Estimate*	*SE*	*95% CI*[a]
WO→ TI (direct)	.23***	.04	
WO→ WIF	.39***	.03	
WIF→ TI	.16**	.05	
WO→ WIF→TI (indirect)	.06**	.02	[.02, .11]
FO→ FS (direct)	-.16***	.02	
FO→ FIW	.33***	.02	
FIW→ FS	-.04	.04	
FO→ FIW→ FS (indirect)	-.01	.01	[-.04, .01]

Note. WO: Work Overload; FO: Family Overload; WIF: Work Interfering Family; FIW: Family Interfering Work; TI: Turnover Intention; FS: Family Satisfaction; $^{*}p < .05$; $^{**}p < .01$; $^{***}p < .001$.
[a] Bias corrected bootstrapped confidence intervals of the standard errors for the indirect effects.

total effect of work overload on turnover intention (b = .29) separated into a significant direct effect (b = .23, SE = .04) and a significant indirect effect through the mediator, WIF (b = .06, SE = .02). This result supports partial mediation with 15% of the variance in turnover intention accounted for by the model. The total effect of family overload on family satisfaction (b = -.17) separated into a significant direct effect (b = -.16, SE = .02) and a nonsignificant indirect effect through the mediator, FIW (b = -.01, SE = .01). This result fails to support the mediation pathway in the family domain. The model accounted for 10% of the variance in family satisfaction (see Table 13.2).

Cross-Cultural Differences: Nested Model Testing

One of the main purposes of this study was to examine cross-cultural differences in the paths of the baseline model. The general expectation was that the relationships in the paths in the baseline model would be stronger for countries characterized by "individualism and egalitarianism" (I-E), followed by those characterized by "mid-level collectivism and mid-level traditionalism" (MC-MT) and finally by "collectivism and traditionalism" (C-T). For each path in Figure 13.1, we set the path coefficient to be equal within each country group and examined the model fit. For example, in step 1, the coefficient for path 1 was set to be equal within I-E countries, within C-T countries, and within MC-MT countries. When this is done, model fit indices are expected to be as good as those in the baseline model. To judge that, we compared the CFI of the baseline model and that of the constraint model. A difference of .01 or smaller between the two CFI values indicated that the model still had good fit (Chueng & Rensvold, 2002). In the next step, we set the coefficient of path 2 to be equal within the same country groups. A difference of .01 or smaller between CFI in step 1 and CFI in step 2 indicated good fit. The same procedure of constraining the coefficients of all 12 paths continued one path at a time.

If the CFI difference was larger than .01 at any point in the nested model testing, we opted for constraining path coefficients to be equal for India and China on the one hand, and equal for all remaining countries, on the other. We opted for this ad hoc strategy by exploring the path coefficient of each country. We refer to this as "Type A modification." If this failed, we opted for constraining the coefficients of all countries to be equal and called it "Type B modification." If this also failed, we set all path coefficients to be freely estimated across countries ("Type C modification").

The findings of the nested model testing are presented in Table 13.1. As can be seen, for 7 out of the 12 paths, the theoretical country groupings yielded good model fit. However, the relative magnitude of path coefficients was as hypothesized for only three of the paths, with the strongest relationship for I-E countries followed by MC-MT and C-T countries. These were the paths from: (1) work overload to WIF (path 1), (2) WIF to turnover intention (path 9), and (3) family overload to family satisfaction (path 12). Although there was good model fit, the reverse order of country groupings was observed for three other paths: (1) family overload to FIW (path 2), (2) family overload to WIF (path 8), and (3) FIW to turnover intention (path 4). For these paths, the strongest relationship was for the C-T country grouping, while the weakest relationship was in the I-E country group. For the last path that had good model fit (path 10), FIW was (negatively) associated with family satisfaction to a greater extent in I-E and C-T countries, compared to MC-MT countries.

Type A modification was employed for two paths: (1) WIF to family satisfaction (path 3), and (2) work overload to FIW (path 7). For India and China, path 3 was positive, whereas it was negative for all other countries. The magnitude of the coefficient for path 7 was much higher for India and China, than for the rest of the countries.

Type B modification was employed for the family satisfaction-life satisfaction relationship. For this relationship, country groupings of all types disrupted model fit. Instead, the model fit was good when the coefficient of all countries was set to be equal. The positive association between family satisfaction and life satisfaction was the only "universal" relationship obtained in this study.

Type C modification was employed for two paths: (1) work overload to turnover intention (path 11) and (2) turnover intention to life satisfaction (path 5). For these relationships, path coefficients had to be allowed to estimate freely for all countries. These paths were those with the maximum level of cross-cultural differences.

Discussion

The study reported in this chapter had two purposes. First, we developed and tested a comprehensive, integrative model of bidirectional and multidimensional

WFC model with within- and cross-domain effects. Second, we explored cross-cultural similarities and differences in the relationships proposed in this model. We will first discuss the findings pertaining to the integrative baseline model, followed by those pertaining to cross-cultural comparisons.

Integrative Baseline Model Featuring Within- and Cross-Domain Effects

The integrative model was first tested at the pan-cultural level (e.g., Heine, 2005) with 2,800+ employees from 10 countries. The integrative model expanded Frone et al.'s basic model (1997) to include crossover effects and multiple outcomes (i.e., turnover intention, family satisfaction, life satisfaction) predicted by role overload through the mediation of WFC. Given the complexity of the model and diversity of the sample to test it, the data provided good fit to the model.

Let us start by discussing the effects of role overload. The findings revealed that overload from both domains was significantly associated with higher levels of both WIF and FIW. However, work overload had a stronger association with WIF than with FIW, and family overload had a stronger association with FIW than with WIF. Feeling overwhelmed and overloaded in one domain increases the risk of time- and strain-based conflict experienced in that domain and the inability to fulfill responsibilities in the other domain. Our findings also suggested that work overload increased the intention to quit one's job, and family overload decreased satisfaction with one's family. However, it should be noted that these direct relationships were modest. It appears that overload by itself is not a strong risk factor for individuals and organizations (i.e., turnover intention and satisfaction with family). Its negative impact on the outcomes is augmented especially when it leads to increased WFC.

Turnover intention was found to increase as a function of both FIW and WIF, although the impact of the former is slightly higher than that of the latter. It appears that employees consider quitting their current job (perhaps with the intention of changing jobs) when the level of time commitment and stress in one domain no longer allows them to fulfill responsibilities in the other domain. Family satisfaction was found to be an outcome marginally, if at all, influenced by FIW and WIF. It seems that satisfaction with one's family is generally high regardless of the level of WFC. Last, but not least, life satisfaction as an indicator of general psychological well-being was strongly and positively associated with family satisfaction and negatively and weakly associated with turnover intention. These findings suggest that satisfaction in the family domain is more important than satisfaction in the work domain in predicting overall psychological well-being of employees.

What does our baseline integrative model tell us about the within- and cross-domain effects? Overall, the model suggests that within-domain effects are stronger than cross-domain effects: (1) family overload was a stronger predictor of FIW than WIF, (2) FIW was a stronger predictor than WIF of turnover intention, and (3) work overload was a stronger predictor of WIF than FIW. The only exception to this general pattern (i.e., within-domain effect being stronger than cross-domain effect) was that FIW was a stronger predictor of family satisfaction than WIF. Employees' sense of satisfaction with the family was reduced when family was perceived to be the source of role conflict (FIW). However, family was not blamed when work was perceived to be the source of role conflict (WIF). This supports the source attribution hypothesis of Shockley and Singla (2011), which asserts that individuals experience dissatisfaction with the domain they perceive to be the source of conflict.

Moderating Effects of Culture and Cross-Cultural Differences

We treated the pan-cultural model as the baseline and culture as the moderator influencing the strength or direction of the relationships in the baseline model (Brett et al., 1997). The general expectation was that relationships among variables in the baseline model would be stronger for "individualistic and gender egalitarian" cultures (I-E: Australia, Canada, Spain, and the United States) than for "medium collectivistic and medium traditional" cultures (MC-MT: Israel and Taiwan) and for "collectivistic and traditional" ones (C-T: China, India, Indonesia, and Turkey).

As expected, the relationship between work overload and WIF, and between WIF and turnover intention was strongest in I-E cultures, followed by MC-MT and C-T cultures. Increased work overload was associated with increased WIF, and increased WIF was associated with higher turnover intention more strongly in individualistic and gender-egalitarian cultures than in collectivistic and traditional cultures. Our findings are congruent with those of previous research, which found that although work demands are predictive of WIF in a wide variety of cultures (Shaffer et al., 2011) the relationship is stronger in individualistic than collectivistic cultures (Lu et al., 2006; Spector et al., 2004, 2007). This is also aligned with the literature showing that the negative relationship between job satisfaction and withdrawal from work (e.g., absenteeism and turnover) is stronger in individualistic compared to collectivistic cultures (Posthuma, Joplin, & Maertz, 2005; Ramesh & Gelfand, 2010; Thomas & Au, 2002).

Higher family overload, on the other hand, was associated with increased WFC (both WIF and FIW) and higher FIW was associated with increased turnover intention more strongly in collectivistic and traditional cultures than in individualistic and egalitarian ones. Our findings call into question findings of Lu et al. (2006) that a stronger relationship between family demands and FIW for British compared to the Taiwanese was due to individualism-collectivism. Our findings may be due to the fact that employees in collectivistic and traditional cultures are more likely to get overwhelmed with family duties and responsibilities (Schwartz et al., 2010). This appears to increase their likelihood of experiencing WFC and of quitting their job to attend more to the family-related responsibilities. Taken together these findings suggest that work overload triggers WIF and turnover intention more strongly/easily in I-E cultures than C-T ones, whereas family overload triggers WFC and turnover intention more strongly/easily in C-T cultures than I-E ones.

Family satisfaction was an important outcome variable in the family domain. Family satisfaction increased with diminishing levels of FIW both in I-E and C-T cultures (the magnitude of this relationship was lower for MC-MT cultures). It may be that employees are pleased with their families to the extent that families do not interfere with work and do not cause low job performance. Alternatively, those employees who are satisfied with their families may be naturally less likely to experience FIW.

Family satisfaction increased with decreasing levels of WIF in all countries except for China and India. For these countries, family satisfaction increased with *increasing* levels of WIF.

There may be three explanations for this counterintuitive finding in China and India. First, the harder employees work in these countries (and therefore experience WIF), the more likely that they provide good living standards for their families. Spector et al. (2005) suggested that extra hours worked is seen as a worthwhile sacrifice for the family in China and Latin countries (see also, Yang, Chen, Choi, & Zou, 2000). Hassan, Dollard, and Winefield (2010) also found a positive relationship between WIF and family satisfaction in Malaysia. These authors propose that in this cultural context, work activities were allowed to interrupt family life because work was seen as a sacrifice for the family. Therefore, although work interferes with family life, it is endured, because in the end, the family would gain and this resulted in higher family satisfaction. This is consistent with the notion that family prosperity is the main agenda in collectivist life (Wang, Li, Xu, & Tian, 2004). It should be noted that China and India were the two countries in our sample with the highest level of income inequality. It is likely that hard work is seen as the only way for upward mobility in these countries. Second, employees in China and India may be satisfied with their family and feel that the family is strong enough to tolerate interference from work; this explanation suggests a reverse causality between family satisfaction and WIF. Third, employees in these cultures may more easily accept the co-existence of contradictory conditions in life (dialectic thinking and Confucianism; cf. Peng & Nisbett, 1999): On the one hand, not fulfilling responsibilities in the family to the extent possible, and on the other hand, being content with the family and pleased with the way it grows and functions.

We would like to end this section by discussing the most "universal" and most "culturally specific" findings of this study. The strongest and culturally most invariant relationship was between family satisfaction and life satisfaction. It appears that family satisfaction plays a very strong role in the psychological well-being of employed individuals, regardless of their cultural background. In contrast, the culturally most variant relationships were between work overload and turnover intention, and between turnover intention and life satisfaction. Employees in some countries appear to tolerate work overload and job dissatisfaction better than others. Cultural context does not appear to be the underlying factor explaining this variation. For example, among the culturally most similar countries, the relationship between work overload and turnover intention (standardized beta weights) was .03 in Australia, .19 in Canada, and -.14 in the United States. The availability of jobs in the market at the time of data collection in each country may have determined the willingness to pursue alternative job options. The same factor may also explain why in some countries turnover intention was a source of dissatisfaction with life, whereas in other countries it was not. For example, in Israel, Spain, and Taiwan work overload was positively associated with turnover intention (.13, .28, and .11, respectively). However, in the same countries, higher turnover intention was associated with lower life satisfaction (-.19, -.21, and -.20, respectively). Employees who suffer from work overload in these countries *can* consider quitting their jobs, probably because there are options in the job market. Knowing that there are options, but continuing to work in the same job/organization seems to lower life satisfaction.

In summary, cultural characteristics as well as country context (e.g., economic development and job market conditions) moderated the relationships found in the integrative model. Several conclusions can be drawn from these analyses. First, work overload was more strongly associated with WIF and turnover intention in I-E cultures, whereas family overload was more strongly associated with WFC and turnover intention in C-T cultures. In competitive individualistic cultures, work role is the primary source of self-identity and self-efficacy, whereas in collectivistic traditional cultures, family role functions the same way. In the former case, it is likely for employees to feel overwhelmed with work and experience the subjective feeling of overload, whereas in the latter case, the same is likely for the family domain.

Second, higher family satisfaction was associated with lower levels of WIF and FIW, with the exception of China and India where family satisfaction increased with *increasing* levels of WIF. We offered several explanations for these exceptions, but for us the most likely explanation was that the harder employees worked in China and India, the more they were pleased with the upward social mobility achieved by their families. Third, culture of country context did not play a role in the relationship between family satisfaction and life satisfaction. Employees' sense of well-being was strongly driven from their satisfaction with their family life, regardless of the cultural characteristics or country context. Finally, turnover intention was associated with higher life satisfaction in countries only when alternative job options were available. The relationships between work overload and turnover intention, and between turnover intention and life satisfaction were not moderated by cultural characteristics; it appeared to be moderated by the country's economic and job market context.

This research is an important step toward testing an integrative model connecting antecedents and consequences of WFC in both the work and family domains. We developed this model based on the results of several meta-analytic reviews (e.g., Allen et al., 2000; Kossek & Ozeki, 1998, 1999; Mesmer-Magnus &

Viswesvaran, 2005) and meta-analytic path analyses (e.g., Byron, 2005; Ford et al., 2007; Michel et al., 2009; Shockley & Singla, 2011). To our knowledge, this is the first time an integrative model using within- and cross-domain effects was tested with such a large and diverse sample. Furthermore, we tested the validity of this model with data from 10 countries to identify culturally generalizable and culture-specific relationships among variables. Collection and analysis of data was conducted as rigorously as possible: The selection of countries was based on theoretical grounds, a standardized sampling scheme was used in each country, questionnaires were developed to represent both etic and emic aspects of the constructs underlying each measure, conceptual equivalence of measures across cultures was tested through measurement equivalence/invariance analyses, and cross-cultural similarities and differences were tested using theoretically sound and empirically justified cultural groups.

There were several limitations of this research. First, our integrative model did not include any constructs tapping "support" in work and family domains. Although social support has been found to play an important role in the W-F interface, we omitted it here because our measures of support did not pass our criterion for measurement equivalence/invariance. It should be noted that there is a chapter in this book devoted specifically to social support (see Chapter 16). Second, data were from organizationally employed individuals with a spouse/partner and at least one child who lived primarily in cities. These sampling criteria may limit the extent to which our findings are generalizable to other family types (e.g., single parents), to the self-employed, or to those living in rural areas. Furthermore, our sample does not fully represent countries with very diverse populations (e.g., India, Indonesia, and Israel). Third, our integrative model featured causal links among variables, but we tested it using cross-sectional, rather than longitudinal data. Finally, we investigated the role of culture, but not the role of gender. The moderating effect of the *interaction* between culture and gender would have given us a more comprehensive picture than the one presented here, but it would have also complicated the analyses and their presentations. We have given gender and gender-role ideology full attention in Chapter 18.

Several implications for policy and practice can be drawn from our findings. First, our findings suggest that domestic or multinational organizations operating in collectivistic and traditional cultures are likely to prevent turnover if they can assist their employees in managing overload in the family. Company-sponsored child care and elder care services, emergency support mechanisms, flexible work arrangements, and extended maternal and paternal leaves are among the practices organizations could adopt. These practices are certainly helpful also for employees in individualistic cultures (see Chapter 3), but our findings suggest that they would be more so for those in collectivistic and traditional cultures. Second, employees should be provided training on how to handle work overload more efficiently, using technology or developing skills, such as time management, delegation/teamwork, support seeking, and communication.

References

Allen, T. D., Herst, D. E. L., Bruck, C. S., & Sutton, M. (2000). Consequences associated with work-to-family conflict: A review and agenda for future research. *Journal of Occupational Health Psychology, 5*(2), 278–308. doi:10.1037/1076-8998.5.2.278

Arbuckle, J. (2006). *Amos 7.0 user's guide.* Spring House, PA: Amos Development Corporation.

Aryee, S., Fields, D., & Luk, V. (1999). A cross-cultural test of a model of the work-family interface. *Journal of Management, 25*, 491–511. doi:10.1177/014920639902500402.

Aycan, Z. (2008). Cross-cultural approaches to work-family conflict. In K. Korabik, D. S. Lero, & D. L. Whitehead (Eds.), *Handbook of work-family integration: Research, theory and best practices* (pp. 353–370). New York, NY: Elseiver.

Baron, R. M., & Kenny, D. A. (1986). The moderator-mediator variable distinction in social psychological research: Conceptual, strategic, and statistical considerations. *Journal of Personality and Social Psychology, 51*(6), 1173–1182. doi:10.1037/0022-3514.51.6.1173

Brett, J. M., Tinsley, C. H., Janssens, M., Barsness, Z. I., & Lyttle, A. L. (1997). New approaches to the study of culture in industrial/organizational psychology. In P. C. Earley & M. Erez (Eds.), *New perspectives on international industrial/organizational psychology* (pp. 75–130). San Francisco, CA: The New Lexington Press.

Byrne, B. (2012). *Structural equation modeling with Mplus: Basic concepts, applications, and programming*. New York, NY: Routledge.

Byron, K. (2005). A meta-analytic review of work-family conflict and its antecedents. *Journal of Vocational Behavior, 67*(2), 169–198. doi:10.1016/j.jvb.2004.08.009

Casper, W. J., Allen, T. D., & Poelmans, S.A.Y. (2014). International perspectives on work and family: An introduction to the special section. *Applied Psychology: An International Review, 63*(1), 1–4. doi:10.1111/apps/12020

Chueng, G. W., & Rensvold, R. B. (2002). Evaluating goodness-of-fit indexes for testing measurement invariance. *Structural Equation Modeling, 9*(2), 233–255. doi:10.1207/S15328007SEM0902_5

Dorio, J. M., Bryant, R. H., & Allen, T. D. (2008). Work-related outcomes of the work-family interface: Why organizations should care. In K. Korabik, D. S. Lero, & D. L. Whitehead (Eds.), *Handbook of work-family integration: Research, theory and best practices* (pp. 157–176). New York, NY: Elseiver.

Emrich, C. G., Denmark, F. L., & Den Hartog, D. N. (2004). Cross-cultural differences in gender egalitarianism: Implications for societies, organizations, and leaders. In R. J. House, P. J. Hanges, M. Javidan, P. W. Dorfman, & V. Gupta (Eds.), *Culture, leadership and organizations: The GLOBE study of 62 societies* (pp. 343–394). Thousand Oaks, CA: Sage.

Ford, M. T., Heinen, B. A., & Langkamer, K. L. (2007). Work and family satisfaction and conflict: A meta-analysis of cross-domain relations. *Journal of Applied Psychology, 92*(1), 57–80. doi:10.1037/0021-9010.92.1.57

Frone, M. R., Russell, M., & Cooper, M. L. (1992). Antecedents and outcomes of work-family conflict: Testing a model of the work-family interface. *Journal of Applied Psychology, 77*(1), 65–78. doi:10.1037/0021-9010.77.1.65

Frone, M. R., Yardley, J. K., & Markle, K. S. (1997). Developing and testing an integrative model of work-family interface. *Journal of Vocational Behavior, 50*(2), 145–167. doi:10.1006/jvbe.1996.1577

Gelfand, M. J., & Knight, A. P. (2005). Cross-cultural perspectives on work-family conflict. In S.A.Y. Poelmans (Ed.), *Work and family: An international perspective* (pp. 401–415). Mahwah, NJ: LEA.

Greenhaus, J. H., & Beutell, N. J. (1985). Sources and conflict between work and family roles. *Academy of Management Review, 10*(1), 76–88. doi:10.5465/AMR.1985.4277352

Hassan, Z., Dollard, M. F., & Winefield, A. H. (2010). Work-family conflict in East vs Western countries. *Cross Cultural Management, 17*(1), 30–49. doi:10.1108/13527601011016899

Heine, S. J. (2005). Where is the evidence for pancultural self-enhancement? A reply to Sedikides, Gaertner, and Toguchi. (2003). *Journal of Personality and Social Psychology, 89*(4), 531–538. doi:10.1037/0022-3514.89.4.531

Hellman, C. (1997). Job satisfaction and intent to leave. *Journal of Social Psychology, 137*(6), 677–689. doi:10.1080/00224549709595491

Hill, E. J., Yang, C., Hawkins, A. J., & Ferris, M. (2004). A cross-cultural test of the work-family interface in 48 countries. *Journal of Marriage and Family, 66*(5), 1300–1316. doi:10.1111/j.0022-2445.2004.00094.x

Hofstede, G. (1990). *Cultures and organizations: Software of the mind.* New York, NY: McGraw-Hill.

Hom, P.W., & Griffeth, R.W. (1995). *Employee turnover.* Cincinnati, OH: South-Western College.

House, R. J., Hanges, P. J., Javidian, M., Dorfman, P. W., & Gupta, V. (2004). *Culture leadership, and organizations: The GLOBE study of 62 societies.* Thousand Oaks, CA: Sage.

Korabik, K., Lero, D. S., & Whitehead, D. L. (2008). *Handbook of work-family integration: Research, theory and best practices.* New York, NY: Elseiver.

Kossek, E. E., & Ozeki, C. (1998). Work-family conflict, policies, and the job—life satisfaction relationship: A review and directions for organizational behaviour-human resources research. *Journal of Applied Psychology, 83*(2), 139–149. doi:10.1037/0021-9010.83.2.139

Kossek, E. E., & Ozeki, C. (1999). Bridging the work-family policy and productivity gap. *International Journal of Community, Work, and Family, 2*(1), 7–32. doi:10.1080/13668809908414247

Loong, L. (2012). *Prime Minister Lee Hsien Loong's National Day Rally 2012 speech.* Retrieved from http://www.pmo.gov.sg/mediacentre/prime-minister-lee-hsien-loongs-national-day-rally-2012-speech-english

Lu, L., Gilmour, R., Kao, S., & Huang, M. (2006). A cross-cultural study of work/family demands, work/family conflict and wellbeing: The Taiwanese vs. British. *Career Development International, 11*(1), 9–27. doi:10.1108/13620430610642354

Lyness, K. S., & Judiesch, M. K. (2014). Gender egalitarianism and work—life balance for managers: Multisource perspectives in 36 countries. *Applied Psychology: An International Review, 63*(1), 96–129. doi:10.1111/apps.12011

MacKinnon, D. P., Lockwood, C. M., Hoffman, J. M., West, S. G., & Sheets, V. (2002). A comparison of methods to test mediation and other intervening variable effects. *Psychological Methods,* 7(1), 83–104. doi:10.1037/1082-989X.7.1.83

MacKinnon, D. P., Lockwood, C. M., & Williams, J. (2004). Confidence limits for the indirect effect: Distribution of the product and resampling methods. *Multivariate Behavioral Research, 39*(1), 99–128. doi:10.1207/s15327906mbr3901_4

Mesmer-Magnus, J. R., & Viswesvaran, C. (2005). Convergence between measures of work-to-family and family-to-work conflict: A meta-analytic examination. *Journal of Vocational Behavior, 67*(2), 215–232. doi:10.1016/j.jvb.2004.05.004

Michel, J. S., Mitchelson, J. K., Kotrba, L. M., LeBreton, J. M., & Baltes, B., B. (2009). A comparative test of work-family conflict models and critical examination of work-family linkages. *Journal of Vocational Behavior, 74*(2), 199–218. doi:10.1016/j.jvb.2008.12.005

Milfont, T. L., & Fischer, R. (2010). Testing measurement invariance across groups: Applications in cross-cultural research. *International Journal of Psychological Research, 3*(1), 2011–2084. doi:10.21500/20112084.857

Milkie, M. A., Denny, K. E., Kendig, S., & Schieman, S. (2010). Measurement of the work-family interface. In S. Sweet & J. Casey (Eds.), *Work and family encyclopedia*. Chestnut Hill, MA: Sloan Work and Family Research Network.

Mueller, C. W., Price, J. L., Boyer, M., & Iverson, R. D. (1994). Employee attachment and noncoercive conditions of work: The case of dental hygienists. *Work and Occupations, 21*(2), 179–212. doi:10.1177/0730888494021002002

Mullen, J., Kelley, E., & Kelloway, E. K. (2008). Health and well-being outcomes of the work-family interface. In K. Korabik, D. S. Lero, & D. L. Whitehead (Eds.), *Handbook of work-family integration: Research, theory and best practices* (pp. 191–214). New York, NY: Elseiver.

Pal, S., & Saksvik, P. Ø. (2008). Work-family conflict and psychosocial work environment stressors as predictors of job stress in a cross-cultural study. *International Journal of Stress Management, 15*(1), 22–42. doi:10.1037/1072-5245.15.1.22

Peng, K., & Nisbett, R. E. (1999). Culture, dialectics, and reasoning about contradiction. *American Psychologist, 54*(9), 741–754. doi:10.1037/0003-006X.54.9.741

Peterson, M. F., Smith, P. B., Akande, A., Ayestaran, S., Bochner, S., Callan, V., . . . Viedge, C. (1995). Role conflict, ambiguity and overload: A 21 nation study. *Academy of Management, 38*(2), 429–452. doi:10.2307/256687

Posthuma, R. A., Joplin, J. R., & Maertz, C. P., Jr. (2005). Comparing the validity of turnover predictors in the United States and Mexico. *International Journal of Cross-Cultural Management, 5*(2), 165–180. doi:10.1177/1470595805054491

Powell, G. N., Francesco, A., & Ling, Y. (2009). Toward culture-sensitive theories of the work-family interface. *Journal of Organizational Behavior, 30*(5), 597–616. doi:10.1002/job.v30:510.1002/job.568Price, J. L., & Mueller, C. W. (1986). *Absenteeism and turnover of hospital employees*. Greenwich, CT: JAI Press.

Pynchon, V. (2011, August). President Obama models work-life balance as dad-in-chief. *Forbes*. Retrieved from http://www.forbes.com/sites/shenegotiates/2011/08/22/president-obama-models-work-life-balance-as-dad-in-chief/#14b002fccdec

Ramesh, A., & Gelfand, M. (2010). Will they stay or will they go? The role of job embeddedness in predicting turnover in individualistic and collectivistic cultures. *Journal of Applied Psychology, 95*(5), 807–821. doi:10.1037/a0019464

Russell, G., & L. Bowman. (2000). *Work and family, current thinking, research and practice (Report prepared for the Department of Family and Community Services)*. Sydney, AU: Macquarie University.

Schwartz, S. J., Weisskirch, R. S., Hurley, E. A., Zamboanga, B. L., Park, I. J. K., Kim, S.Y., . . . Greene, A. D. (2010). Communalism, familism, and filial piety: Are they birds of a collectivist feather? *Cultural Diversity and Ethnic Minority Psychology, 16*(4), 548–560. doi:10.1037/a0021370

Shaffer, M., Joplin, J. R. W., & Hsu, Y. (2011). Expanding the boundaries of work-family research: A review and agenda for future research. *International Journal of Cross Cultural Management, 12*(2), 221–268. doi:10.1177/1470595811398800

Shockley, K. M., & Singla, N. (2011). Reconsidering work-family interactions and satisfaction: A meta-analysis. *Journal of Management, 37*, 861–886. doi:10.1177/0149206310394864

Smith, P. B., Dugan, S., & Trompenaars, F. (1996). National culture and the values of organizational employees: A dimensional analysis across 43 nations. *Journal of Cross-Cultural Psychology, 27*(2), 231–264. doi:10.1177/0022022196272006

Spector, P. E., Allen, T. D., Poelmans, S.Y., Cooper, C. L., Bernin, P., Hart, P., . . . Yu, S. (2005). An international comparative study of work/family stress and occupational strain. In

S.A.Y. Poelmans (Ed.), *Work and family: An international research perspective* (pp. 71–84). Mahwah, NJ: Lawrence Erlbaum.

Spector, P. E., Allen, T. D., Poelmans, S. Y., Lapierre, L. M., Cooper, C. L., O'Driscoll, M., . . . Widerszal-Bazyl, M. (2007). Cross-national differences in relationships of work demands, job satisfaction, and turnover intentions with work-family conflict. *Personnel Psychology*, *60*(4), 805–835. doi:10.1111/j.1744-6570.2007.00092.

Spector, P. E., Cooper, C. L., Poelmans, S., Allen, T. D., O'Driscoll, M. I., Sanchez, J. I., . . . Lu, L. (2004). A cross-national comparative study of work-family stressors, working hours, and well-being: China and Latin America versus the Anglo world. *Personnel Psychology*, *57*(1), 119–142. doi:10.1111/j.1744-6570.2004.tb02486.x

Steibler, N. (2009). Reported levels of time-based and strain-based conflict between work and family roles in Europe: A multilevel approach. *Social Indicators Research*, *93*(3), 469–488. doi:10.1007/s11205-008-9436-z

Tang, S. W., Siu, O. L., & Cheung, F. (2014). A study of work-family enrichment among Chinese employees: The mediating role between work support and job satisfaction. *Applied Psychology*, *63*(1), 130–150. doi:10.1111/j.1464-0597.2012.00519.x

Thomas, D. C., & Au, K. (2002). The effect of cultural differences on behavioral responses to low job satisfaction. *Journal of International Business Studies*, *33*(2), 309–326. doi:10.1057/palgrave.jibs.8491018

Triandis, H. C. (1995). *Individualism and collectivism*. Boulder, CO: Westview Press.

Vandenberg, R. J., & Lance, C. E. (2000). A review and synthesis of the measurement invariance literature: Suggestions, practices, and recommendations for organizational research. *Organizational Research Methods*, *3*(1), 4–70. doi:10.1177/109442810031002

Wagner, J. A. (1995). Studies of individualism-collectivism: Effects on cooperation in groups. *Academy of Management Journal*, *38*(1), 152–172. doi:10.2307/256731

Wang, X. Z., Li, X., Xu, C., & Tian, Z. (2004). State-owned enterprises going public: The case of China. *Economics of Transition*, *12*(3), 467–487. doi:10.1111/j.0967-0750.2004.00189.x

Yang, L. Q., Spector, P. E., Sanchez, J. I., Allen, T. D., Poelmans, S., Cooper, C. L., . . . Woo, J. (2012). Individualism—collectivism as a moderator of the work demands—strains relationship: A cross-level and cross-national examination. *Journal of International Business Studies*, *43*(4), 424–443. doi:10.1057/jibs.2011.58

Yang, N., Chen, C. C., Choi, J., & Zou, Y. (2000). Sources of work-family conflict: A Sino—U.S. comparison of the effects of work and family demands. *Academy of Management Journal*, *43*(1), 113–123. doi:10.2307/1556390

14

POSITIVE SPILLOVER OF THE WORK AND LIFE DOMAINS

Barbara Beham, Anne Bardoel, and Steven Poelmans

Introduction

Work-family research has long been dominated by the conflict perspective (Greenhaus & Beutell, 1985) and the scarcity argument in role theory (Goode, 1960). More recently, the positive aspects of the work-family interface and the examination of antecedents and consequences of concepts such as work-family enrichment (Greenhaus & Powell, 2006), work-family facilitation (Grzywacz, Carlson, Kacmar, & Wayne, 2007), and work-family positive spillover (Grzywacz & Marks, 2000; Hanson, Hammer, & Colton, 2006) have received increasing attention in the literature (e.g., Crain & Hammer, 2013; McNall, Nicklin, & Masuda, 2010). Drawing upon the enhancement argument in role theory (Marks, 1977), scholars argue that engagement in multiple roles can be beneficial for the individual because of enhanced opportunities to generate and transfer resources between domains.

This chapter focuses on the antecedents and consequences of work-family positive spillover in a cross-national context. Work-family positive spillover is defined as "the effects of work and family on one another that generate similarities between the two domains" (Edwards & Rothbard, 2000, p. 180). Positive spillover is an inter-role phenomenon which involves the transfer of developmental, affective, capital, or efficiency gains acquired in one domain to another domain (Wayne, 2009). Like WFC, it is a bidirectional construct, meaning that the transfer of resources can occur from work to family and vice versa (Edwards & Rothbard, 2000; Hanson et al., 2006). Work-family spillover differs from work-family enrichment, as it does not consider an improvement of the quality of life in the other role (Wayne, 2009). Further, work-family enrichment also focuses on a broader set of psychological, physical, social-capital, and material resources that may be transferred by an individual from one role to the other (Greenhaus & Powell, 2006). Work-family positive spillover also differentiates from work-family facilitation since facilitation focuses on improvements in functioning at the system level (e.g., family members, coworkers) rather than on improvements in the other role (Demerouti, Martinez Corts, & Boz, 2013).

Literature Review and Theory

In the last decade, research on the positive work-family interface was mainly concerned with identifying its antecedents and consequences. A large number of nonwork-related variables (e.g., family involvement, support from spouse and family, family salience), work-related antecedents (e.g., job autonomy and control, support from supervisor and colleagues, work-family culture), and personal characteristics (e.g., positive affect, core self-evaluations, extraversion) were found to stimulate work-family enrichment, facilitation, and positive spillover (Crain & Hammer, 2013). Further, these constructs have been linked to a variety of work and nonwork-related outcomes, such as job and family satisfaction, affective commitment, turnover intentions, life satisfaction, and physical/mental health in empirical research (Crain & Hammer, 2013; McNall et al., 2010). The vast majority of these studies were conducted within a single national/cultural context, mainly in Western industrialized nations. More recently, an increasing body of research examining processes of enrichment and its antecedents and consequences in Asia (mainly in China) has evolved (e.g., Lu, Siu, Spector, & Shi, 2009; Siu et al., 2011; Tang, Siu, & Cheung, 2012). Nevertheless, research scrutinizing the positive work-family interface across different countries and cultures is scarce. Although there is good reason to assume that cultural norms and values may influence individuals' experiences of positive spillover between work and family in various ways (Powell, Francesco, & Ling, 2009), we were unable to identify any cross-cultural or cross-national study on work-family positive spillover. Powell and colleagues (2009) argued that societal or national culture, which is likely to influence individuals' experiences of the work-family interface, has been largely unacknowledged in theory and research. They propose a culture-sensitive theory of work-family enrichment that stresses the influence of various cultural dimensions in the enrichment process. More specifically, they suggest that the way in which resources are transferred between domains, and consequently how enrichment is stimulated in the respective domain, is influenced by cultural values and norms. The cultural dimensions of individualism/collectivism, humane orientation, specificity/diffusion, and gender egalitarianism were identified to be important in this enriching process. It is assumed that relationships between variables among the instrumental (direct transfer of resources from one role to another) and the affective path of enrichment (resources generating a direct or indirect effect in the other role through positive affect) are moderated by individualism/collectivism, humane orientation, and specificity/diffusion. Further, Powell et al.

(2009) argue that gender differences in relationships between variables along both paths may be moderated by gender egalitarianism. Please see Chapter 18 for the findings pertaining to gender and gender egalitarianism.

Research Model

To increase our knowledge of the influence of culture on the positive work-family interface, we propose a research model (Figure 14.1) that examines antecedents, outcomes, and the moderating influences of two cultural dimensions for both directions of work-family spillover. More precisely, we focus on the moderating effects of vertical collectivism (VC) and polychronic time orientation (PTO) on the relationships between job and family control as antecedents of work-to family (WTFS) and family-to-work positive spillover (FTWS), respectively. The terms "vertical collectivism" and "polychronic time orientation" are defined later in the chapter. On the outcomes side, we examine the moderating effects of VC on the relationships between both directions of work-family positive spillover and the two outcome variables of turnover intentions and family satisfaction. These relationships are discussed in more detail in the following sections.

Antecedents

In their seminal paper on work-family enrichment theory, Greenhaus and Powell (2006) identified flexibility and control over timing, pace, and location at which role requirements are met, as important resources that can stimulate enriching process between the work and the family domain. Further, they suggested that

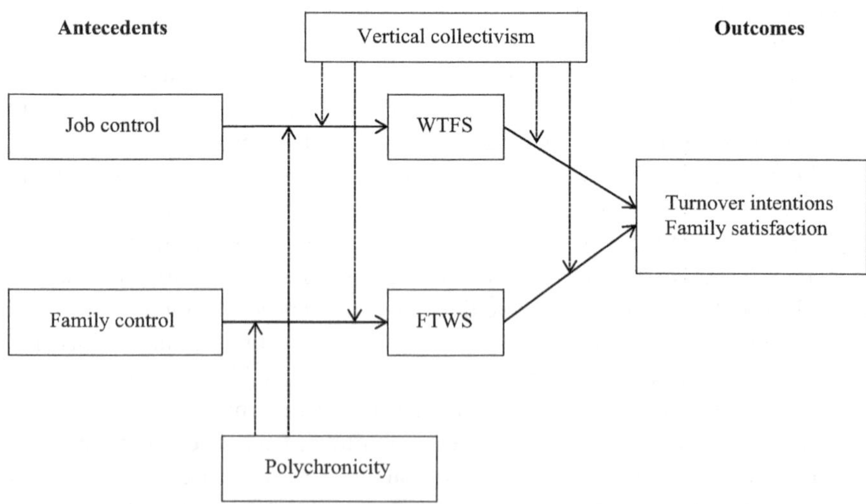

FIGURE 14.1 Research model.

the primary antecedents of enrichment may come from the originating domain. Empirical studies have found job autonomy and control to be positively related to work-to-family enrichment and facilitation, and to a weaker extent or even unrelated to family-to-work enrichment (Butler, Grzywacz, Bass, & Linney, 2005; Carlson, Kacmar, Wayne, & Grzywacz, 2006; Siu et al., 2011). In line with these findings, we assume a positive relationship between job control and WTFS in our sample. In a similar way, we assume that having control over one's family life increases employees' opportunities to transfer resources from the family to the work domain, thereby promoting the experience of FTWS in employees.

Consequences

Whereas family satisfaction has been identified as an important nonwork-related outcome of positive work-family processes, the link between turnover intentions and work-family enrichment has received mixed support in previous empirical studies (Crain & Hammer, 2013). Two competing views regarding outcomes of work-family positive spillover can be found in the literature. The receiving domain view suggests that the positive transfer of moods, skills, and resources from one domain to the other is more likely to generate satisfaction in the receiving domain because the receiving domain experiences an increase in quality (Carlson, Hunter, Ferguson, & Whitten, 2014; Greenhaus & Powell, 2006). The originating domain view in contrast argues that the experience of satisfaction is more likely to happen in the domain in which positive spillover originates because a positive attribution to the originating role of enrichment occurs (Carlson et al., 2014; Greenhaus & Powell, 2006; McNall et al., 2010; Voydanoff, 2005). Empirical results in support of either one of the two competing views are ambiguous. Whereas a recent literature review found support for the originating domain view for family satisfaction (Crain & Hammer, 2013), the study by Carlson et al. (2014) did not find any evidence for family-to-work enrichment having a stronger impact on family satisfaction than work-to-family enrichment. Regarding turnover intentions, the majority of studies showed a negative relationship of work-to-family enrichment with turnover intentions in line with the originating domain view, whereas the findings for family-to-work enrichment and turnover intentions were mixed (Crain & Hammer, 2013). Based on these findings, we assume negative relationships between both directions of spillover and turnover intentions, but we expect the relationship to be stronger for WTFS. Further, we assume that both directions of positive spillover will have a positive relationship with family satisfaction, but for the strength to be equal for both directions.

Culture as a Moderator

Societal or national culture plays an important role in shaping individuals' experiences of the work-family interface. The nature and the strength of relationships between individuals' experiences in both domains may be strongly influenced by norms and values with respect to the meaning and enactment of work and family in their culture (Ashforth, Kreiner, & Fugate, 2000). In their culture-sensitive theory of the work-family interface, Powell et al. (2009) identified the cultural dimension of individualism/collectivism as a potential moderator of the relationships between various antecedents and work-family enrichment. For both directions of enrichment, they assume these relationships should be stronger in collectivist cultures than in individualist cultures. Collectivists should have greater opportunities for enrichment because of the different nature of the employer-employee relationship and a higher level of work-family integration. In collectivist societies the employment relationship is more family-like and the employer often has a paternalistic interest in the employee (Hofstede, 1980, 2001). Further, collectivists are more likely to integrate work and family roles, since they desire to please members of multiple groups (Powell et al., 2009).

Vertical Collectivism

In this chapter, we focus on one aspect of collectivism referred to as "vertical collectivism" in the literature. Vertical collectivism (VC) is a cultural pattern in which "the individual sees the self as an aspect of an in-group, but the members of the in-group are different from each other, some having more status than others" (Singelis, Triandis, & Bhawuk, 1995, p. 244). Vertical collectivists accept inequality to some extent within the group. Serving and sacrificing for the group is an important aspect in vertical collectivist societies. We have chosen this subdimension of collectivism, since it is one of the dominant cultural profiles around the world (Triandis, 1995), and the 10 countries in our study are expected to differ significantly along this dimension.

VC was measured at the individual level in this study (see Chapter 2 for details on measurement). Country level means for VC were obtained by aggregating individual values to the country level. Drawing upon Powell et al.'s (2009) culture-sensitive theory of work-family enrichment, we propose a moderating effect of vertical collectivist values on the relationships between job/family control and WTFS/FTWS (see Figure 14.1). We assume these relationships are stronger in countries with a higher aggregated level of vertical collectivism because of a stronger desire to integrate work and family and a more personal employer-employee relationship in collectivist societies which allows for a better transfer of resources between the two domains (Powell et al., 2009).

Powell et al.'s (2009) culture-sensitive theory of enrichment does not include any theorizing on the impact of culture on the relationships between work-family enrichment and major outcome variables. Further, we could not identify any empirical study which has examined such relationships. We thought it worthwhile to examine whether VC moderates the relationships between WTFS/FTWS and the two outcome variables. Cross-national and cross-cultural research on negative work-family interference provides some cues that the relationships with turnover intentions may be different in collectivist countries. Spector and colleagues (2007) found strain-based work-to-family conflict to be more strongly related to turnover intentions in individualistic countries than in more collectivist societies. They argue that the employment relationship in collectivist societies is more family-like than in individualistic societies, and that collectivists are more loyal toward their employers even if working conditions are less favorable. Employees in individualistic societies, on the other hand, tend to focus more on their own needs and, in a more individualistic manner, respond to adverse working conditions with dissatisfaction and thoughts of turnover. If we extend this argument to positive work-family spillover, one can assume that positive spillover decreases turnover intentions more strongly for employees in individualistic societies, whereas the relationship should be weaker in more collectivist societies. For family satisfaction, we expect the relationships with positive spillover to be stronger in more collectivist societies, since the family is highly valued and work and family roles are more likely to be integrated than in individualistic cultures (Powell et al., 2009).

Polychronic Time Orientation

Although Powell et al. (2009) did not identify polychronic time orientation as one of the cultural dimensions which may influence work-family enrichment, there is a theoretical rationale for partially considering this cultural dimension in our model. Time orientation refers to an individual's preferences to either undertake one task at a time (monochronic time orientation) or engage in multiple tasks simultaneously (polychronic time orientation) (Bluedorn, Kalliath, Strube, & Martin, 1999; Hall & Hall, 1990). Individuals with a polychronic time orientation (PTO) may be more likely to simultaneously engage in activities in both the work and the family domain, work and family roles may be more integrated, and role transitions and boundary crossings may occur more frequently (Korabik, Van Rhijn, Ayman, Lero, & Hammer, in press). Cross-cultural research has conceptualized PTO as a cultural variable (Bluedorn et al., 1999; Hall & Hall, 1990). Consequently, we propose that individuals in polychronic cultures may have more opportunities to transfer resources generated in one domain to the other, thereby increasing the likelihood of positive spillover in both directions. We did not include PTO as a moderator of the relationships with the outcome variables, since we could not suggest an argument as to why these relationships should be different in polychronic/monochronic cultures.

Method

Given the nested structure of our data (employees nested in 10 countries), hierarchical linear modeling is recommended to test the links in our research model (Raudenbush & Bryk, 2002). We estimated baseline models without any predictors for all dependent variables to calculate the intraclass correlation coefficient (ICC) for nestedness within countries. Hierarchical linear modeling is recommended for ICCs exceeding 5%. For WTFS, 13.7% of the variance in WTFS and 8.3% of the variance in FTWS are at the country level. The ICCs for turnover intentions and family satisfaction are 6.5% and 14%, respectively. Consequently, hierarchical linear models are estimated to test our research model.

Few higher-level units can lead to computational problems, and parameter estimates may be biased downward in multilevel models (Bell, Morgan, Schoeneberger, Kromrey, & Ferron, 2015; Raudenbush & Bryk, 2002). Textbooks recommend a minimum number of groups at the upper level of 10 to 50 groups, depending on the number of group-level predictors and whether the focus is on fixed regression predictors or the distribution of random effects (Hox, 2010; Raudenbush & Bryk, 2002). Because our models only contain two group-level predictors, and because we are interested in fixed effects of various predictors rather than parameters to describe the distribution of random effects, we opted for hierarchical random intercept models with employees at the lower level and countries at the higher level. To estimate the impact of cultural values at the country level in our models, individual level assessments of vertical collectivism and polychronic time orientation were aggregated to the upper level. Further, we followed the recommendations of Bryan and Jenkins (2013) to supplement multilevel analyses with a complementary descriptive approach based on the visualization of country differences.

To enhance model estimation and the interpretation of the results (especially cross-level interactions), all independent variables were centered prior to analyses. Following the recommendations of Enders and Tofighi (2007), level 1 variables were group-mean centered whereas level 2 variables were grand-mean centered in all models. Gender, age, number of children, job level (managerial/nonmanagerial), work and family overload were included as individual level control variables in all models. The Human Development Index (HDI) was included as a country level control variable to account for the differences in human development across the 10 countries. The HDI is a composite measure of average achievement in health, education, and standard of living (UNDP, 2007). We opted for the HDI as a country level control variable because it reflects achievements in three key dimensions of human development. Inclusion of a broader range of control variables at the country level is limited due to the small number of countries in our study.

Detailed information about variable measurement and the results of measurement equivalence tests is presented in Chapter 2. Cronbach alphas of some measures used in the subsequent statistical analyses are below the critical value of .70. Cronbach alpha is especially low for vertical collectivism ($\alpha = .55$). Further, some of the measures used in our models have not passed measurement equivalence tests. Job control and family control did not satisfy the stringent criteria of a ΔCFI $< .01$ across our 10 countries. Measurement equivalence tests yielded a ΔCFI of

.05 and .03 for job control and family control, respectively. In addition, we only have measurement equivalence for polychronic time orientation in four out of 10 countries (Australia, Canada, the United States, and Spain). These limitations in measurement must be considered when interpreting the results of data analyses.

Results

Descriptive Statistics

Table 14.1 presents the aggregated country means for the cultural variables of interest in this chapter, both directions of positive work-family spillover, family satisfaction, and turnover intentions. China has the highest aggregated level of vertical collectivism across the 10 countries, followed by Taiwan, Turkey, and Indonesia. The lowest average levels of VC were reported by the study participants in Australia and Israel. Indonesia is the country with the highest aggregated level of polychronic time orientation, followed by India and Turkey. The country mean for PTO was lowest in Taiwan, followed by Canada, China, and the United States. Family satisfaction is lowest in Taiwan and highest in Spain and Australia, whereas turnover intentions are highest in Taiwan and India and lowest in Turkey and Spain.

Table 14.1 and Figure 14.2 show that employees in all countries reported higher mean levels of family-to-work spillover than work-to-family spillover with only small variation in WTFS across countries. Indian, Indonesian, Spanish, and Turkish study participants reported slightly higher mean levels of WTFS than the participants in the other countries. Regarding FTWS, India and Indonesia deviate from the overall trend. Employees in both countries reported significantly more positive spillover from work to family than employees in the other countries. Interestingly, these two countries also deviate from the other countries in terms of WFC. Figure 14.2 also displays the mean levels of both directions of WFC.

TABLE 14.1 Country means cultural values and positive spillover.

Variables	*AU*	*CA*	*IN*	*ID*	*IL*	*US*	*ES*	*TW*	*TR*	*CN*
VC	3.88	4.10	4.42	4.62	3.88	4.09	4.38	4.80	4.63	4.82
PTO	3.34	3.15	3.90	4.01	3.44	3.22	3.49	3.07	3.68	3.17
WTFS	2.73	2.69	3.58	3.30	2.87	2.84	2.62	2.70	2.83	2.69
FTWS	3.55	3.46	3.92	3.96	3.55	3.58	3.92	3.37	3.94	3.56
Fsatis	4.69	4.46	4.31	4.40	4.49	4.56	4.71	3.91	4.40	4.07
Turnover	2.85	2.68	2.90	2.41	2.52	2.51	2.33	2.96	2.08	2.81

Note. N = 2,830. Country abbreviations: Australia (AU), Canada (CA), India (IN), Indonesia (ID), Israel (IL), United States (US), Spain (ES), Taiwan (TW), Turkey (TR), China (CN). VC = vertical collectivism; PTO = polychronic time orientation; WTFS = positive work-to-family spillover; FTWS = positive family-to-work spillover; Fsatis = family satisfaction; Turnover = turnover intentions.

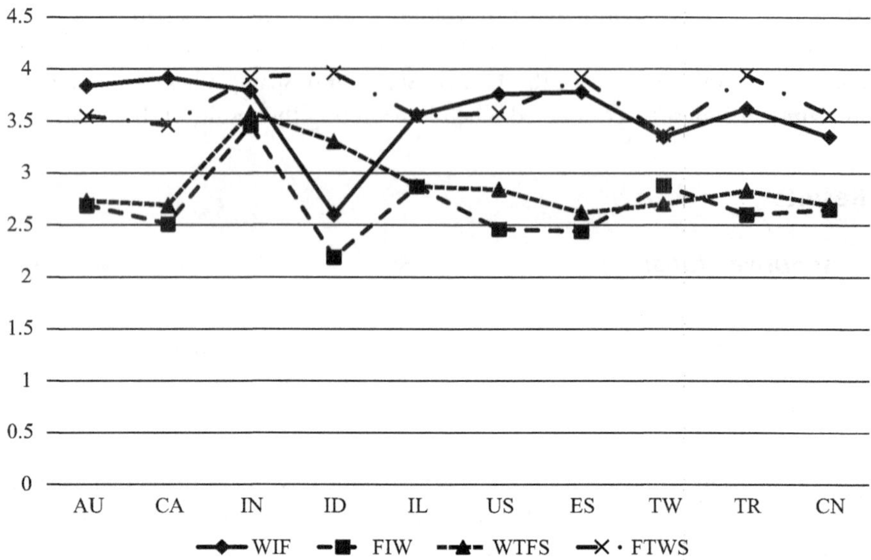

FIGURE 14.2 Mean levels of positive spillover and WFC.

Indonesian employees experience the lowest levels of both directions of conflict, whereas Indian employees seem to experience the highest levels of FIW in our sample, although their average level of WIF is comparable to the Anglo-Saxon countries.

Descriptive statistics and Pearson's correlation coefficients for all individual level variables are reported in Table 14.2.

Multilevel Statistics

Hierarchical linear random intercept models are estimated to test the relationships in our research model. In all subsequent tables, individual level variables are entered in step 1, country level variables in step 2, and interaction terms with cultural values in step 3. Although our research model and the underlying theoretical frameworks conceive culture as a country level variable, cultural values were included both as individual and country level moderators in all models to see whether there are any differences between the levels. Since the power to detect interaction effects is rather low in samples with few countries, findings at the 10% significance level are also reported in the following sections.

Work-to-Family Positive Spillover

Table 14.3 presents the results of the random intercept models for the dependent variable WTFS with job control as the predictor. All models in Table 14.3 reveal

TABLE 14.2 Pearson's correlation coefficients for all variables (full sample).

	M	*SD*	*1*	*2*	*3*	*4*	*5*	*6*	*7*	*8*	*9*	*10*	*11*	*12*	*13*	*14*
1. Gender	1.55	.50	–													
2. Age	38.81	7.44	-.01	–												
3. No. of kids	1.87	1.01	-.02	.33**	–											
4. Job level	1.46	.50	-.02	.08**	.04*	–										
5. Work overload	3.34	1.12	.00	-.03	-.10**	-.03	(.88)									
6. Family overload	3.15	1.13	.18**	-.10**	-.09*	-.09*	.46**	(.86)								
7. Job control	4.28	.76	-.02	.04*	.05**	.03	-.13**	-.03	(.67)							
8. Family control	4.56	.67	.11**	-.01	.02	.00	-.11**	-.12**	.38**	(.67)						
9. Turnover intentions	2.63	1.08	-.03	-.16**	-.12**	-.03	-.30**	.21**	-.30**	-.16**	(.82)					
10. Family satisfaction	4.37	.66	-.04*	.04*	.07**	.01	-.17**	-.26**	.29**	.45**	-.29**	(.79)				
11. WTFS	2.98	.84	.04*	.00	.03	.01	-.05**	.03	.22**	.10**	-.11**	.11**	(.69)			
12. FTWS	3.72	.77	.05*	-.01	-.04	.00	-.16**	-.17**	.19**	.27**	-.19**	.32**	.49**	(.67)		
13. VC	3.51	.78	-.03	-.08**	-.11**	-.06**	.04	.07**	.12**	.13**	-.07**	.05**	.08**	.16**	(.55)	
14. PTO	3.51	.87	-.01	-.10**	.00	.01	.01	.07**	.24**	.12**	-.02	.09**	.26**	.14**	.10**	(.65)

Note. $N = 2{,}830$. $^{*}\ p < .05$; $^{**}\ p < .01$. Cronbach's alphas appear along the diagonal in parentheses. WTFS = positive work-to-family spillover; FTWS = positive family-to-work spillover; VC = vertical collectivism; PTO = polychronic time orientation. Gender is coded 0 = male, 1 = female. Job level is coded 0 = nonmanagerial, 1 = managerial.

TABLE 14.3 Hierarchical linear models—WTFS, job control, and VC.

	Model 1		*Model 2*		*Model 3*	
	β	*SE*	*β*	*SE*	*β*	*SE*
Level 1—Employee						
Gender	.12**	(.03)	.12**	(.03)	.12**	(.03)
Age	.00	(.00)	.00	(.00)	.00	(.00)
No. of kids	.02	(.02)	.03	(.02)	.03	(.02)
Job level	.05	(.03)	.04	(.03)	.04	(.03)
Work overload	-.06**	(.01)	-.07**	(.01)	-.07**	(.01)
Family overload	.01	(.02)	.00	(.02)	.00	(.02)
Job control	.22**	(.02)	.23**	(.02)	.23**	(.02)
VC	.04*	(.02)	.04*	(.02)	.04	(.02)
Level 2—Country						
HDI			-2.66**	(.48)	-2.64**	(.48)
VC_country			-.40*	(.17)	-.40*	(.17)
Interactions						
Job control*VC	.06*	(.02)			.05*	(.02)
Job control*VC_country					.11†	(.06)
Intercept	2.88**		2.96**		2.95**	
Var (intercept)	.09*		.02		.02	
Var (residual)	.54**		.54**		.54**	
Deviance	6,054.24		6,040.86		6,041.67	

Note. $N = 2{,}830$; † < .10; * $p < .05$; ** $p < .01$; VC = vertical collectivism at individual level; VC_country = aggregated vertical collectivism.

a significant, positive relationship between job control and WTFS ($\beta = .22/.23$, $p < .01$). Further, Model 3 shows a significant interaction term job control × VC at the individual level ($\beta = .05$, $p < .05$) and a significant cross-level interaction job control × aggregated VC at country level, although only at the 10% level. Interestingly, both country level variables are negatively associated with WTFS, meaning that employees in countries with a higher human development index and a stronger vertical collectivist value orientation seem to experience less positive spillover from work to family.

We plotted the significant individual level interaction term to illustrate the shape of the moderating effect at the individual level. Figure 14.3 shows that at high levels of job control, employees with more vertical collectivist values experience more WTFS than employees low on VC. Hence, vertical collectivists seem to benefit more from job control. At low levels of job control, employees in our sample seem to experience almost similar levels of spillover from work to family irrespective of their VC value orientation.

Plotting the significant cross-level interaction term (job control × VC country mean) would not allow us to assess differences across countries. Following the suggestion of Bowers and Drake (2005) to visualize country differences, we plotted the within country ordinary least squares (OLS) regression coefficients for

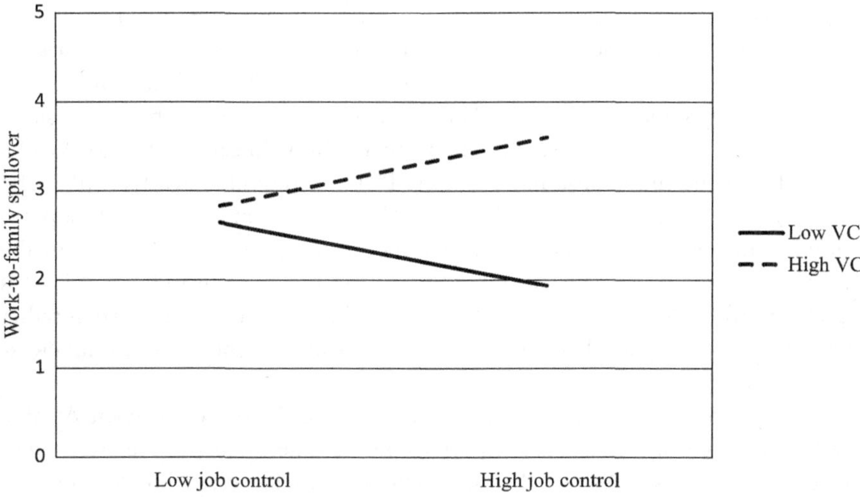

FIGURE 14.3 Interaction of job control and vertical collectivism on WTFS.

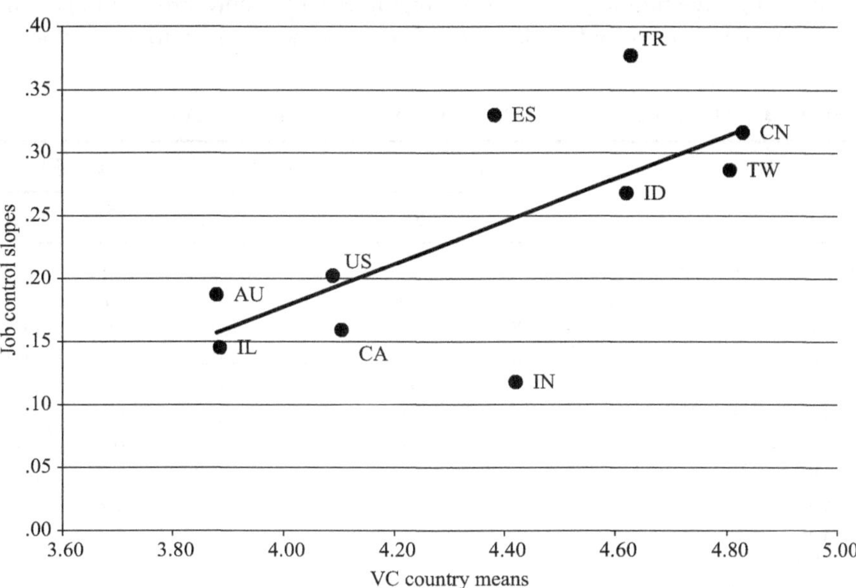

FIGURE 14.4 Job control versus country means vertical collectivism. Solid line from within country OLS regressions. Dependent variable (DV) = WTFS.

job control predicting WTFS (including control variables and VC at the individual level). Figure 14.4 shows the scatterplot and the OLS regression line. In line with our theorizing, the relationship between job control and WTFS becomes stronger as vertical collectivist value orientation at the aggregated country level increases. The Asian countries are mainly at the upper end of the regression line, the

Anglo-Saxon countries with their more individualistic orientation and Israel cluster at the lower end of the regression line. An outlier in our sample is India. Despite medium levels of VC, job control does not seem to contribute as much to positive work-to-family spillover as in the other societies with medium to high VC values.

Table 14.4 presents the results of the hierarchical linear models for WTFS with PTO as the moderator. In all models, PTO at the individual level (β = .10, $p < .01$) is significantly related to WTFS, indicating that individuals with a polychronic time orientation seem to experience more positive spillover from the work to the family domain. Also, the interaction term at the individual level is significant (β = .04, $p < .10$), but only at the 10% level, and the effect size is rather small. At the country level, neither a significant main effect nor a significant cross-level interaction effect was detected.

Figure 14.5 shows the plot of the significant level 1 interaction term. At high levels of job control, employees with a polychronic time orientation seem to experience higher levels of WTFS than monochronic employees. At low levels of job control, the difference between polychronic and monochronic employees is much less pronounced. Polychronic employees only experience slightly more WTFS than their monochronic peers. Hence, employees with a polychronic time orientation benefit more from high levels of job control than monochronic employees.

TABLE 14.4 Hierarchical linear models—WTFS, job control, and PTO.

	Model 1		*Model 2*		*Model 3*	
	β	*SE*	β	*SE*	β	*SE*
Level 1—Employee						
Gender	.11**	(.03)	.11**	(.03)	.11**	(.03)
Age	.00	(.00)	.00	(.00)	.00	(.00)
No. of kids	.02	(.02)	.02	(.02)	.02	(.02)
Job level	.04	(.03)	.04	(.03)	.04	(.03)
Work overload	-.07**	(.01)	-.07**	(.01)	-.07**	(.01)
Family overload	.00	(.01)	.00	(.01)	.00	(.01)
Job control	.20**	(.02)	.20**	(.02)	.20**	(.02)
PTO	.10**	(.02)	.10**	(.02)	.10**	(.02)
Level 2—Country						
HDI			-1.24	(.71)	-1.24	(.70)
PTO_country			.42	(.27)	.42	(.27)
Interactions						
Job control*PTO					.04†	(.02)
Job control*PTO_country					-.05	(.06)
Intercept	2.88**		2.93**		2.95**	
Var (intercept)	.09*		.03		.03	
Var (residual)	.54**		.54**		.54**	
Deviance	6,029.49		6,014.89		6,020.81	

Note. N = 2,830; † < .10; * $p < .05$; ** $p < .01$; PTO = polychronic time orientation at individual level; PTO_country = aggregated polychronic time orientation

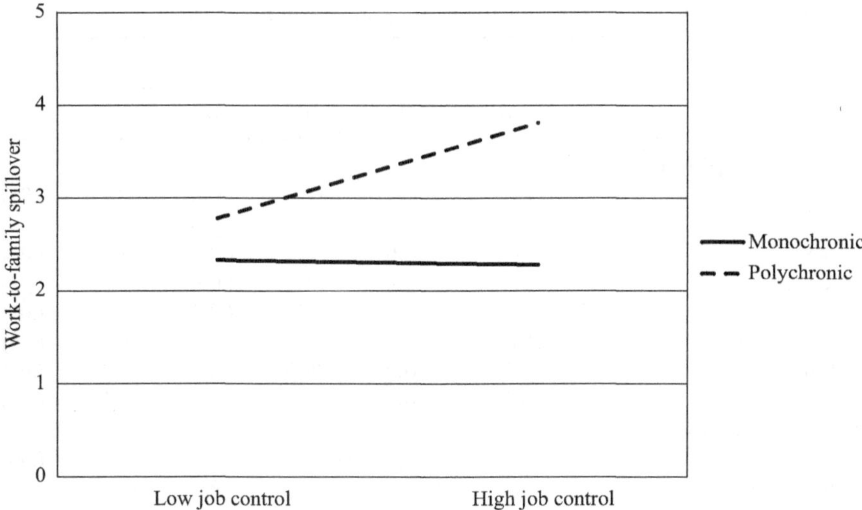

FIGURE 14.5 Interaction of job control and polychronic time orientation on WTFS.

Family-to-Work Positive Spillover

The results of the multilevel analysis for the dependent variable FTWS are presented in Tables 14.5 and 14.6. Family control yields a significant, positive relationship with FTWS ($\beta = .29, p < .01$) in all models in Table 14.5. Further, we found a direct effect of vertical collectivist values at the individual level on FTWS ($\beta = .10$, $p < .01$), meaning that employees with stronger vertical collectivist values seem to experience more positive spillover from family to work. In addition, the level 1 interaction term family control × VC is significant at the 5%-level (Model 3).

Figure 14.6 presents the plot of the significant level 1 interaction. Similar to our findings for job control and WTFS, employees with more vertical collectivist values seem to benefit more from high levels of family control. At low levels of family control the gap between employees high and low on VC gets smaller.

Table 14.6 displays the results for FTWS and PTO as a moderator. Models 2 and 3 reveal a significant main effect for country level PTO ($\beta = .63, p < .01$) and a significant cross-level interaction term ($\beta = -.12, p < .05$). No significant effects were detected for PTO at the individual level. Again, we supplemented our multilevel analyses with a plot of the within-country OLS regression coefficients (Figure 14.7).

Figure 14.7 shows that the relationship between family control and FTWS gets weaker with increasing polychronic time orientation at the country level, which is contrary to our theorizing. Interestingly, Taiwan is the country with the most monochronic time orientation in our sample and family control is a strong predictor of FTWS in this country. Also China seems to have a stronger monochronic time orientation in our sample. Except for these two countries, the Anglo-Saxon countries cluster at the upper end of the regression line, Spain, Israel, and Turkey in

TABLE 14.5 Hierarchical linear models—FTWS, family control, and VC.

	Model 1		*Model 2*		*Model 3*	
	β	*SE*	β	*SE*	β	*SE*
Level 1—Employee						
Gender	.12**	(.03)	.12**	(.03)	.12**	(.03)
Age	.00	(.00)	.00	(.00)	.00	(.00)
No. of kids	-.01	(.02)	-.02	(.02)	-.01	(.02)
Job level	.01	(.03)	.01	(.03)	.01	(.03)
Work overload	-.06**	(.01)	-.06**	(.01)	-.06**	(.01)
Family overload	-.10**	(.01)	-.10**	(.01)	-.10**	(.01)
Family control	.29**	(.02)	.29**	(.02)	.29**	(.02)
VC	.10**	(.02)	.10**	(.02)	.10**	(.02)
Level 2—Country						
HDI			-1.40	(.60)	-1.37	(.60)
VC_country			-.11	(.21)	-.11	(.21)
Interactions						
Family control*VC					.07*	(.03)
Family control*VC_country					-.07	(.07)
Intercept	3.67**		3.72**		3.71**	
Var (intercept)	.05*		.03		.03	
Var (residual)	.48**		.48**		.48**	
Deviance	5,703.44		5,698.92		5,700.64	

Note. $N = 2{,}830$; † < .10; * $p < .05$; ** $p < .01$; VC = vertical collectivism at individual level; VC_country = aggregated vertical collectivism.

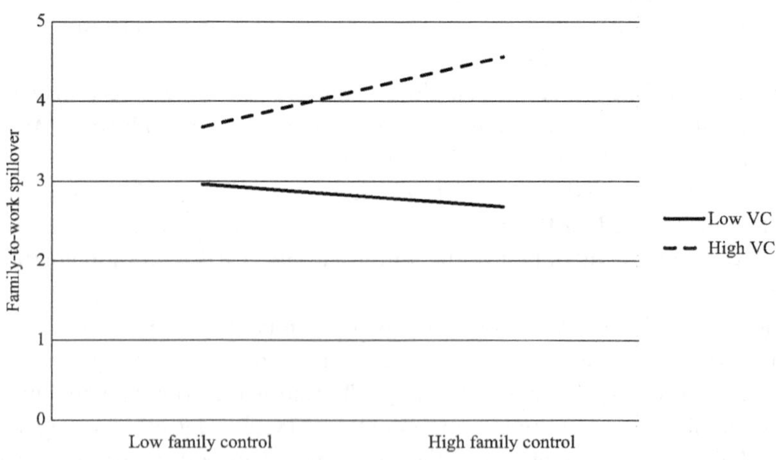

FIGURE 14.6 Interaction family control and vertical collectivism on FTWS.

TABLE 14.6 Hierarchical linear models—FTWS, family control, and PTO.

	Model 1		*Model 2*		*Model 3*	
	β	*SE*	*β*	*SE*	*β*	*SE*
Level 1—Employee						
Gender	.10**	(.03)	.10**	(.03)	.10**	(.03)
Age	.00	(.00)	.00	(.00)	.00	(.00)
No. of kids	-.01	(.02)	-.01	(.02)	-.01	(.02)
Job level	.01	(.03)	.01	(.03)	.01	(.03)
Work overload	-.06**	(.01)	-.06**	(.01)	-.06**	(.01)
Family overload	-.10**	(.01)	-.10**	(.01)	-.10**	(.01)
Family control	.31**	(.02)	.31**	(.02)	.31**	(.02)
PTO	.02	(.02)	.02	(.02)	.02	(.02)
Level 2—Country						
HDI			.01	(.43)	.01	(.43)
PTO_country			.63**	(.16)	.63**	(.16)
Interactions						
Family control*PTO					.02	(.02)
Family control*PTO_country					-.12*	(.06)
Intercept	3.68**		3.71**		3.71**	
Var (intercept)	.05*		.01		.01	
Var (residual)	.48**		.48**		.48**	
Deviance	5,729.32		5,716.46		5,721.14	

Note. $N = 2{,}830$; † < .10; * $p < .05$; ** $p < .01$; PTO = polychronic time orientation at individual level; PTO_country = aggregated polychronic time orientation

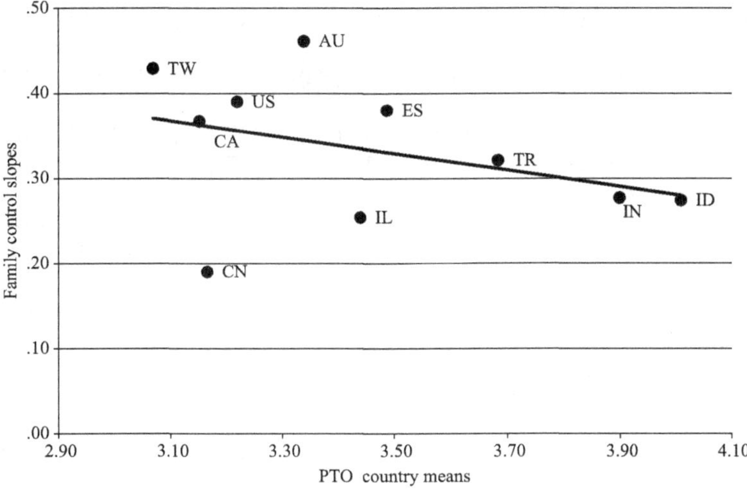

FIGURE 14.7 Family control versus country means for polychronic time orientation. Solid line from within country OLS regressions. DV = FTWS.

the middle, and India and Indonesia at the lower end of the regression line. India and Indonesia are the most polychronic societies in our sample and have the weakest association between family control and positive spillover from family to work.

Outcomes

Table 14.7 reports the results of the hierarchical linear models for WTFS and both outcome variables. WTFS is significantly and negatively related to turnover intentions ($\beta = -.15, p < .01$) and positively related with family satisfaction ($\beta = .10, p < .01$) in all models. Also individual level vertical collectivism is significantly related to both outcome variables. Turnover intentions are negatively related with VC ($\beta = -.13, p < .01$), whereas family satisfaction ($\beta = .15, p < .01$) has a positive link with vertical collectivism.

TABLE 14.7 HLM—outcomes of WTFS and moderating effects of vertical collectivism.

	DV = Turnover Intentions						*DV = Family Satisfaction*					
	Model 1		*Model 2*		*Model 3*		*Model 4*		*Model 5*		*Model 6*	
	β	*SE*	*β*	*SE*	*β*	*SE*	*β*	*SE*	*β*	*SE*	*β*	*SE*
Level 1—Employee												
Gender	-.13**	(.04)	-.13**	(.04)	-.13**	(.04)	-.02	(.02)	.02	(.02)	-.02	(.02)
Age	-.02**	(.00)	-.02	(.00)	-.02**	(.00)	.00	(.00)	.00	(.00)	.00	(.00)
No. of kids	-.04	(.02)	-.04	(.02)	-.04	(.02)	-.02	(.01)	-.02	(.01)	-.02	(.01)
Job level	.01	(.04)	.01	(.04)	.01	(.04)	-.05*	(.02)	-.05*	(.02)	-.05*	(.02)
Work overload	.21**	(.02)	.20**	(.02)	.20**	(.02)	-.01	(.01)	-.01	(.01)	-.01	(.01)
Family overload	.08**	(.02)	.08**	(.02)	.08**	(.02)	-.12**	(.01)	-.12**	(.01)	-.12**	(.01)
WTFS	-.15**	(.03)	-.15**	(.03)	-.15**	(.03)	.10**	(.02)	.10**	(.02)	.10**	(.02)
VC	-.13**	(.03)	-.12**	(.03)	-.13**	(.03)	.15**	(.02)	.15**	(.02)	.15**	(.02)
Level 2—Country												
HDI			-.09	(1.00)	-.09	(1.00)			-.14	(.59)	-.14	(.59)
VC_country			-.03	(.35)	-.03	(.34)			-.57**	(.21)	-.57**	(.20)
Interactions												
WTFS*VC					-.03	(.03)					.05**	(.02)
WTFS*VC_country					.29**	(.08)					-.07	(.05)
Intercept	2.60**		2.60**		2.60**		4.40**		4.39**		4.39**	
Var (intercept)	.07*		.10		.10		.06*		.03		.03	
Var (residual)	.96**		.96**		.96**		.34**		.34**		.34**	
Deviance	7,282.09		7,281.09		7,277.27		4,622.40		4,615.93		4,617.46	

Note. $N = 2{,}830$; † < .10; * $p < .05$; ** $p < .01$; VC = vertical collectivism at individual level; VC_country = aggregated vertical collectivism.

Our analysis revealed a significant interaction effect for WTFS × VC on family satisfaction ($\beta = .05$, $p < .01$; Model 6) on the individual level but not at the country level. The shape of this significant interaction effect is depicted in Figure 14.8. The relationship between WTFS and family satisfaction is stronger for employees with more vertical collectivist values. For employees with strong vertical collectivist values, positive spillover between work and family contributes to a higher extent to family satisfaction than for employees with fewer vertical collectivist values. At low levels of WTFS the effect seems reversed. Employees with low VC values typically report less satisfaction with their family life than employees high on VC.

Figure 14.9, which shows the plot of the within country OLS regression coefficients (turnover intentions regressed on WTFS), facilitates the interpretation of the significant cross-level interaction terms for turnover intentions ($\beta = .29$, $p < .01$; Model 3) and the analysis of country differences. In all countries except India, positive spillover from work to family decreases turnover intentions. Only in India the regression coefficient is positive. The negative relationships between WTFS and turnover intentions are weaker in those countries with a stronger vertical collectivist value orientation, such as the Asian countries and Turkey, and stronger in the more individualistic Anglo-Saxon countries in our sample. Another outlier in our sample is Israel, where the WTFS slope is small despite a low vertical collective value orientation at the country level.

Table 14.8 reports the result for family-to-work spillover. Similar to WTFS, FTWS is significantly linked with both dependent variables. FTWS is negatively related to turnover intentions ($\beta = -.15$, $p < .01$) and positively related to family satisfaction ($\beta = -.23/-.22$, $p < .01$) in all models. Further, VC at the individual

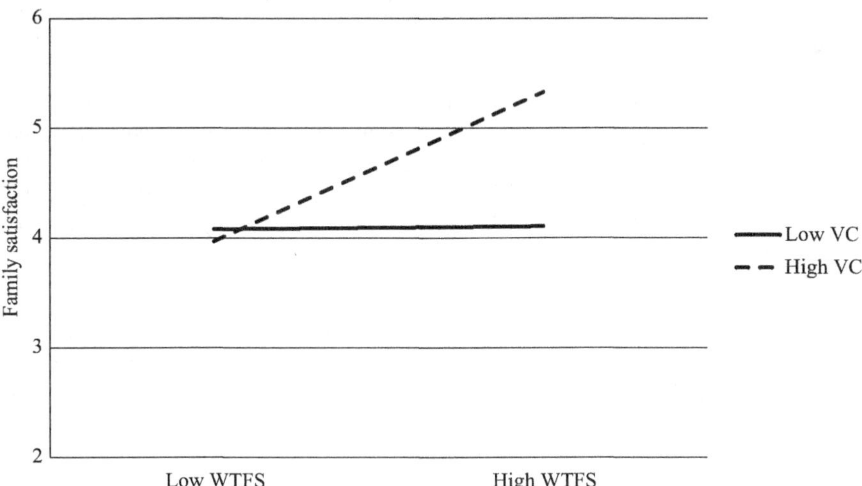

FIGURE 14.8 Interaction WTFS und vertical collectivism on family satisfaction.

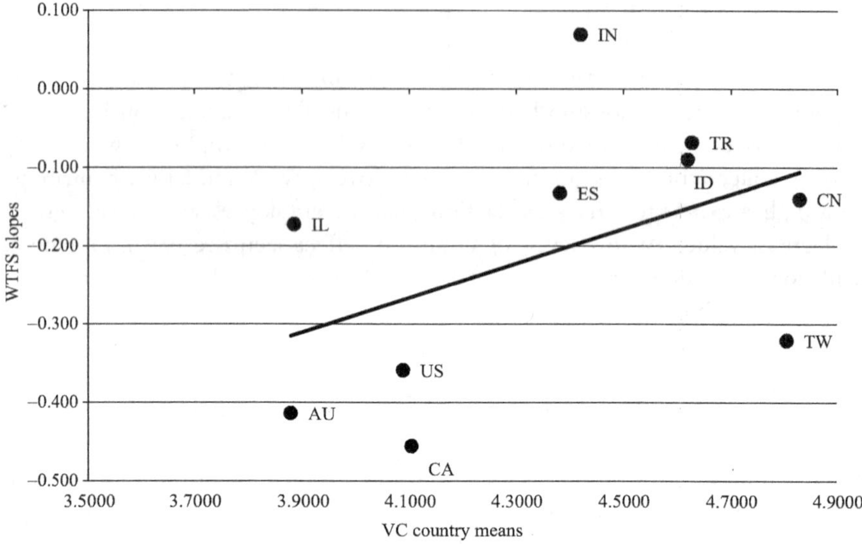

FIGURE 14.9 WTFS versus country means vertical collectivism. Solid line from within country OLS regressions. DV = turnover intentions.

TABLE 14.8 HLM—outcomes of FTWS and moderating effects of vertical collectivism.

	DV = Turnover Intentions						*DV = Family Satisfaction*					
	Model 1		*Model 2*		*Model 3*		*Model 4*		*Model 5*		*Model 6*	
	β	*SE*	*β*	*SE*	*β*	*SE*	*β*	*SE*	*β*	*SE*	*β*	*SE*
Level 1—Employee												
Gender	-.12**	(.04)	-.12**	(.04)	-.13**	(.04)	-.01	(.02)	-.01	(.02)	.00	(.02)
Age	-.02**	(.00)	-.02	(.00)	-.02**	(.00)	.00	(.00)	.00	(.00)	.00	(.00)
No. of kids	-.05*	(.02)	-.05*	(.02)	-.05*	(.02)	-.01	(.01)	-.01	(.01)	-.01	(.01)
Job level	.00	(.04)	.00	(.04)	.00	(.04)	-.05*	(.02)	-.05*	(.02)	-.05*	(.02)
Work overload	.21**	(.02)	.21**	(.02)	.21**	(.02)	-.01	(.01)	-.01	(.01)	-.01	(.01)
Family overload	.06**	(.02)	.06**	(.02)	.06**	(.02)	-.09**	(.01)	-.09**	(.01)	-.09**	(.01)
FTWS	-.15**	(.03)	-.15**	(.03)	-.15**	(.03)	.23**	(.02)	.23**	(.02)	.22**	(.02)
VC	-.11**	(.03)	-.12**	(.03)	-.12**	(.03)	.13**	(.02)	.13**	(.02)	.13**	(.02)
Level 2—Country												
HDI			-.09	(.99)	-.09	(.99)			-.13	(.59)	-.14	(.59)
VC_country			-.04	(.34)	-.03	(.34)			-.56*	(.20)	-.57*	(.20)

	DV = Turnover Intentions						*DV = Family Satisfaction*					
	Model 1		*Model 2*		*Model 3*		*Model 4*		*Model 5*		*Model 6*	
	β	*SE*	*β*	*SE*	*β*	*SE*	*β*	*SE*	*β*	*SE*	*β*	*SE*
Interactions												
FTWS*VC					-.04	(.03)					.05**	(.02)
FTWS*VC_country					.22**	(.09)					-.21**	(.05)
Intercept	2.60**		2.60**		2.61**		4.40**		4.39**		4.39**	
Var (intercept)	.07*		.10		.09		.06*		.03		.03	
Var (residual)	.96**		.96**		.96**		.32**		.32**		.32**	
Deviance	7,285.44		7,284.46		7,284.89		4,469.12		4,462.39		4,447.99	

Note. $N = 2,830$; † < .10; * $p < .05$; ** $p < .01$; VC = vertical collectivism at individual level; VC_country = aggregated vertical collectivism.

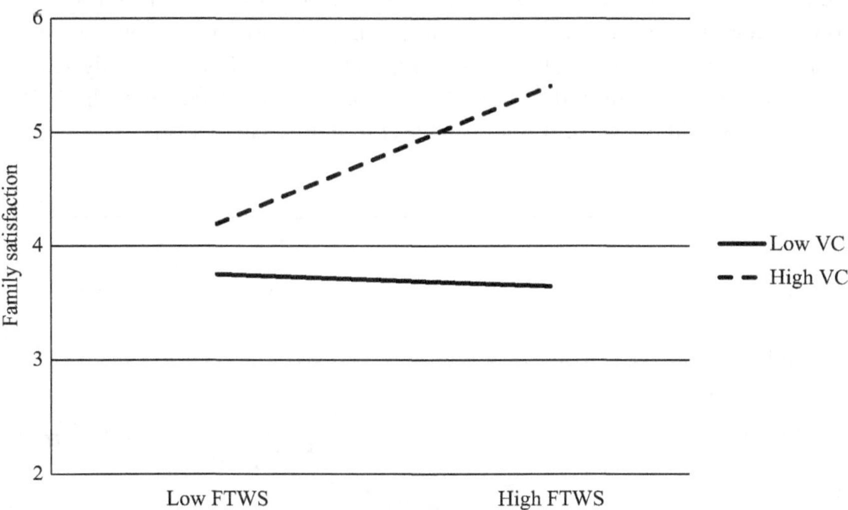

FIGURE 14.10 Interaction FTWS and vertical collectivism on family satisfaction.

level is negatively related to turnover intentions and positively related to family satisfaction in all Models. For aggregated VC at the country level we found a significant, negative effect on family satisfaction (Model 6).

Figure 14.10 shows the shape of the significant interaction term FTWS × VC at the individual level on family satisfaction ($\beta = .05$, $p < .01$; Model 6). The relationship between FTWS and family satisfaction is stronger for employees with more vertical collective values. High levels of spillover from family to work contribute more strongly to family satisfaction for vertical collectivists. Employees with fewer VC values seem to experience similar levels of family satisfaction irrespective of the levels of spillover from family to work.

Models 3 and 6 in Table 14.8 yield significant cross-level interactions for turnover intentions ($\beta = .22, p < .01$) and family satisfaction ($\beta = -.21, p < .01$). Similar to WTFS, the scatter plot in Figure 14.11 shows that the relationship between FTWS and turnover intentions is weaker when country level vertical collectivism is high. Whereas the Asian countries are more at the upper level of the regression line, the Anglo-Saxon countries in our sample and Israel are at the lower end of the regression line. Outliers in this plot are Turkey and Taiwan. Both countries have a high collectivist value orientation in our sample. However, in Taiwan FTWS seems to have the potential to significantly decrease turnover intentions, whereas in Turkey we observe a small but positive correlation for FTWS and turnover intentions.

Figure 14.12 provides information about the shape of the cross-level interaction and country differences regarding family satisfaction (Table 14.8, Model 6). Contrary to expectations and the moderating effect at the individual level, at the country level the effect is reversed. In more collectivist societies, in our case in the Asian countries and Turkey, the relationship between FTWS and family satisfaction seems weaker than in the Anglo-Saxon countries and Israel. In India, FTWS seems to have almost no impact on the level of family satisfaction.

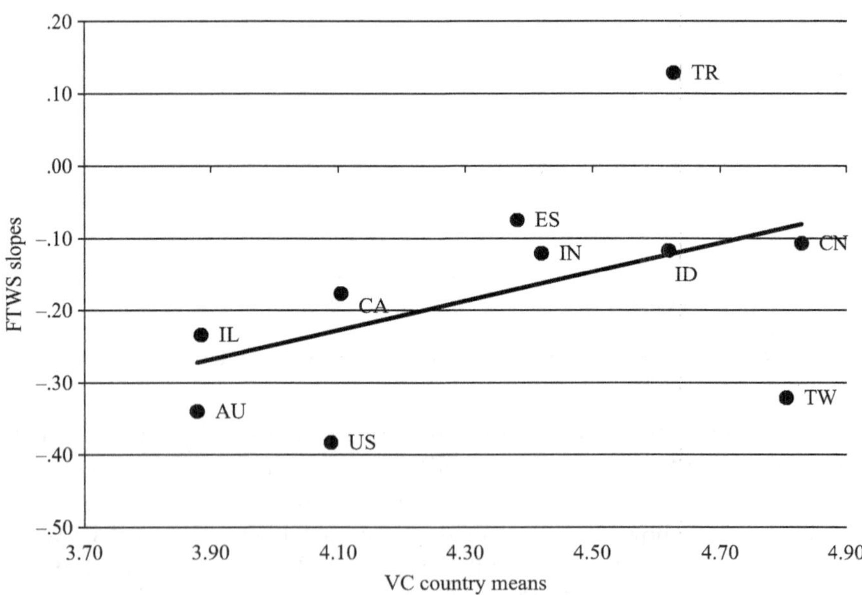

FIGURE 14.11 FTWS versus country means vertical collectivism. Solid line from within country OLS regressions. DV = turnover intentions.

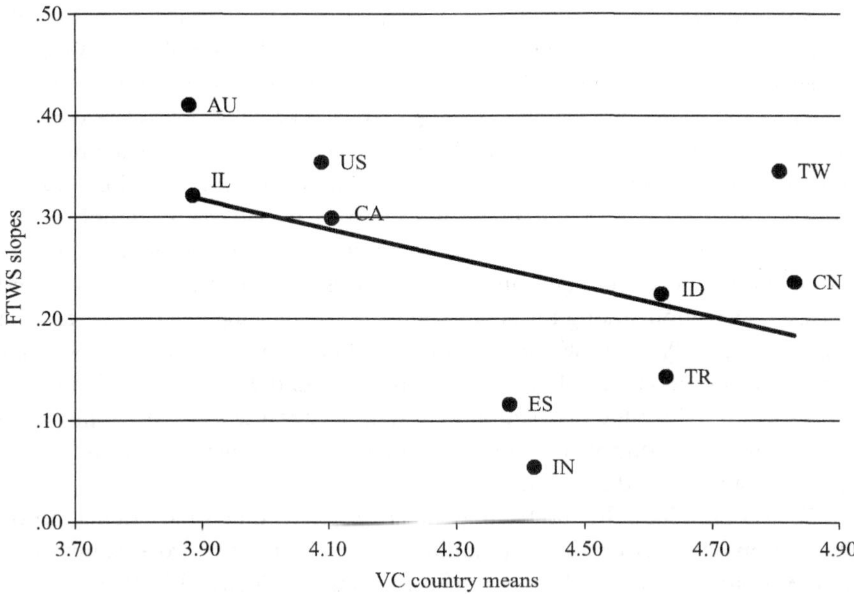

FIGURE 14.12 FTWS versus country means vertical collectivism. Solid line from within country OLS regressions. DV = family satisfaction.

Discussion

Antecedents

Our research model (Figure 14.1) depicts job and family control as within-domain antecedents of WTFS and FTWS, respectively. Statistical analysis using the pooled sample provides support for these relationships. Job control seems to significantly increase positive spillover from work-to-family, whereas family control seems to significantly increase positive spillover from the family to the work domain. In their seminal theory on work-family enrichment, Powell and Greenhaus (2006) suggested that the primary antecedents of enrichment may come from the originating domain, but cross-domain effects cannot be ruled out. A post-hoc analysis revealed positive relationships between job control and FTWS and family control and WTFS in our sample, although the effects sizes were smaller than for the within-domain relationships. We also cannot rule out moderating effects of culture on these cross-domain relationships. However, a detailed analysis of these interactions is outside of the scope of this chapter.

We found both within-domain relationships to be moderated by vertical collectivist values at the individual level. Employees with more vertical collectivist values seem to benefit more from high levels of job and family control than employees with fewer VC values. For aggregated VC at the country level, we only found a significant cross-level interaction effect for family control on FTWS. The moderating effect is in line with Powell et al.'s (2009) culture-sensitive theory of work-family enrichment which suggests that employees in collectivist cultures have more opportunities for enrichment due to a more personal employer-employee relationship and a higher level of work-family integration than in individualistic societies. In our sample, we observed stronger correlations between job control and WTFS in the more collectivist societies of the Asian countries and in Turkey and weaker links in the individualistic Anglo-Saxon countries and Israel. An exception among the Asian countries in our sample is India. Despite a medium level of VC, in India job control has almost no impact on positive spillover from work to family. Nevertheless, companies in the countries with a strong vertical collectivist value orientation may want to pay attention to the provision high levels of job control and autonomy, if they want to increase the well-being of their employees and families.

We also examined the moderating effect of polychronic time orientation on the relationships between job and family control and positive work-family spillover. Although this cultural value dimension was not discussed in Powell et al.'s (2009) culture-sensitive theory of enrichment, research on PTO and negative interference between work and family (Korabik et al., in press) provided clues for potential effects on positive spillover that we considered worthwhile to investigate. For both directions of positive work-family spillover we found a small but highly significant positive main effect of PTO at the individual level. Employees with a polychronic rather than a monochronic time orientation experience more positive spillover in both directions. Due to their simultaneous involvement in multiple activities in different roles, polychronic employees may have more opportunities to generate valuable physical and psychological resources that can then be transferred to the other domain and facilitate positive work-family experiences. We also found a small moderating effect of PTO at the individual level for WTFS, but not for FTWS. Hence, employees with a polychronic time orientation benefit more from higher levels of job control than monochronic employees. Polychronic employees may integrate work and family more than monochronic employees. As a consequence, role transitions and boundary crossings between domains may occur more frequently. Having control over one's job may further facilitate these transitions and boundary crossings, and lead to even higher levels of work-to-family positive spillover. Hence, companies interested in facilitating positive work-to-family spillover in their employees may want to pay attention to the provision of job control to employees with a polychronic time orientation.

Multilevel analysis yielded a significant cross-level interaction effect for aggregated PTO × family control on FTWS. Our graphical analysis (Figure 14.6) shows a small but negative interaction effect, which is contrary to our theoretical assumptions. Family control was more strongly related to FTWS in the monochronic rather than in the polychronic countries in our sample. Indonesia and

India, followed by Turkey, are the most polychronic countries in our sample. The other two Asian countries, Taiwan and China have a more monochronic time orientation, with Taiwan being the most monochronic society in our sample and having the strongest correlation between family control and FTWS. Also China has a rather low aggregated PTO level in our sample, indicating a more monochronic rather than a polychronic time orientation in this country. However, the correlation between family control and FTWS is also weak in China, which is in line with our theorizing. A possible explanation for our surprising findings may be that working conditions in the Anglo-Saxon countries and Taiwan (which has a higher economic development than India and Indonesia) are more favorable and allow a better transfer and application of resources from the family domain into the work domain. In addition, we cannot rule out that the lack of measurement equivalence for our polychronic time orientation measure in 6 of the 10 countries may have influenced our results. Future studies would benefit from using another, more reliable measure for time orientation, such as the full Inventory of Polychronic Values by Bluedorn et al. (1999) rather than a short version of the inventory as used in this study. Further, a larger number of countries may result in more variation in cultural values and yield more precise estimates for the cross-level interactions.

Outcomes

We proposed turnover intentions and family satisfaction as outcome variables in our research model. Both variables have been related to work-family enrichment, spillover, or facilitation in previous research (Crain & Hammer, 2013; McNall et al., 2010). Further, we proposed these relationships to be moderated by vertical collectivism at the individual and the country levels. The discussion on outcomes of positive work-family linkages is dominated by two contrasting views: the originating domain view versus the receiving domain view (see literature review and theory in this chapter for more details). In our sample we found moderate support for the originating domain view. WTFS was more strongly related to turnover intentions than to family satisfaction, but differences in effect sizes were rather small and both links were highly significant. Unlike Carlson et al. (2014), who found no significant relationship between family-to-work enrichment and family satisfaction, we found a stronger association between FTWS and family satisfaction than with turnover intentions, again providing evidence for the originating rather than the receiving domain view.

Like many cross-sectional studies, this study does not allow us to draw conclusions about causality. This becomes especially evident when we look at the outcomes in our research model. Is it the experience of positive work-family spillover which decreases turnover intentions or is it that turnover intentions decrease feelings of positive spillover? Likewise, perhaps employees who are highly satisfied with their family life may also experience higher levels of spillover rather than the other way round, as suggested in our research model and in previous studies (e.g., Carlson et al., 2014; McNall et al., 2010). Ultimately, we cannot rule out converse relationships with our study design. Future research on the positive aspects of the work-family interface would benefit from more longitudinal research designs.

The culture-sensitive theory of work-family enrichment (Powell et al., 2009) does not consider potential moderating effects of culture on relationships between enrichment and outcomes. Nevertheless, we proposed VC as a moderator of the relationships with both outcome variables in our research model. Drawing upon cross-national research on WFC, we expected the links between positive spillover and turnover intentions to be stronger in more individualistic countries. For family satisfaction we suggested the relationship with positive spillover to be stronger in more collectivist countries. At the individual level, our analysis yielded significant interaction effects for family satisfaction and both directions of spillover, but not for turnover intentions. In both cases, we found positive spillover between work and family and vice versa to increase family satisfaction more strongly for individuals with a stronger vertical collectivist value orientation. These findings may be explained by multiple role engagement, a stronger integration of work and family life, and on overall stronger value of the family among individuals with more collectivist values.

Looking at VC as a country-level phenomenon, our analysis yielded significant moderating effects for turnover intentions and both directions of positive spillover and a significant cross-level interaction effect for FTWS and family satisfaction. In line with our theoretical reasoning that in individualistic societies personal needs are central to employees, we found the links between WTFS/FTWS and turnover intentions to be stronger in countries with a weaker vertical collectivist value orientation. In our sample these are the individualistic societies of the Anglo-Saxon countries, but also Israel. In the Asian countries such as Indonesia and China, but also Turkey, the relationships between positive spillover and turnover intentions are less pronounced. Regarding WTFS, India and Taiwan both deviate to some extent from this pattern in our analysis. India was the only country in our sample with a small but positive relationship between turnover intentions and WTFS. In the Taiwanese sample, on the other hand, the relationship was negative (as expected) but almost comparable in size as in the Anglo-Saxon countries.

Looking at FTWS and turnover intentions Turkey and again Taiwan deviated from the pattern outlined earlier. Turkey was the only country in our sample with a positive slope for FTWS despite a rather high average VC at the country level. Hence, in Turkey positive spillover from family to work does not have the potential to decrease, but rather increase, turnover intentions. The pattern for Taiwan is similar to the one outlined above for WTFS. Despite a high level of VC, the link between FTWS and turnover intensions is strong in the Taiwanese sample. If we assume that the direction of the relationship between WTFS/FTWS and turnover intentions is as outlined in our research model, one practical implication would be that organizations aiming at low turnover rates among their staff should provide their employees with working environments rich in opportunities for positive spillover between domains. This possibility seems especially important in individualistic societies where employees may also be less tolerant of unfavorable working conditions.

Finally, our analysis yielded a significant cross-level interaction effect for FTWS × VC on family satisfaction. Contrary to our theoretical assumptions, the positive relationship between FTWS and family satisfaction was weaker in the more collectivist countries in our samples. We found the largest effect sizes in the Anglo-Saxon countries and Israel, all countries with rather low average country values for VC in our study. This finding is also contrary to our finding at the individual level as discussed earlier in this chapter.

In general and for practitioners our findings suggest that work-life functions across nations vary with culture, which is perhaps obvious. Less intuitively, the relatively strong individual-level results for vertical collectivism and polychronic time orientation suggest that employers, employees, and employees' families may benefit from the selection of employees who are relatively (if not absolutely) strong on those orientations. For researchers, the value of accounting for cultural variation in our understanding of the relationship between work and family is highlighted here, and warrants further research.

To conclude, our study is among the first attempts to empirically test the complex influence of societal culture on the positive side of the work-family interface. Despite the small number of countries, the study extends previous theorizing on the impact of culture on positive work-family processes by including new cultural value dimensions (vertical collectivism and polychronic/monochronic time orientation) and by looking at antecedents and outcomes of positive work-family spillover. Previous theory has entirely focused on the impact of culture on the antecedents-spillover/enrichment link. Further, our analysis also enhances our general knowledge on outcomes of positive spillover by providing support for the originating rather than the receiving domain view in the work-family literature. Future research may want to include a wider array of countries and additional cultural dimensions, antecedents, and outcome variables.

References

Ashforth, B. E., Kreiner, G. E., & Fugate, M. (2000). All in a day's work: Boundaries and micro role transitions. *Academy of Management Review, 25*(3), 472–491. doi:10.5465/AMR.2000.3363315

Bell, B. A., Morgan, G. B., Schoeneberger, J. A., Kromrey, J. D., & Ferron, J. M. (2015). How low can you go? An investigation of the influence of sample size and model complexity on point and interval estimates in two-level linear models. *Methodology, 10*, 1–11. doi:10.1027/1614-2241/a000062

Bluedorn, A. C., Kalliath, T. J., Strube, M. J., & Martin, G. D. (1999). Polychronicity and the Inventory of Polychronic Values (IPV). *Journal of Managerial Psychology, 14*(3/4), 205–231. doi:10.1108/02683949910263747

Bowers, J., & Drake, K. W. (2005). EDA for HLM: Visualization when probabilistic inference fails. *Political Analysis, 13*(4), 301–326. doi:10.1093/pan/mpi031

Bryan, M. L., & Jenkins, S. P. (2013). *Regression analysis of country effects using multilevel data: A cautionary tale.* ISER Working Paper Series Institute for Social and Economic Research. University of Essex.

Butler, A. B., Grzywacz, J. G., Bass, B. L., & Linney, K. D. (2005). Extending the demands-control model: A daily diary study of job characteristics, work-family conflict and work-family facilitation. *Journal of Occupational and Organizational Psychology, 78*, 155–169.

Carlson, D. S., Hunter, E. M., Ferguson, M., & Whitten, D. (2014). Work-family enrichment and satisfaction: Mediating processes and relative impact of originating and receiving domains. *Journal of Management, 40*(3), 845–865. doi:10.1177/0149206311414429

Carlson, D. S., Kacmar, M. K., Wayne, J. H., & Grzywacz, J. G. (2006). Measuring the positive side of the work-family interface: Development and validation of a work-family enrichment scale. *Journal of Vocational Behavior, 68*, 131–164. doi:10.1016/j.jvb.2005.02.002

Crain, T. L., & Hammer, L. B. (2013). Work-family enrichment: A systematic review of antecedents, outcomes, and mechanisms. In A. B. Bakker (Ed.), *Advances in positive psychology* (pp. 303–328). Bingley, UK: Emerald.

Demerouti, E., Martinez Corts, I., & Boz, M. (2013). Issues in the development of research on inter-role enrichment. In S. Poelmans, J. H. Greenhaus, & M. Las Heras Maestro (Eds.), *Expanding the boundaries of work-family research: A vision for the future* (pp. 227–253). Basingstoke, UK: Palgrave Macmillan.

Edwards, J. R., & Rothbard, N. P. (2000). Mechanisms linking work and family: Clarifying the relationship between work and family constructs. *Academy of Management Review, 25*(1), 178–199.

Enders, C. K., & Tofighi, D. (2007). Centering predictor variables in cross-sectional multilevel models: A new look at an old issue. *Psychological Methods, 12*(2), 121–138. doi:10.1037/1082-989X.12.2.121

Goode, W. J. (1960). A theory of role strain. *American Sociological Review, 25*(4), 483–496.

Greenhaus, J. H., & Beutell, N. J. (1985). Sources of conflict between work and family roles. *Academy of Management Review, 10*(1), 76–88.

Greenhaus, J. H., & Powell, G. N. (2006). When work and family are allies: A theory of work-family enrichment. *Academy of Management Review, 31*(1), 72–92. doi:10.5465/AMR.2006.19379625

Grzywacz, J. G., Carlson, D. S., Kacmar, K. M., & Wayne, J. H. (2007). A multi-level perspective on the synergies between work and family. *Journal of Occupational and Organizational Psychology, 80*, 559–574. doi:10.1348/096317906X163081

Grzywacz, J. G., & Marks, N. F. (2000). Reconceptualizing the work-family interface. *Journal of Occupational Health Psychology, 5*, 111–126.

Hall, E. T., & Hall, M. R. (1990). *Understanding cultural differences.* Yarmouth, ME: Intercultural Press.

Hanson, G. C., Hammer, L. B., & Colton, C. L. (2006). Development and validation of a multidimensional scale of perceived work-family positive spillover. *Journal of Occupational Health Psychology, 11*(3), 249–265. doi:10.1037/1076-8998.11.3.249

Hofstede, G. (1980). *Culture's consequences.* Beverly Hills, CA: Sage.

Hofstede, G. (2001). *Culture's consequences: Comparing values, behaviors, institutions, and organizations across nations* (2nd ed.). Thousand Oaks, CA: Sage.

Hox, J. J. (2010). *Multilevel analysis: Techniques and applications* (2nd ed.). London, UK: Routledge.

Korabik, K., Van Rhijn, T., Ayman, R., Lero, D. S., & Hammer, L. B. (in press). Gender, polychronicity and the work-family interface: Is a preference for multi-tasking beneficial? *Community, Work, & Family*, 1–20. doi:10.1080/13668803.2016.1178103

Lu, J., Siu, O., Spector, P. E., & Shi, K. (2009). Antecedents and outcomes of a fourfold taxonomy of work-family balance in Chinese employed parents. *Journal of Occupational Health Psychology, 14*(2), 182–192.

Marks, S. R. (1977). Multiple roles and role strain: Some notes on human energy, time, and commitment. *American Sociological Review, 42*, 921–936. doi:10.2307/2094577

McNall, L. A., Nicklin, J. M., & Masuda, A. D. (2010). A meta-analytic review of the consequences associated with work-family enrichment. *Journal of Business and Psychology, 25*(3), 381–396. doi:10.1007/s10869-009-9141-1

Powell, G. N., & Greenhaus, J. H. (2006). Is the opposite of positive negative? Untangling the complex relationship between work family enrichment and conflict. *Career Development International, 11*(7), 650–659. doi:10.1108/13620430610713508

Powell, G. N., Francesco, A. M., & Ling, Y. (2009). Toward culture-sensitive theories of the work-family interface. *Journal of Organizational Behavior, 30*, 597–616. doi:10.1002/job.568

Raudenbush, S. W., & Bryk, A. S. (2002). *Hierarchical linear models*. Thousand Oaks, CA: Sage.

Singelis, T., Triandis, H. C., & Bhawuk, D. P. S. (1995). Horizontal and vertical dimensions of individualism and collectivism: A theoretical and measurement refinement. *Cross-Cultural Research, 29*(3), 240–275. doi:10.1177/106939719502900302

Siu, O., Lu, J., Brough, P., Bakker, A. B., Kalliath, T., O'Driscoll, M. P., . . . Shi, K. (2011). Role resources and work-family enrichment: The role of work engagement. *Journal of Vocational Behavior,* 77, 470–480. doi:10.1016/j.jvb.2010.06.007

Spector, P. E., Allen, T. D., Poelmans, S., Lapierre, L. M., Cooper, C. L., O'Driscoll, M., . . . Widerszal-Bazyl, M. (2007). Cross-national differences in relationships of work demands, job satisfaction and turnover intentions with work-family conflict. *Personnel Psychology, 60*(4), 805–835. doi:10.1111/j.1744-6570.2007.00092.x

Tang, S., Siu, O., & Cheung, F. (2012). A study of work-family enrichment among Chinese employees: The mediating role between work support and job satisfaction. *Applied Psychology: An International Review, 63*, 130–150. doi:10.1111/j.1464-0597.2012.00519.x

Triandis, H. C. (1995). *Individualism and collectivism*. Boulder, CO: Westview Press.

UNDP. (2007). *Human development report 2007/2008*. New York, NY: United Nations Development Programme.

Voydanoff, P. (2005). Social integration, work-family conflict and facilitation, and job and marital quality. *Journal of Marriage and Family, 67*(3), 666–679. doi:10.1111/j.1741-3737.2005.00161.x

Wayne, J. H. (2009). Reducing conceptual confusion: Clarifying the positive side of work and family. In R. D. Crane & J. E. Hill (Eds.), *Handbook of families and work* (pp. 105–140). Lanham, MD: Rowman & Littlefield Publishing.

15

UNDERSTANDING THE ROLE OF PERSONAL COPING STRATEGY IN DECREASING WORK AND FAMILY CONFLICT

A Cross-Cultural Perspective

Anit Somech and Anat Drach-Zahavy

In recent decades, social trends have stimulated a burgeoning interest in work-family conflict (WFC) and its antecedents and consequences (Korabik, Whitehead, & Lero, 2008). However, little research has focused on personal coping strategy for better understanding the WFC phenomenon by specifying the unique styles that individuals use to deal with WFC or identifying among these styles the ones most effective in lowering the conflict level. Moreover, to date, no previous global study has examined cross-national differences in individual coping strategies to ease WFC. Studying coping strategy from a cross-cultural perspective is crucial for several reasons. First, scholars (e.g., Kuo, 2011; Lazarus & Folkman, 1984) have argued theoretically that a person's internalized cultural values, beliefs, and norms affect the appraisal process of stressors, hence the perceived appropriateness of coping responses, although this has not been empirically demonstrated. Second, although coping is a universal experience faced by individuals regardless of culture, ethnicity, and race, members of different cultures might consider and respond to stressors differently with respect to coping goals, strategies, and outcomes (Chun, Moos, & Cronkite, 2006; Lam & Zane, 2004). Further, understanding cultural differences regarding how individuals cope with WFC is necessary for global organizations, but also for domestic organizations with a multicultural workforce. To effectively manage diversity, these organizations seek to develop employees' skills to balance work and family that are sensitive to cultural differences. Studying the influence of culture on WFC and coping will also help managers in non-Western contexts (e.g., emerging economies) who need to understand the applicability of coping strategies that are developed in Western industrialized societies (Gelfand & Knight, 2005).

In this chapter, we sought to help fill a critical void in WFC research by exploring cross-national differences in individual coping strategies to ease such conflict. We developed a classification of countries on two key dimensions that are critical for WFC research: "individualism-collectivism" and "gender-role ideology." Individualism-collectivism (I-C), though well researched in cross-cultural and cross-national studies, and an important variable in the work-family domain (e.g., Spector et al., 2004; Yang, Chen, Choi, & Zou, 2000), as a classification that relies on a single dimension might lead to over-generalization. To capture the complexity of the WFC phenomenon, research needs to move beyond simple dichotomies of individualism-collectivism (Gelfand & Knight, 2005). Specifically, this chapter discuses the role of culture in shaping the strategies employees use to cope with WFC, as well as their effectiveness.

Conceptual Background and Hypotheses

Personal Coping with W-F Conflict—A Cross-Cultural Perspective

Given the extensive study of coping in the stress literature (cf. Folkman & Moskowitz, 2004), it is puzzling to find a relative lack of research on coping in the context of work and family (e.g., Behson, 2002; Somech & Drach-Zahavy, 2007). Coping with WFC is defined here as the cognitive and behavioral efforts individuals make to manage the stresses arising from the conflicting demands of the work and family domains. According to the Conservation of Resources Theory (Hobfoll, 1989, 2001), when stress levels rise, individuals expend internal or external resources to manage the distress. The resources that the person possesses are internal; they encompass personal characteristics such as efficacy, optimism, and coping styles; external resources do not belong to the person but are available from his/her external environment. In the context of this chapter, using personal coping with WFC in an effort to manage conflicting work and family demands might be seen as reliance on internal resources. In this vein, Somech and Drach-Zahavy (2007) developed and refined an eight-strategy typology. The strategies denoted behavioral aspects of coping that specify what individuals actually do at work and/or at home to cope with WFC: *Good enough at home/work*—lowering the performance of family/work responsibilities to a less than perfect level; *Super at home/work*—insisting on doing all family/work duties single-handedly and perfectly; *Delegation at home/work*—managing one's own family/work duties by delegating some to others; and *Priorities at home/work*—arranging family/work duties in order of priority, and undertaking only those with high priority.

WFC is bidirectional, consisting of two components: work interference with family (WIF) and family interference with work (FIW). Given the multiple ways individuals cope with WIF and FIW, we suggest that no coping styles are universally appropriate; some may work better with specific forms of conflict within specific contexts. In particular, we suggest that countries' cluster (operationalized to represent the combination of I-C and gender-role ideology) may moderate the relationship of personal coping and WIF and FIW. WFC and its related issues are inherently a cultural phenomenon (Gelfand & Knight, 2005). Culture has both constitutive and regulatory effects that shape how people act in the domains of work and family. The constitutive effects of culture refer to the way in which the value and significance that individuals attach to different objects and behaviors are shaped by their cultural environment. Thus, what individuals perceive as desirable in terms, for example, of their investment in work and/or family will be influenced by their cultural values and norms. The regulatory effects of culture refer to the way in which social norms, customs, and conventions define the legitimate sets of roles and activities for different individuals in each society (Thein, Austen, Currie, & Lewin, 2010). Work and family pressures reflect social expectations and self-expectations and are most susceptible to values and beliefs internalized through socialization (Parasuraman, Purohit, Godshalk, & Beutell, 1996; Yang et al., 2000). Similarly, divisions of work and family roles tend to differ according to cultural values (Trompenaars & Hampton-Turner, 1998).

Systematic cross-cultural comparisons of WFC are few, and those that exist focus mostly on the antecedents and consequences of WFC (Lu et al., 2009). Many of these studies have adopted individualism-collectivism (I-C) as a general explanatory framework for cultural differences, and found that nation (operationalized to represent I-C) moderated the relation of work/family demands to WFC (e.g., Lu, Gilmour, Kao, & Huang, 2006; Spector et al., 2004; Yang et al., 2000). Although I-C is a construct well researched in cross-cultural and cross-national studies, research apparently needs to move beyond simple dichotomies of individualism—collectivism to capture the complexity of the WFC phenomenon (Gelfand & Knight, 2005). In one of the rare studies that refer to the combination of I-C and power distance, Lu et al. (2009) examined the relation of work resources (supervisory support and organizational family supportive values), WFC, and work- and nonwork-related outcomes, comparing samples of Taiwanese and British employees. They found that supervisory support had a stronger protective effect for Taiwanese than British employees. However, to date, no study has examined the role of individual coping strategy in decreasing WIF and FIW taking a cross-cultural perspective.

Individualism-collectivism is an analytical dimension that captures the relative importance people accord to personal interests and to shared pursuits (Wagner, 1995). Individualistic cultures emphasize self-reliance, autonomy, control, and priority of personal goals, which may or may not be consistent with in-group goals. An individual feels proud of his or her own accomplishments and derives satisfaction from performance based on his or her own achievements. By contrast, in collectivistic cultures people will subordinate their personal interests to the goals of their in-group. An individual belongs to only a few in-groups, and behavior within the group emphasizes goal attainment, cooperation, and group welfare and harmony. Thus, pleasure and satisfaction derive from group accomplishment (Lam, Chen, & Schaubroeck, 2002; Triandis, 1995). In a cultural norm of individualism, people tend to keep work and family relationships separate, while collectivists usually integrate the two realms. The collectivist culture legitimizes giving priority to work, and investing extra effort in work is considered self-sacrifice for the benefit of the family rather than sacrifice of the family for the selfish pursuit of one's own career as in an individualistic culture (Lu et al., 2006).

Gender-role ideology is conceived as beliefs and opinions about the ways that family and work roles do and should differ based on sex (Harris & Firestone, 1998), and these typically lie on a continuum from traditional to egalitarian. Traditional attitudes to gender roles reinforce or conform to expected differences in roles for men and women, while egalitarian attitudes do not believe in role segregation according to gender, and hold more equal views of the roles of women and men at home as well as work. Gender-role attitude, like any other, is learned through experience (Lachman, 1991). Strong forces of socialization and gender-role norms teach children at very young ages that certain roles or jobs are identified with men or with women (Firestone, Harris, & Lambert, 1999). For example, the research of Marini, Fan, Finely, and Beutel (1996) on the influence of job values (i.e., what people want in a job) on youth indicated that these values had a stronger influence on job choice than other background variables.

To classify the 10 countries according to the two dimensions of I-C and gender-role ideology, we conducted a cluster analysis, which is described in Chapter 2. The results revealed three subgroups: (1) high in individualism and a more egalitarian gender-role ideology (I-E group), which includes Australia, Canada, Spain, and the United States; (2) high in collectivism, and a more traditional gender-role ideology (C-T group), which includes China, India, Indonesia, and Turkey; and (3) average ratings in both dimensions (MC-MT), which includes Israel and Taiwan.

Thinking about the implications of these differences suggests that variations in I-C combined with variation in gender-role ideology might serve as a moderator in the relation of coping strategy to WFC. With respect to WFC coping strategies, we expected effective coping to reduce the level of WFC. If an employed parent is coping effectively, his/her perceived WFC should be lower because the conflict is "under control," so to speak. Similarly, perceived conflict should be highest in those who ineffectively or inefficiently manage WFC (Lazarus, 1991; Rotondo, Carlson, & Kincaid, 2003). Given the multiple ways individuals cope with stress, we suggest that no coping styles are universally appropriate; some may work better in specific contexts. In particular, because the combination of I-C and gender-role ideology (represented by group) is expected to affect the extent in which work and family are perceived as distinct domains, and their relative priority, we expected that the effectiveness of specific coping styles in attenuating WIF and FIW would vary depend on cultural differences (Somech & Drach-Zahavy, 2007).

Specifically, the I-E group consisted of people with high individualism together with an egalitarian gender-role ideology. Their self-definition, which is the pursuit of personal gains, emphasizes personal accomplishment and achievement through work (Spector et al., 2004); but they also have a more even attitude to the role of women and men at home as well as at work. Previous studies (Lu et al., 2010) showed that although people in this group value personal achievement through work more than fulfillment of family obligations, they often perceive sacrificing family resources for work as failure to meet their role as parent or spouse. For these individuals (men and women) any coping strategy that allows them personal accomplishment through work (i.e., super at work), but also to function as parents and spouses (i.e., priorities at work/home, delegation at work/home), might serve as an effective technique to lessen WFC. Any technique that distances them from their role at work (i.e., super at home, good enough at work) or at home (i.e., good enough at home) should raise the level of WIF and FIW.

> *Hypothesis 1: For the I-E group, for men and women alike, the coping strategies of super at work will decrease the level of FIW; while priorities at work/home and delegation at work/home will decrease the level of WIF.*

The C-T group consists of people with high collectivism and a traditional gender-role ideology. These employed parents place group interests above individual preferences. Investing extra effort in work is considered as self-sacrifice for the benefit of the family rather than sacrifice of the family for the selfish pursuit of their own career, as it is in an individualistic culture (Lu et al., 2006). However, their more traditional gender-role ideology means that men should invest extra efforts in work for the benefit of the family, while women should sustain their primary role as wives and mothers and invest less effort in work. A coping strategy that allows men to maintain high standards at work (i.e., super at work and good enough at home), and one that allows women to maintain high standards at home (i.e., super at home, and good enough at work), might serve as an effective technique to lessen WIF and FIW. Coping techniques that run counter to their values and beliefs will cause greater WIF and FIW.

> *Hypothesis 2a: For men in the C-T group, the coping strategies of super at work and good enough at home will decrease FIW and WIF.*

> *Hypothesis 2b: For women in the C-T group, the coping strategies of super at home and good enough at work will decrease FIW and WIF.*

People in the third group (MC-MT) evince medium levels of collectivism and of the traditional gender-role ideology, although to some extent, women are expected to be responsible for the home and men for the family's material well-being; men don't want their paid work to distract them from their family, and women don't want their home obligations to distract them from their paid work (Hassan, Dollard, & Winefield, 2010). We expect that any coping strategy that allows these men and women to balance work and family (i.e., priorities at home/work, delegation at home/work) might ease WIF and FIW, while any technique that distances them for one of these roles (i.e., super at home and good enough at work for men, and super at work and good enough at home for women) will raise the level of WIF and FIW.

> *Hypothesis 3: For men and women in the MC-MT the coping strategies of priorities at home/work, delegation at home/work will decrease the levels of WIF and FIW.*

Findings

Figure 15.1 depicts the distribution of coping strategies usage by group, showing that for the I-E group the most common coping strategy was *delegation at home* (M = 3.88), followed by *good enough at home* (M = 3.87), and then *super at work* (M = 3.40); the three least frequently used coping strategies were *priorities at home* (M = 2.78), *super at home* (M = 2.87), and *good enough at work* (M = 2.87). For the MC-MT group, the most common coping strategy was *delegation at home* (M = 4.04), followed by *delegation at work* (M = 3.62), and *super at work* (M = 3.61); the least frequently used coping strategies were *priorities at home* (M = 2.78) and *good enough at work* (M = 2.87). For the C-T group the most common coping strategy was *delegation at home* (M = 3.71), followed by *super at work* (M = 3.62); the least frequently used coping strategies were *priorities at home* (M = 2.78) and *good enough at home* (M = 3.41). Although the results indicated some consistency in the pattern of coping-strategy usage, the findings pointed to significant differences among the three groups in the means. For example, for *delegation at home* the MC-MT group reported the highest mean, followed by the mean of the I-E group, while the C-T group reported it as the least frequently used. Only for *super at work* was there was no difference in means among the three groups.

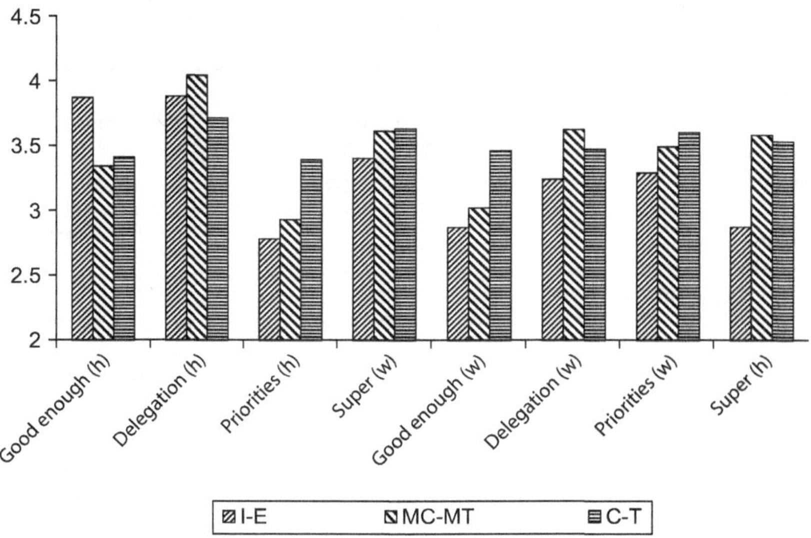

FIGURE 15.1 Coping strategies' means by group.

Testing the Proposed Model

To test our main hypothesis that the interactive effect of culture (group) and gender moderates the relationship between coping strategy and WIF and FIW, we conducted a series of hierarchical regressions to predict WIF and FIW. First, we compared the I-E group with the other two groups, coding I-E as 0 and MC-MT or C-T as 1. Next, we compared I-E (0) with MC-MT (1), and I-E (0) with C-T (1).

In each analysis the control variables (number of children living at home, job schedule, job position) were entered in step 1. The main effect terms of the proposed predictors, namely group, gender, and the eight coping strategies were entered in step 2, the second-order interactive effect of group and coping strategy term in step 3, and the third-order interactive effect of group, gender and coping strategy term in step 4. The models are summarized in Table 15.1 and Figures 15.2 and 15.3.

First, regarding the comparison of I-E group with the other two groups, the results for the prediction of WIF indicated that the control variables accounted for .03% of the variance in this conflict, and the joint main effects of WIF predictors accounted for an additional 24%. The second-order interaction effects between group and coping strategy entered in step 3 accounted for an additional 6.97%, and the third-order interaction effects between group, gender, and coping strategy

TABLE 15.1 Results of hierarchical regression analyses for predicting WIF and FIW.

Step Variables	*I-E vs. Others*		*I-E vs. MC-MT*		*I-E vs. C-T*	
	WIF	*FIW*	*WIF*	*FIW*	*WIF*	*FIW*
	b	*b*	*b*	*b*	*b*	*b*
Step 1: Control Variables						
ΔF	31.34**	6.18**	4.15*	3.92*	31.34**	6.18**
DF	3	3	3	3	3	3
Constant	3.15**	2.69**	3.58**	2.75**	3.15**	2.69**
Number of children	.02	-.05*	.01	.01	.02	-.05*
Schedule of job	.41**	.15**	.23**	-.17*	.41**	.15**
Job position	.15**	-.03	.01	-.07	.15**	-.03
Step 2: Main Effects						
ΔF	94.81**	65.02**	48.91**	28.31**	94.81**	60.12**
DF	13	13	13	13	13	13
Super (H)	-.01	.02	.04	.10**	-.01	.03*
Good enough (H)	.33**	.15**	.38**	.12**	.32**	.15**
Delegation (H)	.05**	.03	.02	.02	.04*	.03
Priorities (H)	.02	.02	-.01	.03	.02	.03
Super (W)	-.01	-.06**	.03	.01	-.01	-.06**

Step Variables	*I-E vs. Others*		*I-E vs. MC-MT*		*I-E vs. C-T*	
	WIF	*FIW*	*WIF*	*FIW*	*WIF*	*FIW*
	b	*b*	*b*	*b*	*b*	*b*
Step 2: Main Effects (cont.)						
Good enough (W)	.05**	.12**	.07**	.18**	.05**	.13**
Delegation (W)	.02	-.05**	- .05*	.03	.02	-.06*
Priorities (W)	-.04*	-.06**	-.05*	-.06*	-.04	-.06*
Group	-.36**	.28**	-.35**	.22**	-.34**	.12*
Gender	-.05	.10*	-.14*	-.02	-.07	.10*
Step 3: Two-Way Interaction						
ΔF	4.75**	5.74**	4.33*	3.34*	4.75**	10.91**
DF	29	29	29	29	29	29
Group × Super (H)	-.14**	-.12**	-.01	-.02	-.08*	-.17**
Group × Good enough (H)	.10**	.07*	-.05	.06	.10**	.10**
Group × Delegation (H)	.01	.01	-.12*	-.07	.05	.03
Group × Priorities (H)	.05	-.01	.07	-.04	-.02	.01
Group × Super (W)	.06	.10**	-.01	.02	.07*	.13**
Group × Good enough (W)	-.024	-.09*	.02	.01	-.04	-.14**
Group × Delegation (W)	-.03	.04	-.11*	.07	-.03	.03
Group × Priorities (W)	-.03	.01	-.01	.02	-.02	-.01
Step 4: Three-Way Interaction						
ΔF	3.89**	3.15*	1.07	0.99	4.03**	3.08**
DF	37	37	37	37	37	37
Group × Gender × Super (H)	-.14*	-.07	.05	-.01	-.13*	-.14*
Group × Gender × Good enough (H)	.24**	.17**	.08	.11	.25**	.15*
Group × Gender × Delegation (H)	-.17**	-.16**	-.06	-.05	-.09	-.01
Group × Gender × Priorities (H)	-.06	.10	-.02	.06	-.02	.07
Group × Gender × Super (W)	.16**	.17**	.10	.04	.14*	.15*
Group × Gender × Good enough (W)	-.08	-.16**	-.10	-.10	-.08	-.16*
Group × Gender × Delegation (W)	-.01	-.07	-.09	-.05	.07	-.03
Group × Gender × Priorities (W)	-.01	.08	.01	.10	.01	-.03
R^2	.34	.26	.33	.23	.33	.27

Note. *$p < .05$; **$p < .01$; ***$p < .001$; unstandardized regression coefficients are shown; I-E = Individualism-Egalitarian; MC-MT= Medium Collectivism-Medium Traditional, C-T = Collectivism-Traditional; H = Home; W= Work. For gender: 0 = male, 1 = female. For schedule of job: 0- part-time, 1-full-time. For job position: 0 = nonmanagerial, 1 = managerial.

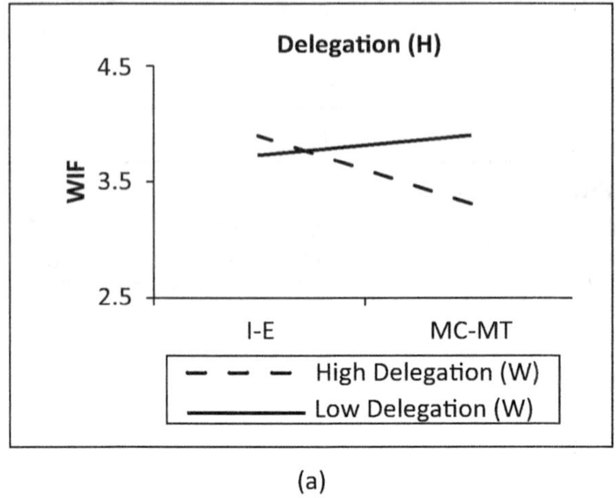

(a)

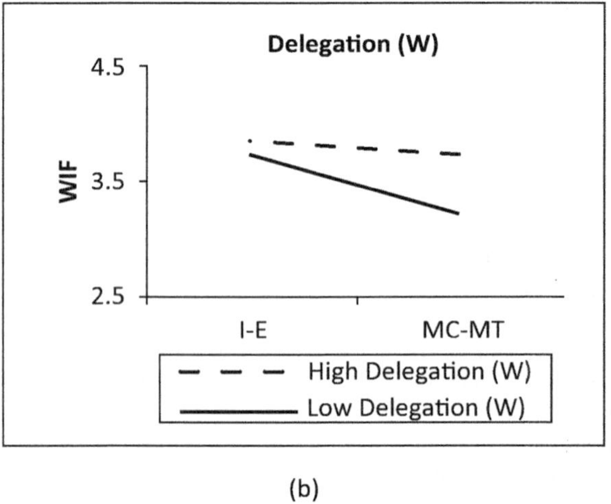

(b)

FIGURE 15.2 Interactive effect of coping strategy and group (I-E vs. MC-MT) on WIF.

entered in step 4 accounted for a further 3%. Of the eight interaction effects between group, gender, and coping strategy on WIF conflict, four were significant: *super at home* ($b = -.14, p < .05$), *good enough at home* ($b = .24, p < .001$), *delegation at home* ($b = -.17, p < .001$), and *super at work* ($b = .16, p < .001$).

The results for predicting FIW indicated that the control variables accounted for .001% of the variance in it, and the joint main effects of FIW predictors accounted for an additional 17%. The second-order interaction effects between group and coping strategy entered in step 3 accounted for an additional 6%, and

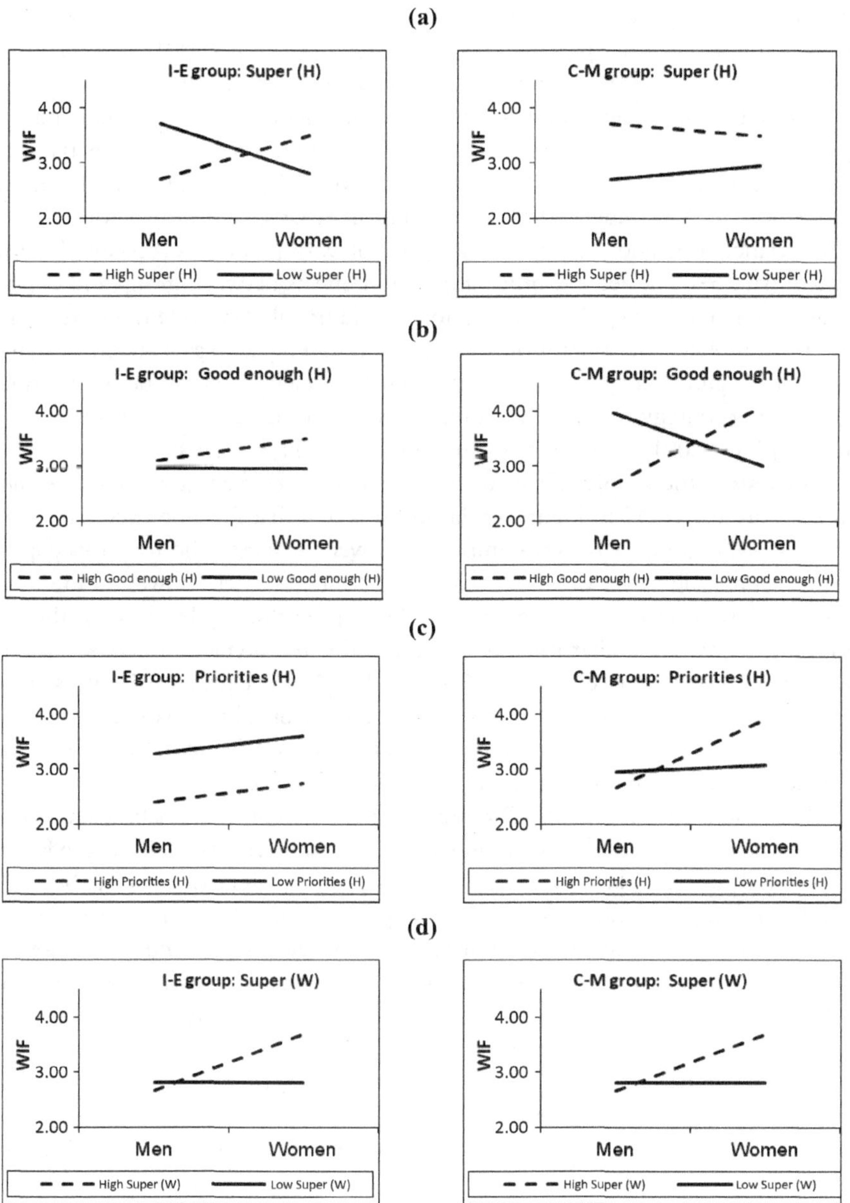

FIGURE 15.3a–d Interactive effect of coping strategy, group (I-E vs. C-T), and gender on WIF.

the third-order interaction effects between group, gender, and coping strategy entered in step 4 accounted for a further 3%. Of the eight interaction effects between group, gender, and coping strategy on FIW, four were significant: *good enough at home* ($b = .17, p < .001$), *super at work* ($b = .17, p < .001$), *good enough at work* ($b = -.16, p < .001$), and *delegation at work* ($b = -.16, p < .001$).

To better understand the pattern of the interactions, we compared the I-E group with the MC-MT group, and the I-E group with the C-T group. Regarding the comparison between I-E group and MC-MT group, the results of the prediction of WIF indicated that the control variables accounted for .01% of the variance in it, and the joint main effects of WIF predictors accounted for an additional 26%. The second-order interaction effects between group and coping strategy entered in step 3 accounted for an additional 4%; while the third-order interaction effects between group, gender, and coping strategy entered in step 4 were not significant ($p > .05$). Of the eight interaction effects between group and coping strategy on the WIF conflict, two were significant: *delegation at home* ($b = -.12, p < .001$), and delegation at work ($b = -.11, p < .001$).

Analysis of the simple effects for the interaction between group and *delegation at home* are presented in Figure 15.2a, and revealed that for employed parents in the MC-MT group, WIF was significantly lower for those who used this coping strategy on a high than on a low level ($t = -10.3, p < .001$); however, no difference in WIF level was found for use of this coping strategy by those in the I-E group ($p > .05$). A similar pattern was found for the interaction between group and *delegation at work* (see Figure 15.2b): For the MC-MT group, WIF was significantly lower for those who used this coping strategy on a high than on a low level ($t = -9.14, p < .001$), but no difference in WIF level was found between high and low use of this coping strategy by the I-E group ($p > .05$).

The results for predicting FIW indicate that the control variables accounted for .003% of the variance in it, and the joint main effects of FIW predictors accounted for an additional 18%. The second-order interaction effects between group and coping strategy entered in step 3 accounted for an additional 4%; however, no third-order interaction effects between group, gender, and coping strategy entered in step 4 was significant. Regarding the comparison between the I-E group and the MC-MT group, the results for predicting FIW revealed no significant three-way interaction effects.

In the comparison of the I-E group with the C-T group, the results of the prediction of WIF indicated that the control variables accounted for .03% of the variance and the joint main effects of WIF predictors accounted for an additional 24%. The second-order interaction effects between group and coping strategy entered in step 3 accounted for an additional 6%, and the third-order interaction effects between group, gender, and coping strategy entered in step 4 accounted for a further 3%. Of the eight interaction effects between group, gender, and coping strategy on WIF conflict, four were significant: *super at home* ($b = -.13, p < .05$), *good enough at home* ($b = .25, p < .001$), *priorities at home* ($b = .19, p < .001$), and *super at work* ($b = .14, p < .05$).

Analysis of the simple effects revealed the following. The interaction between group, gender, and *super at home* is presented in Figure 15.3a. The results indicated that in men and women of the I-E group and in men of the C-T group, WIF was significantly higher for those who used this coping strategy on a high than on a low level ($t = 7.9, p < .001$; $t = 4.75, p < .0001$; $t = 6.63, p < .001$, respectively). However, in women of the C-T group, WIF was significantly lower for those who used this coping strategy on a high than on a low level ($t = -2.95, p < .05$).

For the interaction between group, gender, and *good enough at home* (see Figure 15.3b), in women in both groups WIF was significantly higher in those who used this coping strategy on a high than on a low level ($t = 6.58, p < .001$ for the I-E group, and $t = 8.34, p < .001$ for the C-T group). However, the relation was significantly stronger in the women of the C-T group than in the women of the I-E group. High and low use of this coping strategy by men of all groups yielded no difference between them in WIF conflict level ($p > .05$).

Next, for the interaction between group, gender and *priorities at home* (see Figure 15.3c), WIF was significantly lower in men and women of the I-E group who used this coping strategy on a high than on a low level ($t = -3.06, p < .05$; $t = -6.06, p < .001$, respectively); the opposite pattern was found for the women of the C-T group: WIF was significantly higher in those who used this coping strategy on a high than on a low level ($t = 3.16, p < .05$). Men of the C-T group showed no difference in WIF conflict level whether they applied high or low use of this coping strategy ($p > .05$).

As for *super at work* (Figure 15.3d), in women of both groups WIF was significantly higher in those who used this coping strategy on a high rather than on a low level ($t = 6.51, p < .001$; $t = 7.05, p < .001$, respectively). However, in men of the C-T group WIF was significantly lower in those who used this coping strategy on a high than on a low level ($t = -4.38, p < .05$). Men of the I-E group showed no difference in WIF conflict level whether they applied high or low use of this coping strategy ($p > .05$).

The results for predicting FIW indicate that the control variables accounted for .001% of the variance in it, and the joint main effects of FIW predictors accounted for an additional 16%. The second-order interaction effects between group and coping strategy entered in step 3 accounted for an additional 8%, and the third-order interaction effects between group, gender, and coping strategy entered in step 4 accounted for a further 3%. Of the eight interaction effects between group and coping strategy on FIW, four were significant: *good enough at home* ($b = .15, p < .05$), *priorities at home* ($b = .15, p < .05$), *super at work* ($b = .15, p < .05$), and *good enough at work* ($b = -.16, p < .05$).

Analysis of the simple effects revealed the following. The interaction effects between group, gender, and *good enough at home* are presented in Figure 15.4a. The

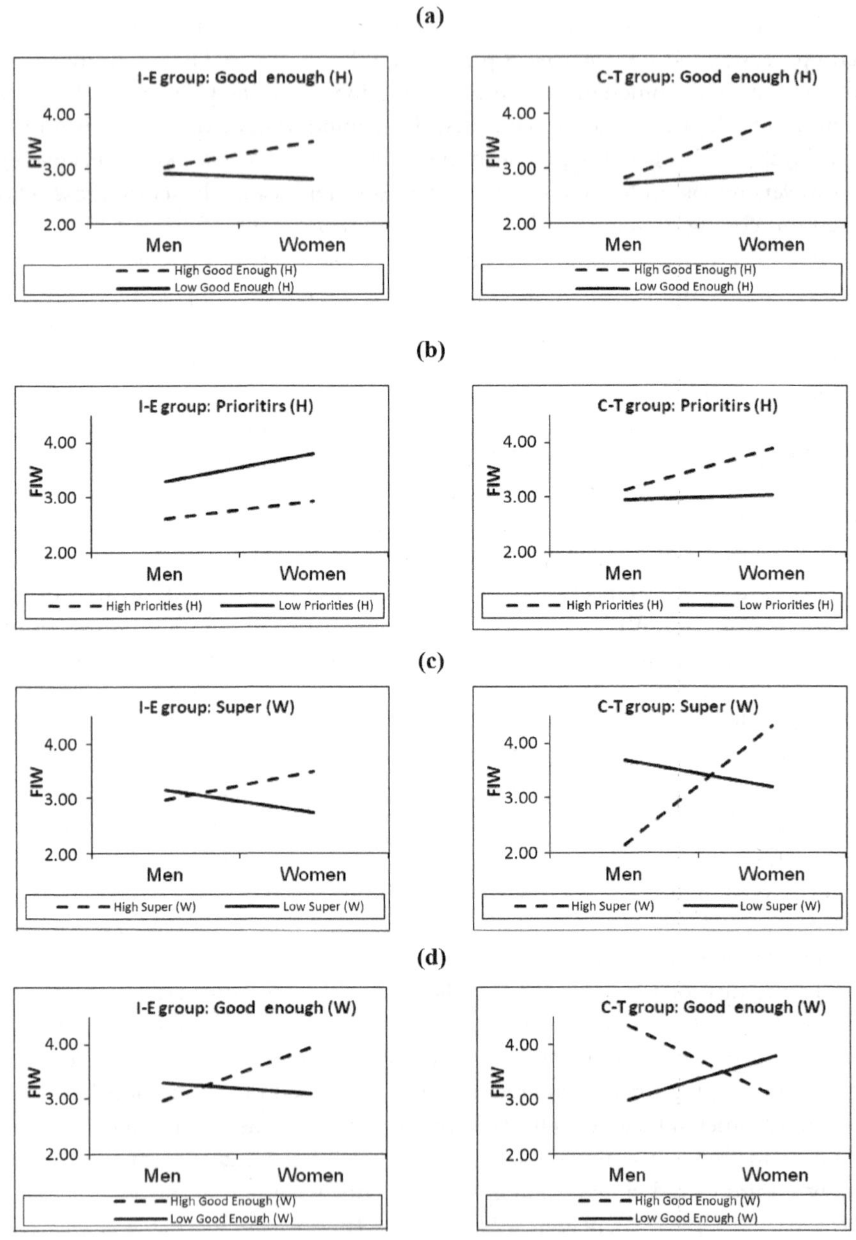

FIGURE 15.4a–d Interactive effect of coping strategy, group (I-E vs. C-T), and gender on FIW.

results indicated that in women of both groups FIW was significantly higher in those who used this coping strategy on a high than on a low level (t = 7.09, $p <$ .001 for the I-E group, and t = 8.27, $p <$ .001 for the C-T group); however, the relation was significantly stronger in the C-T group than in the I-E group. Men of both groups showed no difference in FIW conflict level whether they applied high and low use of this coping strategy ($p >$ .05).

For the interaction between group, gender, and *priorities at home* (see Figure 15.4b), in men and women of the I-E group FIW was significantly lower for those who used this coping strategy on a high than on a low level (t = -6.19, $p <$ .001; t = -6.19, $p <$ .001); however, the opposite pattern was found in the women of the C-T group. FIW was significantly higher in those who used this coping strategy on a high than on a low level (t = 7.30, $p <$ .001). The men of the C-T group showed no difference in FIW level whether they applied high or low use of this coping strategy ($p >$ .05).

Next, for the interaction between group, gender, and *super at work* (Figure 15.4c), in women in both groups FIW was significantly higher for those who used this coping strategy on a high than on a low level (t = 4.69, $p <$ .001 for I-E group; t = 6.61, $p <$ .001 for C-T group); however, the opposite pattern was found in the men of the C-T group: FIW was significantly lower in those who used this coping strategy on a high than on a low level (t = -4.95, $p <$ .001). The men of the I-E group showed no difference in FIW level whether they applied high or low use of this coping strategy ($p >$ .05).

For the interaction between group and *good enough at work* (Figure 15.4d), in men and women of the I-E group and the men of the C-T group FIW was significantly higher in those who used this coping strategy on a high than on a low level (t = 9.58, $p <$ .001; t = 3.50, $p <$ .05; t = 10.03, $p <$ .001, respectively), but the relation was significantly stronger for the men of the C-T group than for the I-E group. However, in women of the C-T group FIW was significantly lower in those who used this coping strategy on a high than on a low level (t = -4.95, $p <$ .001).

Discussion

This chapter focused on the role of personal coping strategy in decreasing WIF and FIW taking a cross-cultural perspective, thereby contributing to bridging the gaps in knowledge of work/family issues from a cross-cultural perspective. First, our results identified distinctive patterns of coping strategies employed by individuals according to cultural differences. These findings support the notion that WFC and its related issues are inherently a cultural phenomenon (Gelfand & Knight, 2005). With respect to coping, investing in a certain set of coping strategies to ease WFC seems susceptible to values and beliefs, and might reflect social expectations and self-expectations internalized through socialization (Somech & Drach-Zahavy, 2007).

Second, we found differences between groups in level of WIF and FIW. The more individualistic/egalitarian group (I-E group) evinced a higher level of WIF than the more collectivistic/traditional groups (MC-MT and C-T); and an opposite pattern emerged regarding FIW, where the MC-MT and C-T groups reported a higher level of FIW than the I-E group. These findings can be explained on the basis of the relative values placed on family and work time in the three groups. For example, Yang et al. (2000) explained that in collectivistic cultures conceding family time for work is viewed as self-sacrifice for the benefit of the family, but in more individualistic cultures, conceding family time for work is often perceived as failure to care for significant others in one's life. Indeed, these researchers found that American employees experienced greater family demands than did Chinese employees. Spector et al. (2004) likewise found a stronger relation of number of hours worked to work-family pressure in individualist regions (Anglos) than in collectivists (Chinese and Latinos); they explained that individualists viewed working extra hours as taking time from the family while the more collectivist employees viewed working hours as a means to support the family.

Third, although all eight coping styles have the potential to reduce WFC, the main argument of the present study was that the effectiveness of certain coping styles might be universal in manner, while the usefulness of others may vary in relation to culture/group. In this study, six out of the eight coping strategies demonstrated cross-cultural differences in easing the WFC, while one strategy was more universal. We found that *priorities at work* contributed to lessening WIF and FIW across cultures, but *super at home* and *super at work*, *delegation at home* and *delegation at work*, *priorities at home*, and *good enough at home* and *good enough at work* were culture-specific. These results highlight the crucial role of culture in predicting the effectiveness of personal coping in managing WFC: when the coping strategy accords with employees' cultural values it facilitates decline in WFC.

Overall, the present results suggest that the effectiveness of a coping strategy style might depend on the congruence between cultural values and the extent of use of a certain style of coping for men and women. For those in the I-E group, in men and women alike *priorities at home* was negatively associated with WIF and FIW. But for women, *super at home* and *super at work*, and *good enough at home* were positively related to WIF, and *good enough at home* and *super at work* were associated with higher levels of FIW. In men, *super at work* was positively associated with FIW. Theoretically, these findings can be explained by the core values of high individualism and a more egalitarian gender-role ideology. Individualists view self-fulfillment and autonomy as core values, and they often reach their self-definition through their work identity; on the other hand, an egalitarian ideology means holding more even attitudes to the role of men and women at home as well at work. Moreover, research has shown that when work and family conflict, individuals in Western societies are expected to give priority to the family and to express themselves through it (Bellah, Madsen, Sullivan, Swindler, & Tipton, 1985; Yang et al., 2000). They are expected to invest time and energy at work, but because family and work are perceived as separated domains, when they do so, they feel guilt for neglecting their family duties (Lu et al., 2010). This can explain why *good enough at home* and *good enough at work* led to higher levels of WIF and FIW, while *priorities at work*, which allowed them to invest in work, but also to devote time and energy to family, led to lower levels of WIF and FIW.

For the MC-MT group, *delegation at home* and *delegation at work* were negatively associated with WIF both in men and women, but no moderating effect was found regarding FIW conflict. First, this group, which is rated in the middle of the individualism-collectivism dimension, and in the middle of the egalitarian-traditional continuum of the gender-role ideology dimension, was less distinctive than the other two groups: the I-C group (high in individualism with a more egalitarian gender-role ideology) and the C-T group (high in collectivism with a more traditional gender-role ideology). Second, the present results can seemingly be understood in the light of cultural values, but also of macro-environmental influences (Joplin, Shaffer, Francesco, & Lau, 2003). Israel and Taiwan, the two countries in the MC-MT group, have undergone fundamental transformations of industrial structures from labor intensive to high tech, as well as rapid social modernization in both work and lifestyles (Cinamon, 2009; Lu et al., 2009). These processes have caused numerous changes in these societies, especially by emphasizing a more individualistic orientation. So for people assuming an active role at work and at home, the effective strategies to handle WFC, and to balance work and family, were to delegate some of their home and work duties to others. These strategies also reflect the role of the extended families in these countries, which usually form a close-knit protective social network that can be called upon to provide support and help in time of need and distress (Lu, 2006). Delegation might be perceived as a legitimate tool to manage multiple roles, and consequently to reduce WIF.

For those in the C-T group, significant differences transpired between men and women in the effectiveness of certain strategies in decreasing WIF and FIW. In women, *super at home* was associated with a lower level of WIF, while *good enough at home*, *priorities at home*, and *super at work* were associated with a higher level of the conflict. As for the FIW, *good enough at work* was negatively associated with it, while *good enough at home*, *priorities at home*, and *super at work* were positively associated with it. For the men of the C-T group *super at work* was effective in decreasing WIF, whereas *super at home* was positively associated with it. As for FIW, *super at work* was associated with lower levels of it, and *good enough at work* was positively associated with it.

In harmony with the cultural values of the C-T group, the combination of high collectivism and traditional gender-role ideology seems to set different expectations for women and men in both the work and the family domains. The traditional gender-role ideology is gender-based, with the wife responsible for the family and the husband assuming the breadwinner's role (Higgins, Duxbury, & Lee, 1994). Accordingly, traditional women, who believe that their main role in life is to be mothers and wives, will invest most resources in the home (*super at home*) or will lessen their performance of work responsibilities (*good enough at work*) so that they can work in the paid labor force but still place family demands first, according to their gender-role attitude, hence experience less WIF. When they use coping techniques that run counter to their values and beliefs, such as setting family duties aside (*priorities at work*) or lowering the performance of family responsibilities (*good enough at home*), they will experience greater WIF. Similarly, when they try to cope with the conflict by investing extra efforts in work (*super at work*) they might experience more FIW. Regarding traditional men, who believe that family functioning is optimized when the husband specializes in market work and the wife in domestic work (Barnett & Hyde, 2001), any coping strategy that allows them to devote their time and energy to work will contribute to lowering the WFC level. Therefore, by investing the utmost effort in work demands (*super at work*) they experience lower levels of WIF. However, a coping strategy such as *super at home*, which means investing extra efforts in the home, might stand in contrast to their traditional values, hence lead to higher WIF levels (Somech & Drach-Zahavy, 2007). These results can be further supported by the collectivist values of this group. In collectivist societies, devotion to work, especially by men, is seen to be for the welfare of the family, but is also tolerated by the family. According to this family-based work ethic, extra work after official hours or on weekends is self-sacrifice for the benefit of the family rather than sacrifice of the family in the selfish pursuit of the person's own career (Lu et al., 2010; Redding, 1993). For example, Spector et al. (2004) found that Chinese demonstrated a weaker positive relation of work hours to work-family stressors than did the Anglo sample.

Limitations and Suggestions for Future Research

While the findings are encouraging for WFC research, there are methodological limitations which should be kept in mind in the interpretation of these results. First, the data were largely self-reported from one source, hence subject to bias, although research suggests that self-reported data are not as limited as was previously believed, and that people often accurately perceive their social environment (Alper, Tjosvold, & Law, 1998). Moreover, regarding workers' strain, Wright and Cropanzano (2000) argue that for any number of reasons self-report measures are and will continue to be an important information source in research. However, future research efforts should incorporate alternative designs, such as incorporating spouses' perspective. Second, the present study focused on the phenomenon of conflict that is experienced by employed parents managing work and family responsibilities; the literature attests that this experience captures only one aspect of the interplay between the two domains. This draws attention to the need to complement the focus on conflict by examining how work and family experiences enrich people's lives in general, and those of employed parents in particular, through the conceptual lens of work-family balance or positive spillover (Aryee, Srinivas, & Hwee Hoon, 2005). Third, albeit the study's focus on white-collar employees might be seen as a methodological strength of study, it is important to note that the cultural values of this subgroup might not fully represent the national cultural values. Finally, in this study we used individualism-collectivism and gender-role ideology as cultural constructs for identifying cross-cultural differences. The conflict and stress inherent in managing work and family responsibilities have proven counterbalanced by the social context. Therefore, cross-cultural research may inspire researchers to identify other cultural constructs to better understand national differences.

Summary and Conclusions

We investigated how working parents in 10 countries maneuver between work and family demands by capturing a certain repertoire of the coping strategies they used to decrease the level of WIF and FIW that they experience. Overall, our results identified distinctive patterns of coping strategies employed by individuals according to culture/group differences. These findings support the notion that the ability to cope with the stress generated from simultaneous demands of work and family is at least partially a function of the individual's capabilities, and the effectiveness of a certain coping strategy to reduce the WFC varies across cultures.

From a practical standpoint, although this study took an individual approach, the overall result that all employed parents, regardless of cultural background, reported a higher level of WIF than of FIW may imply that coping with WFC should be considered the joint responsibility of organizations and employees. Organizations may invest in intervention programs that help employees to manage conflict created by work interfering with family. First, organizational surveys might serve to single out the coping activities used by employees to deal with the variety of work and family stressors, by identifying individual differences. However, organizations, especially international and highly diverse firms, should be aware of cultural differences in how employees perceive the interplay between the two domains of work and family, and the disparate effectiveness of a certain coping strategy in easing WFC. The need for training courses or organizational change could then be determined. If necessary, organizational or training interventions could then be developed and initiated to help individuals identify, and thereafter intensify, the use of adaptive coping strategies in light of cultural differences (Havlovic & Keenan, 1991; Somech & Drach-Zahavy, 2007). However, developing an individual effective coping strategy does not mean that organizations should not be recruited to provide employees with appropriate resources to balance competing and conflicting demands from work and family domains. Organizations should clearly recognize that to "manage the situation" is part of their obligation. They should develop policies and offer benefits that might build more flexibility between work and family.

References

Alper, S., Tjosvold, D., & Law, K. S. (1998). Interdependence and controversy in group decision making: Antecedents to effective self-managing teams. *Organizational Behavior and Human Decision Processes, 74*(1), 33–52.

Aryee, S., Srinivas, E. S., & Hwee Hoon, T. (2005). Rhythms of life: Antecedents and outcomes of work-family balance in employed parents. *Journal of Applied Psychology, 90*(1), 132–146.

Barnett, R. C., & Hyde, J. S. (2001). Women, men, work and family. *American Psychologist, 56*(10), 781–796.

Behson, S. J. (2002). Coping with family-to-work conflict: The role of informal work accommodations to family. *Journal of Occupational Health Psychology*, 7, 324.

Bellah, R. N., Madsen, R., Sullivan, W. M., Swindler, A., & Tipton, S. M. (1985). *Habits of the heart: Individualism and commitment in American life*. Berkeley, CA: University of California Press.

Chun, C. A., Moos, R. H., & Cronkite, R. C. (2006). Culture: A fundamental context for the stress and coping paradigm. In P. T. P. Wong & L. C. J. Wong (Eds.), *Handbook of multicultural perspectives on stress and coping* (pp. 29–53). New York, NY: Springer.

Cinamon, R. G. (2009). Role salience, social support, and work-family conflict among Jewish and Arab female teachers in Israel. *Journal of Career Development, 36*(2), 139–158.

Firestone, J. M., Harris, R. J., & Lambert, L. C. (1999). Gender-role ideology and the gender based differences in earnings. *Journal of Family and Economic Issues, 20*, 191–215.

Folkman, S., & Moskowitz, J. T. (2004). Coping: Pitfalls and promise. *Annual Review of Psychology, 55*, 745–774.

Gelfand, M. J., & Knight, A. P. (2005). Cross-cultural perspectives on work-family conflict. In S.A.Y. Poelmans (Ed.), *Work and family: An international research perspective* (pp. 401–414). Mahwah, NJ: Lawrence Erlbaum.

Harris, R. J., & Firestone, J. M. (1998). Changes in predictors of gender-role ideologies among women: A multivariate analysis. *Sex Roles, 38*(3/4), 239–252.

Hassan, Z., Dollard, M. F., & Winefield, A. H. (2010). Work-family conflict in East vs Western countries. *International Journal of Cross Cultural Management, 17*(1), 30–49.

Havlovic, S. J., & Keenan, J. P. (1991). Coping with work stress: The influence of individual differences. *Journal of Social Behavior and Personality, 6*, 199–212.

Higgins, C., Duxbury, L., & Lee, C. (1994). Work-family conflict: A comparison by gender, family type, and perceived control. *Journal of Family Issues, 15*(3), 449–466.

Hobfoll, S. E. (1989). Conservation of resources: A new attempt at conceptualizing stress. *American Psychologist, 44*, 513–524.

Hobfoll, S. E. (2001). The influence of culture, community and the nested-self in the stress process: Advancing conservation of resources theory. *Applied Psychology: An International Review, 50*, 337–421.

Joplin, J. R. W., Shaffer, M. A., Francesco, A. M., & Lau, T. (2003). The macro-environment and work-family conflict: Development of a cross cultural comparative framework. *International Journal of Cross Cultural Management, 3*(3), 305–328.

Korabik, K., Whitehead, D. L., & Lero, D. S. (Eds.). (2008). *The handbook of work-family integration: Theories, perspectives & best practices*. New York, NY: Elsevier.

Kuo, B. C. H. (2011). Culture's consequences on coping: Theories, evidences, and dimensionalities. *Journal of Cross-Cultural Psychology, 42*(6), 1084–1100.

Lachman, M. E. (1991). Perceived control over memory aging: Developmental and intervention perspectives. *Journal of Social Issues, 47*(4), 159–175.

Lam, A. G., & Zane, N. W. (2004). Ethnic differences in coping with interpersonal stressors: A test of self-construals as cultural mediators. *Journal of Cross-Cultural Psychology, 35*, 446–459.

Lam, S. S. K., Chen, X. P., & Schaubroeck, J. (2002). Participative decision making and employee performance in different cultures: The moderating effects of allocentrism/idiocentrism and efficacy. *Academy of Management Journal, 45*(5), 905–914.

Lazarus, R. S. (1991). Psychological stress in the workplace. In P. L. Perrewé (Ed.), *Handbook on job stress* (pp. 1–13). Corte Madera, CA: Select Press.

Lazarus, R. S., & Folkman, S. (1984). *Stress, appraisal and coping*. New York, NY: Springer.

Lu, L. (2006). The transition to parenthood: Stress, resources and gender differences in a Chinese society. *Journal of Community Psychology, 34*(4), 471–488.

Lu, L., Cooper, C. L., Kao, S. F., Chang, T. T., Allen, T. D., Lapierre, L. M., O'Driscoll, M., Poelmans, S.A.Y., Sanchez, J. I., & Spector, P. E. (2010). Cross-cultural differences on work-to-family conflict and role satisfaction: A Taiwanese-British comparison. *Human Resource Management, 49*(1), 67–85.

Lu, L., Gilmour, R., Kao, S. F., & Huang, M. T. (2006). A cross-cultural study of work/family demands, work/family conflict and wellbeing: The Taiwanese vs British. *Career Development International, 11*(1), 9–27.

Lu, L., Kao, S. F., Cooper, C. L., Allen, T. D., Lapierre, L. M., O'Driscoll, M., Poelmans, S.A.Y., Sanchez, J. I., & Spector, P. E. (2009). Work resources, work-to-family conflict, and its consequences: A Taiwanese—British cross-cultural comparison. *International Journal of Stress Management, 16*(1), 25–44.

Marini, M. M., Fan, P. L., Finely, E., & Beutel, A. M. (1996). Gender and job values. *Sociology of Education, 69*, 49–65.

Parasuraman, S., Purohit, Y. S., Godshalk, V. M., & Beutell, N. J. (1996). Work and family variables, entrepreneurial career success, and psychological well-being. *Journal of Vocational Behavior, 48*, 275–300.

Redding, S. G. (1993). *The spirit of Chinese capitalism*. New York, NY: De Gruyter.

Rotondo, D. M., Carlson, D. S., & Kincaid, J. F. (2003). Coping with multiple dimensions of work-family conflict. *Personnel Review, 32*, 275–296.

Somech, A., & Drach-Zahavy, A. (2007). Strategies for coping with work-family conflict: The distinctive relationships of gender-role ideology. *Journal of Occupational Health Psychology, 12, 1–19.*

Spector, P. E., Cooper, C. L., Poelmans, S.A.Y., Allen, T. D., O'Driscoll, M., Sanchez, J. I., Siu, O. L., Dewe, P., Hart, P., & Lu, L. (2004). A cross-national comparative study of work-family stressors, working hours, and well-being: China and Latin America Versus the Anglo World. *Personnel Psychology, 57*(1), 119–142.

Thein, H. H., Austen, S., Currie, J., & Lewin, E. (2010). The impact of cultural context on the perception of work/family balance by professional women in Singapore and Hong Kong. *International Journal of Cross Cultural Management, 10*(3), 303–320.

Triandis, H. C. (1995). *Individualism and collectivism*. Boulder, CO: Westview Press.

Trompenaars, F., & Hampton-Turner, C. (1998). *Riding the waves of culture*. New York, NY: McGraw-Hill.

Wagner, J. A. (1995). Studies of individualism—collectivism: Effects on cooperation in groups. *Academy of Management Journal, 38*(1), 152–172.

Wright, T. A., & Cropanzano, R. (2000). Psychological well-being and job satisfaction as predictors of job performance. *Journal of Occupational Health Psychology, 5*, 84–94.

Yang, N., Chen, C. C., Choi, J., & Zou, Y. (2000). Sources of work-family conflict: A Sino-U.S. comparison of the effects of work and family demands. *The Academy of Management Journal, 43*(1), 113–123.

16

SOCIAL SUPPORT AND THE WORK-FAMILY INTERFACE FROM A CROSS-CULTURAL PERSPECTIVE

Roya Ayman

Introduction

In understanding the role of social support in a person's life, one could image the role of the roots of a tree. If the tree is deeply rooted and the roots are extended wide, the tree can withstand the demands of the climate and stay strong. Social support has been defined as the personal relationships which give a person support in facing adversity. More specifically, these relationships can accommodate support, and support exchange can give meaning to the relationship (Gottlieb & Bergen, 2010). The social support concept has been evolving and many of the past reviews have shown how it has expanded and how scholars have explored its specificities (Barrera, 1986; Vaux, 1985; Winemiller, Mitchell, Stuliff, & Cline, 1993). In this chapter, a brief review of social support concepts and models will be presented. The focus will be on the results of the multinational study of received social support, satisfaction with support, and its relationship with WFC and facilitation.

Literature Review

Definition of Social Support

In defining the concept of social support, some refer to it as a meta-concept. Social support can be defined by the type of support offered or received, most commonly categorized into instrumental and socio-emotional; some researchers have added other types such as informational, functional, tangible, and companionate (Gottlieb & Bergen, 2010; Ong & Ward, 2005). Scholars have discussed the various methods by which social support is measured. Though the diversity of methods has been the focus of many debates, some believe this diversity of measures is representative of the complexity of the phenomenon (Barrera, 1986). Furthermore, support can also be addressed based on its sources. Some of the sources are at work and some are outside of work. Sources of support are those individuals or institutions that provide the support to an individual as it relates to either their personal or their professional life (Ayman & Antani, 2008). Each of these are elaborated in the following paragraphs.

The nature or type of support given or received has been categorized into esteem support, instrumental support, informational support, and social companionship support (Winemiller et al., 1993). The multidimensionality of this construct has been further validated (Drach-Zahavy, 2004). However, in the majority of research on social support in the workplace, two main categories of social support or helping behavior have been recognized: instrumental/vocational-related and social/emotional (e.g., Adams, King, & King, 1996; King, Mattimore, King, & Adams, 1995). Instrumental and vocational support are assistance given through providing facts, solutions (like career advice), and technical support. Socio-emotional support is represented by demonstrating empathy, listening nonjudgmentally, and being sympathetic to the person's experiences.

Social support has been operationalized through three methods of assessing social support (Barrera, 1986; Vaux & Harrison, 1985):

1. A structural measure that assesses the aspect referred to as **social network** (Gottlieb & Bergen, 2010; Winemiller et al., 1993) or sometimes **embeddedness** (Barrera, 1986; Jiang, Liu, McKay, Lee, & Mitchell, 2012; Sprietzer, Stucliffe, Dutton, Sonenshein, & Grant, 2005).
2. **Enactment** or **received support**, which refers to the type of support provided, or to the supportive behavior of the source of support (Gottlieb & Bergen, 2010; Vaux, 1985).
3. **Perceived support**, which is the general feeling and perception of the availability of support by respondents (Haber, Cohen, Lucas, & Baltes, 2007).

Additionally there has been some discussion about the **directionality of the support** (Gottlieb & Bergen, 2010), that is, whether the person seeks the support or provides it.

The embedded or social network measure of support assesses the number of sources an individual contacts. This construct assesses not only the number of sources used, but also the diversity of the sources, the strength of the relationship, and the reciprocity of the relationship. With this operationalization, the researcher can examine the diversity of the network by studying, for example, the person's use of work or family sources of support, or whether the support system includes people with different backgrounds or expertise. It can also examine the breadth of the individual's support system, that is, how many people do they have to help them. When people have a limited number of sources, it is easier to deplete them as resources of support. Additionally, the strength of the relationship can be gauged to show whether they are interacting frequently or not. Finally, the reciprocity of the relationships can be assessed through this measurement system.

Enactment or received support is the intensity to which each source engages in specific behaviors to assist the target person. Some may be more inclined to provide instrumental support and others more socio-emotional support. Both sources may provide different levels of the type of support. In this case, the individual usually seeks support from various sources: They may ask their parents to provide child care, but ask their boss for deadline flexibility. They may have a heart-to-heart with their friend about their frustration with managing work and family demands, but get help from a colleague to meet a deadline.

Individual differences such as gender and culture can play a role in seeking and providing supportive behavior. For example, the role of gender in providing support and needing support has not been conclusively determined. A study of husbands and wives, through diary and observational data, showed no differences among them in providing support, but there was a difference in the timing of the support (Neff & Karney, 2005). There is also support for the concept that feminine people react more positively and strongly to support than do masculine people (Beehr, Farmer, Glazer, Gudanowski, & Nair, 2003).

Perceived support is the assessment of the individual's feelings and belief in the availability of support. It is a more implicit way of examining support. The majority of research in organizations and with working populations has focused on the measurement of perceived support; most studies have included perceived organizational support (Rhoades & Eisenberger, 2002) and perceived support from supervisor or coworker (Eisenberger, Stinglhamber, Vandenberhe, Scharski, & Rhoades, 2002).

The Work-Family Interface and Social Support

The majority of the research with social support and the work-family interface has been focused on WFC. Most studies on WFC and social support have used perceived social support (Byron, 2005; Kossek, Picheler, Bodner, & Hammer, 2011). Kaufmann and Beehr (1986) argued that when the source of stress and support is the same, the act of support from that source may be construed as a stressor. This can be an issue because most sources—such as family (spouse, parents, and children) or work (supervisor and coworkers)—can be both a support source and a source of stress. It would be interesting to see if providing support for their own domain versus across domains makes a difference. For example, will supervisors providing support for family reduce stress? More recently in regards to sources of support at work, Hammer, Kossek, Bodner, and Crain (2013) have developed a more focused measure of supervisory support that more explicitly assesses the availability of support from the supervisor for managing the work and family interface. A recent meta-analysis showed an improved relationship between WFC and perceived support from the organization or the supervisor when the support was family-focused, instead of it being more general perceived support (Kossek et al., 2011). It also showed that higher supervisory support for WFC can reduce the associated stress.

As already alluded to, sources of support are important. Some studies examining social support and work or family stress have included at least one work source of support, such as organizational support or supervisor support and one nonwork source such as spouse or family and friends (e.g., Blanch & Aluja, 2012; Carlson & Perrewé, 1999; Seiger & Wiese, 2009). Usually the choice of the source of support included in the study has been the researchers' option. Most studies do not have an all-inclusive representation of sources of social support in their investigation. The other issue regarding sources of support is whether they are providing within-domain support or cross-domain support. For example, Blanch and Aluja (2012) examined work support for family issues as well as work issues and family support for work and family issues. But, most studies only examine support for either work or family issues.

In summary, whether we are examining perceived or received support, the source of support and what the support is offered for—whether for work or family issues—become important. In the case of perceived supervisor-provided support, in addition to older measures of supervisor support like Clark (2001) and Kossek and Nichol (1992), the Hammer et al. (2007) measure is more focused on perceived support from supervisor for work-family interface. Also, the nature of support needs to be inclusive and balanced between instrumental/informational support and socio-emotional support. Some scholars have used measures like leader member exchange (LMX). These are used as a proxy to understanding supervisory support and do not have a clear representation of types of support and domains of support (e.g., Bernas & Major, 2000; Lapierre, Hackett, & Taggar, 2006).

Most studies have used concurrent designs with single source surveys to measure perceived social support and WFC (Adams et al., 1996; Aycan & Eskin, 2005; Bhave, Kramer, & Glomb, 2010; Breaugh & Frye, 2008; Carlson & Perrewé, 1999; Casper, Martin, Buffardi, & Erdwins, 2002; Cortese, Colombo, & Ghislieri, 2010; Frye & Breaugh, 2004; Matthew, Bulger, & Barnes-Farrell, 2010; O'Driscoll et al., 2003). Some studies have used longitudinal designs (e.g., Hammer, Neal, Newsom, Brockwood, & Colton, 2005; Nohe & Sonntag, 2014), multiphase designs where data are collected at different times (e.g., Frye & Breaugh, 2004), or longitudinal and multimethod designs (e.g., Ransford, Crouter, & McHale, 2008). Very few studies have used the diary or experience sampling methodology (e.g., Shockley & Allen, 2013; Wang, Liu, Zhan, & Shi, 2010).

In the social support literature, perceived support is the operationalization used the most. However, debate about which measure, perceived or received, best assesses social support is continuing. On one hand, Solomon, Mikulincer, and Hobfol (1985) have argued that subjective measures of social support are the best predictors of the relationship with stress and the reactions. More recently, Haber et al. (2007) reviewed 23 studies and found a moderate correlation of r = .35 corrected reliability between measures of perceived and received social support.

This finding raised concern for them, as only 10–15% of the total variance is shared between these two approaches or measures of social support. This does have implications for future interventions, as it indicated that what people use and what people perceive as being available are not the same. So when introducing interventions, should the concern be about use of support or its availability?

Additionally, concerns were raised about self-report in these assessments and about most studies only using perceived method of assessment of support, making the research method-bound. The meta-analyses have acknowledged that the diversity of measures present in studies are the main moderator of the impact and role of social support (e.g., Viswesvaran, Sanchez, & Fisher, 1999). With this in mind, in this chapter we used received social support and satisfaction with that support, which could be considered as perceived support.

Most studies of social support in relation to WFC were conducted in North America. Other countries were also present, however, such as China (Wang, Liu, Zhan, & Shi, 2010); Germany (Nohe & Sonntag, 2014), Italy (Cortese et al., 2010), the Netherlands (vanDaalen, Willemsen, & Sanders, 2006), New Zealand (O'Driscoll et al., 2003), Spain (Blanch & Aluja, 2012), German-speaking parts of Switzerland (Seiger & Wiese, 2009), and Turkey (Aycan & Eskin, 2005).

Studies on social support and culture (e.g., Chen, Kim, Mojaverian, & Morling, 2012; Glazer, 2006; Goodwin & Hernandez-Plaza, 2000; Pines, Ben-Ari, Utasi, & Larson, 2002; Taylor et al., 2004) have examined the role of culture in providing and seeking (explicit) social support and perceived (implicit) social support. Glazer (2006) demonstrated that cultural values have an impact on the mean differences of perception of support. Her results showed that in individualistic (as compared to collectivist) cultures, people reported more emotional support from the superior and less coworker instrumental support. Goodwin and Hernandez-Plaza (2000) included both perceived and received support. Their sample included British and Spanish students, and their results showed that received support from friends was positively and moderately significantly related to general perceived support among the Spanish students. The study by Chen et al. (2012) was more about providing support rather than receiving support and showed that European Americans provided more support to close others than did Japanese. Also, Kim, Sherman, and Taylor (2008) and Taylor, Welch, Kim, and Sherman (2007) acknowledged that, due to concern for social harmony and mutual obligation, Asians typically will seek less social support than European Americans.

Furthermore, it is more evident when the inquiry on social support addresses seeking support rather than perceiving support, they are referring to explicit rather than implicit social support. Though perceived social support with implicit social support and received social support with explicit social support are not the same, there is a resemblance between the two concepts. As Taylor et al. (2007) explained, as long as the perceived support does not have an element of disclosure—that is, as long as it is about the person's belief and feeling of support—it would be similar to implicit social support.

In examining the role of social support in the relationship between stress (i.e., WFC) and strain (e.g., job satisfaction/dissatisfaction), research has primarily conceptualized social support through the perceived support measurement. As social support scholars have stated, the role of social support in relation to stress—whether it be life stress, work stress, or the interface of work and family—will partially vary based on the measurement and conceptualization of social support (Barrera, 1986). Byron's (2005) meta-analysis supported the role of perceived support as an antecedent. In a meta-analysis on social support and job stress, Viswesvaran, Sanchez, and Fisher (1999) tested three models of social support with relation to stress and strain: social support as a buffer to stress (i.e., WFC), as a mediator between stress and strain, and as a moderator of the relationship between stress and strain. The results showed the strongest support for the role of perceived support in the workplace as a buffer or antecedent to stress, not as a mediator between stress and strain or as a moderator for stress and strain. It seems that most of the 68 studies in their analyses used perceived social support.

The Current Study

This study focused on the reported received support of employed parents in multiple industries across 10 countries. Based on focus groups, the endogenous experts who collaborated for this project listed seven sources of support well represented across these countries. Both instrumental/informational and socio-emotional support types were assessed for each source. Also, while two of the sources were work-related (supervisor and coworker), five were nonwork sources; for each source, however, the respondent reported if they received work-related or family-related support.

Most recent cross-cultural studies have categorized countries by continent: Asian, European, North American, etc. However, as very little is known about social support in all the countries on most continents, we did not categorize the countries, but examined them uniquely. Instead of using the country per se in examining the relation between work-family interface and social support, we used the cultural value of collectivism to examine the nested model of individuals from various countries.

The research questions under consideration were:

1. Are the patterns of received instrumental and socio-emotional support across sources and types parallel across countries?
2. Do the means of received instrumental and socio-emotional support vary across sources and countries?
3. Are the patterns of received support for work and family across sources and types parallel across countries?
4. Do the means of received support for work and family vary across sources and countries?

5. Does the respondents' satisfaction with sources of support show a similar pattern across countries?
6. Is the relation between received support from different sources and WFC moderated by vertical collectivism as a measure of cultural values?

Method

The details of the data collection, the sample, and the measures are provided in Chapter 2. The challenge we faced as mentioned in that chapter was that, on the measure of social support, we did not attain measurement equivalence for most of the sources. This means that the distinction across countries between work and family support or instrumental and socio-emotional support was not clear for most sources. We only have measurement equivalence for the support for supervisor for work issues as mentioned in Chapter 2. Thus, the results of the analysis for this chapter, showing similarity and differences between countries on use of different types of received support and from different sources, should be considered with this in mind.

The nine social support items had a response scale of "Never, Not often, Sometimes, Frequently, and Not applicable (N/A)." For the purpose of our study, we first combined "Never" and "N/A" answers with one another. We combined items related to work and family support separately. Adjusted average work support was calculated from items 1, 2, 6, and 9. Adjusted average family support was calculated from items 3, 4, 5, 7, and 8. We also used an adjusted average to calculate instrumental and emotional support; instrumental support was calculated by combining items 1, 2, 3, 4, and 5, and emotional support was calculated by combining items 6, 7, 8, and 9 (see Appendix for the list of items).

To examine the research questions, profile analysis was used, which is a form of repeated measures MANOVA (Tabachnick, & Fidell, 2010). Thus, we conducted three analyses, one for each of the following dependent variables: the type of social support (instrumental or emotional), the domain for support (work-related or family-related), and satisfaction with the source of support. The within-subject factor was the sources of support and the between-subject variable was the 10 countries.

To examine the moderating effect of culture on the relationship between received social support and WFC, we tested the effects of received support from seven sources and the moderating influence of vertical collectivism (VC) for both directions of WFC and positive spillover across the 10 countries.

A two-level hierarchical linear model assessed the effects of support from different sources and VC on WFC and positive spillover. Multilevel linear modeling is an extension of multiple linear regression, and could be used for examining research questions such as degree of relationship among the dependent variables and various independent variables while the hierarchical structure of the data is taken into account.

In the current study, first-level units were individuals, and second-level units were the 10 countries. Received support from seven sources (i.e., Spouse; Child(ren); Parent(s); Paid household helper; Friends, neighbors, and relatives; Job supervisor; and Coworkers or subordinates) was entered as first-level predictor. Country was entered as higher-level predictor.

Note that there are only 10 different countries, which translates to the current model having a sample size of 10 at the second level. According to a simulation study done by Maas and Hox (2005), a small sample size at level two (i.e., a sample of 50 or less) would lead to bias in estimating the second-level standard error. In addition, small sample sizes at the higher level would also lead to less power (Tabachnick & Fidell, 2013). For these reasons, we report random effects of the intercept (i.e., country) only for reference, and the results in the random-effects part should not be relied on in predicting dependent variables in applied settings.

As a substitute for country differences, we included VC at the country level in the research model to examine its potential moderating effects in the relationship between received support from different sources on the one hand, and WFC and positive spillover on the other. In the current multilevel linear model, VC was measured at the individual-level, aggregated to the country-level, and entered at the first level together with the support variables. Gender, age, type of job, and number of children were entered as control variables. Dependent variables included in the model were WFC (i.e., work interfering with family and family interfering with work, WIF and FIW, respectively) and positive spillover (i.e., work-to-family and family-to-work, WTFS and FTWS, respectively).

The process of analysis was followed as introduced by Tabachnick and Fidell (2013). For each dependent variable, two models were tested and compared. One of them included only country as the intercept at the second level and control variables at the first level, and the other added in received support from the seven sources, aggregated VC, and their interaction terms.

Results of Profile Analyses

The reliability of the two scales of instrumental and emotional received support and two scales of received support for work and family per source per country were calculated. The reliabilities ranges from .44–.98. Three scales had reliability below .5 in different countries: Received parental support for work in Israel (α = .44), received coworker instrumental (α = .50), and received work-related support in the United States (α = .48).

Instrumental and Emotional Support

The results of the repeated measure MANOVA testing parallelism, were rejected, F (13, 2240) = 103.99, $p < .001$. This means that respondents in different countries reported varying levels of received support for instrumental and emotional support. Subsequently, *post hoc* testing of differences of means[1] shows the diversity of level across sources and countries (see Table 16.1). The key finding was that respondents from India and Indonesia reported significantly higher levels of support compared to those from all other countries. The responses of Indonesian and

TABLE 16.1 Means and standard deviations of instrumental/emotional and work/family support across sources.

Source	*Type of support*		*Country*									
			Australia	*Canada*	*China*	*India*	*Indonesia*	*Israel*	*Spain*	*Taiwan*	*Turkey*	*US*
Spouse	Instrumental	*M*	3.08	3.12	3.09	3.39	3.60	2.93	3.23	2.99	3.05	3.00
		SD	0.50	0.51	0.65	0.54	0.48	0.65	0.65	0.59	0.50	0.59
	Emotional	*M*	3.46	3.44	3.05	3.48	3.69	3.33	3.56	3.16	3.29	3.44
		SD	0.55	0.59	0.72	0.52	0.52	0.71	0.69	0.67	0.51	0.62
	Work	*M*	3.66	3.67	3.29	3.52	3.70	3.45	3.64	3.38	3.43	3.48
		SD	0.40	0.47	0.70	0.52	0.47	0.66	0.65	0.64	0.49	0.57
	Family	*M*	2.93	2.94	2.90	3.34	3.59	2.83	3.15	2.80	2.94	2.97
		SD	0.63	0.60	0.71	0.58	0.52	0.71	0.68	0.66	0.55	0.63
Child(ren)	Instrumental	*M*	1.80	1.88	1.95	2.83	2.49	1.88	1.75	1.60	1.63	1.96
		SD	0.61	0.69	0.73	0.77	0.94	0.73	1.13	0.57	0.61	0.69
	Emotional	*M*	2.27	2.27	2.23	2.91	2.43	2.17	2.04	1.80	1.96	2.42
		SD	0.80	0.79	0.82	0.78	1.06	0.93	1.12	0.82	0.68	0.86
	Work	*M*	2.43	2.48	2.28	3.01	2.67	2.34	2.24	1.94	2.04	2.49
		SD	0.78	0.77	0.79	0.72	0.98	0.92	1.25	0.80	0.68	0.80
	Family	*M*	1.68	1.72	1.91	2.74	2.30	1.75	1.67	1.48	1.56	1.89
		SD	0.64	0.70	0.77	0.83	0.98	0.77	1.20	0.58	0.58	0.75
Parent(s)	Instrumental	*M*	1.84	1.82	2.55	2.93	2.69	1.87	2.29	2.22	2.03	1.87
		SD	0.57	0.57	0.75	0.74	0.82	0.60	0.73	0.69	0.56	0.67
	Emotional	*M*	2.33	2.26	2.63	2.94	2.71	2.37	2.76	2.20	2.32	2.42
		SD	0.81	0.83	0.80	0.74	0.84	0.91	0.75	0.74	0.53	0.86
	Work	*M*	2.38	2.32	2.79	3.14	2.83	2.38	2.81	2.58	2.48	2.33
		SD	0.76	0.77	0.77	0.67	0.82	0.87	0.71	0.80	0.60	0.78
	Family	*M*	1.80	1.76	2.42	2.75	2.60	1.87	2.25	1.91	1.89	1.94
		SD	0.63	0.60	0.75	0.83	0.82	0.66	0.77	0.62	0.48	0.68
Paid- household helper	Instrumental	*M*	1.25	1.20	1.17	2.54	1.72	1.52	2.04	1.16	1.44	1.20

		SD	0.44	0.38	0.49	0.78	0.80	0.44	1.25	0.38	0.56	0.39
	Emotional	*M*	1.08	1.07	1.26	2.36	1.33	1.96	1.50	1.12	1.23	1.10
		SD	0.30	0.29	0.57	1.00	0.64	0.64	1.34	0.36	0.54	0.37
	Work	*M*	1.32	1.26	1.22	2.67	1.82	1.82	2.31	1.21	1.60	1.24
		SD	0.56	0.51	0.52	0.79	0.89	0.53	1.39	0.49	0.77	0.47
	Family	*M*	1.05	1.05	1.20	2.31	1.33	1.65	1.49	1.09	1.14	1.08
		SD	0.26	0.22	0.49	0.98	0.60	0.50	1.43	0.28	0.37	0.29
Friends, neighbors, or relatives	Instrumental	*M*	1.61	1.67	1.90	2.69	2.24	1.33	1.86	1.66	1.77	1.69
		SD	0.44	0.52	0.70	0.87	0.72	0.45	0.95	0.52	0.48	0.52
	Emotional	*M*	2.16	2.16	2.10	2.79	2.17	1.22	2.40	1.95	2.06	2.39
		SD	0.75	0.76	0.79	0.88	0.76	0.45	0.76	0.74	0.57	0.86
	Work	*M*	1.97	2.02	1.93	2.74	2.20	1.39	2.14	1.77	2.09	2.05
		SD	0.55	0.62	0.68	0.84	0.69	0.52	0.68	0.58	0.58	0.63
	Family	*M*	1.77	1.79	2.05	2.74	2.22	1.20	2.09	1.81	1.74	1.96
		SD	0.58	0.61	0.75	0.90	0.74	0.41	0.83	0.59	0.49	0.66
Supervisor(s)	Instrumental	*M*	1.87	1.91	2.06	2.67	2.29	1.63	2.15	1.95	1.52	1.94
		SD	0.50	0.46	0.67	0.79	0.66	0.50	0.59	0.51	0.43	0.47
	Emotional	*M*	2.24	2.33	2.23	2.77	2.20	1.97	2.50	2.18	1.72	2.44
		SD	0.72	0.70	0.74	0.78	0.76	0.69	0.68	0.73	0.61	0.79
	Work	*M*	1.40	1.45	1.65	2.48	1.88	1.32	1.56	1.46	1.15	1.54
		SD	0.48	0.44	0.63	0.92	0.75	0.47	0.66	0.48	0.34	0.49
	Family	*M*	2.55	2.62	2.52	2.90	2.55	2.16	2.92	2.53	1.97	2.66
		SD	0.75	0.69	0.82	0.69	0.69	0.76	0.66	0.82	0.71	0.71
Coworker(s) or subordinate(s)	Instrumental	*M*	2.06	2.05	2.21	2.87	2.48	1.78	2.21	2.05	2.09	2.18
		SD	0.47	0.44	0.67	0.83	0.60	0.51	0.70	0.52	0.42	0.44
	Emotional	*M*	2.52	2.46	2.48	2.97	2.44	2.24	2.56	2.42	2.43	2.77
		SD	0.69	0.67	0.77	0.79	0.72	0.73	0.71	0.60	0.52	0.76
	Work	*M*	1.59	1.57	1.90	2.63	2.13	1.51	1.64	1.63	1.65	1.79
		SD	0.47	0.48	0.67	0.96	0.71	0.53	0.69	0.50	0.49	0.53
	Family	*M*	2.81	2.76	2.68	3.10	2.73	2.38	2.95	2.68	2.72	2.97
		SD	0.66	0.62	0.78	0.68	0.61	0.74	0.74	0.70	0.47	0.64

Spanish respondents did not significantly differ from one another. It was interesting to note that Chinese and Taiwanese responses were significantly different, where Chinese respondents reported receiving more support.

Family- and Work-Related Support

The same analysis was conducted for work-related and family-related received social support. There was a difference in the pattern of received support related to work and family across sources and countries, F (945, 20) = 945, $p < .0001$. Also, the test of flatness was rejected, Hoteling $T = 7.76$, F (2244, 13) = 1342.15, $p < .001$. The results showed that use of support by sources was not parallel across countries. Based on the *post hoc* analysis of mean differences, support from spouse for work and family issues was used the most by all respondents. Supervisor support for family was used more than supervisor support for work, except in Canada, where the difference was nonsignificant. Overall, Indian respondents reported using support for work and family more than respondents from all other countries.

Satisfaction with Sources of Support

The between-subject test showed no parallelism for the satisfaction with sources of support across countries, F (1, 917) = 13.37, $p < .0001$, and again, the test of flatness was rejected, Hoteling $T = .22$, F (54, 5462) = 3.72, $p < .0001$. Across the sources of support, spousal support received the highest satisfaction. Respondents from China, India, and Taiwan were less satisfied with their spouse as a source of support than respondents from other countries. Respondents were least satisfied with their paid household helper compared to other sources of support. Chinese respondents seem to be least satisfied with most sources of support. Results of the post hoc analysis of the comparison of means for satisfaction with sources of support showed that respondents from Spain were the most satisfied overall, and were significantly more satisfied than respondents from all countries except Australia and the United States.

Moderating Effect of Vertical Collectivism on Social Support and Work-Family Interface

Correlations among all the variables, as well as the internal consistency reliability of the measures, are shown in Table 16.2.

Work Interfering With Family (WIF)

The full model as a whole was significantly better than one in which only the intercepts and control variables (i.e., differences among countries, gender, age, type

TABLE 16.2 Bivariate correlations among multilevel analysis variables and reliability of measures.

	1	*2*	*3*	*4*	*5*	*6*	*7*	*8*	*9*	*10*	*11*	*12*	*13*	*14*	*15*	*16*
1. Gender	–															
2. Age	-.01	–														
3. Type of job	-.01	.07**	–													
4. Number of children	-.02	.32**	.13**	–												
5. VC	-.04*	-.06**	-.05*	-.10**	(.62)											
6. S_spouse	-.12**	-.10**	.03	-.06**	.11**	(.83)										
7. S_child	.06**	.25**	-.02	.17**	.04	.26**	(.91)									
8. S_parent	.05*	-.35**	-.01	-.22**	.11**	.35**	.33**	(.87)								
9. S_paid helper	.03	-.14**	.02	-.03	-.05*	.14**	.42**	.37**	(.92)							
10. S_friends	.06**	-.19**	-.04*	-.19**	.08**	.27**	.38**	.54**	.45**	(.88)						
11. S_job supervisor	-.00	-.11**	-.01	-.10**	.03	.24**	.38**	.39**	.38**	.60**	(.86)					
12. S_coworker	.05*	-.11**	-.02	-.13**	.07**	.27**	.38**	.43**	.40**	.67**	.73**	(.83)				
13. WIF	-.02	-.05*	-.03	-.01	-.09**	-.12**	-.03	-.03	.06**	.02	-.02	-.02	(.88)			
14. FIW	.04*	-.16**	-.08**	-.05*	-.06**	-.08**	.11**	.14**	.30**	.19**	.15**	.14**	.51**	(.86)		
15. WTFS	.05*	.01	.02	.03	.09**	.25**	.29**	.18**	.20**	.24**	.23**	.25**	-.14**	.05*	(.70)	
16. FTWS	.05**	-.00	.00	-.09**	.22**	.30**	.17**	.16**	.05*	.14**	.08**	.13**	-.14**	-.11**	.54**	(.55)

Note. * $p < .05$, ** $p < .01$. VC = vertical collectivism; S_spouse = support from spouse; S_child = support from child(ren); S_parent = support from parent(s) or parent-in-law(s); S_paid helper = support from paid house hold helper; S_friend = support from friends, relatives, or neighbors; S_job supervisor = support from job supervisor; S_coworker = support from coworker(s) or subordinate(s); WIF = work-family conflict: work interfering with family, FIW = work-family conflict: family interfering with work, WTFS = work-to-family positive spillover, FTWS = family-to-work positive spillover. Cronbach's alpha for each measure is shown on diagonal.

of job, and number of children) were included, χ^2 (15, N = 2172) = 1548.23, $p <$ .01. Thus, support from the seven sources as a group improved the model beyond that produced by considering variability in countries and control variables.

As the number of countries was too small, the results of the random effect for all the dependent variables were at most marginally significant, which means the country differences are not reliable in predicting both WFC and positive spillover. Therefore, we will only present the results of the fixed effects in the following sections.

On average, WIF was negatively related to support from spouse, t = -2.57, $p < .05$, indicating that across countries, WIF is lower when received support from spouse is higher. In addition, WIF was positively correlated to support received from paid household helper, t = 2.32, $p < .05$, showing that there is a positive incremental change in individuals' WIF and their use support from paid household helper. None of the other support variables showed significant correlations with WIF.

Table 16.3 also shows interaction effects between received support and aggregated VC in predicting WIF. Here, the two support variables (i.e., received support from spouse and received support from paid household helper) having significant main effects, also showed significant interaction effects. Figure 16.1 shows the pattern of the significant interaction term between received support from spouse and VC for WIF, t = 2.38, $p < .05$. The relationship between support from spouse and WIF is stronger for individuals in countries with low VC. It seems that for individuals from cultures with lower VC values, received support from spouse was more related to lower WIF than for their counterparts from higher VC value cultures.

The pattern of the interaction between support received from paid household helper and VC, t = -.22, $p < .05$ is shown in Figure 16.2. The relationship between support received from paid household helper and WIF is stronger for individuals in cultures with lower VC values. Specifically, for those from lower VC value cultures, received support from this source shows a strong positive relationship with WIF scores, while for those from higher VC values cultures, WIF tends to be similar irrespective of the levels of received support from paid household helper.

Family Interfering With Work (FIW)

Similar to WIF, for FIW the full model was also better than the intercepts and control variables included model, χ^2 (15, N = 2745) = 1772.58, $p < .01$. This indicated the support variables predict FIW beyond the countries and demographic variables (see Table 16.4).

The results of the fixed effects were that among all the support variables and their interaction terms with VC, only support received from paid household helper and its interaction term showed a significant effect. For the main effect of received support from paid household helper, t = 3.03, $p < .01$; a higher level of support received from this source was associated with a higher level of FIW.

TABLE 16.3 Work interference with family predicted by country, received support, and vertical collectivism.

Random Effects

Parameter	*β Estimate*	*Std. Error*	*Wald Z*	*p*	*95% Confidence Interval*	
					Lower Bound	*Upper Bound*
Residual	.86	.03	32.77**	.00	.81	.91
Intercept (Country)	.12	.06	1.93	.05	.05	.34

Fixed Effects

Parameter	*β Estimate*	*Std. Error*	*Approx df*	*t ratio*	*p*	*95% Confidence Interval*	
						Lower Bound	*Upper Bound*
Intercept	3.47	1.71	8	2.03	.08	-.45	7.39
S_spouse	-.86	.33	2155	-2.57*	.01	-1.51	-.20
S_child	.66	.37	2152	1.78	.08	-.07	1.38
S_parent	-.65	.39	2154	-1.66	.01	-1.43	.12
S_paid helper	1.31	.57	2086	2.32*	.02	.20	2.42
S_friends	.13	.50	2144	.26	.80	-.85	1.11
S_job supervisor	-.62	.51	2153	-1.22	.22	-1.61	.38
S_coworker	.37	.52	2151	.72	.47	-.64	1.38
AggregateVC	-.78	.39	8	-2.03	.08	-1.67	.10
S_spouse* AggregateVC	.18	.08	2155	2.38*	.02	.031	.33
S_child* AggregateVC	-.15	.08	2152	-1.82	.07	-.32	.01
S_parent* AggregateVC	.16	.09	2154	1.81	.07	-.01	.34
S_paid helper* AggregateVC	-.28	.13	2094	-2.22*	.03	-.53	-.03
S_friends* AggregateVC	-.02	.11	2147	-.18	.86	-.24	.20
S_job supervisor* AggregateVC	.12	.11	2154	1.02	.31	-.11	.34
S_coworker* AggregateVC	-.09	.12	2151	-.79	.43	-.32	.14

Notes. *$p < .05$. Approx *df* = approximate degrees of freedom. Aggregate VC = vertical collectivism aggregated at country level. S_spouse = support from spouse; S_child = support from child(ren); S_parent = support from parent(s) or parent-inlaw(s); S_paid helper = support from paid household helper; S_friend = support from friends, relatives, or neighbors; S_job supervisor = support from job supervisor; S_coworker = support from coworker(s) or subordinate(s).

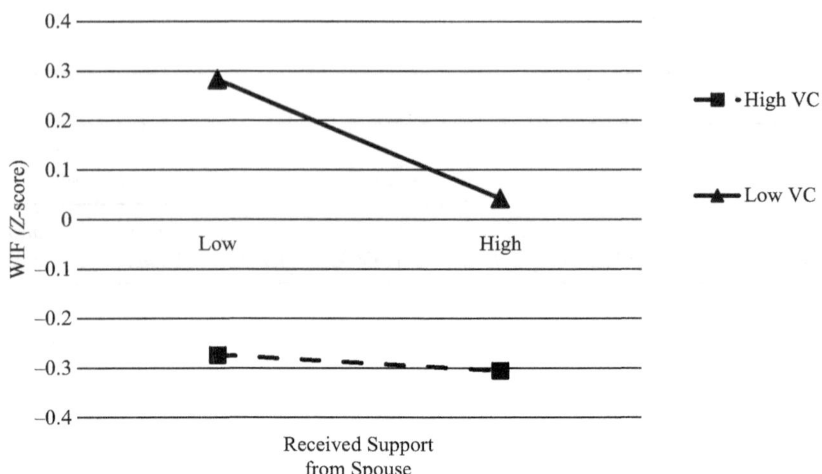

FIGURE 16.1 Interaction between received support from spouse and VC on WIF.

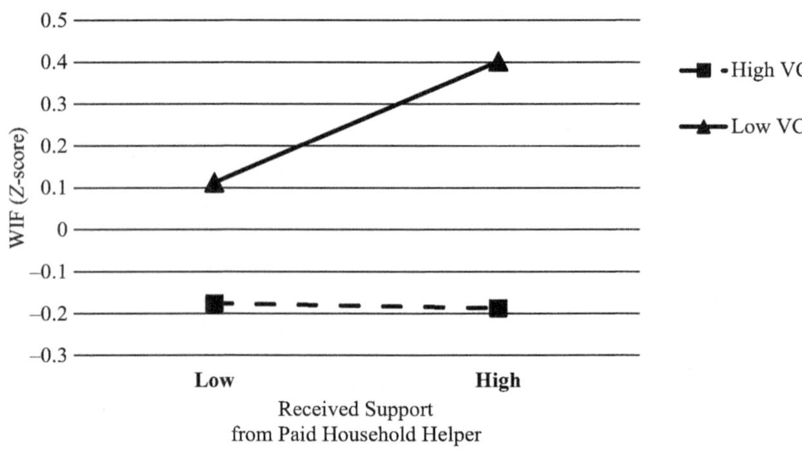

FIGURE 16.2 Interaction between received support from paid household helper and VC on WIF.

Figure 16.3 shows the pattern of the significant interaction between received support from paid household helper and VC for FIW, $t = -2.81$, $p < .01$. The relationship between received support from paid household helper and FIW was stronger for individuals from countries endorsing a lower level of VC than for those from countries with higher VC. It seems that the higher the level of support received from household helpers was related to stronger FIW for participants from countries with lower VC values than for their counterparts. At low levels

TABLE 16.4 Family interfering with work predicted by country, received support, and vertical collectivism.

Random Effects						
					95% Confidence Interval	
Parameter	*β Estimate*	*Std. Error*	*Wald Z*	*p*	*Lower Bound*	*Upper Bound*
Residual	.73	.02	32.77**	.00	.69	.78
Intercept (Country)	.11	.06	1.92	.06	.04	.30

Fixed Effect							
						95% Confidence Interval	
Parameter	*β Estimate*	*Std. Error*	*Approx df*	*t ratio*	*p*	*Lower Bound*	*Upper Bound*
Intercept	.90	1.61	8	.56	.59	-2.79	4.59
S_spouse	-.18	.31	2155	-.58	.56	-.78	.42
S_child	.51	.34	2152	1.49	.14	-.16	1.18
S_parent	.34	.36	2154	.95	.34	-.37	1.06
S_paid helper	1.58	.52	2091	3.03**	.00	.56	2.60
S_friends	-.02	.46	2145	-.05	.96	-.93	.89
S_job supervisor	-.36	.47	2153	-.78	.44	-1.28	.55
S_coworker	-.36	.48	2151	-.76	.45	-1.30	.57
AggregateVC	-.22	.36	8	-.61	.56	-1.05	.61
S_spouse * AggregateVC	.02	.07	2155	.23	.82	-.12	.15
S_child * AggregateVC	-.12	.08	2152	-1.49	.14	-.27	.04
S_parent * AggregateVC	-.06	.08	2154	-.72	.47	-.22	.10
S_friends * AggregateVC	.02	.10	2148	.15	.88	-.19	.22
S_job supervisor * AggregateVC	.07	.11	2154	.70	.48	-.13	.28
S_coworker* AggregateVC	.08	.11	2151	.75	.46	-.13	.29

Notes. $^{*}p < .05$, $^{**}p < .01$. Approx *df* = approximate degrees of freedom. Aggregate VC = vertical collectivism aggregated at country level. S_spouse = support from spouse; S_child = support from child(ren); S_parent = support from parent(s) or parent-inlaw(s); S_paid helper = support from paid household helper; S_friend = support from friends, relatives, or neighbors; S_job supervisor = support from job supervisor; S_coworker = support from coworker(s) or subordinate(s).

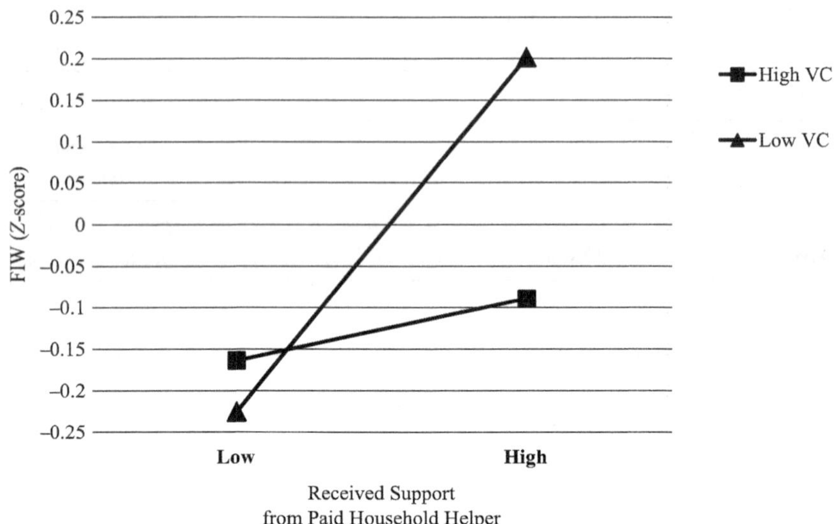

FIGURE 16.3 Interaction between received support from paid household helper and VC on FIW.

of received support from paid household helper, the effect seems to be reversed; individuals from countries with higher VC values reported higher FIW than those from countries with lower VC values.

Work-to-Family Positive Spillover (WTFS)

For WTFS, the model with seven support variables included had better fit than the one including only intercepts and control variables, χ^2 (15, N = 2154) = 1631.61, $p < .01$. In other words, support variables as a whole predicted WTFS beyond country difference and control variables. Among all the main effect terms and interaction terms, the only significant one was support received from child(ren), $t = 2.01, p < .05$. In general, across all countries, higher levels of received support from child(ren) tend to associate with higher levels of WTFS, regardless of VC values (see Table 16.5).

Family-to-Work Positive Spillover (FTWS)

Finally, including support from the seven sources improved the model fit for FTWS, χ^2 (15, N = 2153) = 1858.06, $p < .01$, demonstrating that these support

TABLE 16.5 Work-to-family positive spillover predicted by country, received support, and vertical collectivism.

Random Effects

Parameter	*β Estimate*	*SE*	*Wald Z*	*p*	*95% Confidence Interval*	
					Lower Bound	*Upper Bound*
Residual	.77	.02	32.63**	.00	.72	.82
Intercept (Country)	.08	.04	1.87	.06	.03	.22

Fixed Effect

Parameter	*β Estimate*	*SE*	*Approx df*	*t ratio*	*p*	*95% Confidence Interval*	
						Lower Bound	*Upper Bound*
Intercept	.22	1.37	8	.16	.88	-2.94	3.37
S_spouse	.13	.32	2138	.41	.68	-.50	.75
S_child	.70	.35	2134	2.01*	.05	.02	1.39
S_parent	.63	.37	2137	1.67	.10	-.11	1.36
S_paid helper	-.82	.53	1988	-1.54	.13	-1.87	.23
S_friends	-.12	.48	2102	-.25	.80	-1.06	.81
S_job supervisor	.36	.48	2138	.75	.45	-.58	1.31
S_coworker	.05	.50	2134	.010	.92	-.92	1.02
AggregateVC	-.07	.31	8	-.22	.84	-.78	.65
S_spouse* AggregateVC	-.00	.07	2138	-.02	.98	-.14	.14
S_child* AggregateVC	-.13	.08	2135	-1.66	.10	-.29	.02
S_parent* AggregateVC	-.15	.09	2137	-1.77	.08	-.32	.02
S_paid helper* AggregateVC	.17	.12	2004	1.43	.15	-.06	.41
S_friends* AggregateVC	.03	.11	2111	.30	.77	-.18	.24
S_job supervisor* AggregateVC	-.07	.11	2138	-.64	.52	-.28	.14
S_coworker* AggregateVC	.01	.11	2134	.10	.92	-.21	.23

Notes. *$p < .05$, ** $p < .01$. Approx *df* = approximate degrees of freedom. Aggregate VC = vertical collectivism aggregated at country level. S_spouse = support from spouse; S_child = support from child(ren); S_parent = support from parent(s) or parent-inlaw(s); S_paid helper = support from paid household helper; S_friend = support from friends, relatives, or neighbors; S_job supervisor = support from job supervisor; S_coworker = support from coworker(s) or subordinate(s).

variables predict FTWS beyond country and all the control variables. When considering individual support variables, support received from spouse had a significant correlation with FTWS, $t = 4.26$, $p < .01$. Individuals having higher levels of received support from their spouses tend to report higher levels of FTWS than individuals with lower levels of such support. Apart from the support variables, VC showed a positive significant effect in predicting FTWS, $t = 3.32$, $p < .01$, indicating that individuals in countries with higher VC values generally reported higher FTWS than those from countries endorsing lower VC values (see Table 16.6).

With regard to the interaction terms, received support from spouse interacted with aggregated VC in predicting FTWS, $t = -3.41$, $p < .01$. The pattern of this interaction effect is shown in Figure 16.4. For individuals in countries with lower VC, the positive relationship between received support from spouse and FTWS tends to be stronger than for those from countries with higher VC values. Generally, participants from countries with higher levels of VC reported more FTWS than their counterparts from countries with lower VC values. In addition, the difference in FTWS between individuals from high VC countries and individuals from low VC countries seems to be larger at lower levels of support received from spouse than at higher levels of such support.

Above all, multilevel linear modeling was used to examine effects of country, received support from the seven sources, and interactions of received support and vertical collectivism aggregated at country level, in explaining both directions of WFC, as well as positive spillover in both directions.

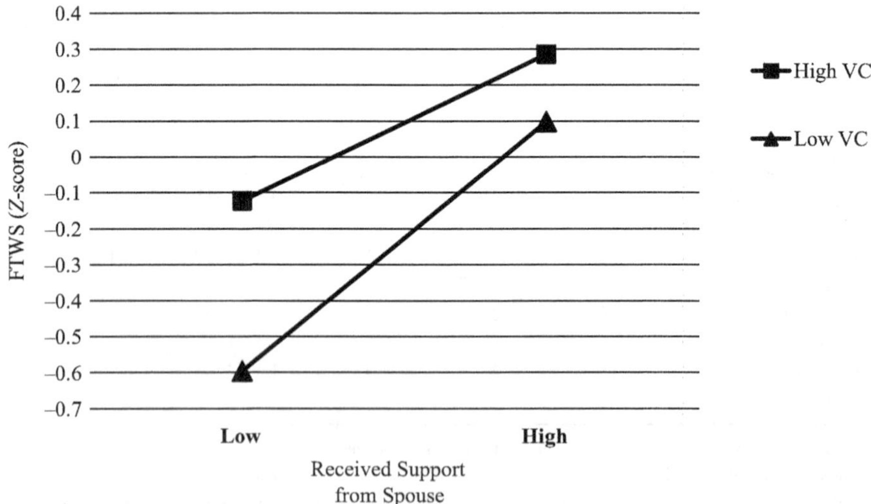

FIGURE 16.4 Interaction between received support from spouse and VC on FTWS.

TABLE 16.6 Family-to-work positive spillover predicted by country, received support, and vertical collectivism.

Random Effects

Parameter	*β Estimate*	*Std. Error*	*Wald Z*	*p*	*95% Confidence Interval*	
					Lower Bound	*Upper Bound*
Residual	.78	.02	32.63**	.00	.74	.83
Intercept (Country)	.02	.01	1.65	.10	.01	.07

Fixed Effect

Parameter	*β Estimate*	*Std. Error*	*Approx df*	*t ratio*	*p*	*95% Confidence Interval*	
						Lower Bound	*Upper Bound*
Intercept	-2.57	.77	9	-3.35**	.01	-4.30	-.84
S_spouse	1.36	.32	2097	4.26**	.00	.74	1.99
S_child	-.31	.35	2137	-.87	.39	-1.00	.39
S_parent	.00	.38	2121	.01	.99	-.74	.74
S_paid helper	-.13	.53	1105	-.26	.80	-1.17	.90
S_friends	.55	.48	1679	1.15	.251	-.39	1.48
S_job supervisor	.33	.49	2118	.68	.49	-.62	1.28
S_coworker	.03	.50	2137	.06	.95	-.95	1.01
AggregateVC	.57	.17	9	3.32**	.01	.18	.96
S_spouse* AggregateVC	-.25	.07	2083	-3.41**	.00	-.39	-.11
S_child* AggregateVC	.09	.08	2137	1.16	.25	-.06	.25
S_parent* AggregateVC	-.00	.09	2119	-.02	.99	-.17	.17
S_paid helper* AggregateVC	.02	.12	1165	.16	.87	-.21	.25
S_friends* AggregateVC	-.13	.11	1748	-1.17	.24	-.34	.09
S_job supervisor* AggregateVC	-.07	.11	2106	-.67	.50	-.29	.14
S_coworker* AggregateVC	-.01	.11	2137	-.06	.95	-.23	.21

Notes. $^{*}p < .05$, $^{**}p < .01$. Approx *df* = approximate degrees of freedom. Aggregate VC = vertical collectivism aggregated at country level. S_spouse = support from spouse; S_child = support from child(ren); S_parent = support from parent(s) or parent-inlaw(s); S_paid helper = support from paid household helper; S_friend = support from friends, relatives, or neighbors; S_job supervisor = support from job supervisor; S_coworker = support from coworker(s) or subordinate(s).

Discussion and Conclusion

This study examined the comparative use of social support in various countries and the impact of the cultural value of vertical collectivism on the relation between the used or received support from various sources with WFC and work-family positive spillover. Lack of measurement equivalence notwithstanding, the results showed that use of emotional and instrumental support and use of support for work- and family-related concerns varied across countries. Also, respondents from countries varied on their reported level of satisfaction with sources of support. Finally, the role of cultural values on the relationship between social support and the work-family interface also varied based on the source of support. Although use of support was universal, and particularly use of support from the spouse or partner and supervisor was very prevalent globally, the results showed more country specificity than any global pattern regarding the use of and satisfaction with support. In comparing received instrumental and emotional support from various sources, results demonstrated that, across almost all countries, respondents received a fairly high level of support from their spouses/partners.

Supervisor support is very critical. O'Driscoll and Beehr (1994) stated that the main source of role conflict is the one with one's supervisor. It is also noted that the supervisor can also be the main source of support. So when the source of stress and source of support is the same, this can potentially intensify the relationship between stress and strain. Mayo, Sanchez, Pastor, and Rodriguez (2012) and Kaufmann and Beehr (1986) suggest that, due to source congruence, support can have a buffering or a reverse buffering effect on the impact of stressors.

Thus, the fact that respondents across countries mostly used supervisor support is reassuring. For both work-related issues and family issues, interestingly, it is the support of the spouse/partner that is called for the most. Compared to other sources, spouses/partners provided that most consistent emotional and instrumental support across countries. It seems that the respondents receive a bit more emotional rather than instrumental support from their spouse/partner.

Overall, respondents from India, Indonesia, and Spain received more support from almost all sources than respondents from other countries. Received support from paid help for the household—though higher for India, Indonesia, and Spain—was overall the lowest-used support across all countries. It was also informative that this paid help was reported to provide both emotional and instrumental support. Additionally, it seems that the spouse provides more work and family support for participants of all countries than does the supervisor. Comparing the support received from supervisors for work and family, interestingly the respondents reported more support for family than for work. This may seem counter intuitive, yet this may be based on our western expectations where the domains of life seem less fluidly connected. There was an anecdote that in Japan, when a worker is sick, the manager or superior who goes to his home with some food and asks of his health is highly regarded. This will not be perceived in the same manner in North American and most Western European countries.

Previous studies mostly identified one or two sources of support: one from the work domain and one from the family domain. Sometimes they used support from only one domain. In this study across countries, we were able to examine the respondents' use of instrumental and emotional support from the work and family domains for work and family challenges across seven sources of support. Contrary to previous findings (Glazer, 2006), we did not find that respondents from Eastern countries were less likely to use support. As a matter of fact, we could not find a pattern based on closeness of the countries or the fact that they were from the same region. It seems many factors play a role in use of support such as economic development, religious belief, educational level, and social values. So it seems the over-generalization that Eastern respondents do not ask for support compared to Western Europeans or North Americans (Tayler, Sherman, Kim, Jarcho, Takagi, & Dunagan, 2004; Taylor, Welch, Kim, & Sherman, 2007) was not supported in our study. We found that Indian, Indonesian, and Spanish respondents were equally reporting that they received support.

Multilevel linear modeling was used to examine effects of country, received support from the seven sources, and interactions of received support and vertical collectivism aggregated at the country level, in explaining WFC in both directions, as well as positive spillover in both directions. There are several conclusions that can be drawn from the results.

First, across all the four dependent variables, incorporating received support and their corresponding interaction terms with VC significantly improved the fit of the model, indicating that the received support from different sources and their interaction terms, as a whole, explained variance in WFC and positive spillover beyond country difference and control variables such as age, gender, type of job, and number of children. Second, country difference generally showed only a marginally significant effect in predicting WFC and positive spillover, leaving within-country variance explaining most of the variance in these dependent variables.

Third, among the seven sources of received support, some are more important than others in explaining variance in WFC and positive spillover. More specifically, support from spouse and from paid household helper had a closer association with WFC than support from other sources. While received support from the former is positively related to reducing WFC, higher levels of received support from the latter tended to relate to a higher level of WFC. With regard to positive spillover, spouse and child(ren) were better sources of received support than any others. Support received from both sources tended to be more positively related to positive spillover. Finally, VC showed a moderating effect in some of the significant relationships between received support and WFC on one hand, and between received support and positive spillover on the other. Generally in these significant moderated relationships, the effect of the received support was related to reduced WFC and increased positive spillover and these findings were stronger for individuals from countries with lower levels of VC than for those from higher VC cultures.

The research implications of these findings are that inclusion of multiple countries and multiple sources of support representing the two domains of life provides a more comprehensive picture of the real life of a person. That said, it also reaffirmed that the spouse/partner and supervisor are the most impactful sources of support. It was clear that respondents from some countries, however, were more dependent on the use of support than others. Yet, we could not use the existing cultural categorizations for these countries. India, Indonesia, and Spain are not culturally, religiously, economically, or educationally very similar. So we recommend that, in the future, researchers be careful in categorizing countries without first testing them separately.

The results of the across country comparisons in this chapter need to be considered with caution, due to the lack of measurement equivalence reported in Chapter 2. The supervisor support measure, however, was among the few sources that did receive some construct validity. Future research on received support needs to develop better measures of support from all sources. It may also be possible that people's experience with support varies across sources, and some may experience a more clear distinction of work and family support and instrumental and emotional support, while others may not make these distinctions. As other scholars have mentioned, social support is contextually and culturally dependent (e.g., Chen et al., 2012).

Practical Implications

From an individual standpoint, the importance of the spouse in providing support, regardless of its type, was very prevalent. Receiving support from children, family and friends, and paid household help varied across countries and type of support. In the workplace, respondents mostly used supervisors to assist with family issues rather than work issues, though the level was not consistent across countries. This could be based on the comment made by Kaufmann and Beehr (1986) about employees not wanting to use the supervisor for work-related issues as supervisors can also be a source of work-related stress. In the case of this source, maybe perception of support availability and providing support is more important and helpful than asking for help. From an individual's standpoint, therefore, some sources are used more readily than others for gaining support to buffer or eliminate stress.

It may be of value to address the use of paid household help across countries. Contrary to the assumption that people use paid help because it is cheap, we found that the use of paid household help varied due to the nature of the type of support. For most respondents across countries, the use of paid household help was low. However, the respondents from three countries using it the most were Australia, India, and Spain, for emotional support. On the other hand, for instrumental support, only participants from India and Spain used paid household help a lot compare to others. Indian respondents also used paid household help for both family issues and work-related issues, whereas Spanish respondents used paid household help primarily for work-related issues. Whether use of paid household help is a norm or economically based is a topic which can be explored in the future. This study showed that when considering the sources of support and their role in the life of the person, context and culture matters. It is important to realize that in all cultures, social support is used and the spouse and supervisor play important roles. However, other sources and the types of support used will vary due to the person's culture and need. From an organizational standpoint, it is necessary to have training programs for managers and leaders to develop skills necessary to attend to individual employee needs. It is also necessary to recognize that the employee's spouse/partner is an important resource in their life. Thus, providing company policies that would facilitate this is vital.

Note

Due to page limitations, all post hoc comparisons among means could not be presented in this chapter. Findings can be obtained from the author.

References

Adams, G. A., King, L. A., & King, D. W. (1996). Relationships of job and family involvement, family social support, and work-family conflict with job and life satisfaction. *Journal of Applied Psychology, 81*(4), 411–420.

Aycan, Z., & Eskin, M. (2005). Relative contributions of childcare, spousal support, and organizational support in reducing work-family conflict for men and women: The case of Turkey. *Sex Roles, 53*(7/8), 453–471. doi:10.1007/s11199-005-7134-8

Ayman, R., & Antani, A. (2008). Social support and work-family conflict. In K. Korabik, D. S. Lero, & D. L. Whitehead (Eds.), *Handbook of work-family integration* (pp. 287–304). San Diego, CA: Elsevier.

Barrera, Jr., M. (1986). Distinctions between social support concepts, measures, and models. *American Journal of Community Psychology, 14*(4), 413–445.

Beehr, T. A., Farmer, S. J., Glazer, S., Gudanowski, D. M., & Nair, V. N. (2003). The enigma of social support and occupational stress: Source congruence and gender role effects. *Journal of Occupational Health Psychology, 8*(3), 220–231. doi:10.1037/1076-8998.8.3.220

Bernas, K. H., & Major, D. A. (2000). Contributors to stress resistance: Testing a model of women's work-family conflict. *Psychology of Women Quarterly, 24*, 170–178.

Bhave, D. R., Kramer, A., & Glomb, T. M. (2010). Work-family conflict in work groups: Social information processing, support, and demographic dissimilarity. *Journal of Applied Psychology, 95*(1), 145–158. doi:10.1037/a0017885

Blanch, A., & Aluja, A. (2012). Social support (family and supervisor), work-family conflict, and burnout: Sex differences. *Human Relations, 65*(7), 811–833. doi:10.1177/0018726712440471

Breaugh, J. A., & Frye, N. K. (2008). Work-family conflict: The importance of family-friendly employment practices and family-supportive supervisors. *Journal of Business Psychology, 22*, 345–353. doi:10.1007/s10869-008-9081-1

Byron, K. (2005). A meta-analytic review of work-family conflict and its antecedents. *Journal of Vocational Behavior, 67*, 169–198.

Carlson, D. S., & Perrewé, P. L. (1999). The role of social support in the stressor-strain relationship: An examination of work/family conflict. *Journal of Management, 25*(4), 513–540.

Casper, W. J., Martin, J. A., Buffardi, L. C., & Erdwins, C. J. (2002). Work-family conflict, perceived organizational support and organization commitment among employed mothers. *Journal of Occupational Health Psychology*, 7(2), 99–108. doi:10.1037//1076-8998.7.2.99

Chen, J. M., Kim, H. S., Mojaverian, T., & Morling, B. (2012). Culture and social support provision: Who gives what and why. *Personality and Social Psychology Bulleting, 38*(1), 3–13.

Clark, L. (2001). La Familia: Methodological issues in the assessment of perinatal social support for Mexicanas living in the United States. *Social Science & Medicine, 53*, 1303–1320.

Cortese, C. G., Colombo, L., & Ghislieri, C. (2010). Determinants of nurses' job satisfaction: The role of work-family conflict, job demand, emotional charge and social support. *Journal of Nursing Management, 18*, 35–43.

Drach-Zahavy, A. (2004). Toward a multidimensional construct of social support: Implications of provider's self-reliance and request characteristics. *Journal of Applied Social Psychology, 34*(7), 1395–1420.

Eisenberger, R., Stinglhamber, F., Vandenberhe, C., Scharski, I. L., & Rhoades, L. (2002). Perceived supervisor support: Contributions to perceived organizational support and employee retention. *Journal of Applied Psychology, 87*(3), 565–573. doi:10.1037//0021-9010.87.3.565

Frye, N. K., & Breaugh, J. A. (2004). Family-friendly policies, supervisor support, work-family conflict, family-work conflict, and satisfaction: A test of a conceptual model. *Journal of Business and Psychology, 19*(2), 197–220.

Glazer, S. (2006). Social support across cultures. *International Journal of Intercultural Relations, 30*, 605–622. doi:10.1016/j.ijintrel.2005.01.013

Goodwin, R., & Hernandez-Plaza, S. (2000). Perceived and received social support in two cultures: Collectivism and support among British and Spanish students. *Journal of Social and Personal Relationship, 17*(2), 282–291.

Gottlieb, B. H., & Bergen, A. E. (2010). Social support and measures. *Journal of Psychosomatic Research, 69*, 511–520.

Haber, M. G., Cohen, J. L., Lucas, T., & Baltes, B. B. (2007). The relationship between self-reported received and perceived social support: A meta-analytic review. *American Journal of Community Psychology, 39*, 133–144. doi:10.1007/s10464-007-9100-9

Hammer, L. B., Kossek, E. E., Bodner, T., & Crain, T. (2013). Measurement development and validation of the family supportive supervisor behavior short form (FSSB-SF). *Journal of Occupational Health Psychology, 18*(3), 285–296. doi:10.1037/a0032612

Hammer, L. B., Kossek, E. E., Zimmerman, K., Daniels, R. (2007). Clarifying the construct of family-supportive supervisory behaviors (FSSB): A multilevel perspective. In P. L. Perrewé, P. (Ed.). *Exploring the work and nonwork interface* (pp. 165–204). NY: Elsevier Science/JAI Press.

Hammer, L. B., Neal, M. B., Newsom, J. T., Brockwood, K. J., & Colton, C. L. (2005). A longitudinal study of the effects of dual-earner couples' utilization of family-friendly workplace supports on work and family outcomes. *Journal of Applied Psychology, 90*(4), 799–810. doi:10.1037/0021-9010.90.4.799

Jiang, K., Liu, D., McKay, P. F., Lee, T. W., & Mitchell, T. R. (2012). When and how is job embeddedness predictive of turnover? A meta-analytic investigation. *Journal of Applied Psychology, 97*(5), 1077–1096.

Kaufmann, G. M., & Beehr, T. A. (1986). Interactions between job stressors and social support: Some counterintuitive results. *Journal of Applied Psychology, 71*, 522–526.

Kim, H. S., Sherman, D. K., & Taylor, S. E. (2008). Culture and social support. *American Psychologist, 63*(6), 518–526.

King, L. A., Mattimore, L. K., King, D. W., & Adams, G. A. (1995). Family support inventory for workers: A new measure of perceived social support from family members. *Journal of Organizational Behavior, 16*, 235–258.

Kossek, E. E., & Nichol, V. (1992). The effects of on-site child care on employee attitudes and performance. *Personnel Psychology, 45*, 485–509.

Kossek, E. E., Picheler, S., Bodner, T., & Hammer, L. B. (2011). Workplace social support and work-family conflict: A meta-analysis clarifying the influence of general and work-family-specific supervisor and organizational support. *Personnel Psychology, 64*, 289–313.

Lapierre, L. M., Hackett, R. D., & Taggar, S. (2006). A test of the links between family interface with work, job enrichment and leader-member exchange. *Applied Psychology: An International Review, 55*(4), 489–511.

Maas, C. J. M., & Hox, J. J. (2005). Sufficient sample sizes for multilevel modeling. *Methodology, 1*(3), 86–92.

Matthew, R. A., Bulger, C. A., & Barnes-Farrell, J. L. (2010). Work social supports, role stressors, and work-family conflict: The moderating effect of age. *Journal of Vocational Behavior, 76*, 78–90.

Mayo, M., Sanchez, J. I., Pastor, J. C., & Rodriguez, A. (2012). Supervisor and coworker support: A source congruence approach to buffering role conflict and physical stressors. *The International Journal of Human Resource Management, 23*(18), 3872–3889.

Neff, L. A., & Karney, B. R. (2005). Gender differences in social support: A question of skill or responsiveness. *Journal of Personality and Social Psychology, 88*(1), 79–90. doi:10.1037/0022-3514.88.1.79

Nohe, C., & Sonntag, K. (2014). Work-family conflict, social support, and turnover intentions: A longitudinal study. *Journal of Vocational Behavior, 85*, 1–12.

O'Driscoll, M. P., & Beehr, T. A. (1994). Supervisor behaviors, role stressors and uncertainty as predictors of personal outcomes for subordinates. *Journal of Organizational Behavior, 15*, 141–155. doi:10.1002/job.4030150204

O'Driscoll, M. P., Poelmans, S., Spector, P. E., Kalliath, T., Allen, T. D., Cooper, C. L., & Sanchez, J. I. (2003). Family-responsive interventions, perceived organizational and supervisor support, work-family conflict, and psychological strain. *International Journal of Stress Management, 10*(4), 326–344.

Ong, A. S., & Ward, C. (2005). The construction and validation of a social support measure for sojourners: The index of sojourner social support scale. *Journal of Cross-Cultural Psychology, 36*(6), 637–661. doi:10.1177/0022022105280508

Pines, A. M., Ben-Ari, A., Utasi, A., & Larson, D. (2002). A cross-cultural investigation of social support and burnout. *European Psychologist, 7*(4), 256–264. doi:10.1027//1016-9040.7.4.256

Ransford, C. R., Crouter, A. C., & McHale, S. M. (2008). Implications of work pressure and supervisor support for fathers', mothers', and adolescents' relationships and well-being in dual earner families. *Community, Work & Family, 11*(1), 37–60.

Rhoades, L., & Eisenberger, R. (2002). Perceived organizational support: A review of the literature. *Journal of Applied Psychology, 87*(4), 698–714. doi:10.1037//0021-9010.87.4.698

Seiger, C. P., & Wiese, B. S. (2009). Social support from work and family domains as an antecedent or moderator of work-family conflicts? *Journal of Vocational Behavior, 75*, 26–37.

Shockley, K. M., & Allen, T. D. (2013). Episodic work-family conflict, cardiovascular indicators, and social support: An experience sampling approach. *Journal of Occupational Health Psychology, 18*(3), 262–275. doi:10.1037/a0033137

Solomon, Z., Mikulincer, M., & Hobfol, S. E. (1985). Objective versus subjective measurement of stress and social support: Combat-related reactions. *Journal of Consulting and Clinical Psychology, 55*(4), 577–583.

Sprietzer, G., Stucliffe, K., Dutton, J., Sonenshein, S., & Grant, A. M. (2005). A socially embedded model of thriving at work. *Organization Science, 16*(5), 537–549. doi:10.1287/orsc.1050.0153

Tabachnick, B. G., & Fidell, L. S. (2010). *Using multivariate statistics* (6th ed.). Boston, MA: Allyn & Bacon.

Tabachnick, B. G., & Fidell, L. S. (2013). *Using multivariate statistics* (International ed.-6th ed.). New York, NY: Pearson.

Tayler, S. E., Sherman, D. K., Kim, H. S., Jarcho, J., Takagi, K., & Dunagan, M. S. (2004). Culture and social support: Who seeks it and why? *Journal of Personality and Social Psychology, 87*(3), 354–362. doi:10.1037/0022-3514.87.3.354

Taylor, S. E., Welch, W. T., Kim, H. S., & Sherman, D. K. (2007). Cultural differences in the impact of social support on psychological and biological stress responses. *Psychological Science, 18*(9), 831–837.

vanDaalen, G., Willemsen, T. M., & Sanders, K. (2006). Reducing work-family conflict through different sources of social support. *Journal of Vocational Behavior, 69*, 462–276.

Vaux, A. (1985). Factor structure of the network orientation scale. *Psychological Reports, 57*, 1181–1182.

Vaux, A., & Harrison, D. (1985). Support network characteristics associated with support satisfaction and perceived support. *American Journal of Community Psychology, 13*(3), 245–268.

Viswesvaran, C., Sanchez, J. I., & Fisher, J. (1999). The role of social support in the process of work stress: A meta-analysis. *Journal of Vocational Behavior, 54*, 314–334. Article ID jvbe.1998.1661, available online at http://www.idealibrary.com

Wang, M., Liu, S., Zhan, Y., & Shi, J. (2010). Daily work-family conflict and alcohol use: Testing the cross-level moderation effects of peer drinking norms and social support. *Journal of Applied Psychology, 95*(2), 377–386.

Winemiller, D. R., Mitchell, M. E., Stuliff, J., & Cline, D. J. (1993). Measurement strategies in social support: A descriptive review of the literature. *Journal of Clinical Psychology, 49*(5), 638–648.

APPENDIX

Scale of Received Support from Different Sources

Please read the following statements and identify the support you have received from ALL the listed sources. Evaluate level of support provided using the following scale. Please use "Not Applicable" for situations that do not apply to you (i.e., you do not have a paid household helper), and please use "Never" when the situation applies to you but never happens.

1. Please indicate how often you receive support with respect to CHILD CARE from:

	Never	*Not Often*	*Sometimes*	*Frequently*	*Not Applicable*
Partner/spouse					
Child(ren)					
Parents or parents-in-law					
Paid household helper					
Neighbors, friends, or relatives					
Job supervisor					
Coworkers or subordinates					

2. Please indicate how often you receive support with respect to HELP WITH HOUSEHOLD TASKS from:

	Never	*Not Often*	*Sometimes*	*Frequently*	*Not Applicable*
Partner/spouse					
Child(ren)					
Parents or parents-in-law					
Paid household helper					
Neighbors, friends, or relatives					

Job supervisor					
Coworkers or subordinates					

3. Please indicate how often you receive support with respect to WORK-RELATED DUTIES from:

	Never	*Not Often*	*Sometimes*	*Frequently*	*Not Applicable*
Partner/spouse					
Child(ren)					
Parents or parents-in-law					
Paid household helper					
Neighbors, friends, or relatives					
Job supervisor					
Coworkers or subordinates					

4. Please indicate how often you receive support with respect to HELPFUL WORK-RELATED INFORMATION (e.g., advice, suggestions) from:

	Never	*Not Often*	*Sometimes*	*Frequently*	*Not Applicable*
Partner/spouse					
Child(ren)					
Parents or parents-in-law					
Paid household helper					
Neighbors, friends, or relatives					
Job supervisor					
Coworkers or subordinates					

5. Please indicate how often you receive support with respect to HELPFUL FAMILY-RELATED INFORMATION (e.g., advice, suggestions) from:

	Never	*Not Often*	*Sometimes*	*Frequently*	*Not Applicable*
Partner/spouse					
Child(ren)					
Parents or parents-in-law					
Paid household helper					
Neighbors, friends, or relatives					
Job supervisor					
Coworkers or subordinates					

6. Please indicate how often you receive support with respect to ENCOURAGEMENT/APPRECIATION regarding events in your FAMILY LIFE from:

	Never	*Not Often*	*Sometimes*	*Frequently*	*Not Applicable*
Partner/spouse					
Child(ren)					

Parents or parents-in-law					
Paid household helper					
Neighbors, friends, or relatives					
Job supervisor					
Coworkers or subordinates					

7. Please indicate how often you receive support with respect to LISTENING TO AND DISCUSSION WORK-RELATED PROBLEMS from:

	Never	*Not Often*	*Sometimes*	*Frequently*	*Not Applicable*
Partner/spouse					
Child(ren)					
Parents or parents-in-law					
Paid household helper					
Neighbors, friends, or relatives					
Job supervisor					
Coworkers or subordinates					

8. Please indicate how often you receive support with respect to ENCOURAGEMENT/APPRECIATION regarding events in your WORK LIFE from:

	Never	*Not Often*	*Sometimes*	*Frequently*	*Not Applicable*
Partner/spouse					
Child(ren)					
Parents or parents-in-law					
Paid household helper					
Neighbors, friends, or relatives					
Job supervisor					
Coworkers or subordinates					

9. Please indicate how often you receive support with respect to LISTENING TO AND DISCUSSING FAMILY-RELATED PROBLEMS (e.g., support, concern for your well-being) from:

	Never	*Not Often*	*Sometimes*	*Frequently*	*Not Applicable*
Partner/spouse					
Child(ren)					
Parents or parents-in-law					
Paid household helper					
Neighbors, friends, or relatives					
Job supervisor					
Coworkers or subordinates					

17

THE ROLE OF WORK-FAMILY GUILT IN THE WORK-FAMILY INTERFACE

A Cross-Cultural Analysis

Karen Korabik

> "Combining work with mothering—the difficult part for me is the balance. I feel guilty a lot of the time that I could be a more attentive mother if I did not work full time."
>
> —(McElwain, Korabik, & Chappell, 2005a)

Work-family (W-F) guilt is an unfortunate fact of life for the majority of today's working parents. Not only does W-F guilt cause workers and their families a great deal of emotional distress, but it also can be extremely detrimental to their physical and mental well-being (McElwain & Korabik, 2004). For example, among the many negative effects that have been associated with W-F guilt are lower family and life satisfaction, and higher psychological distress, and turnover intent (Korabik, 2015). To combat this problem, research that furthers our understanding of when, why, and how people experience feelings of W-F guilt is necessary. This knowledge will not only help working parents cope with their guilt feelings, but it will also lay the foundation upon which effective intervention strategies and human resource policies (e.g., family-friendly policies) can be built.

Although the guilt arising from trying to balance work and family responsibilities has been a frequent topic of interest in the North American media and popular press (Bort, Pflock, & Renner, 2005; Chapman, 1987), it has been relatively neglected in scholarly research (Seagram & Daniluk, 2002). The scant research that does exist indicates that W-F guilt is very widespread. Unfortunately, our ability to fully understand this phenomenon has been restricted due to the methodological limitations inherent in most previous research. In addition, due to the fact that nearly all past studies have been conducted in single countries located primarily in Anglo and European contexts, it is unclear whether their findings are generalizable beyond such settings. This chapter details the findings on W-F guilt from Project 3535, which is unique in that it is the first cross-cultural study to be carried out on W-F guilt and the first to include countries in Asia.

Definition and Conceptualization

Most theory and research on guilt has centered on guilt in general rather than on W-F guilt in particular (McElwain & Korabik, 2004). In the literature on general guilt, guilt is seen as a negative emotion that occurs when individuals believe they have harmed someone else (O'Connor, Berry, & Weiss, 1999). Guilt develops when individuals contravene their internalized standards about the correct way to think, feel, or behave (Kubany, 1994; Zahn-Waxler, Kochanska, Krupnick, & McKnew, 1990). Guilt has been conceptualized as having: (1) a cognitive component or the recognition that harm has been caused, (2) an affective component or the unpleasant feelings experienced, and (3) a motivational component or the desire to undo the damage (Hoffman, 1982). Kubany et al. (1996) propose that more guilt will be experienced to the extent that people behave in a manner contrary to their values, realize their behavior is unjustified, feel responsible for what occurred, and think they could have anticipated and prevented the outcome.

Guilt can be either adaptive or destructive. It can motivate someone to feel empathy, maintain interpersonal attachments (O'Connor, Berry, Weiss, Bush, & Sampson, 1997), control their aggression, or make amends and restore social harmony (Zahn-Waxler et al., 1990). By contrast, it can result in emotional distress, distorted relationships, and psychopathology. Those who externalize their guilt may attempt to minimize the injury they caused, derogate the person they harmed, or treat the precipitating event like an isolated incident (Ausubel, 1955; Baumeister, Stillwell, & Heatherton, 1994). On the other hand, those who internalize their guilt may react by disparaging or punishing themselves (Ferguson, Stegge, Eyre, Vollmer, & Ashbaker, 2000).

The literature on W-F guilt contains a variety of different definitions and conceptualizations (McElwain & Korabik, 2004). W-F guilt has been viewed as an emotional response resulting from the need to choose between work and family (Conlin, 2000; Pollock, 1997), allowing work to interfere with family (Glavin, Schieman, & Reid, 2011), or not being able to effectively balance work and family roles (Napholz, 2000). W-F guilt also has been defined in terms of the difference between one's actual and ideal allocation of home and work responsibilities (Hochwarter, Perrewé, Meurs, & Kacmar, 2007). Some researchers see W-F guilt as arising from behavior that violates internalized norms about how one should balance work and family demands (Morgan & King, 2012). For others, W-F guilt ensues from feeling unable to satisfactorily enact prescribed gender-role norms (Livingston & Judge, 2008; Simon, 1995). Finally, some authors believe that W-F guilt is a consequence of the double standards placed on women versus men (Banarjee, 2003; Bui, 1999).

The Measurement of W-F Guilt

Research into W-F guilt has been hindered by a lack of reliable and valid measures (McElwain & Korabik, 2004). As a result, quantitative research in this area often has relied on single-item (e.g., "In the past seven days, how many days have you felt guilty?") or multi-item measures of general guilt. Meta-analytic findings indicate that W-F specific support constructs are more strongly related to WFC than the more general constructs of supervisor support and perceived organizational support (Kossek, Pichler, Bodner, & Hammer, 2011). This is probably also true for guilt. However, few measures of guilt specific to the W-F context exist, many of which consist of single items (e.g., "I feel guilty that I don't spend enough time with my family"). Others focus only on one aspect of the W-F interface (i.e., only the home context or the work context).

One such measure is the Feelings of Guilt about Parenting Scale (Martinez, Carrasco, Aza, Blanco, & Espinar, 2011). It has 14 items that assess situations that could evoke guilt in employed parents. Two multi-item employment-related guilt scales also exist. One was created by Aycan and Eskin (2005) for use in Turkey (2005), and the other by Hochwarter et al. (2007) for use in the United States.

In addition to the above measures, there are also three multi-item measures that assess W-F guilt as a bidirectional construct. That is, they have separate subscales that assess work interference with family guilt (WIFG) and family interference with work guilt (FIWG). The most recent was developed by Morgan and King (2012) by adding the stem "I feel guilty when" to the eight items on Netemeyer, Boles, and McMurrian's (1996) WFC scale.

McElwain (2008) developed two bidirectional W-F Guilt Scales. The first, the WFGS-F, is a 24-item faceted scale that has six subscales assessing emotional, physical, and psychological WIFG and FIWG. Emotional W-F guilt is defined as the negative feelings that arise from WFC, physical W-F guilt results from the inability to physically attend to both work and family duties, and psychological W-F guilt refers to the psychological spillover from one role to the other. This measure uses a frequency response scale. The second measure is a seven-item nonfaceted version (WFGS) that uses an agreement response scale. This is the measure that was used in the Project 3535 survey, and that is described in more detail in Chapter 2.

Previous Literature on Guilt and the W-F Interface

Qualitative Research

Empirical research in the area of W-F guilt has suffered from a number of methodological limitations. For example, most of the research has: (1) only addressed topics relating to the impact of multiple roles (e.g., maternal employment or role conflict/spillover), (2) used qualitative methods, (3) had very small samples, and

(4) employed samples composed solely of women. Examples of these types of studies are research done on Native American women (Napholz, 2000); women teachers in the United Kingdom (Guendouzi, 2006); and mothers in Australia (Pocock, 2003), Sweden (Elvin-Nowak, 1999), and the United States (Seagram & Daniluk, 2002). Other qualitative research has examined both men and women (Daly, 2001; McElwain, 2008; McElwain et al., 2005a; Simon, 1995).

Many common themes have emerged from this body of research. Both WFC and W-F guilt appear to be widespread concerns for working parents, with men and women being very similar to one another both in the extent to which they admit to experiencing W-F guilt and in the things that make them feel guilty (Korabik, 2015). Although both WIFG and FIWG are frequently mentioned, feelings of guilt about neglecting one's family, particularly one's children, are reported much more often than guilt about neglecting one's work (McElwain, 2008). A recurring theme was that W-F guilt arose when mothers felt they had failed to adequately care for their children (Daly, 2001; Elvin-Nowak, 1999; Guendouzi, 2006; McElwain, 2008; Pocock, 2003; Seagram & Daniluk, 2002; Simon, 1995). This may partially have stemmed from their belief that they were being judged by others (McElwain, 2008). Specifically, Guendouzi (2006) and Pocock (2003) discuss the social pressure the intensive mothering norm puts on mothers to be constantly available and accessible.

In particular, parents tend to feel guilty for working too much, not spending enough time with their children, missing out on their children's important milestones, leaving their children with caregivers, and taking time for themselves (Daly, 2001; Elvin-Nowak, 1999; McElwain, 2008; Napholz, 2000; Pocock, 2003). Parents used several strategies to try to cope with their guilt. For example, they would try to spend more time with their families or do something special for their children (McElwain, 2008; Napholz, 2000; Pocock, 2003). Some resorted to "super syndrome" and attempted to be everything to everybody (Napholz, 2000; Pocock, 2003). This often resulted in a reduction in self-care (Guendouzi, 2006; Napholz, 2000) or the need to devise strategies that allowed them to justify putting their own needs first (Elvin-Nowak, 1999). Many parents spoke about making life choices, such as realigning their priorities or choosing more family-friendly work environments, which allowed them to create better W-F balance (McElwain, 2008). Others merely resigned themselves to the fact that W-F guilt was an inevitable part of their lives (Daly, 2001; McElwain, 2008).

Help seeking was another commonly used strategy. However, reliance on instrumental support from friends, family members, paid helpers, or coworkers often had the effect of amplifying guilt feelings since parents felt they were passing their personal responsibilities off onto others and failing to "pull their own weight" (Guendouzi, 2006; McElwain, 2008). By contrast, receipt of emotional support from others often helped to alleviate guilt feelings (McElwain, 2008). When coping strategies were unsuccessful, they often led to feeling a lack of control, emotional depletion, exhaustion, anger, frustration, and resentment (Elvin-Nowak, 1999; Seagram & Daniluk, 2002).

Quantitative Research

To date, very little quantitative research has been carried out on W-F guilt (Korabik, 2015). Most of the existing literature has focused on how W-F guilt is related to WFC, antecedent and outcome variables, and gender.

W-F Guilt and W-F Conflict

Some previous research has looked at nature of the association between W-F guilt and WFC (McElwain, Korabik, & Chappell, 2005b). Morgan and King (2012) argue that affective emotional reactions, such as guilt, have the capacity to produce both within domain (work or family) and cross-domain effects. Based on this WIFG, as well as FIWG, should be related both to work interference with family conflict (WIFC) and family interference with work conflict (FIWC). Thus far, however, the evidence on this has been contradictory. Livingston and Judge (2008) found that general affective guilt was positively related to FIWC, but not to WIFC. By contrast, Aycan and Eskin (2005) found that among Turkish dual career parents employment-related guilt was positively correlated with WIFC, but not FIWC. Korabik and McElwain (2011) used the WFGS and the WFGS-F with a sample of Canadian women. In support of Morgan and King's proposition, their results indicated that there were both within- and cross-domain effects. For both measures WIFG was significantly and positively associated with both WIFC and FIWC. Likewise, FIWG was significantly and positively related to both FIWC and WIFC.

Antecedents and Outcomes of W-F Guilt

Other research has examined the relationships between W-F guilt and its antecedents and outcomes. In a study of employed parents in Spain, Martinez et al. (2011) found that parents reported guilt primarily when they needed to delegate parenting duties to others or felt they were not paying enough attention to their children. Morgan and King (2012) found W-F guilt to be a precursor of both pro- and anti-social workplace behaviors. In addition, employment-related guilt has been shown to be associated with time inflexibility, depression, and lower emotional spousal support and supervisor support, as well as a lack of satisfaction with life, organizational policies, parenthood, and time spent with children (Aycan & Eskin, 2005).

Korabik and McElwain (2011) used the WFGS and the WFGS-F to examine a comprehensive model of the antecedents and outcomes of W-F guilt. Their results indicated that for both measures, higher work demands were associated with greater WIFC and WIFG, and, in turn, greater WIFG was related to higher turnover intentions. In addition for the WFGS only, higher WIFC predicted greater WIFG, which in turn was related to lower job satisfaction.

Hochwarter et al. (2007) examined whether the ability to manage resources at work could enhance personal control and help to reduce the negative effects of work-induced guilt. They found that work-induced guilt had detrimental effects on job and life satisfaction when individuals did not have ability to manage resources, but these were neutralized when there was an ability to manage resources.

Gender and Age

There has been a large body of research on the issue of gender differences in W-F guilt. In general, there is little evidence of differences between men and women in W-F guilt (see Korabik, 2015 for a review). Two studies have shown that, despite this, women report more W-F guilt than men in some contexts, such as when work tasks must be completed outside of normal working hours (Glavin et al., 2011) or when they must multi-task in certain locations (Offer & Schneider, 2011).

Livingston and Judge (2008) looked at how traditional/egalitarian gender-role attitudes and WFC were related to general guilt. They found that there was a stronger positive relationship between WIFC and guilt for those with more egalitarian gender-role attitudes than for those with more traditional attitudes. By contrast, there was a stronger positive relationship between FIWC and guilt for those with traditional gender-role attitudes than for those with egalitarian gender-role attitudes. However, there was an interaction between gender and FIWC. Traditional men reported the highest levels of guilt, and this was exacerbated when FIWC was high. By contrast, egalitarian men reported the lowest levels of guilt, and this was particularly so when FIWC was high. Traditional and egalitarian women reported moderate levels of guilt.

Age also may be an important moderating variable. Nevill and Damico (1977) found that women between 25 and 39 reported significantly higher levels of W-F guilt than women at other ages, most likely because their children were younger and needed more supervised care.

Project 3535 Results

Qualitative Results

An analysis of the findings from the qualitative data collected as part of Project 3535 revealed that W-F guilt was a frequently mentioned topic in nearly all of the countries for which data were available (see also Chapters 4 through 12 as well as Korabik and Lero (2004) for Canada, Rajadhyaksha and Desai (2004) for India, Mawardi (2004) for Indonesia, Somech and Drach-Zahavy (2004) for Israel,

Huang (2004) for Taiwan, and Velgach, Ishaya, and Ayman (2005) for the United States). Although there were many similarities, women in different countries tended to emphasize somewhat different themes when speaking about what made them feel guilty. Women in India reported experiencing guilt when they were unable to be superwomen and when they ignored the academic achievement of their children (Rajadhyaksha & Desai, 2004). Women in the United States mentioned feeling guilty about having to put their jobs before their families and their inability to be in two places at one time (Velgach et al., 2005). Women in Indonesia, Taiwan, and the Arab women in Israel spoke about feeling guilty for not fulfilling their traditional gender roles (Korabik, 2005). Four of the seven Jewish Israeli women, however, felt that they had moved from guilt to positive spillover as a function of their life stage (Somech & Drach-Zahavy, 2004).

Quantitative Results

Analyses were carried out on the quantitative data to address the following eight research questions:

RQ1: Do levels of W-F guilt differ by country?
RQ2: Is W-F guilt related to individualism-collectivism across countries?
RQ3: Are there differences in W-F guilt attributable to gender or gender-role ideology across countries?
RQ4: What is the impact of demographic factors on W-F guilt across countries?
RQ5: How is W-F guilt related to WFC and positive spillover across countries?
RQ6: How is W-F guilt related to work- and family-related antecedent variables across countries?
RQ7: How is W-F guilt related to work- and family-related outcome variables across countries?
RQ8: Does W-F guilt mediate relationships between WFC and W-F outcomes?

The significance level of statistical tests was adjusted to compensate for the large sample sizes and the numerous correlations computed. To avoid reporting non-trivial effects, only p values $< .001$ and only correlations that exceeded $r > .3$ in magnitude were considered to be significant.

Country and Culture

First, the issue of whether the levels of W-F guilt reported by participants differed by country (RQ1) was examined. The means and standard deviations for WIFG and FIWG by country can be found in Table 17.1. In all countries the mean level of WIFG was higher than the mean level of FIWG. There was a significant main effect for country for WIFG, $F(9, 2806) = 29.68, p < .001$, with Israel and

TABLE 17.1 Means, standard deviations, and correlations of WIFG and FIWG with cultural variables by country.

	Guilt	*M*	*SD*	*VI*	*VC*	*HI at work*	*HI at home*	*HC at work*	*HC at home*	*GRI1*	*GRI2*	*GRI3*
AU	WIFG	3.90	1.09	.16	.13	.13	.06	-.12	-.07	.19	.06	.13
AU	FIWG	2.64	1.06	.15	.06	.16	.20	-.06	-.07	.19	.12	.18
CA	WIFG	3.99	1.09	.27	.18	.10	.06	.07	.15	.27	.16	.14
CA	FIWG	2.40	.86	.10	.09	.00	.05	-.02	-.07	.09	.14	.13
CN	WIFG	4.31	.84	.13	.32	. 17	.12	.20	.26	.10	.03	.13
CN	FIWG	3.22	1.07	.16	.00	.25	.19	.03	.00	.17	.15	.23
IN	WIFG	3.51	1.04	.22	-.01	-.00	.13	.02	.03	.27	.22	.22
IN	FIWG	3.41	1.18	.24	.01	.04	.10	-.05	-.08	.30	.26	.31
ID	WIFG	3.54	1.15	.00	.06	.15	.14	-.04	-.08	.12	.11	.12
ID	FIWG	2.96	1.00	.03	.07	.15	.14	.01	.02	.08	.09	.10
IL	WIFG	3.02	1.19	.10	-.07	.02	-.03	-.19	-.14	.16	.03	.06
IL	FIWG	2.53	1.02	.21	.15	.02	.14	-.04	-.15	.19	.22	.31
ES	WIFG	3.56	1.18	-.08	.09	.11	.07	-.06	.08	.22	.10	.04
ES	FIWG	2.36	.83	.17	.09	-.08	-.07	-.20	-.20	.16	-.02	.01
TW	WIFG	3.73	.87	.09	.09	.10	.03	.06	.13	.24	.15	.25
TW	FIWG	3.06	1.01	.22	.07	.20	.12	-.01	-.04	.18	.23	.19
TR	WIFG	3.33	.91	-.07	-.13	.11	.16	-.17	-.14	-.31	-.33	-.23
TR	FIWG	1.95	.53	-.20	-.09	-.07	-.01	-.12	-.11	-.13	-.24	-.07
US	WIFG	3.55	1.24	.16	.22	.16	.09	-.03	.09	.25	.12	.13
US	FIWG	2.17	.92	.17	.03	-.04	.05	-.08	-.00	.20	.23	.25
Total	WIFG	3.63	1.09	.06	.09	.02	.04	.01	.06	.09	.00	.06
Total	FIWG	2.75	1.10	.18	.10	.10	.01	-.08	-.14	.22	.24	.29

Notes. VI = vertical individualism; VC = vertical collectivism; HI = horizontal individualism; HC = horizontal collectivism, GRI 1 = division of labor, GRI 2 = importance of men's careers; GRI 3 = effects of women's employment; correlations in bold are considered to be significant

Turkey (M = 3.0–3.3) having the lowest levels and Australia, Canada, and China having the highest (M = 3.9–4.3). There was also a significant main effect for country for FIWG, $F(9, 2806) = 79.41, p < .001$. The lowest FIWG was in Turkey (M = 1.95). However, in general, those in the more individualistic Anglo and Latin European countries had lower levels of FIWG (M = 2.2–2.6) than those in the more collectivistic Asian (i.e., China, India, Indonesia, and Taiwan) countries (M = 3.0–3.4) did.

To examine RQ2, correlations were computed by country between WIFG and FIWG and the cultural variables related to individualism-collectivism (i.e., vertical individualism and collectivism and horizontal individualism and collectivism at home and at work). Only one correlation met the criterion for significance (see Table 17.1). In the Chinese subsample, greater vertical collectivism was associated with higher WIFG.

Gender and Gender-Role Ideology

In regard to RQ3, 2 (Gender: man/woman) by 10 (Country) ANOVAs demonstrated that there were no significant main effects for Gender or Gender × Country interactions for either WIFG or FIWG. Gender-role ideology (GRI) refers to the attitudes or beliefs an individual holds about the proper roles of men and women in society. It is generally conceptualized as a unidimensional construct with traditional attitudes at one pole and egalitarian attitudes at the other. Our GRI measure was composed of three subscales assessing beliefs about gendered division of labor, the importance of men's careers, and the impact of women's employment on family well-being, respectively. Table 17.1 presents the correlations of these subscale scores with WIFG and FIWG by country. Almost all of the correlations were positive in sign, indicating that egalitarian GRI was associated with lower WFG. The exception to this was Turkey, where traditional GRI was associated with lower WFG.

To probe these effects further, 2 (GRI: Traditional/Egalitarian) by 10 (Country) ANOVAs were computed. For WIFG there was a significant main effect for GRI, $F(1, 2791) = 25.01, p < .001$, and a significant Country × GRI interaction, $F(9, 2791) = 5.21, p < .001$. Those with egalitarian gender-role attitudes had lower WIFG than those with traditional attitudes did in every country except for China (where there was no significant difference) and Turkey (where traditionals had lower WIFG than egalitarians). For FIWG there was a significant main effect for GRI, $F(1, 2782) = 27.76, p < .001$, and a significant Country × GRI interaction, $F(9, 2782) = 3.80, p < .001$. Those with egalitarian attitudes had lower FIWG than those with traditional attitudes in every country except Spain (where there was no significant difference) and Turkey (where traditionals had lower FIWG than egalitarians).

In a separate study, the Project 3535 data from India, Indonesia, and Taiwan were examined by Rajadhyaksha, Huang, Mawardi, and Desai (2011). In structural equation model (SEM) models GRI was treated as an antecedent variable that impacted on WIFG via work overload and WIFC and on FIWG via family overload and FIWC. GRI predicted W-F guilt in the same way in each country such that more traditional GRI was associated with higher WIFG and FIWG.

Demographics

Next, to address RQ4, ANOVAs were computed to explore whether a number of demographic factors (i.e., living arrangements, job level, job schedule, age, education, and tenure) affected W-F guilt. For WIFG neither the main effect for Type of Living Arrangement (nuclear vs. extended family) nor the Country × Living Arrangement interaction was significant. However, there was a significant main effect for Living Arrangement for FIWG, $F(1, 2369) = 16.26, p < .001$. Those living in extended family situations reported higher FIWG than those in nuclear families. This is consistent with the higher levels of FIWG found in Asian countries (i.e., China, India, Indonesia, and Taiwan), as these are the countries where extended family living situations are likely to be more common. The Country × Living Arrangement interaction was not significant, $p > .05$.

Neither the main effect for Country nor the Country × Job Level (managerial/nonmanagerial) interaction was significant for WIFG or FIWG, $p > .01$. However, there was a significant main effect for Job Schedule on WIFG, $F(2, 2712) = 4.64$, $p < .01$, such that full-time workers reported more WIFG than those working part-time. There was also a significant Country × Job Schedule interaction, $F(9, 2712) = 2.96$, $p < .001$. Full-time employees reported higher WIFG except in China, India, and Taiwan where part-time employees had higher WIFG than full-time employees.

There were no substantial correlations between WIFG or FIWG and age, education, and positional or organizational tenure. However, supporting the findings of Nevill and Damico (1977), the data for some countries (i.e., Australia, Canada, India, Spain, and the United States) showed a pattern such that age was negatively related to FIWG. The magnitude of these relationships was small and ranged from $r = -.26$ for India to $r = -.15$ for Spain.

Relationships With W-F Conflict and Positive Spillover

Next, the results pertinent to RQ5 were examined. Within-domain effects between WFC and W-F guilt were very common (see Table 17.2). Both time- and strain-based WIFC were significantly and positively correlated with WIFG in all countries except Indonesia and China. For China, the correlations ($r = .27$ and .28, respectively) just missed the .3 cutoff for significance. Moreover, both time- and strain-based FIWC were significantly and positively correlated with FIWG in all countries except China, Israel, Indonesia, and Turkey. In China, although there was a significant correlation between FIWG and strain-based FIWC, the magnitude of the relationship between FIWG and time-based FIWC was marginally significant ($r = .27$). Similarly, for Israel the correlation between time-based FIWC and FIWG was significant, but that for strain-based FIWC and FIWG just missed the cut off for significance ($r = .28$). The only country in which significant cross-domain effects occurred was India. For the Indian sample, higher time- and strain-based WIFC and FIWC were significantly related to higher WIFG and higher FIWG. There were no significant relationships between work to family or family to work positive spillover and either WIFG or FIWG for any country (see Table 17.2).

Relationships With Antecedent Variables

To examine RQ6, correlations were computed between WIFG and FIWG and several variables that have been commonly found to be antecedents of WFC,

TABLE 17.2 Correlations of WIFG and FIWG with antecedent and outcome variables by country.

	Guilt	*WO*	*FO*	*JC*	*FC*	*TB WIFC*	*SB WIFC*	*TB FIWC*	*SB FIWC*	*WTFS*	*FTWS*	*EOB*	*SRP*	*Distress*	*TI*	*Fam. Sat.*	*Life Sat.*
AU	WIFG	.37	.24	-.27	-.25	.64	.48	.24	.26	-.18	-.24	-.48	-.37	.34	.19	-.35	-.34
AU	FIWG	.06	.31	.02	-.17	.18	.13	.42	.49	-.05	-.03	-.22	-.16	.29	.07	-.17	-.19
CA	WIFG	.46	.15	-.19	-.27	.68	.47	.20	.07	-.14	-.12	-.45	-.37	.33	.35	-.29	-.29
CA	FIWG	-.05	.12	.03	-.07	-.04	.00	.38	.34	.07	-.04	-.07	-.05	.06	-.03	-.06	-.01
CN	WIFG	.25	.16	.01	.21	.28	.27	.03	.12	.01	.14	-.19	.15	-.10	.15	.34	.02
CN	FIWG	.21	.31	.18	-.03	.16	.15	.27	.34	.11	-.09	.02	.10	.07	.04	.02	.25
IN	WIFG	.35	.40	.06	.04	.46	.40	.50	.47	.11	-.13	.09	-.21	.43	.49	-.21	-.07
IN	FIWG	.39	.59	.10	.06	.45	.44	.60	.59	.03	-.19	.27	-.18	.46	.48	-.27	-.02
ID	WIFG	.16	.06	-.03	.02	.18	.20	.09	.11	-.07	-.08	-.11	-.14	.16	.29	-.10	-.13
ID	FIWG	.14	.09	-.00	.06	.01	.06	.02	.11	-.05	-.05	-.02	-.00	.11	.07	.04	-.05
IL	WIFG	.37	.23	-.19	-.19	.44	.34	.13	.29	-.13	-.24	-.32	-.32	.44	.31	-.31	-.46
IL	FIWG	.08	.20	-.11	-.07	.07	.12	.35	.28	.07	.00	-.15	-.00	.21	.15	-.06	.00
ES	WIFG	.53	.27	-.21	-.14	.58	.59	.25	.16	-.29	.10	-.45	-.31	.42	.32	-.25	-.28
ES	FIWG	.25	.22	-.05	-.22	.09	.29	.43	.45	-.09	-.01	-.22	-.15	.13	.09	-.16	-.18
TW	WIFG	.24	.13	.02	-.02	.36	.34	.27	.27	-.23	-.17	-.41	-.11	.06	.21	-.12	.21
TW	FIWG	.21	.33	.08	-.09	.27	.22	.36	.43	-.03	-.11	-.20	.02	.16	.16	-.02	.16
TR	WIFG	.44	.20	.01	.21	.59	.53	.13	.16	-.24	-.06	-.19	.15	.14	.16	-.35	-.30
TR	FIWG	.08	.18	.18	-.03	.03	.03	.16	.08	-.15	-.11	.02	.10	.27	.15	-.14	-.13
US	WIFG	.45	.21	-.41	-.30	.68	.56	.26	.17	-.19	-.28	-.50	-.41	.41	.43	-.30	-.31
US	FIWG	-.02	.19	-.08	-.31	.15	.06	.40	.51	.04	-.20	-.29	-.21	.19	.17	-.21	-.02
Total	WIFG	.36	.22	-.13	-.09	.44	.37	.22	.17	-.13	-.14	-.18	-.27	.20	.33	-.21	-.26
Total	FIWG	.22	.35	-.02	-.11	.11	.13	.42	.43	.13	.06	.10	-.12	.22	.25	-.18	-.05

Note. WO = work overload; FO = family overload; JC = job control; FC = family control; TB = time-based; SB = strain-based; EPB = ease of balancing; SRP = satisfaction with role performance; Distress = psychological distress; TI = turnover intent; Fam. Sat. = family satisfaction; Life Sat. = life satisfaction correlations in bold are considered to be significant.

namely work and family overload; job and family control; and frequency and satisfaction of social support from spouse, supervisor, coworkers/subordinates, and organization. Within-domain effects between role overload and W-F guilt were common (see Table 17.2). However, these were stronger for the work domain than for the family domain. Thus, higher work overload was positively and significantly related to higher WIFG in all countries except Indonesia, China, and Taiwan. But, higher family overload was associated with higher FIWG only in Australia, China, India, and Taiwan. Cross-domain effects were apparent only for India. Work overload was not significantly related to FIWG nor was family overload significantly related to WIFG except in India.

There were significant effects for job and family control only for the US subsample (see Table 17.2). In the United States, both job and family control were negatively correlated with WIFG, and family control was negatively correlated with FIWG.

For social support, satisfaction with supervisor support was negatively correlated with WIFG only for the Canadian ($r = -.32$) and US ($r = -.27$) subsamples. Greater satisfaction with family-friendly organizational policies was related to lower WIFG in the overall sample ($r = -.24$), as well as in all of the country subsamples, except for China and India. Greater support received from coworkers and subordinates was related to lower WIFG in the Turkish subsample ($r = -.33$). In addition, for the Israeli subsample, satisfaction with supervisor support ($r = -.28$) and coworker/subordinate support ($r = -.28$) were marginally associated with lower FIWG.

Relationships With Outcome Variables

To examine RQ7, correlations were computed between WIFG and FIWG and several outcome variables (see Table 17.2). These included ease of balancing work and family responsibilities (EOB), satisfaction with role performance (SWRP), psychological distress, turnover intent, and family and life satisfaction.

Both higher ease of balancing and greater satisfaction with role performance were significantly correlated with lower WIFG for those in the more individualistic Anglo and Latin European countries (i.e., Australia, Canada, the United States, Spain, and Israel). In addition, there was a significant negative relationship between ease of balancing and WIFG for Taiwan. Similarly, there was a significant positive correlation between WIFG and psychological distress for those in the more individualistic Anglo and Latin European countries. In addition to this, however, for the Indian subsample, greater psychological distress was associated with both higher WIFG and higher FIWG. With the exception of Australia, this pattern also held for turnover intent. That is, there were significant positive correlations between WIFG and turnover intent for Canada, India, Israel, Spain, and the United States and a significant positive correlation between FIWG and turnover intent for India only. There were negative correlations between WIFG and both family and life satisfaction for four countries, namely Australia, Israel, Turkey, and the United States. In the case of Canada and Spain, the correlations were very close to the cut off point. China was an anomaly in that there was a significant positive correlation between family satisfaction and WIFG.

W-F Guilt as a Mediator of the Relationships Between W-F Conflict and Outcomes

Lastly, the issue of whether W-F guilt mediated the relationships between WFC and outcomes (RQ8) was addressed. It was expected that W-F guilt would act as an intervening variable or mechanism that explained why WFC resulted in detrimental outcomes. Because they had been demonstrated to have measurement equivalence/invariance for culture (see Chapter 2), the three particular outcome variables that were chosen for investigation were turnover intent, family satisfaction, and life satisfaction. Previous research, done primarily in Anglo contexts, has indicated that WIFC and FIWC are associated with lower job, family, and life satisfaction (see Korabik, Lero, and Whitehead, 2008). However, with the exception of Korabik and McElwain (2011) no previous research has explored whether guilt mediates these relationships. It was postulated that WFC would result in feelings of W-F guilt, which would then lead to higher turnover intent, as well as to lower family and life satisfaction.

An SEM model, in which it was proposed that WIFG would mediate the relationships between WIFC and each of the three outcome variables, whereas FIWG would mediate the relationships between FIWC and each of the three outcome variables, was tested using AMOS (see Figure 17.1). The data from the baseline sample were fit to this model, and modifications were made to it based on the modification indices provided. A delta chi square test indicated that the modified baseline model fit the data significantly better than the original model did, $\Delta\chi^2$ (12) = 2108.25, $p < .01$.

Model fit tests were conducted to determine the fit indices for each individual country. The fit statistics for the baseline model (after modification) and the individual country models can be found in Table 17.3. The modified baseline model fit the data well. The data for the individualistic/egalitarian Anglo countries (Australia, Canada, and the United States), as well as that for Taiwan, also showed good fit to the model. The fit for Israel was marginal, and that for Spain could not be calculated due to the small sample size. The data from the collectivist/traditional countries, (China, India, Indonesia, and Turkey) did not fit the model well.

Following this, the standardized coefficients for the individual paths in the baseline and individual country models were examined to see if mediation was occurring (see Table 17.4). In the past, the recommended procedure for assessing mediation was that set forth by Baron and Kenny (1986). Recently, this has been called into question by a number of authors (e.g., Rucker, Preacher, Tormala, & Petty, 2011; Zhao, Lynch, and Chen, 2010). They suggest that the decision about whether or not mediation exists should be based solely upon whether the indirect effect is significant and that this should be determined

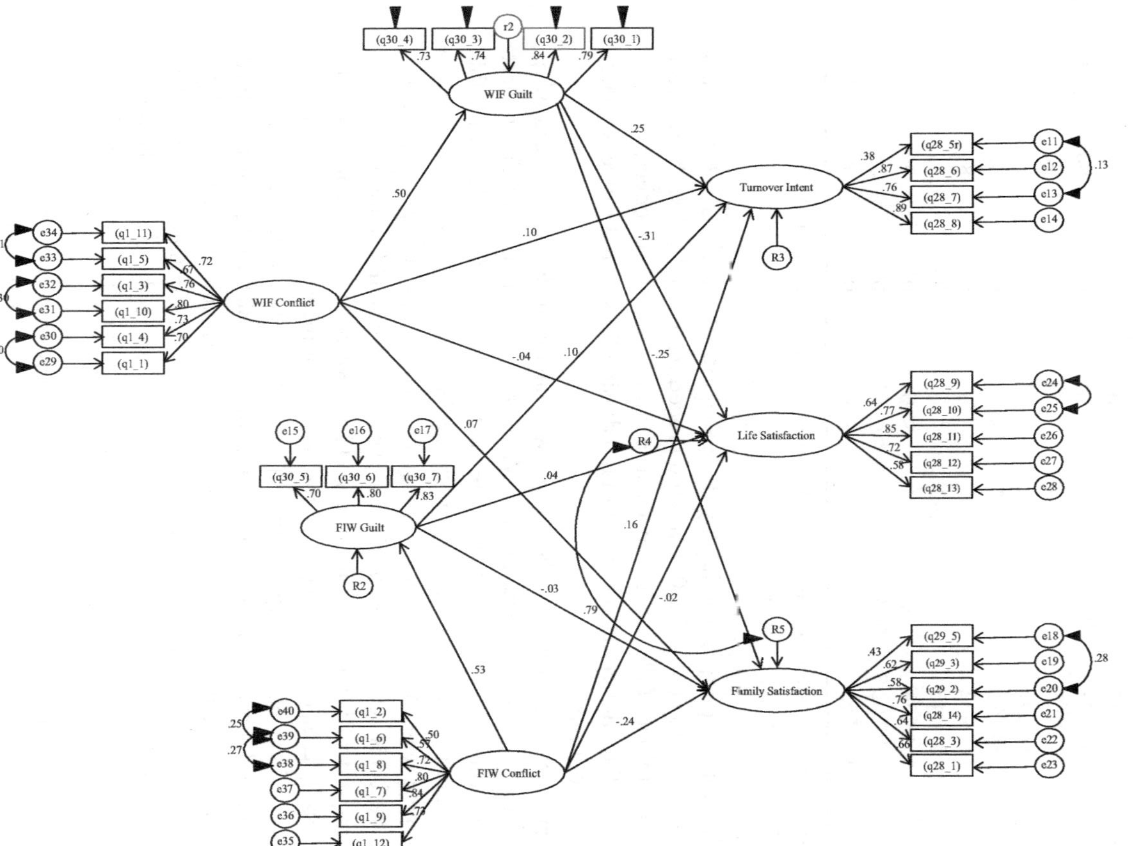

FIGURE 17.1 Standardized paramater estimates for the baseline model of W-F guilt as a mediator of the relationship between WFC and outcomes.

TABLE 17.3 Fit statistics for the single-country confirmatory factor analysis model with mediation.

Country	χ^2	*df*	χ^2/df	*p*	*RMSEA*	*TLI*	*CFI*
Baseline	5242.57	503	10.42	< .01	.06	.91	.90
Australia	917.88	503	1.82	< .01	.06	.90	.91
China	1131.55	503	2.25	< .01	.07	.80	.81
Canada	1183.91	503	2.35	< .01	.07	.90	.90
India	2348.21	503	4.67	< .01	.08	.80	.80
Indonesia	1428.62	503	2.84	< .01	.08	.80	.80
Israel	964.45	503	1.92	< .01	.06	.84	.86
Taiwan	1168.34	503	2.32	< .01	.07	.90	.90
Turkey	1682.02	503	3.34	< .01	.09	.75	.80
US	1017.63	503	2.02	< .01	.07	.90	.90

Note. RMSEA = Root Mean Square Error of Approximation; TLI = Tucker-Lewis Index; CFI = Comparative Fit Index

through bootstrapping rather than by the Sobel test (Rucker et al., 2011; Zhao et al., 2010). Zhao et al.'s (2010) two-step procedure, whereby first the indirect effect is examined, followed by an examination of the direct effect, was followed here. The indirect effect was computed using Shrout and Bolger's (2002) bootstrapping method.

A significant indirect effect indicates that W-F guilt is mediating the relationship between WFC and the outcome variable. When, in addition to this, the direct effect (or the relationship between WFC and the outcome variable) is nonsignificant, full mediation can be inferred. That is, the mediator (W-F guilt) is acting as the mechanism through which WFC is producing the outcome in question. By contrast, when the direct effect is significant, it is indicative of partial mediation. This means that W-F guilt is only a partial explanation for why WFC is predictive of the outcome variable, and for example, that other explanatory mechanisms or mediators might exist.

If the indirect effect is nonsignificant, mediation cannot be inferred. Zhao et al. distinguish between two different types of nonmediation. The first is called direct only nonmediation. This is where WFC is a significant predictor of the outcome variable, but the relationship is not mediated through W-F guilt. The second is called no effects nonmediation. This is where the direct relationship between WFC and the outcome is not significant nor is the relationship significantly mediated by W-F guilt.

As Table 17.4 illustrates, as expected, WIFC was positively and significantly related to WIFG for the baseline sample, as well as for all 10 countries. Furthermore, in six of the 10 countries WIFG appeared to be the mechanism through which higher WIFC resulted in higher turnover intention. With the exception of China, WIFG fully mediated the relationship between WIFC and turnover intent for the countries that were the most collectivist/traditional, which are the Latin European countries (Israel and Spain) and the Eastern/Asian countries (i.e., India, Indonesia, Taiwan, and Turkey). Direct only nonmediation occurred

TABLE 17.4 W-F guilt as a mediator of the relationship between WFC and outcome variables.

Paths	*Baseline*	*AU*	*CA*	*CN*	*IN*	*ID*	*IL*	*ES*	*TW*	*TR*	*US*
WIFC→WIFG	.50*	.68*	.76*	.31*	.59*	.24*	.54*	.64*	.40*	.70*	.79*
WIFG→TI	.25*	.06	.17	.04	.35*	.35*	.31*	.39*	.17*	.28*	.11
WIFC→TI (direct effect)	.10*	.10	.23*	.35*	.12	-.03	-.02	-.12	-.07	-.21	.37*
Indirect effect	.13*	.04	.13	.01	.21*	.08*	.16*	.25*	.07*	.19*	.09
Type of mediation	PM	NNM	DNM	DNM	FM	FM	FM	FM	FM	FM	DNM
WIFG→FS	-.25*	-.27*	-.43*	.47*	-.15	-.12	-.50*	-.02	-.14	-.31*	.10
WIFC→FS (direct effect)	.07	-.05	.14	-.02	.09	-.28*	.04	-.34*	-.12	-.24*	-.43*
Indirect effect	-.13*	-.18*	-.32*	.15	-.09	-.03	1.04*	-.01	-.06	-.22*	.08
Type of mediation	FM	FM	FM	NNM	NNM	DNM	FM	DNM	NNM	PM	DNM
WIFG→LS	-.31*	-.24*	-.23*	-.05	-.22*	-.08	-.51*	-.10	-.08	-.34*	.01
WIFC→LS (direct)	-.04	-.12	-.12	-.15	-.02	-.28*	-.03	-.26*	-.19*	-.04	-.47*
Indirect effect	-.16*	-.17	-.17	.36	-.13*	-.02	-.27*	-.07	.44	-.24*	.01
Type of mediation	FM	NNM	NNM	NNM	FM	DNM	FM	DNM	DNM	FM	DNM
FIWC→FIWG	.53*	.59*	.46*	.39*	.75*	.11	.48*	.52*	.50*	.19	.60*
FIWG→TI	.10*	-.24	-.08	.04	.30*	-.20*	.01	-.15	-.01	-.05	-.01
FIWC→TI (direct effect)	.16*	.34*	.04	.02	.02	.18*	-.15	.23*	.33*	.19*	.08
Indirect effect	.06*	-.14	-.04	.02	.22*	.30	.01	-.08	-.01	-.01	-.01
Type of mediation	PM	DNM	NNM	NNM	FM	DNM	NNM	DNM	DNM	DNM	NNM
FIWG→FS	-.03	.22	.04	-.04	-.32*	.11	.04	-.04	.16	-.12	-.29*
FIWC→FS (direct effect)	-.24*	-.54*	-.30*	-.17*	.07	.00	-.21	-.26*	-.23*	-.14*	.09
Indirect effect	-.01	.13	.02	-.02	-.24*	.01	.02	-.02	.08	-.02	-.17*
Type of mediation	DNM	DNM	DNM	DNM	FM	NNM	NNM	DNM	DNM	DNM	FM
FIWG→LS	.04	.03	.11	.32*	-.11	-.01	.24*	-.08	.04	-.15	.07
FIWC→LS (direct effect)	-.02	-.27*	-.32*	.07	.26*	-.05	-.19*	-.10	-.06	.01	-.11
Indirect effect	.02	-.02	.05	.13	.86	-.00	.11	-.04	.02	-.03	.04
Type of mediation	NNM	DNM	DNM	NNM	DNM	NNM	DNM	NNM	NNM	NNM	NNM

Note. TI = turnover intent; FS= family satisfaction; LS = life satisfaction; FM = full mediation; PM= partial mediation; DNM = direct only nonmediation; NNM = no effects nonmediation; values are standardized estimates; * = $p < .001$

for Canada, the United States, and China, whereas no effects nonmediation was present for Australia.

In addition, WIFG fully mediated the relationship between WIFC and family satisfaction for the baseline sample, Australia, Canada, and Israel, and partially mediated it for Turkey. There was direct only nonmediation for Indonesia, Spain, and the United States, and no effects nonmediation for China, India, and Taiwan. WIFG fully mediated the relationship between WIFC and life satisfaction for the baseline sample, as well as for India, Israel, and Turkey. However, nonmediation was the prevalent pattern in the remaining seven countries. Direct only nonmediation was present for Indonesia, Spain, Taiwan, and the United States, whereas no effects nonmediation occurred for Australia, Canada, and China.

FIWC was a significant predictor of FIWG for the baseline sample and all countries except for Indonesia and Turkey. FIWG partially mediated the relationship between FIWC and turnover intent for the baseline sample and fully mediated it for India. However, the principal pattern was one of nonmediation. Higher FIWC was directly predictive of increased turnover intent (direct only nonmediation) in the case of Australia, Indonesia, Spain, Taiwan, and Turkey. Moreover, no effects nonmediation was present for Canada, China, Israel, and the United States.

This pattern of nonmediation continued for the remaining two outcome variables. FIWG fully mediated the relationship between FIWC and family satisfaction for India and the United States. But, higher FIWC directly resulted in lower family satisfaction (direct only nonmediation) for the baseline sample and six of the countries (Australia, Canada, China, Spain, Taiwan, and Turkey). There was evidence of no effects nonmediation for the remaining two countries (Indonesia and Israel). There was no evidence that FIWG mediated the relationship between FIWC and life satisfaction. Direct only nonmediation was present for Australia, Canada, India, and Israel. No effects nonmediation occurred for the baseline sample and the remaining six countries (China, Indonesia, Spain, Taiwan, Turkey, and the United States).

In summary, the results from the baseline model showed that WIFG mediated the relationships between WIFC and all three of the outcome variables, whereas FIWG only mediated the relationship between FIWC and turnover intent. In all 10 countries, when parents experienced conflict from their work interfering with their family life, it resulted in their feeling guilty about their work interfering with their families. Moreover, for those in the more collectivist/traditional Latin European and Eastern/Asian countries (except China), these guilt feelings were significantly related to a greater intention to quit their jobs. In the United States, Canada, and China, although WIFC was directly related to increased turnover intent, WIFG was not a mechanism through which this occurred. Although WIFG did mediate the relationships between WIFC and family and life satisfaction, it did so in only about a third of the countries. In the case of both Israel and Turkey, feelings of WIFG were a significant mechanism through which the experience of greater WIFC resulted in lower family and life satisfaction. However, for

Australia and Canada, the experience of WIFG was related only to a decrease in family satisfaction and not to life satisfaction, whereas in India, it was related to a decrease in life satisfaction but not family satisfaction. In addition, although there was no mediation by WIFG, higher WIFC had a direct negative effect on both family and life satisfaction in Indonesia, Spain, and the United States, as well as on life, but not family, satisfaction in Taiwan.

There was very little evidence that FIWG was a mechanism through which FIWC affected any of the three outcome variables. The exceptions were that FIWG fully mediated the relationships between FIWC and turnover intent for India and between FIWC and family satisfaction for India and the United States. Instead, the prevailing pattern was that in about half of the countries FIWC was directly associated with the outcome variables, with the remainder of countries showing no effects nonmediation. The failure to find mediation through FIWG could possibly be because family interference with work (whether it be related to conflict or guilt) is far less prevalent than work interference with family.

Discussion

This study was the first to use a multi-method approach that combined qualitative and quantitative methods to investigate W-F guilt. It was also the first to include a cross-cultural comparison of 10 countries from different parts of the globe. Moreover, in contrast to most previous research on W-F guilt, our sample of employed parents consisted of both men and women and those in both managerial and nonmanagerial positions. The quantitative measure used in this research was based on the conceptualization of W-F guilt as a bidirectional construct. The measure not only had excellent reliability and validity, but also was shown to have measurement equivalence for gender and culture.

Paralleling what has been found previously for WFC, the guilt reported because work interfered with family life was greater than the guilt experienced because family interfered with work. Moreover, this was the case in every country that was studied. This is consistent with past qualitative research that has indicated that more guilt is felt about neglecting one's family than about neglecting one's work (McElwain, 2008).

Israel and Turkey had the lowest levels of WIFG, whereas Australia, Canada, and China, three countries with high work demands, had the highest. FIWG was the lowest in Turkey, and it was also lower in the more individualistic/egalitarian Anglo and Latin European countries than in the more collectivist/traditional Asian countries. This may be because of the high importance placed on the family in Asian countries. Surprisingly, except for the association between vertical collectivism and WIFG in China, there were no relationships between either WIFG or FIWG and individualism-collectivism for any countries.

Men and women did not differ in their likelihood of experiencing W-F guilt. This finding is consistent with a recent review of the literature on gender and

W-F guilt, based primarily on literature from North America (Korabik, 2005). It concluded that despite stereotypes that women are more prone to W-F guilt than men, there are few actual gender differences in W-F guilt. The data from Project 3535 demonstrate that this absence of gender differences is generalizable across cultures. Gender-role ideology was significantly associated with W-F guilt, however. In general, except in Turkey, parents with more egalitarian gender-role beliefs reported less WIFG as well as less FIWG.

In terms of demographics, the results of this study indicated that living in an extended family situation exacerbated FIWG but not WIFG. This might be due to the mere fact that when more family members share a household, there is more potential for guilt-provoking situations to occur. Although living in an extended family was positively associated with FIWG in every country, this might help to explain why levels of FIWG were highest in the Asian countries where extended family living arrangements are more common.

Full-time workers had higher WIFG than part-time workers except in three of the Asian countries. Although a weak finding, the data from 5 of the 10 countries (Australia, Canada, India, Spain, and the United States) support the findings of Nevill and Damico (1977) that older women report less W-F guilt than younger women. This is most probably because most W-F guilt is attributable to feeling that one has shortchanged one's children and that child-rearing responsibilities decrease as one gets older.

Within-domain effects between WFC and W-F guilt were very common. Both time- and strain-based WIFC were significantly and positively correlated with WIFG in all countries except Indonesia. Moreover, both time- and strain-based FIWC were significantly and positively correlated with FIWG in all countries except Indonesia and Turkey. Contrary to Morgan and King's (2012) assertion, cross-domain effects for both WIFG and FIWG were present only for India. Surprisingly, there were no significant correlations between work-to-family or family-to-work positive spillover and WIFG or FIWG for any country.

Within-domain effects between role overload and W-F guilt were common, but they tended to be stronger for the work domain than for the family domain. Moreover, the positive relationship between work overload and WIFG did not generalize to three of the Asian countries (i.e., Indonesia, China, and Taiwan). This may be because in these cultures working long hours does not provoke feelings of guilt because it is seen as a way of contributing to the welfare of one's family. Likewise, family overload was associated with higher FIWG only in three of the Asian countries (i.e., India, China, and Taiwan) plus Australia. As with WFC, cross-domain effects were apparent only for India. There were significant effects for job and family control only for the United States, where higher amounts of both job and family control were related to lower WIFG and higher family control was related to lower FIWG.

In terms of outcome variables, there was a general pattern such that for those in the more individualistic/egalitarian Anglo and Latin European countries, higher

WIFG was directly associated with several negative outcomes. These included lower ease of balancing, family satisfaction, life satisfaction, and satisfaction with role performance, as well as greater psychological distress and higher turnover intentions. The exceptions to this were that WIFG was not related to turnover intentions in Australia. It was, however, detrimental to ease of balancing in Taiwan and to family and life satisfaction in Turkey. By contrast, in China there was an association between higher WIFG and greater family satisfaction. Finally, in India both greater WIFG and greater FIWG were associated with greater psychological distress.

Overall, there was some indication that W-F guilt did act as a mechanism that explained why the experience of WFC resulted in detrimental outcomes. This was the strongest for WIFG as it related to turnover intent and weaker for outcomes related to satisfaction. Looked at another way, findings of no effects non-mediation were not very common, and they were primarily confined to FIWG as a mediator of the relationship between FIWC and life satisfaction. In the majority of cases, W-F guilt either acted as a mediator (full or partial) of the relationships between WFC and the outcomes, or, as had been found in previous research, WFC was directly related to the outcomes in the absence of mediation. Only in the instance of WIFG mediating the relationship between WIFC and turnover intentions, however, was there a clear distinction between those countries in which mediation occurred (the more collectivistic/traditional Latin European and Asian ones, except for China) and those where only a direct relationship existed (Canada, the United States, and China). Many factors can impact on whether or not mediation effects are found, including measurement precision, the strength of the relationship between the independent variable and the mediator, sample size and the power to detect effects, and the presence of suppressor variables or other unmeasured mediator variables (Rucker et al., 2011; Zhao et al., 2010). All of these may have affected the present findings. As this is the first study to explore the issue of whether W-F guilt mediates relationships between WFC and outcomes using a cross-national data set, further research is certainly warranted.

There are some limitations to this research. Fewer significant effects were found related to FIWG than for WIFG, perhaps because of a restriction of range on the FIW dimension. In addition, because this research is correlational in nature, causal conclusions cannot be drawn from it. Thus, for example, it cannot be determined whether W-F guilt is an antecedent or an outcome of WFC. In addition, unmeasured variables may have affected the findings, particularly those related to the mediation analysis. Research on W-F guilt is still in its infancy, and much more work needs to be done before we can fully understand its impact.

Conclusion

The results of this study clearly illustrate that W-F guilt affects working parents in all parts of the world. Moreover, with the exception of Turkey, in every country studied, those with traditional attitudes about women's roles were more likely to experience W-F guilt (both WIFG and FIWG) than those with more egalitarian attitudes. These findings imply that the promotion of more egalitarian gender-role attitudes will help not only to elevate women's status, but also to alleviate the W-F guilt experienced by working parents.

In every country in this study, the guilt due to work interference with family (WIFG) was greater than that due to family interference with work (FIWG). The findings presented here suggest that workplace interventions aimed at reducing work demands and overload, as well as the provision of more part-time options, may be effective in helping to decrease WIFG, especially for those in Anglo and Latin European countries. In terms of lessening FIWG, our results indicate that strategies aimed at reducing family demands/overload, as well as those that teach individuals how to better cope with the guilt feelings that arise from extended family living may be beneficial, particularly for those residing in Asian countries where levels of FIWG are the highest.

Overall, within-domain relationships between W-F guilt and both role overload and WFC were stronger than cross-domain relationships. The exception to this was India, where cross-domain relationships were prevalent. This suggests that strategies aimed at reducing within-domain role overload and WFC (e.g., through increased control and social support) may help to diminish W-F guilt. For example, providing greater job control and work-related social support may help reduce one's job overload and WIFC, thereby decreasing WIFG. Likewise, greater family control and family-related social support, by lessening family overload and FIWC, may help to lower FIWG. These possibilities should be explored in future research.

There was an association between WIFG and several negative outcomes (i.e., lower ease of balancing, family satisfaction, life satisfaction, and satisfaction with role performance, as well as higher psychological distress and turnover intentions). This was particularly true for those in the more individualistic/egalitarian Anglo and Latin European countries.

Finally, the very important issue of whether W-F guilt mediated the relationships between WFC and negative outcomes was addressed. There was very little evidence of mediation for family and life satisfaction and what did exist was inconsistent across countries. However, in six countries (i.e., Israel, Spain, Turkey, India, Indonesia, and Taiwan) WIFG fully mediated the relationship between WIFC and turnover intent. Thus, for those in the more collectivist/traditional Latin European and Eastern/Asian countries (except China), their guilt feelings about their work interfering with their family life explained why they wanted to quit their jobs. In the remaining countries there was no evidence of W-F guilt being a mediator. Instead, in the United States, Canada, and China, higher WIFC was directly related to increased turnover intent, but WIFG was not a mechanism through which this occurred. And, in Australia, neither WIFC nor WIFG predicted turnover intent. This finding suggests that in non-Anglo cultures, organizations that wish to reduce their turnover levels need to pay particular attention to reducing the guilt feelings their employees feel when their work interferes with their family lives.

The findings from this study are important for advancing future theory and research on W-F guilt. They also have many implications for the formulation of interventions at the individual, family, corporate, and societal levels. Alleviating the W-F guilt experienced by employed mothers and fathers should improve their health, happiness, and productivity at home and at work, in addition to benefiting the well-being of families as a whole.

References

Ausubel, D. P. (1955). Relationships between shame and guilt in the socializing process. *Psychological Review, 62*(5), 378–390. doi:10.1037/h0042534

Aycan, Z., & Eskin, M. (2005). Relative contributions of childcare, spousal support, and organizational support in reducing work-family conflict for men and women: The case of Turkey. *Sex Roles, 53*(7), 453–471. doi:10.1007/s11199-005-7134-8

Banarjee, S. (2003). Double standards. *Businessline,* November 1–3.

Baron, R. M., & Kenny, D. A. (1986). The moderator-mediator distinction in social psychological research: Conceptual, strategic, and statistical considerations. *Journal of Personality and Social Psychology, 51,* 1173–1182.

Baumeister, R. F., Stillwell, A. M., & Heatherton, T. F. (1994). Guilt: An interpersonal approach. *Psychological Bulletin, 115*(2), 243–267. doi:10.1037/0033-2909.115.2.243

Bort, J., Pflock, A., & Renner, D. (2005). *Mommy guilt: Learn to worry less, focus on what matters most, and raise happier kids.* New York, NY: American Management Association.

Bui, L. S. (1999). Mothers in public relations: How are they balancing career and family? *Public Relations Quarterly, 44*(2), 23–26.

Chapman, F. S. (1987, February 16). Executive guilt: Who's taking care of the children? *Fortune,* 30–37. Retrieved from http://archive.fortune.com/magazines/fortune/fortune_archive/1987/02/16/68675/index.htm

Conlin, M. (2000). The new debate over working moms: As more moms choose to stay home, office life is again under fire. *Business Week, 3699,* 102–104.

Daly, K. J. (2001). Deconstructing family time: From ideology to lived experience. *Journal of Marriage and Family, 63*(2), 283–294. doi:10.1111/j.1741-3737.2001.00283.x

Elvin-Nowak, Y. (1999). The meaning of guilt: A phenomenological description of employed mothers' experiences of guilt. *Scandinavian Journal of Psychology, 40*(1), 73–83. doi:10.1111/1467-9450.00100

Ferguson, T. J., Stegge, H., Eyre, H. L., Vollmer, R., & Ashbaker, M. (2000). Context effects and the (mal)adaptive nature of guilt and shame in children. *Genetic, Social, and General Psychology Monographs, 126*(3), 319–345.

Glavin, P., Schieman, S., & Reid, S. (2011). Boundary-spanning work demands and their consequences for guilt and psychological distress. *Journal of Health and Social Behavior, 52*(1), 43–57. doi:10.1177/0022146510395023

Guendouzi, J. (2006). "The guilt thing": Balancing domestic and professional roles. *Journal of Marriage and Family, 68*(4), 901–909. doi:10.1111/j.1741-3737.2006.00303.x

Hochwarter, W. A., Perrewé, P. L., Meurs, J. A., & Kacmar, C. (2007). The interactive effects of work-induced guilt and ability to manage resources on job and life satisfaction. *Journal of Occupational Health Psychology, 12*(2), 125–135. doi:10.1037/1076-8998.12.2.125

Hoffman, M. L. (1982). Development of prosocial motivation: Empathy and guilt. In N. Eisenberg (Ed.), *The development of prosocial behaviour* (pp. 281–313). New York, NY: Academic Press.

Huang, T. P. (2004, August). *Work-family conflict of employees in business organizations in Taiwan*. Paper presented at the meeting of the International Association of Cross-Cultural Psychology, Xi'an, China.

Korabik, K. (2005, July). *Alleviating work-family conflict for women managers in a global context*. Paper presented at the meeting of the Eastern Academy of Management, Cape Town, South Africa.

Korabik, K. (2015). The intersection of gender and work-family guilt. In M. Mills (Ed.), *Gender and the work-family experience: An intersection of two domains* (pp. 141–157). New York, NY: Springer.

Korabik, K., & Lero, D. S. (2004, August). *A cross-cultural research project on the work-family interface: Preliminary findings*. Paper presented at the meeting of the International Association of Cross-Cultural Psychology, Xi'an, China.

Korabik, K., Lero, D. S., & Whitehead, D. L. (2008). (Eds.). *Handbook of work-family integration: Research, theory, and best practices*. San Diego, CA: Elsevier.

Korabik, K., & McElwain, A. (2011, April). *The role of work-family guilt in work-family conflict*. Paper presented at the annual meeting of the Society for Industrial/Organizational Psychology, Chicago, IL.

Kossek, E. E., Pichler, S., Bodner, T., & Hammer, L. B. (2011). Workplace social support and work-family conflict: A meta-analysis clarifying the influence of general and work-family-specific supervisor and organizational support. *Personnel Psychology*, *64*(2), 289–313. doi:10.1111/j.1744-6570.2011.01211.x

Kubany, E. S. (1994). A cognitive model of guilt typology in combat-related PTSD. *Journal of Traumatic Stress*, 7(1), 3–19. doi:10.1002/jts.2490070103

Kubany, E. S., Haynes, S. N., Abueg, F. R, Manke, F. P., Brennan, J. M., & Stahura, C. (1996). Development and validation of the Trauma-Related Guilt Inventory (TRGI). *Psychological Assessment*, *8*(4), 428–444. doi:10.1037/1040-3590.8.4.428

Livingston, B. A., & Judge, T. A. (2008). Emotional responses to work-family conflict: An examination of gender role orientation among working men and women. *Journal of Applied Psychology*, *93*(1), 207–216. doi:10.1037/0021-9010.93.1.207

Martinez, P., Carrasco, M. J., Aza, G., Blanco, A., & Espinar, I. (2011). Family gender role and guilt in Spanish dual-earner families. *Sex Roles*, *65*(11), 813–826. doi:10.1007/s11199-011-0031-4

Mawardi, A. (2004, April). *Work-family conflict in an Asian cultural context: The case of Indonesia*. Paper presented at the annual meting of the Society for Industrial/Organizational Psychology, Chicago, IL.

McElwain, A. (2008). *An examination of the reliability and validity of the Work-Family Guilt Scale* (Unpublished doctoral dissertation). University of Guelph, Guelph, ON.

McElwain, A., & Korabik, K. (2004). Work-family guilt. In M. Pitt-Catsouphes & E. Kossek (Eds.), *Work and family encyclopedia online*. Retrieved from http://www.bc.edu/bc_org/avp/wfnetwork/rft/wfpedia

McElwain, A., Korabik, K., & Chappell, D. B. (2005a, June). *The work-family guilt scale*. Poster presented at the annual meeting of the Canadian Psychological Association, Montreal, QC.

McElwain, A., Korabik, K., & Chappell, D. B. (2005b, June). *The impact of work-family conflict on work-family guilt*. Poster presented at the annual meeting of the Canadian Psychological Association, Montreal, QC.

Morgan, W. B., & King, E. B. (2012). The association between work-family guilt and pro- and anti-social work behavior. *Journal of Social Issues*, *68*(4), 684–703. doi:10.1111/j.1540-4560.2012.01771.x

Napholz, L. (2000). Balancing multiple roles among a group of urban midlife American Indian working women. *Health Care for Women International, 27*(4), 255–266. doi:10.1080/073993300245122

Netemeyer, R. G., Boles, J. S., & McMurrian, R. (1996). Development and validation of work-family conflict and work-family conflict scales. *Journal of Applied Psychology, 81*(4), 400–410. doi:10.1037/0021-9010.81.4.400

Nevill, D., & Damico, S. (1977). Developmental components of role conflict in women. *The Journal of Psychology: Interdisciplinary and Applied, 95*(2), 195–198. doi:10.1080/00223980.1977.9915879

O'Connor, L. E., Berry, J. W., & Weiss, J. (1999). Interpersonal guilt, shame, and psychological problems. *Journal of Social and Clinical Psychology, 18*(2), 181–203.

O'Connor, L. E., Berry, J. W., Weiss, J., Bush, M., & Sampson, H. (1997). Interpersonal guilt: The development of a new measure. *Journal of Clinical Psychology, 53*(7), 73–89.

Offer, S., & Schneider, B. (2011). Revisitng the gender gap in time use patterns: Multitasking and well-being among mothers and fathers in dual-earner families. *American Sociological Review, 76*(6), 809–833. doi:10.1177/0003122411425170

Pocock, B. (2003). *The work/life collision. What work is doing to Australians and what to do about it.* Sydney, Australia: Federation Press.

Pollock, E. J. (1997, March 10–13). Work and family (a special report): Regaining a balance—This is home; this is work. *Wall Street Journal (Eastern Edition)*.

Rajadhyaksha, U., & Desai, T. P. (2004, April). *Work family conflict in the Asian cultural context: The case of India.* Paper presented at the annual meting of the Society for Industrial/Organizational Psychology, Chicago, IL.

Rajadhyaksha, U., Huang, T-P., Mawardi, A., & Desai, T. P. (2011, July). *Gender-role ideology, work-family overload, conflict and guilt: Examining a path analysis model in three Asian countries.* Paper presented at the meeting of the International Association of Cross-Cultural Psychology, Istanbul, Turkey.

Rucker, D. D., Preacher, K. J., Tormala, Z. L., & Petty, R. E. (2011). Mediation analysis in social psychology: Current practices and new recommendations. *Social and Personality Psychology Compass, 5/6*, 359–371. doi:10.1111/j.1751-9004.2011.00355.x

Seagram, S., & Daniluk, J. C. (2002). It goes with the territory: The meaning and experience of maternal guilt for mothers of preadolescent children. *Women and Therapy, 25*(1), 61–88. doi:10.1300/J015v25n01_04

Shrout, P. E., & Bolger, N. (2002). Mediation in experimental and nonexperimental studies: New procedures and recommendations. *Psychological Methods,* 7, 422–445.

Simon, R. W. (1995). Gender, multiple roles, role meaning, and mental health. *Journal of Health and Social Behaviour, 36*(2), 182–194.

Somech, A., & Drach-Zahavy, A. (2004, April). *Work family conflict in the Middle Eastern cultural context: The case of Israel.* Paper presented at the annual meting of the Society for Industrial/Organizational Psychology, Chicago, IL.

Velgach, S., Ishaya, N., & Ayman, R. (2005, April). *A multi-method approach to investigate work-family conflict.* Paper presented at the annual meting of the Society for Industrial/Organizational Psychology, Los Angeles, CA.

Zahn-Waxler, C., Kochanska, G., Krupnick, J., & McKnew, D. (1990). Patterns of guilt in children of depressed and well mothers. *Developmental Psychology, 26*(1), 51–59. doi:10.1037/0012-1649.26.1.51

Zhao, X., Lynch, J. G. Jr, & Chen, O-M. (2010). Reconsidering Baron and Kenny: Myths and truths about mediation analysis. *Journal of Consumer Research, 37*, 197–206.

18

WORK-FAMILY CONFLICT AND POSITIVE SPILLOVER

Examining the Interaction of Gender, Gender-Role Ideology, and National Gender Equity Culture

Ujvala Rajadhyaksha

Introduction

Recent research on the work-family (W-F) interface has begun to include the positive as well as the negative aspects of relationships between the two domains (e.g., Greenhaus & Powell, 2006; Grzywacz & Marks, 2000). Given a rising trend in the percentage of women in the paid workforce worldwide, W-F research has explored for cross-cultural differences in the role of gender in work and family relationships. Extant literature, however, suggests few consistent gender patterns in the experience of WFC within specific national cultures, as well as in cross-cultural comparisons (Rajadhyaksha, Korabik, & Aycan, 2015). This could be explained partly by the fact that cross-cultural explorations have focused mainly on the cultural dimensions of individualism-collectivism, or the relative neglect of other more relevant dimensions such as gender egalitarianism or gender equity (Powell, Francesco, & Ling, 2009). It also may have to do with a preoccupation in the literature with testing for mean differences between men and women rather than treating gender more broadly as a psychosocial moderator variable and exploring interaction effects (Korabik, McElwain, & Chappell, 2008).

This chapter builds upon analyses in Chapter 13 on WFC and in Chapter 14 on W-F positive spillover by looking at gender-related variables. It also plugs an existing empirical gap in the literature by conducting an examination of the role of gender, gender-role ideology, and national gender equity culture (henceforth referred to as NGE) in both the positive and the negative aspects of the W-F interface. The goal of the chapter is to understand the manner in which the totality of the W-F experience, that is, work-to-family positive spillover (WTFS) and family-to-work positive spillover (FTWS), as well as time- and strain-based work-to-family conflict (TBWIF, SBWIF) and family-to-work conflict (TBFIW,

SBFIW), varies for men and women with different gender-role ideologies or attitudes across countries with varying levels of cultural emphasis on gender equity. In other words, by going beyond simply looking at differences in mean levels of WFC or positive spillover to looking at gender in conjunction with other gender-related attitudinal and culture variables (interaction effects), we are better able to understand the W-F experience.

Literature Review

Positive and Negative Aspects of the Work-Family Interface

The work-family interface is characterized by positive and negative relationships. Negative spillover, or what is commonly referred to as WFC (Greenhaus & Beutell, 1985), has dominated W-F research for many years. Increasingly though, positive relationships between work and family domains, such as positive spillover (Crouter, 1984), enrichment (Greenhaus & Powell, 2006), enhancement (Grzywacz & Marks, 2000), or facilitation (Sieber, 1974) have been identified. There is evidence that these must be distinguished from one another (see Chapter 14). WFC and work-family positive spillover (WFPS) have been found to be bidirectional in nature with work-interfering-with-family (WIF) and family-interfering-with-work (FIW), and similarly work-to-family (WTFS) and family-to-work (FTWS) positive spillover. WFC has been further found to occur along the dimensions of time, strain, and behavior (e.g., Frone, Russell, & Cooper, 1992; Gutek, Searle, & Klepa, 1991), while similar dimensions of WFPS are yet to make an appearance in the literature. Rather than treating conflict and positive spillover separately, empirical studies have increasingly begun to examine positive and negative relationships between work and family within the same study (e.g., Haar & Bardoel, 2008; Hill, 2005; Voydanoff, 2004). In keeping with this research tradition, this chapter examines the positive and negative aspects of the W-F interface simultaneously.

Gender and the Work-Family Interface

An increasing presence of women in the paid workforce has challenged the traditional division of roles, resources, and responsibilities between the work and family domains worldwide. Despite the fact that gender is entrenched within the W-F interface, examination of gender and W-F variables has been limited (Greenhaus & Powell, 2006). Within the literature one comes across several theoretical propositions about the role of gender in the W-F interface, such as the rational versus the gender-role explanations of conflict (Bagger, Li, & Gutek, 2008; Gutek Searle, & Klepa, 1991; Pleck, 1977), and the source attribution versus domain specificity explanations of enrichment (e.g., Shockley & Singla, 2011). As per the rational viewpoint (Gutek et al., 1991), the more the hours that one spends in a domain, the more potential there is for conflict to occur. This theory predicts that men should experience more work interference with family than women because they spend more time at work, whereas women should experience more family interference with work than men because they spend more time at home. According to gender-role theory (Pleck, 1977), individuals tend to identify more with sex-appropriate gender roles, and any interference from the opposite domain likely causes conflict. As a result, family demands will more likely affect work roles for women, whereas work demands will more likely spill over into the family for men. A review of empirical investigations of gender and WFC and WFPS however has shown few meaningful patterns in results of cross-cultural and single nation studies in the North American context and worldwide (Rajadhyaksha et al., 2015).

Moving Beyond Gender: Gender-Role Ideology

Mixed findings in studies on gender and the W-F interface have been attributed to an emphasis in research on exploring for sex-based differences without adequately accounting for gender-related intervening or interacting factors (e.g., Korabik et al., 2008). Rajadhyaksha et al. (2015) suggest the inclusion of "gender-role ideology" in W-F research. Gender-role ideology (GRI) refers to an individual's attitudes toward what are proper societal roles for men and women. According to Gibbons, Hamby, and Dennis (1997) a potential universal dimension of GRI is represented by a modern, egalitarian ideology at one end and a traditional ideology on the other. Individuals with traditional GRI tend to believe that women should give priority to family responsibilities and men to work responsibilities (Gutek, Searle, & Klepa, 1991). By contrast, nontraditional or egalitarian individuals believe in a more equal role distribution for men and women. They are less likely to over-emphasize men's careers or object to women's employment.

As a construct, GRI is distinct from gender in the sense that both men and women can have either traditional or egalitarian attitudes (Korabik et al., 2008). One need not assume that men will be more egalitarian and women more traditional or vice versa. However, role expansion resulting from women's exposure to the labor force and to education could foster more egalitarian GRI (Smith-Lovin & Tickamyer, 1978). In a comparative study of attitudes toward women's employment between Hungary and the United States, Panayotova and Brayfield (1997) found that across the two national contexts, women were more supportive of women's employment relative to men. However, the level of support for women's employment was in general higher for both women and men in the United States as compared to their Hungarian counterparts, despite the Hungarian government's policy of full employment during communist rule.

In a more recent study comparing the GRI of women and men in Taiwan and coastal China, Tu and Liao (2005) found that urbanization had a more significant impact on women's attitudes than on men's attitudes, especially in coastal China as compared to Taiwan since that region had witnessed more growth and development in recent years. Greater propensity for men to have traditional gender-role attitudes relative to women was also found by Pimentel (2006) in his study of husbands and wives in urban China. Pimentel found that over cohorts, while husbands' GRI had become more traditional, possibly as a reaction to decreasing job opportunities for men in reformist China along with increasing expectations of equality among women, wives' GRI had stayed constant and was more egalitarian than that of husbands. An outcome of this difference in GRI of husbands and wives was declining levels of marital satisfaction over time.

An interaction between GRI and gender has been observed in several W-F and dual-earner family studies. For example, Mickelson, Claffey, and Williams (2006) found that GRI, along with gender, can moderate the link between spousal support and marital quality. Emotional spousal support was a better predictor of marital satisfaction and less marital conflict for traditional women and egalitarian men, while emotional and instrumental spousal support was a better predictor of marital satisfaction for egalitarian women and traditional men. Bielby and Bielby (1992) found that the more egalitarian the GRIs of husband-wife pairs was, the less likely they were to adopt gender-stereotypic decisions regarding relocation for jobs such as for instance the wife refusing to accept a job in a different location because it would mean job loss for her husband. Frisco and Williams (2003) found that women with egalitarian GRI in dual-earner marriages were more likely to experience a sense of unfairness when they felt that they were doing more than their spouse. On the other hand, the more egalitarian the husband's GRI relative to the wife, the weaker has been found to be the relationship between job-role quality and distress (James, Barnett, & Brennan, 1998).

To the extent that attitudes are molded by environmental influences, GRI has been found to be affected by national context, cultural values, and economic variables. Harris, Firestone, and Bryan (2006) compared gender-role attitudes between Mexico, Canada, and the United States and found that in general, Mexicans were slightly more likely to exhibit traditional attitudes and gender-role behavior that was congruent with their biological gender. Further, in Canada and the United States, traditional attitudes were more likely to be associated with men rather than women as compared to Mexico. Parboteeah, Hoegl, and Cullen (2008) conducted a cross-national study of national cultural values and managers' traditional gender-role attitudes. They found that managers' traditional gender-role attitudes were positively associated with national cultural values of power distance and uncertainty avoidance, and negatively associated with national cultural values of gender egalitarianism, degree of regulation of the economy, and degree of educational attainment.

Moving Beyond Gender at the Individual Level: Gender Egalitarianism and National Gender Inequality

Confusing results from cross-cultural examinations of gender and W-F variables could be attributed to the fact that culture tends to be viewed in "culture-as-nations" terms relative to "culture-as-dimensions." Even when culture dimensions are used, these tend to focus heavily on the values of individualism-collectivism, to the relative neglect of other cultural dimensions, such as gender egalitarianism, that may have a closer bearing to the W-F experiences of men and women worldwide (Powell et al., 2009).

Gender egalitarianism, defined as "the degree to which an organization or a society minimizes gender role differences while promoting gender equality" (House & Javidan, 2004, p. 12), is likely to cause variations in the WFC and WFPS of men and women through its differential promotion of differences in W-F variables in low versus high gender egalitarianism societies (Powell et al., 2009). In addition to cultural gender egalitarianism, national policy contexts that affect working conditions, especially of women workers, and institutional factors that impact support for work and family demands, could cause variations in the W-F experiences of men and women (e.g., Guan, Rajadhyaksha, & McElroy, 2011; Ollier-Malaterre, Valcour, den Dulk, & Kossek, 2013; Ray, Gornick, & Schmitt, 2010).

Empirical studies support the notion that macro variables, such as gender egalitarianism, national paid leave policies, and national gender inequality are associated with gender differences in W-F experiences. Steiber's (2009) study of 23 European countries found that those countries that had high affluence, high unemployment, and greater "emancipation pressure" displayed higher levels of strain-based WIF conflict. Emancipation pressure was measured in the study as the extent to which respondents in the country agreed with the statement: "Men should take as much responsibility as women for home and children." Steiber's study also found that women were more likely to face time-based WIF in countries that offered good child care support.

Somewhat contrary to Steiber's findings were those found in Öun's (2012) study of four Nordic countries—Denmark, Finland, Norway, and Sweden. Öun found support for a negative relationship between gender equity at the household level and WFC. Although women in general reported higher WFC than men, there were between-country differences. Conflict was higher in Finland compared to the other three Nordic countries. While Öun explained this result in terms of the relatively greater gender inequity and lesser integration of women in to the workforce in Finland, Steiber attributed the higher WFC in countries with higher gender equity to emancipatory pressure.

Allen et al.'s (2014) study of working married parents with children under the age of 5 from 12 industrialized nations found some support for the impact of national paid leave policies on WFC. WFC had a small, but significant, negative relationship with paid sick leave, and almost no significant relationship with paid parental leave or paid annual leave. However, family-supportive organizational perceptions and family-supportive supervision significantly moderated the relationship between national paid leave policies and WFC, with paid leave proving to be more beneficial when employees' perception of support was higher.

Lyness and Kropf (2005), using the survey responses of 505 managers from 20 European countries along with the United Nations Gender Development

Index Scores of national gender equality for these countries, found that national gender equality was positively related to perceptions of organizational W-F support, which in turn created positive work-life balance for the managers in the sample. Similarly, Beham, Drobnič, and Präg (2012), in a study of professional and nonprofessional service employees in five Western European countries, found that utilization of organizational W-F resources varied based on levels of national gender equality and welfare state regimes, being higher in countries with greater gender equality, such as Sweden and the Netherlands, as compared to countries with lower gender equality, such as Portugal.

Studies have indicated that economic gender inequality and cultural gender inegalitarianism are related. Mandel's (2009) study analyzed data from 14 advanced countries on different forms of gender inequality, such as women's labor force participation and continuity of employment, women's economic well-being and financial autonomy, and women's occupational attainments and economic rewards. The study found that distinctive profiles of gender inequality can be obtained shaped by gender-role ideologies and welfare state strategies prevalent within the countries. As a result, different societies could have elements of gender egalitarianism alongside gender inegalitarianism.

In another cross-cultural analysis of 53 countries, Yeganeh and May (2011) found that various aspects of the gender gap, measured in terms of women's economic participation and opportunity, educational attainment, political empowerment, and health and survival, was higher when the cultural value of "conservatism" (that supports a status quo in gender roles among other things) was high. On the other hand, the gender gap was lower for countries higher on the cultural value of "autonomy." Perhaps for this reason, Ollier-Malaterre et al. (2013) recommend considering interactions between cultural and institutional macro factors pertaining to gender in cross-national W-F research.

A few recent studies have examined the impact of "macro" elements of gender on the W-F interface by considering cultural gender egalitarianism and gender inequality together in analyses. For example, Ruppanner and Huffman (2014) conducted a 31-country cross-national study using hierarchical logistic linear models to show that a national context of gender empowerment can affect the likelihood of experiencing nonwork-work and work-nonwork conflict at the individual and national levels. They devised a measure of country-level gender empowerment by relying on UN data from several sources for a variety of measures such as percentage of parliamentary seats held by women, the ratio of female to male earned income, and women's employment status. In another 36-country cross-national study of work-life balance (WLB) that used multilevel hierarchical linear modeling for analyses, Lyness and Judiesch (2014) developed a gender egalitarianism score based on the UN Gender Inequality Index, Project GLOBE research country scores for gender egalitarianism, and a composite measure based on World Values Survey items. Their study examined the relationship between employee gender, supervisor's perceptions of employees' WLB, and societal gender egalitarianism, and found significant interactions between the three variables. In high egalitarian societies, supervisors ratings of men's and women's WLB was similar, however in low gender egalitarianism societies, women's WLB was rated as being lower than men's WLB by supervisors. The cultural value of gender egalitarianism explained the majority of variation in supervisors' appraisals of women's WLB, while economic gender inequality was linked to women's self-reported WLB.

In keeping with current developments in the literature, in this cross-cultural study we aim to organize the countries from which data was gathered on a macro dimension of gender that we refer to as "national gender equity culture" (NGE). We use multiple indicators of a country's values of gender egalitarianism and gender inequality for the purpose.

Studies on the joint effects of gender, GRI, and NGE on WFC and WFPS are almost nonexistent. The literature review earlier in the chapter suggests that macro variables such as national gender equity and cultural gender egalitarianism have the potential to impact WFC and WFPS directly, as well as through their interactions with gender and gender-role attitudes of individuals. However, few researchers have examined the relationship among these variables within the same study. In this study we aim to fill this gap. The main purpose of the study is to explore how the positive and negative aspects of the W-F interface vary as a function of gender, gender-role ideology, and national gender equity culture. In other words, are there significant interactions between gender, gender-role ideology and national gender equity culture that can explain differences in the experience of the positive and negative aspects of the W-F interface? Thus, we aim to ask the question: Are WTFS and FTWS and WIF and FIW along time-based and strain-based dimensions different for men and women, given differences in gender-role attitudes and national gender contexts?

Method

Measures

The measures used in this study were WFC, positive spillover, gender-role ideology, and gender. Please consult Chapter 2 for information about how these were measured. In addition, a composite was created to assess national gender equity culture.

National Gender Equity Culture

Using a recent approach adopted by Lyness and Judiesch (2014) of relying on multiple indicators of a country's gender egalitarianism, a composite measure of national gender equity culture (NGE) was computed for each of the 10 countries. NGE was calculated as the average of the country's score on four different measures. The first of these was the average of Project GLOBE's "as is" (practice) and "should be" (values) score on gender egalitarianism (House & Javidan, 2004). The second was the score on the Gender Equity Index (GEI) 2012 developed

TABLE 18.1 Calculation of national gender equity scores.

COUNTRY	*GLOBE 'AS IS'*	*GLOBE 'SHOULD BE'*	*GLOBE AVG*[6]	*GEI*[5]	*GEI final score—6 point scale*[5]	*GII—score*[3]	*GII-rev*	*GII final score—6 point scale*[5]	*GII—rank*[3]	*WVS*	*WVS final*[9]	*NGE avg*[11]	*Final NGE score*[12]	*Final NGE rank*[13]
AUSTRALIA	3.40	5.02	4.21	80	4.80	.11	.89	5.32	19	2.72	5.43	4.94	2.06	1
CANADA[1,8]	3.70	5.11	4.41	80	4.80	.14	.86	5.18	23	2.83	5.66	5.01	1.99	1
INDIA	2.90	4.51	3.71	37	2.22	.56	.44	2.62	127	2.05	4.09	3.16	3.84	3
INDONESIA[8]	3.26	3.89	3.58	62	3.72	.50	.50	3.00	103	2.29	4.58	3.72	3.28	3
ISRAEL[2,10]	3.19	4.71	3.95	75	4.50	.10	.90	5.39	17	0.00	0.00	4.62	2.39	2
US	3.34	5.06	4.20	72	4.32	.26	.74	4.43	47	2.66	5.32	4.57	2.43	2
SPAIN	2.99	4.82	3.91	81	4.86	.10	.90	5.40	16	2.69	5.38	4.89	2.12	1
TAIWAN[4]	3.18	4.06	3.62	71	4.29	.06	.95	5.67	5	2.43	4.87	4.61	2.39	2
TURKEY	2.89	4.50	3.70	45	2.70	.36	.64	3.84	69	2.03	4.06	3.58	3.43	3
CHINA	3.05	3.68	3.37	64	3.84	.20	.80	4.79	37	2.31	4.63	4.16	2.85	2

Note. [1] = Canada GLOBE scores are for English-speaking population only, French-speaking population scores not available.
[2] = Israel GLOBE scores are total scores, no separate scores for Jewish population available.
[3] = GII scores and ranks are for 2013, lower score means more equal gender culture.
[4] = Taiwan GEI and GII score and rank not available from Social Watch and UN report, taken instead from National Statistics, Republic of China (Taiwan) website.
[5] = For GEI and GII final scores—lower score means less equity between men and women.
[6] = GLOBE average is the average of "as is" and "should be" scores. Lower score means less egalitarian gender culture.
[7] = WVS 2010–2014 questions 45–54, 3-point scale, low score means less equality between men and women.
[8] = Scores for Canada and Indonesia taken from WVS Wave 5 (questions 44, 60, 61, 62, 63).
[9] = Average score of WVS (questions 45–54) * 2 to get on to 6 point scale.
[10] = No data available on WVS for Israel, so final NGE score computed as average of GLOBE, GEI, and GII scores.
[11] = 6-point scale for gender culture—lower scores means less equal culture for men and women.
[12] = Final NGE score reversed to make it consistent with GRI scale used in study—lower scores imply more equal NGE culture.
[13] = Final NGE scores: 1 = High NGE, 2 = Moderate NGE, 3 = Low NGE.

by Social Watch that measures the gap between women and men in education, the economy, and political empowerment (GEI by country, 2012). The third was the score on the Gender Inequality Index (GII) 2013, which is a composite measure developed by the United Nations Development Programme that reflects inequality in achievement between women and men in the three dimensions of reproductive health, empowerment, and labor market (Human Development Reports, 2014). The fourth was the score on the World Values Survey (WVS) measure of patriarchal values. This was based on items such as, "If a woman earns more money than her husband, it's almost certain to cause problems" (World Values Survey Association, 2005–2008, World Values Survey Association, 2010–2014). High scores on the final composite NGE measure indicated a less equal gender culture and a higher gender gap. See Table 18.1 for details on the composite NGE measure.

Analyses

Multivariate analysis of covariance (MANCOVA) was used to assess main and interaction effects of the independent variables of gender, three aspects of GRI (i.e., attitude toward division of work and family roles, attitude toward importance of men's careers, and attitude toward women's employment, or GRI1, GRI2, and GRI3, respectively) and NGE on multiple W-F interface dependent variables, namely TBWIF, SBWIF, TBFIW, SBFIW, WTFS, and FTWS. Covariates included respondent age and number of children. Pearson correlations between all of the dependent variables (see Table 18.2) were found to be significant and in the moderate range thereby ascertaining appropriateness of MANCOVA analyses for the dependent variables (Meyers, Gamst, & Guarino, 2006).

Box's test of equality of covariances was significant (M = 1773.49, $p < .001$), thereby not supporting a required assumption for MANCOVA. However, examination of the inter-item covariance matrix for W-F dependent variables across corresponding levels of subgroups used in analyses indicated that values were within 20–40% of each other for a majority of the variables. Thus, it was assumed that MANCOVA results would be reliable (Huberty & Petoskey, 2000).

Before conducting MANCOVA analyses, the respondents were divided into two groups based on median values for each GRI variable—"1" for low scores on GRI indicating an egalitarian attitude and "2" for high scores on GRI indicating traditionalism. In keeping with the tradition of United Nations, EU, and other reports that classify countries in to high, moderate, and low income countries, the countries in this study were split in to three groups based on percentile NGE values. The resultant groups were "1" for countries with high gender equity culture (Australia, Canada, and Spain), "2" for countries with moderate gender equity culture (the United States, Israel, Taiwan, and China) and "3" for countries with low gender equity culture (Turkey, Indonesia, and India). Table 18.3 gives descriptive statistics across levels of NGE, GRI, and gender.

TABLE 18.2 Intercorrelations among variables.

	TBWIF	*SBWIF*	*TBFIW*	*SBFIW*	*WEF*	*FEW*	*GRI1*	*GRI2*	*GRI3*	*NGE*	*Gender*	*Age*	*NOC*
TBWIF	(.82)												
SBWIF	.66**	(.80)											
TBFIW	.46**	.42**	(.74)										
SBFIW	.34**	.39**	.65**	(.84)									
WTFS	-.11**	-.14**	.08**	.09**	(.69)								
FTWS	-.16**	-.18**	-.13**	-.15**	.49**	(.67)							
GRI1	-.04*	-.01	.14**	.27**	.19**	.10**	(.87)						
GRI2	-.04	.01	.17**	.26**	.12**	.05*	.74**	(.80)					
GRI3	.14**	.15**	.21**	.29**	.10**	.04*	.66**	.60**	(.78)				
NGE	-.10**	-.04	.13**	.27**	.35**	.23**	.68**	.52**	.45**	1			
Gender	-.06**	.03	.06**	.01	.05**	.05**	-.07**	-.03	-.11**	-.03	1		
Age	-.06**	-.04*	-.13**	-.16**	.01	-.01	-.12**	-.13**	-.14**	-.14**	-.01	1	
NOC	-.01	-.02	-.04	-.07**	.02	-.04*	-.13**	-.15**	-.10**	-.19**	-.01	.33**	1
Mean	3.50	3.62	2.83	2.67	2.99	3.71	2.96	3.16	3.20	2.87	1.55	38.86	1.86
S.D.	1.19	1.20	1.05	1.09	0.84	0.77	1.36	1.30	1.20	0.68	0.50	7.48	0.97

Note. $^{*}p < .05$ (2-tailed); $^{**}p < 0.01$ level (2-tailed); reliability scores for scale based measures depicted in parentheses along diagonal, N = 2708

TABLE 18.3 Descriptive statistics across NGE, GRI, and gender.

		NGE = 1—High national gender equity											
		GRI 1—Division of work/family roles				*GRI 2—Importance of men's careers*				*GRI 3—Women's employment*			
		Egalitarian		*Traditional*		*Egalitarian*		*Traditional*		*Egalitarian*		*Traditional*	
		Male	*Female*	*Male*	*Female*	*Male*	*Female*	*Male*	*Female*	*Male*	*Female*	*Male*	*Female*
TBWIF	*M*	4.07	3.70	4.50	4.21	4.08	3.70	4.27	3.93	4.01	3.58	4.27	4.15
	SD	1.06	1.25	0.99	1.25	1.08	1.26	0.90	1.07	1.11	1.25	0.96	1.17
SBWIF	*M*	3.82	3.80	3.91	3.91	3.76	3.81	4.33	3.69	3.69	3.70	4.05	4.14
	SD	1.15	1.26	1.27	1.19	1.15	1.28	1.12	0.87	1.18	1.26	1.08	1.19
TBFIW	*M*	2.72	2.81	2.82	3.09	2.70	2.81	2.97	3.02	2.63	2.78	2.90	2.97
	SD	0.92	1.07	0.89	1.00	0.89	1.08	1.02	0.95	0.90	1.09	0.91	1.00
SBFIW	*M*	2.31	2.31	2.36	2.89	2.27	2.31	2.70	2.82	2.24	2.26	2.46	2.59
	SD	0.94	1.01	0.98	1.02	0.91	1.01	1.09	1.02	0.88	0.98	1.02	1.10
WTFS	*M*	2.63	2.76	2.74	2.43	2.62	2.75	2.79	2.55	2.63	2.81	2.65	2.55
	SD	0.67	0.74	0.81	1.02	0.68	0.75	0.70	0.71	0.67	0.75	0.70	0.72
FTWS	*M*	3.54	3.65	3.39	3.47	3.54	3.63	3.44	3.79	3.53	3.68	3.51	3.53
	SD	0.72	0.75	1.06	1.15	0.73	0.76	0.90	0.80	0.73	0.72	0.79	0.90
	Valid *N*	311	303	26	10	298	296	38	14	212	237	124	73
	Total *N*	650				646				646			

		NGE = 2—Moderate national gender equity											
		GRI 1—Division of work/family roles				*GRI 2—Importance of men's careers*				*GRI 3—Women's employment*			
		Egalitarian		*Traditional*		*Egalitarian*		*Traditional*		*Egalitarian*		*Traditional*	
		Male	*Female*	*Male*	*Female*	*Male*	*Female*	*Male*	*Female*	*Male*	*Female*	*Male*	*Female*
TBWIF	*M*	3.39	3.36	3.49	3.46	3.51	3.37	3.38	3.40	3.40	3.17	3.47	3.73
	SD	1.20	1.17	1.14	1.20	1.28	1.24	1.10	1.13	1.22	1.15	1.12	1.14
SBWIF	*M*	3.47	3.60	3.57	3.68	3.50	3.59	3.52	3.64	3.32	3.43	3.72	3.92
	SD	1.25	1.26	1.21	1.29	1.34	1.28	1.17	1.25	1.23	1.24	1.21	1.25
TBFIW	*M*	2.74	2.70	2.98	3.11	2.76	2.58	2.90	3.00	2.69	2.60	3.00	3.14
	SD	0.95	1.03	1.04	1.18	1.03	1.00	0.97	1.11	0.94	1.00	1.03	1.13
SBFIW	*M*	2.61	2.48	2.85	2.81	2.60	2.36	2.77	2.73	2.55	2.36	2.87	2.90
	SD	1.09	1.03	1.08	1.17	1.15	1.01	1.05	1.10	1.05	0.97	1.11	1.16
WTFS	*M*	2.74	2.80	2.84	2.71	2.74	2.83	2.81	2.73	2.71	2.86	2.87	2.64
	SD	0.75	0.77	0.82	0.71	0.76	0.79	0.79	0.71	0.76	0.79	0.80	0.68
FTWS	*M*	3.51	3.55	3.41	3.52	3.51	3.58	3.45	3.50	3.52	3.62	3.42	3.40
	SD	0.76	0.75	0.76	0.78	0.83	0.72	0.71	0.79	0.72	0.75	0.80	0.74
	Valid *N*	194	422	132	141	132	273	194	290	173	355	153	208
	Total *N*	889				889				889			

(*Continued*)

TABLE 18.3 (Continued)

		NGE = 3—Low national gender equity											
		GRI 1—Division of work/family roles				*GRI 2—Importance of men's careers*				*GRI 3—Women's employment*			
		Egalitarian		*Traditional*		*Egalitarian*		*Traditional*		*Egalitarian*		*Traditional*	
		Male	*Female*	*Male*	*Female*	*Male*	*Female*	*Male*	*Female*	*Male*	*Female*	*Male*	*Female*
TBWIF	*M*	3.08	2.85	3.39	3.46	3.14	2.92	3.39	3.51	3.00	2.71	3.45	3.59
	SD	1.20	1.13	1.10	1.11	1.16	1.07	1.12	1.13	1.13	1.08	1.11	1.07
SBWIF	*M*	3.37	3.14	3.52	3.72	3.34	3.25	3.54	3.75	3.26	3.05	3.57	3.82
	SD	1.22	1.13	1.10	1.12	1.16	1.15	1.11	1.12	1.18	1.15	1.10	1.07
TBFIW	Mean	2.44	2.63	2.83	3.12	2.36	2.68	2.90	3.16	2.35	2.53	2.90	3.21
	SD	0.94	0.96	1.06	1.12	0.77	0.94	1.09	1.14	0.79	0.90	1.09	1.12
SBFIW	*M*	2.44	2.49	2.93	3.11	2.57	2.62	2.92	3.13	2.50	2.43	2.95	3.20
	SD	0.97	1.00	1.11	1.12	0.92	1.05	1.14	1.12	0.88	0.90	1.15	1.12
WTFS	*M*	3.25	3.63	3.21	3.31	3.26	3.51	3.20	3.32	3.15	3.31	3.24	3.40
	SD	1.07	0.88	0.79	0.82	1.00	0.89	0.79	0.82	0.89	0.86	0.84	0.84
FTWS	*M*	4.08	4.14	3.82	3.96	4.06	4.17	3.81	3.92	3.95	3.94	3.85	4.01
	SD	0.88	0.86	0.71	0.67	0.82	0.74	0.72	0.70	0.75	0.81	0.75	0.68
	Valid *N*	121	129	449	491	154	184	416	436	155	178	415	442
	Total *N*	1190				1190				1190			

The following model was examined: main effects of all the independent variables, two-way interactions between gender and each of the GRI variables (gender × GRI1, gender × GRI2, gender × GRI3), as well as between gender and NGE (gender × NGE), and three-way interactions between gender, each of the GRI variables, and NGE (gender × GRI1 × NGE, gender × GRI2 × NGE, gender × GRI3 × NGE).

Results

There were significant multivariate main effects for all of the independent variables (gender, GRI1, GRI2, GRI3, and NGE) and covariates (age and number of children). The two-way interactions were significant for gender × GRI3 (women's employment) and gender × NGE. In addition, the three-way interactions were significant for gender × GRI2 (importance of men's careers) × NGE and for gender × GRI3 (women's employment) × NGE. Table 18.4 summarizes the results of the MANCOVA analysis and as a precaution (given a significant Box's M value) reports observed power of the test as well as Pillai's Trace statistic which is the most robust of all MANCOVA tests to violations of the homogeneity assumption.

Prior to examining tests of between-subjects effects (univariate ANOVAs), the homogeneity of variance assumption was tested for all six W-F subscales. Levene's F tests were statistically significant ($p < .05$) for all subscales. However, tests of normality using skewness and kurtosis values were found to be within acceptable range (z-scores below $\pm$ 2.58, $p < 0.01$). Similarly, results of the Shapiro-Wilk test for subgroups with small sample sizes (e.g., respondents with egalitarian attitudes

TABLE 18.4 MANCOVA analyses—multivariate tests.

Effect	*Pillai's Trace*	*F value*	*Hypothesis df*	*Error df*	*Sig.*	*Partial Eta Squared*	*Observed Power**
Age	.02	8.40	6	2683	.00	.02	1.00
Number of children	.01	2.29	6	2683	.03	.01	.80
Gender	.01	3.41	6	2683	.00	.01	.95
GRI1	.01	2.76	6	2683	.01	.01	.88
GRI2	.03	15.17	6	2683	.00	.03	1.00
GRI3	.01	2.30	6	2683	.03	.01	.81
NGE	.12	29.55	12	5368	.00	.06	1.00
Gender × GRI1	.00	1.57	6	2683	.15	.00	.61
Gender × GRI2	.00	1.71	6	2683	.11	.00	.66
Gender × GRI3	.01	3.64	6	2683	.00	.01	.96
Gender × NGE	.01	2.52	12	5368	.00	.01	.98
Gender × GRI1 × NGE	.01	1.27	24	10744	.17	.00	.93
Gender × GRI2 × NGE	.02	1.85	24	10744	.01	.00	.99
Gender × GRI3 × NGE	.02	2.33	24	10744	.00	.01	1.00

Note. *Computed using alpha = .05

toward division of work and family roles (GRI1) in high NGE countries—see Table 18.2) did not reach significance at $p < 0.01$. This suggested that distributions of the W-F variables were close to normal for each of the subgroups, thereby increasing our confidence in interpreting results of post-hoc analyses (Tabachnick & Fidell, 2013). For all univariate analyses, a Bonferonni correction was used to reduce the possibility of Type 1 error and the significance level was adjusted to $p <.001$.

TBWIF

No significant three-way interactions between gender, GRI1 or GRI2 or GRI3, and NGE were found for TBWIF. The two-way interaction between gender and GRI3 (women's employment) was significant, $F(1, 2688) = 18.24, p = .001$, partial $\eta^2 = .01$ observed power = .79. Simple pairwise comparisons indicated that men with an egalitarian attitude toward women's employment reported significantly higher TBWIF than women with similarly egalitarian attitudes toward women's employment ($M = 3.53$ and $SD = 1.23$ for men; $M = 3.20$ and $SD = 1.21$ for women; mean difference of .33, 99.7% CI [.20, .46], $p = .001$).

There was a significant main effect of NGE on TBWIF, $F(2, 2688) = 41.17$, $p = .001$, partial $\eta^2 = .03$ observed power = 1.00. TBWIF was higher for respondents living in high NGE countries as compared to medium NGE countries (mean difference of .65, 99.7% CI [.23, 1.07], $p = .001$) and as compared to low NGE countries (mean difference of 1.01, 99.7% CI [.60, 1.43], $p = .001$). TBWIF was also higher for medium NGE countries as compared to low NGE countries (mean difference of .36, 99.7% CI [.16, .56], $p = .001$; $M = 3.92$ and $SD = 1.18$ for High NGE countries; $M = 3.41$ and $SD = 1.18$ for Medium NGE countries and $M = 3.33$ and $SD = 1.14$ for Low NGE countries).

SBWIF

No significant three-way interactions between gender, GRI1 or GRI2 or GRI3, and NGE were obtained for SBWIF. In addition, there were no significant two-way interactions between gender and GRI1 or GRI2 or GRI3, or between gender and NGE for SBWIF.

There were significant main effects of NGE on SBWIF, $F(2, 2688) = 11.04$, $p = .001$, partial $\eta^2 = .01$ observed power = .92, and of GRI3 (women's employment) on SBWIF, $F(1, 2688) = 64.97$, $p = .001$, partial $\eta^2 = .02$ observed power = 1.00. SBWIF was higher for respondents living in high NGE countries as compared to low NGE countries (mean difference of .50, 99.7% CI [.06, .93], $p = .001$). SBWIF was also higher for medium NGE countries as compared to low NGE countries (mean difference of .23, 99.7% CI [.02, .43], $p = .001$; $M = 3.81$ and $SD = 1.20$ for High NGE countries; $M = 3.58$ and $SD = 1.25$ for Medium NGE countries; and $M = 3.55$ and $SD = 1.14$ for Low NGE countries).

Further, SBWIF was higher for respondents with high scores (traditional) on GRI3 (women's employment) as compared to low scores on GRI3 (egalitarian) (mean difference of -.35, 99.7% CI [-.48, -.22], p = .001; M = 3.48 and SD = 1.23 for high scores (egalitarian) on GRI3 and M = 3.79 and SD = 1.14 for low scores (traditional) on GRI3.

TBFIW

No significant three-way or two-way interactions between gender, GRI1 or GRI2 or GRI3, and NGE were observed for TBFIW. There was a significant main effect of GRI3 (women's employment) on TBFIW, $F(1, 2688) = 46.02, p = .001$, partial $\eta^2 = .02$ observed power = 1.00. TBFIW was higher for respondents with high scores (traditional) on GRI3 (women's employment) as compared to low scores on GRI3 (egalitarian) (mean difference of -.44, 99.7% CI [-.55, -.32], p = .001; M = 2.61 and SD = 0.97 for low scores (egalitarian) on GRI3; and M = 3.05 and SD = 1.09 for high scores (traditional) on GRI3.

SBFIW

There were no significant three-way or two-way interactions between gender, GRI1 or GRI2 or GRI3, and NGE for SBFIW. There was a significant main effect of GRI3 (women's employment) on SBFIW, $F(1, 2688) = 42.60, p = .001$, partial $\eta^2 = .02$ observed power = 1.00. SBFIW was higher for respondents with high scores (traditional) on GRI3 (women's employment) as compared to low scores on GRI3 (egalitarian) (mean difference of -.57, 99.7% CI [-.69, -.45], p = 0.000; M = 2.38 and SD = 0.95 for low scores (egalitarian) on GRI3; and M = 2.95 and SD = 1.14 for high scores (traditional) on GRI3.

WTFS

There was a significant three-way interaction between gender, GRI3 (women's employment), and NGE for WTFS at $F(4, 2688) = 7.11, p = .001$, partial $\eta^2 = .01$, observed power = .95. Plots of this interaction can be found in Figure 18.1. Post hoc analyses were conducted for high, moderate, and low NGE countries with a Bonferroni adjustment applied and covariates appearing in the model at the following values: age = 38.84 and number of children = 1.86.

For high NGE countries interactions between gender and GRI3 were significant for high scores on GRI3 (egalitarians), $F(1.2688) = 5.414, p = 0.02$. Simple pairwise comparisons indicated that egalitarian women reported significantly more WTFS than egalitarian men, (M = 2.62 and SD = .67 for men; M = 2.81 and SD = 0.75 for women; mean difference of -.18, 99.9% CI [-.40, -.05], t = -2.61, p = .009). For moderate NGE countries interactions between gender and GRI3 were significant for high scores of GRI3 (egalitarian), $F(1.2688) = 4.58, p = 0.03$,

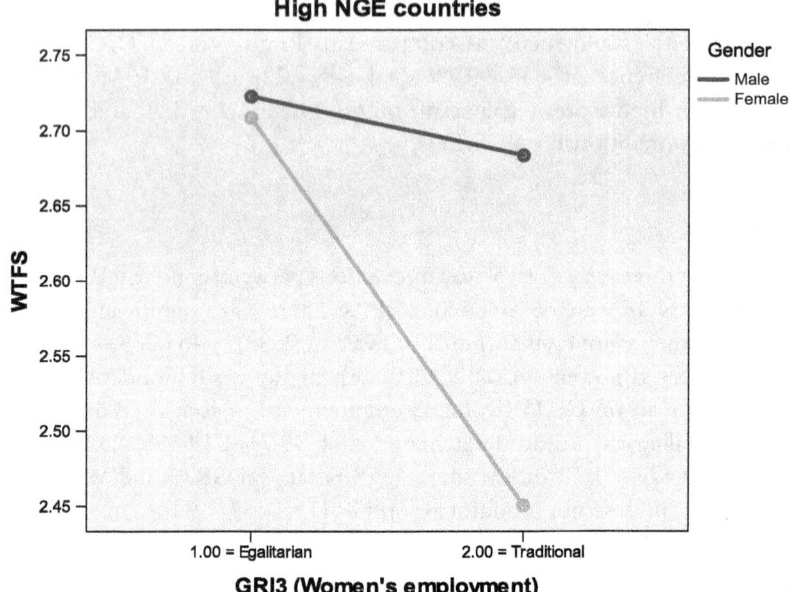

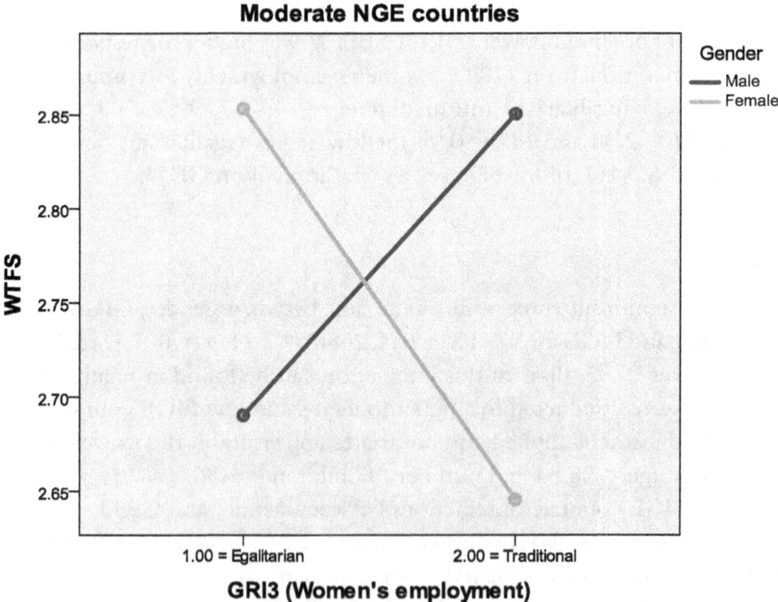

FIGURE 18.1 Profile plots of three-way interaction of gender × GRI3 (women's employment) × NGE on WTFS.

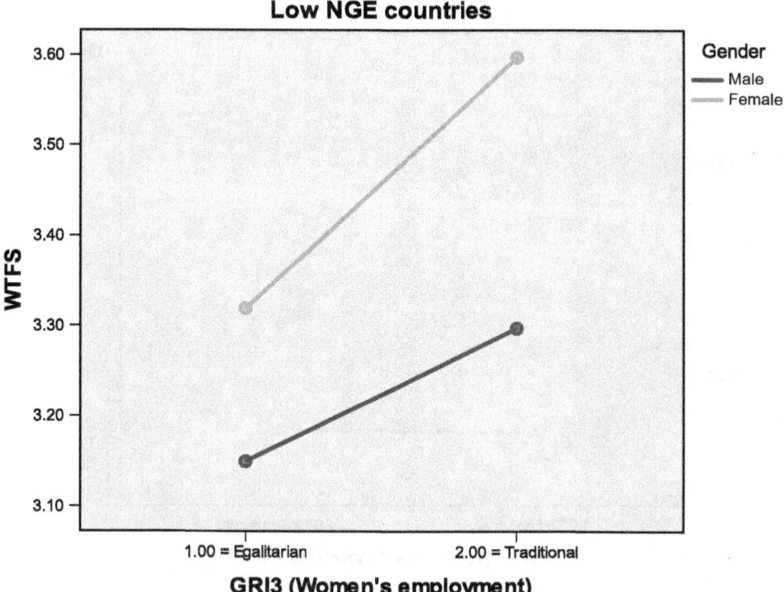

FIGURE 18.1 (Continued)

as well as for low scores of GRI3 (traditional), $F(1, 2688) = 6.41, p = 0.01$. Egalitarian women reported significantly more WTFS than egalitarian men, ($M = 2.86$ and $SD = 0.76$ for men; $M = 2.71$ and $SD = 0.79$ for women; mean difference of -.15, 99.9% CI [-.39, -.09], $t = -2.09, p = .037$) while, traditional men reported significantly more WTFS than traditional women, ($M = 2.87$ and $SD = 0.80$ for men; $M = 2.64$ and $SD = 0.68$ for women; mean difference of .23, 99.9% CI [.02, .49], $t = 3.03, p = .003$). For low NGE countries interactions between gender and GRI3 were significant for low scores of GRI3 (traditional), $F(1.2688) = 9.81$, $p = 0.002$. Traditional women reported significantly more WTFS than traditional men, ($M = 3.24$ and $SD = 0.84$ for men; $M = 3.40$ and $SD = 0.84$ for women; mean difference of -.16, 99.9% CI [.35, .02], $t = -2.87, p = .004$).

There were no significant two-way interactions between gender and GRI1 or GRI2 for WTFS nor any main effects of GRI1 or GRI2 for any of the control variables of age and number of children for WTFS.

FTWS

There was a significant three-way interaction between gender, GRI3 (women's employment), and NGE for FTWS at $F(4, 2688) = 5.61, p = .001$, partial $\eta^2 = .01$, observed power = .86. Plots of this interaction can be found in Figure 18.2. Post-hoc analyses were conducted for high, moderate, and low NGE countries with a

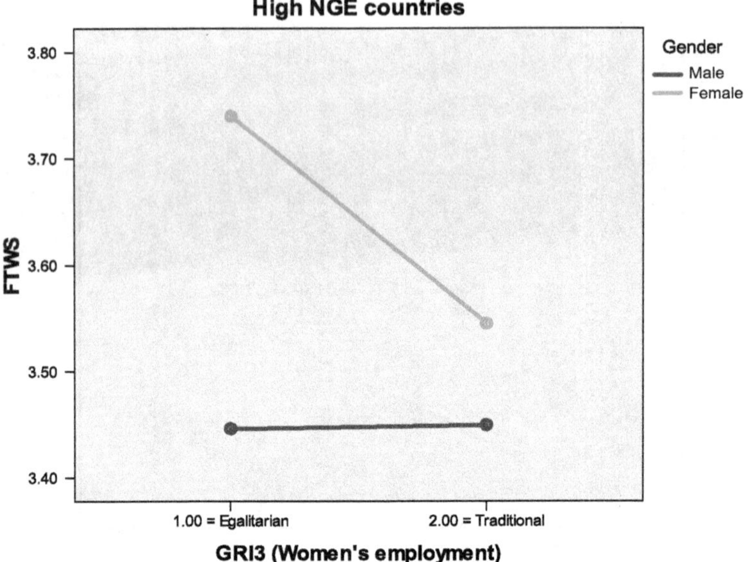

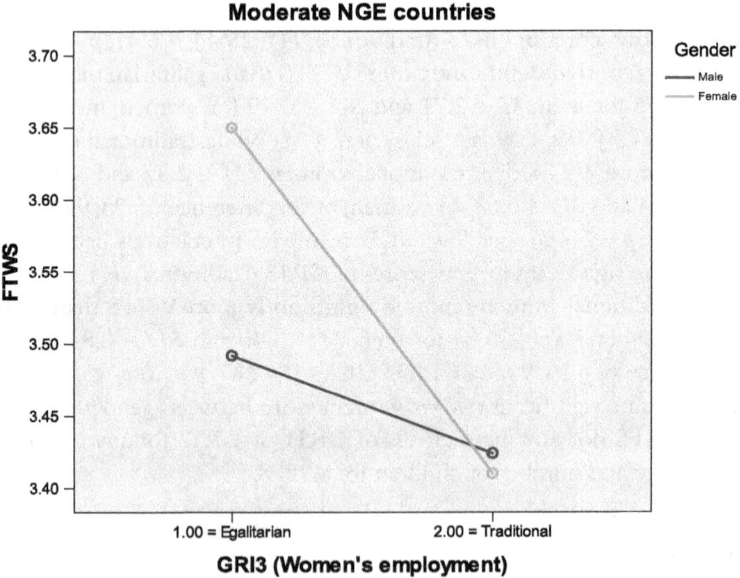

FIGURE 18.2 Profile plots of three-way interaction of gender × GRI3 (women's employment) × NGE on FTWS.

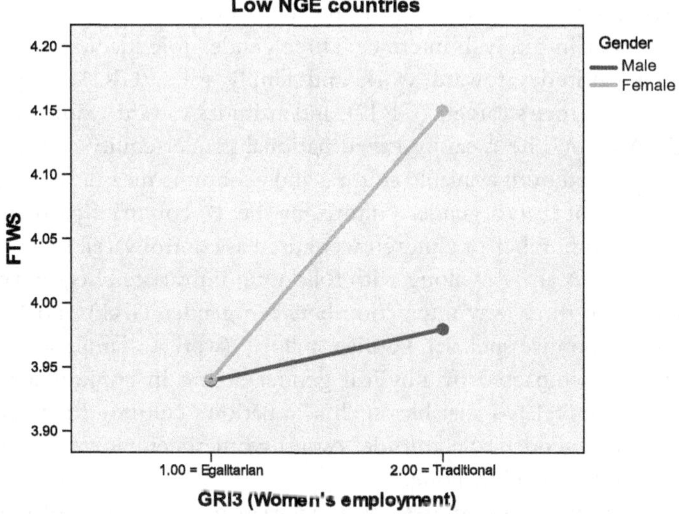

FIGURE 18.2 (Continued)

Bonferroni adjustment applied and covariates appearing in the model at the following values: age = 38.84 and number of children = 1.86.

For high NGE countries interactions between gender and GRI3 were significant for high scores of GRI3 (egalitarians), $F(1.2688) = 4.414, p = 0.04$. Simple pairwise comparisons indicated that egalitarian women reported significantly more FTWS than egalitarian men, ($M = 3.53$ and $SD = .73$ for men; $M = 3.68$ and $SD = 0.72$ for women; mean difference of -.14, 99.9% CI [-.37, -.08], $t = -2.10$, $p = .036$). For moderate NGE countries interactions between gender and GRI3 were not significant for high or low scores of GRI3. For low NGE countries interactions between gender and GRI3 were significant for low scores of GRI3 (traditional), $F(1.2688) = 11.48, p = 0.001$. Simple pairwise comparisons indicated that traditional women reported significantly more FTWS than traditional men, ($M = 3.85$ and $SD = 0.75$ for men; $M = 4.01$ and $SD = 0.68$ for women; mean difference of -.17, 95% CI [-.33, -.00], $t = -3.40, p = .001$).

No significant two-way interactions between gender and GRI1 or GRI2 were found for FTWS. There were no significant main effects of GRI1 or GRI2 for any of the control variables of age and number of children for FTWS.

Discussion

The aim of this chapter was to uncover the main and interaction effects of gender, gender-role attitudes, and macro aspects of a country's gender culture on W-F interface dependent variables. Thus, two broader sets of gender-related variables—gender-role ideology (GRI) and national gender equity (NGE)—were included in analyses, besides physical gender, in order to extend our understanding of the role of gender in the W-F interface. Three gender-role ideologies/attitudes were measured—attitudes toward work and family roles (GRI1), attitudes toward importance of men's careers (GRI2), and attitudes toward women's employment (GRI3). A composite measure called national gender equity culture (NGE) was specially derived from available cultural and economic measures/indices that captured aspects of macro gender culture for the 10 countries participating in the study. Age and number of children were used as control variables.

MANCOVA analyses along with follow-up univariate tests showed that there was significant three-way interaction between gender, GRI3, and NGE for both directions of positive spillover. Positive spillover (work-to-family as well as family-to-work) was impacted by physical gender acting in conjunction with other broader gender-related variables such as a nation's culture of gender equity and an individual's gender-role attitude toward women's employment rather than by physical gender working alone.

Egalitarian women compared to egalitarian men (in terms of their scores on GRI3) reported more WTFS and FTWS in high NGE countries, while traditional women compared to traditional men experienced more WTFS and FTWS in low NGE countries. In moderate NGE countries there was a cross effect with egalitarian women experiencing more WTFS (though not FTWS) than egalitarian men, but traditional men experiencing more WTFS (though not FTWS) than traditional women. These results broadly support the expansionist theory of Barnett and Hyde (2001)—due to role expansion in contexts with rising economic opportunities women (especially) can simultaneously experience strain and positive benefits.

With regard to the negative aspect of the W-F interface, namely, the conflict variables, SBWIF and TBWIF appeared to be influenced by NGE acting as a main effect—being higher in countries that had a higher NGE as compared to countries that had a moderate and low NGE. FIW, on the other hand, was significantly impacted only by gender-role ideology acting as a main effect, especially ideology toward women's employment. Both time- and strain-based FIW were greater for those who had a more traditional as compared to egalitarian attitude toward women's employment (GRI3). The only exception to this was TBWIF, which was influenced by interaction of physical gender and GRI3—men with an egalitarian attitude toward women's employment reported significantly higher TBWIF than women with similarly egalitarian attitudes toward women's employment.

Interestingly, of the various gender-role attitudes that were included, such as GRI1 (attitudes toward division of work and family roles), GRI2 (importance of men's careers) and GRI3 (attitude toward women's employment), the most obvious gender-role attitude pertaining to W-F viz. GRI1, did not significantly affect any of the W-F dependent variables. This could be because attitudes to work and family roles do not directly translate into behaviors, such as hours invested in work or family tasks, since individuals are known to use adaptive strategies, such as scaling back, to avoid WFC (e.g., Haddock et al., 2001).

Attitudes toward women's employment played the most important role in influencing W-F interface variables in the results of this study. GRI3 impacted all the WFC variables as a main effect in such a way that traditional attitudes were more detrimental than egalitarian attitudes, since they increased a respondent's propensity to experience conflict. The exception to this was TBWIF—where egalitarian men experienced more conflict than egalitarian women. Previous research has indicated that there is a general worldwide movement in gender-role attitudes away from traditionalism toward egalitarianism. This is truer for women, especially working women, than men (e.g., Pimentel, 2006; Tu & Liao, 2005). Given that there is wider acceptance for a more progressive stance toward women's employment, anyone with a conservative mindset on this issue may experience more negative societal sanctions and lesser support that could manifest itself in the form of high WFC. Additionally, despite a changing scenario, since egalitarian men still appear to be in a minority, they probably receive the least amount of support for managing W-F demands. There is evidence that awareness and utilization of family-friendly benefits tends to be lower for men as compared to women (e.g., Sprung, Toumbeva, & Matthews, 2015). This may explain the interaction of GRI3 and gender in such a manner that higher levels of TBWIF were associated with egalitarian men as compared to egalitarian women.

The other broad gender variable included in the study—NGE—also had a significant main effect on all W-F variables (except SBFIW) such that countries with a more equitable gender culture experienced greater WFC as compared to countries with lesser national gender equity. This result is similar to the result of Steiber's (2009) study and is suggestive of the higher emancipatory pressure causing greater conflict for individuals in countries with greater national gender equity. Another explanation could be that countries with higher gender equity tend to be more economically developed and have a greater number of women in the paid workforce. As a result, they possibly create work environments characterized by long work hours and high work demands, and therefore also high conflict. The results could also mean that while WFC can vary depending on which country you live in, strain from family and parenting demands varies little for working persons all over the world.

It should be noted, however, that the results obtained here may be due to the manner in which the NGE composite was calculated. Lyness and Judiesch (2014) used separate measures of country level gender egalitarianism and got different results for supervisor's ratings of work-life balance in their study. In the present study, instead of using separate measures, a composite measure of NGE was developed by averaging out GLOBE Project practice ("as is") and values ("should be") scores on gender egalitarianism as well as other measures of cultural and economic gender inequality. This approach was used for the sake of expediency. Future analyses could use multiple measures of gender egalitarianism to yield interesting findings just as multiple measures of GRI have been used in this study.

The ad hoc nature of the NGE composite measure is acknowledged here and is a limitation of the study. It was not intended to be a part of the original Project 3535 study, but was developed in keeping with recent literature, to bring out the broader ways in which gender can affect the W-F interface.

Conclusion

The results of this study provide support for the notion that a more nuanced understanding of the W-F interface requires the inclusion of broader gender variables that go beyond biological gender and the reliance on exploration of interaction effects in addition to main effects (Korabik et al., 2008). To the extent that gender by itself did not significantly affect any of the W-F variables in this study, the results are in keeping with results of previous studies that have found a near zero effect of gender on W-F variables (e.g., Shockley & Singla, 2011). The results of this study also reinforce the case for including culture variables that are alternatives to individualism-collectivism like macro cultural/economic aspects of gender egalitarianism (e.g., Ollier-Malaterre et al., 2013; Powell et al., 2009) in future W-F studies. Finally, a practical implication of this study is that future W-F interventions rather than being targeted toward men or women may need to be based on a person's gender-role ideology. Interventions aimed at W-F attitude change may need to be offered differently for countries with different levels of national gender equity.

References

Allen, T. D., Lapierre, L. M., Spector, P. E., Poelmans, S.A.Y., O'Driscoll, M., Sanchez, J. I., Cooper, C. L., Walvoord, A. G., Antoniou, A.-S., Brough, P., Geurts, S., Kinnunen, U., Pagon, M., Shima, S., & Woo, J.-M. (2014). The link between national paid leave policy and work–family conflict among married working parents. *Applied Psychology, 63*, 5–28. doi:10.1111/apps.12004

Bagger, J., Li, A., & Gutek, B. A. (2008). How much do you value your family and does it matter? The joint effects of family identity salience, family-interference-with-work, and gender. *Human Relations, 61*(2), 187–211. doi:10.1177/0018726707087784

Barnett, R. C., & Hyde, J. S. (2001). Women, men, work and family: An expansionist theory. *American Psychologist, 56*(10), 781–796. doi:10.1037/0003-066X.56.10.781

Beham, B., Drobnič, S., & Präg, P. (2012). The work-family interface of service sector workers: A comparison of work resources and professional status across five European countries. *Applied Psychology: An International Review, 63*(1), 29–61. doi:10.1111/apps.12012

Bielby, W. T., & Bielby, D. (1992). I will follow him: Family ties, gender-role beliefs, and reluctance to relocate for a better job. *American Journal of Sociology, 97*(5), 1241–1268.

Crouter, A. C. (1984). Spillover from family to work: The neglected side of the work-family interface. *Human Relations, 37*(6), 425–442. doi:10.1177/001872678403700601

Frisco, M. L., & Williams, K. (2003). Perceived housework equity, marital happiness, and divorce in dual-earner households. *Journal of Family Issues, 24*(1), 51–73. doi:10.1177/0192513X02238520

Frone, M. R., Russell, M., & Cooper, M. K. (1992). Antecedents and outcomes of work-family conflict: Testing a model of the work-family interface. *Journal of Applied Psychology*, 77(1), 65–78. doi:10.1037/0021-9010.77.1.65

GEI by country. (2012). Retrieved March 31, 2015, from http://www.socialwatch.org/node/14367

Gender Inequality Index. (2013). Human Development Reports, United Nations Development Program.

Gibbons, J., Hamby, B., & Dennis, W. (1997). Researching gender-role ideologies internationally and cross-culturally. *Psychology of Women Quarterly*, *21*(1), 151–170. doi:10.1111/j.1471-6402.1997.tb00106.x

Greenhaus, J. H., & Beutell, N. (1985). Sources of conflict between work and family roles. *Academy of Management Review*, *10*(1), 76–88. doi:10.5465/AMR.1985.4277352

Greenhaus, J. H., & Powell, G. N. (2006). When work and family are allies: A theory of work-family enrichment. *Academy of Management Review*, *31*(1), 72–79. doi:10.5465/AMR.2006.19379625

Grzywacz, J. G., & Marks, N. F. (2000). Reconceptualizing the work-family interface: An ecological perspective on the correlates of positive and negative spillover between work and family. *Journal of Occupational Health Psychology*, *5*(1), 111–126. doi:10.1037/1076-8998.5.1.111

Guan, J., Rajadhyaksha, U., & McElroy, J. (2011). The relation between work conditions and women's socio-economic status: A global exploratory study. *Journal of Research in Peace, Gender and Development* (ISSN: 2251-0036), *1*(10), 271–285. Retrieved from http://www.interesjournals.org/JRPGD

Gutek, B. A., Searle, S., & Klepa, L. (1991). Rational versus gender-role explanations for work family conflict. *Journal of Applied Psychology*, *76*(4), 560–568. doi:10.1037/0021-9010.76.4.560

Haar, J. M., & Bardoel, E. A. (2008). Positive spillover from the work-family interface: A study of Australian employees. *Asia Pacific Journal of Human Resources*, *46*(3), 275–287. doi:10.1177/1038411108095759

Haddock, S. A., Zimmerman, T. S., Ziemba, S. J., & Current, L. (2001). Ten adaptive strategies for work and family balance: Advice from successful dual earners. *Journal of Marital and Family Therapy*, 27(4), 445–458. doi:10.111/j.1752-0606.2001.tb00339.x

Harris, R. J., Firestone, J. M., & Bryan, P. J. (2006). A comparative analysis of sex-role ideology in Canada, Mexico and the United States. *Advances in Gender Research*, *10*, 97–124. doi:10.1016/S1529-2126(06)10005-3

Hill, E. J. (2005). Work-family facilitation and conflict, working fathers and mothers, work- family stressors and support. *Journal of Family Issues*, *26*(6), 793–819. doi:10.1177/0192513X05277542

House, R. J., & Javidan, M. (2004). Overview of GLOBE. In R. J. House, P. J. Hanges, M. Javidan, P. W. Dorfman, & V. Gupta (Eds.), *Culture, leadership, and organizations: The GLOBE study of 62 societies* (pp. 9–28). Thousand Oaks, CA: Sage.

Huberty, C. J., & Petoskey, M. D. (2000). Multivariate analysis of variance and covariance. In H. Tinsley & S. Brown (Eds.), *Handbook of applied multivariate statistics and mathematical modeling* (pp. 183–208). New York, NY: Academic Press.

Human Development Reports. (2014). *United Nations Development Programme*. Retrieved March 31, 2015, from http://hdr.undp.org/en/content/table-4-gender-inequality-index

James, B., Barnett, R. C., & Brennan, R. T. (1998). The psychological effects of work experiences and disagreements about gender-role beliefs in dual-earner couples: A longitudinal study. *Women's Health: Research on Gender, Behavior and Policy*, *4*(4), 341–368.

Korabik, K., McElwain, A., & Chappell, D. (2008). Integrating gender-related issues into research on work and family. In K. Korabik, D. S. Lero, & D. L. Whitehead (Eds.), *Handbook of work-family integration: Research, theory, and best practices* (pp. 215–232). San Diego, CA: Elsevier.

Lyness, K. S., & Judiesch, M. K. (2014). Gender egalitarianism and work—life balance for managers: Multisource perspectives in 36 Countries. *Applied Psychology: An International Review, 63*(1), 96–129. doi:10.1111/apps.12011

Lyness, K. S., & Kropf, M. B. (2005). The relationships of national gender equality and organizational support with work-family balance: A study of European managers. *Human Relations, 58*(1), 33–60. doi:10.1177/0018726705050934

Mandel, H. (2009). Configurations of gender inequality: The consequences of ideology and public policy. *The British Journal of Sociology, 60*(4), 693–719. doi:10.111/j.1468-4446.2009.01271.x

Meyers, L. S., Gamst, G., & Guarino, A. (2006). *Applied multivariate research: Design and interpretation*. Thousand Oaks, CA: Sage.

Mickelson, K. D., Claffey, S. T., & Williams, S. L. (2006). The moderating role of gender and gender role attitudes on the link between spousal support and marital quality. *Sex Roles, 55*(1), 73–82. doi:10.1007/s11199-006-9061-8

Ollier-Malaterre, A., Valcour, M., Den Dulk, L., & Kossek, E. E. (2013). Theorizing national context to develop comparative work—life research: A review and research agenda. *European Management Journal, 31*(5), 433–447. doi:10.1016/j.emj.2013.05.002

Öun, I. (2012). Work-family conflict in the Nordic countries: A comparative analysis. *Journal of Comparative Family Studies, 43*(2), 165–184.

Panayotova, E., & Brayfield, A. (1997). National context and gender ideology: Attitudes toward women's employment in Hungary and the United States. *Gender & Society, 11*(5), 627–655. doi:10.1177/089124397011005006

Parboteeah, K. P., Hoegl, M., & Cullen, J. B. (2008). Managers' gender-role attitudes: A country institutional profile approach. *Journal of International Business Studies, 39*(5), 795–813.

Pimentel, E. E. (2006). Gender ideology, household behavior, and backlash in urban China. *Journal of Family Issues, 27*(3), 341–365. doi:10.1177/0192513X05283507

Pleck, J. H. (1977). The work-family role system. *Social Problems, 24*, 417–427. doi:10.2307/800135

Powell, G. N., Francesco, A. M., & Ling, Y. (2009). Toward culture-sensitive theories of the work-family interface. *Journal of Organizational Behavior, 30*(5), 597–616. doi:10.1002/job.568

Rajadhyaksha, U., Korabik, K., & Aycan, Z. (2015). Gender, gender-role ideology and the work-family interface: A cross-cultural analysis. In M. Mills (Ed.), *Gender and the work-family experience: An intersection of two domains* (pp. 99–117). Cham, Switzerland: Springer. doi:10.1007/978-3-319-08891-4_6

Ray, R., Gornick, J. C., & Schmitt, J. (2010). Who cares? Assessing generosity and gender equality in parental leave policy designs in 21 countries. *Journal of European Social Policy, 20*(3), 196–216. doi:10.1177/0958928710364434

Ruppanner, L., & Huffman, M. L. (2014). Blurred boundaries: Gender and work-family interference in cross-national context. *Work and Occupations, 41*(2), 210–236. doi:10.1177/0730888413500679

Shockley, K., & Singla, N. (2011). Reconsidering work-family interactions and satisfaction: A meta-analysis. *Journal of Management, 37*, 861–886. doi:10.1177/0149206310394864

Sieber, S. D. (1974). Toward a theory of role accumulation. *American Sociological Review, 39*(4), 567–578.

Smith-Lovin, L., & Tickamyer, A. R. (1978). Nonrecursive models of labor force participation, fertility behavior, and sex role attitudes. *American Sociological Review, 43*(4), 541–557. doi:10.2307/2094778

Sprung, J. M, Toumbeva, T. H., & Matthews, R. A. (2015). Family-friendly organizational policies, practices, and benefits through the gender lens. In M. Mills (Ed.), *Gender and the work-family experience: An intersection of two domains* (pp. 227–250). Cham, Switzerland: Springer.

Steiber, N. (2009). Reported levels of time-based and strain-based conflict between work and family roles in Europe: A multilevel approach. *Social Indicators Research, 93*(3), 469–488. doi:10.1007/s11205-008-9436-z

Tabachnick, B. G., & Fidell, L. S. (2013). *Using multivariate statistics* (6th ed.). Boston, MA: Pearson.

Tu, S., & Liao, P. (2005). Gender differences in gender-role attitudes: A comparative analysis of Taiwan. *Journal of Comparative Family Studies, 36*(4), 545–566.

Voydanoff, P. (2004). Implications of work and community demands and resources for work-to-family conflict and facilitation. *Journal of Occupational Health Psychology, 9*(4), 275–285. doi:10.1037/1076-8998.9.4.275

World Values Survey Association (www.worldvaluessurvey.org). World Values Survey Wave 5 2005–2008. Official Aggregate v.20140429. Aggregate File Producer: Asep/JDS, Madrid Spain. Retrieved March 31, 2015, from http://www.worldvaluessurvey.org/WVSDocumentationWV5.jsp

World Values Survey Association (www.worldvaluessurvey.org). World Values Survey Wave 6 2010–2014. Official Aggregate v.20141107. Aggregate File Producer: Asep/JDS, Madrid Spain. Retrieved March 31, 2015, from http://www.worldvaluessurvey.org/WVSDocumentationWV6.jsp

Yeganeh, H., & May, D. (2011). Cultural values and gender gap: A cross-national analysis. *Gender in Management: An International Journal, 26*(2), 106–121. doi:10.1108/17542411111116536

19

EXPLORING THE INTERACTION OF CULTURE AND CONTEXTUAL FACTORS ON THE WORK-FAMILY INTERFACE

Ujvala Rajadhyaksha

Introduction

Work and family research has explored negative aspects of the work-family (W-F) interface, such as WFC (e.g., Eby, Casper, Lockwood, Bordeaux, & Brinley, 2005; Frone, Russell, & Cooper, 1992), as well as positive aspects such as work-family positive spillover (e.g., Greenhaus & Powell, 2006, Grzywacz & Marks, 2000; Shockley & Singla, 2011). Typical W-F antecedents studied have included work and family demands (e.g., Luk & Shaffer, 2005; Voydanoff, 2005) while frequently studied W-F outcomes have covered family satisfaction, life satisfaction, psychological well-being, and turnover intention (e.g., Amstad, Meier, Fasel, Elfering, & Semmer, 2011; Bruck, Allen, & Spector, 2002; Parasuraman & Simmers, 2001). The majority of W-F studies tend to be based in North America or Anglo cultures (e.g., Casper, Eby, Bordeaux, Lockwood, & Lambert, 2007). However, researchers continue to emphasize conducting more cross-cultural W-F research (e.g., Aycan, 2008; Poelmans, O'Driscoll, & Beham et al., 2005; Shaffer, Joplin, & Hsu, 2011) and examining the role of context in addition to culture (e.g., Perrone-McGovern, Wright, Howell, & Barnum, 2014).

This study extends our understanding of the W-F interface by exploring the moderating role of various contextual variables in the impact of societal culture on WFC, work-family positive spillover (WFPS), and W-F outcomes. Three kinds of contextual variables (demographic, work-related, and family-related) were treated as moderators of the impact of Eastern versus Western societal culture (EW) on time-based and strain-based work-to-family and family-to-work conflict (WIF/FIW), work-to-family and family-to-work positive spillover (WTFS/FTWS), and four work-family outcomes—family satisfaction (FS), life satisfaction (LS), psychological well-being (PWB), and turnover intention (TI).

Literature Review

Although a variety of frameworks for studying societal cultures are available in the field of cross-cultural studies, Joplin, Shaffer, Francesco, and Lau (2003) suggest that Anglo and Far Eastern culture clusters capture many dimensions common to other available frameworks (e.g., Hofstede, 1980; Kluckhohn & Strodtbeck, 1961; Schwartz, 1994; Trompenaars, 1993). For instance, countries that fall within the Far Eastern cluster, such as China, Hong Kong, and Singapore, have comparable ratings on Hofstede's (1980) dimensions of power distance, individualism, and masculinity, whereas countries that fall within the Anglo cluster, such as for example the United States, Australia, and Canada, are at the other end of the spectrum on the same dimensions. For the purposes of this chapter, we clustered participating countries into Eastern and Western cultures.

Cross-cultural studies on the W-F interface, although less numerous in comparison to single country studies, have suggested a consistent pattern of results surrounding W-F variables across Eastern and Western cultures. Family variables have tended to play a stronger role in more family-oriented Eastern cultures, and work variables have tended to be more salient in work-oriented Anglo/Western cultures (Allen, French, Dumani, & Shockley, 2015; Aycan, 2008).

Contextual factors have been explored relatively little in W-F research. Perrone-McGovern et al. (2014) recommend that in future studies W-F research consider the following contextual factors: gender roles, cultural background, current economic conditions, workplace environment, and generational status, as well as contextual perceptions and values relating to gender egalitarianism and humane orientation. In this chapter we check to see if the following three categories of contextual variables moderate the relationship between societal culture and W-F interface and outcome variables. The first category was demographic variables, which consisted of respondent age (AGE), respondent education (EDU), number of children (NOC), and age of the youngest child (AYC). The second category, family-related and nonwork variables, included living arrangements (LA), extended family living (EFL), strength of religious beliefs (RB), spouse's job schedule (SJS), and spouse's job type (SJT). The final category was work-related variables, that is, respondent's job schedule (JS), respondent's job type (JT), and organization size. Since findings related to gender are reviewed in another chapter of this book, we hold gender as a covariate in this study rather than treating it as a contextual variable. We review relevant literature pertaining to contextual variables and W-F variables selected for this study.

Demographic Variables and W-F Research

Several studies have examined the relationship between age, life stage, and the W-F interface. Using a subset of data from a survey conducted by a large multinational organization in 79 countries, Hill, Erickson, Fellows, Martinengo, and

Allen (2014) explored the experience of the W-F interface for older (55+ years), middle-aged (35–54 years), and younger workers (< 35 years). Their study found that older workers experienced significantly greater W-F fit, work success, and life success, and significantly lesser WIF and FIW than middle-aged and younger workers. Comparing across gender they found that older men reported lesser awareness of W-F programs as well as lesser FIW than older women. Using data from the same survey, and adopting a life stage approach to segment respondents based on respondent age and age of the youngest child, Martinengo, Jacob, and Hill (2010) reported significant gender differences, with a more strongly negative relationship between family-work spillover and reduced work-family fit for women with a youngest child in preschool, a youngest child in elementary school, or a youngest child who was a teenager.

Allen and Finkelstein (2014) used a cross-sectional sample of full-time dual-earner couples from the 2008 National Study of the Changing Workforce of the United States to investigate the relationship between age, gender, life stage, and WFC. They found a small but negative relationship between age and WFC. WFC was also associated with family stage, with the least amount of conflict occurring during the empty nest stage and the most occurring when the youngest child in the home was five years of age or younger. Comparing across gender they found that women overall experienced greater FIW than men, but men reported more WIF when the youngest child in the home was a teenager.

Using a very similar life stages approach, Rajadhyaksha (2004) examined WFC across the W-F life cycle on a sample of dual-career couples in India and found that conflict was highest in the early stage of the life cycle and subsequently declined across later stages. Men experienced significantly more job-spouse conflict than women across the early (< 35 years and no children), middle (35–45 years and youngest child less than 12 years), and late stages of the life cycle (45+ years and youngest child older than 12 years), while women experienced significantly more job-homemaker conflict and energy-based conflict in the middle stage of the life cycle. By contrast, in a more recent study from India, Jain and Nair (2015) found that W-F enrichment varied significantly across three age groups (< 25 years, 31–35 years, and > 35 years) and that it increased with age across groups.

Several studies have explored the relationship between age, life stage, and commonly studied W-F outcomes such as subjective or occupational well-being, job and life satisfaction, and turnover. In a study of Malaysian working women, Noor (2006) used the life stages approach to examine the effects of roles, conflict, and negative affectivity, across three age groups: 20–29 years, 30–39 years, and 40+ years. Noor (2006) found different predictors of well-being for Malaysian women in each of the age groups. For women below the age of 30, well-being was explained directly by roles, conflict, and negative affectivity, and indirectly by conflict. For women in the 30–39 year age group, well-being was predicted by role and negative affectivity, but not by conflict. Conflict was in turn explained by roles and negative affectivity. For the 40+ year age group, roles and conflict explained health, while negative affectivity had a direct effect only on health and no other variables in the model. Noor explained these results in terms of the differences in child-rearing responsibilities associated with each stage. Contrary to the results of Noor's study, however, in a study of working women primarily from the United Kingdom and Australia, where data was gathered through an online data collection site and by relying on social media, Gervais and Millear (2014) found no relationship between life stage and well-being.

Several studies have examined the relationship between age and commonly examined W-F outcomes such as life satisfaction, job satisfaction, and turnover. Mroczek and Spiro (2005) found based on a study of men who were veterans in the United States that life satisfaction had a curvilinear relationship with age, with life satisfaction peaking at age 65 and declining thereafter. Zacher, Jimmieson, and Bordia (2014) examined time pressure, work-home conflict, and coworker support as mediators of the relationships between age and job satisfaction and between age and emotional exhaustion on a sample of Australian employees in the construction industry and found that those in their late twenties to early forties had lower job satisfaction and higher emotional exhaustion than younger and older employees. Further, time pressure and coworker support fully mediated both the U-shaped relationship between age and job satisfaction and the inversely U-shaped relationship between age and emotional exhaustion. Ng and Feldman (2009) conducted a meta-analysis and established that the correlation between age, and voluntary turnover was −.14. However, the relationship was moderated by race, tenure, and education level such that the age-turnover relationship was stronger when there were more racial minorities in the sample, when organizational tenure was higher, and when education level was lower.

Studies on the relationship between number of children and age of the youngest child on W-F experiences and outcomes have often been subsumed within life stage impact studies such as those reviewed here. Research focusing exclusively on number of children and W-F issues has generally operationalized "number of children" as either "have" or "do not have" children or simply a yes/no check for "parental status." Many of these studies were conducted using samples from countries as spread out as Canada, the United States, Finland, Turkey, and India. The studies found that the presence of children in one's care was generally related to higher WFC (e.g., Gürbüz & Toğran, 2003; Huffman, Youngcourt, Payne, & Castro, 2008; Kinnunen & Mauno, 1998). Presence of children was also related to many negative W-F outcomes, such as higher job stress (e.g., Gürbüz & Toğran, 2003), greater exhaustion or burnout (e.g., Töyry et al., 2004), reduced job satisfaction (e.g., Huffman et al., 2008), and reduced marital satisfaction (van Steenbergen, Kluwer, & Karney, 2011). Presence of children was also related to some positive outcomes, such as reduced turnover or increased length of stay (e.g., Huffman et al., 2008; Padgett, Gjerde, Hughes, & Born, 2005). In recent studies on W-F enrichment conducted in India (e.g., Baral & Bhargava, 2010; Jain & Nair, 2015), both work-to-family and family-to-work enrichment were positively associated with parental status and number of children. In studies comparing parents with preschool-aged versus non-preschool aged/older children, the younger age of a child has been found to be associated with a higher tendency to report conflict and negative outcomes of conflict, whether the sample comprised working women from Turkey (Eastern culture) or working employees from Canada (Western culture) (e.g., Gürbüz & Toğran, 2003; Higgins, Duxbury, & Lee, 1994; Konrad &Yang, 2012).

An exploration of education levels and W-F experiences and W-F outcomes has been relatively less extensive as compared to other demographic variables. Using data from a cohort of young adults in the United States, Ammons and Kelly (2008) found that individuals with low educational levels tended to experience more years of FIW especially when coupled with early family formation and poor working conditions. In contrast, young adults with more education, especially college-educated women, tended to have more WIF. Schieman and Glavin (2011) found, using data from a representative sample of American workers from the 2002 national Study of the Changing Workforce, that well-educated employees experienced more W-F role blurring activities than less-educated employees because they tend to occupy professional jobs with more income and pressures, broadly supporting the "stress from higher status jobs" hypothesis (Schieman, Whitestone, & Van Gundy, 2006). In addition, people with less than a high school degree reported more conflict because of their experience in precarious work with variable shifts. Finally, there was a relationship between WFC and distress, but this relationship was less strong among those with the highest and lowest education. In general, there appeared to be a curvilinear relationship between WFC or work-related stress and education levels. A relationship between WFC and education has been observed in non-Western cultures as well. For example, Anafarta and Kuruüzüm (2012) used logistic regression analysis in a study of WFC of men and women in Turkey, and found that the odds of both men and women experiencing WFC was negatively related to education. Both men and women with higher education levels in the study experienced more WFC compared to those with lower levels of education.

Family-Related Variables and W-F Research

"Family type" in W-F research has tended to focus on traditional heterosexual male-headed (single-income) households with or without children. Studies of dual-income/dual-career couples and their work and family issues in Western and Eastern cultures and in other international contexts have been reasonably frequent, especially with the rise of women in the workforce (e.g., Aryee & Luk, 1996; Duxbury & Higgins, 1994; Kierner, 2015; Lewis, Izraeli, & Hootsman, 1992; Rajadhyaksha & Bhatnagar, 2000). In comparison, examination of female-headed, heterosexual, single-income households or single-parent families has been fairly limited. Studies on single-parent families have shown that single mothers feel more home-to-job conflict than single fathers, married mothers, and married fathers (Nomaguchi, 2012), and single parents benefit less than other employees when using work-life interface options (e.g., Konrad & Yang, 2012). Many family structures are not accounted for in W-F research, such as same-sex couples, multigenerational and extended families (including parents or other elders; members from outside the bloodline or with grandparents providing primary care for grandchildren), and virtual families (Beauregard, Ozbilgin, & Bell, 2009).

Few studies have examined the relationship between religious beliefs and W-F variables. Patel and Cunningham (2012) examined the relationship between the W-F interface and religious involvement of 105 Hindus in the United States. Working within a Conservation of Resources framework, they expected that resource gain/loss from religious involvement would influence coping strategies and perceptions of bidirectional WFC and facilitation. In line with their predictions, resource gain was found to have a significant negative effect on WFC and a positive effect on W-F facilitation.

Another study conducted in the United States by Jensen (2006) compared 120 religiously liberal and conservative lay believers at three life stages—young adulthood, midlife, and older adulthood—on different aspects of family life, including spousal roles, the balance between family and work, and child-rearing approaches. Results showed a marked division between liberal and conservative believers in all three types of beliefs with differences being most pronounced at midlife. Despite this, both groups agreed that people can live happily without marrying and that children should be raised both to be independent and to believe in God. There was also a significant main effect for age group on the three factors—young and older adults within each religious group differed, with younger adults disagreeing that marriage comes with children, and agreeing more that family comes before career and that one can live happily without marrying.

Sav, Harris, and Sebar (2014) conducted a qualitative examination of the manner in which Australian Muslim men attempted to balance work, family, and religion. Findings revealed that relative to external coping mechanisms, such as relying on supervisor support, respondents used routine personal coping strategies, such as time management, as well as making unique permanent changes (e.g., scheduling work around Friday—the holy day for Muslims—and doing it on Saturday instead) in order to deal with immediate conflict. Although some of the strategies used were reflected in existing research, the extent of their usage and reasons for usage differed. Muslim men tended to rely on time management, resource generation, and segmentation strategies in a preventive manner to actively achieve work-life balance rather than to just cope with episodic work-life conflict.

Other nonwork variables examined in W-F research include the impact of spouse's work schedule and spouse's type of job. Spousal employment status (whether working or nonworking) was found to be a consistent predictor of WFC, especially of parents rather than nonparents, in a study conducted by Winslow

(2005) based on data drawn from the 1977 Quality of Employment Survey and the 1997 National Study of the Changing Work in the United States. In a study of 100 couples in China conducted using the diary survey method, Song, Foo, Uy, and Sun (2011) examined the dynamic nature of the relationship of distress levels among spouses (one who was employed full-time and the other who was unemployed). They found that for unemployed spouses, the negative daily financial strain and job search experiences were associated with higher levels of daily distress. For employed spouses, WIF and FIW were factors that were associated significantly with higher levels of distress. Further, marital satisfaction moderated distress crossover from the employed spouse to the unemployed spouse differently for men and women, being significant and positive for female employed spouses but nonsignificant and positive for male employed spouses.

Work-Related Variables and W-F Research

While several work-related contextual variables have been explored in W-F research, for this study we focus on three variables—job type, job schedule, and organization size. Results with regard to job type have been mixed across varied cultural contexts. In some studies higher status jobs, or higher grade occupations have been associated with higher stress and conflict. In other studies, being in a higher status (e.g., professional) job has been associated with higher perceptions of work-life balance, while in still other studies it has been associated with lower satisfaction with work-life balance.

In a study of 18,366 municipal employees in Finland that examined the relationships between occupational grade, domestic responsibilities, age of children, W-F spillover, and registered sickness absence, Väänänen et al. (2008) found that among all white-collar employees (except upper white-collar men), having young children below the age of 7 years was predictive of an increased sickness absence rate. Additionally, the impact of W-F characteristics on sickness absence varied according to gender and occupational grade. Negative spillover from work into family life predicted a heightened rate of sickness absence spells among both women and men in all occupational categories (except upper white-collar men), but especially among blue-collar and lower white-collar employees. Pervasive power status differences across occupational groups affecting perceptions of work-life balance and organizational justice was also observed by Fujimoto and Azmat (2014) in their study of professional/managerial and full-time, nonprofessional Australian employees. However, in their study professional/managerial employees perceived greater rather than lesser organizational justice across all work-life balance/justice dimensions. Beham, Drobnič, and Präg's (2012) study on the other hand found higher levels of work-home interference and lower levels of satisfaction with W-F balance among professional service sector employees as compared to nonprofessional service sector employees, across five Western European countries. A family-supportive supervisor and a family-supportive organizational culture differentially affected work-home interference of professional and nonprofessional workers, with a family-supportive supervisor being more beneficial to nonprofessionals and a family-supportive organizational culture being more beneficial to professional employees.

The impact of various types of job schedules has been examined in W-F research in varied cultural contexts, particularly with occupational groups, such as nurses, that are prone to shift work. Some examples are Kunst et al.'s (2014) study of shift work and W-F spillover of Norwegian nurses; Turk, Davas, Tanik, and Montgomery's (2013) study of the relationship between nonstandard work schedules and W-F spillover of Turkish hospital health care workers; Lembrechts, Dekocker, Zanoni, and Puligano's (2014) study of the relationship between WFC and overtime hours, night shifts, regularity in type of shift and weekend work on a sample of Belgian nurses. Many studies have compared regular work schedules with nonstandard work schedules only to find that the stresses and strains associated with nonstandard work schedules tend to have a more negative impact on work and family aspects and well-being of employees (e.g., Wittmer and Martin's 2010 study of the relationship between nonstandard work schedules, emotional exhaustion, and WFC of US postal workers and Bamberg, Dettmers, Funck, Krähe, and Vahle-Hinz's 2012 study of on-call work of IT service organization employees and well-being). On the other hand, homeworking, flexible schedules, or schedules that are more in the control of the worker have been found to be associated with greater synergies and positive outcomes for employees (e.g., Beutell, 2010; Hill, Erickson, Holmes, & Ferris, 2010; Lee & Duxbury, 1998), especially for women (e.g., Carlson, Grzywacz, & Kacmar, 2008). Comparisons of part-time work versus full-time work have found that part-time work is associated with lesser WFC and fewer negative outcomes such as depressive symptoms, but more positive outcomes such as greater W-F synergy, child care satisfaction, and family success (e.g., Buehler & O'Brien, 2011; Hill, Märtinson, & Ferris, 2004; Seto, Morimoto, & Maruyama, 2006).

The availability and potential benefits of flexible work schedules including part-time versus full-time work, however, can vary across cultures and national contexts. For example, Lyness, Gornick, Stone, and Grotto (2012) in their study of 21 countries from the 1997 ISSP Work Orientations Survey found that workers in more affluent welfare state countries that had greater unionization of the workforce and more workforce regulations reported greater work schedule control than workers from other countries. Lewis (2003) found that voluntary provisions of FWAs (flexible work arrangements) tended to be higher in countries that had medium levels of statutory provisions and legislations for work-life balance, such as Germany and Austria, and lower in countries that had very low (e.g., the United Kingdom, Ireland) or very high levels of statutory provisions or national legislations for work-life balance (e.g., Nordic countries). Masuda et al. (2012) studied managers across countries in Latin American, Anglo, and Asian clusters, and found that Anglo managers tended to most frequently report using FWAs and benefiting positively from these arrangements in terms of W-F outcomes. For Latin Americans, part-time work negatively related with turnover intentions and strain-based WFC, and for Asians, flextime was unrelated to time-based WFC, and telecommuting was positively associated with strain-based WFC.

Studies on organizational size and WFC are fairly limited. In a review of research on FWAs and its implementation, outcomes, and management, Lewis (2003) identified organizational size, and sector and economic factors as being associated with the adoption of FWA policies. Accordingly, Lewis summarized that,

> large organizations are more likely to provide formal FWAs than smaller ones; public sector organizations are more likely to develop initiatives than private sector companies; and, within the private sector, arrangements are more common in the service and financial sector compared with construction and manufacturing. (p. 3)

To the extent that FWAs positively impact WLB, one could expect as has been observed by den Dulk (2005) that larger organizations will be associated with lower WFC. At the same time, smaller organizations can offer informal family-friendly practices that can make employees feel more supported than the formal practices of larger organizations, which even though offered in theory, may be difficult to implement in practice (e.g., Cooper, Lewis, Smithson, & Dyer, 2001). Further, given the variation in availability of FWAs across cultures it is possible that organization size may interact with culture to affect the W-F interface and W-F outcomes.

Variables and Analyses

Dependent Variables

Ten dependent variables were included in the study. There were four measures of WFC: time-based WIF (TBWIF), time-based FIW (TBFIW), strain-based WIF (SBWIF), and strain-based FIW (SBFIW), as well as both directions of WFPS: WTFS and FTWS. Four measures of W-F outcomes were also included: family satisfaction (FS), life satisfaction (LS), psychological well-being (PWB), and turnover intention (TI). Details regarding how the dependent variables were measured can be found in Chapter 2. Measurement equivalence/invariance was established for all the dependent variables except psychological well-being. Please consult Chapter 2 for a detailed explication of this process.

Independent Variables

Societal Culture

Culture was measured by dividing the 10 countries into two categories (East versus West). The Western countries consisted of the five Anglo/European countries (Australia, Canada, Israel, Spain, and the United States), which were coded as 1.

The Eastern countries consisted of the countries in the Asian/Middle Eastern cluster (China, India, Indonesia, Taiwan, Turkey), which were coded as 2. For a more detailed theoretical rationale for measurement of culture along an East-West dimension see Chapter 2.

Demographic Contextual Variables

The following demographic variables were included. Respondent age (AGE) was measured in years and was coded into three categories: 1 = < 35 years, 2 = 35–45 years, and 3 = 45+ years, representing 36.4%, 44.8%, and 18.9% of the sample, respectively. Respondent education (EDU) was measured in terms of total number of years of education and was coded in to three categories: 1 = 0–12 years of education, 2 = 13–16 years of education, and 3 = 16+ years of education, representing 16%, 55%, and 29% of the sample, respectively. Number of children of respondent (NOC) was coded into two categories: 1 = 1 child and 2 = 2+ children, with 56% of respondents having more than one child. Age of youngest child (AYC) was measured in years and was coded into two categories: 1 = less than 3 years and 2 = greater than 3 years, with 67% of the sample being in the latter category.

Family-Related Contextual Variables

Living arrangements (LA) were coded as: 1 = myself, spouse/partner, and kids (nuclear), 2 = extended family, and 3 = other (myself only, myself and kids only, myself and spouse only), representing 69%, 18%, and 13% of the sample, respectively. Extended family living (EFL) was coded as: 1 = not living with extended family, 2 = live in our residence, 3 = live in their residence, and 4 = live close by, representing 50%, 28%, 10%, and 12% of the sample, respectively. Respondent's strength of religious beliefs (RB) was coded as: 1 = not at all important, 2 = somewhat important, 3 = very important, representing 14.4%, 41.3%, and 44.3% of the sample, respectively. Spouse's job schedule (SJS) was coded as: 1 = not working, 2 = working part-time, and 3 = working full-time, representing 14.2%, 21.5%, and 64.3% of the sample, respectively. Spouse's job type (SJT) was coded as: 1 = not working, 2 = non-managerial, and 3 = managerial, representing 11%, 51%, and 38% of the sample, respectively.

Work-Related Contextual Variables

Job schedule of the respondent (JS) was coded as: 1 = part-time, and 2 = full-time, with 72.6% of the sample employed full-time. Job type of respondent (JT) was coded as: 1 = nonmanagerial and 2 = managerial, with 53% of the sample in nonmanagerial positions. Organization size (OS) was coded as: 1 = less than 100 employees, 2 = 100–1,000 employees, 3 = 1,001–5,000 employees,

4 = 5,001–10,000 employees, and 5 = more than 10,000 employees, representing 34%, 25%, 16%, 8%, and 17% of the sample, respectively.

Covariate

Gender (GEN) was held constant as a covariate in the analyses, and was coded as 1 = male and 2 = female.

Analyses

Twelve separate multivariate analyses of covariance (MANCOVA) were run with culture (EW) and each of the 12 contextual variables (AGE, EDU, NOC, AYC, LA, EFL, RB, SJS, SJT, JT, JS, OS) as the independent variables, gender as the covariate, and the 10 W-F interface and W-F outcome variables (TBWIF, SBWIF, TBFIW, SBFIW, WTFS, FTWS, FS, LS, PWB, and TI) as the dependent variables. The significance of the MANCOVA results was ascertained at $p = .05$. Given the large number of dependent variables, the Bonferroni adjustment was used to reduce Type I error, and all univariate test results were examined at the $p \leq .001$ level of significance.

Results

The results of the MANCOVA analyses are summarized in Table 19.1. The multivariate main effects for context, culture, and gender were highly significant for all 12 analyses. The context X culture interactions were also highly significant for all context variables except self and spouse job type, which were nonsignificant.

Univariate Tests[1]

Respondent Age

The interactions between culture and age were significant for TBWIF, $F(2, 2701) = 11.21, p = .001$; SBWIF, $F(2, 2701) = 11.07, p = .001$; and TBFIW, $F(2, 2701) = 6.84, p = .001$. For those in the 35–45 and 45+ age groups, TBWIF and SBWIF were higher when they resided in Western as opposed to Eastern countries, $p < .001$. This culture difference was not significant for those under age 35. TBFIW was significantly lower for those living in the West than for those living in the East, ($p = .001$) for those in the < 35 year age group, $p < .001$, but not for those in the other two age categories.

There were significant main effects of age for SBFIW, $F(2, 2701) = 14.14$, $p = .001$; life satisfaction, $F(2, 2701) = 7.38, p = .001$; and turnover intent, $F(2, 2701) = 18.92, p = 0.001$. Respondents < 35 year of age had significantly higher

TABLE 19.1 MANCOVA results.

Context Variable	*Gender*			*Culture*			*Context*			*Culture × Context*		
	F	*df*	*p*	*F*	*df*	*p*	*F*	*df*	*p*	*F*	*df*	*p*
Age	8.18	10, 2692	.001	64.26	10, 2692	.001	5.62	20, 5386	.001	2.95	20, 5386	.001
Education	8.65	10, 2662	.001	59.67	10, 2662	.001	6.93	20, 5326	.001	4.88	20, 5326	.001
# Children	7.82	10, 2613	.001	65.37	10, 2613	.001	3.28	10, 2613	.001	2.85	10, 2613	.002
AYC	7.70	10, 2599	.001	63.74	20, 2599	.001	7.11	10, 2599	.001	3.84	10, 2599	.001
LA	8.37	10, 2604	.001	17.57	10, 2604	.001	13.14	20, 5210	.001	9.35	20, 5210	.001
EFL	5.41	10, 2052	.001	25.20	10, 2052	.001	2.16	30, 6162	.001	2.94	30, 6162	.001
RB	6.26	10, 2375	.001	42.43	10, 2375	.001	4.43	20, 4752	.001	2.92	20, 4752	.001
SJT	8.09	10, 2389	.001	62.85	10, 2389	.001	2.65	10, 2389	.003	.83	10, 2389	.60
Job Schedule	7.60	10, 2676	.001	52.27	10, 2676	.001	12.07	10, 2676	.001	8.57	10, 2676	.001
Job Type	8.08	10, 2670	.001	73.06	10, 2670	.001	2.10	10, 2670	.02	1.15	10, 2670	.32
Org. Size	7.33	10, 2449	.001	45.88	10, 2449	.001	6.43	40, 9808	.001	3.71	40, 9808	.001

SBFIW than respondents in the 35–45 year age group and respondents in the 45+ year age group, $p = .001$. Respondents < 35 years of age had significantly higher life satisfaction than respondents in the 35–45 year age group, $p = .001$. Respondents < 35 years of age had significantly higher turnover intent than respondents in the 35–45 year and 45+ year age groups, $p = .001$.

Respondent Education

The interactions between culture and education were significant for WTFS, $F(2, 2671) = 9.834, p = .001$; FTWS, $F(2, 2671) = 7.85, p = .001$, and turnover intent, $F(2, 2671) = 10.57, p = .001$.

There were significant differences in WTFS for respondents with less than 12 years of education, $F(1, 2695) = 11.88, p = .001$, as well as those who had 13–16 years of education, $F(1, 2695) = 43.79, p = .001$, and those with 16 or more years of education, $F(1, 2695) = 101.16, p = 0.001$. For those from all educational categories WTFS was significantly lower in the West than in the East, $p = 001$. However, this effect was particularly strong among those with >16 years of education. There was not a significant difference in the WTFS of those with 13–16 years and 16 years or more of education in the West, while for the East, WTFS of those with 16 years or more of education was more than that of those with 13–16 years of education, $p = .001$.

There was a significant difference in FTWS for respondents with 13–16 years of education, $F(1, 2696) = 46.86, p = .001$, and for respondents with 16+ years of education, $F(1, 2696) = 29.28, p = .001$. For these two groups, those living in the West reported significantly less FTWS than those living in the East, $p = .001$. The difference between cultures was not significant for those with less than 12 years education.

There was a significant difference in turnover intent only for respondents with 16+ years of education, $F\ (1, 2758) = 15.82, p = .001$, such that those living in the West experienced significantly less turnover intent than those living in the East, $p = .001$. There was no significant difference between East and West in turnover intent reported by respondents with 13–16 years of education or less than 12 years of education.

There were significant main effects of education for TBWIF, $F(2, 2671) = 12.41, p = .001$; TBFIW, $F(2, 2671) = 13.44, p = .001$; SBFIW, $F(2, 2671) = 8.48, p = .001$; and LS, $F(2, 2671) = 19.27, p = .001$. Respondents with 0–12 years of education had significantly lower TBWIF than both those with 13–16 years of education and those with 16+ years of education. Respondents with 0–12 years of education had significantly lower TBFIW than respondents with 16+ years of education, $p = .001$. Respondents with 0–12 years of education had significantly lower SBFIW than both those with 13–16 years of education and those with 16+ years of education, $p = .001$. Respondents with 0–12 years of education had significantly lower life satisfaction than respondents with 13–16 years of education and with 16+ years of education, $p = .001$.

Number of Children (NOC)

There was a significant interaction between culture and NOC for FTWS, $F(2, 2622) = 16.07, p = .001$, such that those with more than one child living in the West reported significantly less FTWS than those living in the East, $p = .001$. By contrast, there was no difference due to culture for those with one child. There was a significant main effect of NOC for WTFS, $F(2, 2622) = 11.80, p = .001$. Respondents with one child had significantly lower WTFS than respondents with two or more children, $p = .001$.

Age of Youngest Child (AYC)

Although the multivariate interaction effect between culture and AYC was significant, none of the univariate interaction effects were significant. In terms of main effects, there were significant univariate main effects of AYC for TBFIW, $F(2, 2608) = 11.45, p = .001$; SBFIW, $F(2, 2608) = 12.07, p = .001$; and life satisfaction, $F(2, 2608) = 21.97, p = .001$. Respondents with AYC < 3 years had significantly higher TBFIW and SBFIW than respondents with AYC ≥ 3 years, $p = .001$. Respondents with AYC < 3 years had significantly higher life satisfaction than respondents with AYC ≥ 3 years, $p = .001$.

Living Arrangements (LA)

The interactions between culture and LA were significant for WTFS, $F(2, 2627) = 7.38, p = .001$; FTWS, $F(2, 2627) = 33.58, p = .001$; family satisfaction, $F(2, 2627) = 13.45, p = .001$; life satisfaction, $F(2, 2627) = 46.82, p = .001$; and turnover intent, $F(2, 2627) = 11.021, p = .001$.

There were significant differences in WTFS for respondents living both in nuclear families, $F(1, 2649) = 106.23, p = .001$ and in extended families, $F(1, 2649) = 11.67, p = .001$. Those living in nuclear and extended families in the West experienced significantly less WTFS than those in the East, $p = .001$. There was no significant cultural difference for those in other types of family arrangements.

There was a significant difference in FTWS for both respondents living in nuclear families, $F(1, 2650) = 117.75, p = .001$, and for respondents in "other" living arrangements (i.e., myself only, myself and kids only, myself and spouse only), $F(1, 2650) = 13.97, p = .001$. For respondents living in nuclear families, those living in the West experienced significantly less FTWS than those living in the East, $p = .001$. On the other hand, for respondents in "other" living arrangements, those living in the West experienced significantly more FTWS than those living in the East, $p = .001$.

There was a significant difference in family satisfaction for respondents living in nuclear families, $F(1, 2714) = 73.92, p = .001$ and for respondents in "other" living arrangements, $F(1, 2714) = 78.26, p = .001$. Respondents living in both nuclear and "other" families in the West experienced significantly greater family satisfaction than those living in the East, $p = .001$. There was no significant difference for family satisfaction for those in extended family living arrangements in the East versus West.

There was a significant difference in life satisfaction for respondents in "other" living arrangements, $F(1, 2710) = 102.14$, $p = .001$, such that those in the West experienced more life satisfaction than those in the East, $p = .001$. In addition, there was a significant difference in turnover intent for respondents in "other" living arrangements, $F(1, 2713) = 13.66$, $p = .001$, such that those in the West experienced less turnover intent than those in the East, $p = .001$.

There were significant main effects of LA for TBFIW, $F(2, 2627) = 7.15$, $p = .001$; SBFIW, $F(2, 2627) = 27.79$, $p = .001$; and psychological well-being, $F(2, 2627) = 15.77$, $p = .001$. Respondents living in nuclear families had significantly lower TBFIW than respondents living in extended families, $p = .001$. Those in nuclear families had significantly lower SBFIW than those in extended families, $p = .001$, but significantly higher SBFIW than those in "other" family arrangements, $p = .001$. As well, those in extended families had significantly higher SBFIW than those in "other" family arrangements, $p = .001$. Respondents in nuclear and extended families had significantly higher PWB than respondents in "other" family settings, $p = .001$.

Extended Family Living (EFL)

There was a significant interaction between culture and EFL for life satisfaction, $F(2, 2061) = 7.81$, $p = .001$. There was a significant difference in life satisfaction for respondents not living with extended family, $F(1, 2103) = 17.36$, $p = .001$, such that those in the West experienced significantly lower life satisfaction than those in the East, $p = .001$.

Strength of Religious Beliefs (RB)

There were significant interactions between culture and RB for TBWIF, $F(2, 2384) = 6.71$, $p = .001$, and SBFIW, $F(2, 2384) = 13.45$, $p = .001$. There were significant differences in TBWIF for respondents with religious beliefs that were "not at all important," $F(1, 2460) = 15.08$, $p = .001$; "somewhat important," $F(1, 2460) = 11.91$, $p = .001$, as well as respondents whose religious beliefs were "very important" to them, $F(1, 2460) = 68.95$, $p = .001$. Overall, those living in the West reported significantly higher TBWIF than those living in the East, $p = .001$. The differences between those from Eastern countries and those from Western countries increased as their strength of religious beliefs increased.

There was a significant difference in SBFIW for respondents with religious beliefs that were "not at all important," $F(1, 2460) = 13.37$, $p = .001$, as well as respondents whose religious beliefs were "somewhat important" to them, $F(1, 2460) = 75.55$, $p = .001$, such that those in the West reported significantly lower SBFIW than those in the East, $p = .001$. The East versus West difference was not significant for those with "very important" religious beliefs.

There was a significant main effect of religious beliefs for WTFS, $F(2, 2384) = 13.31$, $p = .001$, and for FTWS, $F(2, 2384) = 8.96$, $p = .001$. Respondents whose RB rating was "not at all important" and "somewhat important" had significantly lower WTFS than respondents whose RB rating was "very important," $p = .0001$. Respondents whose RB rating was "not at all important" had significantly lower FTWS than respondents whose RB rating was "very important," $p = .001$.

Spouse's Job Schedule (SJS)

Interactions between culture and SJS were significant for TBWIF, $F(2, 2701) = 9.52$, $p = .001$; TBFIW, $F(2, 2701) = 10.02$, $p = .001$; SBFIW, $F(2, 2701) = 7.71$, $p = .001$; WTFS, $F(2, 2701) = 17.66$, $p = .001$; FTWS, $F(2, 2701) = 7.45$, $p = .001$; and LS, $F(2, 2701) = 7.20$, $p = .001$.

There was a significant difference in TBWIF for respondents whose spouses were working part-time, $F(1, 2793) = 69.75$, $p = .001$; as well as respondents whose spouses were working full-time, $F(1, 2793) = 49.00$, $p = .001$. Respondents living in the West whose spouses were working part-time and full-time reported significantly higher TBWIF than respondents living in the East, $p = .001$, whereas there was no significant difference in TBWIF between East and West reported by respondents whose spouses were not working (see Figure 19.1).

There was a statistically significant difference in TBFIW for respondents whose spouses were not working, $F(1, 2792) = 12.095$, $p = .001$; as well as respondents whose spouses were working full-time, $F(1, 2792) = 11.826$, $p = .001$. Respondents living in the West whose spouses were not working and whose spouses were working full-time reported significantly lower TBFIW than respondents living in the East whose spouses were not working and whose spouses were working full-time, $p = .001$. There was no significant difference in the TBFIW reported by respondents from the East and West whose spouses were working part-time (see Figure 19.2).

There was a statistically significant difference in SBFIW for respondents whose spouses were not working, $F(1, 2794) = 22.150$, $p = .001$; as well as respondents whose spouses were working full-time, $F(1, 2794) = 67.513$, $p = .001$. Respondents living in the West whose spouses were not working and whose spouses were working full-time reported significantly lower SBFIW than respondents living in the East whose spouses were not working and whose spouses were working full-time, $p = .001$. There was no significant difference between West and East in SBFIW reported by respondents whose spouses were working part-time (see Figure 19.3).

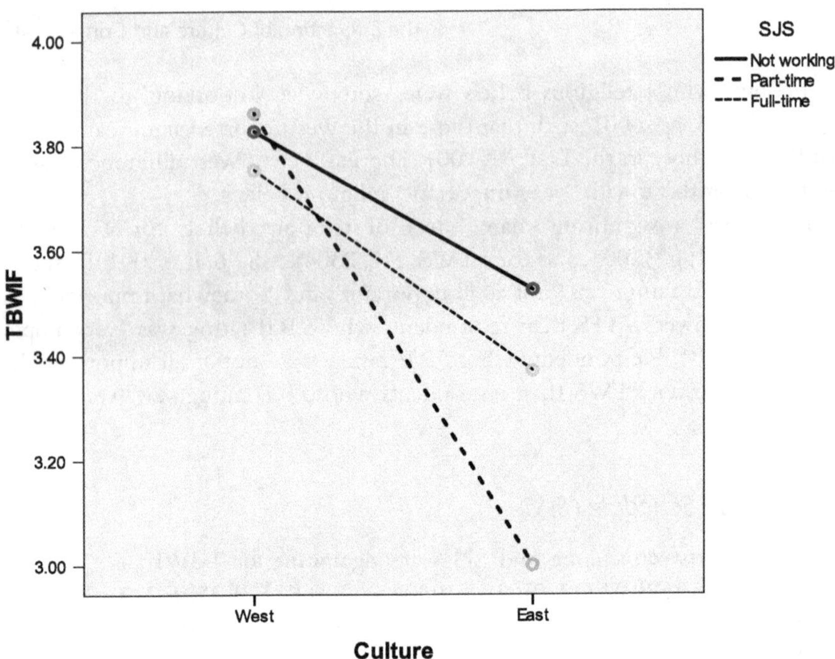

FIGURE 19.1 Profile plots for significant two-way interactions between EW × SJS–TBWIF.

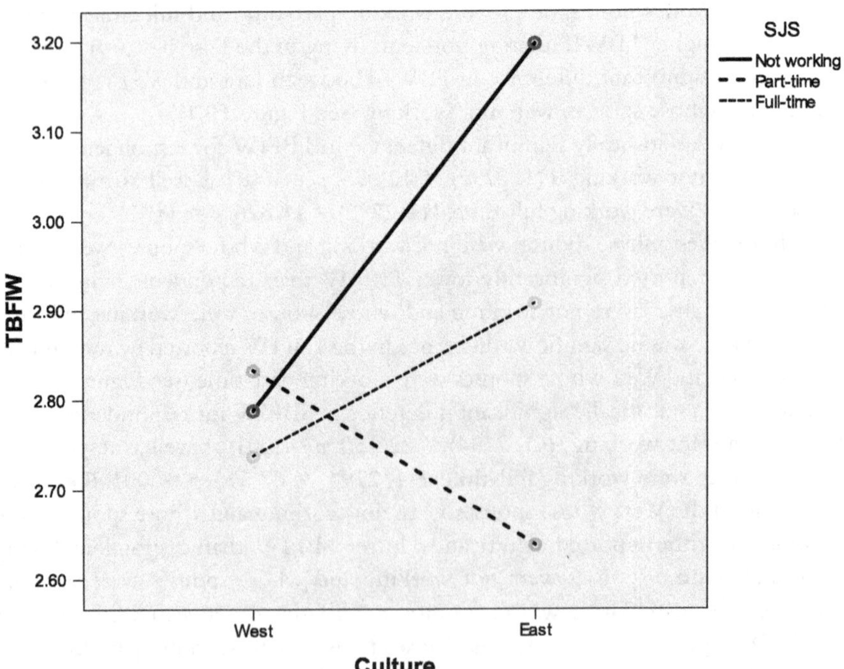

FIGURE 19.2 Profile plots for significant two-way interactions between EW × SJS–TBFIW.

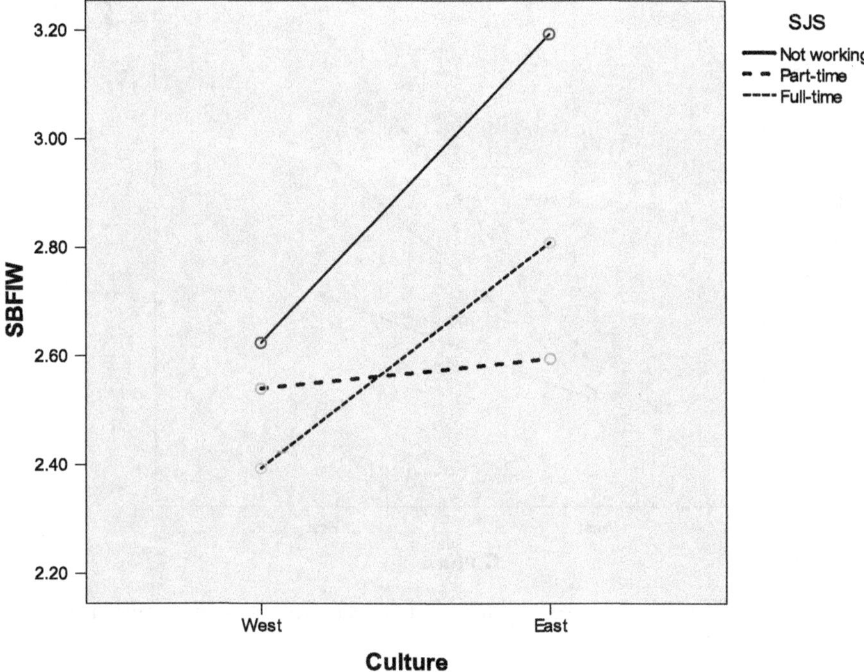

FIGURE 19.3 Profile plots for significant two-way interactions between EW × SJS–SBFIW.

There was a statistically significant difference in WTFS for respondents whose spouses were not working, $F(1, 2725) = 26.541$, $p = .001$, respondents whose spouses were working part-time, $F(1, 2725) = 85.755$, $p = .001$, as well as respondents whose spouses were working full-time, $F(1, 2725) = 98.489$, $p = .001$. Respondents living in the West reported significantly lower WTFS than respondents living in the East, whether their spouses were not working, working part-time or working full-time, $p = .001$. The difference in WTFS between Western and Eastern countries was greatest for respondents with spouses working part-time, followed by respondents with nonworking spouses, and it was least for respondents with spouses working full-time (see Figure 19.4).

There was a statistically significant difference in FTWS for respondents whose spouses were not working, $F(1, 2726) = 17.341$, $p = .001$; respondents whose spouses were working part-time, $F(1, 2726) = 33.247$, $p = .001$; and respondents whose spouses' were working full-time, $F(1, 2726) = 11.596$, $p = .001$. Respondents living in the West reported significantly lower FTWS than respondents living in the East, whether their spouses' were not working, working part-time, or working full-time, $p = .001$. The difference in FTWS between Western and Eastern countries was greatest for respondents with spouses working part-time, followed by respondents with nonworking spouses, and it was least for respondents with spouses working full-time (see Figure 19.5).

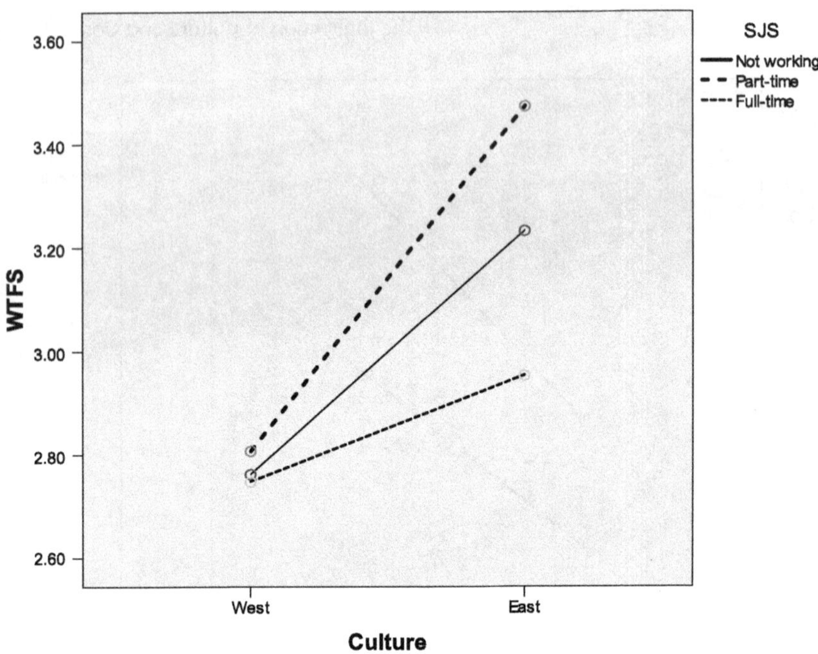

FIGURE 19.4 Profile plots for significant two-way interactions between EW × SJS–WTFS.

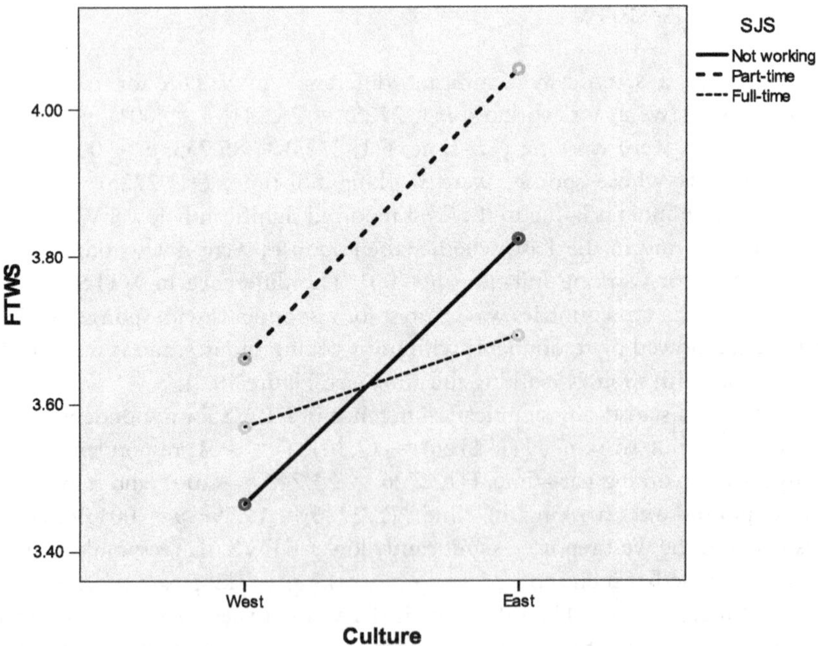

FIGURE 19.5 Profile plots for significant two-way interactions between EW × SJS–FTWS.

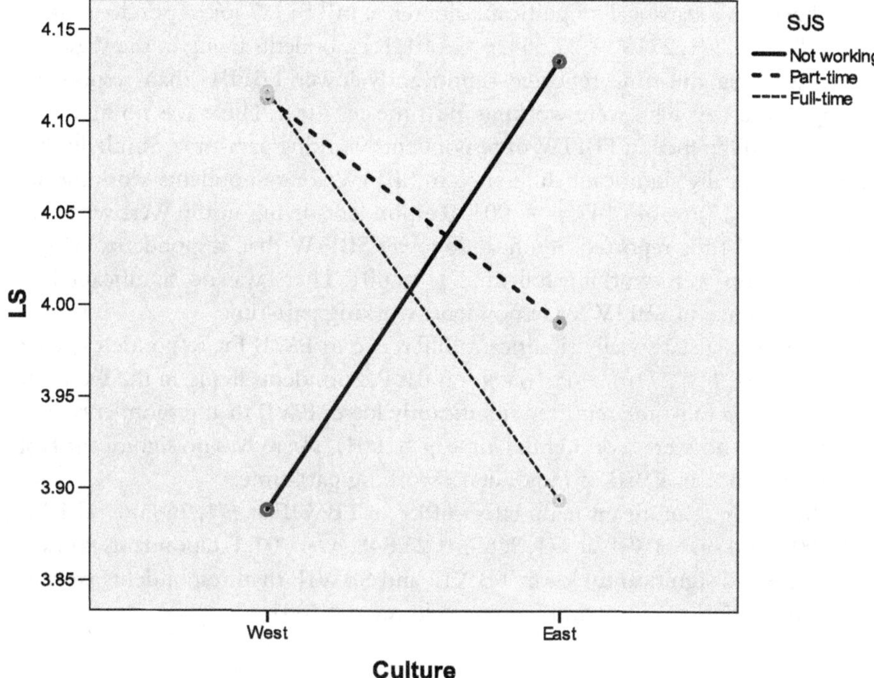

FIGURE 19.6 Profile plots for significant two-way interactions between EW × SJS–LS.

There was a statistically significant difference in LS only for respondents whose spouses were working full-time, $F(1, 2786) = 26.317, p = .001$. Respondents living in the West whose spouses worked full-time reported significantly higher LS than respondents living in the East whose spouses worked full-time, $p = .001$ (see Figure 19.6). There were no significant main effects of SJS on any of the dependent variables.

Spouse's Job Type (SJT)

Results of univariate tests indicated no significant interactions between culture (EW) and SJT for any of the 10 dependent variables. There was a significant main effect of SJT on LS at $F(1, 2398) = 11.466, p = .001$. In both Eastern and Western cultures respondents reported lower LS when their spouses held nonmanagerial rather than managerial jobs, $p = .001$.

Respondent's Job Schedule (JS)

There were significant interactions between culture (EW) and JS for TBFIW at $F(1, 2685) = 17.243, p = .001$, SBFIW at $F(1, 2685) = 56.301, p = .001$, and PWB at $F(1, 2685) = 16.709, p = .001$.

There was a statistically significant difference in TBFIW for respondents working full-time, $F(1, 2715) = 22.554, p = .001$. Respondents living in the West who were working full-time reported significantly lower TBFIW than respondents living in the East who were working full-time, $p = .001$. There was no significant East-West difference in TBFIW of respondents working part-time. Similarly, there was a statistically significant difference in SBFIW for respondents working full-time, $F(1, 2717) = 143.147, p = .001$. Respondents living in the West who were working full-time reported significantly lower SBFIW than respondents living in the East who were working full-time, $p = .001$. There was no significant East-West difference in SBFIW of respondents working part-time.

There was a statistically significant difference in PWB for respondents working full-time, $F(1, 2710) = 65.163, p = .001$. Respondents living in the West who were working full-time reported significantly lower PWB than respondents living in the East who were working full-time, $p = .001$). There was no significant East-West difference in PWB of respondents working part-time.

There was a significant main effect of JS on TBWIF at $F(1, 2685) = 101.716$, $p = .001$, and on SBWIF at $F(1, 2685) = 25.848, p = .001$. Respondents working part-time had significantly lower TBWIF and SBWIF than respondents working full-time in both Western and Eastern cultures, $p = .001$.

Respondent's Job Type (JT)

There were no significant main or interaction effects between culture (EW) and JT at the $p = .001$ level of significance.

Organization Size (OS)

There were significant interactions between culture (EW) and OS for SBWIF at $F(1, 2458) = 4.433, p = .001$, and for LS at $F(1, 2458) = 12.512, p = .001$.

There was a statistically significant difference in SBWIF for organization size of 1,001–5,000 employees, $F(1, 2543) = 22.219$, $p = .001$; and for organization size of 10,000+ employees, $F(1, 2543) = 14.389, p = .001$. Respondents living in the West who were working in organizations employing 1,001–5,000 employees as well as those who were working in organizations employing 10,000+ employees reported significantly higher SBWIF than respondents living in the East who were working in organizations employing 1,001–5,000 employees and those who were working in organizations employing 10,000+ employees, $p = .001$. There was no significant East-West difference in SBWIF reported by employees working in organizations with less than 100, 101–1000, and 5,001–10,000 employees.

There was a statistically significant difference in LS for organization size of 5,001–10,000 employees, $F(1, 2540) = 18.747$, $p = .001$; and for organization size of 10,000+ employees, $F(1, 2540) = 58.426, p = .001$. Respondents living in the West who were working in organizations employing 5,001–10,000 employees and 10,000+ employees reported significantly higher LS than respondents living in the East who were working in organizations employing 5,001–10,000 employees and 10,000+ employees, $p = .001$. There was no significant East-West difference in LS reported by employees working in organizations with less than 100, 101–1,000 and 1,001–5,000 employees.

There was a significant main effect of OS on SBFIW at $F(1, 2458) = 8.989$, $p = .001$ and on FTWS at $F(1, 2458) = 8.112$, $p = .001$. In both Western and Eastern cultures, respondents in small organizations having less than 100 employees had significantly higher SBFIW than respondents working in all other sizes of organizations, $p = .001$. In both Western and Eastern cultures, respondents in small organizations having less than 100 employees had significantly higher FTWS than respondents working in organizations with 5,001–10,000 employees, $p = .001$.

Summary and Discussion

This study explored the moderating effect of three kinds of contextual variables—demographic, nonwork/family, and work—on the relationship between culture and W-F interface and outcome variables. A total of 24 possible effects—12 main effects and 12 interaction effects were examined. See Table 19.2 for a summary of significant main and interaction effects obtained from the MANCOVA analyses.

Results of MANCOVA analyses and follow-up univariate analyses suggested some demographic commonalities as well as differences in W-F experiences across the globe. For instance in terms of the demographic variable of age, younger people (< 35 years of age) experienced greater SBFIW than older people in Eastern and Western cultures, supporting results of the study by Hill et al. (2014). In terms of the demographic variable of age of the youngest child, in both Eastern and Western cultures, similar to results reported by Allen and Finkelstein (2014), people with younger children, reported higher SBFIW and TBFIW than those with older children. Also, people with younger children reported greater life satisfaction and higher turnover intent than those with older children. Since persons with young families are likely younger in age, these results resonate findings of previous studies on the relationship between age and life satisfaction, subjective well-being, and occupational well-being, where life satisfaction is reportedly higher for younger and much older individuals (over 60+ years of age) in a curvilinear relationship (e.g., Mroczek & Spiro, 2005; Zacher, Jimmieson, & Bordia, 2014). Results also support findings of a significant and strong negative relationship between age and voluntary turnover (e.g., Ng & Feldman, 2009). With regard to the demographic variable of number of children, this study indicated that individuals with two or more children experienced higher WTFS than those with one child, in both Eastern and Western cultures. Previous studies have found higher levels of WFC in families with preschool aged children with the level of conflict lessening as children get older (e.g., Higgins, Duxbury, & Lee, 1994). Since families with two or more children are more likely to have older

TABLE 19.2 Summary of results.

		TBWIF	*TBFIW*	*SBWIF*	*SBFIW*	*WTFS*	*FTWS*	*PWB*	*FS*	*LS*	*TI*	*TOTAL (10)*
AGE	M&I	Sig. I	Sig. I	Sig. I	Sig. M	ns	ns	ns	ns	Sig. M	Sig. M	Sig. I = 3 Sig. M= 3 ns = 4
EDU	M&I	Sig. M	Sig. M	ns	Sig. M	Sig. I	Sig. I	ns	ns	Sig. M	Sig. I	Sig. I = 3 Sig. M = 4 ns = 3
RB	M&I	Sig. I	ns	ns	Sig. I	Sig. M	Sig. M	ns	ns	ns	ns	Sig. I = 2 Sig. M = 2 ns = 6
EFL	M&I	ns	ns	ns	ns	ns	ns	ns	ns	Sig. I	ns	Sig. I = 1 Sig. M = 0 ns = 9
LA	M&I	ns	Sig. M	ns	Sig. M	Sig. I	Sig. I	Sig. M	Sig. I	Sig. I	Sig. I	Sig. I = 5 Sig. M = 3 ns = 2
NOC	M&I	ns	ns	ns	ns	Sig. M	Sig. I	ns	ns	ns	ns	Sig. I = 1 Sig. M = 1 ns = 8
AYC	M&I	ns	Sig. M	ns	Sig. M	ns	ns	ns	ns	Sig. M	ns	Sig. I = 0 Sig. M = 3 ns = 7
JT	M	ns	Sig. M (p = .002)	ns	Sig. M (p = .002)	ns	ns	ns	ns	ns	ns	Sig. I = 0 Sig. M = 2 ns = 8

JS	M&I	Sig. M	Sig. I	Sig. M	Sig. I	ns	ns	Sig. I	ns	ns	ns	Sig. I = 3 Sig. M = 2 ns = 5
SJT	M	ns	ns	ns	ns	ns	ns	ns	ns	Sig. M	ns	Sig. I = 0 Sig. M = 1 ns = 9
SJS	I	Sig. I	Sig. I	ns	Sig. I	Sig. I	Sig. I	ns	ns	Sig. I	ns	Sig. I = 6 Sig. M = 0 ns = 4
OS	M&I	ns	ns	Sig. I	Sig. M	Sig. M	Sig. M	ns	ns	Sig. I	ns	Sig. I = 3 Sig. M = 4 ns = 3
TOTAL (12)	M = 12 I = 10	Sig. I = 4 Sig. M = 2 ns = 6	Sig. I = 5 Sig. M = 4 ns = 3	Sig. I = 2 Sig. M = 2 ns = 8	Sig. I = 3 Sig. M = 6 ns = 3	Sig. I = 4 Sig. M = 3 ns = 5	Sig. I = 5 Sig. M = 2 ns = 5	Sig. I = 2 Sig. M = 1 ns = 9	Sig. I = 2 Sig. M = 0 ns = 10	Sig. I = 4 Sig. M = 4 ns = 4	Sig. I = 3 Sig. M = 1 ns = 8	

Note. M = Main effect; I = Interaction effect

children, it is possible that such families are characterized by lower levels of conflict and concomitantly higher levels of WTFS than younger families (with one child). It is also possible that work becomes more meaningful as well as necessary as number of children increases, increasing WTFS alongside. Finally, with regard to the demographic variable of respondent education level, similar to previous studies (e.g., Schieman & Glavin, 2011), across both Eastern and Western cultures, those with graduate and post-graduate levels of education (13–16 and 16+ years) experienced significantly higher conflict (TBWIF, TBFIW, and SBFIW), but also significantly higher life satisfaction than those with high school level of education or less (0–12 years).

Besides the previously mentioned, common East-West W-F experiences across demographic factors, this study found significant interactions between culture and age, number of children, and education, though there were no interactions between culture and age of the youngest child. Middle-aged and older persons in the West reported greater TBWIF and SBWIF than older persons in the East. Conversely, younger persons living in the East reported greater TBFIW than younger persons living in the West. Higher WFC for older persons in the West has been reported previously by Schieman, Milkie, and Glavin (2009). In their study based on data from a 2005 survey of US workers, they found that WIF was greater for men in the 45- to 54-year-old group relative to younger men. They attributed this finding to the greater job authority, skill level, and earnings of the older men. With regards to the interaction between culture and number of children, respondents in the West with more than one child experienced significantly lesser FTWS than those living in the East. These results are testimony of the salience of "family" and "children" in Eastern relative to Western cultures. Family likely places greater time demands, especially on younger individuals in the East, but at the same time potentially creates more meaning in the lives of individuals. With regards to the relationship between culture and respondent education, higher levels of education (both graduate and post-graduate levels) had a more significant impact on W-F positive spillover in Eastern as compared to Western cultures (main effect). There was no significant difference in the WTFS of those with 13–16 years and 16 years or more of education in the West, while for the East, WTFS of those with 16 years or more of education was greater than that of those with 13–16 years of education. Additionally, turnover intention at higher education levels (post-graduate level+) was lesser for those living in the West as compared to those living in the East. Given that countries in the East included in this study (e.g., India, China, Taiwan, and Turkey) have been witnessing high levels of economic growth in recent years, greater job opportunities may be enhancing positive benefits of the W-F interface particularly for the educated. At the same time, frequent reports of job hopping in these countries (e.g., China View, 2008; Khatri, Fern, & Budhwar, 2001; Yiu & Saner, 2014), suggests that higher levels of education could be simultaneously contributing to higher turnover intent in the East.

Results of MANCOVA analyses and follow-up univariate analyses on non-work/family variables of living arrangements (LA) and extended family living (EFL) indicated that the main effect of LA occurred mostly on WFC variables, while interaction effects of LA with East-West culture impacted mainly W-F positive spillover and outcome variables. Across Eastern and Western cultures, nuclear family living created lesser TBFIW and SBFIW than extended family living, but more SBFIW than living in "other" alternative family arrangements. At the same time, psychological well-being (PWB) was higher in nuclear and extended families as compared to "other" alternative family living arrangements. It would seem that the relatively larger family size of extended families and nuclear families (as compared to "other" family arrangements such as single parent living) has the potential to provide greater support and therefore more PWB, but at the same time creates greater family demands and therefore more conflict for respondents.

Interactions between LA and East-West culture indicated that nuclear family living had the potential to increase positive spillover (both WTFS and FTWS) in the East as compared to the West, and similarly extended family living was associated with WTFS more in the East than in the West, whereas there was no significant cultural difference for those in other types of family arrangements. Nuclear families were associated with more family satisfaction in the West as compared to the East. Also, "other" living arrangements were associated with greater FTWS and LS, but lesser turnover intent in the West as compared to the East, whereas other types of family arrangements showed no significant differences in these W-F variables across cultures. These results once again support the importance of family and greater meaning, well-being, and therefore enrichment associated with it in Eastern cultures, especially when family takes on an "acceptable" form such as being nuclear or extended. Less traditional forms of family measured by "other" living arrangements, on the other hand, tend to have more positive W-F outcomes in Western cultures. The results (particularly with reference to the West) also resonate somewhat the findings of Huffman, Youngcourt, Payne, and Castro's (2008) study of US Army soldiers where they found that WFC had a stronger positive relationship with job satisfaction for married employees with children as compared to single, childless employees, and that WFC had a significant positive relationship with turnover intent for married employees with children but a nonsignificant negative relationship for single childless employees. A somewhat confusing finding was that "not living with extended family" was associated with lesser LS in the West rather than the East. It is possible that because extended family living is more than just a physical living arrangement, but rather a "state of mind" in Eastern cultures, "not living with extended family" does not have as significant of a negative impact on life satisfaction in the East as may be imagined. On the other hand, increasing cost of elder care and child care and the rise of the sandwich generation in the West (e.g., Riley & Bowen, 2005) may be increasing the difficulty of balancing work and family responsibilities for employees unless they are close to or living with extended family and therefore in a position to support them or receive support from them.

Strength of religious beliefs (RB) was significantly associated with W-F positive spillover. There was a main effect of RB with lower strength of religious beliefs being associated with lower WTFS and FTWS in both Eastern and Western cultures, similar to the results of Patel and Cunningham's (2012) study. However, RB also interacted significantly with culture to affect WFC variables. For every level of RB, TBWIF tended to be higher in Western as compared to Eastern cultures. However SBFIW was lesser in Western as compared to Eastern cultures for those whose religious beliefs were either "not at all important" or "somewhat important" to them, whereas there was no significant difference across culture for those with "very important" religious beliefs. It is possible that the resource gain/loss from strong religious beliefs has a stronger impact on W-F variables in more materialistic individualistic cultures like the West as compared to cultures of the East marked by the values of Confucianism and collectivism. Future research needs to explore this relationship in greater detail.

Spouse's job schedule (SJS), spouse's job type (SJT), respondent's job schedule (JS) and respondent's job type (JT) presented interesting results in follow-up univariate analyses of W-F variables. Although this paper categorizes SJS and SJT as nonwork/family variables and JS and JT as work variables, results of all four variables are discussed together here to present a more cogent picture of factors impinging W-F variables. It may be noted that gender was controlled for throughout in analyses, and impact of SJT was analyzed only for working spouses (i.e., coded as 2 = nonmanagerial or 3 = managerial).

JT had no interaction effect with culture, but only a main effect on both time-based and strain-based family interference with work. Nonmanagerial jobs in Eastern and Western cultures created lesser TBFIW and SBFIW than managerial jobs. SJT similarly had no interaction effect, but a significant main effect on life satisfaction. Having a spouse employed in a nonmanagerial job was associated with lesser LS than having a spouse employed in a managerial job. Positive association between managerial job type and WFC can be explained in terms of longer work hours and greater pressure associated with managerial jobs, similar to results of Winslow's (2005) study based on data from the West (United States) and Seto, Morimoto, and Maruyama (2006) based in the East (Japan). It is interesting that life satisfaction was related not to respondent's *own* job type, but rather to their spouse's type of job.

Job schedule (JS) interacted with culture to create lesser family interference with work (both time- and strain-based), but also lesser psychological well-being (PWB) for full-time respondents in the West as compared to full-time respondents in the East. JS also had a significant main effect on work interference with family conflict such that in both Eastern and Western cultures, TBWIF and SBWIF was greater for those who worked full-time rather than part-time. Previous studies (e.g., Hill, Märtinson, & Ferris, 2004; Hosking & Western, 2008; Winslow, 2005) have found a similar positive relationship between working full-time/longer hours and WFC. The significant interaction effects once again suggest that family demands may be more pervasive in the East. A larger market for work-family interventions such as day care, elder care facilities, etc., may allow full-time employees in the West to buy more support to buffer themselves from family interference in work. At the same time, the more unforgiving nature of full-time work in the West coupled with greater separation of work and family and lesser accommodation of family into work may be creating lesser psychological comfort and emotional well-being for full-time workers in the West.

A somewhat intriguing result was that respondent's full-time job schedule was associated with lower PWB for the respondent, but spouse's full-time schedule (SJS) was associated with higher LS in the West as compared to the East. In other words, if you were working in the West, your own full-time schedule was more likely to reduce your well-being than if you were working in the East, but your life satisfaction was more dependent upon your spouse's full-time schedule than on your own work schedule. This could perhaps best be explained as follows: Full-time schedules (for self and spouse) potentially provide more income and resources to hire help to reduce conflict and increase LS. At the same time, full-time schedules can cause employees to internalize work devotion and experience "stress from higher status" (Schieman, Milkie, & Glavin, 2009) resulting in lower PWB. This could be truer for individualistic and performance-oriented Western cultures relative to collectivistic and family-oriented Eastern cultures. Future research could compare process models of the work-family interface to test some of these relationships.

Spouse's Job Schedule (SJS) had interaction effects with culture on a range of W-F variables spanning conflict (TBWIF, TBFIW, and SBFIW), positive spillover (WTFS and FTWS), and outcomes (LS), but no main effects at all. Of the 12 contextual variables considered in analyses, SJS had the highest number of significant interaction effects. TBWIF was higher for respondents with part-time and full-time working spouses in the West as compared to the East, and TBFIW and SBFIW was lower for respondents with nonworking spouses and full-time working spouses in the West as compared to the East. WTFS and FTWS was lower in the West as compared to the East for respondents with nonemployed spouses as well as for respondents with spouses who worked full-time and part-time. LS was higher for respondents with full-time working spouse in the West. From these results we gauge that a full-time working spouse is associated with greater WIF (time-based) but also higher LS though lower FIW (time- and strain-based) in the West than a full-time working spouse in the East. A part-time working spouse is associated with greater TBWIF for respondents in the West while a nonworking spouse is associated with greater FIW (both time- and strain-based) for respondents in the East. Once again the results support the emerging pattern of greater interference of work demands in Western cultures and greater interference of family demands in the East. The results further imply that in order to effectively tailor W-F interventions, it is not just enough to know a respondent's spouse's work schedule, but it is also vital to know in which part of the world they reside in or are employed in.

Organization size had a main effect on conflict and positive spillover variables such that in both Eastern and Western cultures, smaller organization size was associated with higher SBFIW as well as higher WTFS and FTWS. Previous studies have shown that larger organizations are likely to offer more work-family initiatives compared to smaller organizations (e.g., Den Dulk, 2005). Smaller organizations on the other hand may compensate by offering a more family-friendly work culture, especially if they are also family-run. Hence, smaller organizations may create conditions where employees may experience greater family interference with work and positive spillover or enrichment at the same time (e.g., Cooper et al., 2001). Organization size also interacted with culture to impact SBWIF and LS. SBWIF was higher for mid-sized (1,001–5,000 employees) and large-sized (10,000+ employees) organizations in the West as compared to the East. Stronger competitive forces in market oriented Western economies perhaps contributed to higher conflict of employees. Interestingly, LS was also higher for employees working in larger sized organizations (5,001–10,000 employees and 10,000+ employees) in the West as compared to the East. It is possible that large sized firms in the Eastern countries included here (China, India, Indonesia, Turkey, and Taiwan) were largely public sector bureaucracies that by offering limited job autonomy, stifled initiative-taking on the part of employees and reduced LS.

Conclusion

MANCOVA analyses of main and interactions effects (with culture) of the contextual variables examined in this study revealed significant interactions for nine of the 12 contextual variables and significant main effects for 11 of the 12 contextual variables. All contextual variables except for AYC, JT, and SJT interacted with culture to impact positive and negative aspects of the W-F interface and W-F outcomes. All contextual variables except for SJS presented significant main effects. It would seem from this that AYC, JT, and SJT are likely to impact the W-F interface and W-F outcomes in a fairly uniform manner *regardless* of where you live, while SJS is likely to impact the W-F interface and W-F outcomes *depending* on where you live.

Post-hoc analyses indicated that of the demographic variables, EDU had the most number of significant effects in total (three interactions and four main effects); of the family related/nonwork variables, LA had the most number of significant effects in total (five interactions and three main effects); and of the work-related variables, OS had the most number of significant effects in total (two interactions and three main effects) on the W-F interface and W-F outcomes. It is important to note that the highest number of significant interactions are attributable to SJS (six) followed by LA (five), both of which are family-related variables.

The highest number of main effects on the other hand (three) are equally attributable to EDU (demographic variable), LA (family/nonwork variable) and OS (work variables).

A dependent variable-wise examination of the total of 12 main effects and 10 interactions effects indicated that LS and SBFIW had the maximum number of significant results (four interactions and four main effects for LS and three interactions and five main effects for SBFIW), whereas FS had the least number of significant results (one interaction and zero main effects). The most numerous interaction effects (four) occurred for FTWS and LS. EW culture interacted with three family variables (SJS, NOC, LA) and one demographic variable (EDU) to significantly impact FTWS. Also, EW culture interacted significantly with three family variables (SJS, EFL, LA) and one work-related variable (OS) to significantly impact LS.

Overall, the results of this study provide overwhelming support for the significant interaction between family/nonwork variables and culture. Future W-F research as well as W-F interventions would benefit from taking cognizance of variations in family structures and gender norms that exist around the globe and how these impact the W-F interface and W-F outcomes.

Note

1 Means, standard deviations and profile plots can be obtained from the author.

References

Allen, T. D., & Finkelstein, L. M. (2014). Work-family conflict among members of full-time dual-earner couples: An examination of family life stage, gender, and age. *Journal of Occupational Health Psychology, 19*(3), 376–384. doi:10.1037/a0036941

Allen, T. D., French, K. A., Dumani, S., & Shockley, K. M. (2015). Meta-analysis of work-family conflict mean differences: Does national context matter? *Journal of Vocational Behavior, 90*, 90–100. doi:10.1016/j.jvb.2015.07.006

Ammons, S. K., & Kelly, E. L. (2008). Social class and the experience of work-family conflict during the transition to adulthood. *New Directions for Childhood and Adolescent Development, 2008*(119), 71–84. doi:10.1002/cd.210

Amstad, F. T., Meier, L. L., Fasel, U., Elfering, A., & Semmer, N. K. (2011). A meta-analysis of work-family conflict and various outcomes with a special emphasis on cross-domain versus matching-domain relations. *Journal of Occupational Health Psychology, 16*(2), 151–169. doi:10.1037/a0022170.

Anafarta, N., & Kuruüzüm, A. (2012). Demographic predictors of work-family conflict for men and women: Turkish case. *International Journal of Business and Management*, 7(13), 145–158.

Aryee, S., & Luk, V. (1996). Work and nonwork influences on the career satisfaction of dual-earner couples. *Journal of Vocational Behavior, 49*(1), 38–52. doi:10.1006/jvbe.1996.0032

Aycan, Z. (2008). Cross-cultural approaches to work-family conflict. In D. S. Lero, K. Korabik, & D. L. Whitehead (Eds.), *Handbook of work-family integration: Research, theories and best practices* (pp. 353–370). San Diego, CA: Elsevier.

Bamberg, E., Dettmers, J., Funck, H., Krähe, B., & Vahle-Hinz, T. (2012). Effects of on-call work on well-being: Results of a daily survey. *Applied Psychology: Health and Well-Being, 4*(3), 299–320. doi:10.1111/j.1758-0854.2012.01075

Baral, R., & Bhargava, S. (2010). Work-family enrichment as a mediator between organizational interventions for work-life balance and job outcomes. *Journal of Managerial Psychology, 25*(3), 274–300. doi:10.1108/02683941011023749

Beauregard, T. A., Ozbilgin, M., & Bell, M. P. (2009). Revisiting the social construction of family in the context of work. *Journal of Managerial Psychology, 24*(1), 46–65.

Beham, B., Drobnič, S., & Präg, P. (2012). The work-family interface of service sector workers: A comparison of work resources and professional status across five European countries. *Applied Psychology: An International Review, 63*(1), 29–61. doi:10.1111/apps.12012

Beutell, N. J. (2010). Work schedule, work schedule control and satisfaction in relation to work- family conflict, work-family synergy, and domain satisfaction. *Career Development International, 15*(5), 501–518. doi:10.1108/13620431011075358

Bruck, C. S., Allen, T. D., & Spector, P. E. (2002). The relation between work-family conflict and job satisfaction: A finer-grained analysis. *Journal of Vocational Behavior, 60*(3), 336–353. doi:10.1006/jvbe.2001.1836

Buehler, C., & O'Brien, M. (2011). Mother's part-time employment: Associations with mother and family well-being, *Journal of Family Psychology, 25*(6), 895–906. doi: 10.1037/a0025993

Carlson, D. S., Grzywacz, J. G., & Kacmar, K. M. (2008). The relationship of schedule flexibility and outcomes via the work-family interface. *Journal of Managerial Psychology, 25*(4), 330–355. doi:10.1108/0268394101103527

Casper, W. J., Eby, L. T., Bordeaux, C., Lockwood, A., & Lambert, D. (2007). A review of research methods in IO/OB work-family research. *Journal of Applied Psychology, 92*(1), 28–43. doi:10.1037/0021-9010.92.1.28

China View. (2008). *Survey: Employers in China face worst staff turnover rate in Asia.* Retrieved from www.chinaview.cn

Cooper, C., Lewis, S., Smithson, J., & Dyer, J. (2001). *Flexible futures: Flexible working and work-life integration* (Report on Phase One). London, UK: Institute of Chartered Accountants England and Wales.

Den Dulk, L. (2005). Workplace work-family arrangements: A study and explanatory framework of differences between organizational provisions in different welfare states. In S.A.Y. Poelmans (Ed.), *Work and family: An international research perspective* (pp. 211–238). Mahwah, NJ: Lawrence Erlbaum.

Duxbury, L., & Higgins, C. (1994). Interference between work and family: A status report on dual-career and dual-earner mothers and fathers. *Employee Assistance Quarterly, 9*(3–4), 55–80. doi:10.1300/J022v09n03_05

Eby, L. T., Casper, W. J., Lockwood, A., Bordeaux, C., & Brinley, A. (2005). Work and family research in IO/OB: Content analysis and review of the literature (1980–2002). *Journal of Vocational Behavior, 66*(1), 124–197. doi:10.1016/j.jvb.2003.11.003

Frone, M. R., Russell, M., & Cooper, M. L. (1992). Antecedents and outcomes of work-family conflict: Testing a model of the work-family interface. *Journal of Applied Psychology*, 77(1), 65–78. doi:10.1037/0021-9010.77.1.65

Fujimoto, Y., & Azmat, F. (2014). Organizational justice of work-life balance for professional/managerial group and non-professional group in Australia: Creation of inclusive and fair organizations. *Journal of Management & Organization, 20*(5), 587–607. doi:10.1017/jmo.2014.45

Gervais, R. L., & Millear, P. (2014). The well-being of women at work: The importance of resources across the life course. *Journal of Organizational Change Management, 27*(4), 598–612. doi:10.1108/JOCM-05-2014-0103

Greenhaus, J. H., & Powell, G. N. (2006). When work and family are allies: A theory of work-family enrichment. *Academy of Management Review, 31*(1), 72–79. doi:10.5465/AMR.2006.19379625

Grzywacz, J. G., & Marks, N. F. (2000). Reconceptualizing the work-family interface: An ecological perspective on the correlates of positive and negative spillover between work and family. *Journal of Occupational Health Psychology, 5*(1), 111–126. doi:10.1037/1076-8998.5.1.111

Gürbüz, F. G., and Toğran, E. (2003). A study on job stress and work-family conflict. *Öneri*, 5(20), 119–130.

Higgins, C., Duxbury, L., & Lee, C. (1994). Impact of life-cycle stage and gender on the ability to balance work and family responsibilities. *Family Relations, 43*(2), 144–150. doi:10.2307/585316

Hill, E. J., Erickson, J. J., Fellows, K. J., Martinengo, G., & Allen, S. M. (2014). Work and family over the life course: Do older workers differ? *Journal of Family and Economic Issues, 35*(1), 1–13. doi:10.1007/s10834-012-9346-8.

Hill, E. J., Erickson, J. J., Holmes, E. K., & Ferris, M. (2010). Workplace flexibility, work hours, and work-life conflict: Finding an extra day or two. *Journal of Family Psychology, 24*(3), 349–358. doi:10.1037/a0019282

Hill, E. J., Märtinson, V., & Ferris, M. (2004). New-concept part-time employment as a work- family adaptive strategy for women professions with small children. *Family Relations, 53*(3), 282–292. doi:10.1111/j.0022-2445-2004.0004.x

Hofstede, G. (1980). *Culture's consequences: International differences in work-related values*. Newbury Park, CA: Sage.

Hosking, A., & Western, M. (2008). The effects of non-standard employment on work-family conflict. *Journal of Sociology, 44*(1), 5–27.

Huffman, A. H., Youngcourt, S. S., Payne, S. C., & Castro, C. A. (2008). The importance of construct breadth when examining interrole conflict. *Educational and Psychological Measurement, 68*(3), 515–530. doi:10.1177/0013164407308472

Jain, S., & Nair, S. K. (2015). Role of demographic variables in work-family enrichment: A study of sales employees in India. *International Journal of Business and Management Invention, 4*(6), 8–18. Retrieved from www.ijbmi.org

Jensen, L. A. (2006). Liberal and conservative conceptions of family: A cultural-developmental study. *The International Journal for the Psychology of Religion, 16*(4), 253–269. doi:10.1207/s15327582ijpr1604_2

Joplin, J. R. W., Shaffer, M. A., Francesco, A. M., & Lau, T. (2003). The macro-environment and work-family conflict: Development of a cross-cultural comparative framework. *International Journal of Cross Cultural Management, 3*(3), 305–328. doi:10.1177/1470595803003003004

Khatri, N., Fern, C.T., & Budhwar, P. (2001). Explaining employee turnover in an Asian context. *Human Resource Management Journal, 11*(1), 54–74. doi:10.1111/j.1748-8583.2001.tb00032.x

Kierner, A. (2015). Dual-income and dual-career couples in international context. In L. Mäkelä & V. Suutari (Eds.), *Work and family in the international context* (pp. 95–116). Cham, Switzerland: Springer.

Kinnunen, U., & Mauno, S. (1998). Antecedents and outcomes of work-family conflict among employed women and men in Finland. *Human Relations, 51*(2), 157–177. doi:10.1177/001872679805100203

Kluckhohn, F. R., & Strodtbeck, F. L. (1961). *Variations in value orientations*. Evanston, IL: Row, Peterson.

Konrad, A. M., & Yang, Y. (2012). Is using work–life interface benefits a career-limiting move? An examination of women, men, lone parents, and parents with partners. *Journal of Organizational Behavior, 33*(8), 1095–1119. doi:10.1002/job.1782

Kunst, J. R., Løset, G. K., Hosøy, D., Bjorvatn, B., Moen, B. E., Magerøy, N., & Pallesen, S. (2014). The relationship between shift work schedules and spillover in a sample of nurses. *International Journal of Occupational Safety and Ergonomics, 20*(1), 139–147. doi:10.1080/10803548.2014.11077030

Lee, C. M., & Duxbury, L. (1998). Employed parents' support from partners, employers and friends. *The Journal of Social Psychology, 138*(3), 303–322. doi:10.1080/00224549809600383

Lembrechts, L., Dekocker, V., Zanoni, P., & Puligano, V. (2014). A study of the determinants of work-to-family conflict among hospital nurses in Belgium. *Journal of Nursing Management, 23*(7), 898–909. doi:10.1111/jonm.12233

Lewis, S. (2003). Flexible work arrangements, implementation, outcomes and management. In C. L. Cooper & I. T. Robertson (Eds.), *International review of industrial and organizational psychology* (Vol. 18, pp. 1–28). Hoboken, NJ: John Wiley & Sons.

Lewis, S., Izraeli, D., & Hootsman, H. (1992). *Dual-earner families: International perspectives.* London, UK: Sage.

Luk, D. M., & Shaffer, M. A. (2005). Work and family domain stressors and support: Within- and cross-domain influences on work-family conflict. *Journal of Occupational and Organizational Psychology, 78*(4), 489–508. doi:10.1348/096317905X26741

Lyness, K. S., Gornick, J. C., Stone, P., & Grotto, A. R. (2012). It's all about control: Worker control over schedule and hours in cross-national context. *American Sociological Review, 77*(6), 1023–1049. doi:10.1177/0003122412465331

Martinengo, G., Jacob, J. I., & Hill, E. J. (2010). Gender and the work-family interface: Exploring differences across the family life course. *Journal of Family Issues, 31*(10), 1363–1390. doi:10.1177/0192513X10361709

Masuda, A., Poelmans, S.A.Y., Allen, T. A., Spector, P. E., Lapierre, L. M., Cooper, C. L., . . . Moreno-Velazquez, I. M. (2012). Flexible work arrangements availability and their relationship with work-to-family conflict, job satisfaction, and turnover intentions: A comparison of three country clusters. *Applied Psychology: An International Review, 61*(1), 1–29. doi:10.1111/j.1464-0597.2011.00453.x

Mroczek, D. K., & Spiro, A., III (2005). Change in life satisfaction during adulthood: Findings from the veterans affairs normative aging study. *Journal of Personality and Social Psychology, 88*(1), 189–202. doi:10.1037/0022-3514.88.1.189

Ng, T. W. H., & Feldman, D. C. (2009). Re-examining the relationship between age and voluntary turnover. *Journal of Vocational Behavior, 74*(3), 283–294. doi:10.1016/j.jvb.2009.01.004

Nomaguchi, K. M. (2012). Marital status, gender, and home-to-job conflict among employed parents. *Journal of Family Issues, 33*(3), 271–294. doi:10.1177/0192513X11415613

Noor, N. M. (2006). Malaysian women's state of well-being: Empirical validation of a conceptual model. *The Journal of Social Psychology, 146*(1), 95–115. doi:10.3200/SOCP.146.1.95-115

Padgett, M., Gjerde, K. P., Hughes, S. B., & Born, C. J. (2005). The relationship between pre-employment expectations, experiences, and length of stay in public accounting. *Journal of Leadership and Organizational Studies, 12*(1), 82–101. doi:10.1177/107179190501200108

Parasuraman, S., & Simmers, C. A. (2001). Type of employment, work-family conflict and well-being: A comparative study. *Journal of Organizational Behavior, 22*(5), 551–568. doi:10.1002/job.102

Patel, S. P., & Cunningham, C. J. L. (2012). Religion, resources, and work-family balance. *Mental Health, Religion & Culture, 15*(4), 389–401. doi:10.1080/13674676.2011.577765

Perrone-McGovern, K. M., Wright, S. L., Howell, D. S., & Barnum, E. L. (2014). Contextual influences on work and family roles: Gender, culture, and socioeconomic factors. *The Career Development Quarterly*, *62*(1), 21–28. doi:10.1002/j.2161-0045.2014.00067.x

Poelmans S.A.Y., O'Driscoll M., & Beham B. (2005). A review of international research in the field of work and family. In S.A.Y. Poelmans (Ed.), *Work and family: An international research perspective* (pp. 3–46). Mahwah, NJ: Erlbaum

Rajadhyaksha, U. (2004). Work-family balance and dual career couples: What do organizations of the future need to know? In R. Padaki, N. M. Agarwal, C. Balaji, & G. Mahapatra (Eds.), *Emerging Asia: An HR agenda* (pp. 333–356). New Delhi: McGraw-Hill.

Rajadhyaksha, U., & Bhatnagar, D. (2000). Life role salience: A study of dual career couples in the Indian context. *Human Relations*, *53*(4), 489–511. doi:10.1177/0018726700534002

Riley, L. D., & Bowen, C. (2005). The sandwich generation: Challenges and coping strategies of multigenerational families. *The Family Journal*, *13*(1), 52–58. doi:10.1177/1066480704270099

Sav, A., Harris, N., & Sebar, B. (2014). Australian Muslim men balancing work, family and religion: A positive look at a negative issue. *Personnel Review*, *43*(1), 2–18. doi:10.1108/PR-07-2012-0130

Schieman, S., & Glavin, P. (2011). Education and work-family conflict: Explanations, contingencies and mental health consequences. *Social Forces*, *89*(4), 1341–1362. doi:10.1093/sf/89.4.1341

Schieman, S., Milkie, M. A., & Glavin, P. (2009). When work interferes with life: Work-nonwork interference and the influence of work-related demands and resources. *American Sociological Review*, 74(6), 966–988. doi:10.1177/000312240907400606

Schieman, S., Whitestone, Y. K., & Van Gundy, K. (2006). The nature of work and the stress of higher status. *Journal of Health and Social Behavior*, 47(3), 242–257. doi:10.1177/002214650604700304

Schwartz, S. H. (1994). Beyond individualism-collectivism: New cultural dimensions of values. In U. Kim, H. C. Triandis, C. Kagitcibasi, S-C. Choi, & G. Yoon (Eds.), *Individualism and collectivism: Theory, method, and application* (pp. 85–119). Newbury Park, CA: Sage.

Seto, M., Morimoto, K., & Maruyama, S. (2006). Work and family life of childrearing women workers in Japan: Comparison of non-regular employees with short working hours, non-regular employees with long working hours, and regular employees. *Journal of Occupational Health*, *48*, 183–191. doi:10.1539/joh.48.183

Shaffer, M. A., Joplin, J. R. W., & Hsu, Y. (2011). Expanding the boundaries of work-family research: A review and agenda for future research. *International Journal of Cross-Cultural Management*, *11*(2), 221–268. doi:10.1177/1470595811398800

Shockley, K. M., & Singla, N. (2011). Reconsidering work-family interactions and satisfaction: A meta-analysis. *Journal of Management*, *37*, 861–886. doi:10.1177/0149206310394864

Song, Z., Foo, M., Uy, M. A., & Sun, S. (2011). Unraveling the daily stress crossover between the unemployed and their employed spouses. *Journal of Applied Psychology*, *96*(1), 151–168. doi:10.1037/a0021035

Töyry, S., Kalimo, R., Äärimaa, M., Juntunen, J., Seuri, M., & Räsänen, K. (2004). Children and work-related stress among physicians. *Stress and Health*, *20*(4), 213–221. doi:10.1002/smi.1009

Trompenaars, F. (1993). *Riding the waves of culture*. London, UK: The Economist Books.

Turk, M., Davas, A., Tanik, F. A., & Montgomery, A. J. (2013). Organizational stressors, work-family interface and the role of gender in the hospital: Experiences from Turkey. *British Journal of Health Psychology*, *19*(2), 442–458. doi:10.1111/bjhp.12041

Väänänen, A., Kumpulainen, R., Kevin, M. V., Ala-Mursula, L., Kouvonen, A., Kivimäki, M., . . . Vahtera, J. (2008). Work-family characteristics as determinants of sickness absence: A large-scale cohort study of three occupational grades. *Journal of Occupational Health Psychology, 13*(2), 181–196. doi:10.1047/1076-8998.13.2.181

van Steenbergen, E. F., Kluwer, E. S., & Karney, B. R. (2011). Workload and the trajectory of marital satisfaction in newlyweds: Job satisfaction, gender, and parental status as moderators. *Journal of Family Psychology, 25*(3), 345–355. doi:10.1037/a0023653

Voydanoff, P. (2005). Work demands and work-to-family and family-to-work conflict: Direct and indirect relationships. *Journal of Family Issues, 26*(6), 707–726. doi:10.1037/1076-8998.13.2.181

Winslow, S. (2005). Work-family conflict, gender, and parenthood, 1977–1997. *Journal of Family Issues, 26*(6), 727–755. doi:10.1177/0192513X05277522

Wittmer, J. L. S., & Martin, J. E. (2010). Emotional exhaustion among employees without social or client contact: The key role of nonstandard work schedule. *Journal of Business Psychology, 25*(4), 607–623. doi:10.1007/s10869-009-9153-x

Yiu, L., & Saner, R. (2014). Talent attrition and retention: Strategic challenges for Indian industries in the next decade. *Elite Research Journal of Accounting and Business Management, 2*(1), 1–9. Retrieved from www.eliteresearchjournals.org/erjabm/index.htm

Zacher, H., Jimmieson, N. L., & Bordia, P. (2014). Time pressure and coworker support mediate the curvilinear relationship between age and occupational well-being. *Journal of Occupational Health Psychology, 19*(4), 462–475. doi:10.1037/a0036995

20

CONCLUSION

Contributions of Project 3535 to Theory, Research, and Practice

Karen Korabik

Significance of Project 3535

Project 3535 is one of the most comprehensive research projects on the work-family (W-F) interface that has been carried out to date. Its purpose was to investigate the universal as well as culture-specific aspects of the W-F interface in a collaborative team environment guided by a best practices approach to conducting cross-cultural research. Project 3535 is ground breaking due to its comprehensive scope, the breadth and depth of its coverage, its advancement of culture-sensitive theory, its incorporation of multiple methods (qualitative, quantitative, and social policy) and multiple approaches (micro-macro, emic/etic, and culturalist/structuralist), and the rigor of its methodology. This book is the culmination of this endeavor.

Country and Participant Sampling

Project 3535 is unique because it included data collected from nearly 3,000 employed married/cohabiting parents in 10 countries on four continents. Although the field of cross-national work-family (W-F) research has been developing rapidly, large-scale global studies of this type are still rare. Most previous examinations of the W-F interface have used samples from North America (Powell, Francesco, & Ling, 2009). A review of 219 W-F studies conducted outside of the United States indicated that only 12 of them compared three or more countries (Shaffer, Joplin, & Hsu, 2011). Although many more multinational studies have recently been carried out, almost all of them have been done solely within a European context (e.g., Beham, Drobnič, & Präg, 2014; Lyness & Kropf, 2005; Steibler, 2009).

We are aware of only a handful of multinational studies that have included countries from more than one continent. However, the sampling criteria used in these studies places limitations on the conclusions that can be drawn from them. For example, although Hill, Yang, Hawkins, and Ferris (2004) sampled employees from 48 countries around the world, all of their participants came from a single corporation (i.e., IBM). Haar, Russo, Sune, and Ollier-Malaterre (2014) examined work-life balance in employees in seven national contexts that included Europe, Asia, and two subcultures in New Zealand. However, their sample contained a mixture of employees who were married and single, as well as those who did and did not have children. The CISMS 2 project by Spector and colleagues (e.g., Masuda et al., 2012; Spector et al., 2007) included 20 countries from five continents that were categorized into three or four clusters (i.e., Anglo, Asian, Eastern European, and Latin American) depending on the particular study. But, their sample was composed only of managers, the majority of whom were men. Furthermore, not all of their participants were married or parents. Therefore, the extent to which the results of such studies are a function of factors such as their participants' organizational affiliation; gender; or marital, parental, or managerial status remains unclear.

By contrast, Project 3535 specifically sampled married/cohabiting parents from a wide variety of different organizations. The participants came from 10 countries, representing five cultural regions (i.e., Anglo, Latin European, Middle Eastern, Confucian Asian, and South Asian) on four continents. We included some countries (e.g., India, Indonesia) on which there had been a dearth of previous information. Since research has shown that managerial and nonmanagerial employees differ in a number of ways that are relevant to the W-F interface (Oliver, Korabik, McElwain, & Lero, 2008), our sample was stratified by job level. Similarly, because men and women have often been shown to be differentially affected by the W-F interface (Korabik, McElwain, & Chappell, 2008) the sample was also stratified by gender.

Culture-Sensitive Theory

Project 3535 also contributed to the literature on the W-F interface through its application of culture-sensitive theory. Most previous cross-national W-F research has been atheoretical (Shaffer et al., 2011) or based entirely on theories formulated in the United States (Powell et al., 2009). Powell et al. (2009) have discussed the necessity of developing culture-sensitive theories that examine how cultural dimensions impact core W-F constructs and their relationships with their antecedents and consequences. Four such cultural values dimensions were identified by Powell et al. (2009). Although the simultaneous use of more than one of these is recommended (Ollier-Malaterre, Valcour, DenDulk, & Kossek, 2013), the few multinational W-F studies that have incorporated a dimension of culture have typically focused only on a single dimension, usually Individualism-Collectivism

(I-C) (e.g., CISMS) or sometimes gender egalitarianism (Ollier-Malaterre et al., 2013). An exception to this is the study by Haar et al. (2014) where both I-C and gender egalitarianism were used together in the same study. Moreover, in almost all studies the information about where countries fall on these cultural dimensions is based on secondary source information (i.e., scores from Hofstede or GLOBE) instead of on information directly obtained from the study's own participants.

Project 3535 focused on advancing the development of culture-sensitive theory in several ways. First, we used cultural dimensions both to select the countries in our sample and to place the countries into categories for analysis. Following the procedure used in the GLOBE project (House, Hanges, Javidian, Dorfman, & Gupta, 2004), we relied on secondary source data for the former and the responses of our survey participants for the latter. More specifically, countries were selected based on the two a priori cultural dimensions of gender egalitarianism (operationalized by the UN Gender Development Index) and type of societal support system. The 10 countries were later empirically classified using a profile analysis based on the two cultural values of I-C and traditional/egalitarian gender-role ideology. This resulted in three country categories: (1) Individualistic-Egalitarian (I-E: Australia, Canada, the United States, Spain), (2) Collectivist-Traditional (C-T: China, India, Indonesia, Turkey), and (3) Mid Collectivist-Mid Traditional (MC-MT: Israel, Taiwan).

Secondly, we contributed to the advancement of culture-sensitive theory by examining the impact of multiple dimensions of culture (e.g., I-C, gender egalitarianism, polychronicity) on the W-F interface. We formulated a state-of-the art, integrative model that specified the many ways in which culture impacted the relationships among: (1) key W-F interface constructs (bidirectional WFC, W-F guilt, and positive spillover), (2) within- and cross-domain antecedents (role overload, coping strategies, and social support), (3) within- and cross-domain outcomes in the work (turnover intent), family (family satisfaction), and well-being (e.g., life satisfaction, psychological distress) domains, and (4) moderating variables (e.g., gender and context). We know of no other multinational study of the W-F interface that has been so comprehensive in its scope.

Multiple Methods and Approaches

Project 3535 is also notable for its utilization of multiple methods and approaches. Data were collected from multiple sources using multiple methods. More specifically, social policy data, qualitative focus group data, and quantitative survey data were collected during the three phases of our project. This ensured both depth and breadth of coverage as well as a focus on both micro- and macro-level processes. Among the advantages of using multiple methods in cross-national W-F research are that they enhance one's ability to triangulate findings (Shaffer et al., 2011) and the different methods can often compensate for each other's weaknesses, resulting in a more thorough understanding of a phenomenon.

Furthermore, throughout Project 3535 we strove to attain a balance between the examination of emic (culturally distinct) and etic (culturally generalizable) processes. The primary focus of Chapters 4–12, which present detailed information about the conditions in the individual countries that were part of Project 3535, was on explicating what was distinctive about each country. With the exception of a study by Joplin, Shaffer, Francesco, and Lau (2003) that examined two North American and three Asian countries using a qualitative focus group methodology, very few previous multinational W-F comparisons have had an emic emphasis. Yet, such in-depth examinations can be useful for understanding the disparate factors that impact the manner in which the W-F interface is experienced in different national contexts (Shaffer & Riordan, 2003). For instance, our focus group results demonstrated that although respondents from all countries spoke about feeling W-F guilt, the particular situations that made them feel guilty differed by country. Moreover, adopting an emic focus can highlight culturally idiosyncratic phenomena like the unique role that festivals play in contributing to WFC in India.

Chapters 13–19 were aimed at explicating both etic and emic processes. Thus, their content was focused not only on articulating which findings generalized over cultures, but also on which ones were representative only of certain national contexts and on using cultural variables in an attempt to explain why. Similarly, Chapter 3 on policies included two types of information. One was emic information from our social policy analysis that was specific to the policies present in each country. The other was the etic findings from our survey regarding the organizational policies in each country and how these were linked to W-F interface and outcome variables.

Few previous studies of the W-F interface have combined emic and etic components within a single study. But, as Project 3535 demonstrates, there were advantages to adopting this approach. For one thing, it helped to ensure that our survey questions were culturally relevant and that they addressed any culture-specific issues that existed. Furthermore, it enhanced our ability to understand the extent to which our results could be generalized across national contexts and gave us a much more complete understanding of the cultural dynamics underlying the W-F interface.

Project 3535 also incorporated both the culturalist and the structuralist approaches to the examination of W-F processes. The culturalist approach focuses on an examination of the impact of cultural values dimensions, whereas the structuralist approach focuses on the impact of legal, economic, and social structures (Ollier-Malaterre & Foucreault, 2017). Although both are important for a thorough understanding of the effects of national context, most studies concentrate on only one approach or the other (Ollier-Malaterre & Foucreault, 2017). Ollier-Malaterre and Foucreault point to Project 3535 as a rare instance of a research project that has involved an integration of the two approaches. As mentioned previously, Project 3535 incorporated several cultural dimensions (e.g., I-C, gender egalitarianism, and polychronicity). However, Project 3535 also had structuralist components. For example, the legal, economic, and social conditions in each country were explicated in Chapters 3–12 and some structuralist questions were included in our quantitative survey.

Attention to Reliability and Validity

As described in Chapter 2, we paid careful attention to using procedures that would ensure the reliability and validity of both our qualitative and quantitative data. We also carried out a detailed measurement invariance analysis on our measures. Shaffer et al. (2011) have called attention to the importance of establishing measurement invariance, stating that by ensuring that the meaning and interpretation of measures is similar across cultures, it improves confidence in a study's results.

Findings From Project 3535

Mean Differences on W-F Interface Constructs

We examined between country differences in the mean levels of three core W-F constructs: WFC, W-F positive spillover, and W-F guilt (see Table 20.1). In all 10 Project 3535 countries mean levels of work interference with family conflict

TABLE 20.1 Means for work-family interface constructs by country.

Country	*WIF*	*FIW*	*WTFS*	*FTWS*	*WIFG*	*FIWG*
Australia	3.85	2.69	2.73	3.55	3.90	2.66
Canada	3.90	2.52	2.69	3.46	3.99	2.40
Spain	3.81	2.44	2.62	3.92	3.56	2.55
US	3.75	2.46	2.84	3.58	3.55	2.17
I-E	3.84[a]	2.52[a]	2.73[a]	3.58[a]	3.79[a]	2.39[a]
Israel	3.55	2.87	2.87	3.55	3.02	2.53
Taiwan	3.38	2.88	2.70	3.37	3.73	3.07
MC-MT	3.48[b]	2.86[b]	2.79[a]	3.45[a]	3.37[b]	2.95[b]
China	3.39	2.65	2.69	3.56	4.31	3.22
India	3.78	3.46	3.58	3.92	3.51	3.41
Indonesia	2.52	2.19	3.30	3.96	3.54	3.96
Turkey	3.56	2.60	2.83	2.94	3.33	1.95
C-T	3.40[b]	2.87[b]	3.20[b]	3.88[b]	3.61[a]	2.78[b]
Total	3.55	2.76	2.98	3.72	3.63	2.76

Note. WIF = work interference with family conflict, FIW = family interference with work conflict, WTFS = work-to-family positive spillover, FTWS = family-to-work positive spillover, WIFG = work interference with family guilt, FIWG = family interference with work guilt; I-E = individualistic-egalitarian, MC-MT = mid collectivist-mid traditional; C-T = collectivist-traditional; column means with different superscripts differ significantly at $p < .001$.

(WIF) were found to be greater than mean levels of family interference with work conflict (FIW). This supports a large body of previous research that has been carried out in Anglo cultures as well as those in the European Union (Amstad, Meier, Fasel, Elfering, & Semmer, 2011; Korabik, Lero, & Whitehead, 2008). Paralleling this, our findings also indicated that the mean levels of work interference with family guilt (WIFG) were higher than mean levels of family interference with work guilt (FIWG) in all 10 countries. By contrast, mean levels of family-to-work positive spillover (FTWS) were higher than those for work-to-family positive spillover (WTFS) for all countries. This is consistent with previous findings based on North American samples reporting higher levels of FTWS compared to WTFS (e.g., Grzywacz & Marks, 2000; Hanson, Hammer, & Colton, 2006).

Next, we looked at whether the means on these constructs were impacted by culture. There has been very little previous examination of this issue. Powell et al. (2009) suggested that WFC should be higher in individualistic than in collectivistic cultures, whereas W-F enrichment should be higher in collectivistic than in individualistic cultures. In line with Powell et al.'s theorizing, Spector et al. (2007) found that both time- and strain-based WIF were higher in Anglo than in Asian cultures. A recent meta-analysis (Allen, French, Dumani, & Shockley, 2015), however, indicated that individualistic and collectivistic cultures did not differ on WIF, but those in Asian collectivistic cultures had higher FIW than those in individualistic cultures.

The results of Project 3535 demonstrated that, consistent with Powell et al.'s (2009) theory and Spector et al.'s (2007) results but contrary to Allen et al.'s (2015) findings, the mean level of WIF was significantly greater for I-E countries than for MC-MT and C-T countries. On the other hand, contrary to Powell et al.'s (2009) theory, but consistent with Allen et al.'s (2015) results, we found that the mean level of FIW was significantly greater for MC-MT and C-T countries than for I-E countries. By contrast, consistent with Powell et al.'s (2009) supposition, we found the mean levels of both WTFS and FTWS to be significantly higher in C-T countries than in I-E and MC-MT countries. For W-F guilt, levels of WIFG were significantly higher in I-E and C-T countries than they were in MC-MT countries. However, FIWG levels were significantly lower in I-E countries than they were in MC-MT and C-T countries.

W-F Conflict

We formulated an integrative model of how bidirectional WFC was related to within- and cross-domain antecedents and outcomes in the work and family domains (see Chapter 13). To our knowledge, this is the first time a comprehensive model has been tested with a large and diverse sample. We found evidence of both cross-cultural similarities and differences.

In regard to cross-cultural similarities, we found support for our hypothesized model using the combined data from all 10 countries. The most culturally invariant relationship was that greater family satisfaction was strongly associated with greater life satisfaction. Our findings indicate that this relationship, which had been found in a previous meta-analytic path analysis (Michel, Mitchelson, Kotrba, LeBreton, & Baltes, 2009), is generalizable across a large range of national contexts.

In general, we found same-domain relationships to be stronger than cross-domain relationships. Thus, consistent with much previous meta-analytic evidence (e.g., Byron, 2005; Ford, Heinen, & Langkamer, 2007; Michel et al., 2009), we found work overload to be more strongly related to WIF than to FIW and family overload to be more strongly related to FIW than to WIF. Our findings also suggested that work overload was directly related to intention to quit one's job, and family overload was directly related to decreased satisfaction with one's family, although the magnitude of these relationships was not great. This is congruent with Michel et al.'s (2009) findings that work and family antecedents were direct predictors of within domain satisfaction irrespective of mediation by WFC and that inclusion of both direct and mediating effects improved the fit of WFC models.

In terms of the relationship between WFC and outcomes, two alternative viewpoints have been put forth in the literature. According to the domain specificity approach (Frone, Yardley, & Markle, 1997), when one role interferes with another, dissatisfaction should occur in the receiving role (i.e., WIF will be associated with family dissatisfaction, whereas FIW will be associated with work dissatisfaction). By contrast, the source attribution hypothesis (Shockley & Singla, 2011) postulates that individuals are more likely to experience dissatisfaction with the domain they view as the source of conflict (i.e., WIF will be related to work dissatisfaction, whereas FIW will be related to family dissatisfaction). Findings from prior meta-analyses and meta-analytic path analyses have been mixed, with some supporting the domain specificity perspective (Ford et al., 2007) and others supporting the source attribution approach (Amstad et al., 2011; Michel et al., 2009; Shockley & Singla, 2011). Consistent with the domain specificity view, we found FIW to be a stronger predictor of turnover intention than WIF. However, consistent with the source attribution perspective, FIW was also more likely than WIF to be related to lower family satisfaction.

In terms of culture-specific effects, in I-E countries there were stronger relationships between work overload and WIF, WIF and turnover intention, and family overload and family satisfaction. By contrast, in C-T and MC-MT countries there were stronger relationships between family overload and both WIF and FIW and between FIW and turnover intention. Taken together, these findings suggest that work overload triggers WIF and turnover intention more easily in I-E cultures than in C-T ones, whereas family overload triggers WFC and turnover intention more easily in C-T cultures than in I-E ones. Our findings regarding work overload are congruent with those of previous research, indicating that although work demands are predictive of WIF in many countries (Shaffer et al.,

2011), the relationship is stronger in individualistic than collectivistic cultures (Lu, Gilmour, Kao, & Huang, 2006; Spector et al., 2004, 2007). However, our results extend this literature by showing that this finding is generalizable to a greater number of national contexts and to employees regardless of their job level. More importantly, however, because Project 3535 incorporated variables from the family domain (i.e., family overload, FIW, and family satisfaction) that had been neglected in previous cross-national model tests, our findings added to the literature by showing that family demands have a lesser impact on family satisfaction, but a greater impact on WFC and turnover intent, in collectivistic than in individualistic societies.

For some relationships, India and China differed from the other countries in our sample. In most countries, as previous meta-analytic research (Ford et al., 2007) has demonstrated, family satisfaction decreases as levels of WIF increase. In India and China, however, this effect was reversed with family satisfaction increasing as levels of WIF increased. In addition, higher work overload was more strongly related to higher levels of FIW in India and China than in the other countries. These counterintuitive findings in China and India may be explained in two ways. First, it is possible that because family duties in these cultures took too much time and energy, respondents might have felt they could not attend to and fulfill work responsibilities, which, in turn, increased their work overload. Looking at it from a reverse causality, it is possible that those who had work overload might have the tendency to attribute it to family responsibilities and their interference with work life.

Work-Family Positive Spillover

Project 3535 was the first cross-cultural study to look at the effects of moderating variables on W-F positive spillover (see Chapter 14). We found that having job control increased work-to-family positive spillover (WTFS), whereas having family control increased family-to-work positive spillover (FTWS). Moreover, job control was more important for promoting WTFS in employees who had more collectivist values and for those in collectivistic societies.

We also examined the effects of monochronic versus polychronic time orientation. Individuals who preferred to handle tasks by multitasking (i.e., those higher in polychronicity) reported less WIF conflict and more positive spillover in both directions (WTFS and FTWS). Moreover, greater job control facilitated WTFS for polychronic employees. By contrast, family control was more related to FTWS in monochronic cultures (Taiwan and China) compared to polychronic cultures (India, Indonesia, and Turkey).

A meta-analysis (McNall, Nicklin, & Masuda, 2010) and a meta-analytic path analysis (Shockley & Singla, 2011) have examined the relationships between W-F enrichment and outcomes. They both found support for the source attribution hypothesis. That is, outcomes were more a function of the role from which the enrichment originated than they were of the role in which the enrichment was received. Our finding that within-domain relationships between job/family control and W-F positive spillover were stronger than cross-domain relationships suggests that this applies to antecedents as well as outcomes of W-F enrichment.

McNall et al.'s (2010) meta-analysis indicated that although there were significant positive relationships between both directions of W-F enrichment and job and family satisfaction, there were no significant effects for turnover intent. Our findings were more nuanced. We found that although both directions of positive spillover were associated with lower turnover intent, this relationship was stronger in individualistic than in collectivistic societies. Surprisingly, we found the relationship between W-F positive spillover and family satisfaction to be stronger for those who held more collectivistic values, but weaker for those from collectivistic countries.

Work-Family Guilt

Project 3535 was the first study to use a multi-method approach that combined qualitative and quantitative methods to investigate W-F guilt (see Chapter 17). It was also the first to include a cross-cultural comparison of 10 countries from different parts of the globe. We used a newly created quantitative bidirectional measure of W-F guilt that was found to have reliability, validity, and measurement invariance for culture and gender. The availability of this measure should do much to advance research in the field of W-F guilt.

Our results demonstrated that W-F guilt affects working parents in all parts of the world. We also found that, contrary to popular stereotypes, men and women did not differ in either work interference with family guilt (WIFG) or family interference with work guilt (FIWG). Similar to the findings for WFC, those with egalitarian gender-role attitudes reported lower W-F guilt than those with traditional attitudes, except for Turkey, where traditionals had lower W-F guilt, probably due to the fact that work is perceived as an obligation to the family (rather than an individualistic pursuit) by those who hold traditional views. Guilt due to family interfering with work was highest in Asian countries and among those living in extended family situations.

Positive relationships between WIF and FIW conflict and WIF and FIW guilt were very common, but they tended to be stronger for the work domain than for the family domain. Higher work overload was associated with higher WIFG except for the Asian countries, whereas higher family overload was associated with higher FIWG only in the Asian countries and Australia.

In I-E countries higher WIFG was associated with many negative outcomes including lower ease of balancing, family satisfaction, life satisfaction, and satisfaction with role performance and higher psychological distress and turnover intentions. Furthermore, WIFG acted as a mediator or mechanism that explained why the experience of WFC resulted in these detrimental outcomes. This was the strongest for WIFG as it related to turnover intent and weaker for outcomes related to satisfaction. In Israel, Spain, Turkey, India, Indonesia, and Taiwan, WIFG fully mediated the relationship between WIFC and turnover intent. Thus, for those in the more collectivist/traditional Latin European and Eastern/Asian countries (except China), their guilt feelings about their work interfering with their family life were the reason they wanted to quit their jobs.

Coping Strategies

Project 3535 was the first cross-cultural study to examine how the coping strategies used by employed parents impacted on the amount of WFC they experienced (see Chapter 15). The effects of eight coping strategies were examined. These were setting priorities at home and at work, delegation at home or at work, being "good enough" at home or at work, and being a superman/woman at home or at work.

The strategies that were associated with both lower WIF and lower FIW were: (1) setting priorities at work (for everyone), (2) setting priorities at home (for I-E men and women), and being a superman at work (for C-T men). The strategies that were related to lower WIF, but not lower FIW were: (1) delegation at home and at work (for men and women in MC-MT cultures) and (2) being a superwoman at home (for C-T women). The strategy of being good enough at work was related to lower FIW, but not lower WIF, for women in C-T cultures.

Three strategies (i.e., being good enough at home, setting priorities at home, and being a superwoman at work) were associated with both higher WIF and higher FIW for women in C-T cultures. The strategies that were related to higher WIF, but not higher FIW, were being a superman at home (for C-T men) and being a superwoman at home and at work and being good enough at home (for I-E women). Finally, the strategies that were related to higher FIW, but not to higher WIF, were: (1) being good enough at work (for C-T men), (2) being a superman at work (for I-E men), and (3) being good enough at home or a superwoman at work (for I-E women).

In general, these results indicate that setting priorities at work was a universally helpful strategy for managing WFC. However, the strategies that were the most effective also differed as a function of country category. For those in MC-MT cultures, delegation at home and at work was related to lower WIF. For those in I-E cultures, setting priorities at home was associated with lower WFC, whereas trying to be a superman at work or a superwoman at home or at work was associated with higher WFC. For those in C-T cultures, gender-congruent coping strategies (i.e., being a superman at work for men and being a superwoman at home for women) appeared to be the most helpful for lowering WFC. By contrast, in these settings gender-incongruent strategies (i.e., being good enough at home, setting priorities at home, and being a superwoman at work for C-T women and being a superman at home or only good enough at work for C-T men) were related to higher WFC.

Social Support

Project 3535 is one of the relatively few studies that have examined received support across different cultures, as well as the only cross-national study to the best of our knowledge to look at support from work and family sources for both work- and family-related issues (see Chapter 16). Across all countries spouses provided high levels of support for both work and family and respondents expressed high levels of satisfaction with the support they received from their spouses. Job supervisors also provided high levels of support, but it was more for family issues than for work issues. Paid household helpers provided the least amount of support of all sources, and respondents were least satisfied with the support received from them. Overall, spouse support was related to lower WFC and higher FTWS, whereas support from paid household helpers was related to higher WFC. In general, these effects were stronger for individuals with less collectivistic values.

Organizational and Government Policy Support

Project 3535 examined how organizational and government policies were related to W-F interface and outcome variables (see Chapter 3). With the exception of Masuda et al. (2011), who compared managers from Anglo, Latin American, and Asian country clusters, ours is one of the only multinational comparisons of the effects of organizational policies to be conducted outside an Anglo or European context. We examined the use and perceived helpfulness of nine family-friendly (FF) organizational policies.

Our results indicated that government policies to support W-F reconciliation were uncommon and that satisfaction with FF organizational policies was greater than satisfaction with government policies. The most widely used policies were permission to leave work in a personal or family emergency, employer-provided health insurance, and flexible scheduling. Comparisons across countries indicated that FF workplace practices were used least often by employed parents in Turkey, Spain, and Taiwan, and most often by employed parents in China, India, and Israel. This is somewhat at odds with the findings of Masuda et al. (2011) that managers from Anglo countries were more likely to report working in organizations that offered FF benefits (i.e., flextime, compressed working week, part-time work, and telecommuting) compared with managers in collectivistic (i.e., Asian and Latin American) countries. The discrepancy in results may be due to several methodological differences between our study and theirs, including the nature of the sample (employed parents versus managers), the countries studied, the specific policies included, and the fact that we looked at policy use, whereas they looked at policy availability.

Overall, we found that women reported significantly greater satisfaction with FF organizational policies than men did, except in India, China, and Taiwan, where men were more satisfied than women. Among both policy users and nonusers, women were more likely than men to feel that organizational supports that allowed greater flexibility and additional support for their family roles (i.e., longer maternity/parental leave, child care support, leave to care for sick family members) were or would be beneficial in helping them attain greater W-F balance.

There were substantial cross-national differences in the extent to which each specific organizational policy or practice was used and in the extent to which users rated these policies as helpful to them for improving their W-F balance. However, overall, we found that across national contexts greater satisfaction with FF policies was related to many positive outcomes, including lower WIF, higher WTFS, higher life satisfaction, and lower turnover intent.

Gender

In Project 3535, gender was conceptualized as a multidimensional construct. We examined the effects gender (whether someone was a man or a woman), gender-role attitudes or ideology (GRI), and national gender equity (NGE) on WFC and W-F positive spillover (see Chapter 18). Cross-national research that includes all three of these components of gender together in one study is almost nonexistent. There were few significant effects that were due to the influence of gender alone. Instead, gender interacted with GRI and NGE to impact the W-F interface.

In terms of GRI, we looked at traditional versus egalitarian gender-role attitudes toward: (1) division of work and family roles, (2) the importance of men's careers, and (3) women's employment. Of these, attitudes toward women's employment (GRI3) figured the most prominently, particularly in regard to W-F positive spillover. In countries with high national gender equity, women with more egalitarian GRI3 reported higher positive spillover (both WTFS and FTWS) compared to egalitarian men. By contrast, in countries with low national gender equity, women with traditional GRI3 reported more positive spillover (both WTFS and FTWS) compared to men with similar attitudes. For moderate NGE countries, there was a cross-effect with men with traditional GRI3 reporting significantly more WTFS than women with similar attitudes, and women with egalitarian GRI3 reporting significantly more WTFS than men with similar attitudes.

For WFC, WIF was higher in countries that had a higher NGE as compared to countries that had a moderate and low NGE. FIW, on the other hand, was significantly impacted only by GRI3. FIW was greater for those who had more traditional as compared to egalitarian GRI3.

Context

In Chapter 19, the moderating role of three kinds of contextual variables (demographic, work, and family) on the relationship between culture (East versus West) and a number of W-F interface and outcome variables was examined. All contextual variables except for age of youngest child, job type, and spouse's job type interacted with culture to impact the dependent variables. The most numerous interaction effects between culture and the contextual variables occurred for FTWS and life satisfaction. For example, there were significant interactions between culture and FTWS for spouse's job schedule, living arrangements, and extended family living. The most common contextual moderator variables were the family variables of spouse's job schedule and living arrangements.

Those with young children reported higher FIW and higher turnover intent, but also greater family satisfaction, indicating that children can be both a source of stress and a basis for satisfaction. Overall, nuclear family living created less FIW than extended family living. Although extended family living was associated with WTFS more so in the East than in the West, nuclear families were associated with more family satisfaction in the West as compared to the East.

In both Eastern and Western cultures, participants with stronger religious beliefs reported higher positive spillover (both WTFS and FTWS) than those with beliefs that were not as strong. However, strength of religious beliefs also interacted significantly with culture such that the same level of religious beliefs tended to be associated with higher levels of time-based WIF, but lower levels of strain-based FIW, in Western as compared to Eastern cultures.

In both Eastern and Western cultures, WIF was higher among full-time than among part-time employees, whereas FIW was higher for those in managerial than for those in nonmanagerial positions. Full-time workers in the West had lower FIW, but also lower psychological well-being than those in the East. Culture interacted with spouse's job type and job schedule to influence a range of W-F variables, including conflict (WIF and FIW), positive spillover (WTFS and FTWS), and life satisfaction. Having a spouse employed in a nonmanagerial job was associated with lower life satisfaction than having a spouse employed in a managerial job. In Western cultures, having a spouse who worked full-time was more likely than in Eastern cultures to be associated with greater time-based WIF, but also lower FIW and higher life satisfaction. Having a part-time working spouse was associated with greater WIF for respondents in the West, while a nonworking spouse was associated with greater FIW for respondents in the East. These results support the emerging pattern of greater impact of work demands in Western cultures and greater impact of family demands in Eastern ones.

In both Eastern and Western cultures, working for an organization that was smaller in size was associated with higher strain-based FIW, but also greater positive spillover (both WTFS and FTWS). This may be because larger organizations are more able than smaller ones to offer W-F initiatives that can reduce FIW. Smaller organizations, on the other hand, may compensate by offering a more family-friendly work culture that can enhance positive spillover.

Implications for Theory, Research, and Practice

Due to its comprehensive nature, Project 3535 has advanced our knowledge about the W-F interface and allowed us to gain a better understanding of the processes that underlie WFC, guilt, and positive spillover as they pertain to a wide variety of national contexts. Our results have contributed to the development of culturally sensitive theory in several ways. First, Project 3535 has expanded WFC theory by examining how national context influences the relationships between conflict and its antecedents and outcomes in both the work and the family domains. Previous multinational studies of WFC often have excluded family domain variables (i.e., family overload, FIW, and family satisfaction). Our results, however, demonstrate that the inclusion of these variables is vitally important for a complete understanding of the effects of culture on WFC. Second, prior theory in the area of W-F guilt has been virtually nonexistent. The results of Project 3535 make a major contribution to the literature on W-F guilt by delineating a theory that conceptualizes W-F guilt as an affective mediator that helps to explain why WFC results in detrimental outcomes and by demarcating the national contexts in which it does so. Third, Project 3535 has contributed to advancing culturally sensitive theory in the area of W-F positive spillover by investigating how the previously unexplored cultural dimensions of collectivism and polychronicity impact on the experience of positive spillover.

Fourth, Project 3535 has added to our preexisting knowledge by looking at how gender and context interact with culture to affect WFC and positive spillover and by including an examination of how some important, but previously neglected factors, such as coping strategies and social and organizational support, influence the W-F interface in different national contexts. Finally, Project 3535 is one of the only cross-national studies to have examined turnover intent instead of job satisfaction as a work-related outcome. This is important because turnover intent is not only a more distal outcome of WFC, but it is also of more practical relevance to organizations. Our many significant findings linking various aspects of the W-F interface to turnover intent speak to the importance of examining this variable.

Our findings make it very clear that WFC and W-F guilt have a detrimental effect on working parents in all parts of the world. By contrast, we found widespread evidence pertaining to the benefits of W-F positive spillover. In all 10 countries, WIF conflict and guilt were greater in magnitude than FIW conflict and guilt, whereas FTWS was greater than WTFS. This points to working conditions being the main driver of WIF conflict and guilt and to the ability of family circumstances to buffer work stress.

In line with previous research, we found that WIF and FIW were higher among those with heavier work and family demands, respectively. Thus, WIF was higher among full-time than among part-time employees, whereas FIW was higher among those whose children were younger. These findings applied to working parents regardless of where in the world they resided. Furthermore, our results suggested that interventions aimed at reducing within-domain overload (e.g., through increasing autonomy and control) may assist employed parents in dealing with WFC and guilt, as well as in enhancing their positive spillover and well-being.

Our results suggested some behavioral strategies that individuals could adopt to help reduce their work and/or family overload. For example, our findings indicated that those employed parents who set priorities at work had lower WIF and FIW conflict. As well, parents who preferred to multitask (i.e., had a polychronic time orientation) had lower WFC and higher W-F positive spillover, and these beneficial effects appeared to be accentuated when polychronic employees were given greater job control.

We also found that in some instances individuals' attitudes and beliefs were important to their experience of the W-F interface. Thus, employed parents with egalitarian gender-role attitudes reported lower WFC and W-F guilt in both directions (i.e., WIF and FIW) than those with traditional attitudes. Moreover, participants with stronger religious beliefs reported higher positive spillover (both WTFS and FTWS) than those whose beliefs were not as strong.

Social and organizational support also played a very important role. Our results suggested that employed parents should try to capitalize upon their social support networks at home and at work. Furthermore, our findings indicated that across all countries employed parents who reported greater satisfaction with FF policies also reported many positive outcomes, including lower WIF, higher WTFS, higher life satisfaction, and lower turnover intent. Although workplace policies and practices can have favorable effects for employees in diverse national settings, we found that women were more likely than men to feel that policies that allowed greater flexibility and additional support for their family roles would be most beneficial. Thus, our findings strongly suggest that organizations offer FF benefits as a way of preventing turnover, particularly among women. However, companies should make sure that their policies are formulated in such a way as to satisfy the needs of their employees and that they are offered in the context of a hospitable climate.

Individualistic-Egalitarian Cultures

The Individualistic-Egalitarian (I-E) cultures in our sample included the United States, Canada, Australia, and Spain. Compared to those in C-T countries, employed parents in I-E countries reported experiencing higher conflict as a result of their work interfering with their family lives. Furthermore, in these cultures, both WIF and WIFG were triggered by high work overload and both resulted in higher turnover intent. By contrast, higher positive spillover, both from work-to-family and family-to-work, was associated with lower turnover intentions.

Turnover is very costly for organizations. Our results suggest that to help prevent turnover in I-E cultures, there is a need for organizations to foster working conditions that will help their employees reduce their WIF conflict and guilt by lowering their work overload. Workplace interventions aimed at reducing work demands and overload, as well as the provision of more part-time options may be particularly effective in these national contexts. For example, greater job autonomy and control may help diminish one's job overload and WIF, thereby decreasing WIFG and increasing WTFS. Employees also can be provided with training on how to handle work overload more efficiently by using technology or developing their skills in areas such as time management, delegation/teamwork, support seeking, and communication.

We found that in I-E cultures, setting priorities at home was associated with lower WFC for both men and women, whereas trying to do everything at home and at work was related to higher WFC for women. This suggests that training individuals in how to prioritize might be beneficial. Moreover, it speaks to the need to reduce the social pressure on women to be perfect in all roles, a norm that has also been shown to induce W-F guilt for those in I-E cultures. Spouse support was also found to be very important for decreasing WIF and increasing FTWS in I-E cultures. Efforts should be made to work with married couples to give them strategies that they can use to support their partners.

Collectivist-Traditional Cultures

The Collectivistic-Traditional (C-T) cultures in our sample included China, India, Indonesia, and Turkey. Compared to I-E cultures, mean levels of FIW and FIWG were significantly greater for C-T countries. In addition, in these cultures family overload was associated with many negative effects, including greater FIW and FIWG, decreased life and family satisfaction, and higher turnover intent. Moreover, for those in C-T countries (except China), their guilt feelings about their work interfering with their family life were the reason they wanted to quit their jobs.

Our results indicate that strategies aimed at directly reducing family demands/overload should be helpful in reducing the FIW conflict and guilt and increasing FTWS for employed parents in C-T cultures. As well, teaching individuals how to better cope with the guilt feelings that can arise from the extended family living situations, close family ties, and the network of reciprocal social obligations that characterize these societies may be beneficial in terms of lessening their FIWG. It appears from our results that the coping strategies that are most effective in C-T cultures are those that are congruent with gender-role norms. For men, this means being an overachiever at work, whereas for women it involves being an overachiever at home.

To prevent turnover in collectivistic and traditional cultures, there is a need for organizations to help employees reduce the conflict and guilt that arises when their family interferes with their work. In these national contexts, FF policies aimed at reducing demands and overload in the family would be most helpful. Company-sponsored child care and elder care services, emergency support mechanisms, flexible work arrangements, and extended maternal and paternal leaves are among the practices that organizations could adopt.

It should be recognized that although FIW conflict and guilt are higher in C-T cultures than in I-E ones, positive spillover (both WTFS and FTWS) is also significantly higher in these national contexts. However in C-T countries it is also important for employers to provide their employees with job control to ensure WTFS.

Conclusion

This volume presents some of the many results from Project 3535. As with our project as a whole, preparing this book has been a team effort. To come to fruition, Project 3535 has required many years of sustained dedication from a large team of researchers. Along the way, we encountered every sort of work-life challenge imaginable (e.g., death or illness of family members, divorce, job changes, natural disasters). In addition, we have had to come to terms with the realities that a collaborative approach is more time-consuming, communication across distance is more difficult, and doing research well takes longer. In the end, we hope that our research pays homage to the proverb: "If you want to walk fast, walk alone; if you want to walk far, walk together."

The aim of Project 3535 was to further our understanding about how to lessen WFC and guilt and enhance W-F positive spillover for employed parents in different parts of the world. Alleviating the WFC and guilt experienced by working mothers and fathers should improve their health, happiness, and productivity at home and at work and benefit the well-being of families and of society as a whole. However, our results speak to the importance of taking national context into account and tailoring recommendations based on culture and other factors such as gender and job level. Understanding the influence of culture on the W-F interface in this way will help organizations deal with a diverse workforce. It also is important for managers in non-Western contexts (e.g., emerging economies), who need to understand the applicability of strategies that have been developed in Western industrialized societies. Although we have advanced the state of knowledge regarding the W-F interface, our work has raised many new questions and opened many future directions for research.

References

Allen, T. D., French, K. A., Dumani, S., & Shockley, K. M. (2015). Meta-analysis of work-family conflict mean differences: Does national context matter? *Journal of Vocational Behavior, 90*, 90–100. doi:10.1016/j.jvb.2015.07.006

Amstad, F. T., Meier, L L., Fasel, U., Elfering, A., & Semmer, N. K. (2011). A meta-analysis of work-family conflict and various outcomes with a special emphasis on cross-domain versus matching-domain relations. *Journal of Occupational Health Psychology, 16*(2), 151–169. doi:10.1037/a0022170

Beham, B., Drobnič, S., & Präg, P. (2014). The work-family interface of service sector workers: A comparison of work resources and professional status across five European countries. *Applied Psychology: An International Review, 63*(1), 29–61. doi:10.1111/apps.12012

Byron, K. (2005). A meta-analytic review of work-family conflict and its antecedents. *Journal of Vocational Behavior, 67*(2), 169–198. doi:10.1016/j.jvb.2004.08.009

Ford, M. T., Heinen, B. A., & Langkamer, K. L. (2007). Work and family satisfaction and conflict: A meta-analysis of cross-domain relations. *Journal of Applied Psychology, 92*(1), 57–80. doi:10.1037/0021-9010.92.1.57

Frone, M. R., Yardley, J. K., & Markle, K. S. (1997). Developing and testing an integrative model of work-family interface. *Journal of Vocational Behavior, 50*(2), 145–167. doi:10.1006/jvbe.1996.1577

Grzywacz, J. G., & Marks, N. F. (2000). Reconceptualizing the work-family interface: An ecological perspective on the correlates of positive and negative spillover between work and family. *Journal of Occupational Health Psychology, 5*(1), 111–126. doi:10.1037/1076-8998.5.1.111

Haar, J., Russo, M., Sune, A., & Ollier-Malaterre, A. (2014). Outcomes of work-life balance on job satisfaction, life satisfaction and mental health: A study across seven cultures. *Journal of Vocational Behavior, 85*(3), 361–373. doi:10.1016/j.jvb.2014.08.010

Hanson, G. C., Hammer, L. B., & Colton, C. L. (2006). Development and validation of a multidimensional scale of perceived work-family positive spillover. *Journal of Occupational Health Psychology, 11*(3), 249–265. doi:10.1037/1076-8998.11.3.249

Hill, E. J., Yang, C., Hawkins, A. J., & Ferris, M. (2004). A cross-cultural test of the work-family interface in 48 countries. *Journal of Marriage and Family, 66*, 1300–1316.

House, R. J., Hanges, P. J., Javidian, M., Dorfman, P. W., & Gupta, V. (Eds.). (2004). *Culture leadership, and organizations: The GLOBE study of 62 societies.* Thousand Oaks, CA: Sage.

Joplin, J. R. W., Shaffer, M. A., Francesco, A. M., & Lau, T. (2003). The macro-environment and work-family conflict. *International Journal of Cross Cultural Management, 3*(3), 306–327. doi:10.1177/1470595803003003004

Korabik, K., Lero, D. S., & Whitehead, D. L. (Eds.). (2008). *Handbook of work-family integration: Research, theories and best practices.* San Diego, CA: Elsevier.

Korabik, K., McElwain, A., & Chappell, D. B. (2008). Integrating gender-related issues into research on work and family. In K. Korabik, D. S. Lero, & D. L. Whitehead (Eds.), *Handbook of work-family integration: Research, theories and best practices* (pp. 215–232). San Diego, CA: Elsevier.

Lu, L., Gilmour, R. Kao, S., & Huang, M. (2006). A cross-cultural study of work/family demands, work/family conflict and wellbeing: The Taiwanese vs. British. *Career Development International, 11*(1), 9–27. doi:10.1108/13620430610642354

Lyness, K. S., & Kropf, M. B. (2005). The relationships of national gender equality and organizational support with work-family balance: A study of European managers. *Human Relations, 58*(1), 33–60. doi:10.1177/0018726705050934

Masuda, A. D., Poelmans, S. A. Y., Allen, T. D., Spector, P. E., Lapierre, L. M., Cooper, C. L., . . . Moreno-Velazquez, I. (2012). Flexible work arrangements availability and their relationship with work-to-family conflict, job satisfaction, and turnover intentions: A comparison of three country clusters. *Applied Psychology: An International Review, 61*(1), 1–29. doi:10.1111/j.1464-0597.2011.00453.x

McNall, L. A., Nicklin, J. M., & Masuda, A. D. (2010). A meta-analytic review of the consequences associated with work-family enrichment. *Journal of Business and Psychology, 25*(3), 381–396. doi:10.1007/s10869-009-9141-1

Michel, J. S., Mitchelson, J. K., Kotrba, L. M., LeBreton, J. M., & Baltes, B., B. (2009). A comparative test of work-family conflict models and critical examination of work-family linkages. *Journal of Vocational Behavior, 74*(2), 199–218. doi:10.1016/j.jvb.2008.12.005

Oliver, T., Korabik, K., McElwain, A., & Lero, D. (2008, June). *The effects of family-friendly workplace policies on work interference-with-family and organizational outcomes.* Poster session presented at the annual meeting of the Canadian Psychological Association, Halifax, NS.

Ollier-Malaterre, A., & Foucreault, A. (2017). Cross-national work-life research: Cultural and structural impacts for individuals and organizations. *Journal of Management, 43*(1), 111–136. doi:10.1177/0149206316655873

Ollier-Malaterre, A., Valcour, M., Den Dulk, L., & Kossek, E. E. (2013). Theorizing national context to develop comparative work-life research: A review and research agenda. *European Management Journal, 31*(5), 433–447. doi:10.1016/j.emj.2013.05.002

Powell, G. N., Francesco, A., & Ling, Y. (2009). Toward culture-sensitive theories of the work-family interface. *Journal of Organizational Behavior, 30*, 597–616. doi:10.1002/job.v30:510.1002/job.568

Shaffer, B. S., & Riordan, C. M. (2003). A review of cross-cultural methodologies for organizational research: A best practices approach. *Organizational Research Methods, 6*(2), 169–215. doi:10.1177/1094428103251542

Shaffer, M., Joplin, J., & Hsu, Y.-S. (2011). Expanding the boundaries of work-family research: A review and agenda for future research. *International Journal of Cross Cultural Management, 12*(2), 221–268. doi:10.1177/1470595811398800

Shockley, K. M., & Singla, N. (2011). Reconsidering work-family interactions and satisfaction: A meta-analysis. *Journal of Management, 37*, 861–886. doi:10.1177/0149206310394864

Spector, P. E., Allen, T. D., Poelmans, S. Y., Lapierre, L. M., Cooper, C. L., O'Driscoll, M., . . . Widerszal-Bazyl, M. (2007). Cross-national differences in relationships of work demands, job satisfaction, and turnover intentions with work-family conflict. *Personnel Psychology, 60*(4), 805–835. doi:10.1111/j.1744-6570.2007.00092.

Spector, P. E., Cooper, C. L., Poelmans, S., Allen, T. D., O'Driscoll, M. I., Sanchez, J. I., . . . Lu, L. (2004). A cross-national comparative study of work-family stressors, working hours, and well-being: China and Latin America versus the Anglo world. *Personnel Psychology, 57*(1), 119–142. doi:10.1111/j.1744-6570.2004.tb02486.x

Steibler, N. (2009). Reported levels of time-based and strain-based conflict between work and family roles in Europe: A multilevel approach. *Social Indicators Research, 93*, 469–488. doi:10.1007/s11205-008-9436-z

INDEX